U.S. Aerial Armament in World War II Vol. 3

U.S. Aerial Armament in World War II

The Ultimate Look:

Vol. 3
Air Launched Rockets, Mines, Torpedoes, Guided Missiles and Secret Weapons

William Wolf

Schiffer Military History
Atglen, PA

Book Design by Ian Robertson.

Printed in China.
ISBN: 978-0-7643-3658-4

We are interested in hearing from authors with book ideas on related topics.

Published by Schiffer Publishing Ltd.
4880 Lower Valley Road
Atglen, PA 19310
Phone: (610) 593-1777
FAX: (610) 593-2002
E-mail: Info@schifferbooks.com.
Visit our web site at: www.schifferbooks.com
Please write for a free catalog.
This book may be purchased from the publisher.
Please include $5.00 postage.
Try your bookstore first.

In Europe, Schiffer books are distributed by:
Bushwood Books
6 Marksbury Avenue
Kew Gardens
Surrey TW9 4JF, England
Phone: 44 (0) 20 8392-8585
FAX: 44 (0) 20 8392-9876
E-mail: Info@bushwoodbooks.co.uk.
Visit our website at: www.bushwoodbooks.co.uk

Contents

Preface

While researching and writing my "Ultimate Look" series of bomber books, including the B-29, B-32, B-18, and B-25, I realized two things. One, that there was no definitive book available concerning American World War II aerial armament and ordnance. Two, I had a large source of technical manuals, microfilm, books, and magazines in my library on the various aspects of the subject on which I had to spend hours and hours digging out research material for these Ultimate Look bomber books. It was not long into my gathering of data that I realized that the massive subject would have to be divided into two books: Volume 1 on Guns, Ammunition, and Turrets (which is available), and a second volume on US Air-Dropped Weapons. Then, while I was gathering material for Volume 2, I found it also would have to be divided into two volumes: the volume on Bombs, Bombsights, and Bombing (which is available), and this Volume 3 on Air-Dropped, Air-Launched, and Secret Weapons. In the early 1970s I became fascinated with WWII guided missiles and compiled 100s of photos and copied 100s of pages of manuals, reports, and academic papers on the subject for an unpublished manuscript which I have finally used for this book. I hope this volume will serve as an easy to use reference and definitive work on the subject for WWII aviation historians, modelers, and enthusiasts.

Acknowledgments

My lifelong hobby has been WWII aerial combat, and over the past 35 years I have collected over 16,000 books and magazines, along with over a thousand reels of microfilm on the subject. I probably have nearly every book written on WWII aviation and complete collections of every combat aviation magazine published since 1939. Also included in my collection are hundreds of aviation unit histories; intelligence reports; pilot, crew, flight, and training manuals; and technical, structural, and maintenance manuals for aircraft ordnance, armament, engines, and equipment. My microfilm collection includes vintage intelligence reports; hundreds of USAF, USN, and USMC group and squadron histories and After Combat Reports; complete Japanese Monograph series; and complete US Strategic Bombing Surveys, as well as complete USAF Historical Studies. Over the years I have been fortunate to meet many fighter aces, other pilots, and fellow aviation buffs who have shared stories, material, and photographs with me (I have over 5,000 photos of fighter aces alone). I have made numerous multi-day expeditions to various military libraries, museums, and photo depositories with my copy machine and camera, accumulating literally reams of information and 1,000s of photographs. Also, in particular, I wish to thank George Eaton, ASC Command Historian at the Rock Island Arsenal, for his invaluable help in securing access to several Bombing Technical Manuals.

Over the past decade I have completed 11 books on WWII aviation that included many hundreds of photos and drawings, many in color. Most of the photos gathered for this volume and the others were from the WWII era and before, and over the years were not well cared for and showed their age. As described above, almost all were copies or copies of copies made before the Digital/Photoshop Age by a standard film 35mm camera on a copy stand; many hundreds at a time over several days while visiting various facilities. At one time I had a photo darkroom where I developed 1,000s of rare photos from microfilm negatives which were not of the best quality. Many photos were copied from printed dot-type photos from contemporary World War II publications. The reproductions of the many technical drawings were made by my non-digital drum copy machine 20 years ago or more from yellowed manuals that originally were poorly printed on poor quality wartime paper. So I apologize in advance for the quality of some photos and drawings in this book (despite being photo-shopped), but I feel rare photos of marginal quality are better than no photos in describing topics in this book. Many of the photos in this book are stills reproduced from training and operational films, microfilm, and manuals and are of poor quality, but are the only sources available on the secret weapons of the era.

The author wishes that every person who contributed photos and materials to his collection over the past 35 years could be specifically mentioned. Over the years the origin of some of the 1,000s of photos I have been lent to copy or have copied and collected have become obscured. Most are from military and government sources, but many are from private individuals, so I also apologize if some of the photos are wrongly credited.

And last but not least, for the eleventh time thanks go to my persevering wife, Nancy, who allows me to spend many hours researching and writing, and patiently (mostly) waits while I browse bookstores and visit air museums in search of new material and photos. Also, I thank her because her car sits out in the hot Arizona sun as my WWII library luxuriates in the remodeled, air-conditioned three-car garage.

1

The American Fighter Plane Becomes a Fighter Bomber

USAAC/USAAF Fighter Bomber Development

Gen. William "Billy" Mitchell, a well-known pilot in WWI and an air power activist, confronted the infantry-minded Army Senior Staff by stating that the next war would be won by air power, and challenged the accepted military doctrine of the day that proclaimed that the Navy ruled the waves. After the First World War the US Congress ruthlessly slashed military appropriations, and of what little funding was doled out a disparity was allotted to the Navy. Mitchell stated that a thousand bombers could be built at the same cost as one battleship and could sink that battleship, and in 1921 a test was scheduled in which Army bombers led by Mitchell sunk captured German capital ships. The Navy saw Mitchell's success as an affront, and decided any future air attacks on naval targets would be the sole province of the Navy. Meanwhile, the Army Senior Staff also saw Mitchell's success as an affront, as he had the audacity to question his superiors, and then when put to the test demonstrated he was right. But in being right he had committed the intolerable; he had proven Senior Staff wrong. Instead of receiving promotions and decorations Mitchell was relieved of command, court-martialed, reduced in rank, and expelled from the Army for five years. Mitchell resigned from the service and would only be vindicated when the next war did break out. There were a few, but fortunately influential, air power advocates in Congress that prompted the Army to separate its air arm and establish the Army Air Corps in 1926. Despite this apparent independence, the Air Corps remained a non-entity for the next decade due to the lack of funding and high-ranking officers. In a weakened Army, Senior Staff Officers could only attain star rank in the time-honored branches of the Army: the infantry, the artillery and, in those days, even the cavalry, but not in the new unproven Air Corps.

By the mid-1930s, the Army's thinking on the role of air power changed, and they decided that the airplane's primary role in the next war would be to support the infantry. The Air Corp's Tactical School at Maxwell Field, AL, ordered Army infantry and the command of close air support elements to be directed by a ground commander as if it were artillery or armor. While the AAC generals didn't agree with this directive, it was a moot point, as there were no aircraft or trained pilots to carry out close air support, no matter who was in command.

The stunning defeat of Poland in less than a month by German Panzer columns supported by ruthless Stuka dive bombers was seen as the definitive use of a coordinated assault by air and ground units, and put a new term in the military dictionary, "Blitzkrieg." The defeat of Poland and then the Blitzkrieg in France alarmed the senior American commanders, who had developed no close support aircraft, and now insisted on a Stuka-

Gen. William "Billy" Mitchell was a well-known WW-I pilot and an air power activist who confronted the infantry-minded Army Senior Staff by stating that the next war would be won by air power. Mitchell challenged the accepted military doctrine of the day that proclaimed that the Navy ruled the waves. (AAF)

In November 1943, the Allies established tactical air forces for the impending invasion of Europe. The RAF established the 2nd Tactical Air Force from experienced personnel from the RAF Mediterranean Air Forces. The USAAF transferred the entire 9th Air Force HQ from the MTO to England. Shown is the devastation on retreating German troops caused by Allied fighter bombers in closing the Falaise Gap. (AAF)

type dive bomber. Gen. H.H. Arnold, Commander of the AAC, countered their choice with orders to utilize the twin-engine light attack bomber, the Douglas A-20 Havoc, which was already in production for export to England. By this time the *Luftwaffe* had found the Stuka to be vulnerable to enemy interceptors and ground fire and had turned to the Junkers Ju-88 twin-engine light bomber. The dive bomber faction in the ACC persisted, and in early 1941 US Army Chief of Staff, Gen. George C. Marshall, ordered Arnold to develop an Army Air Corps dive bomber. The belated product was a hybrid. The North American Aviation Company had developed and was producing a single-engine (Allison V-1710) close support fighter, the Mustang I, for the English. To convert it to a dive bomber it was modified to Navy dive bomber specifications with dive brakes and bomb racks and designated the A-36. Even with the A= Attack designation it was to be no more than a mediocre dive bomber. In March 1943 a conference was held at Wright Field, OH, to finally determine whether to use the dive bomber or the fighter bomber in the ground support role. It was decided that the A-36 was to be employed operationally, as its fighter capabilities allowed it first to establish the absolute air superiority that needed to be achieved before first-line fighters could be safely consigned to the fighter bomber role. The fighter bomber also enjoyed the tactical flexibility that the dive bomber did not possess; it was not restricted to attack a singular target with bombs. It was able to strafe, launch rockets, and drop Napalm and bombs in high speed, low level passes, which gave it the element of surprise and a degree of protection from AA fire. A fighter bomber squadron was able to perform multiple duties on the same mission, such as flying a close air support mission and then move on to an interdiction mission. The fighter bomber squadron also was able to respond to sudden changes of the intended target and be re-briefed by radio to the changes.

Establishment of the Tactical Air Forces

By the end of 1943 the worth of close air support had been firmly demonstrated by both the Germans and Russians on the Eastern Front and by the Allies over North Africa. In November 1943 the Allies established Tactical Air Forces for the impending invasion of Europe. The RAF established the 2nd Tactical Air Force from experienced personnel from the RAF Mediterranean Air Forces. The USAAF transferred the entire

9th Air Force HQ from the MTO to England. However, initially the 9th Air Force operated under the control of Fighter Command in a fighter escort role. It was not until April 1944 that two Tactical Air Commands were instituted to support the two US Armies slated to take part in the D-Day invasion. The IX TAC (seven P-47 groups/21 squadrons and three P-38 groups/nine squadrons) was to support the First US Army, while the XIX TAC (five P-47 groups/15 squadrons and two P-38 groups/six squadrons) was to support the Third US Army. In early October 1944 the XXIX TAC was established from the merger of the 303rd and 84th Fighter Wings of the 9th Air Force. During the same month the First Tactical Air Force (Provisional) was established to provide tactical air support for the Franco-American Army group over the southern ETO. The mission of these TAC Air Forces was threefold:

1) Gain air superiority by destroying enemy aircraft in the air and by attacking enemy aircraft on their airfields.
2) Isolate the battlefield by destroying enemy motor and rail transportation, cutting rail lines and bridges, and attacking supply depots and troop concentrations in the rear to prevent or delay their movement to the battlefront.
3) Give direct support to ground forces by hitting troop concentrations, strong points, armor, and gun positions.

The increasing effectiveness of 9th Air Force TACs can be illustrated by comparing the **monthly**, June 1944, performance figures to a **one-day** figure, 25 March 1945, when the Allies pushed across the Rhine.

Target

(Destroyed/Damaged)	All June 1944	25 March 1945
Enemy Aircraft in Air	180/96	3/0
Enemy Aircraft on Ground	33/15	15/26
Locomotives	91/55	76/26
Railway Cars	427/513	858/1,351
Tanks/Armored Vehicles	22/24	118/76
Motor Transport	1,288/583	742/649
Artillery	14/10	27/16

(Note: My book, *USAAF Jabos in the MTO and ETO* (Schiffer, PA, 2004) gives a detailed look at the AAF fighter bomber and operations in the MTO and ETO.)

USAAF Fighter Bombers in the Pacific

In the Pacific almost any medium and attack bomber or fighter aircraft could provide effective close support. At the beginning of the war, medium and attack bombers were of necessity used for ground attack, but as the need for fighters for defense against enemy aircraft declined, fighters took over the greater portion of close support assignments. Heavy bombers proved useful, however, when close support had to be conducted at long range, or when a great number of heavy bombs were needed to saturate an area.

Early in the Pacific war light demolition bombs, fragmentation bombs, and machine guns were considered the best armament for close support strikes by land-based aircraft. These weapons continued to be used, but heavier bombs came to be favored, and the 1,000 pound bomb became a standby. In the Central Pacific, partly because of the lesser carrying capacity of the carrier-based aircraft engaged there, smaller bombs were used more often. Rocket fire came to supplement strafing during the invasion of the Marianas, and assumed greater importance in the Central Pacific as the war continued. Napalm was an important addition to close support armament, but it was most effective when used in conjunction with fragmentation bombs, strafing, or ground fire.

Generally, ground support in the Pacific was not as effective as in Europe; but could often be critical in determining the outcome of portions of the main battle. Shown is a F4U of VMF-323 attacking a Japanese position on Okinawa with rockets and Napalm. (Author)

Coordination was essential to effective close support, and that good liaison was essential to coordination. There was continual progress toward more comprehensive air liaison after the failures in early campaigns (i.e. Tarawa); concluding in the establishment of an air officer, either AAF, USN, or USMC, as Commander Support Aircraft (CSA) or Commander Air Support Control Unit (CASCU). In the Southwest Pacific Area (SWPA), where ground operations were likely to continue long after the amphibious phase was concluded, the Air Commander recovered operational control of support aircraft when the assault phase ended. This was not always the case in the Central Pacific, as the Tactical Air Force (TAF) came under the control of the Ground Army (i.e. in the Philippines and Okinawa). However, the direct command of aircraft was always controlled by air officers everywhere in the Pacific.

Control of air support tended toward locally centralized control. In the SWPA, the three 5AF Bombardment Wings, XIII Fighter Command, and Marine Air Groups, although originally established to permit decentralized control of airpower in areas removed from air headquarters, were instruments for locally centralized control of air support. Other agencies for centralized control of air support were CASCUs, LFASCUs (Landing Force Air Support Control Units), and TAF in the Central Pacific. As air and ground operations in the Pacific became larger in scale, coordination and centralization became increasingly critical so that air support would not be misused or injure friendly forces. Centralization of air control was more important in the Central Pacific, where ground action was confined to small areas than in the larger islands of the SWPA. However, it was also important that decentralized air control be possible, for an attack by one flight of fighters in support of a battalion of infantry could be just as vital to the outcome of the battle as an attack by a hundred aircraft in support of an entire division. In the Central Pacific, the Air Liaison Parties (ALPs) were unsuccessful in effectively performing in decentralized control as the air coordinator, frequently aided by the ALPs, were the primary method of controlling small numbers of aircraft in close support. On Iwo Jima and Okinawa, forward observer teams from the LFASCUs sometimes moved into the lines to control planes engaged in close support. In the SWPA support aircraft parties and forward observer teams were more prominent than air coordinators in controlling support strikes.

While ground support in the Pacific was not as effective as in Europe, it could often be critical in determining the outcome of portions of the main battle. Close support was less effective against Japanese defending from caves, but these caves could be vulnerable to sustained air bombardment combined with infantry and artillery action, as was established on Iwo

Jima and Okinawa. Fighter bomber attacks on enemy troops were more effective during attacks on rear areas than attacks on the front lines, but even when enemy troops were not incapacitated by accurate frontline strikes, they were often so stunned that a carefully coordinated infantry/air attack could capture their positions before they could begin to resist.

Fighter Aircraft Ordnance Pylons
Wing Center Section Pylons
The two wing center section pylons were used for carrying bombs, external auxiliary fuel, and Napalm tanks, or rockets on the lower surface of the wing center section, inboard of the wheel. Each pylon was designed to carry a maximum load of one 1,600 pound bomb. In January 1944 D-15 and D-16 pylon adapter kits were sent to P-47 units to be installed in the field and were installed on all current aircraft in production. The streamlined pylon containing the Interstate B-10 Bomb Shackle rated at 2,000 pounds was positioned outboard of each wheel well. The pylon was capped by a fairing when no bombs were attached and the fighter bomber was to revert to a fighter and needed the increased performance. Later, the smaller D-22 pylon with anti-sway braces was introduced.

The D-15, D-16, and D-22 pylon assembly consisted primarily of a casting that supported the bomb rack, with each end of the bomb rack bolted to the casting. The entire pylon assembly was fastened to the center section of the wing by a bolt and retaining nut. The bolt passed through a special fitting in the wing and fit into a hole in the pylon. Two studs projecting from the top of the casting fit into receptacles in the wing, which prevented lateral movement of the pylon after installation. Two coat hanger type sway braces were mounted to the forward and aft ends of the D-22 pylon. The sway brace shanks were inserted into receptacles in the casing and held in place by set screws. The position of the braces could be reversed when necessary. Adjustable sway brace pads prevented lateral play of the bomb, and secondary holes in the sway braces allowed relocation of the pads to accommodate 100 to 200 pound small bombs. The pylon was provided with an electrical lead that was "plugged" into the bomb rack receptacle to allow electrical arming and release of the bombs. The pylon assembly also incorporated a mechanical bomb release linkage that was made up of a bellcrank connected to a turnbuckle that was attached to the bomb rack manual release trigger. This linkage was actuated by another bellcrank and plunger assembly located in the inner compartment of the wing center section. A fuel line for the external auxiliary fuel tank was attached to the aft end of each pylon by two clamps. A special plug had to be inserted in the bottom opening of the

A wooden scale silhouette mock up of a P-40 wing and center fuselage bomb release mechanism. (AAF)

Wing Pylon

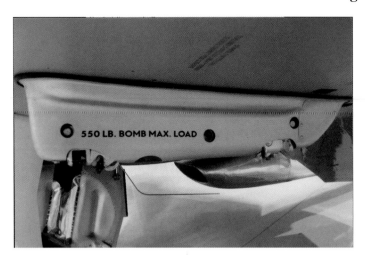

Pylon Fairing Assembly

fuel line when the external tank was not installed. The left hand pylon was provided with a pressurizing line that maintained pressure in the left external tank at high altitudes.

The entire pylon assembly, with the exception of the sway braces, was covered by a boot type fairing that was attached to the pylon by screws. The fairing assembly incorporated a spring-loaded hinged access door which was held closed by two snap fasteners. The sway braces had to be removed prior to installation or removal of the fairing. When the pylon was not in use a fairing could be attached to the bottom of the pylon.

Centerline Pylon

The centerline pylon was located on the underside of the fuselage between the two center section pylons. It was designed for carrying a bomb, external auxiliary fuel or Napalm tank, or a *Tiny Tim* rocket, and to support a maximum load of one 2,000 pound bomb. The pylon was a casting that supported a bomb rack which was bolted at each end to the pylon. The pylon was mounted at the front end to a fitting that was bolted to the engine mount, while the rear end was attached to a fitting

A pilot checking the 500 pound size **T4B3 Cluster** that contained twenty fused 20 pound AN-M41 Fragmentation Bombs attached to the wing pylon of a P-47. (AAF)

D-22 Sway Brace

Loading a Wing Pylon

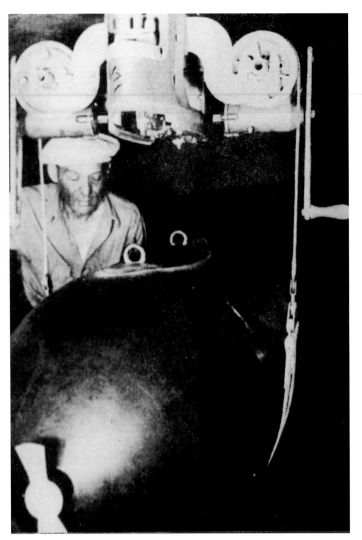
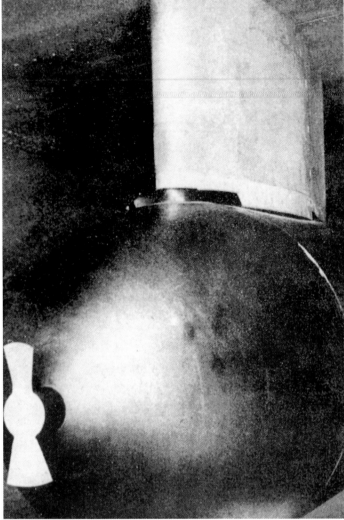

that was bolted to the main beam. The front fitting incorporated a hook assembly that was retracted into the fuselage by a spring when the pylon was not installed. Before mounting to the pylon, the hooks were pulled down by hand and automatically locked in the extended position by a spring-loaded plunger. The hooks secured the forward end of the pylon by engaging a cross pin located on the front end of the pylon casting. An arm that extended up from the aft end of the pylon and was integral with the casting, incorporated a barrel and pin assembly that was similar to a turnbuckle. The end of the pylon was secured to the fuselage centerline when the barrel pins were extended and engaged two holes in the fuselage rear fitting (trunnion). The pins were extended to engage the holes or retracted to clear them by turning the barrel with a special wrench that was permanently attached to the barrel and pin assembly. The coat hanger type sway braces were mounted just forward and aft of the bomb rack, and the position of the braces could be reversed when necessary. The sway brace shanks were inserted into recesses in the pylon support casting and held in place by set screws. The adjustable sway brace pads prevented lateral movement of the bomb. The secondary holes on the sway braces permitted the relocation of the pads to accommodate small 100 to 200 pound bombs. The pylon was provided with an electrical lead that was "plugged" into the bomb rack receptacle to permit electric arming and

release of the bombs. The pylon assembly also incorporated a mechanical bomb release linkage that consisted of a bellcrank and an adjustable cable attached to the bomb rack manual release trigger. The linkage was adjusted in conjunction with the manual release system Teleflex cable that was connected to one end of the pylon bellcrank by a quick-disconnect fitting. A fuel line for the external auxiliary fuel tank was attached to the pylon aft fairing by two brackets welded to the fuel line that was bolted to supports located on the inside of the fairing. The upper bracket on the fuel line was slotted to allow alignment of the fuel line with the opening in the fuel inlet fitting located in the fuselage. A special plug stowed in a hole in the lower horizontal rib of the pylon aft fairing had to be placed in the bottom opening of the fuel line when the external fuel tank was not installed. The entire pylon unit, with the exception of the sway braces, was covered by three fairing assemblies which incorporated two access doors that facilitated installation, removal, and servicing of the pylon.

USAAF Dive and Fighter Bombers
At the time of Pearl Harbor the AAC had a large number of the Douglas A-24 Banshee (the USN SBD Dauntless) dive bombers on order, and had placed other contracts for the Curtiss A-25A (USN SBC-2 Helldiver). In January 1942, the AAC appropriated 300 Vengeance and 192 Bermuda

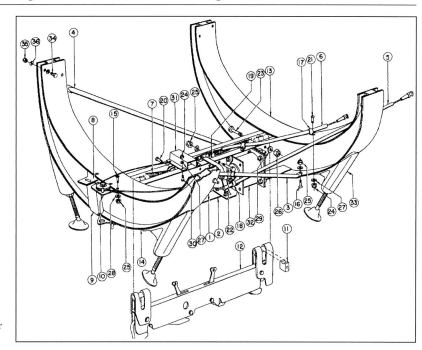

An illustration of the mechanism of the centerline fighter bomber pylon with a B-10 shackle. (AAF/P-47 E&R Manual)

A **Centerline Hook and Cable Adapter** containing a centrally-mounted 500 pound GP bomb flanked by two bundles of five 23 pound fragmentation bombs on each side. (AAF)

(**Left**) Armorers use a small automotive-type cart to load a 250 pound bomb under a P-47 center pylon (**Right**) Sway brace pads are being adjusted to prevent the lateral movement of the bomb. (AAF)

The **North American A-36 Apache/Invader**, the by-product of P-51 Mustang development, was the only AAF-designed aircraft to be designated as a dive bomber. Note the extended dive brake under the wing-sitter's feet. (AAF)

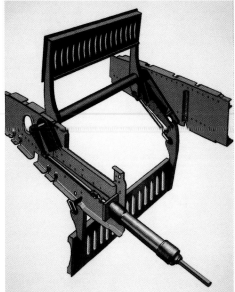

Four cast aluminum alloy lattice-shaped **dive brakes** were installed outboard of the ammunition bays in the wing panels of the A-36. A selector lever to extend and retract the dive brake was located on the left side of the cockpit behind the throttle lever. (AAF)

(the USN Buccaneer) dive bombers on order by the British. However, in combat AAC dive bombers had proven to be a disappointment. Early operations by the 91BS based in the Dutch East Indies and the 8BG based in northern Australia were notably unsuccessful. The major action in which AAC dive bombers participated was an attack by the 27BG(L), when seven A-24s attacked a Japanese naval squadron off Java on 29 February 1942, in which they lost two dive bombers and caused no damage. More unsuccessful dive bombing missions were flown in April 1942 against Laue and Salamaua, but the mission on Buna on 29 July was a total failure, when six out of seven A-24s were lost, confirming the AAC's deep-rooted belief that dive bombers and dive bombing was futile and costly, and thereafter the AAC withdrew the dive bomber concept from combat for the time being.

North American A-36 Apache/Invader: Want-to-be Dive Bomber

The A-36, the only AAF-designed aircraft to be designated as a dive bomber, was a by-product of P-51 Mustang development. Even before Louis Wait made the first flight in the XP-51 fighter on 29 May 1942, funding for AAC fighter aircraft had been expended for the fiscal year June 1942. But there was money in the budget for attack aircraft, and to get the P-51 in production, North American Aircraft Company designer Dutch Kindelberger added bomb racks and dive brakes to the P-51 Apache (the RAF designation "Mustang" was substituted in July) airframe and designated it as an attack bomber, the A-36. The installation of the bomb racks (which also could carry external fuel tanks) and dive brakes required a total redesign of the wing. The racks were located outboard, close to the landing gear strut, to minimize structural load during taxiing and takeoff. The bomb rack placement permitted prop clearance when releasing the bombs. The high diving speed of the A-36 presented a particular problem for the North American engineers, but the solution was literally next door. The Vultee factory, which produced the A-31 Vengeance dive bomber, was located next to the North American factory and visiting NAA engineers took the hydraulic dive brake system of the A-31 and adapted its design for the A-36. Four cast aluminum alloy lattice-shaped brakes were installed outboard of the ammunition bays in the wing panels. A selector lever to extend and retract the dive brake was located on the left side of the cockpit behind the throttle lever. A selector valve and hydraulic actuators, that upon activation extended the brakes out of the top and bottom of each

wing, controlled the dive brakes. The retracted brakes were housed in a faired recessed well in the wing contour. The diving speed with the dive brakes deployed was about 300 mph.

Republic P-47 Thunderbolt: Ultimate AAF Fighter Bomber

It was ironic that the P-47 that was originally designed as a high altitude escort became the premier fighter bomber, while the P-51, designed as a ground support fighter as the Mustang I for the RAF, would become the premier bomber escort. At the end of 1943 Gen. H.H. Arnold declared war on the *Luftwaffe* both in the air and on the ground in his "Down to earth" edict. Eighth Air Force Jugs returning from their escort missions dropped to the deck to expend their remaining ammo strafing ground targets of opportunity. The fuselage shackle, which could be used for a 500 pound bomb, was used to carry a drop tank for the escort mission. Republic consequently redesigned the wing after the so-called "universal" British wing by strengthening the mainplane and adding several external ventral

The **Republic P-47 Thunderbolt** was originally designed as a high altitude escort fighter and became America's premier fighter bomber while the P-51 was designed as a ground support fighter as the Mustang I for the RAF and would become the premier bomber escort. The P-47's robust construction and rugged air-cooled Pratt & Whitney engine made it an ideal fighter bomber. (AAF)

This P-47 is loaded for ground support with eight .50 caliber machine guns in the wings, two 500 pound bombs hung on the wing shackles, two triple M-10 bazooka launchers each firing three 4.5 inch RP M-8 rockets. On shorter missions bombs of various sizes could be carried on the fighter's centerline pylon instead of the auxiliary fuel tank. (AAF)

would replace the belly bombs, or the two underwing bombs would be replaced by 150 gallon auxiliary tanks and a 500 pound bomb would be carried on the belly shackle.

In the fall of 1943, the VIII FC was evaluating the role of the Thunderbolt as a fighter bomber. Maj. Loren McCollom, CO of the 353rd Fighter Group, tested the P-47's dive bombing capabilities flying training sorties over the 353rd base at Metfield. On 25 November the first 8th Air Force dive bombing mission of the war was scheduled for St. Omer-Fort Rouge airdrome. McCollom led four bomb carrying flights of the 351st Squadron escorted by the 350th and 352nd Squadrons and some fighters from the 78th Fighter Group. The plan was to dive from 15,000 feet following McCollom down in flights of four, dropping their 500 pound bombs at the altitude McCollom determined best for accuracy. However, five miles south of the airdrome the initial point was passed and heavy AA fire began. As McCollom rolled to approach the target a flak burst hit his fuel tank, engulfing his fighter in flames. McCollom bailed out, suffering serious burns, and was captured by *Luftwaffe* personnel on the ground. The remaining P-47s dropped their bombs from 8,000-10,000 feet, scoring only three hits on the target, and AA fire damaged six more P-47s.

Maj. Loren McCollom, CO of the 353rd Fighter Group, tested the P-47's dive-bombing capabilities on 25 November 1943 leading the first 8th Air Force dive-bombing mission of the war which was unsuccessful with only three bomb hits on target, six P-47s damaged by AA fire while McCollom was shot down and taken prisoner by the Germans. (Author)

pylons. The Thunderbolt could carry a variety of armament: either two underwing 1,000 pound bombs or three 500 pound bombs (one under each wing and one on the fuselage shackle), or a variety of bombs, drop tanks, and rocket clusters. Meanwhile, the 9th Air Force had been reformed as a tactical air force to support the invasion and subsequent land battles. But the 8th was beginning to transition its P-47 units to the P-51s, which were considered the better long range escort, and by March 1944 its P-47s were being mentioned in official reports as fighter bombers.

The Air Proving Grounds Command (APGC) at Eglin Field, FL, supervised extensive tests using various combinations of bombs and drop tanks that changed the P-47 from a fighter to a fighter bomber. In late 1943 several technical developments were introduced to enhance the P-47's lackluster low altitude performance. Water injection increased the horsepower of the Pratt & Whitney engine by 15%, horsepower from 2,300 to 2,535, and its top speed from 406 to 433mph. The so-called 13 foot "paddle blade" propeller replaced the 12 foot two inch propeller, increasing the rate of climb by 600 feet per minute and the speed as much as 10 mph.

The attachment of underwing shackles to carry bombs or drop tanks gave the P-47 new flexibility in its missions. The two-point suspension bomb rack/drop tank with sway braces had B-10 shackles that were mounted on small pylons extending from the underwing which, in the first types, decreased maximum speed by as much as 45 mph. Subsequent pylons were streamlined to reduce the speed loss by two-thirds. Initially the M series triple cluster rocket launchers were fitted, but were very inaccurate and slowed the fighter significantly. Later, the 5 inch HVAR rockets using Zero Length Launchers were fitted with better results. Rockets were not used in the ETO by the AAF to the extent of the RAF's 2nd TAF.

The configuration of ordnance and fuel tanks used varied to fit the target type and distance. A short mission allowed the use of maximum armament: two underwing 500 pound or 1,000 pound bombs, one belly-mounted 260 pound Fragmentation Bomb or 500 pound bomb, eight or ten 4.5 inch rockets, and eight .50 caliber machine guns. A longer mission required more fuel than the 305 gallons carried internally, so external fuel tanks replaced some or all three bombs. A 200 gallon external fuel tank

The Republic P-47 was the preeminent fighter bomber in the USAAF inventory, and probably one of the best of World War II (along with the Soviet Ilyushin Il-2 Sturmovik), because of its firepower and bomb carrying capacity and ruggedness. The P-47 was sturdily built and could withstand damage from the heaviest and most accurate AA defenses of World War II. It could withstand cannon hits from *Luftwaffe* fighters, and was particularly indestructible from the standard rear attack, and *Luftwaffe* victories over the P-47 were usually by deflection shots. However, four top P-47 aces in the ETO were lost to enemy AA fire during fighter bomber missions: Francis "Gabby" Gabreski (28 victories), Glenn Duncan (19.5v.), Walter Beckham (18v.), and Gerald Johnson (16.5v.), and were taken prisoner or evaded and escaped (Duncan). Between March 1943 and V-J Day the P-47 flew 546,000 sorties with a loss rate of 0.7%. Between June 1944 and the end of the war against Germany T-bolts destroyed 9,000 locomotives and 86,000 railway cars, 6,000 armored vehicles, and 68,000 road vehicles, and had an air combat kill ratio of 4.6 to 1.

Lockheed P-38 Lightning: Jack-of-All-Trades

The P-38 was Lockheed's first military project and had many innovative features. First design work began in 1937 under Clarence "Kelly" Johnson and H.L. Hibbard to meet the USAAC specifications for a high-altitude interceptor that also spawned the P-40 and P-39. The first USAAC twin-engine, single seat interceptor was the first to have a turbo-supercharger, the first to exceed 400 mph, and the first to use the twin boom configuration, and it was to be powered by the 12 cylinder Allison V-1710, which had recently passed its 150 hour approval tests. However, these innovations conspired to delay the development of the fighter and caused problems throughout its Mediterranean and European combat career. Early in its career it was plagued by a compressibility problem that was eventually overcome by re-engineering. It was claimed that every P-38 in the ETO had at least one unscheduled complete engine change. The turbo-superchargers were difficult and required attentive handling by experienced pilots. The AAF just didn't have the time to train newly arrived pilots to overcome the Lightning's peculiarities in combat. Most P-38 pilots were happy to transition to the less demanding P-47s and P-51s when they came available. Winston Churchill facetiously remarked that the P-38 was a blessing "quite effectively disguised."

The P-38 has been described as a jack-of-all-trades, master of none. In the early stages of the war in the ETO and MTO the P-38 performed adequately as a bomber escort and fighter aircraft, but the transformation of the P-38 into an effective fighter bomber/dive bomber came about as its previous escort responsibility was taken away. Early in its career in the ETO its Allison engine limited its effectiveness as both a fighter and escort. However, because the twin Allisons were located in two outboard nacelles, the fighter was a very stable gun platform and heavy armament could be concentrated in the nose of the fighter without the need of a propeller synchronizing gear. The nose compartment mounted four .50 caliber machine guns with 500 rpg firing for 41.5 seconds and a 20mm Hispano-Suiza cannon with 150 rounds that fired for 13.5 seconds. The ordnance carried could be two 500 or 1,000 pound bombs or ten 4.5 inch rockets or ten 4.5 inch rockets with two 500 pound bombs, or up to a 4,000 pound load of external stores.

In the ETO, as P-47s and then P-51s took over escort duties, the 8th Air Force decided to use the P-38 in ground attack and short-range escort missions. After D-Day P-38 units were flying escort and attacking targets of opportunity. As the *Luftwaffe* was driven from the air, the Lightning's role moved more and more to the fighter bomber role. When Gen. James Doolittle assumed command of the 8th Air Force in mid-1944 he decided that P-47 and P-38 groups would be equipped with the P-51 for both escort and ground attack missions. P-47 commanders did not agree with the decision, as they felt the Thunderbolt's great diving speed, heavy armament, and rugged airframe gave it an advantage over the Mustang. ETO P-38 commanders, on the other hand, felt that their J-models were not yet an effective aircraft, and that the P-51 had more potential. Since the Italian campaign had become a secondary theater, 15th Air Force Commander Nathan Twining and MAAF commander ACM Sir Arthur Tedder were happy to receive the P-38s downgraded in the ETO. So was Gen. George Kenney, commander of the Fifth Air Force in the Pacific, where the P-38's long range capability, high altitude performance, and speed made it the ideal fighter against Japanese fighters in the widespread and warmer Pacific island-hopping campaign.

P-38 Droopsnoots

An interesting P-38 development was the "Droopsnoot," which was a modified P-38J having its nose guns and metal nose gun fairing removed and replaced by a Plexiglas nose fairing with a flat bomb-aiming window on its underside. Entry and exit was through a hatch located on the top of the nose and an escape hatch was provided at the bottom. Two additional windows on each side behind the Plexiglas nose fairing furnished additional light. The bombardier, who had previously completed a tour in bombers, "sat" in a reclining seat in the cramped compartment. The shorter time of the short-range missions usually flown by the Droopsnoot compensated for this discomfort. Crammed into the front of the snoot was a Norden Bombsight with a PDI (Pilot's Directional Indicator) and a panel on the lower left side containing bomb indicator lights and arming and selector switches. Forward of this panel was an altimeter, airspeed indicator, air temperature gauge, and clock. The bombardier had an interphone connection with the pilot, and was able to transmit on the radio if the pilot's radio was set to do so. The snoot had its own independent oxygen system with a demand-type regulator and flow meter. For the bombardier's comfort there was a relief tube and a heating duct and bombing window defroster. For the bombardier's safety there was an armor-plated seat and floor, a crash pad, and a bombing window defroster. A K-24 camera was mounted in the 20mm cannon shell ejector chute to take bomb strike photos.

Droopsnoot, "B-38" mission bomb loads varied according to target distance. External fuel tanks were carried on longer missions that decreased the bomb load. During operations the Droopsnoot led eight conventional P-38s carrying bombs. The mission was flown in a normal fighter formation until ten minutes from the initial point, at which

The nose compartment of the **Lockheed P-38 Lightning** mounted four .50 caliber machine guns with 500rpg and a 20mm Hispano-Suiza cannon with 150 rounds. These guns combined with up to a 4,000 pound load of external stores made the P-38 a potent fighter bomber. (AAF)

The **P-38 Droopsnoot** was a modified P-38Js having its nose guns and metal nose gun fairing removed and replaced by a Plexiglas nose fairing with a flat bomb-aiming window on its underside. The bombardier sat in a reclining seat in the cramped nose compartment operating a Norden Bombsight with a PDI. (AAF)

time the formation closed up to the tight, wing tip to wing tip bombing formation. On the way to the target the formation cruised at an altitude about 2,000 to 3,000 feet above the bombing altitude. On the turn at the bomb run altitude was lost at a rate of 1,000 feet per minute until the desired bombing altitude was attained. The bombardier took over at the bomb run turn and a 30 second bomb run at 210 to 270 mph at 10,000 to 20,000 feet. Several methods of bomb release were used. While lining up the target on the Norden bombsight the bombardier counted down from ten on the radio to all P-38s for bomb release. Or on sight the formation would simultaneously release their bombs when the bombardier released. Or by connecting the automatic release on the Norden to the VHF radios of the formation so that when the Norden bombsight indices crossed the target all bombs in the formation were released by radio signal.

The Droopsnoots had some success against large military and industrial installations, airfields, and marshaling yards. Post strike analysis showed the Droopsnoot to have comparable results against these targets as heavy and medium bombers. The fighter bombers did more damage to airdromes when they dropped several tons of fragmentation bombs on the runway and facilities. They were ineffective against pinpoint targets, such as bridges and buildings, as the bomb patterns were too dispersed. The reason for its lack of success was attributed to the lack of training of the fighter pilot in flying the tight, wing tip to wing tip formations necessary to attain a good bombing pattern. Another factor was the inability of the lead pilot to make corrections as given by the bombardier from the PDI. Also the P-38's design as a fighter and its speed made it difficult to be a stable bombing platform and maintain formation when making the corrections indicated by the PDI. Another drawback of the Droopsnoot was that it carried fewer bombs and had a shorter range than a medium bomber, and certainly a heavy bomber. The ideal target for the Droopsnoot formation was one having light AA defenses, whose destruction did not require a heavy bomb tonnage, was relatively large and was within 500 miles. It was determined that the P-38 could be better employed as a dive bomber.

North American P-51 Mustang: Fighter Bomber turned Fighter Escort
In April 1940, the British approached North American Aviation to build the Curtiss P-40 for the RAF. However North American had other ideas, and proposed that it would build a better fighter using the P-40 Allison V-1710 engine. The British agreed, stipulating that due to the grave war

situation in Europe the prototype had to be completed in 120 days. North American president J.H. "Dutch" Kindelberger and his design team, Raymond Rice and Edgar Schmued, incredibly completed the NA-73 in 117 days, although the engine was not ready for an additional six weeks. The NP-73 flew for the first time on 26 October 1941, and it demonstrated notable performance due to its innovative laminar flow wing that was to become the standard for most future high speed fighter designs. AAF test pilot Robert Chilton tested two NA-73s designated as the XP-51, and the USAAF was impressed enough to order 150. The RAF ordered 620 as the Mustang I, with deliveries starting in November 1941, and another 150 were ordered as the Mustang II (55 were repossessed by the AAF to be converted to the F-6A photo recon aircraft). The low altitude Allison engine made the Mustang I unsuited for air to air combat, which took place at higher altitudes in the ETO, and these models were relegated to ground attack by the RAF. In England the Rolls Royce Merlin 60 was fitted to the Mustang I airframe, which was to establish the Mustang as the "Cadillac of the Air" and ultimate long range escort fighter, relegating the P-47 to ground support missions. In England the Rolls Royce Merlin 60 was fitted to the Mustang I airframe, which was to define the Mustang as one of, if not the elite fighter of the war. In the meantime, the Air Force had accepted 500 Allison-powered A-36s, the ground attack version of the P-51, and 310 Allison-powered P-51As. The RAF received 50 Allison Mustangs as the Mustang II and 35 others to be modified to F-6Bs. The A-36 was briefly named the "Invader" and the first P-51s the "Apache," but the RAF designation "Mustang" was the adopted name for all P-51 models. The first Merlin-powered Mustangs were the P-51B and C (RAF Mustang III). The American-built Merlins were licensed to Packard, and the USAAF ordered 2,200 before its Merlin Mustang had ever flown. The B and C models were identical, with the B being built in Inglewood and the C in Dallas, and both began operations in December 1943. A combined total of 3,749 (1,999 Bs and 1,750 Cs) were built, of which 910 were shipped to the RAF and 91 were converted to the F-6C (a total of 482 F, photo recon, versions were completed to F-6A/B/C/D/K from P-51/51A/C/D/K respectively). The P-51D was the first major design change that was to give the Mustang its classic lines. The fuselage cockpit fairing was cut down to the tail plane to permit the elegant teardrop canopy to be fitted and thus eliminate the blind spot created by the faired cockpit. A dorsal fin was added to compensate for keel loss. The D carried six .50 machine guns instead of four, moved the wing slightly forward, and provided

The **North American P-51 Mustang** lacked the massive firepower of the P-47 as the P-51D was armed with six .50 caliber wing guns and could carry two 1,000 pound bombs or ten underwing rockets or six bazooka rockets and two 500 or 1,000 pound bombs. Its inline, liquid-cooled Merlin engine made it vulnerable to AA and ground fire. (AAF)

rocket launchers. The D was the most numerous P-51 model with 7,956 being produced, including 876 Mustang IVs for RAF. The 1,337 K models were similar to the Ds. The H was the last production model (555 built), and was the fastest with a speed of 487 mph. Neither the K nor H saw operational service, as the war ended in the Pacific and contracts for an additional 3000 were canceled. Some 15,367 Mustangs were built and helped to change the course of the war in the ETO, allowing American bombers to penetrate into German-held territory under continuous escort protection.

The *Luftwaffe* had been virtually driven from European skies, and an VIII Fighter Command HQ decision was made to allow its pilots to drop to the deck to strafe targets of opportunity after their escort duties ended. The P-51s lacked the massive firepower of the P-47, as the P-51D was armed with six .50 caliber wing guns carrying 1780 total rounds: 350 rpg (32 seconds) for each inboard gun and 270rpg (22 seconds) for each center and outboard gun. The Mustang could carry two 1,000 pound bombs or ten 4.5 inch rockets or six 4.5 inch rockets and two 1,000 pound bombs.

The Mustangs did considerable damage to *Luftwaffe* airdromes and targets of opportunity, but suffered about four times the losses in ground attack than they did in aerial combat. If the pilot closed to 250 yards or less on his target the six MGs were sufficient, but at that range the pilot had to evade the AA and flying debris during the attack. P-51 pilots would fly seven to eight hours of tedious and tiring bomber escort duty and then drop down to spend a dangerous hour as a fighter bomber. Later, when more Mustangs reached the ETO, P-51s were sent on longer range (than the P-47) pure fighter bomber sorties against *Luftwaffe* airfields strongly protected by experienced *Luftwaffe* AA batteries. The Mustang's liquid-cooled Merlin engine, its radiator, and web of coolant-carrying hoses and pipes were vulnerable to even small arms fire. A pilot whose Mustang received a hit in the cooling system had only a short time to convert his 400 mph diving speed into enough altitude to bail out. Although many P-51s returned to base with considerable damage, many crashed into the ground at 400 mph when the aircraft's control surfaces or control mechanisms were damaged by AA fire. The P-47 and P-38 were much better suited for ground attack than the Mustang. Again, it was ironic that the Mustang that was ordered by the RAF as a ground attack fighter would become a superlative high altitude escort and the Thunderbolt that was designed as a high altitude escort would become the superlative ground attack fighter!

The **Bell P-39 Airacobra** was an overweight, underpowered, high maintenance fighter that was useless over 12,000 feet and needed to be protected on its ground support missions by medium and high cover fighters. The P-39 had limited bomb-carrying capacity but did have heavy armament; a 37mm cannon and two .50 machine guns in the nose and four .30 caliber machine guns in the wing which the Russians used to good advantage as a ground strafer. (AAF)

The Mustang was an amazing aircraft from the time of its inspired creation until the end of the war, when it was probably the best piston-engined fighter of World War II. In its 13 months of combat the Mustang recorded the destruction of nearly 5,000 Axis aircraft in the air. Although its superb interceptor and escort qualities precluded it from becoming an equally superb fighter bomber, through sheer numbers it did destroy an additional 4,000 Axis aircraft on the ground, which when combined with its aerial victories accounted for more than half of the aircraft destroyed by all AAF units in Europe in 1944-45.

The Tally: 8th and 9th Air Force P-47s, P-51s, and P-38s

Aircraft Type	Sorties	Air Victories	Ground Victories	Losses
P-47	423,435	3,082	3,202	3,077
P-51	213, 873	4,950	4,131	2,520
P-38	129,849	1,771	749	1,758
Total	**767,157**	**9,803**	**8,082**	**7,355**

Bell P-39 Airacobra: Soviet Fighter Bomber

Bell Aircraft's art deco P-39 Airacobra has a place in World War II aviation history as a symbol of America's being unprepared for war and its overconfidence in its aircraft designs. The P-39 possessed two unique features that were dictated by its heavy nose armament, the most unusual of which was the placement of the engine behind the pilot, while the second was that it was the first AAC fighter with retractable tricycle landing gear. From the onset of the design the Bell people were enamored with the American Armaments Corporation's T-9 37mm cannon, which was to be fired through the propeller hub. To do so meant that the engine needed to be placed in the fuselage, directly above the rear half of the wing. A ten-foot drive shaft passed under the cockpit floor to couple the engine to the propeller reduction gear.

The power plant was the Allison liquid-cooled, 12 cylinder inline V-1710 with an integral single-stage, single-speed supercharger that produced 1,100 to 1,300hp. The deletion of the turbo-supercharger on the early Allisons has always been brought into question. At the time of its development America had no reliable turbo-supercharger, and P-39 wind tunnel tests showed it to have numerous aerodynamic and technical problems that precluded it from becoming an interceptor without expensive and time consuming changes. During its production run the P-39's performance remained constant, as Bell engineers checked the weight increases which beset other fighter designs. The Q model was only 200 pounds heavier (empty) than the D.

With the development of other fighter types, the AAF decided to banish the P-39 to an advanced training role and many pilots remembered its performance as a trainer. The Airacobra did see limited AAF combat in North Africa and Italy, and more so in the Pacific, but was generally held in low regard. There were 2,150 Airacobras in inventory in early 1944 and these were released for sale or lend-lease. However, the Soviets utilized their Lend-Lease P-39s and P-63 Kingcobras that they used in large numbers (4,743 P-39s and 2,400 P-63s) to great effect in its proper role as a low level attack aircraft against German Panzer columns.

The P-39 Ds (923 built) and Ns (2,095 built) were the versions most used by the AAF (there were 4,905 Q models built but the majority went to Russia, 75 went to the AAF). The P-39D-1 and P-400 equipped the 81st and 350th Fighter Groups in North Africa and Italy, where they saw considerable action as they supported the Allied advance up the Italian boot attacking German infantry, armor, transport, and supply depots. The 322nd Fighter Group, the Black "Tuskegee Airmen" unit, flew the P-39Q models while flying routine patrol missions over Italy during the first months of 1944. The D model was equipped with self-sealing fuel tanks, extra armor plate, and a shackle for a 500 pound bomb or drop tank. The armament on the D-2 was a 37mm cannon, two .50 machine guns in the nose, and four .30 caliber machine guns in the wing. The D-1 was armed with a 20mm cannon in place of the 37mm. The D-3 and -4 models were special ground attack models with extra armor plate. The Q model retained the nose 37mm cannon and two .50 caliber machine guns in the nose, but deleted all wing guns, which were sometimes replaced by a pod under each wing that held one .50 caliber machine gun. The P-39 was originally designed to be America's principal fighter, capable of intercepting any enemy fighter, but developed into an overweight, under powered, high maintenance fighter that was useless over 12,000 feet and needed to be protected on its ground support missions by medium and high cover fighters.

The 81st Fighter Group equipped its 91st and 92nd Squadrons with the P-39 Airacobra, but the aircraft was to play only a minor role in the air fighting in the MTO, as there was a shortage of spare parts and their mechanics had no training in P-39 maintenance. At the end of January 1943 there were no more than 25 P-39s combat ready between the two squadrons.

Curtiss P-40 Warhawk: Used Everywhere for Everything
Because it appeared there was little chance that high-altitude bombers could attack the continental US, 1930s AAC strategy was influenced by the theoretical need for long range bombers, while pursuits (fighters) were to meet the need for ground attack and coastal defense. Pursuit aviation was characterized by low-altitude performance and rugged construction. When the war broke out for America on 7 December 1941 the P-40, which dated back to early 1937, was already obsolete, but implausibly remained in production until December 1944, by which time over 14,000 were produced. Throughout the war the design was continuously upgraded and improved, and the production numbers and longevity of the P-40 reveal that Donovan Berlin's design had something going for it. But the weight increases associated with these changes kept P-40 performance below that of the P-38, P-47, or P-51. The Curtiss P-40 and the Bell P-39 design, both under the "bombardment over pursuit" concept, were to make up over half of AAF overseas fighter strength until July 1943. By July 1945 one P-40 group was still operational, but the P-39 had seen very little combat anywhere. Throughout the war, from Chennault's Flying

The **Curtiss P-40 Warhawk** was a stable gun platform and its six .50 caliber machines guns were more than adequate and the centerline bomb shackle could mount a 500 pound bomb and external stores could be carried on the underwing racks. The P-40 was the only fighter available at the time and its virtues kept it flying with the Allied air forces in all theaters, in a variety of roles until the end of the war. (AAF)

Tigers onward, P-40 pilots were able to utilize the fighter's strengths to advantage against superior performance, maneuverability, and firepower. With the introduction of the P-38, P-47, and P-51, the P-40 was not needed as a fighter, but the strength of its airframe and firepower and armament load allowed it to continue as a journeyman fighter bomber in secondary theaters, such as Italy and the CBI.

Like the P-39, the P-40 languished in the poor performance of its Allison engine above 12,000 feet, and the lack of a supercharger consigned the fighter to low and medium altitude operations. It couldn't climb or run and its range was limited, but it could dive and turn with a Me-109. The cockpit was cramped and noisy but did offer good visibility. To maintain a straight and level course the rudder needed constant attention. The fighter was a stable gun platform, and its six .50 caliber machines guns were more than adequate. The P-40 was the only fighter available at the time, and its virtues kept it flying with the Allied air forces in all theaters in a variety of roles until the end of the war.

The installation of the Packard-built Rolls-Royce Merlin in the P-40Fs did increase performance, but not as much as it did for the P-51 Mustang, as the Warhawk's mid-1930s engineering prevented modifications to increase performance. The RAF Desert Air Force utilized the good low level performance of their export P-40E Kittyhawks and Tomahawks to good advantage in North Africa, hitting Rommel's critical fuel and supply depots, infantry, and even Panzers. They fitted a centerline bomb shackle that could carry a 500 pound bomb, and some versions carried a wing rack that could carry four 50 pound bombs. On USAAF models nose guns were deleted in the D-model, but four .50 caliber machine guns were mounted in the wing. The E-model carried six. .50 caliber machine guns in the wing with 280rpg at 24 seconds duration, and the centerline bomb shackle could mount a 500 pound bomb; external stores could be carried on the underwing racks. The AAC 57th Fighter Group went into combat in North Africa and adopted the successful ground attack tactics used by the RAF. To maintain that any other fighter bomber could have performed better than the P-40 over North Africa and Italy has no meaning, because the aircraft and its pilots were available when they were needed and did the job required of them until the better fighter bomber came along.

Northrop P-61 Black Widow: Night Interdiction Unused
After the war began in Europe and the *Luftwaffe* was bombing English cities at night, American military planners envisioned enemy long range bombers attacking US coastal cities at night. The Emmon Board of the AAC drew up a preliminary proposal in late 1940 for a twin-engine aircraft to operate at night, manned by a pilot and an "operator of a device to detect aircraft in the dark" (the designers were not told any details about radar). On 21 October Northrop was presented the proposal, and on 17 December, less than two years after the company's founding, Northrop Aircraft designers John Northrop and Walter Cerny had their design proposal for an AAC design specification for a large radar-carrying, long range, high performance night fighter approved. Northrop's reputation led to a contract for two XP-61 prototypes on 11 January 1941. Even before the XP-61's first flight, the necessity for the development of an operational night fighter led to the order of 13 YP-61s on 10 March, 150 more on 1 September, and 410 on 12 February 1942. Finally, on 21 May 1942 test pilot Vance Breese flew the XP-61 on a successful initial flight. The XP-61 was a twin boomed, cantilever mid-wing fighter powered by two Pratt & Whitney R-2800 radial engines and armed with four fixed ventral 20mm cannons and a dorsal GE turret with four .50 cal. machine guns. The twin engines were housed in twin nacelles that tapered towards the vertical tailplanes that were connected by a horizontal tailplane with control flaps. It was crewed by three: the pilot, the radar operator in the nose, and the observer/gunner situated above the pilot. At 25,000 lbs it was as large as

The Northrop P-61 Black Widow was America's only purpose-built night fighter and as such had only limited use during nocturnal interdiction missions against enemy road and rail transport. There are few photos available of P-61s carrying ordnance; shown is a one mounting four 5 inch HVAR rockets on Zero Length Launchers. (AAF)

a medium bomber, but had fighter speed and maneuverability. The aileron surfaces were very small, and were mounted at the wing tip to give the necessary roll for a turn. A small set of retractable spoilers located forward of the flaps performed as ailerons, so the P-61 was able to quickly reverse direction. The test fighters were painted black, hence the name "Black Widow." The first of 200 P-61As were delivered in November 1943. The first 37 had dorsal turrets, and the remainder was delivered without, as they caused buffeting (the observer/gunner position was deleted). The problem was solved, and all P-61s from 201 onward had the dorsal turret. Throughout its operational life the P-61 maintained its original appearance with little external change. The Pratt & Whitney R-2800 engines were minimally upgraded in the A and B models, and the supercharged -73 increased the maximum speed from 370 to 430 mph in the P-61C models. The first operational P-61s were delivered in the Pacific in early 1944 and in the ETO in May 1944. The P-61 was a successful night fighter design, but it entered service too late to have any serious effect on the outcome of the air war, as neither the *Luftwaffe* nor Japanese were able to raise any night attacks. Of the 706 Black Widows produced, there were 200 P-61As, 450 P-61Bs, and 517 P-61Cs, of which only 41 were produced before the contract for the remaining 476 was terminated as the Pacific war ended. The P-61 was the forerunner for post war all-weather fighters and remained in front line service until the early 1950s.

In March 1944 the 9th Air Force was in the process of building up to full strength when it was assigned the 422nd Night Fighter Squadron (NFS), followed by the 423rd and 425th. It wasn't until July that any of the squadrons became operational because of delays in receiving the fighter from America, getting its crews ready for operations, and also due to a much belated controversy about its superiority to the Mosquito. Its first missions were chasing V-1 Buzz bombs. It was not until the Black Widow units moved to the Continent in late July that they would operate primarily against *Luftwaffe* night intruders and take part in some nighttime interdiction sorties against road and rail movement. Since the Allies ruled the daytime skies the Germans were forced to move troops and supplies at night. The P-61 was ineffective in its nighttime interdiction role, as radar to detect transport movement on the ground had not been developed and flare and searchlight missions were ineffective. It was unfortunate that the Allies never developed a large night fighter force equipped with radar to harass the German transportation around the clock.

USAAF Fighter Bombing Tactics
Dive Bombing Attack

Dive bombing was an attack from 8,000 to 15,000 feet at angles of 20 to 50°, with the bombs being released from 6,000 to 1,500 feet. Since the bomb release was over 1,000 feet instantaneous fuses were used. Dive bombing tactics were determined by target type, AA concentration, and weather/wind. High-level dive bombing attacks were made at steep angles, usually between 60° and 70°, which were imperative for accuracy. It was difficult for the pilot to see straight down to the target without tipping the wing. Target identification needed to be precise but was difficult, and often the leader would use the R/T to ID the target to his pilots. As he was about to dive the leader would R/T "Bomb switches on," followed by "Diving in 10 seconds" and "Diving now." The dive was slowed by dropping the main gear, whose fairing acted as a dive brake (except in the A-36, which had wing-mounted dive brakes). This would allow the pilot time to line up the target before releasing his bombs. The attacking aircraft had to be properly trimmed, and the aileron as well as rudder trim had to constantly be used. Following their leader into the attack, the pilots released their bombs at 2,000 to 3,000 feet. After releasing the bombs an intense evasive turn was

A P-47 (arrow top left) in a low level dive bombing attack which was most accurate dive attack but also the most dangerous unless AA was not present or had been suppressed by strafing or a ground-based artillery anti-flak barrage. (AAF)

made in a predetermined direction before reforming in line abreast. If the target was heavily defended, the attack would be made out of the sun and/or from two directions in order to reduce the AA proficiency.

Low and Minimum Level Dive Bombing
Low level dive bombing attacks were usually from 20° to 30°, with the bombs being released at 800 feet at high speed and short range in order to evade small arms and light flak, as well as the burst and debris from the explosions of the dropped bombs. Minimum altitude bombing was attacking on the level and on deck. It was the most accurate, but also the most dangerous, unless AA was not present or had been suppressed by strafing or a ground-based artillery anti-flak barrage.

Skip Bombing/Glide Bombing
Skip and glide bombing were used extensively in the Pacific by 5AF medium bombers. In the ETO after D-Day the type of targets and the bad weather prohibited the use of vertical dive bombing, and as a consequence glide bombing and skip bombing were used by AAF fighter bombers.

Skip bombing was a variation of minimum bombing, but the attacking aircraft went into a 10°-20° dive and pulled out just over the target. When instantaneous fuses were used the pilot was warned that it was for 250 pound bombs, 800 feet for 500 pound, and 1,500 feet for 1,000 pound. However, when using delay fuses (usually four second) the pilot could skip the bomb later in the dive. After releasing their bombs, pilots were to take immediate evasive action by turning sharply to the left or right; otherwise, they would stand a chance of being blown up by their own bombs which may skip along underneath the plane.

Glide bombing was a high speed, accelerating attack delivered at 30° to 55° without the use of flaps. It was soon found by operational experience that glide bombing had to be at least 30°; otherwise, even 1,000 pound bombs tended to bounce. This method gave the pilot more visibility, but also made him even more vulnerable to flak, so the initial element of surprise and the built up speed made the attacker a more difficult target for enemy AA fire going in and out.

Shortcomings of USAAF Fighter Bombers
The significant drawback of USAAF fighter bombers was their combat radius. With 2x500 pound bombs (thus unable to carry external fuel tanks) the P-38 and P-47 had a combat range of 260 miles, while the P-51 had a range of 325 miles. The short-range factor necessitated that fighter bomber airfields be located near the battle front.

Radius of Action: P-51, P-47, and P-38*

Aircraft	Take-off Weight (lb.)	Bomb Weight (lb.)	Fuel (US gal.) Internal	External	Radius (mi.)
P-38L	19,500	1x1,000 (uw)	410	1x165 (uw)	400
	18,500	2x500 (uw)	410	--------	260
	19,500	2x1,000 (uw)	410	--------	250
	19,500	----------	410	2x165 (uw)	600
	17,500	----------	410	---------	290
P-47D	14,500	----------	370	---------	280
	15,150	----------	370	1x108 (cl)	400
	16,150	2x500 (uw)	370	1x108 (cl)	360
	15,500	2x500 (uw)	370	---------	260
	16,500	2x1,000 (uw)	370	---------	230
	16,400	----------	370	2x150 (uw)	575
P-51B/C/D	9,800	---------	269	--------	350
	10,800	2x500 (uw)	269	-------	325
	10,800	--------	269	2x75 (uw)	650
	11,200	---------	269	2x108 (uw)	750

(uw) = underwing (cl) = centerline
* Conditions (from AAF Proving Ground at Eglin data):
(a) Warm-up and takeoff at 10 minutes at normal power
(b) Climb to 10,000 feet at normal rated power
(c) Cruise to target at 10,000 feet at 200 mph (P-47) 220 mph (P-38 & P-51)
(d) Jettison drop tanks at target
(e) 5 minute combat at war emergency power and 15 minute combat at military power
(f) Cruise back to base at 10,000ft. at 210 mph (P-47) and 230 mph (P-38 & P-51)
(g) No account taken for decreased fuel consumption during descent
(h) Allowance made for 30 minute reserve fuel at minimum cruising power
(i) No allowance made for formation flight or evasive action other than 20 minutes combat

A 5th Air Force B-25 swoops over a Japanese destroyer at mast height during a strafing-skip bombing attack in the Pacific. (AAF)

The P-51 had the lowest fuel consumption of the three main USAAF fighters: P-51B: 65 gallons per hour; P-47D: 140 gph; and the P-38J: 144 gph

Comparing the Fighter Bomber to the Light and Medium Bomber

In addition to its strafing/ground attack role, the adaptable fighter bomber was able to carry out a number of tasks: light and medium bomber escort, short and long range interdiction missions, short and long range fighter sweeps, and anti-shipping sorties. In contrast to light and medium bombers, the fighter bomber was mission-adaptable and not confined to one target. They could go from an interdiction target and proceed to a ground support target on the same mission. The fighter bomber could be rearmed, refueled, and its pilot briefed more quickly than a bomber crew, which enabled fighter bomber units to carry out three or four missions per day as compared to the usual two for light and medium bombers. The fighter bomber boasted imposing firepower and ordnance, and compared to medium bombers could deliver more ordnance per day and inflict more damage for effort expended. The fighter bomber was able to attack targets with more precision than medium bombers, with the exception of targets

In terms of damage caused for effort expended the fighter bomber was more efficient than light or medium bombers and was able to attack most targets with more accuracy. A 12 plane Mustang squadron was three times more effective as a six plane **B-26** squadron on a daily mission basis. (AAF)

requiring pattern bombing, such as extensively prepared positions or gun areas. Being able to deliver their ordnance at lower altitudes, they were less vulnerable to heavy enemy AA than the higher flying bombers. Enemy fighters were of little consequence at this stage of the war, but small-caliber flak was a major concern, as it was effective to 3,000 feet and not visible.

When comparing the number of missions that could be flown in a day, the weight of bombs delivered per mission and the number of aircrew and ground crew required per mission, the fighter bomber was more efficient than the medium bomber. A 12-plane Mustang squadron carrying a maximum 2,000 pounds of bombs per aircraft was able to fly three squadron missions per day and deliver 72,000 pounds of bombs. To achieve this tonnage delivered approximately 300 officers and men were required, giving a tonnage/personnel factor of 240. A six-plane B-26 Marauder squadron carrying 4,000 pounds per aircraft could fly two missions per day and deliver 48,000 pounds of bombs, requiring approximately 600 personnel for a tonnage/personnel factor of 80. The fighter bomber could be refueled and armed and the pilot briefed more quickly than the medium bomber. After D-Day, fighter bomber and light/ medium bomber squadrons moved to forward airfields on the Continent. These fields were newly constructed or quickly repaired former *Luftwaffe* fields, and therefore had small dispersal areas and narrow taxiways, which favored the fighter bomber.

In terms of damage caused for effort expended the fighter bomber was more efficient than light or medium bombers, and was able to attack most targets with more accuracy. The fighter bomber was particularly effective against targets such as motor vehicles, armor, rail transport, and strong points, but was less effective against targets requiring pattern bombing, such as heavily defended positions. The major threat to the fighter bomber was not the *Luftwaffe*, which rarely appeared over the battlefield in daylight, but German flak. However, the fighter bomber formation was less vulnerable to heavy flak. Fighter bomber squadrons required slightly more maintenance than the pure fighter squadrons. More armorers were needed for the fusing and maintenance of bombs, and the bomb racks, fusing, and release apparatus required only regular maintenance and were mostly trouble free.

USN/USMC Dive Bombing and Bombers

Of the three services, the Navy and Marines pioneered and then utilized dive bombing to the greatest extent. The first use of dive bombing should be probably credited to Leonard Warden Bonney, an American soldier of fortune who was taught to fly by the Wright Brothers. Bonney flew a Moisant pusher biplane for the Mexican government headed by Gen. Venustiano Carranza during the Civil War of 1913-15. During 1913 Bonney threw small bombs armed with shotgun shell detonators developed by Mexican mining engineers against revolutionaries in Tampico and Vera Cruz. While in shallow diving attacks from about 1,500 feet, Bonney would aim his aircraft directly at the target without using any sighting device, dropping the bombs just as he pulled out of his dive. Bonney claimed to hit his target about half the time while being hit by numerous bullets from the Revolutionaries on the ground. During WWI Bonney became a USN flight instructor and an early proponent of dive bombing.

It seems that dive bombing evolved in a number of air services during World War I, as both Allied and German pilots were reported to have used it in combat. The earliest successful dive bombing attack of World War I occurred in October 1914, when Royal Naval Air Service pilot Flt.Lt. R.G. Marix in a Sopwith Tabloid flew a surprise attack against the German Zeppelin hangars near Dusseldorf. Marix dropped 20 pound Cooper bombs with contact fuses and caused the hangar to collapse, destroying Zeppelin L.IX. Soon the possibility of destroying moving warships with a

The first use of dive-bombing should be probably credited to **Leonard Bonney**, an American soldier of fortune, while flying a Moisant pusher biplane for Mexican government during the Civil War of 1913-15. (Author)

single well-aimed bomb was investigated. Nonetheless, dive bombing saw haphazard use in World War I. US Air Service fliers training at Ellington Field, TX, practiced it during 1917-1918, dropping their bombs from wing racks controlled by wires leading to the pilot's cockpit. There is no record of the fliers of the AEF using dive bombing in the war.

After the war the dive bombing concept was sustained by a few devoted international disciples who maintained that dive bombing provided both aircraft survival and bombing accuracy, since the high altitude initial approach escaped enemy AA defenses and attained surprise, while the low altitude bomb release maximized accuracy. In the immediate postwar, when the Congress restrained the budgets of Army, Navy, and Marine aviation, these services sent their pilots to demonstrate dive bombing's potential with spectacular exhibitions performed at air shows.

The Marine Corps is credited with the first American combat use of dive bombing when in 1919 Lt. Lawson Sanderson, CO of VO-9M, flying a DH-4B, began experimenting with dive bombing against the guerrillas in Haiti and the Dominican Republic. Until that time aircraft had dropped their bombs from a level attitude, but Marine fliers found that they could achieve a far greater degree of precision by releasing their bombs while aiming their planes directly at their targets in a dive. After trying a number of methods to improve bombing accuracy, Sanderson decided on dropping his aircraft's nose in what was then considered a steep 45° dive directly at the target and releasing the bomb manually at an altitude of approximately

250 feet. Soon his squadron adopted the technique, using large canvas mail sacks to carry the bombs under the fuselage and releasing the bombs during the dive by pulling a draw rope around the end of the sack.

It is probable that Sanderson's attacks and those of World War I were, as defined by today's standards, actually glide bombing attacks of 40 to 70° from horizontal flight, not dive bombing attacks of 70 to 90° from the horizontal, as true, steep, powered dives were not possible in existing aircraft. Biplanes could dive bomb without wing flaps or diving brakes because the inherent speed impediment of struts, wires, fixed landing gear, etc. kept their speed under 150 miles per hour even in a wide-open vertical dive.

The first organized dive bombing attack occurred on 17 July 1929 when five De Havilland DH-4M aircraft of the Marine VO-1M under the command of Marine Maj. Ross Rowell flew a mission against guerilla forces under Augusto Sandino, which had surrounded the Marine garrison at Ocotal, Nicaragua. At 1230 Rowell and his flight took off from Managua with each aircraft carrying a full combat load of 600 rounds of ammunition for each of its machine guns, but only a partial load of 17

The first organized dive-bombing attack occurred on 17 July 1929 when aircraft of the VO-1M squadron under the command of Marine **Maj. Ross Rowell** flew a mission against guerilla forces which had surrounded the Marine garrison in Nicaragua. (USMC)

Luftwaffe **General Ernst Udet** attended the 1932 Cleveland Air Races and was so impressed by an American dive bombing demonstration that Germany adopted the technique and developed the famous JU-87 Stuka dive bomber. (Author)

pound fragmentation bombs could be carried as the aircraft had to carry a heavy fuel load for the long two hour flight.

Rowell had previously trained in dive bombing with the Army Air Service 3rd Attack Group at Kelly Field, TX, in 1923, and trained his pilots in dive bombing. He led the four DH-4s into a column formation and circled the town at 1,500 feet trying to locate the rebel and Marine positions, and then dove, firing their front machine guns on the way down and dropping bombs when targets presented themselves. As they pulled out of their dives the observers strafed the enemy with their rear cockpit machine guns. After the second passes the Sandinos began to withdraw from the onslaught of the first Marine air-ground combined action. Rowell later successfully demonstrated his dive bombing technique at the 1932 Cleveland Air Races, which was also attended by *Luftwaffe* General Ernst Udet, who was so impressed that Germany adopted the technique and developed the famous JU-87 Stuka dive bomber. Rowell retired from the Marine Corps as a Lt. General in 1946 after 40 years of distinguished service.

Combat missions in Nicaragua and fleet exercises had showed the potential of dive bombing. During Fleet Exercises it was found that solid cloud cover made high altitude bombing impossible, allowing ship gunners to concentrate their fire on attacking torpedo bombers. BuAer pointed out that the average low cloud ceiling throughout the world was approximately 4,000 feet, which put the continuation of the high altitude horizontal bombing by the Navy in question. But the Navy had too much tradition and too many resources invested in battleships and torpedo and horizontal bombers to rely solely on still unproven dive bombing. During the 1920s the military services used any scout or observation plane for dive bombing, including Jennies and DH-4s. But when more robust aircraft, such as the Curtiss F6C series, appeared they began to approximate modern dive bombing, and the USN initiated their quest of dive bombing in exercises to achieve greater bombing accuracy. In 1925 Capt. Joseph M. "Bull" Reeves took command of the Pacific Fleet's aviation squadrons and received seven new Curtiss Hawk F6C-ls for VF-2 on the carrier *Langley*. Reeves worked with Lt. Frank Wead to develop bombing techniques for attacking beach defenses during amphibious assaults. The exercises demonstrated that at the low altitudes required to minimize the dangers of bombing friendly forces, enemy AA fire would devastate any attacking aircraft. To minimize AA fire pilots were to approach the target at 10,000 feet, diving at high speed at up to 70° to minimize exposure to surprised ground fire.

On 13 December 1926 Reeves, then a Rear Admiral and commanding Aircraft Squadrons, Battle Fleet, observed the first formal dive bombing exercises ("light bombing," as it was then called) during annual fleet gunnery competition. VF-2, commanded by Lt.Cdr. Frank Wagner, flying the Curtiss F6C-2 and FB-5s, simulated a dive bombing attack on the Pacific Fleet in the first Fleet demonstration of the technique. One Marine and two Navy fighter squadrons and three Navy observation squadrons participated, making 45° dives (technically glides) from 2,500 feet and dropping 25 pound practice bombs at 400 feet. Wagner's VF-2 squadron scored 19 hits out of 45 drops on a 100 by 45 foot target, and dive bombing took a giant step on becoming the standard method of attack for the Navy's air force.

Meanwhile, dive bombing continued to prove itself, as during exercises late in 1933 two squadrons made simulated dive bombing attacks on the *USS Lexington* and *Saratoga* and were credited with 68 hits, while the simulated torpedo bomber attacks were considered not only ineffective but dangerous. In 1936 Adm. Reeves, promoted to head the US Fleet, outlined the responsibilities of carrier aircraft to limiting torpedo attacks to just before the main engagement and assigning dive bombers the primary responsibility for the destruction of enemy capital ships.

On 13 December 1926, **R.Adm. Joseph Reeves** (left) commanding Aircraft Squadrons, Battle Fleet, observed the Navy's first formal dive bombing exercises during annual fleet gunnery competition. (USN)

Each carrier group would include four aircraft squadrons: one squadron of VBFs (fighters with dive bombing capability), two squadrons of VSBs (scout bombers with dive bombing capability), and one squadron of VBs (dive bombers) or VTBs (torpedo bombers). The VBs were to carry 1,000 pound bombs. The VTBs would be capable of carrying torpedoes or 1,000 pound bombs to be dropped from high altitude using Norden bombsights.

Fleet Exercise 74, held in April 1938, finally and clearly vindicated the Navy's position on dive bombing in operations. Dive bombers off the *Lexington* attacked three cruisers and the battleships *Tennessee* and *Oklahoma*, hitting them with "nearly total surprise" and against "ineffective" AA fire. Five minutes later the *Lexington's* torpedo bombers attacked these two battleships, but encountered "heavy and effective" AA fire. The *Saratoga's* dive bombers attacked several cruisers and the battleship *California*, again with complete surprise, but the torpedo bombers from the *Saratoga* met very heavy anti-aircraft fire. Aircraft from the *Ranger* attacked the three cruisers with the same results as the other two carrier's attacks. Land-based PBYs and VPBs bombed the *Tennessee* and *New Mexico* horizontally from above 10,000 feet against very heavy and accurate AA fire. The Exercise not only demonstrated the vulnerability of the torpedo bombers, but also the vulnerability and the poor accuracy of the horizontal bombers that signaled an end to the Navy's reliance on high altitude horizontal bombing with the Norden bombsight. The Fleet Commander concluded by saying that he would not be able to defend his ships against a dive bombing attack.

Dive bombing feasibility took a further quantum leap as the first of the purpose-built dive bombing aircraft were designed in the early 1930s. While procurement quantities would be limited to smaller allocations of 40 to 100 units, these aircraft were the high tech developments of the day, featuring a variety of new aerodynamic designs, such as dive brakes, flaps, wing slots, enclosed cockpits, trim tabs, and spoilers, which gave pilots more control over their aircraft in every phase of the dive, as did retractable landing gear and controllable pitch propellers. But increased diving speeds caused a number of problems. The correct free fall of the bomb became critical, as larger bombs suspended between the landing gear legs showed an inclination to occasionally wobble in the slipstream and hit the gear struts when released. The small 25 pound fragmentation bombs carried under the wing well outboard of the propeller arc posed no problems, but 300 to 500 pound bombs mounted on the centerline had a tendency to hit the landing gear undercarriage upon release, causing the bomb's trajectory to deviate or to damage the gear. Since centerline bombs had to be carried near the bomber's longitudinal center of gravity, a method had to be developed to make sure that the bomb swung clear of the landing gear and propeller arc. A trapeze-like clutch was developed which mechanically swung the bomb well clear of the gear and propeller.

Dive bombing took a physical toll on the pilot, as faster diving speeds resulted in high-gravity "G" forces being imposed upon the pilot's body, with momentary black outs occurring due to the drainage of blood from the brain. The angle of the dive and its duration, plus the gravitational forces exerted during the pullout from the dive, dictated the extent and severity of the blackout. Protracted blackouts could cause the total loss of aircraft control, which was more or less remedied by the use of automatic devices that would take over the controls and pull the nose up. Attempts were made to keep blood from draining to the pilot's lower extremities, but it would not be until 10 years later inflatable abdominal dive belts and the "G" suit were introduced to effectively reduce gravitational forces on the human body.

The US Navy had the predilection of having every aircraft in its inventory to be capable of multiple uses. Dive bombing had become so important that Boeing redeveloped its stumpy little high performance

F4B-1 fighter, which had a top speed of 176 mph and a service ceiling of 27,000 feet in 1929. It was the first fighter capable of carrying a 500 pound bomb and was fitted with the new retractable carrier landing hook. It was easy to fly, and an entire cadre of 1930's USN pilots learned the basics of dive bombing in the Boeing F4B series of open cockpit fighter/bombers. The fixed gear F4Bs continued as the Navy's standard shipboard fighter until the late 1930s.

Also in 1929 the Curtiss F8C Helldiver was hastily adapted as a dive bomber, and the Helldiver designation would soon to become synonymous with dive bombing, and would ultimately be applied to three successive generations of Curtiss-built scout/dive bombers. It soon became evident purpose-built dive bombers would be required, and in 1929 the Navy drew up new specifications for what was to become its first true dive bomber.

By 1932 several manufacturers submitted promising designs, including the Curtiss-Wright XSBC-1 Helldiver II, which was a retractable-geared, parasol-winged monoplane with a canopy enclosing the two man crew. The single parasol wing created higher landing speeds and was incompatible with dive bombing, so in 1934 the Helldiver was made into a biplane with full-span lower wing flaps and a larger 700 hp engine, which allowed it to carry a 1,000 pound bomb. The new design was redesignated as the SBC-3, but continued to be called the Helldiver (II). When the first deliveries began to VS-5 on board the *USS Ranger* (CV-4) in July 1937 the second Helldiver was a vast improvement, and the nearly 200 SBC-3 and 4s would operate aboard several carriers, but by the time of Pearl Harbor the Helldiver II was already obsolete and largely relegated to the utility/training role.

In 1934 Chance Vought submitted a design for its Vought SB2U-1 Vindicator, a very advanced scout bomber that was to become the foundation for the entire next generation of naval combat aircraft. With a maximum 250 mph speed this tandem two-place enclosed cockpit retractable gear aircraft was the Navy's first monoplane scout bomber, boasting a number of innovations, such as a 1,500 pound bomb load, folding wings for easier deck stowage, and unique Venetian blind type leading edge slats to control diving speeds. The Vindicator was first flown in January 1936; the Navy was so impressed by its performance that a total of 169 were ordered and eventually flew from the *USS Lexington, Wasp, Saratoga*, and *Ranger*, setting new records in dive bombing accuracy.

By the late 1930s most of the supposition and problems associated with dive bombing had been resolved, and although the AAC still wavered on its commitment to dive bombing the Navy was confident that its commitment was headed in the right direction. Although its aircraft were not as numerous, fast, or modern as their Japanese and German opposite numbers, USN training and tactics were equal, if not better.

In 1939 Maj. Vernon Megee, USMC, presented an exceptionally comprehensive white paper at the War College which hypothetically

The **Curtiss Wright SBC-3 Helldiver II** was the Navy's first effective dive bomber when it came on board the USS *Ranger* in July 1937 but was obsolete and superceded by the time of Pearl Harbor. (USN)

In 1939 Marine Corps **Maj. Vernon Megee** presented an remarkably comprehensive white paper at the War College which hypothetically assessed the potential of dive-bombing which post-WWII combat records basically confirmed (USMC)

the Northrop BT-1 by the Northrop Corporation, which was a Douglas Aircraft Corporation subsidiary. Northrop was dissolved in September 1937, and Northrop designs continued production under Douglas. In November 1937 the BT-1 underwent many major modifications and the new model, the XBT-2, was the forerunner of the Dauntless. In 1939 both the US Navy and Marine Corps had placed orders for the new dive bombers, designated the SBD-1 and SBD-2 (the latter had increased fuel capacity and different armament). The former went to the Marine Corps in late 1940, and the latter went to the Navy in early 1941. The SBD-3 and -4 were followed by the -5, which was the most produced version. Over 2,400 of all versions were built.

The bomb displacement gear was a bomb cradle that carried bombs up to 1,600 pounds that was located on the bottom of the fuselage below the cockpit. Prior to the release of the bomb, the forked clamp would swing down and forward so that the bomb would clear the prop during dive bombing maneuvers. A 100 pound bomb or a small depth charge could be carried on racks on each wing. In the SBD-5 the bomb load was increased to 2,250 pounds with a 1,600 pound bomb under the fuselage and a 325 pound bomb or depth charge under each wing.

On 10 December 1941, VS-6 flying SBDs off the *Enterprise* were on an early morning patrol and made contacts with three Japanese submarine I-Boats. Ens. Perry Teaff attacked the diving I-70 and inflicted enough damage that it had to resurface later and was unable to dive again. At 1130, three SBDs of VB-6 took off from the *Enterprise* to check on the earlier I-Boat contacts. The Dauntless dive bombers flew a search pattern at 800 feet and discovered the surfaced I-70 moving northeast at high speed. One of the pilots was Lt. Clarence Dickinson, who had been shot down by

assessed dive bombing. Megee compared dive bombers to horizontal bombers and conclusively showed that dive bombers were on average three times more effective while likely to suffer only 10% higher losses. Horizontal bombers inflicted only 13% hits on battleships, whereas dive bombers scored better than 40%. These figures were worse against fast-moving destroyers, which were hit less than 2% of the time by high-altitude bombers and nearly 10% by dive bombers. Megee also investigated the effects of attacks from different dive angles and altitudes, and concluded that the Navy's preference of beginning steep dives from 8,000 feet and releasing bombs, depending on their size, from 3,000 to 1,000 feet provided the highest probability of a hit and the maximum security against AA fire. Post-WWII combat records basically confirmed these hypothetical findings.

The Douglas SBD Dauntless was arguably the preeminent American dive bomber of World War II while serving with the USN and USMC, and became the symbol of American resurgence after the Pearl Harbor attack. It earned the affectionate nickname of "**S**low **B**ut **D**eadly" (to signify her designation) in the Battle of the Coral Sea and the Battle of Midway. The SBD (Scout Bomber Douglas) monoplane was designed as a light bomber and reconnaissance aircraft. The Dauntless originated with the design of

The **Douglas SBD Dauntless** was arguably the preeminent American dive bomber of World War II while serving with the USN and USMC and became the symbol of American resurgence after the Pearl Harbor attack. (USN)

On 10 December 1941, *Enterprise* VS-6 SBD pilot, **Lt. Clarence Dickinson**, sunk the Japanese submarine I-70; scoring the first successful USN dive bombing attack of the war. (USN)

Zeros during the Pearl Harbor attack three days earlier. Dickinson climbed to the dive bombing altitude of 5,000 feet and dove into enemy AA fire to drop his bomb close amidships and saw the submarine sink as he left the area. Post-war Japanese records confirmed this first successful USN dive bombing attack.

The development of USN dive bombing reached its zenith in 1940, when Curtiss was allotted a contract to produce a heavyweight attack aircraft called the SB2C Helldiver, the third and last using this celebrated name to serve the Navy. Because of the challenging new specifications Curtiss, with its extensive experience in building Naval aircraft, first flew the XSB2C-1 in December 1940, after which it was delayed due to a number of aerodynamic and systems problems and by an entirely new factory at Columbus, OH, largely operated by inexperienced aircraft workers. Even after the prototype crashed the Navy still ordered nearly 600 Helldivers, but the program was halted until many changes were made, all of which tended to enlarge the already overweight airframe. When dive tests were resumed in November 1941 the XSB2C-1 crashed again, bringing the entire program to a halt for many months while the wing underwent a major redesign. Many other delays, including factory

labor problems and Congressional investigations, further delayed the SB2C's development. It would not fly its first combat mission until late 1943, flying with VS-9 from the *USS Essex*. The SB2Cs would take part in many of the late combats in the Pacific, and the Helldivers would bring to a close the era of the prop-driven dive bombers in USN and USMC service. Many would continue in service for many years with postwar reserve squadrons after nearly 4,000 variants of six different marks had been built in the United States and Canada.

During World War II horizontal bombing continued, but AA fire forced horizontal bombers ever higher, with each increase in altitude negatively affecting bombing accuracy, and the dive bomber continued its move to the vanguard of naval aerial warfare. Official Navy policy was to use high altitude precision bombing or torpedo bombing first to surprise enemy ships, and to divert attention from the dive bombers that would carry out the main attack. Against maneuvering targets, BuOrd concluded, the dive bomber "held a practical monopoly on effective attacks" but, nonetheless, dive bombing never completely displaced horizontal or torpedo bombing in Navy use. The Navy had spent two decades developing these three techniques for sinking ships from the air, and it was unwilling to give up on any of them. Navy carriers carried Douglas TBD Devastators, dual-purpose torpedo/dive bombers equipped with Norden bombsights for horizontal bombing; Vought SB2U Vindicators, dual-purpose scout aircraft capable of dive bombing; Grumman F4F Wildcats, fighter aircraft capable of dive bombing; and Douglas SBD Dauntless dive bombers. At the Battle of the Coral Sea in May 1942 the *Lexington* and *Yorktown* combined carried 42 F4F Wildcat fighters, 25 TBD Devastator torpedo bombers, and 74 SBD Dauntless dive bombers.

A typical combat strike attack was by a division of six SBDs in two sections of three aircraft in V formation. The first section was the "lead," and the second section was free to move to the left or right of the lead section, according to conditions. But often, the dive bomber force would consist of two or three divisions, along with TBD Avengers and fighters. In late 1944, SB2C Helldiver VB units adopted the four-plane division (two two-plane sections) for easier maneuvering and flexibility, similar to the fighter pilot's "Thatch Weave." The flight to the target was usually at 12,000 to 15,000 feet, depending on the weather. About 15 to 20 miles from the target the SBDs would decease altitude at about 5°, maintaining the same power setting, picking up speed while approaching the area above the target. The SBDs would then begin to break at very

The **Curtiss SB2C Helldiver** had many teething problems which delayed its introduction until late in 1943. The Helldiver participated in many of the late combats in the Pacific and brought to a close the era of the prop-driven dive bombers in USN and USMC service. (USN)

short intervals, quickly establishing the dive angle of 65° to 70°, and dove on the target as if sliding down a very narrow 5° cone where enemy AA guns could not track effectively. Ideally each attacker was at 70°, but each aircraft following at a slightly different angular path with respect to the target couldn't dive down the same path, or pull out in the same path. Anything less than 65° was too shallow and the bombs would fall short, while over 75° the pilot was leaning way over in the seat and very uncomfortable in seat straps, and not likely to retain accurate control and obtain a satisfactory hit and recovery.

During the bombing of the by-passed Japanese garrisons on the Marshall Islands during 1944-1945 the Fourth Marine Aircraft Wing plotted the fall of almost every bomb dropped. The measure of accuracy was called "Circular Error of Probability" (CEP), expressed as a radius within which half the bombs struck. The Wing's three SBD squadrons recorded a composite CEP of 175 feet, in which 50% of the SBDs bombs hit within 175 feet of the target. Of course, the CEP was somewhat influenced by the size of various targets. In the Marshall Island analysis the targets ranged from gun positions of 25 to 50 feet in diameter to buildings of up to 250 feet. Vought F4U Corsair fighters were also widely used as dive bombers, and performed well with an average 195 foot CEP and near-identical direct hit ratios on the varied targets: from 5.4% on 50 foot targets for the SBD to 4.5% for the Corsairs. Against well defended targets, capable of putting up flak, the Marine pilot increased their release altitude from 1,700 feet to 3,000, but still maintained most of their previous accuracy. On larger

targets Dauntless pilots scored three hits out of four bombs, while Corsair pilots were two of three.

USN Dive Bombing Sights
BuOrd contracted Sperry Gyroscope to further develop an earlier project to build a sight that would determine the proper diving angle. The new dive bombing sight, the Aiming Angle Sight Mark I, was a combination of the dive-angle indicator, a telescope, and an altimeter reading into the telescope. The Mk I was to correct for dive angle, lift angle, release altitude, and diving speed, but did not correct for wind and target motion because these calculations would increase the complexity, and thus the size and weight of the Mk I. It was thought that because calculations were being done by the Mk I the pilot would be free to concentrate on those two important adjustments. In May 1935 Sperry delivered 16 experimental Mark Is to BuOrd for testing. The device consisted of an aircraft gun sight linked to a gyroscope-driven computer and altimeter. The pilot preset the required altitude for bomb release, the expected air speed at the point of release, and the expected lift angle derived from tables based on the preset air speed. A gyroscope fed the dive angle to the computer, which automatically set the sighting arm in the gun sight. The pilot flew the aircraft at the preset speed, keeping the sighting arm fixed on the target while compensating for target motion, the effects of wind, and deflection. USN VB-4 tested the experimental Mk I against moving targets and concluded that it did "not afford a complete solution of the dive

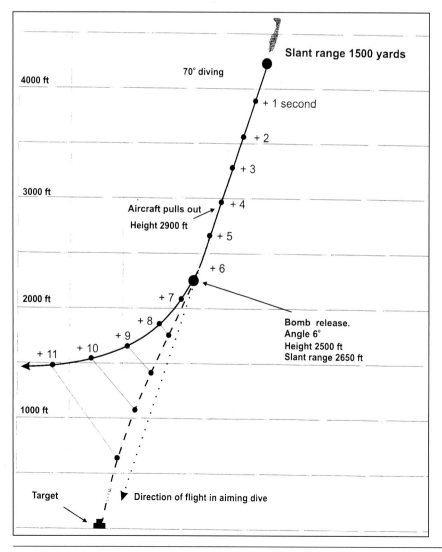

Dive Bombing Technique (USN)

bombing problem, but it does correct for variations in angle of dive and incorporates a warning light to indicate when the proper release altitude is reached." The Mark I achieved 64% hits on a maneuvering target, which was only marginally more than the gunsight without the Sperry computer, gyroscope, and altimeter.

Sperry worked four years to modify the Mk I with little progress, and in April 1941 BuAer Chief R.Adm. John Towers canceled the Mark I Aiming Angle Sight project, stating:

"In view of the slight improvement in bombing performance, the restrictions inherent in its use, and the installation difficulties involved, it is recommended that none of these sights be procured, but that a more vigorous effort be made to perfect the Aiming Angle Sight Mark II."

In July 1933, as part of its move toward dive bombing, the BuOrd asked Carl Norden to reduce work on improvements on his Mark XV bombsight and to concentrate on developing an "aiming angle sight," designated the Mark II, for dive bombers. On 2 January 1934 BuOrd contracted with Carl L. Norden, Inc., for a stabilized dive bombing sight, the Aiming Angle Sight, Mark II, in cooperation with the Army. Norden spent two years in Zurich working on the mathematical equations of dive bombing and their mechanical analogs, mailing blueprints to the New York Norden plant in the diplomatic pouches of the American Swiss embassy. The experimental Mk II was ready and sent to the Dahlgren Naval Proving Ground in late 1936 for testing.

These tests revealed faults, as the pilot's angle of vision was too small, and the required steep diving angles did not give the pilot enough time in dives to compensate for the total amount of drift involved. The barometric altimeter gave readings that were significantly behind the actual altitude, which became dangerous during the high speeds at which the aircraft approached the ground in a dive. Norden's design showed promise over the Sperry design because, after entering the dive, adjustments were automatic, except for the pilot having to release the directional gyroscope. Four prototypes were purchased for $95,000.

The Norden bombsight design continued to be too complicated; the pilot needed to focus too much on its use; and it allowed too little variation from a constant speed and steady course. Norden made little progress on improving this sight, because with the prospect of war the company received a flood of orders for its Mark XV/M-series bombsight and new Army demands for modifications to it. Work continued slowly until the Army and Navy finally canceled the project in 1944.

In the pre-war Carl Norden was developing the automated Aiming Angle Mark II dive bombing sight but due to his preoccupation with its famous Mk9 bombsight Navy dive bombers entered World War II equipped with the simple **Mark III line-of-sight telescopic gun sight** for aiming their bombs. (USN)

So Navy dive bombers entered World War II, not with an automated dive bombing sight, but equipped with the simple Mark III line-of-sight telescopic gun sight for aiming their bombs. The pilot kept the cross hairs on the target and used a turn-and-bank indicator to maintain level flight. AAC dive bombing in support of ground forces used the N-3A gun sight equipped with an adjustable reflector Model A-l and a Norden-style gyroscopic stabilizer.

2

Rockets

General

The rocket incorporated a warhead and a motor that was a propellant powder and made up most of the rocket's length. The rocket motor was comprised of the propellant charge, motor tube, nozzles, and powder trap or grid. The motor propellant was a smokeless powder composed of nitrocellulose and ingredients to generate high pressure gases rapidly. The mass of smokeless powder used in a rocket motor was called a grain no matter its size. The popular misconception is that a rocket is propelled by the push of the escaping gases against the atmosphere, but it is Newton's Third Law of Motion which is responsible for its movement. This Law, formulated in the late 1600s, states "For every action, there is an opposite and equal reaction." The action of the exhaust of the burning propellant inside the rocket is equaled by the reaction which pushes the rocket in a forward direction opposite the exhaust flow. Rocket warheads included high explosive in thin and thick-walled heads, solid shot, incendiary, smoke, and chemical. Depending on the target, the rocket was nose and sometimes base-fused.

The advantages of the aircraft rocket were:

1) Rockets gave an aircraft potentially heavier striking power over gun fire with a greater lethal area.

2) Rockets were not nearly as heavy as the large bore 37mm and 40mm aircraft cannon then in use and had the advantage of simpler installation.

3) The caliber of cannon was limited by the ability of the carrying aircraft to withstand its recoil. For example, 40mm cannon firing its 31 pound shell had a recoil force of 6,000 pounds. Therefore, the aircraft structure had to be built to withstand this recoil force. To counteract this recoil specially built underwing pods were designed, which left the carrying aircraft vulnerable to enemy fighters due to the greatly decreased aerodynamics and performance caused by the pods. Rocket-firing aircraft, though encumbered by the rockets, were, once they salvoed them, again normal, effective aircraft fully able to defend themselves.

4) Rockets, by virtue of Newton's Third Law, had no recoil.

5) The upgrading of German tank armor decreased the effectiveness of the 40mm "Tank Buster" cannon. Rockets attained a maximum velocity of approximately 1,200 feet per second which, when combined with the speed of the launching aircraft, yielded great penetrative qualities.

6) The use of bombs against armor was precluded by their relative inaccuracy and the need for a direct hit to put the tank out of action. To increase accuracy, the fighter had to fly low over the target, which subjected it to anti-aircraft fire and also the blast of its own dropped bomb. To eliminate the threat of bomb blast damage delayed fuses were tried, but unfortunately a direct hit on a tank would cause the bomb to bounce off and explode harmlessly away from the target.

7) Rocket production utilized less machinery and raw material and was faster, cheaper, and required less manpower, especially of the highly skilled variety used in cannon manufacture.

8) Rocket manufacture could more easily be modified to incorporate technical advances. This factor, along with ease of installation on aircraft, allowed these advances to be brought into operational use more rapidly.

9) In combat, rocket armament required fewer personnel and less time for maintenance when compared to cannon.

10) Wear and tear on the rocket launching mechanism was not nearly so great as that on gun mechanisms, especially barrels which wore out quickly and had to be replaced. Therefore, the need for spare parts was decreased and the down time of the carrying aircraft was also less.

The disadvantages of the aircraft rocket were:

1) The external launchers and the rockets caused increased aerodynamic drag and concomitant decrease in performance *until* the rockets were fired, making the carrying aircraft vulnerable. Even after rocket release the design of early launching rails decreased aircraft performance to some extent, but the development of smaller rail-type launchers eventually eliminated this problem.

2) Unlike cannon mounted in light bombers, rockets could not be reloaded in flight. Fighters carrying cannon in pods were able to fire more rounds of ammunition when compared to the eight rockets usually carried by fighters.

3) Because of their lower velocity and weight, and weight distribution, rockets had a greater gravity drop (a curved trajectory) when compared to cannon. Therefore, it needed to be fired at a range of 1,000 to 2,000 yards, which put the pilot in jeopardy from AA and ground fire. Beyond that range the trajectory became too pronounced for any hope of accurate fire. Pilots had to be specially trained to compensate for this drop in trajectory, as unlike a fired gun or cannon shell, the rocket followed the line of aircraft flight rather than the line of sight. Since this was the case, rocket-firing aircraft attacking a target could take no evasive actions during their pre-firing run-in on the target.

4) The rocket was difficult to fire accurately and demanded a high degree of skill. In operations, the distraction of having to identify an

often camouflaged or moving target under AA fire was reason enough to diminish accuracy.

5) The fighter bomber needed to remain stable as it launched the rocket. If the pilot skidded or turned the aircraft at launch, the rocket's low launching speed would cause a large error in aiming it at a target. Pilots were likely to undershoot their targets either because they launched their rockets at too long a range or flew too slowly at the lower dive angles.

6) Wind also needed to be considered accurately, as a 10 mph wind could cause a 15 foot miss in line and a nine foot miss in range, which was the difference in scoring a hit or a near miss as in the case of a tank or gun position. The modification of the gyroscopic gunsight in late 1944 compensated for the gravity drop of the rocket, and also for the effect of the wind and target movement.

7) New principles and mechanisms had to be developed for arming rocket fuses.

Complete Rocket Round

The complete round consisted of all components of the rocket necessary for it to function and could be issued as a single assembled unit, or as separate components to be assembled in the field. The complete round was made up of the head and motor:

1) The rocket head was that component which contained the high explosive charge or other filler, the booster, and the fuse. Its purpose was to produce the desired effect on the target.

2) The motor, which propelled the rocket contained the propelling charge and the igniter, and was assembled to the rear of the head. It consisted of a tube closed at the end and having one or more nozzles (venturi) at the rear end. The propelling charge, usually in stick form, was held in place by a trap, grid, or cage. Provision was made in the form of contact rings, fixed connections to fin shrouds, or cable and plug, dependent upon the design of the launcher, for electrically connecting the igniter to the external firing circuit.

Rocket Classification, Identification, and Markings

Classifications as to
1) Use:
Rockets were classified according to use as aircraft or ground.
2) Purpose:
Rockets were classified according to purpose as service, practice, target, and drill.
a) Service rockets were used in combat;
b) Practice rockets were used for training and target practice;
c) Target rockets were used to provide a fast moving aerial target for practice firing of automatic anti-aircraft weapons;
d) Drill rockets were used for training and handling.
3) Filler:
Rockets were classified according to the filler in the head as high explosive, chemical, and inert.
a) High explosive rockets contain a filler of high explosive for blast, fragmentation, mining, or demolition effect. The high-explosive antitank (HE, AT) rocket, which contains a filler consisting of a shaped charge of Pentolite or other high explosive, is used for penetration of armored targets, (The designation HE, AT identifies ammunition utilizing the shaped charge principle.)
b) Chemical rockets contain a chemical agent; and a burster; or an igniter to disperse or ignite the agent at the target. The chemical agent may be

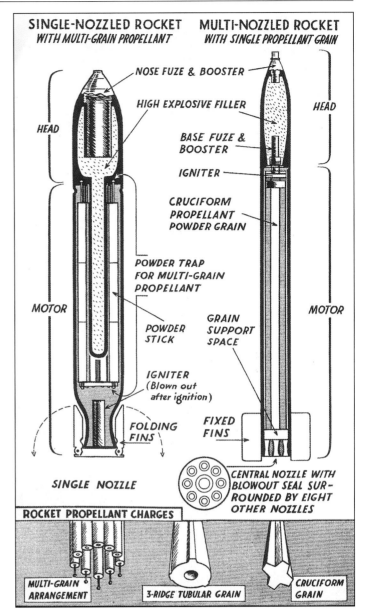

Complete Rocket Round (USN)

a gas for producing a toxic or harassing effect, a smoke producer for screening or signaling, an incendiary, or a combination of these.
c) The head of inert rockets which are intended for target practice contains inert filler; the motor contains a standard propellant charge. Drill rockets, intended for practice and training have both the head and motor as completely inert.

Identification
Rockets, like other types of ammunition, were identified by the standard nomenclature and a lot number of the item. Such identification was marked on all containers and, unless the item was too small, on the ammunition itself.

Markings
Rockets were marked by stamping in the metal or by stenciling with the type, size, model, and lot number. The safe temperature limits for storage and use was shown on the rocket motor.

Data Card

A 5x8 inch card for each lot was supplied with each rocket shipment. This card gave the ammunition lot number of the item, the lot number of each component of the item, and other pertinent data, such as expected muzzle velocity, AIC symbol, and assembling and firing instructions when required.

Development

The use of aircraft rockets in World War II was not the creation of a new weapon, but rather the updating of one which was first utilized in the middle ages and then used sporadically throughout history. In the mid-nineteenth century rocket development reached an impasse due to the propelling fuel available, and more importantly due to the improvement in conventional artillery, such as increased accuracy due to barrel rifling and progress in recoil absorbing mechanisms. Though some minor work was done during World War I in rocket warfare, development languished afterward through the 1920s and early 1930s. In Europe and America most rocket development concentrated on the liquid fueled models developed by Walter Dornberger and Werner von Braun in Germany and Robert Goddard in America. By the mid-1930s, either through budding official interest or individual initiative, initial development began on rockets which were eventually to be mounted on aircraft.

British Rocket Development

The airborne rocket of World War II was the progeny of the early work of Dr. Allwyn Crow and a small group of British scientists who investigated ground-to-air anti-aircraft rockets in the spring of 1935. After three years of work Crow's group developed a practical though low performance, cordite solid-fuelled, two inch rocket. Design problems occurred, as many of the specifications were either incompatible or contradictory. Strength was needed but so was lightness. Stability was required for accuracy, but the need for small size allowed for no elaborate fin configuration. A large payload was desired, but was limited by the size of the rocket motors then available. The regulation of gas pressure and thrust was determined by allowable temperature ranges. Drawing on the experience gained in two inch rocket development, Crow developed the three inch rocket. The rocket, or "UP" ("Unrelated Projectile") as it was coded, measured 76 inches in length, 3.25 inches in diameter, and weighed 54 pounds with a 4.3 pound warhead and self-destruct fuse. The UP was propelled to 1,041 mph and 22,000 feet by 12.7 pounds of SCRK cordite propellant. Crow had designed the three inch UP for the so-called "Z" anti-aircraft batteries, but again, the basic specifications mentioned previously, along with the lack of proximity fuse development, delayed their introduction until April 1941, by which time the *Luftwaffe* was no longer particularly active over England.

In the early phases of the war RAF ordnance experts were pre-occupied with conventional guns and bombs, as these weapons had proven effectiveness and there were no compelling reasons to investigate other ordnance. However, in North Africa, the Germans introduced new tanks of improved armor design and thickness which were resistant to RAF fighter assault. In August 1941, Gen. Mason MacFarlane was given a demonstration of the anti-tank use of airborne rockets by the Russians. Impressed by this demonstration, meetings were held in September between the CDP (Controller of Projectile Development, Dr. Crow) and the Ministry of Aircraft Production. During the course of these meetings the relative advantages and disadvantages of the aircraft rocket were discussed.

Since the rockets used in the anti-aircraft Z-batteries were immediately available, early air-to-air tests were begun with them using Armor Piercing heads similar to those used with the 2.5 pounder guns. These rockets were adapted by G/C Dixie Dean, Experimental Gunnery Officer at Boscombe Down, and Dr. Cook at the Ministry of Supply Experimental Station at Abergorth. It soon became obvious that the Z-battery rockets were unsuitable for aircraft use, as they were designed to reach great heights at a constant velocity. An aircraft rocket needed a motor to propel it over a relatively short distance at a high initial velocity to yield the maximum penetrating power. The logical answer to this problem was to develop a new design, but this request was officially denied, as it would hamper current Z-battery rocket production. Orders were issued to redesign existing rockets, and so the better part of a year passed before the old rocket was redesigned into a satisfactory aircraft rocket.

Since aircraft rocketry was a new field, initial tests investigated several potential problems regarding a suitable method of carriage and launch and the effect of the rocket's ignition blast and propelling exhaust of the mother aircraft. On 25 October 1941 a Hawker Hurricane fired the first aircraft rocket since World War I, when it launched a three inch rocket over Chichester Harbor. The test was considered a success, as it did not destroy the launching aircraft! Testing for range and accuracy then commenced, but range created a problem, as the first test saw a rocket overshoot, setting a distant sawmill on fire. In another test the rocket would not fire, but as the pilot attempted to return to base the rocket ignited, striking a seawall protecting a small town some five miles away. Finally, the rocket was modified and deemed ready for operational testing. The modified version of the rocket carried a solid steel warhead capable of penetrating four inches of armor and was carried four under each wing. Operational tests carried out over the North African desert were disappointing, as the new German Panzers were protected by up to seven inches of armor. Tests requested by the Royal Navy against merchant vessels were also disappointing, as the Semi-Armor Piercing explosive warhead would penetrate a ship's hulls above its waterline but would cause very little damage. Reports from North Africa from army howitzer gunners showed good results using low velocity, thin-cased shells of low explosive charge, and this report was investigated and applied to aircraft rockets with great success.

By early December 1941 aircraft rocket development shifted emphasis in Great Britain. At this time German U-Boats were threatening to cut Britain's material lifeline from the outside world, and meetings were held with the Air Staff to discuss the use of rockets against submarines and merchant shipping. Since these U-Boats presented a long lateral surface, initial tests were conducted attacking targets above the waterline. During these tests a target was imbedded in a sand bank which at high tide resembled a surfaced submarine and at low tide allowed hits to be inspected. Rockets with 25 pound solid steel warheads were launched from steeply diving aircraft. One morning low-lying clouds made these steep dives too dangerous and 20° dives were tried. Post-test observation found several unexpected additional holes in the target because the rockets striking short in the water curved upwards under the water and pierced the target under the waterline. This serendipitous set of circumstances greatly speeded anti-submarine rocket technical development by utilizing underwater trajectory.

Meanwhile, in November and December 1941 ballistic trails were conducted in wind tunnel and flight tests to gather data on dispersion and trajectory, along with sighting methods. Data was collected on the size and type of projectile, along with the size and type of stabilizing fin. Developmental work continued throughout 1942, and in December of that year the Air Ministry issued a comprehensive report on aircraft rockets as a result of trials at Pendine Range and Boscombe Down Experimental Station. By this time the three inch motor mounted by either a 60 or 25 pound warhead was selected as the standard British aircraft rocket. The motor consisted of a three inch diameter steel tube, measuring 4.58 inches long and containing 11 or 12 pounds of cordite propellant depending on the size of warhead used. Four 8x5 inch cruciform rectangular fins were placed at the rear of the rocket. The solid propellant charge burned from the front end and exhausted through a rear orifice which passed through the center of the rocket. This method of exhaust discharge was utilized so as not to change the rocket's center of gravity during burning when using the 25 or 60 pound or concrete practice heads. The rocket launcher consisted of four pairs of seven foot fixed rails mounted under each wing. Initially steel blast plates were bolted under the wings, but the fear of rocket exhaust damage was unfounded and the use of these plates was discontinued. The rockets were held to the rails by two saddles of which two types were available; one for the 25 pound head and one for the 60 pound head.

The 25 pound rocket head was a three inch long Armor Piercing shot. When fired the rocket accelerated along the seven foot rail at 50 Gs, and by the time it left the rail it was traveling at 150 fps over the speed of the carrying aircraft (350 fps at 240 mph). It attained a maximum speed of 1,700 fps in 1.5 seconds and had a gravity drop of 40 to 50 feet over 600 yards. This rocket had excellent penetrating characteristics, as it could pierce four inches of armor at 600 yards. The head exhibited good underwater characteristics and was used extensively in anti-shipping and anti-submarine roles.

The 60 pound rocket head measured six inches and was a Semi-Armor Piercing shell that contained 18 pounds of high explosive. This head was larger, and thus slower in attaining a maximum speed of 1,200 to 1,300 fps, and had a larger gravity drop of 80 to 100 feet over 600 yards. This head could not be used for underwater anti-shipping attacks, as the head often broke away from the motor or tended to explode upon hitting the water. The fuses for these heads were thermally armed by the heat of the burning cordite and incorporated a short delay element for the percussion base.

The first recorded maritime use of rockets by the British occurred on June 1943 when Hurricane IVs of 184 Squadron under Typhoon escort attacked German coastal shipping. In May the Beaufighters of Air Vice-Marshal A.B. Ellwood's No. 18 Group received their rocket projectiles. Originally these "Rover" flights (single aircraft, or small formations not exceeding five aircraft) ranged along the German held European coasts hunting enemy convoys, but by late June 1943 the Group changed its tactics, operating in force to utilize the rocket to its best advantage. Throughout 1943 RAF Typhoon squadrons were withdrawn from combat to be outfitted with rocket launching apparatus and to allow their pilots to fire a few practice rounds. At this time there were many German

maritime targets available for practice: German trawlers, E-Boats, flak ships, blockade runners, mine layers, and mine sweepers. Soon German airfields, railways, vehicles, and bridges located just across the channel in France, Belgium, and Holland came under rocket attack.

American Rocket Development

Meanwhile in America, work on rockets was at a virtual standstill at the outbreak of the war in 1941, with the US considered a poor fourth in aircraft rocket development, behind Britain, Germany, and Russia. In 1918 Dr. Robert Goddard, the father of American rocketry, and Clarence Hickman, then a physics graduate student, undertook the study of artillery rockets for the US Army at Aberdeen Proving Grounds. In the course of their tests they proposed a four inch rocket to be carried under the wings of an airplane. The weapon was to be an air-to-air missile with HE burster tubes to fragment the rocket body and motors in addition to the warhead to increase the lethal effect. The First World War ended before the proposal could come into fruition. In the 1930s little, if any, rocket development took place in America. However, Lt. Leslie Skinner of the Army Ordnance Department foresaw the rocket's potential as a weapon and undertook independent experimentation during this period.

On 20 June 1940 Dr. Hickman, then working for Bell Telephone Labs, pleaded the rocket's case in a letter to Dr. Frank Jewett, the head of Bell Labs and also the President of the National Academy of Sciences. Among Hickman's proposals were for rocket deployment from aircraft, land vehicles, and boats; furnishing heavy, mobile fire support for the Army. Hickman also proposed to add rocket motors to standard bombs to increase their armor piercing capacity. These proposals were offered to the Army and Navy, which exhibited only lukewarm interest. However, on 26 July the National Defense Research Committee felt that Hickman's proposal in regard to rocket-propelled bombs merited attention and established Section H of Division A to be headed by Hickman to study the problem. Hickman was joined by Army Captain Leslie Skinner at the Naval Proving Ground at Dahlgren, VA, but since their work was of low priority and received little support–the two scientists fabricated their rocket from a fire extinguisher! The extinguisher's bottom became the rocket's head and its tapered top was used to construct the nozzles. The first test shots of America's first US military "rocket" were conducted at Dahlgren in September 1940.

In the fall of 1940 the British sent a scientific mission to America, headed by Sir Henry Tizard, to discuss English rocket development, especially in the field of high altitude anti-aircraft rockets. This mission established the free exchange of rocket data between the two countries, which was to greatly enhance the development of the weapon. The future major breakthrough in rocket development would be the adaptation of the British dry-extrusion process for manufacturing high performance large grain propellant rocket motor.

In the summer of 1941 Dr. Charles Lauritsen of the California Institute of Technology (CIT/Cal Tech) and vice chairman of Division A of NDRC traveled to England to study British rocket development. Lauritsen realized the potential of the military rocket and made recommendations to NDRC offering major CIT involvement in the development of a five inch aircraft rocket with a proximity fuse and the firing mechanism, along with the development of the 3.25 inch anti-aircraft rocket with a proximity fuse and the necessary launching apparatus.

In late 1941 the NDRC let further research and development contracts to selected parties. CIT and George Washington University were contracted to carry out overall rocket development while the Universities of Wisconsin, Minnesota, and Duke, along with Hercules Powder Company, were to conduct propellant research. Budd Company and Bell Labs were to engineer and design rocket components and equipment.

Dr. Charles Lauritsen of the California Institute of Technology and Vice Chairman of Division A of NDRC was instrumental in American rocket development in World War 2. (Author)

The 38 pound **4.5 inch M8 rocket** was the product of the Army's work in developing the infantry bazooka in 1940 and was first ground test-fired on 29 May 1941. (AAF)

The first air launch of forward-fired rockets was conducted on 14 July 1943 by **Lt.Cdr. Thomas Pollock**, the Commander of Headquarters Squadron 14 (flying a Grumman TBF-1 Avenger. (USN)

It was at this time that American Rocketry divided into Eastern and Western Establishments. The Eastern group under Hickman, Skinner, and NDRC Section H became "Army oriented," even though it was then relocated at the Naval Powder Factory at Indian Head, MD. The Eastern program concentrated on the bazooka, recoilless gun, and the five inch aircraft rocket. The Western faction also worked on the aforementioned projects beginning in September 1941, and were to become Navy oriented under the Bureau of Ordnance.

In 1940 Army Captain Leslie Skinner and Navy Lieutenant Edward Uhl developed a simple and very effective anti-tank weapon designated as the M1 Rocket Launcher, but its resemblance to the Bob Burns' musical instrument, the bazooka, gave the weapon its common nickname. In early 1941 Skinner, working at the Ordnance Department at Indian Head Powder Factory, developed the first US aircraft rocket, which was first ground test-fired on 29 May 1941. The extension of Skinner's work led to the Army's development of the 4.5 inch M8 rocket, which weighed 38 pounds and carried a five pound HE head; it was propelled by a motor that carried a multiple charge of 39 grains of solvent extruded powder. Early designs had fixed fins, but were later replaced by folding fins so that tubes, instead of rails, could be used for launchers. Capt. Harry Donicht of the AAF Wright Field Armament Lab headed the team to adapt these rockets for operational use.

Once America was drawn into war there was a renewed interest in aviation ordnance requirements and the rocket was considered as a promising solution. At the time the 4.5 inch plane-to-plane rocket was being developed for the Army by the NDRC under Clarence Hickman and Leslie Skinner. By April 1942 Hickman and Skinner reported that the 4.5 inch "projectile is in an advanced stage of development and that it could be applied in actual warfare in the very near future if sufficient direction of its production were undertaken by those having the necessary authority." On 6 July 1942, at the Aberdeen Proving Ground, an Army fighter aircraft launched the first American *forward*-firing aerial rockets (three days earlier the Navy fired its first aerial rocket, a Cal Tech <u>retro</u>-rocket at Goldstone Lake/AAF Camp Haan). Meanwhile, Cal Tech began to privately work on aircraft rockets in 1942 after Dr. Charles Lauritsen's visit to the UK when he secured 50 for experimental purposes.

In November 1943, BuOrd requested the Dahlgren Naval Proving Ground to develop and install underwing rocket "projectors" (launchers)

for Douglas SBD bombers assigned to the Proving Ground and to conduct experimental ground and air firing tests. After two months Capt. David Hedrick, the Inspector of Ordnance at Dahlgren, informed the Chief of the Bureau of Ordnance that the installation of the requested launchers on the SBD would necessitate extensive structural changes, and that another aircraft was needed or the tests would be suspended indefinitely. The BuOrd was adamantly against suspending the tests and ordered another aircraft be modified in order to start the tests ASAP. The Brewster SB2A-4 Buccaneer was chosen, and between 24 February and 29 March 1943 a series of ground and air tests was conducted. During the air tests 15 rockets were successfully launched by three different pilots with only several misfires, which led Capt. Hedrick to report:

"It is believed that the rocket type of projectile has unlimited possibilities as a weapon against either airplanes, troops or vehicles on the ground, or lightly armored vessels....More research should be done to increase the velocity to at least 2,000 feet per second before its service use is contemplated."

However, the BuOrd's position at this time was to only monitor the AAC's air-to-air rocket program. The US Army Ordnance "Eastern Faction" had designed the M-8, a 37 pound, three foot, 4.5 inch diameter rocket for use by ground forces as the "Bazooka." This 4.5 inch RP (Rocket Projectile) had an explosive filling of five pounds, a launching speed of 800-850 fps, and a maximum range of 4,600 yards. By the spring of 1943 the AAF had adapted the infantry weapon to aerial use and began limited production of 15,000 4.5 inch aircraft rocket rounds per month. R.Adm. John McCain, Chief of the Bureau of Aeronautics, requested that the BuOrd obtain 2,000 of these rockets for experimental and developmental squadron use, and that two carrier squadrons per month be equipped with the rockets in the next fiscal year.

Soon a number of unforeseen rocket explosions occurred during testing which were traced to the functioning of the ballistic propellant powder due to hot summertime temperatures. While the rocket was having technical problems it continued to receive administrative support, with some factions expecting that one million of these rockets to be produced per month by mid-1943. However, there were many in the Bureau that understood that the development of a successful operational aircraft rocket depended on using a dry-extruded propellant.

Rocket development at Cal Tech (CIT) was spurred by the German U-Boat threat against Atlantic convoys, as during May 1943 *Kriegsmarine* U-Boat commanders were ordered to remain on the surface to fight it out with attacking aircraft. In several top secret reports from the English, nine verified successes of rockets against U-Boats were mentioned using a modified version of the three inch fin-stabilized rocket fitted with a solid steel head to penetrate the U-Boat's pressure hull. These British anti-submarine rocket successes brought about a meeting between Lauritsen and other Cal Tech scientists with BuOrd, BuAer, and representatives of Adm. King. The meeting's agenda was to explore the possibility of a crash program for Cal Tech to develop and produce anti-submarine rockets comparable to the British rockets. During the meeting Lauritsen vigorously lobbied for this project and outlined what measures would be needed to bring it to fruition. On 7 June 1943, USN C-in-C Adm. Ernest King issued a significant memorandum which would totally alter the scope and importance of US rocket use and be responsible for launching the huge future US aircraft rocket program. Basically, the memorandum stated that not only did King want US Navy rockets to be the equivalent to the British rockets, but he wanted them in service as soon as possible. R.Adm. Julius Furer requested that Lauritsen and Cal Tech adapt the 3.25 inch chemical rocket for aircraft use, but new types of launchers and the tactical use of the weapon still needed to be developed and tested. To meet King's demand for a maximum rocket effort Cal Tech possessed the organization, the technology, and military support necessary. Importantly, Cal Tech also had Cdr. Jack Renard available with the authority to make decisions and commitments, cutting time consuming red tape. On 19 June Cal Tech received approval for the development of the forward-fired anti-submarine rocket. Previously, Cal Tech had completed experimental work on its version of a similar weapon and had made substantial progress toward its development, but it would be some time before it would be available for testing.

On his earlier trip to England, Dr. Lauritsen had procured 50 English three inch aircraft rockets for study and testing. By summer 1943 the rocket, officially designated 3.25 Rocket Motor Mark 6 and 3.5 inch Rocket Body Mark 1, was ready for flight testing. The round was about a foot shorter than the British version, but was expected to be faster and more accurate at 1,175 fps (plus aircraft launch speed). The rocket came in two versions: the 3.5 inch Model 1, anti-submarine model, which weighed 53.8 pounds and carried a 20 pound solid steel warhead; and the 3.5 inch Model 10, which weighed approximately the same and carried a warhead of 2.2 pounds of TNT detonated by a Mark 148 point-detonating fuse. Both versions were powered by the 3.25 inch rocket motor which weighed about 34 pounds.

The first air launch of forward-fired rockets was scheduled for 14 July 1943 by Lt.Cdr. Thomas Pollock, the Commander of Headquarters Squadron 14 (Hedron 14) Experimental Unit, flying a Grumman TBF-1 Avenger. As the Cal Tech version of the rocket had not been checked for reliability the British rockets were to be fired. Pollack had to improvise aiming as there was no sight in the aircraft. Previously, Pollock sat in the TBF cockpit while it was on the ground and fired several rounds out over Goldstone Lake, and as he observed the airborne rounds he took a piece of tape and placed it on the windshield to serve as a sight for future air firings. The test firings went well, and marked the turning point in the Navy rocket program, despite the AAF success in firing 4.5 inch rockets on 6 August 1942. The AAF 4.5 inch rockets were considered to be inaccurate, and were limited in their penetration of steel hulls and the water's surface.

In early August 1943, BuOrd contracted Cal Tech to produce 10,000 rounds per month for four to six months. The Cal Tech CIT Type High Velocity Rocket 3A12 round was officially designated the 3.25 inch Rocket Motor Mark 6 and the rocket was the 3.5 inch Rocket Body Mark

1. The principal difference between the British round and the first Cal Tech model was that the American round was 12 inches shorter, and by using Cal Tech dry-extruded propellant there would be an anticipated increase of 200 fps in velocity above that of the British round, which would translate into increased accuracy. These rockets were to be used for extensive service testing until the Navy contracted private industry to mass produce the weapons. Despite the fact that the Cal Tech designed rocket had yet been fired from an aircraft, and that final engineering drawings had not been made, the rocket went into production. The confidence of those individuals devoted to this program was confirmed as test results were received. In mid-August a Navy aircraft took off from Goldstone Lake with four of the Cal Tech rockets under each wing. Those on the right wing were mounted on Mark 4 American rail launchers, those on the left on British launchers. Two firing runs were made with the CIT rocket, and then for comparison 16 rounds of the British rockets were fired. The majority of both rocket types hit within the lethal range of the target, and a proposal was tendered that all anti-submarine aircraft, including fighters aboard escort carriers, were to be equipped with rockets.

Navy officials were so impressed with the 3.5 inch rocket tests that on 26 August 1943 the Navy decided that it would need to contract Cal Tech to manufacture 200,000 of the high velocity aircraft rockets per month as soon as "practicable." Added impetus for the US rocket program was furnished by intelligence reports which stated that the *Luftwaffe* had begun operational use of air-to-air rockets against Allied bomber formations. Although the final production drawings were incomplete and only a handful had been flight tested, the rocket went into production, and by September Cal Tech made its first deliveries. By comparison the monthly estimated figure for the 4.5 inch barrage rocket was 20,000 per month, and 45,000 for the 7.2 inch anti-submarine rockets. The Navy also planned to request 600,000 high velocity aircraft rockets from the British at the rate of 50,000 per month, but subsequently the British declined, as they found that they would require all the rockets they could produce. In September 1943 Cal Tech began regular delivery of the rockets. In October 1943 HQ, C-in-C of the US Fleet, asked that plans be made to equip 1,500 aircraft with rockets for Atlantic deployment and 4,500 for the Pacific by 1 June 1944, along with a comprehensive pilot training and retraining program. The first of these aircraft were 12 rocket-equipped TBF-1s assigned to the Naval Air Station, Quonset Point, RI. Although the forward-firing rocket program had started on the West Coast, most of the early rockets were shipped to the East Coast because of the urgent situation of anti-submarine warfare in the Atlantic.

After the first rocket launching success the Navy celebrated with this sign under Pollock's Avenger equipped with a wing-mounted **3.5 inch Model 10 rocket** and rail. (USN)

After the development of the 3.5 inch rocket, natural evolution turned to the development of a larger and improved aircraft rocket, using the 3.25 inch motor and a larger warhead. No special design problems were involved in modifying standard 5 inch 38 caliber AA shells with instantaneous, air-arming, impact-firing nose fuses and a delay base fuse. The 3.25 inch solvent base, wet extruded, multiple grain motor screwed into the base of the projectile. The rocket, designated 5 inch Aircraft Rocket Model 5, weighed 80 pounds and was 5.42 feet long. The use of the standard 3.25 motor allowed this rocket to be fired from existing launchers before the end of 1943. However, due to rapid 1/10th second burning time velocity performance decreased from 1,175 to 750 fps because the standard 3.25 inch motor was being used with a larger payload. Therefore, there was a decrease in range (to only 2,400 feet) and accuracy, and the launching aircraft had to release the rockets closer to the target to take advantage of the high acceleration and have a high enough velocity at target to achieve adequate penetration. Even so, at 2,400 feet

the warhead was able to only penetrate an inch of armor plate and one foot of reinforced concrete. A feature incorporated in this rocket was the use of "zone charges" in the propellant to compensate for temperature changes in various combat theatres. As issued the rocket propellant could be adjusted for external firing temperatures between 20° to 90° F. If a rocket was used in high tropical temperatures internal pressures on burning could build up, affecting the rocket's performance. Accordingly there were three marked grains among the 30 grains of propellant. Removal of any of the three grains modified the propellant for the firing temperature. Later improvements eliminated the marked grains altogether, giving an operating temperature range/between - 20° to 120°F.

Rocket Motor/Propellant Development
As mentioned previously, when rocket development began the only project which aroused any interest was Aictzman's proposal to the NDRC to develop rocket-propelled bombs. To design the rocket motor to

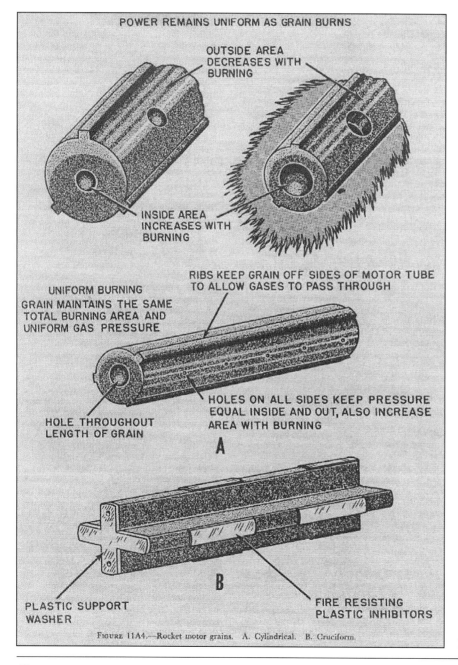

POWER REMAINS UNIFORM AS GRAIN BURNS

OUTSIDE AREA DECREASES WITH BURNING

INSIDE AREA INCREASES WITH BURNING

UNIFORM BURNING GRAIN MAINTAINS THE SAME TOTAL BURNING AREA AND UNIFORM GAS PRESSURE

RIBS KEEP GRAIN OFF SIDES OF MOTOR TUBE TO ALLOW GASES TO PASS THROUGH

HOLE THROUGHOUT LENGTH OF GRAIN

HOLES ON ALL SIDES KEEP PRESSURE EQUAL INSIDE AND OUT, ALSO INCREASE AREA WITH BURNING

A

PLASTIC SUPPORT WASHER

FIRE RESISTING PLASTIC INHIBITORS

B

FIGURE 11A4.—Rocket motor grains. A. Cylindrical. B. Cruciform.

Rocket Motor Grains (USN)

drive this bomb, scientists had to first establish the principles of interior rocket ballistics. The flight of a rocket is determined by its size, shape, weight, manner of launching, and thrust developed by the burning of the propellant charge. The thrust (lbs), burning time (sec), burning rate (inch per second), pressure (psi), initial temperature (°F.) of the propellant, and ratio of burning surface of the propellant to the area of the nozzle orifice are among the factors known as interior ballistics.

Laying this groundwork required the development of special instruments and methods of study which delayed the production of a suitable full size motor until spring 1941 and an improved, standardized version a full year later. Though the rocket-powered bomb never became a tactical necessity, experience pointed out a major obstacle in the US rocket program; the propellant. The British used their standard smokeless powder called cordite to manufacture rocket propellant. The cordite powder was not a powder but a plastic-like substance composed of primarily nitrocellulose and nitroglycerine. The advantage of cordite was that when its ingredients were mixed they could be rolled into a sheet which was in turn was wound into a roll. This roll was then put into a press and extruded through a die at medium heat and high pressure to produce a grain of propellant. A grain is any mass of propellant of any shape and weight. The British method of propellant manufacture allowed them to produce a grain of minimal cross-sectional thickness between two surfaces called a web. The web thickness dictated the time required to burn the grain. The rate at which gases were generated by the burning of the propellant depended upon the area of exposed grain surface. It was desirable to have the gas pressure remain constant during burning without high pressure peaks so that the rocket motor body could be constructed of minimal strength, thickness, and weight. To accomplish this, the grain needed to burn without changing its total exposed area where all the burning occurred. Burning occurred in parallel layers thus maintaining the basic grain shape without decreasing its thickness. The easiest method of producing a constant burning area was to have the grain tube-shaped.

The exposed tube surface remained fairly constant as the burning progressed and the exterior surface area of the tube decreased and the interior area increased. Another method was to use a cross-sectional configuration of a thick-armed cross with areas of the arm surfaces treated to prevent burning. A grain of ordinary gunpowder was generally a perforated cylinder up to an inch in diameter and rarely over two inches long. A five foot, 40 pound cruciform (cross shaped) rocket grain would be the equivalent of 13,600,000 grains of .30 caliber rifle powder.

In the US the only available powder was ballistite which also consisted of nitrocellulose (60%) and nitroglycerine (40%) along with a small quantity of diphenylamine added as a stabilizer. Nitrocellulose powder and nitroglycerin were used as rocket propellant as they were especially well-suited for that purpose because of its chemical composition and its surface-burning property. When ignited, burning took place over its exposed surface and progressed in a direction perpendicular to those surfaces. The burning time depended upon the chemical composition of the propellant, the initial temperature of the propellant, and the surrounding pressure. The burning rate increased with the increase of pressure and temperature.

Ballistite was the only commercial powder which had a high enough energy content required to be a rocket fuel. The principal method of manufacturing smokeless powder in America was by the solvent extrusion process. The powder ingredients were suspended in a volatile solvent to form dough in which state it could be extruded through dies into the desired shape. However, this method limited the cross-sectional thickness (web) because it was necessary to dry the solvent out of the extruded grain and thin-webbed grains restricted the performance of the motor. In order to initiate the US rocket program as quickly as possible; rather than waiting

to develop a new powder industry, the NDRC concentrated on rockets using solvent-extruded powders which were available in large quantities. Upon his return from England, Dr. Lauritsen petitioned Dr. Vannevar Bush, chairman of the National Administrative Committee on Aeronautics (NACA) to allow CIT to expand the US rocket program using the British solventless, dry-extrusion technique using ballistite. Also, research was to continue to improve solvent extruded ballistite and soon, Section H developed what was called "New Technique" (NT) powder which was a substantial improvement. However, the dry-extrusion method continued to hold the most promise for the manufacture of thick-webbed grains. A $200,000 contract was let to Cal Tech for "studies and experimental investigation in connection with the development, adapting, and testing of ordnance devices." This was to be the first of over $80 million allotted to the rocket program. The contract was to begin in February 1942 but CIT trustees advanced the $200,000 so work could start 1 September 1941. By March 1942, CIT had spent half a million dollars without being reimbursed and Dr. Ernest Watson, organizer of the Institute's program, went to Washington to plead for the much needed funds. Finally a check for $250,000 was approved and was promised to arrive by registered mail. Watson knowing the dire need for funds asked to have the check sent at least by air mail but there was a regulation against unnecessary use of airmail! Watson volunteered to purchase an air mail stamp and so the check arrived at Cal Tech a few days sooner. When NDRC expanded the rocket program in late 1941 CIT was given the task of developing the equipment and technique for dry extrusion of thick web grains and the rockets using them. Except for *Tiny Tim* rockets, the war's largest aircraft rockets, all Cal Tech rocket motors had a single grain charge. Although Section H began studies on dry-extrusion in 1941, the expansion of the rocket program delegated the design of rockets using multiple grain, solvent-extruded thin web charges to them.

CIT scientists designed a press to demonstrate the feasibility of dry-extruding ballistite grains from trench mortar sheet powder. Soon production technique and larger more efficient, presses were devised and were used to produce dry-extruded ballistite for testing purposes and later in amounts sufficient for operational testing and use. The Army built a pilot factory at Radford, VA, which was operated by Hercules Powder Co. Later Hercules opened plants at Badger, WI, and Sunflower, KS. It is interesting to note that initially the Sunflower plant was built to fill Russian requests for dry-extruded powder as most of their powder factories had been over run by the Germans. In late 1944 the Russians had built new factories and this plant was available for US needs. The Navy also built a dry-extrusion factory in 1943 at its Indian Head Powder Factory, MD. Generally, rocket research and development progressed rapidly only to be hindered by the lack of production facilities to realize these advances. This situation was particularly evident in the manufacture of thick web powder grains; a predicament which persisted until the end of the war.

The manufacture of ballistite and its transformation into a rocket motor combined chemical and physical processes. To produce the raw material, cotton was shredded and bathed in hot acid and then purified into a watery nitrocotton "slurry." Meanwhile fats and nitric acid combined to form nitroglycerine. The nitrocotton slurry and nitroglycerine along with other chemicals were combined into a dough which was placed into sacks to dry in warm air for three to four days. After drying, the dough was rolled into sheets which were slit into strips that were, in turn, cut and rolled into bundles. These bundles were put into a 5,000 pound per square inch hydraulic press and extruded into long cruciform rods. These rods were then cut into the approximate grain length and x-rayed for uniformity. A small bubble or defect in the texture of the grain could cause an explosion or a deviation in flight. The grain was then milled to exact specification to a surface tolerance of 1/1000 inch. Some 40 inspections were made

Finished rocket shell and burst tubes loaded into baskets on production line. (USN)

and initially every tenth grain was test-fired in special rooms where temperature and humidity could be controlled to simulate operational atmospheric conditions. In this room the grain was bolted to a concrete stanchion and connected to gauges and photographed. Gas pressure was measured by the gauges while the cameras showed the rate of burning. The finished grains were wrapped in cellophane, sacked, and then packed into insulated metal containers for shipment.

In the context of today's rocket technology it would seem a relatively easy matter to design a solid fuelled rocket of such seemingly little complexity. But as is the case with most new technology, the establishment of the fundamental principles required time and patience, and trial and error. Once these basic premises were determined, development proceeded at an accelerating rate. Such was the case with the airborne rocket. Rocket scientists had to determine the relationships of many variables and their limits.

If the warhead size was to be enlarged then speed, range, and accuracy would be reduced unless a larger grain motor was used or the motor's metal casing lightened. If the casing were lightened then it would necessarily be weaker and a decrease in maximum burning temperature would be required. The use of stronger and lighter metal alloys would be more expensive and usually require metals which were in short wartime supply. If an increased speed was required for better trajectory and accuracy; there were several possible remedies. First the grain size could be increased by using a heavier motor. If more propellant were packed into the same motor area then gas flow would be retarded increasing operating temperatures and decreasing the maximum temperature limits. The use of a thicker web grain with less surface area and longer burning time enabled more propellant to be used in the same area without decreasing gas flow. But the manufacture of thicker web grains was a bottle neck throughout the war. Burning and pressure were directly proportional; the higher the pressure, the faster the grain burned. So the rate of gas production by burning and the rate of gas exhaust through the nozzle had to be in balance at a pressure below the limit of motor strength. The effect of burning temperature was a critical factor on rocket performance and safety. The

higher the initial temperature the faster the grain burned. At temperatures below operating limits the rocket could fail to ignite or burn intermittently ("chuff"). At increasingly higher temperatures, up to operating maximum, range and speed varied only slightly but acceleration increased; improving accuracy. At temperatures above operating maximums, many rockets exploded soon after launch. The operating temperature limits were printed on all rocket rounds. Nozzle design also required extensive investigation as the nozzle had to control the pressure and direct the gas discharge in a smooth rearward flow. The burning grain generated gases in the rocket motor which exerted equal pressure in all directions.

The burning rate of the powder was a surface phenomenon and the pressure developed within the motor could be controlled by the design of the grains of propellant powder. If the perforated grains were coated on the outside with a very slow burning substance and the inside were ignited, the inside surface would increase as burning progressed and pressure would increase at an accelerated rate; called progressive burning. If the inside surface of the grain were coated, the outside surface would decrease as burning progressed, and pressure would increase at a decelerating rate; called degressive burning. If neither the inside nor the outside were coated, the decrease in burning area on the outside would be offset by the increase in burning area on the inside, and the burning area would be constant. Thus, by grain design and by the use of coatings, called inhibitors or deterrents, it was possible to control the burning surface of the grains to obtain the desired burning time for the propellant charge, to obtain high density of propellant loading, and to protect the motor walls from the effects of intense heat. Cellulose acetate in a thin layer generally was used as an inhibitor in connection with star-perforated and cruciform (in cross section) grains in order that the burning area would remain constant, giving the desired burning characteristics and assuring uniform flight and motor protection.

The rate at which gases were generated by the burning of the propellant depended on the amount of the exposed surface of the grain. Even burning was best achieved by manufacturing the grain in the shape of a tube. The grain was contained in the motor tube that had to withstand the gas pressure exerted equally in all directions. Since the grain was held in a metal casing and supported by a powder trap or grid during burning the gases could only escape toward the rear of the rocket providing an

2-8 Rocket bodies being formed on presses. (USN)

An electric current was introduced through a pig tail to the **electrical ignition wire** leads that sent the current to a filament or Platinum wire bridge that contacted the black powder igniter and then ballistite grain; firing the rocket. (USN)

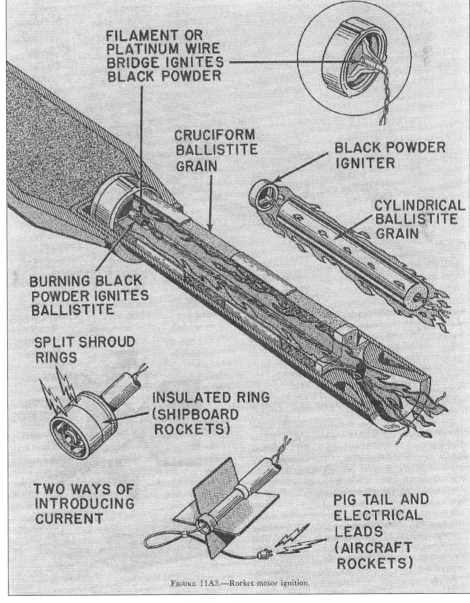

FILAMENT OR PLATINUM WIRE BRIDGE IGNITES BLACK POWDER

CRUCIFORM BALLISTITE GRAIN

BLACK POWDER IGNITER

CYLINDRICAL BALLISTITE GRAIN

BURNING BLACK POWDER IGNITES BALLISTITE

SPLIT SHROUD RINGS

INSULATED RING (SHIPBOARD ROCKETS)

TWO WAYS OF INTRODUCING CURRENT

PIG TAIL AND ELECTRICAL LEADS (AIRCRAFT ROCKETS)

FIGURE 11A3.—Rocket motor ignition.

Rocket Motor Ignition (USN)

unbalanced forward force yielding approximately 70% of the thrust. When exhausting through the nozzle, the gases expanded to a lower pressure, with increased speed, and by pushing against the outwardly flaring portion of the nozzle providing the remaining 30% of the thrust. Once these fundamental building block problems were remedied and the design frozen for production the rocket became relatively trouble free.

There was concern over, the effect of AA fire or a fighter interceptor bullet hitting either the rocket or launching rail. A hit to the rocket was not devastating as the damaged rocket would fire normally but fly erratically, or explode usually without severe damage to the wing. With the introduction of Zero Length Launchers there was little chance of damage to them because of their small size. A rocket was usually powerful enough to ride over the damaged rail section or straighten it out; of course, rocket accuracy was altered.

Rocket Launcher Development

Launchers

The rocket launcher was to carry and aim the rocket, to provide a source of electric power for firing, and sometimes to protect the aircraft against the blast of the rocket. The launcher proper (separate from the mount) consisted of a tube or a set of tubes, rails, and finally studs with a means of holding the rocket in place and a system of electrical contacts. There was no recoil since the propulsion of the rocket was accomplished by the jet action of the propellant powder in the stabilizer tube of the rocket and did not depend upon gas pressure built up inside the launcher tube.

Mark 4

For both the British and Americans the rocket launchers initially were large and cumbersome significantly decreasing the performance and maneuverability of the carrying aircraft. The first British launchers were pairs of seven foot rails bolted to a metal blast plate, four pair per wing. Cal Tech copied the British design using six foot rails designated as the Mark 4 for use with the 3.5 inch rocket.

"Bazooka" Types

Next, the US Army Ordnance had designed the M-8, a 4.5 inch diameter rocket for use by ground forces as the "Bazooka." The first airborne 4.5

inch RP M-8s were fired from aircraft from the original 'Bazooka-type' metal M-14 launching tubes but were found to be too unwieldy at 10 feet and too heavy at 190 pounds. The launcher tube needed to only heavy enough to prevent denting or bending during handling and to prevent excessive heating at normal rates of fire. Lightweight tubes manufactured from flameproof M-10 plastic soon replaced the M-14. Plastic was used as initially lightweight metals such as magnesium and aluminum were in short supply. General Electric and the Ordnance Department developed the M-10 plastic which was a special paper impregnated with a plastic compound and developed the 80 pound "Launcher, Rocket, three-tube, 4.5 inch Aircraft, M-10. However the flaming rocket exhaust limited the life of these composite plastic tubes and when light metals became available the three-tube interchangeable M-15 magnesium tubes of comparable weight (86 pounds) replaced them. The rockets were fired by individual electrical circuits from three or four (per wing) six foot underwing tubes mounted in either in M-10 or M-15 clusters and had an effective range of 800 to a 1,000 yards. The rocket had folded fins attached to the rear of the motor that opened when it left the tube to stabilize it in flight. Field trials revealed that the launching apparatus severely decreased performance and could be dropped after use. Since the tubes were in fairly short supply further development was necessary. The first American aircraft to fire rockets (M-8s in tubular cluster launchers) in combat were B-25s of the 10th Air Force in Burma in early 1944. The final report on these tests and field trials was dated 28 February 1944. It concluded that the 4.5 inch, M-8/M-10 rocket and launcher combination was effective in frontal attacks against area targets but was not suitable for use against point targets such as armor or pillboxes due to the wide dispersion and inaccuracy of fired rockets.

"Rail" Type

Further testing concluded that the P-47D was to be the AAF rocket-carrying fighter bomber and that the launching tubes were to be replaced by slightly modified British MK I rail launchers under the supervision of RAF personnel in December 1943. These British launchers were the prototypes for later American RP launchers. In tests the harmonization of the rockets was achieved by aligning the rails with the wing guns with the pilot using in MK VIII gunsight for both weapons. Between December 1943 and July 1944, none of the P-47 groups stationed in Italy or England used the rail type launcher.

The first British rocket launchers were pairs of seven foot rails bolted to a metal blast plate, four pair per wing. Cal Tech copied the British design using six foot rails designated as the **Mark 4** for use with the 3.5 inch rocket. (USN)

The American **Rail Launcher** was a slightly modified British MK I rail launcher and was used in tests but was never used operationally due to the successful ntroduction of the Zero Length Launcher. (AAF)

Bazooka Aerial Rocket Launcher

P-51D carrying a triple 80 pound **M-10 Bazooka Launcher** for the 4.5 inch rocket. Special flameproof M-10 plastic was used in the manufacture of the tubes because of the shortage of metal. (AAF)

Fuselage-mounted M-10 Bazooka Launcher on a B-25 medium bomber. (AAF)

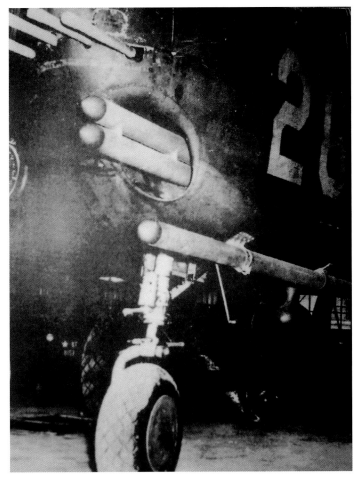

Still another innovative placement of the M-10 Bazooka tubes was on the bomb bay doors of a B-25. (AAF)

Pictured is a very unusual mounting of the M-10 Bazooka tubes on a B-25G. In addition to the single fuselage-mounted M-10 tube some inventive armorer inserted two tubes in the tunnel usually reserved for the 75mm cannon on the G-model B-25. (AAF)

Armorers loading the **M-8 or M-10 type rocket** that was 4.5 inches in diameter, about three feet long, and weighed 40 pounds. (AAF)

Armorers fixing the ignition wires to a 4.5 inch rocket which was fired electrically through a small cockpit control box and Intervalometer. Contact was made with the ignition circuit through two metal rings on the closure at the back end of the motor on the early type rockets. Later models had a double contact, single prong plug attached to the rear end. The plug was inserted in jacks on the launchers. (AAF)

"Zero Length" Launcher

In late 1943, the Bureau of Aeronautics assumed control over all launcher development and manufacture and ordered large scale replacement of all rail launchers with the Zero Length Launcher. To make use of the already available M8 rockets with the new launcher in the field; Section H, Army Ordnance, and the Air Force worked together to devise a field conversion kit for their use with the Zero Length Launcher. The M8s were fitted with larger fins and the encompassing bands and lugs. As new rocket models were produced it was a simple matter to install different adapter slots on the launcher studs.

Experimentation established that the launching rails could be shortened without affecting rocket performance or accuracy. The logical conclusion of this investigation was the so-called "Zero Length" launcher

which was so-named because the rocket was free of the launcher after a half to three inches of flight. The Mark 5 was two small streamlined posts or studs weighing 2.5 pounds per set (20 pounds for an eight rocket installation). The Mark 5 was easily installed, consisting of four button-type posts mounted on a forward plate and four loop-type lugs on a rear plate attached by screws on the outer wing surface. Lugs attached to bands encircling the rocket and fitted into slotted plated on the bottom of the posts, one at the forward end of the rocket and the other at the rear. The zero-rail attached the rocket about six inches below the wing surface, parallel to the long axis of the aircraft and only reduced the maximum aircraft speed by six to nine mph. The length of travel of the ignited rocket was nil as compared to the six or seven feet on early launching rails. There was no loss of accuracy using Zero Length Launchers as the affect of the

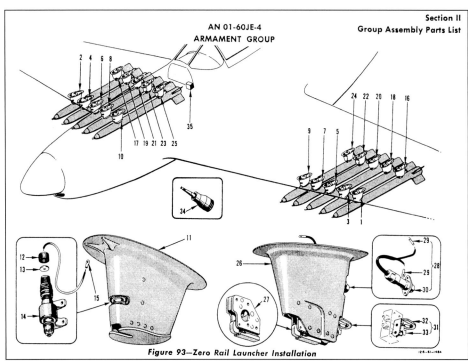

Opposite: **Posterior Mark 5 Post** An aft-facing socket in the rear post accommodated the rocket ignition wire that connected to the rocket motor for electrical ignition similar to that firing the 4.5 inch rocket. (AAF)

Zero Length Rail Launcher Installation (P-51 Parts Manual)

Zero Length Launcher

Anterior Mark 5 Post The Mark 5 Post was a streamlined stud weighing 2.5 pounds per set (AAF)

The **Mark 5 Zero Length Post** was easily installed, consisting of four button-type posts mounted on a forward plate and four loop-type lugs on a rear plate attached by screws on the outer wing surface. (AAF)

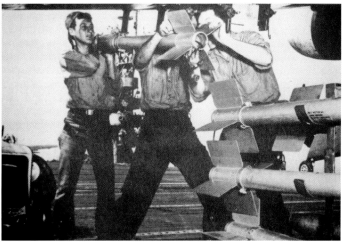

Navy armorers loading the 140 pound, six foot 5 inch HVAR rocket onto Zero Length posts. (USN)

Lugs attached to bands encircling the rocket and fitted into slotted plated on the bottom of the posts, one at the forward end of the rocket and the other at the rear. The zero-rail slung the rocket about six inches below the wing surface, parallel to the long axis of the aircraft and only reduced the maximum aircraft speed by six to nine mph. (AAF)

A **"Christmas Tree" multiple rocket launcher** could carry three or five (shown) rockets. (AAF)

A loaded five rocket Christmas Tree Launcher flanked by three standard wing-mounted Zero Length Launchers. (AAF)

airstream at speeds of over 200 knots was to act as a weather vane to direct the rocket into the aircraft's line of flight. The rocket's forward mounting lug fit into a slot on the bottom of the Mark 5's forward post while the rocket's rear section mounting lug fit into the lower front of the post. An aft-facing socket in the rear post accommodated the rocket ignition wire that connected to the rocket motor for electrical ignition similar to that firing the 4.5 inch rocket. The launcher fixed the initial direction of the rocket's flight by limiting the motion of its center of gravity until it left the launcher. The fin-stabilized rocket fired from the zero rail launcher flew a "line of flight" attitude and its trajectory could not be harmonized with the guns. A different sight setting was required for firing guns and rockets. There was no danger if both machine guns and rockets were fired at the same time.

The launchers were numbered one, two, three, and four starting from inboard. Each launcher was attached to the wing by a single hangar bolt that screwed into a wing fitting. The correct fore and aft alignment of the launcher and electrical connections was provided by an aligning tube that incorporated an electrical connector that fit into the wing receptacle. A T-Slot slideway on the bottom of the launcher accommodated the mounting lugs on the rocket. The front end of the T-Slot was open to allow the entrance of the lugs. After the lugs were inserted into the front end of the T-Slot the rocket was pushed aft, causing a latch to engage the rear lug and lock the rocket in place. This latch could be manually released by a lever that extended the rear end of the launcher. During rocket firing the latch was unlocked by a solenoid that was actuated when the rocket firing button on the control stick was depressed. After the latch was unlocked the rocket had to overcome the pressure of the latch spring to leave the launcher. Each rocket and a "pig tail" electrical lead that led from the rocket to a telephone jack-type plug that was inserted into a special wing receptacle located behind the launcher. When the rocket firing button on the control stick was pressed, electrical current passed through the pig tail to a squib that exploded and initiated the burning of the power in the rocket motor. The pig tail was blown off by the rocket discharge as the rocket left the launcher. The T-Slot latch that retained the rocket in the launcher was unlocked by the latch solenoid that was energized simultaneously with the rocket firing circuits. The rocket motor had to build up sufficient pressure before it could overcome the latch spring and leave the launcher. A safety pin was included in the latch assembly unit. If the latch did not release, the pin sheared with a force of about 2,000 pounds,

The design of some rocket breaker heads allowed either instantaneous or delayed detonation depending on whether the rocket nose fuse was armed or not. A rocket arming solenoid located in the front of the launcher allowed the insertion of the loop end of a standard arming wire that extended from the solenoid to the rocket nose fuse. Once the arming solenoid was energized by the rocket arming switch, the solenoid plunger extended and locked the arming wire to the launcher. When the rocket was fired from the launcher, the arming wire was pulled from the rocket fuse and armed it. The general principal of rocket arming was similar to arming bombs with the only difference being that under no circumstances could the rocket be fired in "SAFE" condition because the inside of the rocket contained a base fuse that armed automatically and caused a delayed detonation of the rocket.

Multiple Launchers
In the late war a number of multiple launchers appeared which included the three and five rocket "Christmas Tree" and the ten rocket enclosed pod.

The jury-rigging of 10 small (3.5 inch?) rockets bound by hooks and straps into pods carried on standard underwing pylon of a P-38. (AAF)

Rocket Sights

Initially, in the early 1940s, little attention was paid to the development of a rocket sight as the philosophy of the time was to aim the aircraft at the target and the rockets would follow. The first rocket sight during early tests was a small piece of tape positioned on the windshield after observing previous rocket trajectories. But the Navy needed something more sophisticated to sight their new rockets so the Bureau of Ordnance modified its outstanding Mark 8 Illuminated Sight which was used to sight forward-firing fixed machine guns. An adjustable (by the pilot) reflector was added that permitted the line of sight to be raised to compensate for the rocket's greater gravity drop. This modification had the disadvantage of having the pilot perform another manual task in the frenzy of making an attack; often in the face if anti-aircraft fire. This problem was rectified in mid-1944 by replacing the adjustable reflector by a sight whose reticle had a vertical ladder of crossbars that allowed the pilot's eye to raise or lower his line of sight. The pilot had to be familiar with the different rocket types to select a particular line on the crossbar also with the sighting tables that would indicate the necessary sighting information for his particular aircraft, rocket, airspeed, dive angle, and slant range. These tables were developed by Cal Tech scientists who used range data from thousands of rocket firings at the Naval Ordnance Test Station (NOTS) at China Lake, CA.

During the last year of the war, Dr. Horace Babcock of Cal Tech developed four "CIT Aircraft Rocket Sights" which were assigned the type numbers, 1 through 4. The first test of the Cal Tech Type 1 Sight occurred on 4 June 1944 was successful but the sight never went into service use because the improved Type 2 was soon successful. The Type 2 had a two-way throw switch that enabled the pilot to select either of two types of rockets even after beginning a diving attack. Neither the Type 1 nor Type 2 was completely automatic as the pilot had to set dials in advance for predicted airspeed and propellant temperature; plus he had to make his diving attack at a predetermined angle. However, the changes in altitude were automatically fed into the sight from a barometric altimeter that continuously readjusted the sight and allowed the pilot to fire at any point within the effective range of his rockets. Types 3 and 4 became more automatic and were used effectively by experienced pilots.

As the war progressed, it became apparent that the accuracy of forward-firing rockets could stand much improvement. The Bureau was already working hard to enhance the accuracy of fixed machine guns with a sophisticated system of fire control. Once the gyroscopic lead computing Gun Sight Mark 14 was available it was adapted to sighting rockets. When using the Mark 14 in air-to-air combat the pilot only had to keep a constant view of his target while controlling an expandable circle of dots to continually surround the target's wingspan. Any pilot sighting inaccuracy was compensated for the mass volume of fire from the multiple fixed machine guns but this was not true for individual rocket projectiles. The ballistic characteristics for conventional ammunition were well-known; but rocket ballistics was not which stifled modifying the Gun Sight Mark 14 for rocket use. This was eventually accomplished but the sight was not ready for operational use with rockets until late in the war.

Fighter Bomber Rocket Use in Ground Support

Generally aerial ground support rocket targets were those targets which would be put under artillery fire if they were in range of artillery. The topography of the target area was a major factor in considering the suitability of a target as a low approach and attack angle were necessary. Targets situated in flat open areas were easiest to attack while targets in valleys or surrounded by hills were difficult or impossible to attack as the target had to be recognized at one mile out. Targets located in hills or mountains could be successfully attacked but surprise was often lost in the attack. Rocket attacks created a morale problem for the enemy that was more of a factor than the actual destructive damage they caused. Scuttlebutt spread among German troops that exaggerated the effect of the rocket attack. The noise and the sight of the diving fighter bomber and then of the launched rockets unnerved the German troops on the receiving end of the attack.

It was estimated that the salvo of all eight rockets would result in a one-in-twenty chance of hitting a target the size of a Panzer tank. Despite their inaccuracy, the rocket was more accurate than the free-fall bomb but much less than strafing with machine gun or cannon, which, in turn, when compared to a rocket had much less striking power to inflict significant damage when hitting the target (the HVAR had the explosive effect of a 155mm shell).

Against heavily defended targets pilots were advised to make a steep 60° dive at 7,000-8,000 feet and fire all rockets in salvo at about 4,000 feet altitude and at a range of 5,000 feet. On these strongly defended targets, doctrine stated that they should only be attacked once. If the target were lightly defended, the pilots were to make a shallow dive of 20°-30° at 3,000-4,000 feet and to fire them in pairs from 1,500 feet altitude at a range of 3,000 feet and return to fire the other pair. However, in practice

The Navy Bureau of Ordnance modified its outstanding **Mark 8 Illuminated Sight** which was used to sight forward-firing fixed machine guns for rocket firing by adding an adjustable reflector that permitted the line of sight to be raised to compensate for the rocket's greater gravity drop. (Author's Equipment Collection)

the pilots disregarded the prescribed tactics and developed their own tactics.

The advantages of the rocket used in ground support operations were that rocket attack tactics were easily learned by pilots already experienced in dive or glide bombing attacks and the installation of the equipment was as simple as installing bomb racks and the rockets were easier to handle by ground crews than the bulkier bombs. Compared to glide or dive bombing attacks, a much higher degree of accuracy was attained especially later in the war when aircraft with increased speeds and rockets with longer burning times and increased velocity were introduced. The rocket had a greater destructive effect per maximum load than the maximum bomb load carried by the same aircraft. The maximum rocket velocity of 1,000 to 1,200 fps plus the aircraft's speed gave great penetration and decreased the time for a mobile target to maneuver. Rockets were regarded with fear by enemy troops far in excess of their destructiveness. The speed of the rocket attack was faster than other bombing techniques thereby reducing the risk to AA fire.

The major disadvantage of the rocket in a ground support role was its sensitivity to pilot errors especially in the face of anti-aircraft fire. Incorrect airspeed or glide angle along with any errors in range or wind estimation would cause inaccuracies. It was not possible to set the launching rails, tubes, or studs parallel to the line of flight for all speeds and loadings. If the rocket was fired at an angle to the aircraft's flight path then a force acted on the tail fins tending to make the rocket swing back into the relative wind causing an inaccuracy. The pilot had to fly at the speed for which the sight was harmonized. Side slipping and last minute aiming corrections were not possible without subjecting the rocket to G-forces. While experienced ground attack pilots could easily master rocket technique, intensive training was required for new pilots. Generally, rocket training was deficient in both the USAAF and RAF (except the 2TAF later) scheme as air-to-air combat was concentrated upon rather than ground attack practice. Premature firing was commonplace and pilot aiming errors were proportional to launching range. The average error was six feet per every 1,000 feet in range (vertically and horizontally). Since the rockets caused decreased aircraft performance pilots often fired their rockets first to get rid of them. Pilots were often unable to identify small pin-point targets which were suited to rocket attack. Since accuracy rather than weight of explosives was the major asset of the weapon, it was imperative to have a thorough preflight briefing with low level photo recon studies.

In a typical ground attack a combination of strafing and rocket launching was employed. Approach angles of 20° to 55° were used and these angles could be steeper than those used in anti-shipping attacks because underwater trajectory was not a consideration. If the glide were begun at 4,000 feet the pilot had sufficient opportunity to aim at the target and launch at an optimum slant range of 750 to 1,000 yards. There was no limitation on glide speed except the maximum speed of the aircraft. In attacks on specific targets the flight leader and his wingman carried eight phosphorous marker rockets which were launched first. The rockets would fall into machine gun bullet pattern when released at 2,000 feet with slant ranges of 1,000-1,500 yards in angles of 35° or more. As the glide angle decreased then compensation had to be made for the drop of the rocket trajectory. Therefore, a proper approach allowed the attacker to strafe accurately to decrease the effect of anti-aircraft fire and permit a closer launch increasing accuracy. As mentioned previously, since the rockets followed the line of flight of the firing aircraft, it was imperative for the pilot to hold the aircraft steady before launch without any evasive maneuvers. In coordinated attacks, sufficient intervals between aircraft were necessary to permit each aircraft to steady on the target, launch, and withdraw.

The release of bombs and rockets simultaneously was discouraged as the pilot needed to have further extensive training to become proficient. Combat studies demonstrated that pilots failed to close sufficiently to launch for two major reason: failure to estimate range correctly and fear of target reaction (e.g. AA fire or explosion of the target, or colliding with the ground). The withdrawal from the target after launch could be accomplished by turning away before the aircraft was too close to the exploding target or by flying over the target at a height sufficient (800 to 1,000 feet) to avoid the explosion.

The following rocket firing procedure taken from the pilot's manual of a P-51D. The rocket armament switches were located on the special rocket panel insert located at the lower left of the front cockpit. The firing sequence was as follows:

1) Turn rocket counter dial to 1

A rocket counter was incorporated into the rocket panel and had a control knob located adjacent to its number window which showed the rocket to be fired by number. The firing order of rockets singly or in train was:

1-3-5-7-9 on the left wing and 2-4-6-8-10 on the right wing

Rockets 7, 8, 9, and 10 were not installed when bombs or drop tanks were carried. The type of target determined the number of rockets fired during the attack run. Against smaller targets the rockets were usually fired in pairs while against larger targets such as bridges or trains all were fired at once.

2) Turn the Bomb-Rocket Selector dial to the ROCKETS position.

This dial was located on the front switch panel and completed the rocket firing circuit making the bomb release circuits inoperable.

3) Turn the Rocket Arming switch to DELAY

The two-position Rocket Delay Switch, nose armed the rockets for instantaneous delay upon impact. The alternative setting was INST (instantaneous)

4) Set the gunsight (rocket sight) to the FIXED position

5) Set the Rocket Release control switch

This switch had OFF-SINGLE-AUTO positions and was located on the front switch panel

6) Aim the aircraft at target through the gunsight

7) Depress three ORB-ROCKET RELEASE switch

This control was a button located on top of the joy stick and could fire rockets singly when set on SINGLE (one rocket was fired per press of the button) but to fire all rockets in train, the setting was AUTO and the button was pressed for one second.

The rocket was fired electrically through a control box and Intervalometer. While cannon and machine gun fire could be heard by the pilot above the noise of the engines the rocket launch was a small whip-like crack signifying the release of the rockets as the propellant gases blew out the end plugs.

The rocket was used for both day and night low level operations, however, the difficulty encountered in depth perception on dark nights made accuracy difficult. Pilots using rockets for the first time during nighttime needed to be aware of the rocket flash that caused momentary partial blindness immediately after firing. Various methods were recommended to eliminate this problem. One was to close one eye during the time the rocket was being fired and then to use this eye after the flash diminished. Another method recommended closing both eyes a split second before the rockets were released, then allowing one or two seconds for the flash to subside before opening the eyes again. This latter method was not to be used when operating below 1,000 feet.

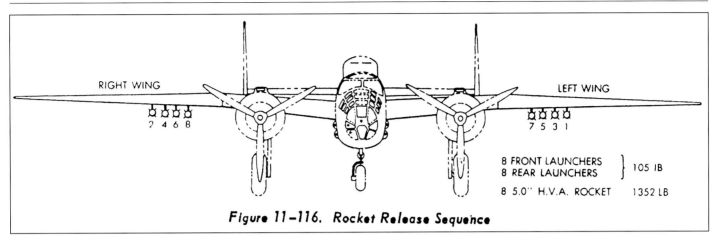

Figure 11-116. Rocket Release Sequence

RIGHT WING

LEFT WING

2 4 6 8

7 5 3 1

8 FRONT LAUNCHERS
8 REAR LAUNCHERS } 105 IB

8 5.0" H.V.A. ROCKET   1352 LB

The **Rocket Firing Sequence** singly or in train was: 1-3-5-7-9 on the left wing and 2-4-6-8-10 on the right wing. (B-25 Flight Manual)

The Rocket's Effectiveness Against Varied Ground Targets
Buildings: In attacking groups of buildings, bombs were found to be twice as effective as rockets due to their blast effect on large exposed surfaces However; rockets were more accurate and could deliver a heavier concentration of firepower. Rockets were much more effective in destroying small isolated buildings (up to 10 times better) than bombs and fewer attacking planes were risked; four to five against 27 to 28 in a conventional bombing attack.

Armored Vehicles: The effectiveness of rockets against tanks and armored vehicles depended on the courage of the attacking pilot in closing on the target. The lower and closer the launch of the rockets was to the target; the more accurate and destructive the hits. It was best to attack tanks before they took shelter or began to move. The anti-tank rocket technique was for the aircraft to fly straight, level, and steady at 250 to 400 feet and launch at under 600 yards. The attacking aircraft had to quickly climb or sharply veer away immediately after launch to avoid the shrapnel of the exploding rockets.

Locomotives: Strafing was more effective in stopping the target by releasing steam through the perforated boiler. However, a rocket hit caused much more extensive, permanent damage to the locomotive.

Parked aircraft: Rockets were better than bombs on widely dispersed aircraft as they were more accurate than bombs and caused more damage than strafing.

Trucks: Strafing with cannon was more accurate and economical.

Personnel: Fragmentation Bombs were much more effective than either rocket or strafing attacks.

Gun Emplacements: The gun itself was difficult to damage or destroy by any means even in open emplacements. The best method to attack gun emplacements was to attack the manning personnel, fire control equipment, or ammunition. Rockets compared favorably with bombs.

Bridges: Rockets were not powerful enough to affect the concrete supporting pillars. An accurate rocket launch could go through or bounce

P-47 attack on German rail traffic. A rocket hit could devastate a locomotive and stop a train for further attacks, or destroy rails and rail beds in marshaling yards, or in remote locations cause long delays until repair crews arrived. (AAF)

Japanese coastal freighter undergoing a rocket attack. (USN)

off the bridge girders and superstructure to explode 10-15 feet away without damage.

Shipping: Rockets were effective against shipping, especially when used in conjunction with strafing.

By the end of the war the aircraft ground support rocket had become an effective weapon when used in experienced hands. On Okinawa Marine Corps F4U Corsairs outfitted with two 500 pound bombs or Napalm bombs under their center sections and four HVARs mounted on Zero Length Launchers on each outer wing panel provided close ground support on "cab rank." Aircraft flew on station and were called by a controller on VHF/RT to a target identified on an especially gridded map carried by pilots. The map (1:100,000) was divided into squares representing 500x400 meters and lettered A to Z horizontally across the map and numbered vertically. Japanese strong points were reported and the air controller called them to the waiting Corsairs. The technique was so successful that the F4Us were called the "Sweethearts of Okinawa" by grateful infantry troops.

Medium Bomber Rocket Attack
The tactics used for a rocket attack by a medium bomber were identical to those used in the low level and high angle strafing attacks. However, this technique required a better than average judgment of range and could only be achieved through comprehensive instruction and constant practice. Procedures for setting up the Rocket Intervalometer needed to be thoroughly understood and the rocket checklist was to be used before the rocket attack.

Lt.Col. Jack Cram's VMB-612, was commissioned 1 October 1943 as a conventional North American PBJ (Navy/Marine B-25) daylight unit, but in February 1944 it was chosen for experimental work in night bombing and torpedo launching. The B-25J was equipped with eight 5 inch HVAR rockets weighing approximately 1,100 pounds on launching racks mounted outboard each engine. After routine but intense training on the East Coast the Squadron was ready to move into night combat. During August 1944, a prototype PBJ was equipped with Zero Length Rocket

During the battle for Okinawa Japanese strong points holding up Marine infantry advances were reported to an air controller who called in waiting Corsairs (VMF-323 shown). The technique was so successful that grateful Marines called the F4Us the "Sweethearts of Okinawa." (USMC)

Lt.Col. Jack Cram was the CO of VMB-612, flying North American PBJ which was the Navy and Marine Corps version of the B-25. The innovative Cram pioneered night bombing, rocket, and torpedo launching in the Pacific. (USMC)

Launchers at San Diego and then another 15 aircraft were similarly equipped when the Squadron reached Oahu.

In an interview with Air Intelligence (15 March 1945) Squadron Commander Cram described a rocket attack:

"We figured that by flying at a definite altitude, say 300 feet, in level flight and knowing the ballistics of the rocket, we could predict where it would hit the water. ....By making a temperature correction, a correction for the weight which affects the attitude of the rocket, using a constant altitude and figuring in the wind drift and the velocity, we had a correction that gave us a very accurate range."

To put its training to a test the Squadron deployed to Eniwetok and targeted a small coral outcropping that was no larger than the many Japanese ships which sailed at night. The Squadron fired about 250 rockets at this island and scored 56% hits. They were equipped to use the 5 inch rocket in combat, sometimes in conjunction with the large *Tiny Tim* rocket, but by that time Japanese shipping and large ground targets were scarce.

Anti-shipping Rocket Attack

The aiming procedure for an anti-shipping attack was similar to a glide bomb attack. The principles of a bombing and rocket attack were similar; even though the rocket's trajectory was different from a bomb's (being along the aircraft's flight path) and the rocket technique required successive acts of sighting and firing. When attacking a lone surface ship or surfaced submarine with rockets the point of aim was to be just below the waterline. Attacks on a partly or fully submerged submarine the point of aim was slightly lower (e.g. the visible portion of the target was sighted, slightly above the mark in the sight reticle used in normal firing). The pilot was to hold the target in the sight for as long as possible without deviating from the glide angle. He had to maintain steady flight for two seconds before launching so as not to bind the rockets on the launching rails or tubes used at that stage. Therefore last second corrections were not feasible. The firing button was pressed and ignition and launch occurred one tenth second later. The first pair of rockets was launched at 1,200 yards as a sighting salvo and to disorganize the ship's crew. The second pair was launched at 800 yards as a final sighting salvo which would also have a fair chance for a hit. The third pair was launched for a hit at 400 yards. The steeper the glide angle the better the accuracy and rocket stability in flight but if the angle of entry into the water was too great there was a loss of underwater trajectory. The optimum angle of water entry was 20° or less. The 3.5 inch solid head rocket projectile had a lethal underwater range of 50 to 60 feet and within this range it maintained a velocity of 600 fps which was sufficient to penetrate a merchant ship's hull or the pressure hull or saddle tanks of a submarine. If the attacking aircraft were carrying both depth charges and rockets they both were not be released on the same attack rim as the low altitude pull out of the aircraft for the rocket attack could subject it to damage from the blasts of the depth charges. Strafing was helpful in reducing return anti-aircraft fire from the target but its accuracy was poor as the gunsight was set for the rocket attack. When the wind velocity was known aiming allowances could be made (e.g. a 30 knot wind was corrected for by aiming 40 to 50 feet in the proper direction). Premature launching was fairly common especially in the face of stiff anti-aircraft fire.

Anti-shipping attacks against convoys utilized both torpedo and rocket-carrying aircraft. Anti-flak strafing escorts, usually comprising two-thirds of the attacking aircraft, would attack first turning to attack the beam of the convoy firing throughout their entire run to intimidate and destroy AA fire. If the convoy consisted of deep draught merchantmen

and warships the rocket-carrying aircraft would be used first to further suppress AA fire and the torpedo planes were used as the main force. In attacking shallow draft convoys which usually consisted mainly of barges protected by small warships the rocket carrying aircraft were used to sink the convoy as torpedoes were ineffective as they would pass under the barges. During anti-shipping attack the rocket-carriers would peel off into a 20° dive and at 1,000 yards open machine gun or cannon fire, salvoing all their rockets at 600 yards. The rocket rails were set to give above and below waterline hits. Gunfire would continue to 200 yards or less where upon the attacker would zoom over the target or turn off.

On 24 September 1944 the 51,000 former Italian passenger ship *Rex* became the largest vessel in World War II to be solely sunk by rockets. The ship was being used as a block ship in Trieste harbor when it received 123 3.5 inch rocket hits by eight RAF Beaufighters of 272 Squadron.

Types of Rockets and Their Operational Use
3.5 inch Rocket

The 3.5 inch fin-stabilized AR that used a modified 3.25 inch Mk7 motor set in a tube which was 3.5 inches in diameter, hence the designation. The motor contained a single cruciform propellant grain supported internally on a grid. At the front end of the grain was a black powder igniter and electric squib contained in a plastic case. The electrical connector from the squib ended in a plug. At the rear was a nozzle sealed in a moisture-proof closure. The reversible fin assembly was a metal sleeve with four equally-spaced rectangular fins. The sleeve slid over the rear end of the motor and was attached by screwing it into the tail ring. The motor was attached to a 20 pound solid steel head giving the projectile a 65 inch length and 54 pound weight. Front and rear shipping caps were supplied to protect the motor during shipping and storage. Its maximum velocity was 1,175 fps (plus the speed of the carrying aircraft) and its accurate range was 1,000 yards. The primary use of this rocket was against submarines as the solid steel head could easily penetrate the hull of a sub even if it was traveling at periscope depth.

Early Operational Use

The first rockets taken into combat by the Navy were sent aboard two small escort carriers that were assigned to offensive ASW in the Atlantic. The *USS Mission Bay* was one of these carriers and accounts from Lt. Frank Habicht, the aviation ordnance officer in charge of aircraft rockets, indicate after a period of learning stowage, handling, mounting techniques the pilots and crew became proficient in keeping the German U-Boats

The **3.5 inch fin-stabilized AR** used a modified 3.25 inch Mk7 motor set in a tube which was 3.5 inches in diameter, hence the designation. The motor was attached to a 20 pound solid steel head giving the projectile a 65 inch length and 54 pound weight. (USN)

The first rockets taken into combat by the Navy were sent aboard two small escort carriers that were assigned to offensive ASW in the Atlantic. Shown are armorers on the **USS Mission Bay** preparing 3.5 inch rockets. The ignition wires and very large tails are noticeable. The four fins were attached to a sleeve that fit over the aft rocket body. (USN)

from surfacing to recharge their batteries. It would not be until 16 January 1944, before the first confirmed submarine kill with a rocket occurred.

In December 1943, Marine Corps Squadron VMTB-134 received experimental Mk 4 rocket launching rails that were to be followed a month later by 1,500 rockets. Eight rails were installed on each of 22 Grumman TBF Avengers with no blueprints, drawings, or instructions to help and the initial installation required more than 300 man hours for the first TBF which was decreased to only 16 man hours when the last aircraft was equipped. However, the rockets did not arrive as promised as the supply was limited by problems with fusing and those released for operations were sent to carriers in the Atlantic. The rockets did not arrive in January and the TBF pilots had to contend with the drag of the 70 inch rocket launchers which decreased not only speed by five mph but also range. When the rockets finally arrived in Noumea Harbor by cargo ship, they were packed at the bottom of hold and would take days to unload. Orders were issued to use an acetylene torch to cut through the ship's bulkhead and then air freight them to Bougainville where VMBT-134 had transferred.

The unit was allowed very limited time for training and practice with their new weapon and on 15 February 1944, only a week after their arrival at Noumea the first American aircraft rockets were launched in the Pacific. VMBT-134 TBFs, led by Maj. A.C. Robertson, attacked large Japanese transport ships in Keravia Bay, near Rabaul, New Britain. The Avengers pressed their attack through heavy enemy anti-aircraft fire, launching their rockets at practically point-blank range (500 to 600 feet) but post-mission reconnaissance showed that the damage was not as great as thought and the transports escaped heavy damage. An investigation of this failure discovered that the rockets fired were of two types, neither was designed to attack shipping. One batch of 1,000 rockets were 3.5-inch aircraft rockets with solid steel heads designed for use in perforating submarine pressure hulls. However, when used against transports the same hole that was disastrous to a submarine was not of the same consequence, especially since it usually hit above the waterline. The other 500 rockets in the Noumea shipment were 5 inch ARs with high explosive heads and fast acting fuses for antipersonnel use. This fuse was designed to detonate

immediately upon impact and would not penetrate the hull of a large vessel. If a delay fuse had been used, the rocket would penetrate the hull and then explode. Once the rockets were used for their correct tactical deployment the Marine TBFs had great success against AA emplacements, radar installations, and troop bivouac and concentrations.

On 29 February, Navy Composite Squadron 7 raided the Marshall Islands where four attacks were made by TBFs loaded with three 500 pound GP bombs and eight rockets (four HE and four solid heads on the first attack but all HE heads on the remaining three attacks). Three attacks were made against ground targets and one against shipping. Damage done by the rockets was difficult to access due to the extensive bombardment of the area. CAP did report the violent explosion of a large ammo dump during one rocket attack. The Intelligence Summary (HQ 7AF) of the raid stated the pilots reported an (overly) optimistic 80 to 100% of the rockets on target for the four attacks.

4.5 inch Rocket

On 6 July 1942 an AAF fighter fired a number of 4.5 inch rockets at the Aberdeen Proving Ground to mark the first AAF firing of an aerial rocket. The first combat aerial rocket was the 4.5 inch M-8 or M-10 types that was 4.5 inches in diameter, about three feet long, and weighed 40 pounds. The forward (head) portion contained a nose fuse and five pounds of HE. The aft portion consisted of the motor that contained the propellant charge that was a solvent base, wet extruded grain with zone charges. The charge was a rapid-burning type, lasting about one-tenth second that gave it excellent acceleration characteristics making it an ideal medium range weapon (800 yards). Its accurate range was about 750 yards at a maximum velocity of 865 fps (plus the speed of the firing aircraft). At this range the 4.5 inch rocket could penetrate one inch of homogenized face-hardened steel and about one foot of reinforced concrete. The rocket was carried in three bazooka-type launching tubes clustered together and suspended under each wing so as not to interfere with the normal bomb load or external fuel tanks. Armorers tried to bore-sight the launcher tubes to harmonize the rockets with the machine guns so that one gunsight setting could be used for both. Each rocket carried a nose fuse that could only be adjusted on the ground for a .015 second delay or for instantaneous setting. The round was placed in the tube from the rear and fastened in place and then the electrical firing connections were made. The rocket was fired electrically through a small cockpit control box and Intervalometer. This allowed selective firing or salvo firing with a one-tenth interval. Contact was made

The **4.5 inch M-8 or M-10 rocket** was 4.5 inches in diameter, about three feet long, and weighed 40 pounds. The forward (head) portion contained a nose fuse and five pounds of HE. The aft portion consisted of the motor that contained the propellant charge that was a solvent base, wet extruded grain with zone charges. (AAF)

with the ignition circuit through two metal rings on the closure at the back end of the motor on the early type rockets. Later models had a double contact, single prong plug attached to the rear end. The plug was inserted in jacks on the launchers.

4.5 inch Rocket Operations
In early 1944, under the ATSC, the AAF Army Ordnance established a rocket-testing center at the Army Air Field at Dover, DE with 200 rocket scientists and technicians under Col. Donald B. Diehl. The Navy and NDRC also did further work. Rockets were tested, launching installations and methods were developed and refined and the effectiveness of rockets against various targets was evaluated. The aircraft best suited for rocket attacks was one with good maneuverability at high speed: fighters then dive bombers, finally, and torpedo bombers. It was found that rocket accuracy depended on pilot aiming ability, altitude, and rocket dispersion after launching. Inaccuracies decreased as the speed of the firing aircraft increased. The AAF claimed that at 250 mph a trained pilot was able to put half of his rockets within a 16 foot circle at 400 yards!

By February 1944, only four months before D-Day, the "rocket question" remained unresolved in the USAAF. On 5 May 1944 the 9th Air Force finally began trials using the P-47 equipped with prototype MK V rocket projectors. These jettisonable installations were attached to standard bomb shackles and could carry four M-8 or M-10 rockets on each carrier. There was not enough time to conduct effective trials, standardize the fittings or train pilots before D-Day so the 9th Air Force P-47s carried no rockets into combat on D-Day.

In August, four 8th Air Force fighter groups were supplied with four sets of 4.5 inch triple-tube bazooka-type rocket launchers with 60 M-8/M-10 rockets. The 56th and 353rd Fighter Groups were immediately equipped with trial installations but the 78th and 356th Groups met delays due to lack of installation tools. All four 8th Air Groups participated in a few lackluster, half-hearted ground attack rocket missions. First and foremost, 8th Air Force pilots thought of themselves as fighter pilots and if they had to be ground attack pilots they preferred strafing and the 500 pound bomb that was easier to use and had a lower AA fire risk. On 17 August the 56th Fighter Group, led by deputy group CO, Lt.Col. David Schilling, conducted the first organized rocket mission when the Group attacked Braine-le-Compt area firing M-10 rockets with mixed results. Schilling was able to destroy four rail cars but he only proved that a

highly experienced pilot could achieve good results. The P-47s had no special sight to aim the rockets but needed to use machine gun fire to aim the rockets. Success was correlated to combat experience and pilot skill and 8th Air Force bomber escort pilots had received no training for ground attack. Again despite the potential of the rocket by mid-September the rocket tubes were removed from 8th Air Force P-47s. The inevitable disagreements within the USAAF high command occurred. XIX TAC commander, O.P. Weyland, correctly favored saving the rockets for use against tanks and armored targets but throughout the summer of 1944 the limited rocket supply was wasted haphazardly.

Despite this moderate success that equaled bombing results, American pilots preferred bombing targets to "rocketeering." The rockets were found to be inaccurate on pinpoint targets and the tubes reduced the Thunderbolt's performance after the rockets were salvoed. Pilots found other faults with the rocket. When the pilots received their new rockets they were given a chart that listed the sight settings as a function of dive angle, air speed and distance to the target. Pilots found it very difficult to correlate all these factors during a firing pass. Rocket installation on the P-47 had a serious disadvantage, as the machine guns could not be fired until the rockets were salvoed. The rockets were located under the chutes that ejected the machine gun belt links and shell casings that would break the rocket firing wire. Probably the biggest fault was that a rocket had to be fired within a 1,000 yards of the target to attain any accuracy and this range exposed the fighter bomber to accurate AA and ground fire which could have been suppressed by the eight .50 caliber machine guns.

However, the RAF 2nd TAF was equipped with RP-equipped (RP=Rocket Projectile) Typhoons which were instrumental in preventing German tanks from reaching the front. Studies of the 2nd TAF's rocket-equipped 124 Squadron showed that it only destroyed 12 tanks in June using 3,700 rockets for an immense expenditure of 308 rockets per tank destroyed! The RAF used long rails to give the rocket its initial accuracy but experience found that the fixed fin rocket tended to align itself with the air stream, much like a weathervane. Tests showed comparable accuracy could be obtained with "Zero-rails" which referred to the lack of guide rails as the rocket was actually attached by small posts and guided for only about an inch. With these posts the top speed of the fighter was only decreased six to nine miles per hour. The rockets were aligned parallel to both the centerline of the fuselage and the aircraft's line of thrust and were fired in pairs, one from each wing, to maintain equal wing loads. The Zero-rail launcher went into US service in the spring of 1944.

On 17 August 1944, Deputy 56th Fighter Group CO, **Lt.Col. David Schilling** led the first organized rocket operation when it attacked the Braine-le-Compt area firing M-10 rockets with mixed results. (Author)

The rocket-equipped **Hawker Typhoon** of the RAF's 2nd TAF was the premier rocket fighter bomber of World War 2 as the RAF emphasized the use of rockets far more than the 8th Air Force. (AFHRC)

In spring 1943 the California Institute of Technology and the US Navy under a contract to the Office of Scientific Research and Development actively pursued an aerial rocket development program. Their research quickly produced a number of rockets and launching techniques. The three rocket types were: the 3.5 inch aircraft rocket (AR), the 5 inch aircraft rocket (AR) and the 5 inch high velocity aircraft rocket (HVAR) which were all fin-stabilized and intended for an assortment of different targets. A few P-47 squadrons were equipped with eight HVARs and were particularly effective against the Germans at St. Lo. During this period the HVAR was produced by CIT and about 100 rockets per day were air-shipped from California to the east coast then to USAAF airfields in France. So it was that civilian scientists and Navy developers and testers would have the Air Force use the HVAR in combat.

5 inch AR and HVAR Rocket

The 5 inch AR used the same motor as the 3.5 inch rocket. The 5 inch AR had a 5 inch diameter warhead that increased its weight to 80 pounds but was about the same length as the 3.5 inch AR. The larger head slowed the weapon to about 850 fps. This rocket was intended for use against targets where high explosive effect, not penetration, was important. The celebrated 5 inch HVAR was developed from the 5 inch AR, employing the warhead of the 5 inch AR attached to the 5 inch diameter motor. The rocket's length was standardized at six feet and weighed 140 pounds that included eight pounds of HE in the warhead. The propellant was a non-solvent base, dry extruded grain. It had a comparatively slow burning time (1.2 seconds) that gave it a slower acceleration with a higher maximum velocity (1,375 fps plus the speed of the firing aircraft) and greater accurate range (1,000 yards) than the 4.5 inch rocket. At 1,000 yards it was able to penetrate 1.75 inches of homogenized face-hardened steel and three feet of reinforced concrete. The Armor Piercing plug in its head was capable of penetrating reinforced concrete and armor and could be replaced with

a nose fuse set for instantaneous detonation on impact. A lightweight (15 pound for a six rocket installation) Zero-rail launcher was developed to launch these rockets and was made up of two streamlined posts attached to the underside of the wing. The Mark 5 rocket launcher consisted of four posts mounted on a forward plate and four on a rear plate attached by screws on the outer wing surface. Lugs attached to bands encircling the rocket and fitted into slotted plated on the bottom of the posts, one at the forward end of the rocket and the other at the rear. The Zero-rail slung the projectile about six inches below the wing surface, parallel to the long axis of the aircraft. The HVAR's forward mounting lug fit into a slot on the bottom of the Mark 5's forward post. The rockets rear section mounting lug fit into the lower front of the post. An aft-facing socket in the rear post accommodated the rocket ignition wire that connected to the rocket motor for electrical ignition similar to that firing the 4.5 inch rocket. The launcher fixed the initial direction of the rocket's flight by limiting the motion of its center of gravity until it left the launcher. The fin-stabilized rocket fired from the zero rail launcher flew a "line of flight" attitude and its trajectory could not be harmonized with the guns. A different sight setting was required for firing guns and rockets. There was no danger if both machine guns and rockets were fired at the same time.

ETO AAF Rocket Trials and Use
The Ordnance Department of the USAAF had conducted trials using the 4.5 inch rocket for nearly two years but rocket accuracy was inconsistent and the bulky launching tubes so reduced aircraft performance even after rocket launch that P-47 pilots preferred dive bombing attacks as once a bomb was released the shackles had little effect on aircraft performance. It was decided that operational trials could resolve the "rocket issue". Col. H.L. Donicht of the AAF, Drs. C.C. Lauritsen and Carl Anderson of CIT and RAF GC H.W. "Dixie" Dean flew to England to personally supervise the installation and combat tests. In July 1944, several P-47Ds

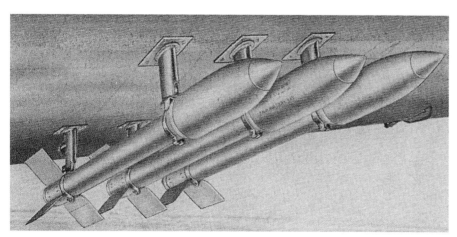

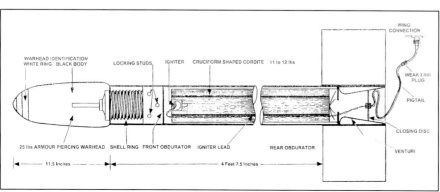

5 inch HVAR Rocket

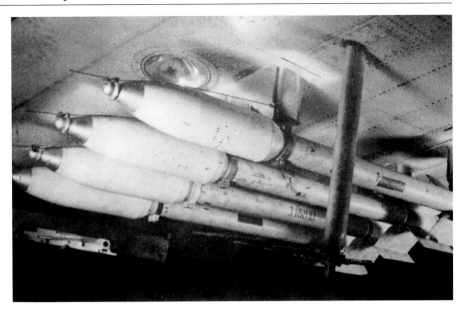

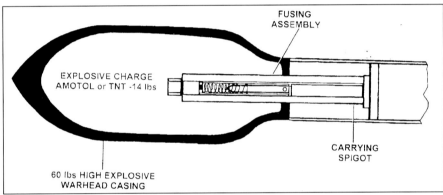

5 inch HVAR Warhead

FUSING
ASSEMBLY

EXPLOSIVE CHARGE
AMOTOL or TNT -14 lbs

CARRYING
SPIGOT

60 lbs HIGH EXPLOSIVE
WARHEAD CASING

of the "rocketeer" 513th Fighter Squadron of the 406th Fighter Group were equipped to carry four HVAR 5 inch rockets, two under each wing, instead of the eight normally installed on Navy aircraft. The initial production of the rocket was set at a 100 rounds a day, manufactured under Cal Tech direction, and was ferried daily by air directly from the production line in California to England until 1,400 had been delivered and stockpiled.

The first operational use (officially scheduled as a "safe practice run") of American HVARs in the ETO occurred on 7 August 1944 when Col. Anthony Grossetta led three flights of four P-47s from their base at Ashland, England to attack marshaling yards (Tiger-Quail) near Nevers, France. The first pass was made on a flak tower protecting the yards that suffered a direct hit, putting it out of commission. The Thunderbolts dove on a concentration of over 50 locomotives, firing 48 rockets, 38 of them disabling 25 valuable locomotives. Three repair shops and a roundhouse were also damaged. On the 26th the first American rocket attacks against German armor were made with nine tanks destroyed (four by rockets, three by strafing and two by bombs) and three damaged (all by rockets). On the next day three rocket-equipped flights attacked German airdrome at Coulommiers. A total of 37 rockets were fired at 1,000 yards at a 30° dive. Moderate damage was done as one large hangar; four small hangars, a fuel dump, and one Me-110 were hit. A rail bridge at Montford was also claimed destroyed by seven rockets as a target of opportunity. In a later mission several *Luftwaffe* FW-190s attacked rocket-carrying P-47s and four Thunderbolts were shot down. On 13 August, the 513FS attacked four heavy Mark V Panther tanks and one light German tank moving

along a road near Marigny, France. The attack, led by RAF rocket expert Group Captain H.W. Dean, destroyed all five Panzers. By September the 513th Squadron had flown 323 sorties firing 1,117 rockets and claimed:

Drawing from the AAF's October 1944 issue of the intelligence magazine *Impact* of the 26 August 1944 P-47 rocket attack by 8AF P-47s on German armor in France. These August rocket missions were scheduled to test the new American HVARs in the ETO (AAF)

Thunderbolt fighter bombers destroyed nine tanks (four by rockets, three by strafing and two by bombs) and damaged three others (all by rockets). (AAF)

Target	Destroyed	Damaged	Totals
Tanks	85	29	114
Armored Cars	15	1	16
Motor Vehicles	164	23	187

The success of the 513th's rocket attacks drew praise and optimism for the rocket's future in the ETO. Lt.Gen. Carl Spaatz, CG of US Strategic Air Forces in Europe, wrote, "The success of the equipment has resulted in a requirement from the Ninth Air Force to equip all of their P-47 fighter aircraft with rockets." Maj.Gen. Bennett Meyers head of the Air Technical Service Command to describe the 5 inch HVAR as the "best anti-tank weapon of the war." Maj.Gen. Elwood Quesada, CO of the 9AF requested: "We want rockets, repeat; we want Cal Tech rockets, not Army Ordnance" (e.g not the AAF's 4.5 inch M-10 rockets).

With the good results of the 513th's rocket attacks and the glowing appraisals, one would expect that the new rocket would be in great demand by the AAF in the ETO and become as successful as it would be in the Pacific. But the 513th's experience was not the norm, as the squadron benefited from the direct supervision of scientists like Anderson and Lauritsen and the combat officers like Dean and Donicht, who were able to quickly train the squadron's pilots. Their minimal training gave other units the impression that rocket technique was easy to master, and that there would be no detailed operational manuals distributed to help them. The result was poor results and disillusionment in the use of rockets by the AAF in Europe. Despite its potential, the 8th and 9th Air Forces in the ETO and MTO, the US never used the rocket to any large degree as did the RAF Second Tactical Air Force that preferred the rocket as its primary anti-tank and ground support weapon. The 9th Air Force utilized only 13,959 during the war as compared to 222,515 used by the RAF 2TAF.

MTO AAF Rocket Use

The 79th Fighter Group was the first group to use rockets in Italy during an 86th Squadron armed recce led by Col. Melvin Neilsen along the east Italian coast. The Squadron was assigned to use three 4.5 inch bazooka tube rockets mounted under each wing on a combat trial basis. Initial missions were ineffective as these rockets were found to be generally unreliable, as their fins would not always deploy and their HE explosive warheads were ineffective against the heavy armor of the German Panzer. The pilots found that aiming was difficult and took time and skill to accomplish. A hit could easily destroy M/T, railway rolling stock, locomotives and gun

positions and against larger targets such as buildings they also could be very effective. The first successful use was on 6 November 1944 during an attack on the Brenner Rail Line at Verona which claimed 18 direct hits on the main buildings and 23 hits on the transformer stations in a combined attack by Desert Air Force (DAF) P-40s. Three days later, the 86th and 87th Squadrons attacked the German stronghold at Forli where the British 4th Infantry Division was being held up. The attack hit the fortress with 26 rockets and it was taken a few hours later. However, during its attack, a diving P-47 had its rocket tubes become fouled in its ailerons and turn the fighter over on its back and crash into the ground. During the operational trials the group fired 444 rockets with 97 claimed as direct hits. The group continued to use rockets intermittently throughout the remainder of the war. A 9th Air Force Report (No. 59) entitled "Rocket Status in the 9th Air Force (19 Sept. 1944)" concluded that rockets could be fired at longer range than .50 machine guns reducing the threat from AA fire. Rockets had more penetration capability than machine gun rounds or general-purpose bombs that tended to break up upon contact with the target and were more accurate than dive bombing and the report advocated further use of rockets.

CBI AAF Rocket Use

In March 1944 the 10AF and 14AF utilized the M8 rocket with the tubular Bazooka launchers in Burma. The 10AF outfitted B-25s with tubular cluster launched M8s and flew nine missions against trains, dumps, etc. in early March 1944 reportedly scoring 55 hits with the 99 rockets fired. On 4 March 23 P-40s carrying six rockets each escorted six B-25s carrying 12 parafrag clusters to Kiungshan Airdrome on Hainan Island. The post-mission debriefing reported 17 Japanese aircraft were destroyed on the ground, one probable and six damaged in the raid.

USN/USMC Use of the HVAR
First USN Operational Use of Rockets

In late 1943 Navy TBM Avenger Squadron VC-7 stationed at Ream Field, San Diego under Lt.Cdr. William Bartlett had flown a few rocket tests for the CIT program at Inyokern. Their Avengers were equipped with rockets when the unit boarded the carrier *Manila Bay* for the 22 January 1944 invasion of the Marshall Islands where the unit successfully tested their rockets against enemy positions on Kwajalein Island destroying ammunition dumps and ground installations during the first USN use of rockets in combat.

First USMC Operational Use of Rockets

Marine Squadron VMTB-134's Capt. Arthur "Bill" Patterson and his "*Rockettes*" were assigned to conduct trials using 5 inch HVARs launched

A P-51A carrying Bazooka-type rocket launchers in the CBI. (AAF)

Marine Squadron VMTB-134's **Capt. Bill Patterson** (kneeling second left) and his *"Rockettes"* made the first combat use of the 5 inch HVAR in the Pacific on 15 February 1944. (USN)

aerial rockets was that there was no satisfactory doctrine established for training, handling, maintenance, and use in combat. Cal Tech published a number of operating and procedural manuals and sent civilian scientific advisors to theaters that were using rockets.

In the Pacific, where the war was basically a naval war, the rocket benefited from its development by the Navy as involved scientists and naval officers became its ambassadors. The early 3.5 inch and 4.5 inch aerial rockets had shown the rocket's potential, but the new 5 inch HVAR with its Zero length launchers, improved fuses, and effective sights was promoted at every echelon in the combat theaters, from the C-in-C to the lowly sailor loading the rocket launchers. Promises were made that rockets would sink Japanese shipping, the lifeline of the Empire, and support the infantry on the ground by destroying enemy personnel and fortifications. By early 1944 rockets were quickly establishing themselves in the Pacific as an effective and soon to be ubiquitous weapon. While the AAF was acquiring rockets at $150 million per year the Navy's 1,200 rocket manufacturing plants were producing rockets at $1.2 billion per year in 1945. If the war had continued to the point of invading the Japanese Homeland, the vast use of rockets would have added exponentially to the already enormous damage inflicted by the fleets of B-29s that bombed Japan.

from rails welded to the wings of their TBF Avengers. The new rockets saw their first combat use in the Pacific on 15 February 1944 when the Squadrons TBFs flew from their Green Island base in the Solomons against the Japanese airfields on Rabaul.

Capt. T. B. Hill, Admiral Nimitz's Gunnery Officer, had been previously impressed by the accuracy of rockets in tests conducted in Honolulu and with the reported successes of VTBM-134 and VC-7 Nimitz requested 100,000 rockets per month. Nimitz's request could be met as Cal Tech had just completed the emergency production of the first 100,000 rockets, and the rocket factories under Navy contract were beginning to mass produce them. However, the fundamental problem with

First Successful US Aerial Rocket Attack vs. a U-Boat

The first recorded rocket attack (eight Model 5 3.5 inch) against a U-Boat occurred on 11 January 1944 by TBFs of VC-58 piloted by Lt.(jg.)s John McFord and Willis Seeley off the *USS Block Island*. Although the crew claimed a kill post war Kriegsmarine records documented no U-Boat losses on that day.

During the late afternoon of 16 January 1944, Ensigns Bert Hudson and William McLane were flying ASW patrol northeast of the Azores in their TBF Avengers of VC-13 off the *USS Guadalcanal* when they came upon three surfaced U-Boats. The "milch kau" tanker U-544 was refueling

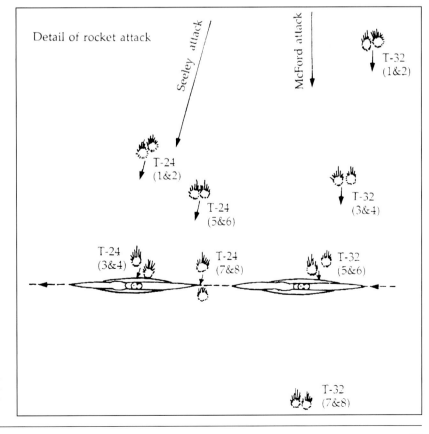

The first recorded USN rocket use against a U-Boat occurred on 11 January 1944 by TBFs of VC-58 piloted by Lt.(jg.)s John McFord and Willis Seeley off the USS *Block Island*. The schematic of the attack shows the results of the eight rockets fired by McFord (T-32) and Seeley (T-24). (USN)

Photo of McFord and Seeley's first rocket attack on a U-Boat with two rockets splashing short and two rockets (small bright circles near the U-Boat) streaking in. (USN)

Photo of Hudson and McLane's first sinking of a U-Boat with two rockets falling short (lower right) and two boring toward the U-Boat (two bright circles in middle third of frame). (USN)

U-516 with U-129 waiting close by and diving immediately upon spotting the closing Avengers. U-544 and U-516 were forced to remain on the surface while their crews struggled to disconnect the fuel lines connecting the two boats.

Ens. Hudson attacked from the starboard beam firing two rocket salvos at a range of 500 to 800 yards. The first two rockets fell short of U-516 but U-544 was hit by the second pair. Continuing on his attack run, Hudson fired his remaining four rockets and dropped two MK47 depth charges as he passed over the wounded U-Boat. U-544 was hit again by the rockets and one depth charge detonated about 50 feet from U-516 and the second exploded between the two U-Boats. U-516 was observes to settle slowly by the stern with it bow rising high into the air. Meanwhile the crew of U-544 began to abandon ship, jumping overboard.

Ens. McLane followed Hudson's attack by firing his rockets in three salvos; then dropping his two MK-47s as he salveod his last two rockets. One depth charge detonated too far away to be effective but the other exploded close to U-544. McLane saw U-516 disappear stern first and assumed that it had been sunk but the Kapitan of the damaged U-516 was able to regain control and escape. When the two TBFs left they reported

During the late afternoon of 16 January 1944, **Ensigns Bert Hudson** and **William McLane** were flying ASW patrol northeast of the Azores in their TBF Avengers of VC-13 off the *USS Guadalcanal* when they came upon three surfaced U-Boats, the tanker U-544 refueling U-516 with U-129 waiting close by. (USN)

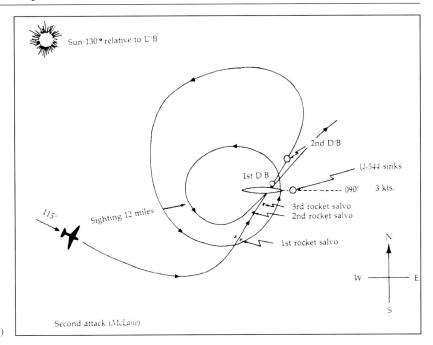

Second attack (*McLane*)

Schematic of the sinking of U-544. (USN)

seeing 20-30 men awash in a large pool of oil. Two destroyers were dispatched to pick up survivors but none was found when they arrived.

As the eight patrolling TBFs were returning to the *Guadalcanal* they were low in fuel and night was falling. The first four were landed successfully but the next Avenger landed but its tail blocked the flight deck. The flight deck crew was unable to completely clear the deck and despite the report of another U-Boat in the area the flight deck was illuminated and the remaining three pilots made repeated unsuccessful attempts to land and were waved off. Finally one Avenger pilot hit the deck but bounced over the side and fell into the water. The last two TBF piloted decided to ditch alongside and all three crewmen were rescued.

There are several other reports of rockets (aided by depth charges) sinking U-Boats:

On 10 April 1944 TBF Avenger and F4F Wildcats of VC-58 also off *Guadalcanal* attacked U-68 northwest of Madeira, Portugal. On 15 June 1944, F4Fs and TBFs off the *USS Solomons* (TF22.10) were on South Atlantic patrol off St. Helena Island when they attacked and sunk U-860. (Note: The first U-Boat sunk by rockets was U-752 on 23 May 1943 off the Irish coast. The U-Boat was hit by three inch RP-3 rockets launched from a Fairey Swordfish of 819 Squadron off the HMS *Archer* and was scuttled as escort vessels approached.)

US Rockets

Characteristic	3.5 inch	5 inch AR	5 inch HVAR
Head Length (in)	17.0	17.0	16.73
Head Diameter (in)	3.5	5.0	5.0
Head Weight (lbs)	20.0	40.0	45.5
Filler Weight (lbs)	20 (solid steel)	8.6 TNT	7.5 TNT
Motor Length (in)	45.0	45.0	52.0
Motor Diameter (in)	3.25	3.25	5.0
Motor Weight (lbs)	36.4	36.4	86.3
Propellant Weight (lbs)	8.5	8.5	24.0
Rocket Length (in)	62.0	62.0	69.0
Rocket Weight (lbs)	56.0	76.4	131.8
Maximum velocity (fps)	1,140	715	1,360
Burning time (sec)	0.6-1.5	0.6-1.5	0.9-1.4

11.75 inch *Tiny Tim* Rocket

In early 1944, after working on developing the 5 inch HVAR "Holy Moses" aerial rocket, Dr. Charles Lauritsen, head of the California Institute of Technology and USN rocket program, proposed a larger rocket which could be fired from higher altitudes and longer ranges than the smaller rockets and aerial torpedoes. Since Navy air power was limited to single-engine carrier-based aircraft a large rocket promised to give the Navy more punch against Japanese ground fortifications and shipping larger than destroyers.

Also, at the time aerial reconnaissance had discovered that the Germans had developed the V-1 Buzz Bomb which was to be launched from fixed "Ski" sites located on the French Channel coast. It was determined that these sites would be vulnerable to a large rocket and the Joint Chiefs if Staff conceived an aerial counteroffensive codenamed *Crossbow*. Using this opportunity Lauritsen presented his large rocket proposal to Capt. H. B. Temple who convinced Adm. Ernest King, Chief of Naval Operations, to give the new rocket the highest priority against the V-1 sites.

Description

The new weapon was to be a large, high explosive; unguided, fin stabilized, air to ground rocket that was a standard 500 pound Semi-Armor Piercing M58A1 bomb filled with 150 pounds TNT and attached by only a spanner wrench to a steel tube fitted with a rocket motor and cruciform fins. The head and motor were 11.75 inches in diameter, had an overall length of 10.25 feet, and weighed 1,255 to 1,283 pounds. The motor tube comprised the aft half of the projectile and contained a 150 pound four grain cruciform propellant charge and a 0.5 pound black powder igniter in a metal case with two electric squibs in parallel that were wired to the receptacles in the nozzle plate. The thrust through the 25 nozzles was 37,000 pounds (vs. 60,000 pounds for the V-2, 700 pounds for the V-1, and 5,000 pounds for the Me-262 jet). The aluminum fins were 10 inches by 24 inches attaching to two bands which were clamped around the motor when the rocket was assembled in the field.

The large rocket was nicknamed, for unknown reasons, by unknown persons, the "*Tiny Tim*." Perhaps the name was an incongruity referring to one of Charles Dickens' smallest and most mild-mannered fictional

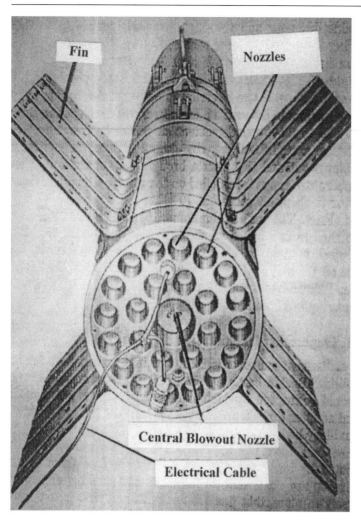

11.75 inch *Tiny Tim* Rocket

Armor Piercing bomb. New casings were in short supply but could be salvaged from abandoned oil wells. Also, at the time there was no existing press for extruding a smokeless powder propellant grain large enough for the *Tiny Tim*'s solid propellant motor. A new multigrain motor was developed using four grains weighing about 37 pounds each. When the huge rocket was test fired in a static test firing bay at Eaton Canyon, CA it lifted the concrete roof off the walls which were blown out. Afterward, further ground static tests were conducted in the open desert at Inyokern. Of course, the tremendous power of large rocket raised a no little concern about the effect of the rocket's blast on the launching aircraft.

Testing Launching Methods
To test the blast effect on aircraft structure a special ground launcher constructed of a steel girder was built at Inyokern and the fuselage of a TBF torpedo bomber was positioned so that the rocket was fired under the open bomb bay. In mid-May 1944, three test rounds were fired without damage and during the following five weeks work proceeded frantically on developing an aerial launcher. The first launcher, designated as a displacement launcher was a large design consisting of two tubular frames that retained the rocket. On an electrical signal from the pilot the launcher pivoted down from the aft end of the bomb bay and at the bottom of the arc the rocket was fired. For the first test of this launcher on 9 June, a TBF, equipped with a launcher, was placed on top of a 12 foot platform with its engine running and the launcher was remotely lowered and the *Tiny Tim* fired across the open desert. The test report stated that the only damage to the test aircraft was to the elevator that had each rib buckled five inches from the trailing edge. The report concluded that the damage was caused by the reflection of the blast off the ground and that this would not occur during air firing.

The next launching technique was the "lanyard method" in which a steel cable lanyard attached to the rocket paid out from a reel located in the bomb bay for a predetermined "safe" distance of 60 to 70 inches, at which time an electrical impulse ignited the rocket motor. The lanyard method seemed to be the simple and practical but the displacement launcher was too far along in development to be abandoned and air drop tests had not been conducted.

As the development of the displacement launcher continued it became apparent that the installation of this launcher on some aircraft types would be problematical and entail significant structural modifications. Also, there were doubts about its aerodynamics and accuracy during the launching procedure. Ground tests had showed a marked tendency for the aircraft nose to pitch downward at the end of the launcher's extension into the firing position. With these problems taken into account an alternative

characters. Because it was to be carried by single-engine aircraft capable of carrying 1,000 pound bombs the rocket was designed to weigh around 1,000 pounds. Also to facilitate production the size was limited to steel tubing that was available and compatible with existing bombs or shells that could be adapted for use as a warhead. The 11.75 diameter was chosen as it was the size of standard oil drilling casings and the 500 pound Semi-

Test film stills of a *Tiny Tim* being launched from a PBJ. A steel cable lanyard attached to the rocket paid out from a reel located in the PBJ bomb bay for a predetermined "safe" distance of 60 to 70 inches, at which time an electrical impulse ignited the rocket motor. (Both USN)

Among the locations for mounting the red and white striped test *Tiny Tim* on the PBJ were on the underwing outboard of the engine nacelle and along the side of the fuselage adjacent to the bomb bay. (Both USN)

launcher was studied. Among the locations for mounting the *Tiny Tim* on the test PBJ were on the underwing outboard of the engine nacelle and along the side of the fuselage adjacent to the bomb bay. When aimed and released from these positions the rocket fell free in a horizontal position aligning itself relative to the air stream of the bomber (e.g. the predetermined aiming angle) and fired.

On 20 June 1944, the first *Tim* firing tests were scheduled with Lt. Donald Innes flying a F6F-3. When Innes dove his Hellcat on a target floating in the Salton Sea for unknown reasons the rocket exploded on its launcher decimating his aircraft. Two days later another attempt was made by the highly experienced Lt.Cdr. Thomas Pollock as the pilot. Pollack had been with the Navy's aerial rocket program from its beginning and had test fired the first forward firing rockets and the first 3.5 and 5 inch rockets. For the tests, representatives from the Navy, Cal Tech, Washington, and even Churchill's chief scientific advisor, Lord Cherwell were on hand and all were initially awed by the size of the rocket. Pollock flew a TBF-1 mounting a *Tiny Tim* on four test flights with the tests to be filmed for analysis. On the first two test flights inert rockets were to be lowered and dropped without igniting to assess the mechanism of the launcher and, if it was satisfactory, then two "live" rockets were to be lowered and fired. Pollock climbed to 8,000 feet and successfully launched one inert *Tiny Tim* and then followed with another successful inert launch. For the critical third "real" test a bulldozer had marked a target line in the desert sands of the C-1 Test Range. At 1230 Pollock climbed to 10,000 feet and released the first successful air-launched *Tiny Tim*. Navy armorers rearmed the cumbersome second rocket onto the launcher in the hot desert sun and Pollock duplicated his first test. The British spectators were especially impressed as they considered the big rocket as a potential weapon to destroy the launching sites of the German V-1s that had began falling on London only five days before. After returning from the last test Pollock noticed that the TBF's controls were sluggish and upon inspection it was found that one elevator was missing a large section. Nonetheless, Pollock sent the following telegram to Lauritsen in Washington:

HAVE THIS DAY GIVEN BIRTH TO TWIN *TINY TIMS* WITHOUT ADVERSE EFFECT. (signed) MOTHER POLLOCK

The film of the testing was developed and sent to Washington and immediately the Navy Chief of Staff increased the weapon's developmental priority, especially for use on other Navy aircraft such as the TBM, SB2C, F6F, and F4U. In the meantime, the AAF 4146th Base

Unit (Experimental Projects) at Dover, DE, maintained a detachment at the Air Materiel Command's Flight test base, Muroc, CA to test *Tiny Tims* for use on its A-20 and A-26 attack bombers and the P-47 fighter bomber. Testing found the A-20 and A-26 unsuitable for *Tiny Tim* operations due to elevator damage from the rocket's ignition blast.

Although the viability of an air launch had been established further development was needed on ballistics, fusing, and warheads, particularly for underwater use. But during the next three months the displacement launcher caused problems and eliminated all aircraft but the TBF, TBM, and F4U. During firing tests the pilot lined up the aircraft on the target and released the launcher which thumped down into firing position. There was a long one second delay from the time the launcher was released and the rocket fired. During this time the launcher release pitched the aircraft nose down at a critical moment in aiming and firing causing a significant sighting error. Also, the blast caused damage, mostly minor, the elevators (particularly on the A-26) and sometimes to the tail structure and caused concern. The solution was to increase the distance of the propellant blast from the aircraft but that meant increasing the length of the already too long launcher. Service testing of the *Tiny Tim* was scheduled for 1 November and unwilling to delay development, further tests, both air and ground, were conducted to determine the characteristics of the rocket blast.

On 20 June 1944, the first *Tim* firing tests were scheduled with Lt. Donald Innes flying a F6F-3. When Innes dove his Hellcat on a target floating in the Salton Sea, the rocket exploded for unknown reasons on its launcher decimating his aircraft. (USN)

Meanwhile, the lanyard launcher concept was resurrected in August and drop tests using inert rockets began. The tests showed that the nose down attitude on dropping the rocket no longer occurred and that the rate and angle of free fall were uniform for any airspeed and dive angle. Two lanyard launcher tests on 17 and 18 August using live rockets mounted on a SB2C were successful and a third test was scheduled for 21 August. On the fourth test on that day, at 1,500 feet Lt. John Armitage dropped the rocket which cleared the aircraft and at three feet the lanyard ignited the rocket which sped away. On the ground shocked observers watched as Armitage's aircraft nosed over and dove steeply into the ground.

Further air testing of the *Tiny Tim* was postponed until an investigation determined the cause of the accident. Initially, the investigation found that the trim tabs of the SB2C had been tied together as the aircraft was considered to have too much trim under "normal circumstances" but the shock wave created by firing the large rocket was not a normal circumstance. It was not until late September that the investigation concluded that the cause of the accident (e.g. the shock wave) was the igniter rather than the propellant and the solution was to decrease the amount of igniter from 1,200 grains to 235 grains which would decrease the shock wave that sent the SB2C into its fatal spin. Also, the length of the lanyard was increased for greater separation of the rocket and aircraft at ignition. (Note: the new airfield at China Lake was named Armitage Field in honor of the deceased pilot).

Tiny Tim-Equipped F4U Corsairs
F4Us Against German V-Weapon Sites.
On 1 July 1944, 96 pilots of the F4U equipped Marine Aircraft Group 51 (MAG-51), which was already undergoing intensive training at Cherry Point, NC, were given highest priority for *Tiny Tim* rocket training to use them against the German V-1 launching sites on the French Channel coast as part of *Crossbow* with the Marine component of the operation codenamed *Danny*. The plan was to load the Corsairs and the *Tiny Tims* aboard an escort carrier and transport them to the North Sea where they would be take off for attacks against the V-1 launching sites. However, at this time there were no USMC squadrons aboard carriers. The F4U had been tested with the Tiny Tim at Inyokern initially using the displacement yoke which proved unsatisfactory. Further testing determined that the lanyard method was the solution to clear the arc of the large F4U propeller before firing and still retain reasonable accuracy.

Because the rocket was not in mass production, training was conducted with dummy and 5 inch rockets. On 11 July 1944 MAG-51 (VMF-513, VMF-514, and SMS-51) was given the order to stand by for shipment to the ETO with 60 aircraft in six days. The group's Forward Echelon materials were transported to Norfolk while flying units, were completing their training. At the end of July the Marines completed their training in the *Tiny Tim* technique, but the permanent Channel V-1 "Ski' launching sites had been captured causing the Germans to replace these sites with smaller mobile launchers or air-launched V-1s. The V-1s launched by these means were shot down in large numbers by the British developed SCR-584 radar and proximity fuses for AA shells. The *Danny Project* was cancelled and the first three squadrons went on to become the first Marine Corps fighter squadrons to be assigned to carriers during WWII.

Further F4U/*Tiny Tim* Deployment
In spring 1945, the F4U squadrons of Air Group 5: VMF-214 (Pappy Boyington's old Black Sheep Squadron) and VMF-452 equipped with *Tiny Tim*s, were deployed with Task Force 58. According to Major R.L

In July 1944 Marine Air Group 51, flying F4Us had been selected to be trained to use *Tiny Tim*s against the German V-1 launching sites on the French Channel coast. A MAG 51 Corsair is shown with a centerline fuselage *Tiny Tim* mounting. (Both USN)

Davis of the Air Ordnance Office, 108 *Tiny Tim*s were fired in the pre-invasion bombardment of Okinawa by F4U Corsairs. It was noted that the large size of the weapon created storage and deck handling problems on carriers. Evaluation of the weapon's effectiveness was masked by the extensive damage caused by naval guns and aerial bombs on the same targets. The records of the *Tiny Tim* sorties were lost in the subsequent bombing of the *Franklin*.

On 18 March the *Franklin* was preparing to launch 31 aircraft with 14 Corsairs to be armed with *Tiny Tim*s which were on handling carts on the flight deck waiting to be loaded. When the carrier was hit by two enemy 500 pound bombs, detonating the *Tiny Tim*s armed with high explosive warheads which added to the devastation that led to the heroic fight to save the carrier and its subsequent return to America.

Tiny Tim Equipped PBJs

After flying combat in D-model PBJs from Saipan in the Marianas beginning in October 1944, VMB-612 was transferred to Iwo Jima in early April 1945, equipped with new PBJ-1Js. On Iwo the Squadron flew patrol missions around the island, long range anti-submarine patrols, harassing missions to the Bonin Islands, and anti-shipping missions. In May, popular former Squadron CO, Lt.Col. Jack Cram, returned to the unit with orders to test the *Tiny Tim* which were to be shipped to Iwo Jima for operational testing by VMB-612. The *Tiny Tim* motors and bodies and the lanyard launching mechanism shipment intended for the VMF-612 PBJs were transported on the *Intrepid* and were delayed when the carrier was hit by a kamikaze attack off Okinawa on 16 April. When the shipment finally reached Iwo Jima a dump fire destroyed some of the rocket motors and bodies.

"Cram's Rams," as the VMB-612 was nicknamed, aided by a team of five specialists, led by 1Lt. R.C. Johnson, immediately started work to modify the new PBJ-1Js, and some of the residual older D-models, to carry the large new rocket. A two rocket rack system was adapted from a Mk 51 bomb rack and the lanyard rocket launching system developed during the Inyokern tests installed to prevent damage to the aircraft from the rocket's ignition blast. The rocket was attached to a reel and steel cable lanyard which swung down to delay the rocket's ignition until the weapon had dropped free of the aircraft. A PBJ loaded with two *Tiny Tim*s experienced 10 knot drag which meant that patrol range was slightly reduced. After launch, the bomb bay doors could be opened for conventional bomb drops. To load the large heavy rockets a modified hoist was developed to lift them onto a special, four wheel, standard bomb trailer fitted with

The large 10.25 foot and heavy 1,270 pound *Tiny Tim* being transferred from the dump by a large transporter to a smaller hand truck equipped with a hydraulic pump to raise the rocket into the bomb bay of a PBJ. (Both USN)

sway braces and two screw jacks that would raise the rocket up to be attached to the PBJ's bomb bay shackles for a lanyard launch. Other modifications included the installation of AN/APQ-5 gunsight/bombsight and AN/APS-3 search radar equipment and several K-19 cameras to film the test attacks. The AN/APS-3 search radar equipment would allow the squadron to function as a low altitude night unit against enemy shipping which primarily moved at night. Once the target was detected, the bomber would head towards the target and the AN/APQ-5 would be set up for an attack which was to be straight and level at an altitude of approximately 500 feet. During the attack, the pilot controlled air speed, the co-pilot maintained altitude, and the navigator-bombardier guided the plane. After the attack, the pilot took full control of the aircraft and proceeded to take evasive action away from the target. The cameras were fitted in the vacant waist gun positions and in the ventral hatch aft of the bomb bay to follow the flight of the rockets from every angle. Meanwhile, during *Tiny Tim* firing tests, it was found that the 500 foot altitude for firing the rockets was too dangerous and it was amended to 700 feet. During May and June 14 PBJs aircraft were converted to carry *Tiny Tim*s and two 5 inch HVAR underwing launchers, each carrying four rockets; for a total 3,800 pound rocket payload.

By June the aircraft had been modified and the equipment installed, and the Squadron was ready to pioneer attack techniques and fine-tune

A Marine PBJ-1J of VMB-612 carrying AN/APS-3 search radar equipment and two *Tiny Tim*s. (USMC)

the *Tiny Tim* equipment. On 11 June, the weapon was ready for its first operational training flight and afterward Lt.Col. Cram reported that the PBJ handled acceptably but with the anticipated 10 knot drag. During June, with the US Navy operating off Honshu, a joint USN/USMC zone was set up which affected VMB-612's patrol area which was temporarily west of the new zone, along the southern coast of Kyushu. In this area the squadron continued normal combat operations consisting mainly of patrols that encountered increasingly fewer and smaller Japanese vessels. During June the squadron flew 74 low altitude sorties and made 23 anti-shipping attacks using conventional bombs and .50 caliber machine gun strafing and occasionally 5 inch HVAR underwing rockets but the targets did not justified *Tiny Tim* attacks. There were no losses during combat or on operational training flights. The squadron was to deploy to Okinawa and its supply of *Tiny Tim*s was shipped to Okinawa which would locate them closer to the Japanese mainland, reducing the operational range and also putting them nearer combat. In the meantime the air and ground echelon remained on Iwo Jima, awaiting official deployment orders.

In early July 1945, the VMB-612 air echelon flew into Chimu Field on Okinawa while the ground echelon arrived by LST some days later. In general, the squadron suffered logistically from its moves from Saipan to Iwo Jima to Okinawa and at these locations often suffered from inadequate billeting from the weather. The radar and other electronic equipment were fragile and complicated, its maintenance difficult, and its operators were often under trained. The squadron was under the operational control of Fleet Air Wing 1, and was to conduct anti-shipping sweeps along the northwestern coast of Kyushu and at the same time conduct live *Tiny Tim* firing tests. On the evening of 21/22 July, Cram flew the first operational *Tiny Tim* mission, a search which took the aircraft over the China Sea to the northern tip of Korea but only a few small inconsequential fishing boats were located. On 28 July the squadron's first losses of the Okinawa campaign took place when a PBJ-1J carrying a crew of seven was lost.

As the war was nearing its end worthwhile targets, not only for the two *Tiny Tim*s and the eight conventional underwing 5 inch HVARS, were becoming scarce and Cram was eager to fire the rockets. (The *Tiny Tim*s and HVARs were the Squadron's only offensive weapons, and its PBJs were armed with only the defensive twin .50s in the tail turret as the waist guns were replaced with cameras and the dorsal turret had been removed previously). During the night of 11/12 August, Cram flew another *Tim* mission; again with disappointing results as no ships large enough even to create a radar return were located. On his way back to base the impatient Cram took a radar fix on a protruding rock in the sea off Okinawa that had previously served as a practice target. Using the radar return he fired a *Tim* on the rock and film of this practice run proved that *Tiny Tim* was "quite a weapon."

On 13 August, Capt. Theodore Boutwell took off for the Tsushima Straits carrying eight 5 inch HVARs and two *Tims*. His radar operator located several ships and Boutwell fired his wing rockets hitting two ships. With two *Tiny Tim*s remaining, Boutwell ordered his navigator-bombardier MT/Sgt. Robert Reed to recalibrate his sights and be ready for the launch signal. At launch there was a loud explosion that jolted the PBJ, as the rocket had misfired and exploded, riddling the bomber with shrapnel. Luckily, Boutwell and his crew were unhurt and the aircraft was able to fly safely back to base.

On the 14th, a PBJ spotted a 200 foot ship and attacked immediately, firing its HVARs first; resulting in a large explosion that sank the vessel. A second PBJ attacked a group of three ships consisting of two 150 foot and one 250 foot vessel, running parallel. The larger vessel was attacked first resulting in a HVAR hit but the *Tiny Tim*s fired prematurely and missing. A third Mitchell attacked another vessel with its *Tiny Tim*s, both of which

missed. A repeat run firing 5 inch rockets resulted in three hits from five rockets, which set the vessel on fire.

On the night of 15-16 August, six PBJs patrolled into the Tsushima Straits on an anti-shipping mission, and attacked a 250 foot vessel with their *Tiny Tim*s. The first attacker missed with both rockets while a second PBJ also missed another vessel with both its *Tims*. A third PBJ fired all eight HVARs at a 200 foot vessel but was unable to observe the results. A fourth PBJ attacked a 150 foot target with six rockets and scored one hit. This aircraft then made a run on a 350 foot vessel and scored one hit with a *Tim* causing extensive damage; the first and only operational hit by a *Tiny Tim* as the war had ended and the six crews on this mission had missed much of the victory celebration taking place while they were gone on the nine hour mission. During the final days of the war, 1 August to 15 August, there were very few Japanese ships remaining to attack but the unit flew 31 sorties and claimed to have damaged 20 enemy vessels around the waters of Japan and Korea but with only one confirmed *Tiny Tim* hit.

After four days of celebrating the war's end, VMB-612 was back in the air as many of the squadron's men didn't have enough points to rotate home and air crew were transferred in to replace those who qualified to go home. *Tiny Tim* test runs were made on 24 and 26 August, with Cram flying a further six on the 27th, expending nine more Tims. The rockets were test fired over bombing ranges, with data being compiled as to release points, missile behavior, and aircraft altitudes with photographs taken to record the results obtained. Lt.Col. Lawrence Fox took over as squadron CO when Cram was transferred to the MAW-31 HQ, on 1 September. Aircraft were maintained for a few more weeks, and by the end of October VMB-612 still had an inventory of 31 PBJs but the *Tiny Tim* inventory was depleted.

But for the general lack of suitable targets by the time it entered service, *Tiny Tim* would surely have found greater deployment; and only VMB-612 had time to use it in action, without proving its potential. The pioneering work of the Marine Mitchell crews in the use of the big rocket was followed up in the immediate postwar years with test launchings from Hellcats, Corsairs, Tigercats and several other types. Navy aircraft naturally had priority on a weapon developed for that service, and the PBJ-1H figured in further practice firings involving medium bombers over the range at Inyokern. What is believed to be the only other combat use of *Tiny Tim*s (probably those originating from Navy World War II stocks in Japan) took place in Korea when USAF F-51s, F-84s, and Navy F4Us expended a number against ground targets.

14 inch *Big Richard*

A sidelight to the *Tiny Tim* story was the 14 inch *Big Richard* which was an enlargement of the *Tiny Tim* design. The low priority prototypes were completed in spring 1945 but none had been air fired by the end of the war. After the war the *Big Richard* program continued as low priority and by January 1947 was completed but never was deployed. However, a few developmental rounds were used as rocket boosters for the test track for *Lark* missiles.

"Super 4.5 inch Round"/ 115mm Aircraft Rocket

The Air Force had wanted a rocket with a higher velocity and better accuracy than the M8, especially against moving targets at longer ranges. Research by the NDRC Allegheny Ballistics Laboratory at Cumberland, MD developed a new solvent process propellant which exceeded the performance of the existing propellant, particularly at extreme temperatures. This propellant was applied to a new rocket designated the "Super 4.5 inch Round" or 115mm aircraft rocket. The rocket was design-frozen in December 1944 but the war ended before it could be used in combat. The 115mm aircraft rocket specifications were 6.0 feet long, 103 pounds, (of which 40 pounds was contained in one of two warhead choices), a velocity of 1,000 fps over the speed of the launching aircraft, and stabilization by four fixed fins. The warheads were improved with the Semi-Armor Piercing head that could penetrate five inches of armor plate while the fragmentation head contained 8.5 pounds of HE (nearly double that of the M8). The light weight of the 115mm rocket made it possible to carry the rockets in the "tier" method, in which two of the rockets were carried on each post, one over the other.

2.25 inch SCAR (Sub-Caliber Aircraft Rocket) Practice Rocket
With rocket supplies so critical, BuOrd wished to develop a rocket substitute to provide rocket training. In late 1943 work was begun to use a .50 caliber reduced charge tracer bullet to approximate the velocity and trajectory of the 3.5 inch and 5 inch rockets. This method was a failure and it was decided to develop a true rocket for training. Cal Tech was given the specification for this training rocket using a motor already in production, using as little propellant as possible, be adaptable to launchers in service, and, of course, duplicate the velocity and trajectory of 3.5 and 5 inch rockets. However, to match both 3.5 and 5 inch performance characteristics complicated the design problem. At first two head sizes were used but later development shifted to two different propellant sizes which delayed work until 19 July 1944 when drawings were finally available. When the HVAR became operational the practice rocket program received higher priority due to shortages of that rocket due to its effectiveness and consequent popularity. The opinion was that training objectives could be served with one practice rocket simulating the HVAR since the general rocket firing principles remained the same whatever the performance. By January 1945, the practice rocket was standardized as the 2.25 inch SCAR (Sub-Caliber Aircraft Rocket). Its simple design made the SCAR immediately available and by the end of the war over 500,000 per month were being manufactured.

Spinner Rockets
The US had no "spinner" rocket developmental program until 1943 when Cal Tech and the OSRD began independent research to develop rotational stabilization in which several nozzles would produce a rotational as well as a forward thrust, thus canceling out the effects of any eccentricity in the rocket, reducing dispersion, and eliminating the fragile and bulky fins which made rockets difficult to handle and store.

The advantage of spinner rockets was their smaller size as finned rockets needed to be considerable longer in relation to their diameter for stable flight characteristics. The 5 inch finned rocket was about 70 inches long while the M8 5 inch spinner was only 32 inches long (a 4.5 inch spinner rocket was also developed). The rocket was fired through launching tubes and its rotation was caused by directing the exit gases through canted exhaust nozzles. At the request of the Marine Corps Cal Tech began a study to replace the 75mm cannon used in the B-25G and H with a spin stabilized rocket launcher. Later the Navy requested the development of a 5 inch spinner rocket launcher to arm PT boats and multiple launchers for pre-invasion barrage landing craft. These projects were followed by a wide range of surface fired spin stabilized rockets. The Naval Ordnance Testing Station (NOTS) soon developed aerial spinner rockets. There were three types of Aerial Spinner Rockets (ASR): CASR: common; GSAR: general purpose; and PASR: pyrotechnic.

Launchers
While tube launching was not a particular problem for ground or ship installations; the installation of the multi-tube launchers on aircraft reduced their airspeed and maneuverability. In their development of the spinner rocket the NOTS designers considered the advantage that the aerial rocket had because of the substantial forward velocity imparted to them by the forward speed of the launching aircraft. This head start launching velocity allowed the launching tubes to be shorter than those of similar diameter used for static surface launching. The aerial design was a three foot long; six inch diameter wing mounted launching tube that was shorter and more aerodynamic than the earlier 5 inch tubes but was much less aerodynamic than the conventional Zero length launching rails.

Tests and Lowered Priority
The first aircraft spinner rockets were ground tested on 7 October 1944 at Inyokern using a static F6F-3. During the first test eight rockets were fired with no damage to the aircraft or launcher while the spinner's flight was reasonably accurate and its dispersion was about the same as that of fin stabilized rockets. Three days later the first spinner rocket flight test was made using a PV-1. The results very disappointing as many rockets left their launchers in increasing spirals and at the end of burning tumbled to the ground. NOTS scientists realized that spinner development would be a complicated and lengthy process and with many other projects under development and the Zero Length launching rails satisfactory the spinner rockets were to be allocated a low priority unless another launching method could be developed. The obvious answer seemed to be the development of a reloadable in flight internal launcher that housed a larger number of the smaller spin stabilized rockets.

Internal Rocket Launchers
To eliminate the aerodynamic drag caused by the underwing rockets and their launching mechanism an internal launcher was developed by the United Shoe Machinery Corporation (USM). The device was a six round launcher for 4.5 inch M8 spinner rockets that were housed in a series of paper/plastic carrier tubes in a vertical magazine located in the nose. An electrical drive indexed the tubes successively downward to the bottom of the magazine and into alignment with a launching barrel and exhaust tube at which time it was fired and the empty carrying tube jettisoned. The automatic launcher fired its six rockets, two at a time in three seconds and was to be the forerunner for an improved reloadable (in flight) model that could carry 16 rockets. Near the end of the war, Bell Laboratories had developed a revolver-type launcher under NDRC contract and was testing it at Dover in May 1945. After ground and air testing a B-25H was equipped with the unit and deployed to the CBI for combat testing by the 10th Air Force against targets in northern Burma but little is known about this revolver-type launcher.

In mid-1945, an automatic launcher for 5 inch spin stabilized rockets was jointly developed by the Naval Ordnance Test Station (NOTS) at China Lake, CA and the Harvey Machine Company using PBJ-1J 35849 (ex USAAF 44-30980) as the test aircraft for the program. The nose of a PBJ-1J was equipped with two compact rotating drums, one on either side of the centerline, which carried five spin-stabilized rockets each which could be released in salvoes of five or singly at 3/10 second intervals. The rockets were fitted with fins that were to create a stabilizing spin to the rocket as it passed through the short launching tube. The unit was to be reloadable in flight either manually or mechanically, depending on the type of carrying aircraft. The exhaust of the fired rockets was vented downward out of the airplane at the aft end of the nose section via a deflector tube. The ground and aerial firing tests were unimpressive and this rocket launcher concept was discontinued.

Several other internal units were developed. One had a stationary barrel and blast deflector with either horizontal or vertical magazines and a motor driven breech and loading system. Another unit utilized a

In mid-1945, an automatic launcher for 5 inch spin stabilized rockets was jointly developed by the Naval Ordnance Test and the Harvey Machine Company using PBJ-1J as the test aircraft for the program. The nose of a PBJ-1J was equipped with two compact rotating drums, one on either side of the centerline, which carried five spin-stabilized rockets each which could be released in salvoes of five or singly. (USN)

motor driven, rotating drum with five chambers containing rockets each aligning, in turn, with a single launching tube that extended out of the aircraft's nose. A blast deflector tube vented the rocket's detonation downward out the aft of the nose section. In tests the rocket was unstable until the optimal launch tube length was determined. During ground and aerial testing, neither of these concepts was proven to be effective and was not put into production.

X2R-1

In 1944 Dr. Horace Babcock proposed a spinner rocket concept designated as the X2R-1 was to be installed in the tails of B-17s and B-24s to ward off *Luftwaffe* fighters which lobbed rockets out of the range of .50 caliber machine guns. In tests at NOTS this retro-firing rocket showed a great dispersion and inconsistent ballistics and the project was abandoned on favor of the priority of forward-firing spinners.

Tail Mounted Bomber Rocket Installations

4.5 inch Rocket /M-10 Triple Launch Tube

In 1944, in view of the inability of heavy bombers to deal with mass rear quarter attacks of *Luftwaffe* fighters heavily armed with 30mm cannon the 8AF began experimenting with rocket launchers mounted in the tail of a B-24. These defenses were designed to break up enemy fighter formations and force individual fighter attacks. The initial 8AF field installations were completed by mid-December 1944 on a B-24H donated by the 489BG. The Liberator's rudder was marked with a white square which was a "stay clear" identification for tests. Preliminary tests showed the need for a fast burning rocket and long tubular launchers in order to insure good initial acceleration and to protect the bomber from the blast of the rocket. The 4.5 inch HE rocket and the ten foot M-10 triple launch tube were adopted. The launcher was jettisonable but tests showed that this was unnecessary as it produced negligible drag. The unit had a fire selector switch in the tail turret and an elevation adjustment in the waist position. Trials over the Wash Bombing Range showed the unit to be successful, especially when combined with a T-5 proximity fuse which armed one second after launching and detonated automatically when passing within 50-75 feet of the target. Sighting was simple as the three 4.5 inch rockets were fired in a spread salvo into the massed formation of enemy fighters where the proximity fuse and the large bursting area of the exploding charge encompassed a very large lethal area. Operational installation was completed just as the war ended.

Rockets were fitted with fins that were to create a stabilizing spin as it passed through the short launching tube. When the rocket was fired from the launcher, the arming wire was pulled from the rocket fuse and armed it. The exhaust of the fired rockets was vented downward out of the airplane at the aft end of the nose section via a deflector tube. (USN)

Tail Mounted Bomber Rocket Installations

3

Napalm for Fighter Bombers

Incendiary weapons were useful in tactical air missions which were those flown in the combat zone for the purpose of influencing the local tactical situation. Enemy strongholds, motorized vehicles, troop concentrations, and military stores were targets that were particularly vulnerable to fire. Occasionally tactical aircraft (Fighter Bombers) used M47 and M50 bombs against these targets and occasionally they dropped an M76. However, another type of incendiary weapon called the fire, blaze, or Napalm bomb proved to be the most effective against tactical targets. During the war Napalm bombs was most commonly referred to as the "fire bomb" in press releases.

Escort fighters carried jettisonable auxiliary fuel tanks for long range missions and it became routine for the pilots on the homeward trip to drop these tanks, if used, on targets of opportunity, returning to ignite the gasoline with tracer ammunition. It was only a small step to provide these gasoline-filled tanks with igniters which more convenient and reliable than hitting the tank with tracer ammunition.

It was soon realized that these fire bombs could be thickened with a filler and would provide a more intense fire than ordinary gasoline, Chemical Officers in Europe initially thickened gasoline with oil, or rosin oil and lime, and when they became available, with the approved thickeners, British Perspex and American Napalm. (The development of Napalm is discussed in detail in US Aerial Armament in World War II: Volume 2 with incendiary bombs.) Initially, the CWS devised an igniter from a shortened section of a two pound magnesium bomb which was clamped on the side of the drop tank but later an all-ways fuse was inserted into the filler opening.

The first fire bombs began as a field improvisation and were simply large capacity containers of a variety of sizes which happened to be on hand, such as 55 gallon drums. Spare auxiliary fuel (drop) tanks, often made of processed paper, were stocked in quantity and were the container of choice. The containers which saw the most use were of 75, 100, 108, 110, and 165 gallon capacity with the latter two the most popular. In the field Napalm tanks were hung on the aircraft empty and then filled with petroleum jelly usually pumped from 50 gallon drums or a special fuel bowser. The percentage of gasoline or Napalm filling to the total weight of the (paper container) bomb was high. Safety issues were always a problem in mixing and filling the bombs with gasoline or Napalm, and then during their handling and mounting. Napalm filling drums were usually painted flat yellow although dark red and natural metal drums were common.

The high accuracy with which the fire bomb could be placed on small targets was a major advantage, although this precision was possible

only when the bombs were released from a low altitude, which pilots under heavy antiaircraft fire could not always safely accomplish. For best effect, the Napalm bombs were to be tumbled onto the target as when the Napalm bomb burst on the ground the thickened fuel splashed, spreading it over a large area. A white phosphorous igniter set fire to Napalm when it hit the ground creating a large, intense fireball that was fueled by the gelled gasoline mixture that would adhere to anything it touched as it spread forward upon impact. Besides its incendiary effect Napalm rapidly deoxygenated the available air as the oxygen was replaced by carbon monoxide (CO) as a result of incomplete combustion. As little as 0.4% CO can be fatal within one hour because of the high affinity between carbon monoxide and blood hemoglobin. Napalm created a localized atmosphere of at least 20% carbon monoxide either causing the victim to suffocate or pass out and burn to death.

A 165 gallon tank filled with Napalm could burn out a 100x150 foot area and its fires were extremely difficult to extinguish. During attacks on personnel, Napalm tank(s) were carried mixed with bombs or rockets. Initially Napalm was considered most effective for the incineration of entrenched enemy troops but it was also used to destroy enemy camouflage and expose the target prior to rocket and bombing attacks. On flat terrain Napalm was dropped from level flight at minimal altitude that produced

The high accuracy with which Napalm could be placed on small targets was a major advantage, although this precision was possible only when the bombs were released from a low altitude as shown by this Marine F4U dropping a Napalm on Japanese caves during the Battle for Peleliu, 15 September to 27 November 1944. (USMC)

A 165 gallon auxiliary fuel drop tank converted to a Napalm bomb is transferred from a hand cart for attachment onto the wing pylon of a P-51. Napalm tanks were hung on the aircraft empty and then filled (AAF)

A towed pumping unit used to transfer gasoline from drums was also used to pump Napalm into the various containers that were used operationally: 75, 100, 108, 110, and 165 gallon capacity. (AAF)

long swaths of fire that engulfed the selected target such as trenches, foxholes or gun positions. Napalm attacks on defensive positions made up of rubble and shattered buildings drove enemy troops into the open. Until Napalm was introduced enemy troops in jungle areas were attacked with Fragmentation Bombs but their caves, trenches, and foxholes afforded them good cover. Dropped Napalm spread and rushed into the trenches and foxholes causing horrific casualties by burning or asphyxiation. In attacking hilly or mountainous areas, the pilot dropped the Napalm tank from a shallow angle, tumbling the tanks into enemy positions that produced concentrated oval areas of fire along the ground.

Although personnel were more vulnerable than material to Napalm; motorized vehicles, marshaling yards, warehouses, and other combustible buildings also made excellent Napalm targets. Concrete, stone, and steel reinforced buildings and pillboxes could be compromised if the Napalm engulfed the ventilation systems. It had a significant demoralizing effect on troops defending the area around fortifications when they were forced to take refuge inside them to escape the Napalm. This allowed US infantry to flank the fortifications and get to their rear to utilize satchel charges, pole charges, or grenades to neutralize them. At times Napalm was used

in combination with artillery or high explosive bombs in attacks against fortified towns or strongpoints consisting of open emplacements and earth and log fortifications. These positions were first subjected to artillery fire or high explosive bombing and then fighter bombers dropped fire bombs on the rubble forcing the enemy into the open and just before the infantry assault an artillery barrage placed its fire on the exposed enemy troops. The fire bomb, however, had little or no effect against heavy fortifications such as the pillboxes of the Siegfried Line. During the introduction of Napalm in the ETO there was extensive positive news coverage of its extensive use to reduce the surrounded fortress of St. Malo on the French coast. However, analysis of the damage and interviews with enemy POWs determined that fire bombs were not instrumental in the causing the German's surrender.

Napalm Use in the ETO and MTO
In the ETO in March 1944, the IX TAC conducted experiments on methods of dropping and exploding (not igniting) gasoline but it burned off too quickly on contact and the tests were discontinued. In the Pacific flame throwers were achieving surprising successes against heavily

Hand-pumping Napalm from 55 gallon drums into the 165 gallon Napalm bombs. Safety issues were always a problem in mixing and filling the bombs with gasoline or Napalm, and then their handling and mounting. (AAF)

A filled 165 gallon Napalm bomb with the external igniter evident. Initially, the CWS devised an igniter from a shortened section of a two pound magnesium bomb which was clamped on the side of the drop tank but later an all-ways fuse/white phosphorus ignitor was inserted into the filler opening. (AAF)

The use of Napalm, called "fire bombs" was limited in the ETO. On 17 July 1944 the first aerial Napalm bombs were ready for operations when Col. Howard Nichols led a flight of 370th Fighter Group Napalm-carrying P-38s to a German command post near Coutances, St. Lo, France. (AAF)

fortified Japanese positions and Bradley's First Army advancing toward Germany was supplied with these flame throwers with the improved Napalm to use against German positions on the fortified Siegfried Line. Gen. Pete Quesada requisitioned some of this Napalm and directed the 370th Fighter Group to conduct operational trials and by 16 July 1944 the aerial Napalm bombs were ready for operations. Unfortunately on the first test, one of the Napalm-filled tanks exploded while a ground crew was hanging it to a P-38 and two men were killed and the Lightning was fused into a molten lump. The next day Col. Howard Nichols led a flight of Napalm-carrying P-38s to a German command post near Coutances, St. Lo, France. Nichols led his group in at low altitude toward the German headquarters that was located in a small forest. About a mile from the target the Lightnings formed up and descended to 1,000 feet and dropped their Napalm tanks. Returning to inspect the damage, Nichols saw the target scorched with smoke rising to 2,000 feet and the surrounding trees turned into burned out stumps. Back at base Nichols praised Napalm but later reconnaissance showed the actual damage to the cement buildings was less than reported.

Fighter bombers carrying fire bombs flew frequent missions against the Germans attempting to escape encirclement at Falaise in August 1944. During this period P-38s and P-47s armed with bombs, rockets, and Napalm attacked fleeing concentrations of enemy trucks and armor, causing Eisenhower to described the carnage as being able to walk hundreds of yards, walking only on dead bodies. At the time of the Battle of the Bulge AAF fighter bombers used fire bombs effectively against German motor transportation and armored concentrations in the wooded sections of the battleground. In one of the most effective uses of Napalm in the ETO occurred when fighter bombers dropped 72 fire bombs on the marshaling yards at St. Quentin, France, destroying 400 of the 500 railway cars in the yards. An example of the effectiveness of the fire bomb against point targets took place on 25 August 1944 when 16 fighter bombers carrying 24 165 gallon Napalm bombs and eight 500 pound HE bombs, attacked the headquarters of Feldmarschall Guenther von Kluge, German Army Group commander, at Verzy, France. Twenty-two of the Napalm tanks made direct hits on the headquarters buildings completely destroying eight houses.

Production and supply problems limited ETO Napalm use until early 1945. Once there was an adequate supply of Napalm and auxiliary

fuel tank containers the rapid Allied advance into Germany reduced the number of practical targets and so Napalm saw limited use in the ETO in 1945.

Napalm Use in the Pacific

The Navy's first use of fire bombs occurred during carrier aircraft attacks on the Marshall Islands in the Pacific. Armorers jury-rigged the bomb by attaching a practice bomb filled with gasoline instead of water to a 100 pound GP bomb and then dropping the two together. The Navy pilots saw that the blast of the GP bomb ignited the fuel and quickly spread it over a large area. BuOrd tested variations of this bomb at Dahlgren Proving Grounds to decide whether it was suitable for procurement. Tests did not duplicate the enthusiastic combat reports as it failed to inflict any more damage than a 100 pound GP bomb alone as the gasoline burned off spectacularly but instantly. Fire bomb development and testing continued and later in the war when Napalm was developed the Navy used old jettisonable fuel tanks filled with the gelled gasoline and fitted with igniters. The first true Napalm bombs were first used by the Navy during the the pre-invasion attacks on Tinian in the Marianas on 23 July 1944 when the bombs spread a devastating sheet of flame over Japanese bunkers which offered no real protection to its occupants.

During the Luzon campaign American air units dropped a total of 1,054,200 gallons of Napalm-thickened gasoline, of which an estimated 989,000 gallons were effectively placed on targets. The failures were the result of defective igniters and of faulty release mechanisms but generally the fire bomb functioned effectively. One of the most effective uses of Napalm during World War II took place during the fight for Ipo Dam, north of Manila, northern Luzon. After the Philippine capital was recaptured the low water supply to the city made the capture of the dam essential. During attacks during 16 to 18 May 1945, Thunderbolts, Lightnings, and Mustangs of 5th Fighter Command harassed the Japanese who withdrew to the Ipo Dam area taking advantage of natural defensive barriers; wooded knolls, hills, and valleys and enhancing them with fortified caves, an interlocking system of trenches, and artillery weapons. The enemy defenses slowed the 43rd Infantry Division's advance with the prospect of suffering heavy casualties. Plans were made for the 5th Fighter Command to contradict Japanese opposition. Five large enemy strong points, each consisting of about three million square yards, were selected as target areas with sufficient bomb coverage on each to wipe out enemy opposition. From 200 to 250 5FC Fighter Bombers were to come in low at 75 to 150 feet, wave after wave, at 10 to 15 second intervals, four to eight abreast, with air and ground controllers providing target information and regulating the air strikes. Initially, the closely following fighters found that smoke from preceding waves obscured the target but the problem was overcome by directing the bombing runs downwind, with each successive wave dropping its Napalm on the near side of the bursts from the wave which preceded it. A-20s followed saturating the area with parafrags and then all aircraft involved thoroughly strafed the area. Over 200,000 gallons of Napalm were dropped by the 144 P-38s, 48 P-47s, and 64 P-51s. American infantry closely followed the air strikes and overran all target areas with a minimum of casualties. The Japanese, not killed in the Napalm attack, tried to escape the fire in terror and were caught in the open by a combined barrage of A-20 fragmentation bombs, and ground artillery and mortar fire. At least five large gasoline dumps were destroyed and the enemy abandoned food and ammunition supplies in his flight to safety. In addition, approximately 75 to 100 caves were sealed by bombs or their occupants suffocated by the Napalm. The 43rd Division counted over 2,100 Japanese dead in their area.

During World War II the AAF dropped about 37,000 CWS supplied fire bombs (14,000 tons) on German and Japanese targets. Two thirds of

Both the AAF and USN used Napalm in the Pacific. Extensive use of Napalm in the Pacific occurred during the mopping up operations against entrenched Japanese forces in central and northern Luzon by Thunderbolts, Lightnings, and Mustangs of 5th Fighter Command during May 1945. (AAF)

the bombs and an even higher percentage of the tonnage were used in the Pacific. No matter where the fire bombs were used reaction to their method of employment seemed to be the same. To insure the best results they had to be dropped in adequate numbers and from altitudes ranging from 50 to 100 feet; the efficiency of a Napalm strike was increased when coordinated with HE bombs, artillery fire, or strafing; the most effective targets for Napalm were enemy strongholds and troop concentrations, extremely inflammable material, and motorized vehicles. While Napalm was used widely in the Pacific by Army, Marine, and Navy aviators; by far the most effective and deadly use of Napalm was by the thousands of incendiary bombs dropped by the B-29s of the XX Air Force gutting inflammable Japanese cities.

4

Torpedoes

Development

The first use of the term "torpedo" was by renowned American inventor Robert Fulton when he referred to naval explosive launched from his submarine *Nautilus*. However, Fulton's torpedo more resembled a mine as it was towed to the target.

Whitehead Torpedoes
The inventor of the first true torpedo was Robert Whitehead, the English director of a metal foundry that produced ship steam engines in the then Austrian (now Croatian) port of Fiume. Here he met local engineer Giovanni Luppis who had retired from the Austrian Navy and the two developed a small self-propelled torpedo (minenschiff) which they offered to the Austrian Imperial Navy on 21 December 1866. The torpedo carried only 18 pounds of dynamite and was launched from barrels mounted on a gunboat. The rudimentary new weapon was to establish the mechanical principles on which future torpedo development was based.

Whitehead returned to England in 1870 to successfully demonstrate a 14 inch model that traveled at seven knots per hour to the Royal Navy. (Note: From that time, torpedoes were generally categorized by the diameter of their cylindrical bodies e.g. the main types used by the Royal Navy during the First and Second World Wars were the 18 and 21 inch models). On 16 January 1878, the Turkish steamer *Intibah* became the first vessel to be sunk by a torpedo which was launched from a Russian torpedo boat during the Russo-Turkish War. The torpedo was manufactured by the German firm, L. Schwarzkopf, which used a design similar to Whitehead's. Over the next two decades Whitehead incorporated a number of innovations in his torpedo increasing its speed to 30 knots and size to 19 feet long and 18 inches in diameter. He equipped it with a 200 pound gun cotton warhead and a self-regulating device that kept the torpedo at a constant pre-set depth. The Whitehead torpedo was propelled by a small two cylinder, reciprocating, 90 degree V-engine powered by compressed air that drove a single propeller which needed a long vane connected to the torpedo to keep from turning in a circle. In 1898, Whitehead purchased the newly conceived gyroscope from its Austrian inventor, Ludwig Obry, and used it to give his torpedo directional stability.

Whitehead Torpedo Specifications:
Length: 11 feet
Diameter: 18 inches
Weight: 836 pounds
Speed: 26 knots
Maximum Range: 1000 yards
Charge: 110 pounds
Explosive: Guncotton
Motive Power: Three cylinder engine driven by compressed air
Launch: Small powder charge

The first Whitehead torpedoes used a simple bellows arrangement to measure the hydrostatic pressure and deduce the operating depth of the torpedo. This depth data controlled the horizontal rudders to correct any error in depth but this design was unstable. The creative Whitehead added a pendulum to sense the pitch angle and combined the pitch and depth information to control the horizontal rudder which was referred to as "Pendulum and Hydrostat" control.

Englishman **Robert Whitehead** and Austrian Giovanni Luppis developed what is considered the first true self-propelled torpedo which was presented to the Austrian Imperial Navy on 21 December 1866. (Author)

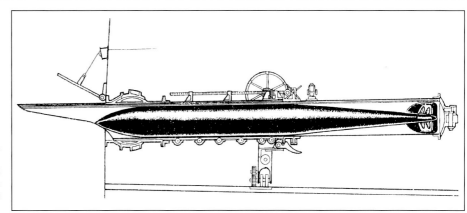

The 836 pound **Whitehead Torpedo** introduced in 1870 was 11 feet long and had an 18 inch diameter. From that time, torpedoes were generally categorized by the diameter of their cylindrical bodies as the main types used during the First and Second World Wars were described by their 18 and 21 inch diameters. (Author)

The Royal Laboratory at Woolwich assumed the development of Whitehead's weapon and by 1911 Woolwich had produced an effective 17 foot long, 18 inch diameter torpedo capable of traveling through the water at 35 knots to a target at 2,000 yards.

US Torpedo Development

The US Naval Torpedo Station (USNTS) was established on Goat Island, Newport, RI in 1869 as the first organization in any of the world's navies that was mainly concerned with the development of torpedoes, torpedo equipment, explosives, and associated electrical equipment. The first NTS undertaking was to improve existing spar torpedoes and mines ("stationary torpedoes") and initiate work on automobile torpedoes ("movable torpedoes"). These automobile torpedoes were to move underwater "for a considerable distance at a fair rate of speed".... and "to make a straight course and maintain a constant immersion, whether started at the surface of the water or any point below it."

Fish Torpedo

The NST did not attempt to design a new torpedo but essentially duplicated the contemporary Whitehead torpedo. Outwardly, the first automotive torpedo was very similar to the Whitehead torpedo in shape but somewhat shorter at 12.5 feet long and 14 inches in diameter. The engine consisted of two, 2x4 inch, cylinders with their axes parallel to the torpedo axis. The first NTS "Fish Torpedo" was tested in 1871 with poor results as the hull was not water tight, air flasks leaked, and the engine's power was inadequate. The Navy BuOrd tested an improved Fish Torpedo in June 1874 but this torpedo also did not meet expectations.

By 1891 some 1,500 proven British Whitehead torpedoes had been sold to other navies and had been offered to the US Navy in 1869 and 1873 and had been declined. So due to limited government funding, from 1874 until 1891, the development of the American automobile torpedoes passed to civilian inventors with the role of the NTS to mainly provide the test and evaluation facilities. A number of inventors (Lay, Ericsson, Haight) submitted designs which culminated in the Howell torpedo design.

Howell Torpedo

Lt.Cdr. John Howell began his torpedo design in 1870 which was not completed until 1889 at which time the US Navy ordered 50 from the Hotchkiss Ordnance Company, Providence, RI and placed it in service the next year. The 580 pound Howell Torpedo Mark 1 was 14.2 inches in diameter, 10.8 feet long, and contained a 96 pound explosive charge 400 yards at 25 knots with good course keeping and the absence of a revealing wake. Howell's torpedo was distinctive in that it stored propulsive power

in a heavy cylinder rotating at high speed. The torpedo had propellers at both ends tied to a common shaft together with a cylinder that contained the explosive charge. The entire rotating structure, except for the propellers, was contained in an exterior cylindrical shell. The rotating structure was given a large angular velocity, thus storing energy for propulsion, after the torpedo was launched. The Howell torpedo was one of the few realistic challengers to the Whitehead torpedo and other navies made some inquiries. The Howell torpedo would be the Navy's only torpedo until the Whitehead torpedoes produced by Bliss and Williams came into US Navy service in 1894 and continued in service into the turn of the century.

US Navy Bliss-Leavitt (Whitehead) Torpedoes
Mk1 through Mk3, 1891-1906.

The Navy did not obtain the Whitehead torpedo directly from its British manufacturer but Bliss and Williams (later the E.W. Bliss Company), with the USN as its only customer, negotiated a contract with Whitehead to provide drawings, sample torpedoes, and a manufacturing license. The Navy finally decided to use the Whitehead torpedo as its range and speed were somewhat better than the Howell torpedo and it was considered to have much greater developmental possibilities. Besides, it was proven and all the other major navies were using it. The first 100 were ordered in 1891.

E.W. Bliss produced three types of Whitehead torpedoes for the US Navy: the 11.5 foot, 21 inch diameter, Marks 1, 2, and 3. Pictured is the **Mk3** being tested at NTS in 1894. (USN)

US Navy Torpedo Models Mark 7 through Mark 36

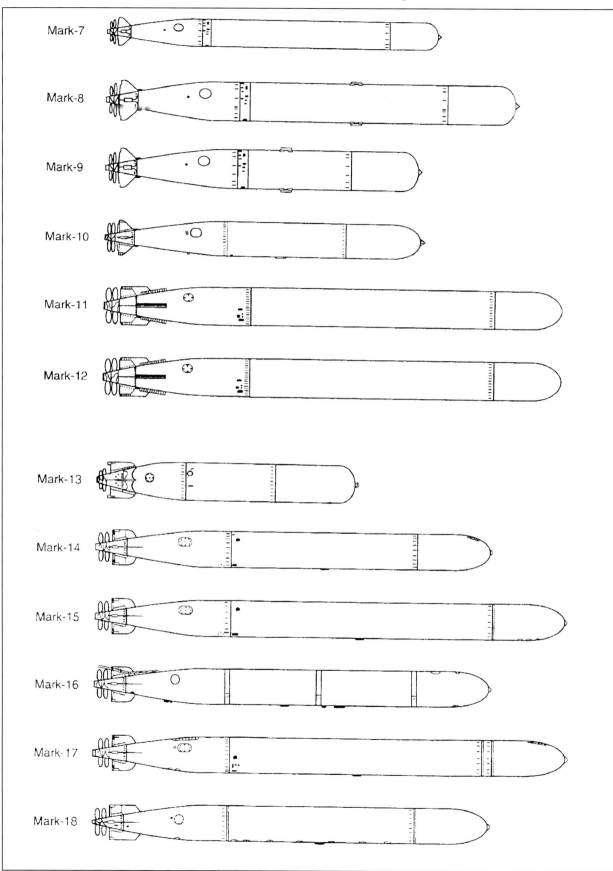

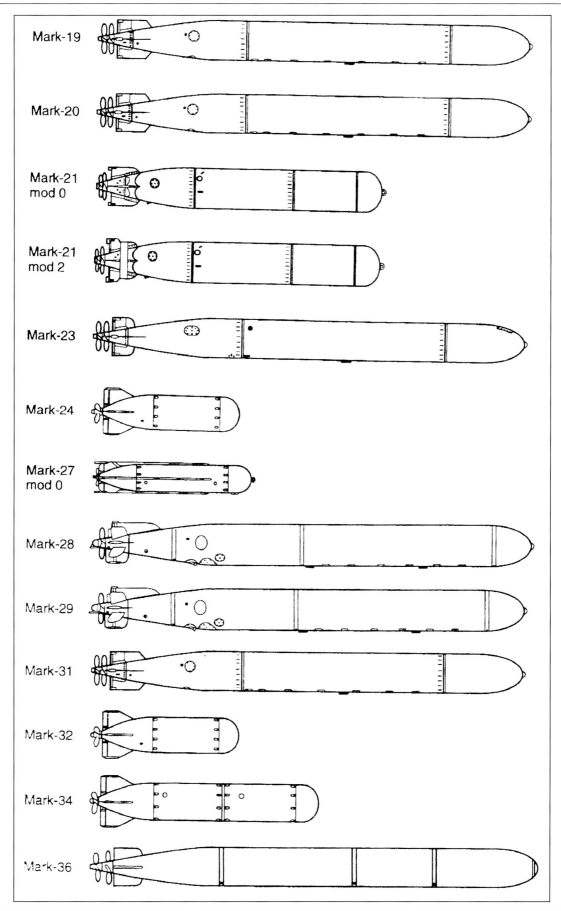

Mark-19

Mark-20

Mark-21
mod 0

Mark-21
mod 2

Mark-23

Mark-24

Mark-27
mod 0

Mark-28

Mark-29

Mark-31

Mark-32

Mark-34

Mark-36

E.W. Bliss produced three types of Whitehead torpedoes for the US Navy: the 11.5 foot, 21 inch diameter, Marks 1, 2, and 3. The propulsion system was an air flask, cold running compressed air powered, three cylinder, radial Brotherhood engine. All used the standard Whitehead pendulum and hydrostat depth control system and the Obry gyro for course control.

E.W. Bliss torpedo project engineer Frank Leavitt improved the Whitehead torpedoes which were to be known as the Bliss-Leavitt torpedoes. Leavitt's improvements were larger at 21 inches diameter, had larger warheads, and used turbine engines, innovative alcohol-fired dry heaters, and higher air pressures. The Bliss-Leavitt Mk1 torpedo had and much longer range, 4,000 yards at 27 knots vs. 1,500 yards at 28.5 knots for the best US Navy Whitehead (16.5 foot Mk2). About 750 Bliss-Leavitt torpedoes Mk1 through Mk3 were procured by the US Navy and entered service between 1904 and 1906 and remained in service until 1922. To overcome the unbalanced torque of the Mk1, the Mk2 introduced two counter-rotating turbine wheels and propellers which eliminated the rolling at a slight cost in range and speed. This propulsion arrangement was used on all subsequent Navy torpedoes through World War II.

Bliss-Leavitt Mk4 through Mk12, 1908-1940

The standard 21 inch torpedo was adequate for large surface warships but was too heavy and large for contemporary torpedo boats, destroyers, and particularly submarines; so Bliss-Leavitt designed four 16.3 foot, 17.7 inch torpedoes. The Bliss-Leavitt Mk4 was similar to the Mk3, but designed especially for submarines. Mk5 was a Whitehead design manufactured by Vickers and the new torpedo factory at Newport. The Mk4 could be set for any one of three speeds with equivalent maximum ranges with the slower speeds for longer ranges. The speed had to be set before the torpedo was loaded into the tube which restricted its tactical flexibility. The Mk4 was propelled by a dry heater system using a four cylinder reciprocating engine and was the last piston engine used in US torpedoes until the Mk46. Beginning with the Bliss-Leavitt Mk4 torpedo the Navy system of assigning a series of Marks to each manufacturer was changed to a single series of Marks for all manufactures. Accordingly, from the Mk4 onward, the Mark number alone, or in a few cases the Mark and Mod exclusively identified each torpedo.

The Bliss-Leavitt Mk6 pioneered a new turbine design in which the wheels were horizontal which would be the universal US Navy torpedo turbine system since.

Although the Bliss-Leavitt Mk7 was the last 17.7 inch torpedo contracted by the US Navy it introduced several innovations. It introduced a new method of cooling the combustion chamber by spraying water into it along with fuel and air. The ensuing mixture of steam and combustion products was an improved operational fluid for the turbine than the previous heated air and significantly improved the torpedo's range. These torpedoes logically would be labeled as "steam torpedoes." Another improvement in the Mk7 was the use of TNT as the explosive charge. This torpedo could be launched from submarines or destroyers and was used later in experimental air launchings. The Mk7 entered service in 1911 and after 1922 it was the only US Navy 17.7 inch torpedo in service and with numerous modifications continued was used by older submarines through 1945. The Mark 8 was the 21 inch version of the Mk7 and was designed to be launched by destroyers against surface vessels.

E.W. Bliss Marks 7 and 8 were the main torpedoes used by the US Navy ships during World War I. While 5,910 torpedoes were ordered; only 1,982 were delivered between 1 January 1917 and 30 November 1918 as torpedo manufacture fell behind schedule, mainly due to a shortage of forgings for air flasks. Torpedoes were not significant weapons for the US Navy during World War I as there were few enemy surface vessels available after America entered the war.

Marks 9 through 12 were 21 inch steam turbine powered torpedoes, which were basically similar to the Mk7 and 8 except in details. The Mk9 was the last torpedo manufactured by E.W. Bliss while the Mk10 was the last designed by the company. Torpedo manufacture and design was then taken over entirely by the Newport Torpedo Station on Goat Island on 1 July 1923. Until 1940 no new US Navy torpedoes, or even parts for torpedoes, were designed or produced by any other US Navy entity or private industrial concern.

The Mk11 instituted multiple speeds that could be selected after loading into the tube. The Marks 9 through 12 continued in service through 1945 but with only several hundred built did not see much operational service.

Mark 13 through 15

The development of the Mk13, Mk14, and Mk15 was completed in 1936, 1931 and 1935 respectively, with their purpose being to offer a modern weapon for each of the three weapons delivery systems; aircraft, submarines, and surface vessels. These new torpedo designs incorporated the physical, performance, and manufacturing improvements of the earlier designs, especially the Mk7 through 12. The commonality of the three new torpedoes was the turbine and other mechanical parts of the propulsion system, the depth engine and gyro, and the contact part of the exploders. Once the Newport Torpedo Station's monopoly on torpedo research and development was ended; NDRC sponsored university and industrial laboratories became involved. These organizations appreciably expanded both the intellectual and industrial capacity committed to torpedo research and development. Torpedo production was expanded by using manufacturing companies and GOCO (Government Owned Contractor Operated) plants in addition to the established Navy facilities. Of the nearly 64,000 torpedoes produced during World War II the Naval Torpedo Stations produced about 46%, the GOCOs about 31%, and industrial firms about 23%.

Torpedo Basics
Requirements of a Torpedo
A torpedo is a self-propelled weapon containing an explosive charge and a power plant. A torpedo must have a number of features including the following:

1) A shell, or housing, that was strong enough to carry the explosive charge, power plant, and related mechanisms, and to withstand the shock of launching.

2) A source of energy for the power plant and for the torpedo control mechanisms.

3) An exploder that would detonate the explosive charge when the torpedo reached its target but which would remain inoperable while the torpedo was close to the firing ship.

4) Control mechanisms that held the torpedo on a preset course, at a preset depth.

5) One or more propellers to drive the torpedo through the water.

6) Tail vanes and rudders, to control course and depth.

Sections of a Torpedo
Warhead: Consisted of 550 pounds of explosive, Detonator (firing pin), water inlet pipe, and ballast. A bulkhead separated the warhead from the aft sections.

Mid-Body: The majority of this section was occupied by the large compressed air flask which held air at 2,800 pounds psi. A smaller tank in this section contained fuel.

Engine: This compartment contained the combustion chamber, electric motor, small water and alcohol flasks, along with a depth-setting pendulum and gyro mechanism. This compartment was the heart of the torpedo as at launch there were a chain of events which took place in rapid succession. The jolt caused by the torpedo entering the water released the starting lever that released a burst of compressed air that turned the engine over; a valve opened to spray a mist of alcohol in the combustion chamber; the alcohol was ignited by a pair of cartridges that combusted into flame. Meanwhile, a water pot began to spray water into the flame; generating an explosion of steam that simultaneously provided the force to generate about 400 hp and kept the firebox temperature down to about 1,250°F.

Tail: This aft section included a set of elevators for depth control, a set of rudders for direction, and twin contra-rotating four-bladed propellers on a single shaft (propellers rotating in one direction tended to spin the torpedo). The direction of the torpedo's run was computed beforehand by the fire-control officer and set by a torpedoman and was held by a gyro, The gyro was a six to eight inch bronze disk which was spun at approximately 18,000 rpm by a compressed air jet. The gyro regulated a small motor that then operated the directional rudders. Depth was maintained by the pendulum controlled by a hydrostat that measured water pressure through a port, and thus depth. The pendulum controlled the elevators through a second small motor. The exit for the exhaust was through the hollow propeller shaft.

History of Torpedo Energy Sources
Compressed Air

This first successful self-propelled Whitehead torpedo of 1866 used compressed air as its energy source. The air was stored under pressure and fed to a piston engine which turned a single propeller at about 100 rpm. It was able to travel about 200 yards at an average speed of 6.5 knots with the speed and range of later models improved by increasing the pressure of the stored air. In 1906 Whitehead-built torpedoes were able to travel nearly 1,100 yards at an average speed of 35 knots.

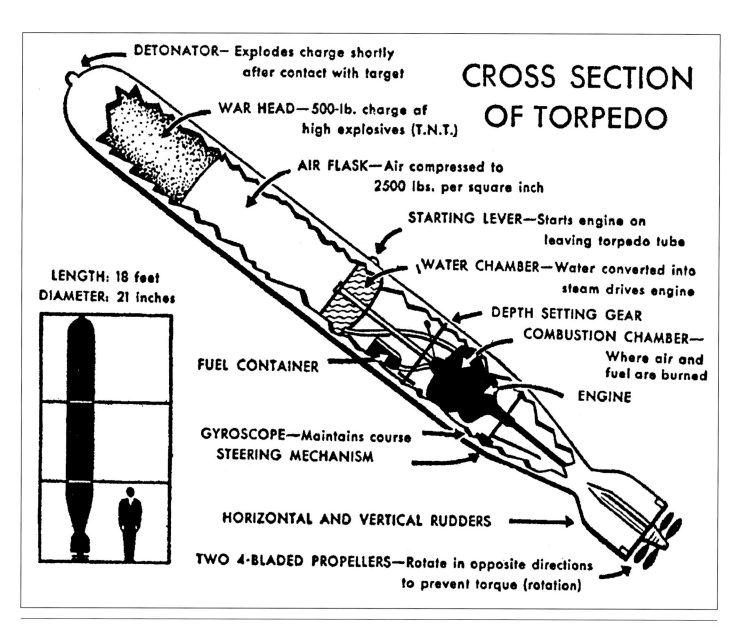

Flywheel

The Howell torpedo used by the US Navy in the late 1800s featured a heavy flywheel which had to be spun up before launch. It was able to travel about 400 yards at 25 knots. The Howell had the advantage of not leaving a trail of bubbles behind it, unlike compressed air torpedoes. This feature gave the target vessel less chance to detect and evade the torpedo and avoided giving away the attacker's position. Additionally, it ran at a constant depth, unlike the very early Whitehead models.

Electric batteries

Electric propulsion systems also avoided tell-tale bubbles. John Ericsson invented an electrically propelled torpedo in 1873; it was powered by a cable from an external power source, as batteries of the time had insufficient capacity. The Sims-Edison torpedo was similarly powered. The Nordfelt torpedo was also electrically powered and was steered by impulses down a trailing wire.

Heated torpedoes

Injecting a liquid fuel, like kerosene, into the air and igniting it; heated the air up more and expanded it even further, while the burned propellant added more gas to drive the engine. Construction of such heated torpedoes began about 1904 by Whitehead's company.

Compressed oxygen

The amount of fuel that could be burned by a torpedo engine was limited by the amount of oxygen it could carry. Since compressed air contains only about 21% of oxygen, engineers in Japan developed the Type 93 (nicknamed *Long Lance* postwar by historian Samuel E. Morison) for destroyers in the 1930s. The Type 93 used pure oxygen instead of compressed air and had unmatched performance in World War II. During the war, Germany experimented with hydrogen peroxide for the same purpose.

Steam

A derivative of the compressed-air torpedo was the steam torpedo. Developed by British company, Vickers Ltd, it mixed alcohol (first ethanol, later methanol) with compressed air in the combustion chamber, producing steam. But as this increased speed, it also produced a visible wake.

Wet-heater

A further enhancement was the use of water to cool the combustion chamber. This not only solved heating problems so more fuel could be burned, but also allowed additional power to be generated by feeding the resulting steam into the engine together with the combustion products. Torpedoes with such a propulsion system became known as w*et heaters*, while heated torpedoes without steam generation were, retrospectively, called *dry heaters*. A less complicated system was developed by the British Royal Gun factory in 1908. Most torpedoes used in World War I and World War II were wet-heaters.

Torpedo Identification

Dummy: Black warhead with the standard green body separated by a blue stripe painted at the warhead juncture.

Exercise: Red warhead head with the standard green body.

Explosive: Black warhead with the standard green body separated yellow stripe painted at the warhead juncture.

Development of the American Mark 13 Air-Dropped Torpedo

During World War II submarines were shown to be the most successful users of torpedoes with aircraft a close runner up both in the quantity expended and in effectiveness. The inherent problems of using aircraft torpedoes precluded the long experience of using torpedoes in submarines. The common limitations on torpedo design, such as the requirements for light weight and small size combined with the highest power commensurate with reliability, were increased for aircraft torpedoes. Over and above these normal requirements were the need of the aerial torpedo to withstand the severe impact of high altitude, high speed launches, the need to conform with both the principles of aero- and hydrodynamics. Another problem which had to be addressed was to develop control mechanisms that could take effect despite the forces of cavitation and deceleration which affected torpedo performance as it transformed from an airborne projectile to an underwater weapon. The specifications for aerial torpedo speed and range and weight were frozen but the rapid development of the airplane at the time necessitated flexibility in design not required of torpedoes for surface or submarine employment.

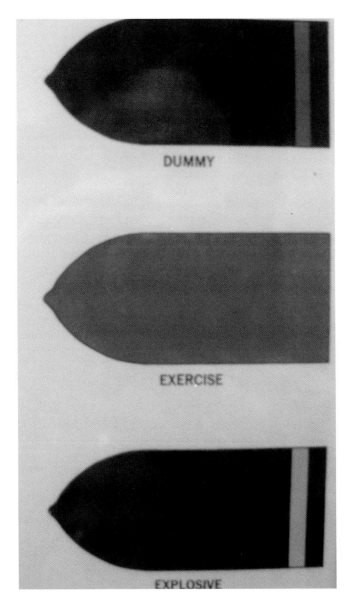

US Torpedo Identification (USN)

During World War I the Navy Bureau of Ordnance became interested in the potential of torpedo aerial warfare and in 1915 conducted experiments by launching torpedoes lowered on a cable and then released at a predetermined altitude but that seemed to be the extent of American interest in the aerial torpedo. During the inter-war years airborne torpedo testing generally was a haphazard occurrence as stringent military budgets caused most navies to cutback or forego torpedo development and testing. At the beginning of World War II only the Japanese had a fully-tested and operational aerial torpedo as the American battleships at Pearl Harbor would discover.

The Mk7 was designed in 1910 and accepted into service in 1912 and continued in use by some old submarines during World War II. It was the first wet-heater (water spray into combustion chamber) torpedo used by the Navy. The 18 inch Mk7 was 17 feet long, weighed 1,628 pounds, and carried a 326 pound TNT explosive charge 6,000 yards at 35 knots. The Mk7 was built for use in submerged submarine tubes and lacked the structural strength to withstand the shock of high altitude release but some Mk7 torpedoes were modified for use by aircraft. The first experimental USN aircraft drops were made by two DT-2 float planes in May 1920 at the Naval Air Station, Anacostia, Maryland, using two Mark 7 Mod 5 torpedoes. Air speed for these drops was at 50 to 55 knots at altitudes of 18 and 30 feet. The torpedo dropped from over 30 feet was badly damaged while the one dropped from 18 to 30 feet was not. The first mass torpedo practice against a live target was conducted off the Virginia Capes on 22 September 1922 by 18 PT aircraft of Torpedo and Bombing Plane Squadron One. The Squadron attacked the *Arkansas* which was one of a formation of three battleships that were maneuvering while running at full speed. The attack lasted over a 25 minute period during which time the aircraft approached the ships from both sides and released 17 Mark 7 Mod 1 A torpedoes at distances of 500 to 1,000 yards. Eight hits were made and subsequent analysis emphasized the "artificialities which prevented the practice from demonstrating combat capability of either the surface or air units," but nothing was noted about aircraft being able to launch torpedoes that could be made to run straight. In 1924 further tests at NTS Newport showed that a structurally modified Mk7 could be successfully dropped from about 32 feet at 110 mph. The experimental addition of a nose drogue to improve the MK7's flight characteristics so diminished its structural strength, that the benefits of the structural changes were almost totally lost.

Meanwhile, the Navy BuOrd doubted the practicability of aircraft using torpedoes against ships due to their vulnerability to AA fire during the low release altitudes. However, the BuOrd considered that radio-controlled aircraft could use the torpedo effectively. In 1925 a joint Army-Navy Board resolved the question and the BuOrd began the total redesign of the semi-successful Mark 7 Aerial Torpedo. The new specifications called for a 2,000 pound torpedo, measuring 21 inches by 18 feet, to be capable of carrying a 350 pound warhead 4,000 yards at 35 knots. It was to be tough enough to withstand a dropping speed of 140 miles per hour at an altitude of 40 feet.

While the BuOrd embraced the new weapon that was designed with the particular requirements of aircraft in mind; the Naval Torpedo Station at Newport opposed the new design. From 1923, all development of the air-dropped torpedo had been under the control of NTS Newport and during this time that station had total US torpedo monopoly in almost complete isolation from the influence of any outside technical development. NTS Newport preferred to further modify the Mk7 in order to more easily standardize the weapon and decrease production problems. After eliminating the nose drogue and by employing balanced rudders NTS Newport had made successful drops from 65 feet at 120 knots; causing the BuOrd to put its new specifications on hold. Late in 1929 a General Board finally recommended the development of a new torpedo for aircraft and their provisional specifications were even more stringent than those in the BuOrd's shelved plans. The length was not to exceed 13.5 feet; the diameter was increased by two inches; the overall weight was reduced to 1,700 pounds; while the explosive charge was increased to 400 pounds. Once the General Board decided the issue a contract NTS Newport abandoned its opposition to the project and built a rough model that approximated the BuOrd specifications in August 1930.

The chronic limitation in the airborne torpedo was that it had to be dropped low and slow (a maximum of 50 feet at about 110 mph); otherwise it would be destroyed. Scientists at Cal Tech and Columbia were requested to determine baselines for the basic data on the aerodynamic and hydrodynamic characteristics of standard torpedo shapes and to develop a torpedo design that could enter the water at a high speed from high altitudes and then move toward the target while maintaining the correct course and depth.

The Mark 13's development was held up by a number of factors including the delay in the completion of the torpedo bombers which were to carry it and by the time taken to eliminate the usual developmental bugs. Once the European war began the value of the torpedo bomber became evident and the BuOrd accelerated work to improve and complete the Mark 13. Before Pearl Harbor the MK13 was put into Navy inventory approximating the original specifications. Although its weight of 1,927 pounds did not meet the 1929 General Board weight specification of 1,700

Newport Naval Torpedo Station was established in 1869 and is located on Goat Island near Newport, RI (in background) located near the mouth Narragansett Bay. Torpedo production reached its peak during World War II, when more than 13,000 persons were employed on three shifts in the manufacture of 80% of American torpedoes. (USN)

The Battle of Midway on 4 June 1942, though a astounding victory for America when four Japanese carriers were sunk, showed the shortcomings of torpedo bombers. Of the 41 **Douglas TBD torpedo bombers** dispatched 35 of were lost and the six surviving bombers were badly damaged without causing any damage to the Japanese. Shown is a VT-8 TBD leaving the carrier *Hornet*. (USN)

pounds the range was increased to 5,000 yards at 33.5 knots and it could be dropped at least 60 feet by a bomber flying at 115 knots.

Even though the Mk13 was available for operations it would not be until another three years before it was used to any degree or with any effect. Early in the war, pilots thoroughly disliked torpedoes and much preferred bombs. One reason was due to their lack of experience with torpedoes; another was due to the large number of defective torpedoes; and a third reason was that the technique required for launching airborne torpedoes effectively was at low altitudes and slow speeds which were considered suicidal. On 4 June 1942, all three drawbacks became heartbreakingly apparent during the Battle of Midway when 35 of 41 TBD torpedo bombers were lost (10 out of 12 from VT-3, 10 out of 14 from VT-6, and 15 out of 15 from VT-8) with the six surviving bombers badly damaged without doing any damage to the Japanese. The Douglas Devastators armed with Mk13 torpedoes had attacked at a speed of 110 knots and an altitude of 50 feet, with little fighter protection against strong enemy fighter attacks and in the face of intense anti-aircraft fire. The pilots surviving the run in were dismayed that torpedoes launched at any altitude or speed higher than that specified in the "low and slow" procedure would porpoise or just disappear after hitting the ocean's surface.

To make matters worse, at the beginning of the war there was a critical torpedo shortage and in February 1942, the Chief of BuOrd chief recommended that Navy patrol planes use Mark 15 torpedoes outfitted with special stabilizers. The Mark 15 was a 1931 weapon designed to be launched from destroyers and needed to be dropped even lower and slower than the Mk7. It was found that "30% to 40% suffered structure failures or dove too deep or ran cold (failed to explode)."

Much has been written about the so-called "Great Torpedo Scandal" which occurred between December 1941 and August 1943. USN submarine skippers reported a distressing number of premature detonations, duds, and inexplicable misses during the first full year of the war. The Mk14 submarine torpedo suffered from three distinct problems which involved depth control, the magnetic influence exploder, and the contact exploder; whose collective effects reduced the performance of these torpedoes. The Mk13 being a slower speed torpedo had a smaller depth error and did not use the contact exploder but used the Mk4 exploder which did not utilize the magnetic influence element. The impact portion of the Mk6 exploder

used by the 46.5 knot Mk14 torpedo was exactly the same as that which was used very satisfactorily in the Mk4 exploders used by the 33.5 knot Mk13. However, the inertial forces in striking a target at normal incidence at 33.5 knots and 46.3 knots were almost doubled. These greatly increased inertial forces were sufficient to bend the vertical pins that guided the torpedo's firing pin block. This displacement sometimes caused the firing pins to miss the percussion caps which resulted in a dud. When a torpedo hit a target obliquely, the forces were smaller and the impact exploder functioned normally.

By the end of 1942, USN torpedo engineers at Newport worked on the problem and determined that by cutting off the nose and welding on a dome of strengthened 0.375 inch steel would allow drops of up to 250 knots. However, pilot complaints continued as many torpedoes were defective. BuOrd investigated the data from more than 100 torpedoes dropped at more than 150 knots and found that two thirds were defective and of these 33% ran cold (e.g. failed to ignite); 20% just sank, and the rest had either poor deflection performance or depth problems. The Pacific Fleet demanded the development of a new, well-built torpedo that could be launched from higher altitudes and at greater speeds.

It appeared that the resolution of the air-drop difficulties could be remedied by retro-rockets which could be mounted on a small aircraft torpedo and exert rearward thrust during its fall, slowing it so that the high speed release would result in a moderate or even slow speed water entry. Cal Tech engineers developed a 12 retro-rocket/torpedo array that would fire after dropping a safe distance from the aircraft; separating from the torpedo before entry into the water. The concept had some worth as tests in early 1943 showed that torpedo air speed could be cut by about 100 knots but was too complex in use and simpler solutions were being investigated.

Other Cal Tech researchers were working on simpler solutions using data collected during the basic studies of the hydrodynamics of high speed water entry. Their investigation uncovered several factors that led them closer to an answer but the effect of the wind on the falling torpedo remained to be a major problem. They observed that in a headwind, a torpedo tended to enter the water nose-up while in a tailwind it entered with its nose down, and in a crosswind it entered with a yaw.

Many of the failures were blamed on the poor design of the torpedo components but were actually due to the failure to aerodynamically control the angle of torpedo entry into the water. Until the angle of entry was controlled the delicate control mechanisms could not be designed to be strong enough to survive the impact of water entry nor could other deficiencies be uncovered and corrected. Changes were made in the tail surfaces, rudders, and the shape of the nose but were unsuccessful in solving the fundamental angle of entry problem.

As a remedy, plywood extensions were bolted to the horizontal vanes of the torpedoes. Tests found that the extensions did improve stabilization, different extensions had to be used for different aircraft and each had its own speed and altitude limitations. It was found that if the extensions were not freed soon enough, they disrupted the underwater run of the torpedo; if they were freed to soon, air stabilization was lost before water entry. In the spring of 1942 the best expedient, but not solution, appeared to be biplane extension stabilizers bolted to the torpedo vanes.

The forces acting on a torpedo as it entered the water were found to be extraordinarily complicated. Upon hitting the water there was the initial impact force along the torpedo longitudinal axis which was followed almost immediately by a number of forces acting in other planes, depending on the entry angle. The result of these forces was an indeterminate nose-up or nose-down attitude just below the water surface. Simultaneously, for a number of torpedo lengths, the torpedo was traveling not in water but in a conical cavity containing a partial vacuum; with only

Mk13 Aerial Torpedo

Standard Mk13 (with original finned tail) (USS *Hornet* Museum)

Mk13 Torpedo (USS *Hornet* Museum)

Ring Tail Mk13-1A (USS *Hornet* Museum)

The **David Taylor Model Basin (DTMB)** opened in 1939 at Carderock, MD, for the study of depth-control mechanisms. DTMB contained three basins: a shallow water basin, a deep water basin, and a high speed basin equipped with sophisticated towing carriages, wave-makers, and measuring equipment that tested the sea worthiness and propulsion characteristics of vessels and weapons. (USN)

Interior view of the Towing Tank at the DTMB (USN)

its nose in contact with water. During this time, depending on the shape of the nose, the torpedo tended to upend if it entered nose down or dropped its tail if it entered nose up. When the tail touched the top or bottom of the vacuum cavity, attitude changed and became even more erratic, and if it slammed against the bubble side the fins could be destroyed.

Researchers found that they could not do much correction while the torpedo was in the vacuum cavity so their studies were concentrated on calculating the trajectory after collapse of the vacuum, predicting the actions of the torpedo at the beginning of its run, and on developing a corrective action after underwater stabilization was achieved. A two-position method of horizontal control was investigated using full and scale model torpedoes in wind tunnels and towing tanks and was found to be the best solution.

The study of depth-control mechanisms was undertaken by researchers at Columbia University assisted by MIT, Cal Tech, and the David Taylor Model Basin (DTMB). The DTMB was named in honor of David Watson Taylor, the gifted naval architect who developed the Navy's first "Model Tank for Experiments" in 1896. The DTMB was built by the USN and opened in 1939 at Carderock, MD. The facility contained three basins: a shallow water basin (303 feet Long x 51 feet Wide x 10 feet Deep), a deep water basin (1,886L x 51W x 22D), and a high speed basin (1,168L x 21W x 10D) equipped with sophisticated towing carriages, wave-makers, and measuring equipment that tested and analyzed the sea worthiness and propulsion characteristics of vessels and weapons. The deep water basin contained 15.82 million gallons of water.

The torpedo's controlling elevator per se presented no problems but some type of sensor had to be developed that would note any stimulus that could turn the torpedo nose up or down and would apply counter forces before the torpedo significantly changed depth; resulting in large fluctuations of the torpedo's path. After a number of trials the Columbia University researchers determined that the pendulum principal first developed by Robert Whitehead in 1869 was the simplest and only workable solution despite some disadvantages. Among these disadvantages was the pendulum's frequent reaction to striking the water with the violent raising of the elevator and its innate periodicity that occasionally too closely approached that of the torpedo and could cause oscillation.

BuOrd assigned Cal Tech to completely revamp the Mk13 and ultimately they thoroughly redesigned the torpedo to solve the operational difficulties. The problem of erratic runs was determined to be caused by

the depth mechanism diaphragm which would rupture when the torpedo entered the water so the diaphragm was redesigned and strengthened. The rudder contours were changed to solve deflection problems. Depth failures were proved to be the result of weak propeller blades that bent upon impact with water and were also redesigned and strengthened. The exploder mechanism was redesigned to arm upon water entry rather than in the air. Despite all the strengthening and repositioning of interior mechanisms they still weren't strong enough to survive water entries until the impact of the entries were lessened.

The BuOrd was now faced with two alternatives: it could acknowledge that the Mark 13 was an interim weapon with recognized tactical limitations and begin the development of a new torpedo, or it could concentrate on eliminating the known defects in the Mk13. To develop a new torpedo would require two years while to correct the 12 major Mk13 defects would not be an immediate solution either. BuOrd decided to increase its resources and to attempt to pursue both alternatives together. In late 1942 the National Defense Research Committee granted unlimited funds produce a new aircraft torpedo, the Mark 25, for tactical use at 350 knots launching speed, and it agreed to aid the Bureau in making immediate improvements to the Mk13.

Despite the improvements and modifications of 1942 and 1943, the Mk13 continued to perform poorly and was generally disliked. In mid-1943 an analysis of 105 torpedoes launched at speeds in excess of 150 knots showed that 36% ran cold, 20% sank, 20% had poor deflection performance, 18% gave unsatisfactory depth performance, 2% ran on the surface, and only 31% were satisfactory. The attentive reader will see that the total percentage exceeds 100% which was due to many torpedoes having more than one of the defects. Most of the problems continued to be traced to the effects of poor air stabilization prior to their entry into the water. For better torpedo performance combat pilots were instructed to approach the target at reduced speeds! This dictum put the pilot in harm's way and when they did reduce their approach speed the torpedo went into recurrent hooking and broaching runs.

Much of Cal Tech's testing equipment was jury-rigged to meet the requirements of testing new concepts. A large, water-filled, glass tank was built in which small scale model torpedoes were launched by a cross bow or a large blow gun to investigate nose shapes and the air bubble each model would produce when it entered the water. To study the performance of a full-scale mockup, particularly the various configurations of bomb-

The Mk13 Torpedo Problems with the Mk13's water entry led to the development of the first ring assembly, known as the **"pickle barrel."** Constructed of plywood, the ring was attached to the nose of a torpedo and served as a stabilizer for the time that the weapon was airborne. The wooden shroud ring termed the **"ring tail"** fit over the rear of the torpedo and added stability while the torpedo was in the water and also minimized broaching and underwater rolls. (USN)

type fins designed to smooth out the water entry, a 300 foot, 22.5 inch diameter tube was constructed near the Morris Dam running down the side of the mountain at 19°. The scientists would lug the torpedo to the top of the mountain and send it down the tube and, upon leaving the end, it would become airborne and finally smash into the water where an assortment of hydrophones and submerged high speed cameras recorded its performance. An additional 4,300 air drops were done at Newport to test various Mk13 tail fin configurations designed to slow and dampen water entry. In early 1943 after trying many configurations, Cal Tech scientists finally found the right combination which was a pair of wooden rings.

The Mk13 Ring Tail Development

In 1944 the performance of the Mk13 was improved dramatically by minor changes to the propeller blades and a reduction in gyro damage improved performance, but the greatest improvement came from the stabilizing effects of the drag ring and the shroud ring developed by the California Institute of Technology.

The first ring assembly fitted to the Mk13's nose, known familiarly as the "pickle barrel," was ready for use by 1944. Early experiments with parachutes attached to aircraft torpedoes had demonstrated that a drag had a beneficial effect on the in air characteristics of the weapon. While parachutes did not appear the solution to the problem, discovery of the principle involved led to the development of the drag ring. Constructed of plywood, the ring was attached to the head of a torpedo and served as a stabilizer for the time that the weapon was airborne. Oscillations were reduced and the ring effected a 40% deceleration in air speed and then acted as a shock absorber when the torpedo struck water. Better water entry, a byproduct of air stabilization, reduced damage so substantially that pilots were able to increase the heights and speeds at which torpedoes were released.

The addition of the drag ring greatly enhanced the Mk13 but its underwater performance required improvement which was achieved by the shroud ring. The shroud ring was almost an exact copy of an assembly developed by Newport in 1871. The wooden shroud termed the "ring tail" fit over the rear of the torpedo and added stability in the water similar to the feathers on an arrow and also minimized broaching and underwater rolls. Also when the torpedo struck the water the tail fin of the shroud ring broke off and absorbed some of the entry shock. Further deep water testing at Ft. Lauderdale demonstrated that the Mk13 could be launched at altitudes up to 800 feet instead of the conventional 50 feet, and at air speeds as high as 300 knots instead of 110. The Mk13 generated stable water runs by reducing hooks and broaches and eliminating most of the water roll which had previously characterized this torpedo. These improvements came at only slightly reduced speed and range.

In early 1944 the Ring Tail, as it was commonly called in the field, was flight-tested by VT-13 of the *USS Franklin* commanded by Lt.Cdr. Larry French. Tests were conducted off Point Loma, San Diego using dummy warheads and depth regulators set to pass under the *Franklin*. Sixteen TBM Avengers simultaneously attacked the carrier from ahead and 30°-45° on port and starboard bows. They were launched at 500-800 foot altitudes and at speeds of 275-325 mph both of which varied order to

A Mk13 being transported to a TBF Avenger. The wooden tail shroud is in good view in this photo. (USN)

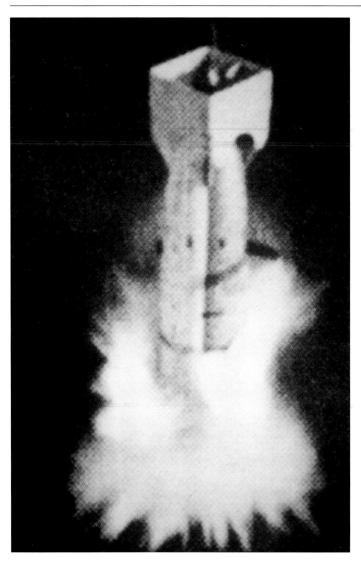

A dramatic still photo taken from test films. The plywood nose ring acted as a shock absorber as the torpedo entered the water. (USN)

gain correct entry angle into the water. The results were very good with all the new ringtails running hot, straight and normal, scoring many "hits." The only problem revealed was that the initial dives were too deep but refinements of controls shortly solved this last problem. The only flight restriction was that the aircraft had to be in straight and level flight at time of release. Finally, by mid-summer 1944, the wooden pickle barrel and shroud ring developed by CIT and along with the strengthening and relocation of internal structures arguably made the Mk13 the best aerial torpedo of the war; invariably running straight and true and wreaking havoc on Japanese shipping.

To speed the availability of the modified Mk13 torpedo BuOrd built the ring tail assemblies with the shroud ring attached and shipped them to the fleet to replace the Mk13s on hand and by the fall of 1944 the overhauled weapon had a wide circulation. The first use of the ring-tail Mk13 was on 4 August 1944 by VT-13, led by Cdr. Larry French off the *Franklin*, against a Japanese convoy of six transports escorted by nine destroyers cruising about 70 miles west of Iwo Jima. The attack included 12 F6F Hellcats which strafed and suppressed AA fire, 30 SB2C dive bombers , and 16 TBMs. The dive bombers attacked first but scored no direct hits. VT-13 then dove over the AA fire from the destroyer screen

and released their ring tails at 400 feet and sunk all six transports.

Another development was the lanyard was attached to the Mk13 tail. When dropped, the lanyard tripped a starting lever with a water trip delay valve prevented the combustion flask from lighting until the torpedo entered the water. When dropped at 150 knots or more, the torpedo entered the water at an angle of between 26 and 30°. The water needed to be at least 150 feet deep and the torpedo began its pre-set running depth (maximum 50 feet) after traveling 300 yards in the water while the exploder mechanism was armed after 200 yards.

When a Mk13 torpedo was launched from an aircraft, a starting lever opened a valve admitting compressed air to the engine, turning it over and igniting a mixture of fuel and air, providing gas and steam to rotate the driving shaft and two propellers. These were mounted one behind the other revolving in opposite directions, an arrangement which enhanced running evenness and balance. Once running at the selected speed, the torpedo was kept on course by a gyroscope together with vertical and horizontal rudders, the appropriate depth being maintained by a hydrostatic control mechanism.

Initially, Mk13 torpedoes used a magnetic-type firing mechanism but with varied success. The intention was to have the intrinsic magnetism of the target vessel trigger the torpedo's firing mechanism as it passed below under the target's hull and explode directly underneath, fatally rupturing the weak bottom. But for a number of reasons the magnetic trigger did not always succeed. Firing pistols were then installed in the warhead to initiate detonation on impact either mechanically or electrically. All pistols were fitted with safety devices to ensure safe handling or jettisoning in an emergency. Furthermore, they were programmed not to arm until

The **first operational use of the ring-tail Mk13** was on 4 August 1944 by VT-13, led by Cdr. Larry French off the *Franklin*, against a Japanese convoy cruising about 70 miles west of Iwo Jima. (USN)

the torpedo had traveled a selected distance (from 100 to 1,000 yards) through the water. Before the torpedo aircraft took off, a safety clip was removed from the firing pistol; which along with a preventer ensured the torpedo vanes did not rotate during handling or flight. On impact with the water, the preventer lever between the vanes was forced back out of contact. Travel through the water caused the impeller to rotate, enabling the internal mechanism to push the detonators into contact with the primers, cock the strikers, and push aside three safety bolts to clear the striker's path to the detonators. Should the boss of the pistol or any one of the six vanes impact with the target, the strikers would be forced on to the detonators, instigating an instantaneous detonation chain. If the torpedo did not strike its target it literally ran out of steam and sank.

Mk13-1A

Through further development the unwieldy wooden tail shroud was replaced by a circular metal ring about the same circumference as the propeller arc and welded to four fins just forward of the propeller. Soon authorization was given for Mk13-1A torpedo drops at altitudes up to 800 feet and at speeds up to 300 knots and combat experience soon revealed that these limits could be increased even more. The aft rings and the

The unwieldy wooden tail shroud was replaced by a circular metal ring of the **Mk13-1A.** It had about the same circumference as the propeller arc and was welded to four fins just forward of the propeller. (USN)

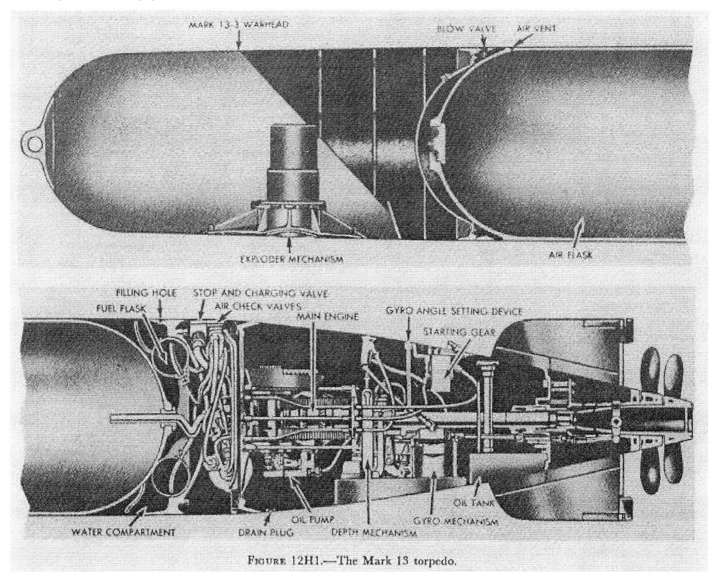

FIGURE 12H1.—The Mark 13 torpedo.

strengthening and repositioning of interior components were the panacea and the Mk13 was transformed into a reliable torpedo; with hot, straight, and normal runs approaching 100% reliability and at the war's end the Mk13 was considered by many as the best air-launched torpedo in the world.

Mark 13 Modifications

The four modification of the Mk13 were: 1) The Mark 13, 2) the Mark 13 Increased Warhead, 3) the Mark 13 Modification 1, and the 4) the Mark 13 Modification 2. The Mark 13 and the Mark 13 Modification 1 were standard sized torpedoes. The Mark 13 Increased Warhead and the Mark 13 Modification 2, both had an increased warhead size, having a CG that was nine inches further forward, thus necessitating alternate positions of the release mechanism

Mark 13 Torpedo Specifications

Width	22.4 inches
Overall Length	13 feet, 5 inches
Total Weight	1,927 pounds (early Mk13s)
	2,216 pounds (later Mk13s)
Negative Buoyancy	523 pounds
Explosive Charge	410 pounds (early Mk13s) TNT
	600 pounds (later model Mk13s) Torpex
Powerplant	98 hp Wet-Heater engine (33 knots)
	17 pounds alcohol
	130 pounds air
	48 pounds fresh water
	Expendable consumption 17.3lbs/hp/hr
Range	6,300 yards at 33.5 knots (39 mph)
Dropping Conditions	110 knots at 2,400 feet (later models)
Number Manufactured	17,000

A History of US Torpedo Production

During World War I torpedoes were produced by the Naval Torpedo Stations at Newport and Alexandria, and by the E.W. Bliss. Between 1 January 1917 and 30 November 1918, a total of 5,910 Mk7 and Mk8 torpedoes were ordered with 1,982 being actually delivered during this time period.

When the war ended Navy contracts with Bliss were terminated, though all Navy facilities were kept in operation to supply the massive

Mk13 torpedo production at NTS Newport which held a virtual monopoly on US torpedo output until war broke out in 1939 when other facilities were opened. (USN)

numbers of flush-deck destroyers completed during and after the war which resulted in a total production of about 3,000 Mk8 torpedoes. After the Washington Naval Conference of 1922 reduced the number of capital ships for the world's major navies, an additional reduction in torpedo production occurred. NTS Newport was chosen as the only production and development facility and NTS Alexandria Station was deactivated. So for the next decade from 1923 NTS Newport had the monopoly on American torpedo development and production. During this period Congressional allocations and general lack of interest kept torpedo development and production minimal.

During the mid-1930s with Japan and Germany building their navies Congress authorized funds. In 1933 the Vinson Shipbuilding Program increased the output of torpedoes for the new ships and expanded the Newport facilities and personnel. The Newport work force increased from 1,000 in 1933 to triple that in 1937. During the next five years nearly $750,000 was allocated for new construction and over $500,000 for new machine tools. By 1936 the total annual expenditure for NTS Newport increased $7.45 million and then to $9.31 million in 1937 (equaling an increase of 2.5 torpedoes per day). Nonetheless, production could not fill demands and by the beginning of 1938 there was a $29 million backlog at Newport. NTS Newport had long been a monopoly and the facility showed little creativity in torpedo technology or manufacture and was impeded by labor union problems and local politics.

Once the war in Europe broke out a serious consideration of the state of US torpedo development and production was undertaken. BuOrd considered a 50% expansion of NTS Newport but that would require $4.5 million and one and a half years to complete and being near the East Coast also required expensive defensive installations. The other alternative was to open new facilities and Alexandria and San Diego were considered. San Diego was eliminated as the estimated three year completion date was judged to be too long. BuOrd then was left with the most economical and expeditious alternative was to reopen NTS Alexandria as it had facilities in existence and a first-rate proving ground available nearby at Piney Point. Since NTS Alexandria was close to Washington DC, its defense would be provided by that already allocated to the Capital. Despite heavy opposition from politicians and labor leaders NTS Alexandria was approved. So after over $7 million was spent to increase torpedo production, by September 1939 US torpedo production was only three per day.

This expenditure did not include the expansion of private business for the production of complete torpedoes. Soon the heavy forging facilities of Bethlehem, Crucible, and Midvale steel companies, and American Locomotive were expanded to produce air flasks and bulkheads. In July 1941, the A. O. Smith Company welded air flask production technique was adopted by the BuOrd. This technique saved incalculable man and machine hours, freed vital forging facilities for other crucial programs, and saved enormous amounts of precious high alloy steel. A large NTS spare parts facility was also opened in Keyport, WA.

Torpedo deliveries increased significantly but shipbuilding accelerated and small torpedo-equipped vessels were being built faster than the weapons they were designed to carry. In order to meet the torpedo demand BuOrd decided to contract private firms to mass produce torpedoes. However, at the time US torpedo requirements were at 50 torpedoes per day, so until private companies came on board, NTS Newport and Alexandria were to increase their production by installing additional machinery and personnel to three shifts 24/7 which would increase production to about 23 torpedoes a day.

Once America entered the war torpedo requirements had to be revised sharply upwards. Because Japan, the new enemy, was a naval power, America's only weapons for the near future in the Pacific were aircraft bombs and torpedoes launched from the few aircraft carriers available and submarines. So when the demand for aircraft torpedoes increased the Naval Ordnance Plant (NOPF) at Forest Park, IL, which was managed by Amertorp, an American Can Co. subsidiary was contracted to build a modern production line to manufacture complete Mk13 aerial torpedoes. Forest Park would eventually produce 70 Mk13 torpedoes per week as compared to 25 to 30 per week for Newport and seven to ten week for Alexandria. However, initial production was hindered by poorly performing torpedoes which was eventually remedied by better quality control and torpedo design modifications. Later, complete torpedo manufacture contracts were let to International Harvester, Westinghouse, Western Electric, and Pontiac. In addition to the Illinois Forest Park plant, the American Can St. Louis plant which was under construction was to be devoted to torpedo production. In February 1942, Pontiac Motor and International Harvester were contracted to manufacture the British aerial torpedo for which large requisitions had been placed. Meanwhile, E.W. Bliss and Precision Manufacturing, two manufacturers with contracts for the British torpedo, were contracted to accelerate their programs. During the war no other companies were contracted to manufacture complete torpedoes as demands were met by expanding facilities at existing plants and by widespread subcontracting. NTS Newport was supplied by over 750 subcontractors and NTS Alexandria from over 550 subcontractor suppliers.

US Torpedo Production during World War II
By Manufacturer
From 1 January 1939, to 1 June 1946, BuOrd produced 57,653 torpedoes at a cost of close to $700 million, including the expansion of facilities. NTS Newport produced 18,751; NTS Alexandria, 9,920; Westinghouse, 8,250; American Can, Forest Park. 8,391; American Can, St. Louis, 6,257; Keyport, 795; and Pontiac and International Harvester, 5,289.

By Type
Mark 13 (aircraft)-17,000; Mark 14 (submarine) -13,000; Mark 15 (surface) - 9,700; Mark 16 (hydrogen peroxide) -1,000; Mark 18 (electric) - 9,600; Mark 23 (a Mark 14 variant) - 9,600. (The numbers are rounded off and include all torpedoes produced during the 1930s.) The three service torpedoes, the Mk13, Mk14, and Mk15, which were the majority of the US Navy torpedoes developed in the 1930's became excellent weapons and had long service lives. The Mk13 remained in service until 1950, the Mk14 was a valuable service weapon until 1980, and Mk15 served as long as 21 inch torpedoes were carried on destroyers.

MkXXIV Torpedo Director shown installed in a TBD with a MkIII Mod2 gunsight above (USN)

The Aircraft-Torpedo Problem
Using the Torpedo Director
The fundamental problem in launching a torpedo from an aircraft was to put the torpedo in the water on a collision course with the target. To accomplish this objective pilots could obtain satisfactory accuracy using Torpedo Directors which allowed the pilot to be able to 1) estimate target angle 2) estimate target speed, 3) estimate and utilize proper lead, and 4) release the torpedo at the sighting angle to produce a collision course with the target.

Torpedo Directors
MkXXIV USN Torpedo Director
The pilot used the MkXXIV Torpedo Director sight which was mounted on the top of cockpit cowl below the MkIII Mod2 gunsight which protruded out of the windscreen. The MkXXIV operated by estimating the target's size, speed, and distance which were entered into the sight providing the pilot with the correct release point.

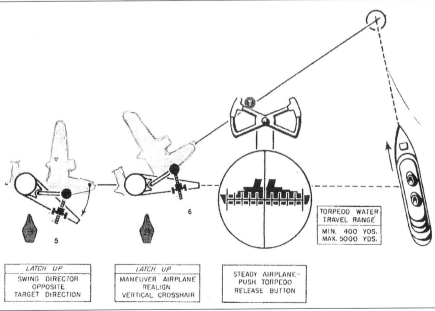

The operational use of a **Type B-2 AAF Torpedo Director** for a B-25. (Aircraft Torpedo Sighting and Launching Data)

Type B-2 AAF Torpedo Director

The Type B-2 torpedo director was an instrument operated by the pilot that enabled him to approach a moving target so that a torpedo could be launched on a course to intercept the moving target. The instrument was mounted on a bracket that moved laterally on a square support rod across the cockpit in front of the pilot. It was easy to use as the pilot could make any adjustment with one hand and fly the aircraft with the other. The torpedo director consisted of a reflector-type of collimator sight similar to, but slightly smaller than a gunsight. The electrically illuminated sight projected a luminous crosshair pattern with a stadia line scale into the field of vision. A darkened Polaroid filter reduced glare or blinding when working against reflected or direct sunlight. The rim of the sight was covered with rubber for protection to the pilot and instrument.

Using the "Estimated Aiming Point Method"

After the Mk13 was improved so that it could be launched from higher altitudes and greater speeds there was more flexibility and a wider range in making torpedo attacks that necessitated many changes in torpedo aiming and launching techniques. After extensive scientific study to develop new methods a 50 page booklet entitled <u>Aircraft Torpedo Sighting and Launching Data</u> was published. This booklet provided the essential practical data to the pilot known as the "Estimated Aiming Point Method" that provided a means of sighting aircraft torpedoes without using a torpedo director. The heavily illustrated booklet contained 16 tables and six appendices. The first eight tables were basic sighting tables for various altitudes in 200 foot increments from 200 to 2,200 feet at an airspeed of 100 to 360 knots against 400 and 600 foot ships moving on a straight course at 10, 20, and 30 knots allowing for a torpedo run of 400 yards. The other eight tables consisted of two tables for the effect of air resistance; two for aiming allowance for cross winds; two for maneuvering targets; and two for best target angles of attack. Rules of thumb were given for various situations. The Estimated Aiming Point Method proved to be accurate and very rapid to learn and use with a minimal amount of memorization of information by the pilot.

The **<u>Aircraft Torpedo Sighting and Launching Data</u>** booklet provided the essential practical data to the pilot known as the "Estimated Aiming Point Method" that provided a means of sighting aircraft torpedoes without using a torpedo director. (Author)

Typical Aerial Torpedo Attack

Ideally during a torpedo attack, dive bombers should attack first and then pull off the smoking target, while hordes of fighters strafed the decks with machine guns to keep the anti-aircraft fire down. At this point, the torpedo bombers, escorted by fighters, protecting them from above, make their runs. After an approach from altitude the leader took his squadron down and they scattered, closing on their targets, launching their torpedoes so they would converge from the rim of a semi-circular pattern ahead of the ship selected. Target selection usually was; carrier, battleship, heavy cruiser and transport. Battleships and carriers did not remain stationary and in addition to violent circling and twisting maneuvers to block coordinated runs on their bows, these enemy trophies were usually surrounded by destroyers and lesser ships which would take the torpedo intended for the larger ships. Additionally, the skies were not always cloudless with unlimited visibility and the enemy was difficult to locate in the vast oceans and limited revealing radio transmissions. By dropping their torpedoes fanwise to converge, the squadron was able to bracket both bows. If the enemy turned to "comb" one group of converging wakes, he was hit from the other side. The pattern was ideal but, unfortunately, a textbook layout and practice theory did not always succeed.

When a dive bomber pilot "pushed over," his aircraft reached speeds in excess of 300 mph; making his exposure to AA fire in the dive momentary and after he dropped his bomb he left the danger behind. The torpedo bomber pilot had to attack at less than half that speed exposing him to anti-aircraft range for twice as long. At six miles, the torpedo bomber pilot encountered fire from five and seven inch guns; at three miles, 40 mm cannon cut in, and from there on, everything was firing at him. The entire run was made while skimming low over the water where there was virtually no room to maneuver. Once the pilot determined his aiming point and proceeded toward it, any skidding, jinking, and short turning maneuvers had to cease and the aircraft had to be held straight and level for the torpedo to drop accurately. If the torpedo was released too high it could turn over and reverse course; dropped too low it could fracture when it struck the water. If the bomber was not properly aligned with the target, the torpedo which characteristically hooked left when it entered the sea; could broach and porpoise. If the pilot had a reasonable expectation of a hit; he had to press home his attack to at least within 1,200 yards of the target and many courageous pilots released at less than

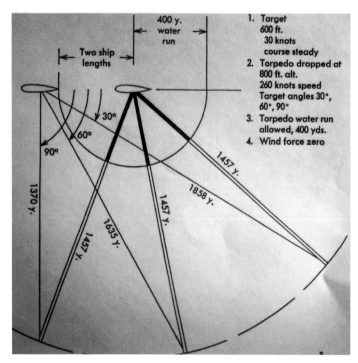

One of the many diagrams used in the <u>Aircraft Torpedo Sighting and Launching Data</u> booklet to illustrate the use of the 16 Tables it contained. (Author)

800 yards. All the while the committed torpedo bomber pilot was on the deck vulnerable to enemy fighters and AA fire and the pilot's skill became secondary to the enemy's aim and the vagaries of chance. The only advantage the TBF had over the older TBD was that it would have made the dangerous passage somewhat faster.

It took the Midway torpedo bomber debacle to highlight the difference between theory and practice and a result future torpedo actions waned. The torpedo squadrons were just too vulnerable, no matter what aircraft, TBD or TBF, they were flying. The success at Midway was due to the SBD dive bombers which sunk four Japanese carriers, partially because the TBD attacks had brought the Japanese fighters down on the deck, and they had reached their targets quickly. After Midway, the TBD was retired and the Grumman went out to attack with bombs more often than it did with torpedoes. By 1943, major torpedo operations were over and at war's end the Navy dropped aerial torpedoes from its inventory.

Torpedo Bomber Development
The Torpedo Bomber in World War I
Italy

In 1912, Pateras Pescara, an Italian lawyer, contacted the Italian Marine Ministry with the proposal for launching torpedoes from an aircraft. Lt. Allessandro Guidoni of the Italian Navy was assigned to assist in the design and testing of air-dropped torpedoes. Guidoni, flying a British Farman float biplane equipped with hydro-vanes, conducted the first takeoffs and landings in Venice harbor. Because there were no Italian aircraft suitable for carrying a torpedo, the response of Italian officials and designers was indifferent to their torpedo bomber proposal. Guidoni and Pescara, designed a float-equipped monoplane to carry torpedoes called the *Pateras Pescara*, which had a wingspan of 71.5 feet and also had hydro-vanes. The aircraft was completed in 1914 and during the tests an 820 pound torpedo was successfully launched. After World War I erupted in August 1914, Italy was initially neutral, and Guidoni continued with his testing using his *Pateras Pescara* against the *Elba,* moored in Venice harbor. After Italy entered the war in 1915 on the Allied side, the *Pescara* project was abandoned.

The Italians' major enemy in the war was the Austro-Hungarian Empire and they renewed the development of the torpedo bomber in order to attack the Austro-Hungarian fleet plying the Adriatic Sea. During August 1917 the first successful torpedo launchings were carried out from the single-engine pusher Caproni Ca.33s and the Ca.34s which were followed by the tri-motor Caproni Ca.46 and Ca.47. On 20 September 1917, the ammunition base at Pola was attacked by an Italian torpedo

bomber piloted by Giovanni Ridolfi and in 1918 Gabriele D'Annunzio formed the first torpedo bomber unit.

Great Britain

The Royal Navy also developed the torpedo bomber at the outbreak of World War I. Lt. A.M. Longmore (later Air Chief Marshal Sir Arthur Longmore) successfully tested the 14 inch, 810 pound Whitehead torpedo at Calshot on 28 July 1914 flying a Short Folder seaplane. The chief British advocate of the torpedo bomber was Commodore Murray Sueter who collaborated with the Short Brothers Airplane Company to develop the renowned Short 184 two-seat, biplane, seaplane. It had a wingspan of 63.5 feet, an overall length of 40.6 feet and could carry a single 14 inch torpedo. The first deliveries of the Short 184 were made to the Royal Naval Air Service at Mudros in June 1915 and the Royal Navy made its first successful torpedo bombing attacks during the Dardenelles campaign in August. Operations from the seaplane carrier *Ben my Chree* were made on 12 August from the Gulf of Xeros. While flying over the Sea of Marmara, Flt./Cdr. C.H.K. Edmonds sighted a large steamer and glided down to within 300 yards before releasing his torpedo which struck the vessel at the mainmast. However, Edmonds was unable to confirm that the sinking. On 17 August, he made an attack on a three vessel convoy proceeding for Ak Bashi Liman and hit a steamer which was set on fire and although it was towed to Constantinople it was a total loss. Flt./Lt. G.B. Dacre, making his attack while taxiing across the water after engine failure sunk a tug and subsequently made his escape under fire from Turkish coastal batteries. Later in the war enemy shipping targets were infrequently encountered and there were few opportunities for the fragile and underpowered seaplanes to launch the heavy torpedoes.

Germany

Possibly the first use of a synchronized torpedo attack occurred in September 1916, launched by a German Seeflieger Abteilung based on the Gulf of Riga. The unit flew reconnaissance and pursuit aircraft fighting Russian aircraft but plans were laid to use its four torpedo aircraft. On 12 September 1916, the Russian battleship *Slava* and destroyer escorts were lured into leaving their protected anchorage. At 1745 the four German torpedo aircraft, led by a single engined floatplane, and accompanied by conventional bombers left for their attack. The bombers were to bomb the Russian warships to distract their attention while the torpedo bombers turned on a parallel course to the warships to maneuver into the optimum position to make a stern attack at sea level. At 1,600 yards the torpedo bombers turned 90° in order to release their torpedoes broadside to the battleship. One of the torpedo bombers aborted its attack due to engine failure but the remaining three attacked at four seconds intervals through intense AA fire. The torpedo launched by the first bomber failed to run as it was damaged when it hit part of the aircraft when released. The second ran short before diving to the bottom of the sea. The third ran straight and true but one of the destroyers crossed its track before it reached the *Slava* which escaped damage.

The Torpedo Bomber in US Navy Service
USN Torpedo Bomber in World War I

Several years after the Wright Brothers at Kitty Hawk some of the more innovative USN officers envisaged aircraft carrying a torpedoes against enemy warships. However, at the time airframes and engines were not adequate to transport the heavy torpedoes of the time. In July 1912 Adm. Bradley Fiske was granted a patent for a proposed Naval torpedo aircraft but met opposition from old line admirals and their unshakable belief in the invincibility of the battleship. Nonetheless, Fiske was able to modify a hulking Curtiss R-6 float biplane for torpedo testing and on 14

A.M. Longmore made a successful aerial torpedo drop at Calshot on 28 July 1914 flying a **Short Folder** seaplane; testing the 14 inch, 810 pound Whitehead torpedo. (AFHRC)

A **R-6** during an unsuccessful torpedo test at Pensacola, May 1920, in which the torpedo hit the water a poor angle and then began to porpoise. (USN)

August 1917 the first aerial torpedo drops were conducted. The tests were unsuccessful as both speed and altitude had to be precise to ensure that the torpedo entered the water without porpoising.

The USN continued some limited work on the aerial torpedo and on 22 November 1918, the Navy made a successful torpedo drop when a Curtiss F-5L flying boat launched a 400 pound dummy torpedo. The Navy next turned to the Curtiss R-6 which had been the first American-built combat aircraft to serve overseas with US forces during World War I, patrolling off the Azores for German U-Boats using 50 pound bombs.

The last 40 of the 76 R-6s contracted had the newly developed 400 hp Liberty V-12 engine installed and were designated as the R-6L. These engines gave the aircraft increased load carrying capability to carry the new light 1,036 pound torpedo. Successful tests were conducted during the spring of 1919 and at the Navy formed two torpedo squadrons at Hampton Roads. Forty R-9s (basically an R-6 airframe specifically built for the Liberty engines) were ordered but its airframe was not sturdy enough for protracted operations.

Post World War I
With the failure of the R-9, in September 1919 the Navy ordered ten of the Air Service's land-based Martin MB-1 which was modified to carry a 1,618 pound torpedo between its landing gear. The aircraft was redesignated MT-1 and was moderately successful but not the ideal solution. The Naval Aircraft Factory, Philadelphia, built a hybrid torpedo bomber that consisted of the fuselage of an R-6, wings from an HS-2, and a Liberty engine which became the PT-1/-2 series. Torpedo and Bombing Squadron One conducted the first massive aerial torpedo practice on a live target on 27 September 1922. The *USS Arkansas* steaming at high speed was attacked by 18 PTs which scored eight hits with their Mk8 aerial torpedoes.

However, the jury-rigged PTs left much to be desired and the Navy issued five prototype contracts for torpedo-carrying aircraft of which two were for twin-engine three-place aircraft featuring a low-wing layout. One was the ST-1 and the second was the Curtiss CT-1 that had two 300 hp Wright-Hispano engines each mounted above the twin floats. The CT-1 had a short wooden fuselage with the pilot and navigator in tandem ahead of a rear gunner while a biplane tail was suspended from twin tail booms. The Navy's initial contract specified nine CT-1s but only the one was completed which was first flown in March 1921 and due to insufficient power these engines were replaced with 350 hp Curtiss D-12s. However,

during further testing numerous problems were found and the D-12 was cancelled on 9 November 1923.

The Navy also considered two foreign-built single-engine aircraft. Three twin-float monoplane Fokker FT-1s were purchased from Holland and 400 hp Liberty engines were installed. Two Swift biplanes were also purchased from the Blackburn Company in England. Donald Douglas had modified his *Cloudster* biplane into the DT-1 torpedo-bomber and the Navy ordered three. The first DT-1 delivered on 10 November 1921 could carry a 1,835 pound torpedo between twin floats that could be removed and wheels added for land operations. The DT-1 was exhaustively tested and was successful enough that 38 improved DT-2 two-seat versions (including the two original DT-1s which were converted) were ordered and delivered in 1922 to the San Diego Naval Air Station, joining VT-2. By 1925 it had replaced the R-6L in Navy service and was the main USN's principal torpedo plane.

Development in the "Golden Age"
The so-called "Golden Age" of American aircraft design lasted from 1934 until Pearl Harbor, during which time the American Army and Navy air arms demanded and aircraft manufacturers supplied a seemingly endless variety of specific types of aircraft to fill specific missions ranging from torpedo bombing to four engine and twin engine horizontal bombardment, dive bombing, reconnaissance, scouting, observation, and patrol missions, utility usage, long range and air superiority fighter duties, and so on.

In 1934, despite lack of funds and facilities, aircraft designers began to quickly evolve the aviation industry, both military and commercial, from the biplane stagnation of the twenties into revolutionary metal monoplane concepts. At this time prototype aircraft cost less than $100,000 to build and test and then billed out at $25,000 each in quantity production runs of 50 or more. This tended to keep many manufacturers viable, even though they never received a substantial contract. The Navy, after years of being limited by biplanes, now had a variety and diversification of new aircraft designs at its disposal.

However, as the aircraft industry improved and diversified its merchandise, it also gradually deteriorated its position. The multitude of aircraft types built before the war to accommodate the combat theories developed during the thirties, quickly proved inadequate in actual combat in the new European war. Combat experience demonstrated that what was required was less variety and more standardization of sound designs. The Navy found that their multitude of dive bombers, torpedo bombers, scouts, long range fighters, air superiority fighters, and observation aircraft, caused a disorganized Fleet inventory and chaotic maintenance problems. Finally, in the late 1930s the Navy settled on the Douglas TBD as its primary torpedo bomber and the Douglas SBD as its dive bomber, but by this time both aircraft were on the verge of being obsolete.

Donald Douglas had modified his *Cloudster* biplane into the DT-1 torpedo-bomber which were developed into the two-seat **DT-2** delivered in 1922 when it replaced the R-6 as the Navy's first line torpedo plane. (USN)

Douglas TBD-1 Devastator

The three-man Douglas TBD-1 Devastator was first introduced in 1935, when it was considered the ultimate in torpedo bomber design and was the first USN aircraft to carry the TB, torpedo bomber designation. (USN)

The TBD-1 had no bomb bay as such but had an opening in the ventral fuselage between the wings to fit the Mk13 torpedo was hoisted into the aircraft with its tail section inside the aircraft's belly and its nose angled downward. (USN)

The TBD-1 bombardier's station was located below the pilot's seat and was equipped with a aft-angled, forward-facing viewing window located forward of the torpedo bay over looking the nose of the angled torpedo. (USN)

View from the interior of the bombardier's window down onto closed bomb aiming doors (no torpedo present). (USN)

Douglas TBD Devastator

The US Navy World War II dive bomber had many precursors; Northrop's BT-1, Vought's SB2U, Brewster's SBA but the World War II torpedo bomber had only one, the Douglas TBD. When the three-man TBD-1 Devastator was first introduced in 1935, it was considered the ultimate in torpedo bomber design and was the first USN aircraft to carry the TB, torpedo bomber designation. In February, 1936, 114 were ordered with 15 more added in August of 1938.

The TBD 1 had no bomb bay or bomb bay doors as such but had an opening in the ventral fuselage between the wings. The Mk13 torpedo was hoisted into the TBD-1 with its tail section inside the aircraft's belly and its nose angled downward. Two wire cables strapped around the torpedo's middle attached it to the aircraft. A release device was located on the starboard side of the bomb opening and clips attached to one end of each cable attached to the release device.

The bombardier's station on the TBD-1 was located below the pilot's seat. It was equipped with a aft-angled, forward-facing viewing window located forward of the torpedo bay and was enclosed by a pair of bomb aiming doors which opened similarly to standard bomb bay doors. The bomb aiming doors were opened and closed by the crank handle at the bombardier's right hand. The interior skin of the original bomb aiming doors was of the so-called weight-saving Swiss cheese-type with holes and three hinges. Because of buffeting caused by the holes the inner skin was replaced with solid skins and were attached by two hinges. The Norden bombsight, when installed, was mounted on the shock absorber pads in front of the left bomb aiming window while the altitude and air speed instruments were located above the window to the left and right respectively. Even though these doors could be opened when a torpedo was carried, they were not used because the down-sloping nose of the torpedo obstructed the view through the Norden bombsight.

The TBD-1 scored the Navy's first torpedo victories. The first USN torpedo attacks on enemy shipping were carried out on 1 February 1942 on Japanese shipping in the Kwajalein Atoll, Marshall Islands by VT-6 off the carrier *Enterprise*. The TBD-1s, led by Lt.Cdr. Lance Massey claimed four hits on a transport and two oilers but post-strike reports credited the unit with only one non-lethal ship hit. The first successful USN torpedo attack occurred on 10 March 1942 when TBD-1s of VT-2 based on the *Lexington* hit enemy shipping in the Lae-Salamaua area. Led by Lt.Cdr. James Brett, three TBDs attacked the *Yokohama Maru* off Salamaua at

All Torpedo Squadron 8's 15 TBDs led by **Lt.Cdr, John Waldron** were destroyed at Midway and the TBD was retired and the Grumman TBF was introduced as the Navy's first line torpedo bomber. (USN)

0938. Despite torpedo problems, one torpedo hit the transport which sank into the mud of the harbor. Other VT-2 TBDs attacked transports near Lae but their torpedoes malfunctioned or ran too deep.

During the Battle of the Coral Sea on 4-8 May 1942 the USN torpedo bomber would reach the pinnacle of its success, albeit shared. At 1040 on 7 May USN strike aircraft sighted the Japanese light carrier *Shoho* near Misima Island and deployed to attack with 53 scout bombers , 22 torpedo bombers , and 18 fighters from *USS Lexington* and *USS Yorktown* The enemy carrier was protected by only eight fighters flying combat air patrol (CAP) because the rest of the carrier's aircraft were being prepared below decks for a strike against the American carriers. The *Lexington's* Air Group attacked first, hitting the Shoho with two 1,000 pound bombs and five torpedoes, causing severe damage. At 1100, *Yorktown's* Air Group attacked the burning and stationary carrier, hitting it with at least 11 more 1,000 pound bombs and two torpedoes. The crippled *Shoho* sank at 1135 with only 203 of the carrier's 834 man crew recovered. At 1210, *Lexington* SBD pilot Robert Dixon radioed the famous exclamation, "Scratch one flat top!" Three American aircraft were lost in the attack, including two SBDs from *Lexington* and one from *Yorktown*.

However, by mid-1942 the Devastator remained as the only torpedo plane the Navy inventory in any quantity and was shown by combat experience to be extremely vulnerable as it was utterly obsolete and outclassed. This was categorically proven during the Battle of Midway which was to be the Devastator's last important combat encounter. During the attack on the Japanese carriers all of Torpedo Squadron 8's 15 TBDs led by Lt.Cdr, John Waldron were destroyed without scoring a torpedo hit and Torpedo Squadrons Three and Six lost 24 aircraft out of 26 launched without success. The debacle was due mainly to the TBD's slow speed, lack of fighter protection on the run in, and faulty torpedoes.

Although it was not fast at 200 mph and its range carrying a torpedo was a mediocre 435 miles; the TBD was reliable with its huge 422 square foot wing area giving safe low speed maneuverability and the ability to execute steep reversals. The TBD did help introduce many new innovations such as is all-metal, low-wing monoplane design. It was equipped with a hydraulically powered wing-fold system, operable from the cockpit, a retracting landing gear, automatic pilot, full radio and intercom equipment. The TBD-1 carried the first torpedo designed for aerial use (modified destroyer torpedoes were used previously) which was the wretched 2,000 pound 21 inch Bliss-Leavitt Mk13. After Midway, the

During the Battle of the Coral Sea on 4-8 May 1942 the USN dive bomber would reach the pinnacle of its success when torpedo bombers from USS *Lexington* and USS *Yorktown* helped sink the Japanese carrier **Shoho** with seven torpedo hits. (USN)

Grumman TBF Avenger

The large three-place TBF/TBM was the Navy's foremost torpedo bomber after Midway and was named the Avenger because of the Japanese attack on Pearl Harbor. (USN)

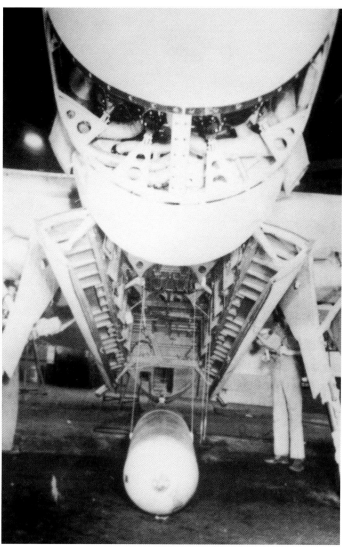

The four tandem 500 pound bombs could be carried giving the TBF the versatility of being a horizontal bomber using the Norden Bombsight. (USN)

The TBF was the USN first torpedo bomber to carry an internal load of a 2,000 pound torpedo or four 500 pound bombs. The torpedo or bombs were hoisted into the bomb bay by the standard apparatus. (USN)

A TBF on a Mk13 Ring Tail torpedo run during the Battle of the Philippine Sea, 20 June 1944 where Avengers from *Belleau Wood* torpedoed the light carrier *Hiyo*. (USN)

TBD was retired and the Grumman TBF was introduced as the Navy's new torpedo bomber even though it attacked with bombs more often than it did with torpedoes.

TBF/TBM Avenger

The TBF Avenger was created by Grumman in 1939, as a design to replace the older Douglas TBD Devastator, which was already obsolete at the time of Pearl Harbor. It was the second (after the F4F Wildcat) of what was to become a venerable line of dependable, sturdy combat aircraft that would give Grumman a virtual monopoly in Navy aircraft procurement during the war years. The design was so successful that after the first 2,546 were built, Grumman licensed it to General Motors Eastern Aircraft Division, Trenton, NJ which built 7,290 more as the TBM with only minor modifications made during the five years of production. (Note: Grumman needed to have its TBF production line freed for manufacture of the new F6F Hellcat.)

The TBF/TBM was the Navy's foremost torpedo bomber after Midway and was named the Avenger because of the Japanese attack on Pearl Harbor. It was a large (weighing two tons more than the TBD), three-place torpedo bomber, the first to carry an internal load of a 2,000 pound torpedo or four tandem 500 pound bombs. The bombardier sat on a folding bench facing forward to operate the radio and to sight in torpedo/bombing runs (using the Norden Bombsight). The Avenger's maximum speed was increased by 60 mph to 270 mph and its range with a torpedo was more than doubled from less than 500 miles in the TBD, to more than 1,100 mph. The aircraft had overall ruggedness and stability, docile handling, long fully-loaded range of 1,000 miles range.

During its operational time the Avengers took part in the destruction of six Japanese carriers but only two were sunk entirely or mainly by torpedoes. On 24 August 1942, during the Battle of the Eastern Solomons 24 TBFs from the *Saratoga* and *Enterprise* sank the Japanese aircraft carrier *Ryujo*. Avengers from *Belleau Wood* torpedoed the light carrier *Hiyo* during the Battle of the Philippines Sea on 19-20 June 1944. Three battleships and 14 cruisers were sunk in entirely or in part by Avengers using bombs and torpedoes. During the Battle of Truk Lagoon (*Operation Hailstone*) on 17-18 February 1944 Avengers from five USN Fleet Carriers and Light Carriers took part in sinking three cruisers, four destroyers, eight other smaller warships and 32 merchant ships. The torpedo bomber era lasted for less than a decade, 1934 to 1943, and by which time, pure

During the Battle of Truk Lagoon on 17-18 February 1944 Avengers from five USN Fleet Carriers and Light Carriers took part in sinking three cruisers, four destroyers, eight other smaller warships, and 32 merchant ships. The photo shows a torpedo from an *USS Enterprise* TBF striking a Japanese cargo ship with another torpedo on its way (lower right corner). (USN)

torpedo actions had virtually ceased to occur and the question arose: What could a torpedo bomber like TBF/TBM or a dive bomber like Douglas SBD do, that the new, heavier fighter, Vought's F4U Corsair, couldn't do as well and faster? At the war's end, the Navy dropped pure torpedo aircraft from its inventory.

However, it must be pointed out that during the 1930s, in both the Navy and Army Air Corps, the innovation of torpedo bombing and high altitude daylight precision strategic bombing techniques, respectively, was accomplished from the ranks below Admiral and General. In the relatively young AAC, traditions and a hierarchical rank structure were not ingrained and the revolutionary high altitude precision bombing doctrine evolved into a potent weapon. But in the tradition-bound Navy, the hierarchical rank structure discouraged such innovation from below; leaving the Navy with no integrated operational doctrine for torpedo attacks. Consequently, hundreds of Navy torpedo bomber crews were left exposed to be slaughtered enemy AA defenses while the Navy felt compelled to hoard thousands of unused Norden bombsights it developed at great expense when the AAF strategic high altitude bombing program had a critical need for them. (See <u>Vol. 2: Bombs, Bombsights, and Bombing</u>)

SB2C Helldiver

In mid-December 1941, Lt. Cdr. J.N. Murphy, the head of VSB design, considered future Navy dive and torpedo bomber guidelines. It was obvious that fighter protection would be essential and escorted dive bombers would become single-seat and have the speed of a fighter and would not require flexible gun defense and gunners. Torpedo bombing and scouting (dive bomber) functions could be merged and would continue to be two-seat aircraft and require flexible gun defense. VT-3 held trials dropping torpedoes in a diving attack but it was found that increased structural strength and dive brakes were required and the aircraft which had both was the dive bomber. Murphy suggested that the scout dive bomber (VSB) become a combination dive bomber/torpedo bomber (VBT) and the torpedo bomber would have scouting added to its responsibilities to become a VTSB (this latter suggestion was never adopted).

Murphy's suggestions were developed by Lt. A. B. Metsger, the head of the VTB design. Metsger considered the strength and range requirements for this type aircraft and came to the same conclusion; because both a dive bombing and torpedo attack used a diving approach, the aircraft needed to be strong and be equipped with dive brakes. He concluded that the obvious solution was to design strong aircraft for the dive/torpedo bomber role and on 21 January 1943 the BuAer Planning and Engineering Division met to confer on the issue. On 4 February 1942 Admiral Towers approved a contract for Curtiss to develop a single-seat dive bomber with a speed of 390 mph carrying a 1,000 pound bomb for 1,600 miles.

Beginning 30 November 1942, BuAer decided to equip the Helldiver for torpedo dropping and tests were conducted at the NAS Quonset Point, RI, and at the NTS, Newport, RI. SB2C (#00013) was used for torpedo test launchings that were initially made with the aircraft in normal horizontal flight but no diving approaches were made before winter weather postponed the tests. The tests showed that there were no takeoff, flying, or landing problems while carrying a torpedo and the release of the torpedo did not have any undesirable effects upon flight. A major problem was the long time required for loading the torpedo and switching back to bomb-carrying configuration.

Further tests to configure the Helldiver as a torpedo-carrying aircraft were continued at the Naval Dahlgren Proving Ground, VA at the end of May 1943. SB2C (#00149) was equipped with a Mk13 Mod 1 torpedo with a Mk2 wooden stabilizer. Again conversion from and to torpedo configuration was time and manpower consuming and a complete redesign of the torpedo mounting was required and completed. The Helldiver was

Curtiss SB2C Helldiver

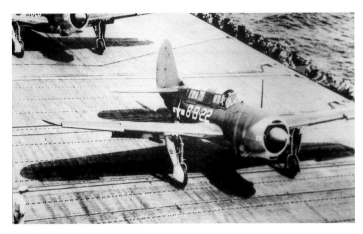

The **SB2C Helldiver** was designed as a bomber to be used both in a dive-bombing and torpedo attacks. However, the Helldiver was never used as a torpedo bomber in combat as the Grumman TBM Avenger was so successful that it could not be replaced. (USN)

The Mk13 torpedo did not completely fit into the bomb bay of the SB2C. (USN)

A major problem encountered by the SB2C torpedo/dive bomber was loading the torpedo (the torpedo carrying frame is shown) and then switching back to bomb-carrying configuration. (USN)

never used as a torpedo bomber in combat as the Grumman TBM Avenger continued to be so successful that it could not be replaced; especially at a time when dangerous torpedo attacks were abandoned and attacks on warships had been virtually taken over by dive bombers .

US Navy Torpedo Expenditure in World War II
% of Torpedoes to Total Ordnance
Expended on Shipping by Weight

Year	Carrier VTB	Land-Based VTB
1942	73%	94%
1943	68%	5%
1944	32%	3%
1945	16%	0%

USN Torpedo Expenditure on Shipping Targets

Date	# Torpedo	Carrier	Land	VPB	Aircraft Type Armored	Vessel Type Unarmored	Merchant	UID
2/42	9	9	0	0	9	0	0	
3/42	13	13	0	0	0	0	13	
5/42	64	64	0	0	64	0	0	
6/42	24	17	4	3	21	0	3	
8/42	12	12	0	0	11	0	1	
9/42	5	0	5	0	5	0	0	
10/42	32	8	24	0	23	5	4	
11/42	48	8	40	0	39	0	9	
12/42	7	0	7	0	7	0	0	
1942	**214**	**131**	**80**	**3**	**179**	**5**	**30**	
1/43	15	0	15	0	0	6	9	
2/43	3	0	3	0	0	3	0	
7/43	4	0	4	0	0	4	0	
11/43	77	73	0	4	59	14	4	
12/43	44	43	0	1	35	0	9	
1943	**143**	**116**	**22**	**5**	**94**	**27**	**22**	
1/44	56	48	6	2	16	16	6	18
2/44	67	66	0	1	14	16	36	1
3/44	35	35	0	0	0	16	16	3
6/44	22	22	0	0	20	1	1	
8/44	39	39	0	0	4	11	19	5
9/44	72	72	0	0	0	0	70	2
10/44	354	354	0	0	239	13	74	28
11/44	136	136	0	0	34	13	89	
1944	**781**	**772**	**6**	**3**	**327**	**86**	**311**	**57**
1/45	109	109	0	0	3	28	78	
3/45	73	72	0	1	0	10	60	3
4/45	114	111	0	3	103	9	2	
5/45	12	0	0	12	4	4	2	2
6/45	8	0	0	8	0	8	0	
7/45	6	0	0	6	0	0	6	
1945	**322**	**292**	**0**	**30**	**110**	**59**	**148**	**5**
Totals	**1,460**	**1,319**	**103**	**38**	**710**	**173**	**515**	**62**

Note: No torpedo expenditure in months not listed. UID=Unidentified

The table shows, monthly, the targets against which torpedoes were expended, and the types of planes carrying them.

Torpedoes accounted for 12% of the total weight of bombs, torpedoes and mines expended by USN and USMC aircraft against enemy shipping during the war. In carrier-based attacks they accounted for 14%, in land-based attacks only 5%.

In shipping attacks by carrier VTB units torpedoes represented 29% of the total weight of heavy ordnance carried, and in shipping attacks by land-based VTBs only 15%. The proportion of torpedoes to total weight of ordnance carried by VTBs against shipping declined throughout the war.

Torpedoes constituted over one quarter of the total weight of ordnance expended against armored warships, slightly over 10% of expenditures against unarmored warships, and slightly less than 10% of expenditures against large merchant vessels. Nearly half of the total torpedo expenditures were directed against armored warships.

All but 3% of total aircraft torpedo expenditures were by VTB units, mostly TBFs or TBMs.

The Torpedo Bomber in Army Air Corps Service

After Pearl Harbor the US Navy had no long range twin engine torpedo bombers as did the British (Blenheim and Beaufort) and the Germans (Ju-88 and He-111). The Navy's current TBD Devastators were slow and obsolete while its replacement, the TBF Avenger were beginning to come off the Grumman assembly line and only a few trickled into operational units. So, despite the Navy's long-standing fear of encroachment on its

A B-26 of the Minimum Altitude Bombardment and Torpedo Unit (Medium) at Eglin Field, FL, testing a Mk13 torpedo. (AAF)

Serious consideration of the medium bomber's potential as a torpedo bomber can seen in this photo of a wooden scale model B-25 being readied for aerodynamic testing in a wind tunnel. (Loc/Palmer)

aerial province, Navy engineers cooperated with the AAF to develop the AAF's medium bombers, the B-25 and B-26, in particular, for torpedo operations.

The Minimum Altitude Bombardment and Torpedo Unit (Medium) was formed at Eglin Field, FL in 1942 to formulate torpedo tactics for medium bombers. It was found that that to achieve good accuracy the medium bomber had to be in level flight and the height of release had to be equal to the air speed; all of which was difficult to attain in the heat of combat. The torpedo needed to enter the water at an angle of 25° (not to breach) to 30° (not to dive too deeply).

B-25

In the transitional pre-to-early war period in which aircraft such as the B-25 were developed for the US Army Air Corps, some items of equipment were specified but would not find much use in combat. One such item was the aerial torpedo release and carrying gear which was developed rapidly soon after Pearl Harbor and introduced on the B-25C-1 to carry the Mark 13 aerial torpedo. Its large size necessitated that it be carried externally with the B-25 bomb bay doors open. Tests with a B-25B (40-22740) named *Jonah* were performed in the spring of 1942 and revealed that the drag of a torpedo, suspended on a bomb bay rack by cables and semi-enclosed by the partially shut bomb bay doors, reduced aircraft's cruise speed by 14 mph but otherwise no adverse effects were found in the way the B-25 handled. Torpedo release gear remained standard on

the AAF B-25s through to the J model. All variants of the PBJ, the Navy/USMC B-25 version, were equipped to carry the Mk13 Aerial Torpedo although it was never used operationally.

A-20

The A-20G had provisions to carry the (too) long Mk13 in its bomb bay by having its bomb doors removed and hoisting the torpedo into the bomb bay with its nose slightly low and protruding somewhat below the fuselage. The Havoc had a torpedo director installed in the cockpit for use by the pilot. There is no record of the A-20 using the torpedo operationally but the Russian Navy did modify their Lend-Lease A-20Gs to become their main torpedo bomber carrying one or two torpedoes. The Soviets designed special reinforced torpedo racks to fit to the lower sides of the fuselage under the wings just above the bomb bay doors. Two torpedoes could be carried but normally only one was carried on the starboard side. The Russian Baltic and Black Sea Fleets recorded a number of successes against German transports and small warships.

B-26

The B-26 was the more suitable option for carrying a torpedo because it was strongly built and the torpedo cradle could be mounted on the bomber's keel former. The Marauder performed well carrying the 2,000 pound weapon; however, during takeoff when the bomber nose was lifted the clearance between the ground and the torpedo was only about four

The aerial torpedo release and carrying gear was introduced on the B-25C-1 to carry the Mk13 aerial torpedo. The torpedo's large size necessitated that it be carried externally with the B-25 bomb bay doors open. Tests with a B-25B named *Jonah* were performed in the spring of 1942. (AAF)

The Russian Navy modified their **Lend-Lease A-20Gs** to become their main torpedo bomber that was capable of carrying one or two torpedoes. (AHFRC)

inches so a tire failure could be devastating. All new B-26s had torpedo carrying provisions built in on the production line.

B-26s at Midway: The Only AAF Use of Torpedoes in Combat
In May 1942 two B-26s from the 22BG were joined by three Marauders from the 38BG at Ford Island, Pearl Harbor, after the first ever flight of B-26s from the mainland. Exterior racks to carry the Mk13 torpedo below the bomb bay doors were installed on the five B-26s in addition to an improvised torpedo release system. The pilots and crews were briefed on torpedo attack techniques and flew a few practice missions and found that the B-26 was not too adversely affected by the torpedo.

On 29 May four B-26s (one crashed during tests) were rushed to Midway where their torpedoes were to be waiting for them but upon arrival they were told that the torpedoes would arrive six hours later. Once the torpedoes arrived it was found that the B-26's internal bomb hoists could not hoist the 2,000 pound torpedoes and the armorers worked feverishly to jury-rig the necessary equipment to load the torpedoes. The B-26 crews were unaware of the reason for the hectic activity at Midway; the Japanese code had been broken and an imminent attack was expected.

On 4 June the Japanese Fleet had been discovered and the four B-26s were to be dispatched at 0625, only 15 minutes behind the six Navy TBDs of VT-8. The B-26s were led by 38BG pilot Capt. James Collins accompanied by the Marauders piloted by 1Lt. Herbert Mayes (22BG/408BS), 2Lt. William Watson (38th BG), and 1Lt. James Muri (408BS).

At 0710, the B-26s had caught up with the VT-8 TBDs as they were about to attack the Japanese carriers *Akagi, Kaga, Hiryu,* and *Soryu* which were surrounded by protecting cruisers and destroyers. The Devastators

targeted the *Hiryu* while the Marauders closed towards the *Akagi*. The attackers were intercepted by 30 Zeros and five of the six TBFs were quickly shot down with the two torpedoes they managed to launch missing the *Hiryu* (the other TBD was badly damaged and escaped). As the Zeros closed on the B-26s Collins led them to 500 feet to just 200 feet to prevent the Zeros from making diving firing runs on them but Watson's bomber was shot down.

Collins' B-26 continued through the fighter attacks and defensive fire toward the *Akagi* and launched his torpedo which appeared to run true. Collins then dashed for cloud cover at 2,000 feet to elude the pursuing fighters and flew his badly damaged bomber safely back to Midway. Mayes' B-26 was hit many times by AA fire and flew just above the water and passed over the top of the carrier's bridge by a few feet and crashed into the sea beyond. Muri began his run on the enemy carrier, dodging the Zeros and AA fire at 200 feet. As he neared the *Akagi* he throttled back to keep his airspeed below the critical launch speed for the torpedo. The carrier was turning into the oncoming B-26 and Muri headed in at an angle of 20° to the bow, at an altitude of 185 feet, and an air speed of 210 mph. The bombardier pushed the release trigger to launch the torpedo but the torpedo did not seem to launch and he pushed the release several times until Muri jammed the throttles full-forward to climb to avoid hitting the carrier and roared over the deck from bow to stern. As Muri passed over the *Akagi,* the bombardier manned the nose gun and sprayed the carrier island and deck with bullets. Muri's B-26 was seriously damaged and its crew seriously injured or dead as he turned back toward Midway. When Muri made his landing approach on Midway he was fired on by nervous Marine gunners and had to make another approach in which he came to a hair-raising skidding stop, snapping off the landing gear.

Of the ten torpedo bombers that flew the first strike against the *Akagi* and *Hiryu* seven were lost: five TBFs and two B-26s. Their torpedoes scored no hits and the only damage done was by the strafing of the *Akagi*'s deck by Muri's nose gunner. However, their sacrifice caused Japanese Admiral Nagumo to change his battle plans. His carrier bombers were being prepared for a strike against the American carriers but Nagumo became convinced that another strike on Midway Island would be necessary first. He ordered that the torpedoes and armor piercing bombs be removed from his planes and that ordnance for attacking ground targets be loaded in their place. This delayed the takeoff of his striking force and allowed US Navy carrier dive bombers to hit Nagumo's four carriers before they could launch another strike. The crew members of the four B-26s were awarded the Distinguished Service Cross in recognition of their heroic actions.

Torpedo-carrying B-26s were dispatched to the Aleutians (77BS and 28BG) and the SWPA (42BG and 69BS and 70BS) but encountered no targets. Operational trials with torpedoes were also carried out by B-26 units in Australia and North Africa but the weapon was quickly abandoned in preference for the more effective and safer skip bombing of shipping.

The only recorded combat use of the aerial torpedo by the AAF was by B-26s during the opening attack on the carrier *Akagi* during the Battle of Midway. (AAF)

The **crew of the Muri B-26** attacker posing for publicity photos on their return to Hawaii from Midway. Muri is kneeing second left. The severely wounded gunner remained in the hospital. (AAF)

Torpedo-carrying B-26s were dispatched to the Aleutians (77BS and 28BG) and the SWPA (42BG and 69BS and 70BS) but encountered no targets. Pictured is a ground crew preparing a Mk13 for loading at Cold Bay, Alaska. (AAF)

However, for the year after torpedo-carrying operations had been abandoned, Marauders continued to leave the factory with provisions for carrying this weapon.

Description of Medium Bomber Torpedo Mechanisms
For a weapon that was little used, the torpedo occupied an inordinate amount of space in B-25 and B-26 Parts, Maintenance, and Pilot's Manuals. The B-25 or B-26 could be fitted for the installation of a torpedo to be used as an alternate bomb load; the carrying of the torpedo precluded the carrying of bombs except on wing racks. Torpedo carrying equipment was not furnished with the aircraft but could be obtained as a kit. Because anti-shipping patrols were usually long range; to increase the cruising radius of the aircraft while carrying the torpedo, a 215 or 240 gallon self-sealing fuel tank could be installed above the torpedo rack in the bomb bay.

B-26 Torpedo Suspension
The Mk13 could not be installed into the B-26 bomb bay but made use of the strong centerline keel of the fuselage to hang the special torpedo suspension rack that resembled a standard bomb shackle. The torpedo was

The Mk13 could not be installed into the bomb bay of the **B-26** and required a special rack. (AAF)

A Mk13 suspended by two cables under a semi-closed **B-25** bomb bay doors from a special internal rack. A stabilizer bar can be seen under and to the rear of the torpedo. (AAF)

hung on lugs and the rack had metal stabilizer bar located at the fore and aft ends.

B-25 Torpedo Suspension

The torpedo was mounted below the fuselage centerline of the Mitchell on a semi-external rack, suspended by two transverse cable slings fastened to the two lower bomb rack stations #1 and #2. When the torpedo was loaded no bombs could be carried in the bomb bay but wing racks could be loaded with bombs or depth charges. The center of gravity of the torpedo was almost directly in line with the CG of the aircraft. With the torpedo installed, the bomb bay doors could be only partially closed and in this position, the doors rested against pads on the torpedo rack. The torpedo was released either mechanically or electrically and the torpedo was released similar to that of a bomb. Immediately after the torpedo was released, protruding parts of the torpedo rack automatically retracted, after which the bomb bay doors could be completely closed. The torpedo was released either by the electrical (selective) release or by moving bomb control handle to salvo.

US Homing Torpedoes
Mark 21 Aerial Homing Torpedo

The MK21 (22.4 inches) was originally intended as a 25 knot electric anti-shipping torpedo. Successful dropping trials were conducted in 1943, but the Mk21 was soon cancelled and replaced by the Mod 2 which was turbine-powered unlike other US homing torpedoes of the time and was a passive homing version of the MK13. The turbine was too noisy at homing frequencies and it was scheduled for cancellation in the spring of 1944, when Neoprene gaskets and rubber mountings allowed homing at 33 knots. During testing only a few hits were made due to poor maneuverability in the final approach and the problem was not solved until after the war when 312 were produced and used as the payload of the Petrel missile in 1955.

Mark 21 Specifications:

Length	13.42 feet
Weight	2,130 pounds
Explosive	350 pounds Torpex
Range	24,000 feet
Speed	33.4 knots

Mark 24 Fido Torpedo: The First American ASW Acoustic Homing Torpedo

Introduction

Homing torpedoes were significantly different from the conventional gyro-controlled, set-depth torpedoes used against surface ships in that once they acquired their target; they homed on it only using onboard controls. In addition to the obvious advantage of homing in the horizontal plane in attacking surface targets, homing could also operate in the vertical plane; providing an important capacity against submerged submarines or shallow draft escorts.

A successful homing torpedo had to:

1) Detect the target and indicate its direction relative to the torpedo axis
2) Process this directional information to generate orders to the vertical and horizontal rudders
3) Be provided with propulsion apparatus and other mechanisms that did not interfere with the homing system
4) Be provided with adequate safety features to prevent attacking the launching platform or other friendly forces
5) Be sufficiently strong to withstand launching, water entry, and other impediments inherent in its use

Requirements

The development of a homing torpedo had been considered by torpedo designers during World War I but the physics of underwater sound generation and transmission was not well understood at the time. In September 1941, the US Navy solicited the National Defense Research Committee to investigate the feasibility of a small, anti-submarine, acoustic homing torpedo which could be air-launched and be capable of tracking a target in depth in addition to azimuth, fit within size and weight limitations imposed by the launching aircraft, and be able to withstand the shock experienced in an airdropped water entry. Essentially the Mk24 was to replace air-dropped depth charges.

In mid-December 1941 the Navy's request was scheduled to be discussed by representatives from science and industry at a series of conferences at Harvard University's Underwater Sound Lab (HUSL) led by its brilliant administrator, Frederick "Ted" Hunt. The following initial requirements were established:

1) The dimensions were limited to seven feet in length and 19 inches in diameter to fit 1,000 pound bomb racks.
2) Had to be droppable from 200 to 300 feet at about 120 knots.
3) Electric propulsion using lead acid storage batteries that could withstand power-draining high temperatures. A small motor would turn the propeller.
4) Speed of 12 knots which was sufficient to catch a submerged submarine but slow enough not to emit too much noise.
5) Duration of the run was to be 10 to 15 minutes.
6) Contain a 90-100 pound high explosive charge which was small when compared to the 500 pounds of a conventional torpedo. However, the homing device would lead the torpedo to explode directly against the submarine's unarmored hull.
7) Use a passive acoustic homing with the greatest possible range.
8) The torpedo had to begin a predetermined search pattern as soon it entered the water and until its hydrophones were close enough to the target to hear it. When the homing device had no signal to follow; it was under hydrostatic control operating at a depth controlled by water pressure. The torpedo would continue to circle with its acoustic homing device scanning for a noise source of an adequate threshold. Once a target was acquired; control was switched to the homing device which led to torpedo to the target.

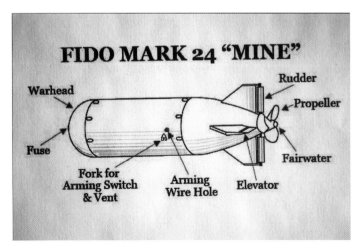

FIDO MARK 24 "MINE"

Warhead

Rudder

Propeller

Fuse

Fairwater

Fork for Arming Switch & Vent

Arming Wire Hole

Elevator

Within a few days after the meetings, the HUSL and Bell Telephone Labs (BTL) submitted formal proposals for the homing torpedo's development to the Office of Scientific Research and Development (OSRD) which were accepted and ultimately became OSRD Project 61 "*FIDO*." The origin of the codename "*FIDO*" can not be determined, as it doesn't appear to be an acronym but perhaps it is an endearing term as it always headed home like a pet dog, *FIDO*? According to Alan Carey in US Navy PB4Y-1 (B-24) Liberator Squadrons in Great Britain during World War II (Schiffer, PA, 2003) the Mk24 was called the *Zombie* by both US and British. The Mk24 was also nicknamed "Wandering Annie" by the British. The Mk24 was officially designated as the "Mk24 Mine" as a security cover name. The existence of the Mk24 was kept top secret as it was shipped under armed guard in three boxes (nose, hull, and tail) that were stored in a secure area of the ship. It was only to be used in daylight operations and then not against surfaced submarine so that the enemy did not realize he was being chased by a homing device. Use in the Mediterranean was very restricted so that if a torpedo that missed or malfunctioned would not run on shore and be captured.

Mark 24 *Fido* Torpedo Development

The wartime development of homing torpedoes was accomplished almost entirely under the backing of the OSRD and its NDRC subsidiary. Wartime production of homing torpedoes was achieved by standard BuOrd procurement contracts with industrial firms, principally Western Electric, Westinghouse, and General Electric. The main research and development contracts were let under the authority of the Office of Emergency Management (OEM) to Harvard University, Western Electric (Bell Telephone Laboratories), General Electric, and Westinghouse with smaller contracts to other universities and commercial firms. Many subcontractors worked for the major contractors on special aspects of torpedoes. Each of the major contractors and the Brush Development Company developed one or more homing torpedoes through the prototype stage. In several cases two contractors developed competing models designated by the same Mark. For instance, the Bell Telephone Laboratories (BTL) and the Harvard Underwater Sound Laboratory (HUSL) developed competing versions of the MK24 and HUSL and GE developed rival types of the Mk32. Other competing torpedoes had different Marks. The Brush Company developed the Mk30 was as a backup separately with its work on the Mk24, while there was intense rivalry there also was a lot of cooperation which created the first operational US homing torpedo in the extraordinarily short time period of 17 months from initial concept to the first operational success.

In December 1941, Bell Lab was engaged to design the torpedo, to be manufactured by Western Electric. The project manager was Charles Weibusch, who was instrumental in managing the design of the body, propulsion gear, steering, hydrophones, etc. for the Bell design. In January 1942 the DTMB was to develop a prototype hull. Engineers modified the Mk13 torpedo body by shortening the hull, reducing its diameter and weight, and designing a new hemispherical nose section to contain the explosive charge, and a conical tail unit with four stabilizing fins and rudders and a single propeller.

Homing torpedoes developed along two lines: torpedoes based on straight runners, primarily Mk13, Mk18, and Mk19 with standard 21 inch x 20.5 foot or 22.5 inch x 13.5 foot envelopes and smaller torpedoes with 10 inch or 19 inch diameter envelopes which were seven to eight feet in length. To produce a homing torpedo the primary new technologies integrated into the torpedo were underwater acoustics (hydrophones); hydrodynamic and mechanical quieting; electronic controls and servomechanisms. The number of torpedoes under development was large but only three; Mk24,

Mk27, and Mk28 became operational during World War II. All but the Mk21 MOD2 (a homing version of Mk13), used electric propulsion which was the prevailing form of propulsion for new US Navy homing torpedoes until the emergence of high submerged speed nuclear submarines which forced the return to thermal, propulsion during the Cold War.

Homing Systems

The analyses of target signatures and probes for use by homing torpedoes were repeatedly conducted and the acoustic signature was found to be the best and the only practical, means. The use of underwater sound for target detection and tracking had been developed during the inter-war years for use by surface vessels in the antisubmarine role and for offensive and defensive employment by submarines.

Two types of sonar systems were used; passive, which basically listened for noise created by the target, and active, which detected the reflection or echo of a probing sound pulse emitted by the system. These shipboard systems were the basis for developing torpedo homing systems but their size and weight were much too great for torpedoes. The problems of miniaturizing and installing an entire sonar system, using the contemporary vacuum tube technology, into a torpedo body while allowing space for the propulsion system and a significant warhead were very challenging. The first US homing torpedoes used passive systems that detected ship noise, primarily the cavitation noise from the enemy's propellers. Hydrophones mounted around the circumference of the torpedo (using body shadow and hydrophone directivity) or an array of hydrophones mounted in the nose of the torpedo (relying primarily on hydrophone directivity) provided the direction data toward the target to provide the torpedo's homing rudder the information to direct it toward the target. It was not until early 1944 that the first active homing torpedo made a three dimensional acoustically controlled run.

In late December 1941, Harvard (HUSL) and Bell (BTL) were directed to begin *FIDO* development with each assigned to engage in independent but parallel torpedo development programs with the principal emphasis to be on the development of the passive acoustic homing and control system and torpedo integration. Western Electric was to develop a light weight, shock resistant, 48-volt lead acid storage battery providing 110-amps for 15 minutes. General Electric was to design and build the propulsion and steering motors and investigate an active acoustic homing system with the assistance of the David Taylor Model Basin with hydrodynamics and propulsion.

Target detection and direction data had to be converted to rudder motions that directed the torpedo to the target which was theoretically relatively straightforward. However, in the pioneering days of electronics this theoretically simple process caused many problems. The balancing of the left and right amplifiers was so difficult that early systems used a single amplifier that switched back and forth between the left and right channels.

The hydrophone array of the torpedo consisted of four hydrophones symmetrically located flush in the hull at mid-body, spaced around the hull in a circle at the 0°, 90°, 180°, and 270° positions where 0° was the topmost hull position at the centerline. The signals from the pair of hydrophones located at the 90° and 270° positions supplied steering data in the horizontal plane (i.e. the left or right steering). The hydrophone signals were compared and processed to provide steering commands to the rudders which would steer the torpedo in the direction of the hydrophone receiving the strongest signal. When both hydrophone signals were of equal amplitude the torpedo would be steered straight ahead. Therefore one pair of hydrophones at 90° and 270° provided the signals necessary for "turn left", "go straight ahead," or "turn right" steering.

Correspondingly, the hydrophone signals from the pair located at 0° and 180° were compared and processed to provide the steering commands to the elevators for "down", "straight ahead," or "up," steering in the vertical plane. The combined net effect of both the rudder and elevator commands was to steer the torpedo in the direction from which the target's noise signals were arriving.

The Harvard homing system utilized magnetostrictive hydrophone sets and provided for non-proportional steering in which the rudders responded to the amplitude of the acoustic signals received and were positioned either in the straight ahead position or hard over in the full "turn left" or "turn right" position. The Bell Labs system used piezoelectric hydrophone elements that were based on proportional steering; in which the rudder deflections were proportional to the difference in the amplitude of the paired hydrophone signals. In both systems the torpedo was turned in the direction of the hydrophone producing the strongest signal. After comprehensive in-water testing, by the end of July 1942, both the HUSL and BTL guidance systems were found to have satisfactory sound control in both the vertical and horizontal planes.

Noise Control

The conventional steam-driven torpedo was very noisy and it was considered that any attempt to quiet it or to develop electronics that would ignore the noise would not be possible at that time. The acoustic homing torpedo had to be quiet enough that its own noise did not mask the target signal noise or echo. The hydrodynamic and the propulsion machinery noise had to be minimized especially from cavitation. The solution was a battery-powered electric torpedo whose concept had been under development intermittently for years but was last shelved in 1931. The electric torpedo which while extremely quiet and leaving no tell tail bubbles, was inherently slower and had a shorter range than steam-driven models. The so-called "self-noise" emanating from an electric torpedo was from its propeller noise (cavitation) and from the water rippling over the torpedo's hull which was to be overcome by the hydrophone design. The self-noise of a torpedo was reduced in steps; component by component. Fairprene, a canvas coated with Neoprene, insulated housings from the

hull while propellers and motors were modified to reduce vibrations. Cavitation and the noise from water flow presented more complex scientific solutions. A conventional 7.5 horse power washing machine motor was modified by General Electric to drive the propeller. Finally, these problems and the restrictions of electrical propulsion used with in most World War II homing torpedoes were solved, creating relatively slow, short range torpedoes that were mostly effective only against submerged submarines or slow moving actively searching escorts.

Safety Measures

During World War II, as with conventional torpedoes, there were three launching platforms for acoustic torpedoes: aircraft, submarines, and surface vessels, and two classes of targets; surface vessels and submarines. These platform/target combinations obliged design requirements on homing torpedoes that were not in effect, or at least much less important, in the case of conventional torpedoes. The major new safety requirement was that the torpedo should not home on the launching platform or other friendly vessel. This requirement was satisfied in a variety of ways. To protect surface vessels, ceiling switches disabled the homing system of air-launched weapons when the depth was less than a preset value (i.e. 40 feet). Floor switches similarly protected submerged submarines from their own anti-escort torpedoes. Straight enabling runs to the vicinity of the target; anti-circular run devices, and other safety features were also added to some of these new torpedoes. Further, during WW II Allied aircraft did not drop homing torpedoes when operating in conjunction with surface ASW forces. The Royal Navy Escort carrier HMS *Biter* was pursued by a homing torpedo which was described as "*Biter* bitten by *FIDO*" in press releases.

Mk24 Production

In October 1942, the Navy was confident that the *FIDO* was viable and "froze" the design for production despite the need for air-drop and in-water testing of pre-production prototypes to continue on into December 1942. The BTL prototype, which integrated many HUSL concepts and developments, was selected for production which began immediately and the first production models were delivered to the Navy in March 1943.

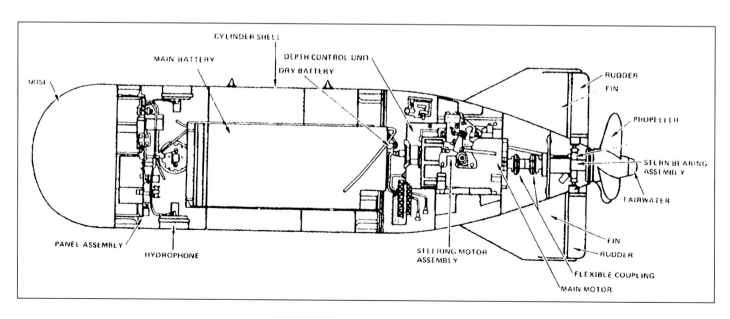

FIDO Mk24 Torpedo Mechanism (USN)

The first production model MK24 *FIDO* had the following features:

Size	19 inches diameter x 84 inches long
Weight	680 pounds
Propulsion	Single propeller driven by a GE 5 hp electric motor
	48-volt lead acid battery
Speed and Endurance	12 knots for approximately 15 minutes
Range	12,000 feet
Warhead	92 pounds HE Torpex
Homing System	4 piezoelectric (crystal) hydrophones operating at 24 kHz providing signals to a vacuum tube signal processing system with proportional steering. The hydrophone positions were moved slightly forward of mid-body about eight inches behind the joint ring between the hemispherical nose s ection and cylindrical body section.
Max. Drop Altitude	200-300 feet
Aircraft Launch Speed	120 knots
Search Pattern	The initial circular search was approximately 150 feet, diameter at a depth of 50 feet; and shifted to acoustic homing upon detection of the target (the initial search depth was later changed to 150 feet).

On 29 June 1942, Bell Telephone's manufacturing division, Western Electric (Kearny, NJ, factory) was awarded the prime production contract for 5,000 of the BTL prototype Mk24 which was soon increased to 10,000. General Electric was the subcontractor for the propulsion and steering motors while the battery which was developed by Western Electric was subcontracted to Electric Storage Battery Co., while the production of the torpedo hull was subcontracted to a bathtub manufacturer. The original production order was for 10,000 torpedoes but was reduced to just over 4,000 units with the final production per unit at $18,000 each. The reason for the reduction was that *FIDO* and other anti-submarine methods proved so effective in reducing the U-Boat threat that fewer were needed. The first production torpedoes were delivered to the Navy in March 1943; the first 500 units were ready in May 1943; and the first U-Boat was sunk by a *FIDO* that month, only 17 months from the first planning stage.

The MK24 in Combat

The Mk24 was supplied to most USN Composite Squadrons based on escort carriers operating anti-submarine patrols in the Atlantic from mid-1943. It also equipped USN some land-based PBY squadrons and was sent to the Royal Navy and the Canadian Navy.

The Mk24 was to be only used against submerged U-Boats as its homing heads were steered by the U-Boat's cavitation sounds (the popping sounds of the bubbles produced by a rotating propeller underwater). So the Mk24 was dropped on the area where the diving U-Boat left a swirl of water after it had been spotted. When it entered the water the *FIDO* was to begin a circular search pattern at a predetermined depth controlled by a standard bellows/pendulum system. The circular search pattern continued until the target's acoustic signal exceeded a predetermined threshold level when control was transferred to the acoustic homing system. The initial *FIDO*s were set to search at depth of 45-50 feet in a drifting circle with a 35 foot radius until it was able to home acoustically. The depth was later changed to 150 feet when operational use showed that setting to be optimal as enemy submarines were running deeper. The Mk24 was a

relatively slow torpedo so that the sounds from its own propellers would not obscure the sounds from the target. The performance of the homing device varied greatly with conditions. It functioned most efficiently against a U-Boat traveling at high speed just under the surface when the target could be picked up from three quarters of a mile. This was the most frequent operational condition as the U-Boat commander would attempt to escape by diving and then moving away from the revealing white swirl. A U-Boat commander could escape by slowing down after diving to eliminate the cavitation bubbles. The Mk24 could not be used against U-Boats in deep water. Also the Mk24 was too slow for the new Type XXI U-Boats. The production of the Mk24 was planned to be terminated at the end of 1943 as by that time the Germans would have discovered its existence and taken counter measures.

FIDO Torpedo Attack Tactics by CVE Hunter-Killer Groups

US Navy torpedo attack doctrine used the analogy of movement out along the spokes of a wheel with the CVE as the hub with a team composed of fighter bomber teams of TBFs and F4Fs sweeping out in an area enclosed by two adjacent spokes and the portion of the rim joining them. The movement was out along a spoke to the rim, then along the rim to the next spoke, and then inward along it. The area covered also included that immediately outside the spokes and rim.

Once contact with a U-Boat was made the fighter bomber teams began a coordinated attack; breaking radio silence to inform the CVE of the range and bearing of the action. The Wildcats went into a strafing run first in order to divert the U-Boat's AA gun crews if present but except for the rarely encountered special AA U-Boat, the return fire was relatively innocuous. At this time in the war the U-Boat except for a few tenacious captains usually headed into a crash dive when spotted. The TBF followed closely behind the F4F but usually at an angle to its course. The Avenger launched its *FIDO* at 200 to 300 feet at 120 to 150 mph into the swirling dive wake. While the initial attack was being carried out, the CVE launched an attack group of F4Fs and TBFs to the U-Boat contact point which were joined by other fighter bomber teams from adjacent sectors. As soon as the U-Boat submerged and was under attack surface warships were also dispatched to the scene.

The first USN confirmed sinking by a Mk24 torpedo appears to have occurred on 14 May 1943 when a PBY Catalina of VP-82 flown by Lt. P.A. Bodinet sank U-657 or U-640 east of Cape Farewell, Greenland. However, the first FIDO success occurred two days earlier, RAF Flt.Lt. J. Wright, flying a Liberator of No. 86 Squadron, dove on a diving U-Boat (U-456) that was stalking Convoy HX 237 northwest of Cape Ortegal. Wright's *FIDO* hit the U-Boat which was forced to surface but had sunk by the time RN destroyers arrived. During July and August 1943 an escort carrier group comprised of the *Bogue, Card, Core,* and *Santee* were congregated around the Azores to introduce the Mk24 into a large scale organized combat. Searching in sectors, TBFs carrying the torpedoes flew in pairs; one to force the U-Boat to dive and the other to drop the torpedo just ahead of the diving wake. *Santee* VC-29 Avengers accounted for U-160 (by Lt.(jg) John Ballantine) on 14 July, U-509 the next day, and U-43 on 30 July.

In October Adm. Doenitz again sent his U-Boats to the area around the Azores and they were again met by USN escort carriers. On 4 October 1943 Avengers of VC-9 from the *Card* came across a U-Boat refueling operation in progress: the submarine tanker U-460 had just finished refueling U-264 while U-422 and U-465 waited nearby. The four U-Boats sent up a determined AA defense making the air attack unproductive and the U-Boats remained surfaced. Lt. R. Stearns was forced to orbit out of range of the U-Boat's AA fire and wait until reinforcements arrived to make the U-Boats dive so he could use the homing torpedo remaining in his bomb bay. Soon U-465 dived but Stearns could not attack fearing that one of the three U-Boats remaining on the surface might see the top secret Mk24 in action and determine it was a homing device. Two Wildcats and an Avenger from the *Card* arrived but again, the heavy AA fire stymied their attack and the three U-Boats submerged. Stearns was then safe to drop his homing torpedo in front of the swirl left by the largest U-Boat and soon large bubbles and then oil and debris from the U-460 began to float to the surface. Later that day the captain of U-422 surfaced only three miles from the morning's action and came under almost immediate air attack and when the U-Boat dived, Lt.(jg.) S.B. Holt dropped a homing torpedo which hit its mark.

Mk24 Success in Combat

US Navy OEG Study No. 289, 12 August 1946 gives the following data for the Mk24 in combat against German and Japanese submarines:

Number of launching attacks	264
Total number of torpedoes launched (all targets)	340
Number launched against submarines	204
Number of attacks on submarines by US aircraft	142
Number of submarines sunk by US	31
Number of submarines damaged by US	15
Number of attacks on submarines (primarily British)	62
Number of submarines sunk by Allies	6
Number of submarines damaged by Allies	3
Total number of submarines sunk	37*
Total number of submarines damaged	18

*Includes 5 Japanese (1 in the Atlantic and four in the Pacific)

The success rate of the Mk24 was 32% (i.e. 142 launches yielded 31 kills and 15 damaged) which was three times better than the 9.5% success rate of air-dropped depth charges. The *FIDO* was so successful that contracts were reduced to 4,000 that initially cost $50,000 each but was reduced to $18,000 on the final versions as compared to $12,000 average for non-acoustic types.

A later submarine launched version of *FIDO*, the Mk27 ("*Cutie*") was developed for use against surface vessels and saw action in the Pacific in mid-1944 and were very successful with a 31% success rate. The Torpedo Mk24 *FIDO* continued in service with the US Navy until 1948 when it was superseded by the Mk34 which was an improved Mk24 with a 30 minute search at 17 knots.

The Mark 22 Active Homing Torpedo

Active homing was significantly more complex than passive homing and only two torpedoes of this kind, the Mk22 and Mk32, were developed during WW II. The Mk22 started as an attempt to integrate active homing into the Mk14 torpedo but was completed as a standard Mk18 electric torpedo design modified by Westinghouse and Bell Telephone Laboratories to include active homing in azimuth only. The homing system transmitted a pulse of 28 KHz sound using both halves of a left-right split transducer. Echoes received by the two halves were handled separately and their relative phase was used to determine the direction of the target. From the relative phase a course correction signal was generated and this signal controlled a change in the gyro angle. The gyro maintained course control between "pings" of the sonar. The realization of this system with only minimal modification of the basic Mk18 torpedo required ingenuity including, specifically, a complex mechanical device called the "translator" which received signals from the servo amplifiers and power from the propeller shaft to drive the course input for the gyro.

One of the problems encountered in active acoustic homing systems, but not in passive systems, was reverberation, which were the reflections of the transmitted sound pulse from random features in the surface, body, and bottom of the ocean. Reverberations were false targets and without special devices an active acoustic torpedo would often home on them but fortunately, reverberations diminished quickly. In the Mk22 system, the receiver was blanked for 40 milliseconds after the transmitted pulse and the amplifier gains programmed to increase with time in order to avoid the reverberation problem. The guidance system was successful, but by 1944 azimuth only homing, even for 21 inch torpedoes, was less attractive than the combination of vertical and horizontal homing offered by competing systems. Development of the Mk22 was terminated before production designs were completed.

Mark 32 Active Homing Torpedo

In 1942, the HUSL and General Electric developed two contending designs for the other World War II active homing torpedo, the MK22 and Mk32. The Mk32 used the Mk24 body and that weapon's passive homing system was replaced by a small active sonar. To accomplish the conversion the size and weight constraints were stringent with the total available volume less than two cubic feet and the weight were limited to less than 50 pounds. These space and weight restrictions meant that the best choices of equipment could not be used if there were a lighter or smaller alternative. The second problem was to devise a control system that functioned on the basis of short, widely spaced inputs rather than the continuous inputs characteristic of passive homing systems.

The GE system that was selected used a magnetostrictive transducer, four elements wide and eight elements high, that was split into an upper half and a lower half. This configuration made it possible to use phase comparison and proportional control in the vertical plane where it was necessary to home on a submarine hull that measured about 25 feet from keel to deck. In the horizontal plane, where the target was about 225 feet wide (long), a simpler ON-OFF control was used. In the absence of an echo the rudders moved hard over to port and the torpedo circled in that direction. When an echo was received the rudder was shifted to hard over starboard and remained in that position until about one second after the last echo was received. At this time the rudder was reversed and the procedure repeated. The torpedo thus apparently homed on either the bow or stern of the target, but the dynamics of the torpedo and the electronic time constants shifted the actual homing point toward the center of the target. The chief advantage of this homing system was that it used the same amplifiers as the vertical control system without adding complex circuitry and saved weight and space.

Homing signals in the vertical plane were acquired by comparing the phase of the signals from the two halves of the transducer. The up or down signals were used to drive a pendulum frame in which the pendulum was suspended. Electrical contacts connected the horizontal (diving) rudder motor to its power source to keep the pendulum centered in the frame. The system then controlled the pitch angle and accordingly the rate of climb, directly. A hydrostat was installed, but it was used only to control the mode of operation, (e.g., set the depth ceiling), and did not provide servo inputs that affected the horizontal rudder. Reverberation and other false target problems were managed by a combination of time variation of gain and blanking.

Only 22 months after the concept was first presented to the NDRC an experimental General Electric Mk32 made a successful sound-controlled, three-dimensional run in February 1944 and in July successful tests against target submarines were conducted. Leeds Northrop was contracted to manufacture the GE Mk32 and 10 pre-production units were completed

During World War II the USN initiated a top secret program using frequency hopping radio controlled torpedoes based on a patent by beautiful Hollywood star **Hedy Lamarr**. (Author)

the first nude scene and facial depiction of an orgasm in cinematic history. Lamarr's first husband (of six) was the much older, Fritz Mandl, a Berlin munitions manufacturer and Nazi sympathizer, who in the 1930s became interested in control systems for aircraft and the jamming of radio control systems. Lamarr was not only beautiful but she was also brilliant and while she was married to Mandl they attended hundreds of dinners and meetings with arms developers and manufacturers where she learned of radio jamming and radio hopping. Being an anti-Nazi of Jewish descent Lamarr escaped to London in 1937.

Lamarr met neighbor George Antheil, an avant-garde musician, in 1940, and during their relationship Lamarr somehow proposed the idea of using radio frequency hopping to reduce the danger of detection or jamming for radio-controlled torpedoes. Although the idea of radio control for torpedoes was not new, the concept of frequency hopping was. Broadcasting over an apparently random series of radio frequencies and switching from frequency to frequency at split second intervals prevented radio signals from being jammed. The receiver could be synchronized to the transmitter to allow the two to jump frequencies together. If both the transmitter and receiver were hopping in sync, the message was clearly transmitted. However, anyone trying to intercept the message would hear only random noise. Lamarr developed the theory of radio frequency hopping into synchronization, while Antheil's contribution was to suggest the device by which synchronization could be achieved as he had once coordinated 16 synchronized player pianos in his *Ballet Méanique*. Antheil's device was a roll of paper with holes punched in it, like a player piano roll; both radios would be controlled by the same pattern of holes on the paper.

Lamarr and Antheil worked on their idea for several months and in December 1940, sent a description of it to the National Inventors Council, whose chairman was Charles Kettering, the Research Director of General Motors. Kettering suggested that they consult the Electrical Engineering Department of the California Institute of Technology to perfect the engineering portion of their concept. On 11 August 1942 Lamarr and Antheil obtained their patent on a "Secret Communication System" which specified that a high altitude observation aircraft that could steer the torpedo from above. The two patriotically gave their patent rights to the US Navy but the Navy was never able to develop their idea as the device was too large to fit into a torpedo. After the war the concept of frequency-hopping was forgotten.

In 1957 Sylvania Electronics adapted the patent by using transistors and it was first used on ships sent to blockade Cuba during the 1962 missile crisis. Today the concept is called "Spread Spectrum" and more than 1,000 Spread Spectrum patents have referred back to the Lamarr-Antheil patent. Spread Spectrum is the basis for wireless communication technology such as WiFi and Bluetooth, helping these devices to operate in the same radio spectrum without interfering with each others' signals.

and tested before the project was canceled at the end of the war. Beginning in 1950, Philco produced a substantial number (about 3,300) of the somewhat different MK32-2 torpedoes for fleet use by destroyers.

The HUSL system differed in that its transducer was symmetrically divided into four quadrants. The echo signals in these four quadrants were processed in an inventive electronic system to obtain rudder orders. The system also contained a Doppler-enabling system that prevented homing on reverberation and other false targets including wakes. While the HUSL system was not selected for the Mk32 torpedo, many of its features were incorporated into the Penn State Ordnance Research Laboratory (ORL) Project 4 system which was the basis for the very successful Mk37 torpedo.

During World War II active and passive acoustic homing torpedoes became well-developed and their most important practical set the stage for subsequent post-war Navy torpedo development.

Hedy Lamarr and the Radio-Controlled Torpedo

An interesting addendum to the USN World War II torpedo program are experiments with frequency hopping radio controlled torpedoes using matching pairs of punched card rolls based on those of player pianos which were patented by beautiful Hollywood star, Hedy Lamarr!

Lamarr was born as Hedwig Eva Maria Kiesler in Vienna, and as teenager starred in the controversial film "Ecstasy," which contained

5

Depth Charges

Development

British

In their early attacks on U-Boats the RAF and Coastal Command found that their 500 pound anti-submarine aerial bombs originally developed in World War I were often more dangerous to the user than to the enemy as they had to be dropped at low speeds and altitudes exposing them to enemy AA fire and the explosion of an inaccurate drop could bring down the attacker. In 1940, the British developed an improvised aerial depth charge based on the well-proven standard Mark VII 450 pound drum-shaped naval depth charge. It was fitted with a conical fairing on one end and fins on the other to stabilize it as it fell from the aircraft. This device used the reliable hydrostatic pistol that would detonate at a preset water pressure (depth) and prevented it from detonating in the air if it bounced off the ocean's surface. The weight and shape of these depth charges restricted their use and they proved to be ineffective and improvements were needed. During almost two years of war, September 1939 to June 1941, Coastal Command calculated that a paltry 1% of the U-Boats that had been attacked were sunk. Attacking aircrews were disgruntled when U-Boats were seen to be bracketed by these depth charges; only to emerge from the spray of the explosions unscathed.

In early 1941 the British had created the Operational Research Section of the Coastal Command headed by Dr. Patrick Blackett and his assistant Dr. E.J. Williams. One of their first projects was to analyze attacks on U-Boats by studying attack records and photographs. By the summer of 1941, the Research Section had determined that an aircraft's best chance of causing significant damage to a U-Boat was to depth charge it while it was on the surface or at the latest when it was in the first 15 seconds of its dive. There were two methods to improve a depth charge that had to be of a given size and weight so that it could be accommodated inside an aircraft. The first was to use a more powerful explosive and the second was to have the depth charge detonate closer to the U-Boat. The early Coastal Command depth charges were filled with Amatol but by the end of April 1942, Mark XI depth charges were filled with Torpex, a mixture RDX, TNT, and aluminum, which was 30 to 50% more powerful than Amatol-filled types and became the British depth charge explosive of choice. The preset hydrostatic pistols detonated at 100 to 150 feet which was the hypothetical average depth the U-Boat would reach during a crash dive initiated at the hypothetical average distance at which the attacking aircraft was first seen by the U-Boat. Since the aircraft dropped the depth charges on the eddy of diving bubbles the U-Boat would actually be too far ahead of this hypothetical position to be damaged. The only U-Boats

likely to be attacked successfully were those caught on the surface or just initiating their dive but these U-Boats escaped because the depth charges were set too deeply at 100-150 feet. The apparent remedy was to preset the hydrostatic pistols at a more realistic depth using a depth charge that sank slowly so it would explode at the desired depth. The ideal depth for detonation was determined to be 25 feet but the existing hydrostatic pistols had been designed for shipboard use where the minimum safe detonation depth was 50 feet. A new shallow firing device needed to be developed and the Mark VIII detonator was introduced in spring 1942. However, it had a minimum depth setting of 34 feet that was not shallow enough to contend with a surfaced U-Boat considering that the Torpex-filled depth charge's lethal range was 19 feet. Also a dropped depth charge had tendency to form a coating of bubbles upon impact that delayed the action of water pressure on the pistol. By July 1942, the Mark XI depth charge had been adapted to use the Mark XIII Star pistol, a break-away tail, and concave nose spoiler that allowed the depth charge to detonate at 15 to 25 feet.

American

When the US entered the war it had no depth bombs in inventory but had designs from the 1930s and could draw on proven British designs. The Naval Gun Factory designed and tested a new American depth charge dropped from warships after which BuOrd undertook designing a depth bomb to be dropped from an aircraft. Initially, the BuOrd developed a number of inadequate makeshift types before the 325 pound Mark 17 series appeared in spring 1942; followed three months later by the 650 pound Mark 29 series. After their introduction there were reports that the bombs exploded when they contacted the water subjecting the dropping aircraft to dangerous shock waves; especially from the heavier 650 pound Mark 29. BuOrd launched an immediate investigation and found that while definite shock waves did occur; they were not dangerous nor the result of a malfunction. The depth bombs had reached their preset depth so quickly that the explosion occurred before the water could close in around the column of air dragged down by the sinking bomb. When detonation occurred; this shaft of air provided a path of escape for the shock waves that were projected upwards into the air.

Ricochet was a common problem to all air-dropped depth bombs, especially when dropped at increasing attack speeds. The combination of high speed and low altitude resulted in an unfavorable entrance angle for the round nosed depth bombs. BuOrd developed flat nose attachments that could be attached to existing bombs until the redesign could be incorporated into the production line. The blunt ends were able to dig into the water when they entered at low entrance angles. Operational experience led to other improvements. The tail assemblies were strengthened to avoid the distortion that gave previous bombs unpredictable underwater trajectory. Torpex and then HBX was substituted for TNT which increased the explosive power of the bombs without changing the bomb's dimensions. New and more reliable fuses were developed. These changes led to a gradual multiplication of depth bomb mark numbers in the American arsenal.

In August 1943, the American aerial depth charge arsenal consisted of 14 Marks which were derived from two basic types, the 325 pound Mark 17 and the 650 pound Mark 29. The Mark 17 design yielded the Marks 41, 44, 47, 53, 54, and 75; while the Mark 29 design yielded the Marks 35, 37, 38, 48, 49, and 71. The first operational depth charge was the Mark 17 which became available in quantity in April 1942. The round nosed Mark 17 was 15 inches in diameter and 52.5 inches long, weighed 325 pounds including 234 pounds of TNT (the Mark 44 was a Torpex-filled version) which gave it had lethal range of approximately 17 feet from the U-Boat's pressure hull. The 1st Sea Search Attack Group (1SSAG) helped to test this depth charge that initially had a tendency to skip or ricochet due to its rounded nose. A flat-nosed attachment was added to cure this problem in the TNT-filled Mark 41 and the later Mark 47 which was filled with Torpex. The TNT-filled Mark 53 armed with a hydrostatic fuse was introduced late in the war and was followed by the similar Torpex-filled Mark 54 that remained in service for 30 years (the Mark 75 was a thicker cased limited version). The Mark 29, introduced in May 1942, was the other main US depth charge. It weighed 650 pounds, was filled with approximately 425-450 pounds of TNT, and measured 18 inches in diameter and 67 inches in length. This Mark was plagued by a weak tail, unstable underwater course, and its round nose also caused surface skipping. This surface skipping could detonate the explosive charge and endanger the attacking aircraft due to its larger charge and resulting explosion but the problem was also remedied by the attachment of a flattened nose. The TNT-filled Marks 35 (no data), 37 (new tail) and 38 (shorter at 61 inches with more explosive at 425 pounds of TNT) were versions of the basic Mark 29 which remained as the main 650 pound type depth charge. The Marks 48 (enlarged, 18.6 x 68 inch Mark 29 weighing

850 pounds), 49 (a Mark 38 filled with 472 pounds of Torpex), and 71 (a modified 525 pound M64GP bomb version armed with hydrostatic fuse) were later 650 pound type depth charges. By the end of the war 400,000 depth bombs had been loaded at a cost of $31 million.

General Description
The depth bomb was a cylindrical, flat nosed, light case light case type of bomb design; for use against submarines. Older models with hemispherical (round) noses were provided with flat nose attachments in order to reduce ricochet. There were three methods of delivering depth bombs: low altitude release, dropping (toss) bombing, and glide bombing. It averaged 70% explosive and was loaded with HBX, HBX-1, or TNT. The depth bomb was fused with a hydrostatic fuse which functioned at a predetermined depth rather than on impact. Depth bombs were designed for a nose fuse, a transverse fuse, and, in the case of larger bombs, a tail fuse. The nose fuse was an impact fuse, for use when surface blast effect was desired under certain tactical conditions. The transverse fuse was a double-headed hydrostatic fuse which was assembled in a tube running diametrically through the bomb body. The tail fuse, when used, also was a hydrostatic fuse. Small depth bombs were shipped in metal crates while larger depth bombs were shipped in shipping bands.

Components of a Depth Bomb Complete Round
1) Bomb, unfused, without fin assembly included:
   a) Bomb body with single and double suspension lugs attached.
   b) Explosive charge.
   c) Nose fuse adapter and fuse seat liner with two auxiliary boosters.
   d) Transverse fuse seat.
   e) Fin lock nut or cap screws for attachment of fin assembly.
2) Fin assembly (attached with cap screws to light bombs, with fin lock nut to heavy bombs).
3) Nose fuse (used for blast effect. Nose and hydrostatic fuses both used only when selective arming was available),
4) Transverse fuse.
5) Arming wire assembly or assemblies.
6) Trunnions (large bombs) or trunnion band.
7) Tail fuse and arming bracket (large bombs only).
8) Flat nose attachment (for round nose bombs only).

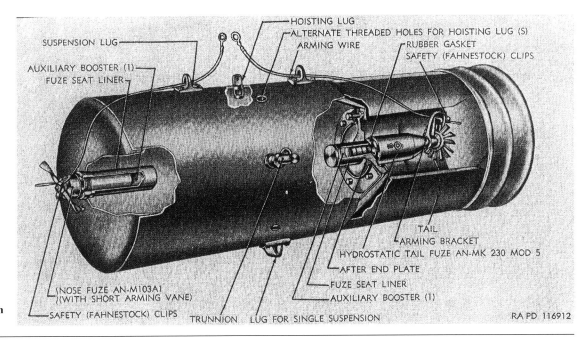

Description of the Depth Charge (USN)

RA PD 116912

Assembly of a Complete Round

The bomb was removed from its packing case and, if it was the older round nose type, the round nose attachment needed to be installed by first standing the bomb on its base. The fuse seat adapter was removed and the round nose attachment was placed over the nose of the bomb. The fuse seat adapter was then replaced and securely tightened. The space between the attachment and the bomb was filled with Plaster of Paris cement or some other quick-setting material and allowed to set.

The shipping plugs or cover plates were removed from the fuse cavities to be used and the cavities were cleansed of the gun-slushing compound with which they were coated and of any other foreign material. The threads were inspected to be sure that they were clear and the fuse cavities were not distorted. The transverse tube was gauged by sliding a dummy booster completely through it. The fin assembly was attached so that one fin aligned with the suspension lugs. The correct fuse or fuses were assembled and inserted.

If bomb was not dropped and if it was to be returned to storage, the above steps were reversed, coating the fuse cavities with Compound, Rust-preventive, light. All components were to be returned to their original packing those which were originally sealed were to be resealed.

Function

Depth bombs were intended for attack on submarines and so had to be equipped with hydrostatic fuses but to attack surface targets they were also adapted for impact fuses. Since the anti-submarine mission was primary, only hydrostatic fuses were to be used unless selective arming was available (so that the bomb may be dropped with the impact fuse on SAFE and the hydrostatic fuse armed). The blast effect from a depth bomb fused for impact was slightly greater than that from a GP bomb of equal weight, since the percentage of explosive was greater. The radius of underwater effectiveness which was the distance from the explosion at which a submarine would probably suffer fatal damage, was approximately 45 feet for 325 pound bombs and 56 feet for 650 pound bombs.

Limitations

Depth bombs could not be used for penetration of solid material. They could not be used from high altitude because the hydrostatic fuses would function at depths greater than those for which they were set. In addition, impact with the water from high altitudes would warp the bomb body and fuse cavities so that the fuses could not function. Depth settings had to be made in advance and were difficult if not impossible to change in flight.

Bomb, Depth, 350 Pound, AN-Mk44 (USN)

Conditions for Storage of Fused Bombs

Depth bombs with transverse hydrostatic fuses could be stored in the open for overnight or similar temporary storage under certain conditions (especially weather proofing) and with permission. Permission was given to avoid damage to fuses from repeated fusing and defusing of the bomb.

Types of Depth Bombs

350 Pound Depth Bombs
Bomb, Depth, 350 Pound, AN-Mk47
The AN-Mk47 was a round nose Light Case type. It measured 53.1 inches long and weighed 355 pounds, as released. The bomb body was 28.46 inches long and 15 inches in diameter, weighing 354.5 pounds of which 252 pounds, 71% of the complete round, was a high explosive Torpex charge.

Other 325-350 Pound Depth Bomb Models
Bomb, Depth, 325 Pound, AN-Mk41
The AN-Mk41 was the same as the AN-Mk 47 except that it was loaded with 221 pounds of TNT.

Bomb, Depth, 350 Pound, AN-Mk44
The AN-Mk44 was the same as the AN-M47 except that it was a round nose type but required attachment of the flat nose.

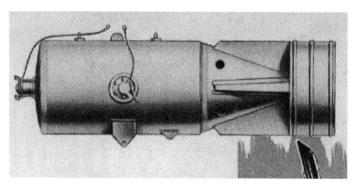

Bomb, Depth, 350 Pound, AN-Mk47 (USN)

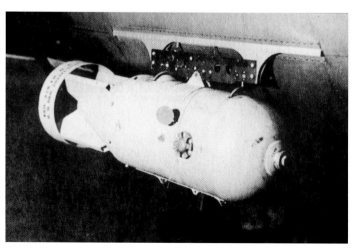

Bomb, Depth, 350 Pound, AN-Mk47 (USN)

Bomb, Depth, 350 Pound, AN-Mk17 (Wing Mount PBY) (USN)

Bomb, Depth, 350 Pound, AN-Mk17 (Bomb Bay B-25) (USN)

Movie still of the 22 May 1943 Mk17 depth charge attack on U-569 by *USS Bogue* Avengers. (USN)

Bomb, Depth, 350 Pound, AN-Mk17
The AN-Mk17 was a round nose type loaded with 243 pounds of TNT. This type usually required the attachment of the flat nose but was sometimes issued with the round nose attached.

On 22 May 1943 U-569 a Type-VIIC U-Boat captained by Oblt. Hans-Peter Hinsch was attacked by two VC-9 TBF-1 Avengers off the USN escort carrier *USS Bogue*. Lt. Howard Roberts dropped four Mk17 depth charges badly damaging the U-Boat which was scuttled leaving 21 dead and 25 survivors.

Bomb, Depth, 350 Pound, AN-Mk54 MOD1
The AN-Mk54 MOD1 was a round nose, Light Case type bomb which was 52.5 inches long and weighed 346 pounds as released. It contained 248 pounds of HBX which was 71.7% of complete weight. Alternative loading was 225.5 pounds of TNT, 70% percent of the complete weight which was 324 pounds.

Authorized Fuses for the 350 Pound Bombs
1) Fuse, Bomb, Hydrostatic, AN-Mk234 (transverse) with the Fuse, Bomb, Hydrostatic, AN-Mk224 (all models) as a substitution.
2) Fuse, Bomb, AN-Mk219 (nose)
This fuse was only used when surface demolition effect was desired. Fuse, Bomb, AN-Ml03 (nose) was preferred when the special arming vane for use with round nose bombs was available. This fuse would not arm if the regular vane was used on the fuse when it is used in round nose bombs.

650 Pound Depth Bombs
Bomb, Depth, 650 Pounds, AN-Mk29
The AN-Mk29 was a round nose type, 70 inches in length weighing 729 pounds as released, of which 72 pounds represented the weight of the round nose attachment. The bomb body was 42.25 inches long and 17.7 inches in diameter and contained an explosive charge of 464 pounds of TNT.

Other 650 Pound Models
Bomb, Depth, 650 Pounds, AN-Mk37 had the same body with a shorter (Mk37) fin assembly.

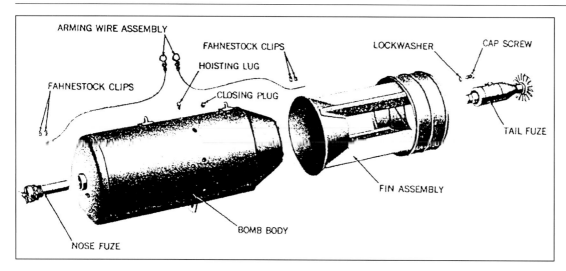

Bomb, Depth, 350 Pound, AN-Mk54 (USN)

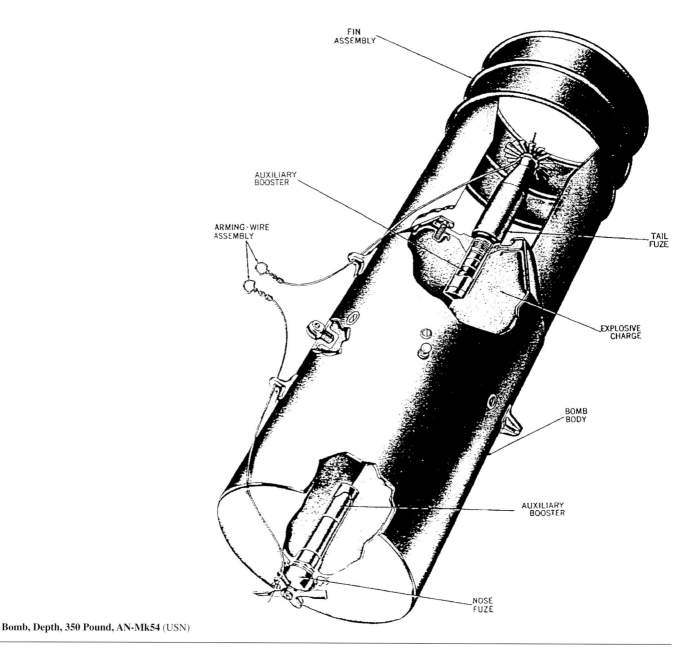

Bomb, Depth, 350 Pound, AN-Mk54 (USN)

Bomb, Depth, 650 Pounds, AN-Mk37 (USN)

Bomb, Depth, 650 Pounds, AN-Mk38 was a round nose type loaded with TNT.

Bomb, Depth, 650 Pounds, AN-Mk49 was a round nose type loaded with Torpex.

Authorized Fuses for the 650 Pound Bomb
1) Nose
The preferred nose fuse was the Fuse, Bomb, AN-M103 with special arming vane. This fuse will not arm on round nose bombs if equipped with the standard vane. Consequently, if the special arming vane is not available then Fuse, Bomb, AN-M103 and one additional auxiliary booster was to be used. When equipped with the special vane, FUSE, bomb, AN-M103 will arm in 1,800 feet of air travel. The AN-Mk. 219 arms in 2,500 feet of air travel.

2) Transverse
The preferred transverse fuse was the Fuse, Hydrostatic, AN-M234 but the Fuse, Hydrostatic, AN-Mk224 (all models) could be substituted.

3) Tail
Fuse, Hydrostatic, AN-M229 was authorized when the Mk 37 fin assembly was used but this fuse would not arm when the Mk29 fin was used.

Depth Bomb Fuses
Fuse, Bomb, Hydrostatic, AN-Mk 224 (Transverse)
The 14 pound AN-Mk 224 was an arming pin type, double-headed fuse which was assembled in a transverse tube in the bomb body. Upon withdrawal of the arming wire, the jump-out arming pins were ejected, leaving the fuse free to arm and fire by hydrostatic pressure at a depth determined by the springs assembled in the fuse. This fuse was designed for use in the 325 and 350 pound depth bombs, and could also be used in the 650 pound depth bombs by adding a spacer which was issued with the bomb. As issued, the fuse was set to function at a depth of 25 feet which could be changed, as described below, for 50, 75, 100, or 125 feet.

Description:
(Note: Since the fuse of the depth charge was its most important functional component this fuse will be described in detail as a representative hydrostatic fuse.)

The AN-Mk 224 was issued in three parts, a pistol, a booster, and a booster extender.

Pistol
The pistol consisted of a head, a body, and a primer and detonator holder. The head was dome-shaped and was bolted to the mouth of the transverse tube and contained the arming pin and water ports. The body was cylindrical and contained the firing pin and guide piece, hydrostatic piston and bushing, and a firing pin spring. The firing pin was held in place against the firing pin spring by two balls which pressed on a groove in the firing pin, and were held by the hydrostatic piston bushing. The end of the guide piece extended through the end of the body and was threaded for the attachment of the primer and detonator holder. The primer and detonator holder was shaped like a flattened cone and was assembled to the end of the firing pin guide piece. It contained two L-shaped slides held apart by the action of two springs. One slider contained the primer, the other contained the detonator. In the unarmed position, the firing pin, primer, and detonator were out of line with each other. When the fuse

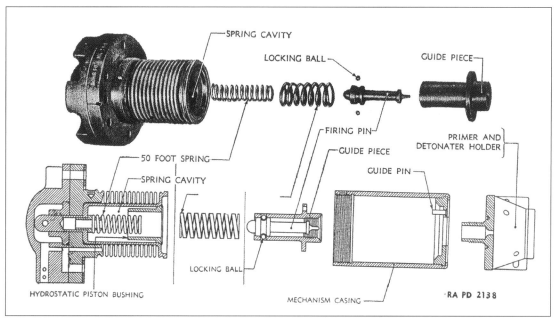

Fuse, Bomb, Hydrostatic, AN-Mk 224 (Transverse) (USN)

armed, these elements were brought into line with each other and with the booster lead which was assembled in the outer end.

Booster

The booster was assembled in a cylindrical metal container which had a slip joint on one end for attachment to the booster extender and on the other, a funnel-shaped metal skirt for engaging the sliders in the primer and detonator holder.

Booster Extender

The booster extender consisted of a head and body. The head was similar to that of the pistol. The body contained a hydrostatic bellows, an extender rod, and a release mechanism similar to that of the firing pin in the pistol. When assembled to the bomb, the heads of the pistol and booster extender protruded slightly. A branch of the arming wire was required for each head and both branches had to be withdrawn to permit the fuse to function.

Function of the Fuse

When the arming wires were withdrawn the arming pin in the pistol and booster extender were ejected by their springs. This action released the hydrostatic piston in the pistol and the extender rod in the booster extender. As the bomb sunk, the water entered the ports in the heads and hydrostatic pressure built up. When the depth for which the fuse was set was reached that pressure caused the following. In the pistol, the hydrostatic piston advanced to the end of the body carrying with it the bushing which held the firing pin locking balls in place. In the booster extender, the extender rod advanced against a spring, compressing it. When the rod advanced about 0.6 inch, the balls which locked the rod to the spring were released and the rod snapped forward, pushing the booster ahead of it. The skirt on the booster engaged the sliding blocks in the pistol extender, moving them to line up the primer and detonator with the firing pin and booster lead. The booster continued to advance, forcing the primer and detonator holder and the firing pin guide piece toward the pistol head. This action was opposed by the firing pin spring. When the set depth was reached, the firing pin guide piece was pushed through the piston bushing sufficiently to clear the locking balls which flew out releasing the firing pin which was driven by its spring into the primer initiating the explosive train.

Fusing

The fuse was assembled into the bomb in this sequence:
1) Unseal the container and inspect the fuse and the gaskets.
2) Remove the pistol with its gasket from the container and apply a thin coat of grease to both sides of the gasket. The pistol was inserted in either end of the tube, with the gasket in place between the pistol flange and the head of the tube. Care had to be taken that the assembly entered freely and was located properly upon the locating dowel pin so that the arming pin pointed toward the tail of the bomb. The holding screws were inserted and drawn up evenly. They were checked two or three times, in rotation, after the initial tightening. A "P" was stenciled or otherwise marked on the bomb body to indicate the pistol end of the fuse. It was extremely important that a watertight seal be obtained between the flange of the fuse and the head of the tube; otherwise a deeper functioning or a dud will result.
3) Remove the booster and the booster extender from the container. Apply a thin coat of grease to the extender gasket, as in 2) above, Attach the booster to the extender by the provided slip joint. (When fusing a 650 pound depth bomb, a spacer was attached to the extender and the booster to the spacer.) The assembly was inserted into the end of the tube opposite the pistol and bolted in place observing all the precautions specified in 2) above. This step could conveniently precede (2) above.

4) Thread a branch of the arming wire through each head of the fuse. Cut off the excess wire so that no more than six or seven inches protruded. Remove all kinks and burs. Slip two safety clips up each wire until they touched the head of the fuse.
5) If necessary, weatherproof the fuse against icing.
6) Remove the safety cotter pins. (In fuses of later manufacture there was only one hole through the pin and housing and the arming pin needed to be held in place while removing the cotter pin and replacing it with the arming wire.)
7) Reverse the above steps when it was necessary to defuse the bomb to return it to regular storage.

Preparation for Use

If the required depth of functioning was that marked on the fuse or its container, the fuse was ready for use when removed from its packing. If another depth was required, it could be changed. (see next)

Depth Setting

Five depth settings were possible with this fuse. Unless otherwise marked, the fuse, as issued, functioned at 25 feet which could be changed to 50, 75, 100, or 125 feet by the insertion of the appropriate springs which were supplied in the can in which the fuse was packed. The 50 foot setting was used for all ordinary anti-submarine operations while the other settings were not to be used except on instructions from the Chief of Ordnance or on direction of the officer in charge of operations.

To Change Depth Setting

The primer and detonator holder were unscrewed after forcing it counter-clockwise by hand to break the staking. The set screw in the mechanism casing was removed and the casing was unscrewed from pistol-carrying flange. The guide piece, firing pin, and locking balls were removed as a unit from the hydrostatic piston bushing, exposing the spring cavity. The appropriate depth spring was to be inserted: for function at 25 foot depth: the yellow spring; for function at 50 foot depth: the black spring; for function at 75 foot depth: the black spring in place and the larger green spring inserted over it; for function at 100 foot depth: the small yellow spring with the larger red spring inserted over it; for function at 125 foot depth: the black spring with the larger red spring over it. The firing pin and locking balls were assembled in the guide piece and inserted as a unit into the hydrostatic piston bushing, with the firing pin resting on the 0.5 inch spring. The mechanism casing was assembled to the pistol carrying flange, taking care that the guide pin entered the hole in the guide piece. The mechanism casing was screwed tight and the set screw replaced. The primer and detonator holder were reassembled to guide piece taking care that the end of the firing pin was centered and screwed tightly. The pistol head was marked to indicate the depth setting and if the fuse was repacked, the packing can and data card were also marked.

Precautions

In addition to the general precautions, the following were to be observed. If a fuse or any part was dropped on a hard surface from a height less than five feet, the fuse was to be examined for superficial damage, if none was evident, it was to be considered serviceable. If a fuse was dropped from a height greater than five feet, it was to be tagged and turned in as unserviceable. If the arming pins were accidentally ejected, they were to be replaced and the fuse was to be inspected by the Ordnance officer before being replaced in service. When a fuse was removed from an unused bomb, notes were to be made on its complete history, recording all actions and installations from its first assembly to the time it was turned in or expended.

Fuse, Bomb, Hydrostatic, AN-Mk 234 (Transverse)
The AN-Mk 234 was a double-headed fuse similar to the AN-Mk 224
except as it could be set for the depth required, from 25 to 125 feet in steps
of 25 feet, without disassembly of the fuse. It was issued in three parts,
pistol, booster, and booster extender. The booster and booster extender
were similar to those of the AN-Mk 224, and were assembled to the bomb
in the same manner. The pistol differed in the shape of the head and the
method of arming but was assembled in the same manner as that of the
AN-Mk 224 except for manner of attaching the arming wire.

The head of the pistol was cylindrical. A lock screw with a safety clip
projected through a slot in one side of the head. Projecting through a slot
in the other side was the depth-setting knob which also served as a water
port to the firing mechanism of the pistol. When the pistol was unarmed,
this port was closed by a small plug and a neoprene tubing connector.
Depth settings are graduated on the head.

Fuse, Bomb, Hydrostatic, AN-Mk 229 (Tail)
The AN-Mk 229 was a vane-type tail fuse which armed after 110
revolutions of the arming vane. It was 16.37 inches in length and 2.36
inches in diameter and weighed 14.5 pounds. It acted in response to
hydrostatic pressure to detonate the bomb at a depth set by a handle or
disk on the fuse body. This fuse was authorized for use with the 650 pound
depth bomb, AN-Mk 37.

This fuse was bottle-shaped with a booster cup assembled to the base
and a 16 blade arming vane assembled to the outer end. The depth setting
control was attached to the side of the body. The fuse body was marked
with depth graduations around the hub of the depth setting handle but on
earlier models lock screw did not have these markings. On later models,
the depth setting was indicated on the disk. A safety cotter pin, which
had a ring and tag attached, passed through the neck of the fuse body and
arming vane shaft preventing rotation of the vane and consequent arming
of the fuse. A safety bar which was held in place by a cotter pin passed
through the booster cup and kept the detonator carrier from moving toward
the firing pin. A J-shaped arming bracket, furnished separately, clamped
around the neck of the fuse to provide for installation of the arming wire.

When the arming wire is withdrawn the air stream rotates the arming
vane (1). The rotation is transmitted through a reduction gear train (2) to
the arming shaft (3) which is threaded into the arming cup (4). The arming
cup progresses upward and, after 110 revolutions of the vane, clears the
arming pins (5) which are ejected by their springs from the groove in the
head of the firing spindle (6). Upon impact with the water, the inertia
counterbalance weights (7) prevent function by set-forward. As the bomb
sinks, the water enters the ports (9) in the body of the fuse and builds up
hydrostatic pressure in the bellows (10). When sufficient pressure is built
up to compress the firing spring (11) and auxiliary depth spring (12), the
firing spindle is forced downward so that the locking balls (13) fly into a
recess and the firing spring forces the detonator carrier (14) against the
fixed firing pin (15). The resultant explosion is transmitted through the
booster leads (16) to the booster (17). Variation in depth setting is obtained
by varying the compression of the auxiliary depth spring by means of a
cam on the inner end of the depth setting control (18).

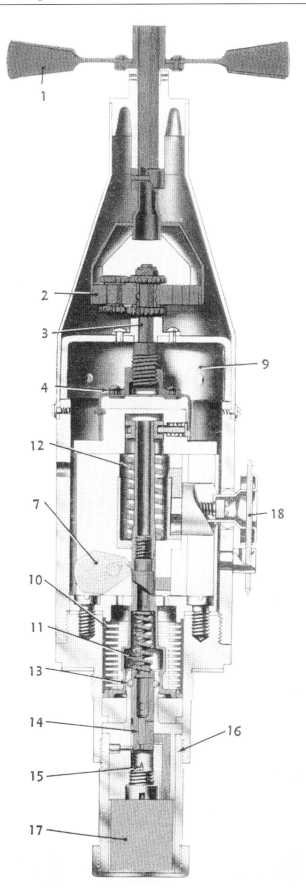

Fuse, Bomb, Hyrdostatic Fuse AN-Mk229 (USN)

Tactical Aerial Depth Charge Attack on a U-Boat

Because the British were at war against the U-Boat since September 1939, the Coastal Command had completed extensive studies on formulating an anti-submarine doctrine in relation to depth charges much of which would be adopted by American ASW units. In July 1942 it had prescribed that its policy was "to concentrate efforts on sinking those U-Boats which are still on or near the surface." A "stick" of six dropped depth charges spaced at 36 foot intervals yielded a hypothetical "lethal area" of approximately 20 feet wide by 220 feet in length. The Type VIII U-Boat was 220 feet long and the Type IX was 254 feet long. The lethal area of each depth charge was the diameter of a circle (20 feet) around its explosion and the lethal area of a stick of depth charges would vary with the interval (spread) of the charges, the greater the interval the less overlapping of explosive charges. This depth charge interval was to allow for the average range error that occurred when a pilot was attempting to maneuver his aircraft at 150 mph or more while descending to 50 feet across a moving target. To further complicate matters while aiming the plane and preparing to release the depth charges the pilot and bombardier had to compensate for the forward movement of the U-Boat and for the trajectory of the depth charges as they fell through the air and then into the sea, each having a different density that affected their speed. With experience the initial 36 foot interval was later lengthened to 60 feet which increased the lethal area to 20 by 340 feet that gave the pilot more much needed leeway in adjusting for range error. There were two types of error when making an attack; range error and line error. Typically range error (150 to 180 feet) was two to three times that of line error (60 to 90 feet). Coastal Command attack policy also recommended that the route of attack should be the shortest possible even if the angle of attack would be more difficult as it was much better to attack while the U-Boat was still on the surface. Depth charges were to be dropped from 50 feet not only for a more accurate attack but also to preclude the depth charges from breaking up when hitting the surface when dropped from higher altitudes. Depth charges dropped from 50 feet took less than two seconds to hit the water's surface and then two to three seconds to reach 25 feet and to explode. During this time it was determined that the forward movement of the depth charges was about 40 feet from their point of release using the conning tower used as the center of the drop by the attacking aircraft. The speed of a crash diving U-Boat was about 10 feet per second. A U-Boat that submerged entirely with its conning tower leaving a swirl on the surface would have moved forward about 150 feet beyond the head of the swirl in 15 seconds which was the

maximum period of submergence for an effective attack. First the pilot would have to initiate an immediate attack, hoping to catch the U-Boat on the surface or in the preliminary act of a crash dive and then he had to make an estimate of the U-Boat's movement when calculating the time to drop the depth charges. There was no accurate low level bombsight available and attacks on U-Boats were more of an art than science and constant practice was required to become proficient.

When the USAAF First Bomber Command initially investigated the depth charge bombing of submarines it believed that a bombsight was not necessary for optimal attacks from 50 to 100 feet. But tests showed that the average range of error using this dead reckoning type of attack was 175 feet. When the standard round nosed depth charges were found to be erratic both the Army and Navy pushed to develop a low level ASW bombsight. By the summer of 1943, several efficient bombsights were developed and with the more accurate flat nosed depth charges produced improved results.

The AAFAC Anti-submarine SOP Manual of 29 July 1943 began by noting that attacks on a U-Boat were very uncommon but reassured the aircrews that their efforts were successful, nonetheless, because their presence overhead forced the U-Boats to stay submerged and reduced their operational effectiveness. The American anti-submarine attack directives issued for patrolling aircraft followed the British methods. Ideally the patrol aircraft was to patrol at 1,000 feet as flying above that altitude was ineffective because the aircraft could not dive quickly enough to the 50 foot attack level before the U-Boat submerged and escaped. Surprise was essential to catch the U-Boat in time to drop a stick of depth charges near enough to be lethal and an attack via the most direct route was recommended even if it was not the most efficient. Attacks on U-Boats that had submerged more than 15 seconds were deemed useless. With experience and new types of depth charges the American procedure of spacing dropped depth charges differed from the British method. The American 325 pound-type depth charge was dropped at 50 foot intervals while the more powerful 650 pound-type was dropped at 70 feet intervals. The Americans felt that patrols over five hours were unproductive (the Coastal Command conducted much longer patrols) and that 30 minutes was the radar watch duration limit (vs. 45 minutes in the Coastal Command).

Initially, American ASW patrol aircraft were inadequate. The Navy's PBY Catalina had a long range of up to 2,500 miles but had a limited bomb capacity and flew so slowly that the U-Boat could easily crash dive before the lumbering amphibian could reach it. After Pearl Harbor the

The Navy's **Consolidated PBY Catalina** (pictured dropping a depth charge) had a range of up to 2,500 miles but had a limited bomb capacity and flew so slowly that the U-Boat could easily crash dive before the lumbering amphibian could reach it. (USN)

During a **depth charge attack** the pilot first would have to initiate an immediate attack, hoping to catch the U-Boat on the surface or in the preliminary act of a crash dive and then he had to make an estimate of the U-Boat's movement when calculating the time to drop the depth charges. (USN)

After Pearl Harbor the only bomber the AAC had in adequate numbers was the **Douglas B-18 Bolo** medium bomber which had only barely adequate range, speed, and bomb capacity for ASW patrols. But the B-18 was all that was available until the B-24 could be produced in sufficient numbers to meet all its operational obligations. (AAF)

only bomber the AAC had in inventory in adequate numbers was the B-18 medium bomber which had only barely adequate range, speed, and bomb capacity but was all that was available until the B-24 could be produced in sufficient numbers to meet all its other operational obligations. The four-engine Liberator in its long range configuration (LR) could patrol to 1,800 miles with 10 to 12 depth charges and its very long range version (VLR) could fly 2,400 miles carrying six or eight. Also its larger crew (ten) allowed for watch rotation which meant shorter and more efficient visual searches.

In responding to the U-Boat offensive the US developed and implemented tactics that took advantage of the U-Boat's need to surface daily, usually at night, when it was necessary for the U-Boat to recharge its batteries (usually requiring four hours for a full charge), ventilate the boat, and to allow the crew some fresh air time. The U-Boat only had a limited submerged battery speed of four knots and a surface diesel speed of 15-18 knots. Because their surfaced speed was five knots faster than most merchant vessels U-Boats had to maneuver on the surface to intercept a convoy and then fire their torpedoes or deck guns at a target and only submerge to escape pursuing surface ASW warships that soon had to return to escort the convoy. After its escape the U-Boat would surface and race ahead to make another attack on the convoy. The use of round-the-clock aerial patrols caused the U-Boats to dive frequently and remain submerged for long intervals and prevented them from catching up to the convoys. When the air patrols extended into the night the two to four hour battery recharging procedure became dangerous for the U-Boat from nine days before and five days after the full moon. When patrol aircraft were fitted with ASV radar recharging became even more dangerous and had to be accomplished even further off shore.

When an aircraft was using radar to detect a surfaced U-Boat that was using its *Metox* radar warning set to detect aircraft radar; the two opposing radar operators were confronted with different liabilities for detections and false alarms. If the aircraft radar operator made a contact he could ask the pilot to investigate without misgivings because if the contact was a false alarm the aircraft would continue its patrol. However, if the U-Boat *Metox* signaled an alarm its operator had to risk an air attack weighing the option of a crash dive and stopping recharging of the batteries to the option of a false alarm and remaining on the surface to recharge the batteries and continue on a quicker and more comfortable voyage. When centimetric radar became available, negating *Metox*, the U-Boats spent much more time submerged.

Types of Anti-submarine Search and Patrol Procedures
Routine Aerial Patrol
Early in the war the AAF utilized the aerial patrol to contain and obstruct U-Boat operations in areas where they were known to be operating. During this phase air patrols had to be flown using accurate navigation and dependable communications that were often neither accurate nor dependable. The air crews had to be able to quickly and accurately identify surfaced vessels so as not to attack friendly vessels. It was to be assumed any submerged vessel was a U-Boat as Allied submarines did not operate in the Caribbean. In early 1942, Capt. C.D. Meadowcroft of the 90BS out of Zandery Field, Surinam was flying a patrol to search for a reported U-Boat when the crew spotted a dark shape moving slowly beneath the surface. Meadowcroft turned and dove into the attack dropping four depth charges in a perfect pattern. As the crew watched for a result they saw an oil slick come to the surface but closer inspection identified it as the mangled remains of a whale. There were at least three confirmed "whale kills' in the Caribbean but how many other whale oil slicks seen after a depth charge attack were reported as a possible U-Boat sinking? In reality the large majority of patrols were routine and thousands of hours were flown looking over an empty ocean, especially after the summer of 1942 when the Germans withdrew most of their U-Boats from American waters.

Aerial Escort of Convoys
Aerial convoy escort while universally loathed by aircrews because of its defensive nature became essential to keep the U-Boats at bay especially after the establishment of the coastal convoy system which initially ran from Chesapeake Bay to Key West and before long extended into the Caribbean and Latin America.

Killer-Hunt/Hunter-Killer Search Operations
Later, the Air Force favored the offensive killer-hunt search operations using their newly developed anti-submarine tactics and equipment. These patrols extended hundreds of miles from the coast in an attempt to keep reported U-Boats submerged and on the defensive, away from the convoys. Accurate navigation, dependable communications, and constant vigilance by either human eye or radar was again required and then the ability to make quick and decisive attacks when the rare U-Boat was encountered. With experience and time navigation, communications, and radar equipment and their use all improved. If the patrolling Army aircraft was unsuccessful in its attack it would radio the position of the U-Boat, not only to other AAF units, but also to the Navy that would post-warships and aircraft to the area to maintain contact and continue its unremitting hunter-killer operation. The offensive killer-hunt and hunter-killer operations required large numbers of aircraft and shipping which had to be taken from defensive convoy escort and patrols and so it was not used extensively until mid-1943 when patrolling aircraft off escort carriers very successfully employed this tactic in conjunction with the Ultra code breaking U-Boat intelligence. The Navy killer-hunt and the Army Air Force hunter-killer systems required close collaboration of the two armed forces which was difficult due to the unfortunate inter-

service rivalry that had existed early in the war and continued on to a lessening degree as the war progressed. The Navy had control over the American anti-submarine organization and thus the use of the AAF's land-based patrol aircraft. To Army aircrew's chagrin, the Navy had employed AAF aircraft on everlasting and fruitless search and convoy patrols off the eastern US coast and then over the Caribbean. The important story of the Army/Navy contest for administrative control will be discussed at length.

First U-Boat Sunk by US Depth Charges
On 1 March 1942, Ens. William Tepuni was piloting a Lockheed Hudson PBO-1 (A-28B) of VP 82/Patrol Wing 7 (PatWing-7) from his base at NAS Argentia, Newfoundland in support for convoy ON-72. The Hudson was one of 20 diverted Lend-Lease Hudson IIIA's used by the USN to equip one ASW squadron. U-Boat U-656 was spotted in the North Atlantic south of Cape Race and was sunk by the Hudson's two 325 pound depth charges with all hands for America's first U-Boat sinking. Two weeks later VP-82 pilot, Chief Aviation Machinist's Mate Donald Mason, sank U-503 southeast of the Virgin Rocks in the North Atlantic. (Note: VP-82

Lt. Robert Williams, piloting his Grumman TBF Avenger of VC-13 off the *USS Core*, was credited with sinking three U-Boats within a six week period to become America's leading aerial U-Boat "Ace." (Author)

claimed that it had sunk a U-Boat off Cape Race on 28 January 1942, but postwar examination of German records do not indicate any losses during this period.)

Lt. Robert Williams, USN Depth Charge "Ace"
Lt. Robert Williams piloting his Grumman TBF Avenger of VC-13 off the *USS Core* was credited with sinking three U-Boats within a six week period. His first success occurred on 13 July 1943, when the his TBF and F4F attack team came upon "milk cow" supply U-487 that was detected southwest of the Azores after a planned refueling was reported by an ULTRA code-breaking unit. The Wildcat piloted by Lt.(jg.) Earl Steiger made the initial strafing run on the completely surprised U-487 as some crewmen were seen sun-bathing on deck so no AA fire was encountered. Williams made his attack and placed four depth charges that straddled the boat which came to stop in a large patch of oil; mortally wounded. Steiger went into a second strafing attack but was hit by AA fire and crashed fatally nearby. Two other Wildcats arrived and strafed the U-Boat allowing a second Avenger piloted by Lt.(jg.) J.F. Schoby to drop four depth charges directly on target, sinking it. The 33 rescues survivors reported that their boat was the U-487.

The next day Williams attacked another U-Boat with one depth bomb exploding near enough to cause an oil slick but the U-Boat submerged and escaped with "possible damage." Then two days later on the 16th Williams spotted a surfaced U-Boat (U-67) at nine miles and raced in, releasing his depth charges, one exploding directly under the German causing it to rapidly sink. Williams continued to circle the scene to direct a destroyer to rescue the three survivors.

After five and a half weeks on routine patrol, Williams scored his third victory when his radioman reported spotting a U-Boat. After the Wildcats strafed the German, Williams dropped his four depth charges causing black smoke to pour from the conning tower and to list sharply. The F4Fs made a number of strafing attacks after which the crew abandoned ship. The 30 survivors of the U-185 were rescued suffering from the effects of the chlorine gas that had escaped when William's depth charges ruptured the U-Boat's battery room. (Note: S/L Terence Bullock of Britain's Coastal Command flying in B-24 Liberators sunk four U-Boats and damaged two others.)

USN Depth Bomb Expenditure by Aircraft Type, Tonnage, and Year

Carrier-Based				Land-Based			
Tonnages				Tonnages			
1942	1943	1944	1945	1942	1943	1944	1945
8	60	668	36	6	19	N/A	368

6

Aerial Mines

History of Mines and Mining

Ralph Rabbards formulated the first plan for a sea mine and presented his design to English Queen Elizabeth I in 1574 but it was not implemented. Later the Dutch inventor Cornelius Drebble was engaged by English King Charles I to work in the Office of Ordnance to develop weapons, including a "floating petard" which was tried unsuccessfully by the English at the Siege of La Rochelle in 1627.

The earliest reference to the successful use of mine warfare occurred in the 16th century when the Chinese used floating timed explosives loaded in wooden boxes sealed with putty against Japanese Wokou Pirates. The "The Exploitation of the Works of Nature" (Tiangong Kaiwu) treatise, written by in 1637 AD, described mines released by an individual hidden on the shore who pulled a rip cord that instigated a mechanism that produced sparks and ignited the fuse of the mine.

During the American Revolutionary War David Bushnell invented the first practical mine, "Bushnell's Keg" which was called a torpedo. It was a watertight keg filled with black powder and a flintlock percussion detonator suspended from a float. It was first used in 1777 when Gen. George Washington directed that a number of the kegs to be set adrift in a failed attempt to destroy a fleet of British warships anchored in the Delaware River off Philadelphia.

In 1812 Russian engineer Pavel Shilling exploded an underwater mine using an electrical circuit. In 1854, during the unsuccessful attempt by the Anglo-French fleet to seize the Kronstadt fortress, British steamships HMS *Merlin*, *Vulture*, and *Firefly* were damaged by underwater explosions of Russian naval mines designed by Moritz von Jacoby in the Gulf of Finland during the Crimean War.

Early mines continued to be called torpedoes into the American Civil War as self-propelled torpedoes had not yet been invented. These torpedoes were contact mines, floating on or below the water surface using an air-filled demijohn (glass vessel used for fermenting alcoholic beverages) or similar flotation device. In this period, torpedoes floated freely on the surface or were bottom-moored just below the surface. They were detonated when struck by a ship, or after a set time, but were generally unreliable. R.Adm. David Farragut led his ironclad, *USS Tecumseh*, into Mobile Bay and was sunk by a tethered contact mine (torpedo). When his squadron halted, afraid of hitting additional torpedoes, Farragut encouraged his men to push forward, with his famous "Damn the torpedoes, full speed ahead!"

During the Civil War mines were first successfully used by both sides. The first ship sunk by a mine was the Union ironclad *USS Cairo* on 12 December 1862 in the Yazoo River, near Vicksburg. In 1863, the

Confederate Congress established the Torpedo Service, whose mission was to sow Southern waterways with Bushnell's Kegs. These mines were susceptible to leaking and defective detonators but were easy and inexpensive to manufacture. Confederate mines struck 43 Union ships during the war of which 27 sank. A spar torpedo was a mine attached

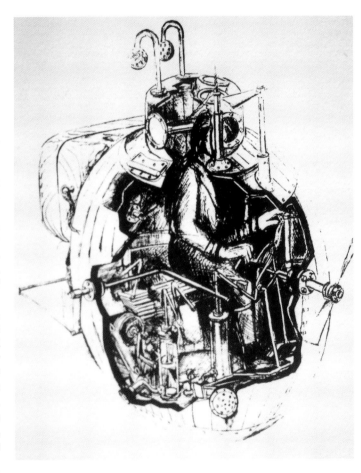

During the American Revolution **David Bushnell** invented the first practical mine, "Bushnell's Keg" which was called a torpedo. It was a watertight keg filled with black powder and a flintlock percussion detonator suspended from a float. (Author)

to a long pole and detonated when the ship carrying it rammed another one which is what Confederate submarine *Hunley* used to sink the *USS Housatonic* on 17 February 1864.

The next major use of mines was during the Russo-Japanese War of 1904 when on 13 April the Russian battleship *Petropavlovsk* was sunk killing the fleet commander, Adm. Stepan Marakov and most of the crew during the siege of Port Arthur. Later two Japanese battleships were sunk by Russian mines in one day. Many of these early mines were fragile and dangerous to handle, with glass containers filled with nitroglycerine or mechanical devices that activated them upon tipping causing several mine-laying ships to be destroyed when their cargo exploded.

Naval mines became well-developed and widely used during World War I. Initially contact mines were used in which a ship had to physically strike one of the mines to detonate it. These mines were usually tethered at the end of a cable just below the surface of the water but drifting mines were also used. In five months during 1918 American and British ships sowed over 72,000 mines in a 250 mile wide minefield between Scotland and Norway to stop German U-boats.

Prior to and during World War I most of the Royal Navy mines were of the spherical, moored, horned type. Direct ship contact with any one of the horns initiated an electrical current which detonated the mine. The British were credited with inventing the first magnetic mine and using it operationally off the Belgian coast in August and September 1918. They were not a great success with many of them unintentionally detonating shortly after deployment. They were categorized as influence ground mines because they were laid on the sea beds of shallow inshore waters where they waited until the firing system was triggered by the inherent magnetism of an unsuspecting enemy vessel.

British mine development virtually ceased when the war ended and little progress was made until rearmament demands in the mid-1930s influenced the Admiralty to authorize developmental work on a moored magnetic mine for use against submarines which had posed a major threat during World War I and were seen as a similar threat in any future war.

Air Laid Mines: A Background

The first recorded aerial minelaying in combat occurred during the night of 20 November 1939, when nine Heinkel 59 floatplanes were dispatched to lay mines in the Thames Estuary. Five had navigation difficulties and returned to base but the other four aircraft laid seven mines that night and 34 more in the following two days. However, two of the mines dropped on the third attempt fell into shallow water and the British recovered Germany's new secret magnetic mine.

During the war, Germany was probably the most innovative user of mines; however the Nazis never had a mining strategy that allowed the

weapon to be decisive. The Germans were the first to lay mines by aircraft; first to put each new type of influence mine (magnetic, acoustic, pressure, and their combinations) into combat; and first to use ship counters and delayed arming features on mine fuses. The Nazis airdropped mine program suffered from the perpetual rivalry between the German Navy and Goering's *Luftwaffe* which controlled all strategic aircraft, including those assigned maritime duties. The chronic dispute over missions and the unenthusiastic nature of *Luftwaffe*'s support for the anti-shipping role, limited the success of German naval war although overall, the Germans laid an imposing 223,000 mines in World War II, mostly from surface ships, which sank 576 British vessels. The total could have been much higher if aircraft would have laid mines in the busy waters off the English coast which could not be approached by Kriegsmarine vessels.

Almost all Allied aerial mining in the ETO was done by the Bomber Command which laid 47,307 mines, 80% of the total offensive effort. In 1936, Arthur Harris, then a young officer in the Air Ministry, had been the first to advance the idea of air dropped magnetic mines. The first order for 30 air-dropped, trial magnetic mines was placed by the Admiralty in July 1939. This mine was intended to be free-dropped from torpedo bomber aircraft but trials showed that the dropping aircraft (Beauforts, Swordfish, or Albacore) did not have the necessary range to reach enemy sea lanes. The longer range Hampden aircraft were tried which necessitated a major mine modification to accommodate the increased speed and height of dropping. In 1939, Harris was the CO of the Hampden-equipped No.5 Group which became the only aerial minelaying bomber unit. To reduce damage from impact with the water the mine was fitted with a nose fairing and drogue parachute which slowed its rate of descent. The trials were completed in March 1940, and production MkI 1,500 Pound A (Airborne), model of the modified mine, became available to the RAF in early April. The first British aerial minelaying operation was carried out by the Hampdens of 5 Group, Bomber Command, on the night of 13/14 April 1940, when they laid 14 mines off the Danish coast five months after the *Luftwaffe* had dropped its first magnetic mines in British waters. Once Harris became Bomber Command Commander-in-Chief in 1942 he increased the number of mines delivered to just over 1,000 total in all of 1941 and to an average of 1,000 per month for the remainder of the war. The expertise of British aerial minelaying development was shared with the Americans who expanded and improved them for their needs. For about 5% of all Bomber Command sorties flown during the war, the RAF claimed 762 Axis ships sunk and 196 damaged. Altogether 260,000, mostly defensive, British mines were laid by air and sea in the ETO causing 1,590 ship losses. As well as sinking ships, mines disrupted goods and weapons shipment on inland and coastal waterways and tied up a large German minesweeping force, which comprised 40% all German naval operations by 1945.

For much of the war, the British led the Americans in mine technology, tactics, and employment. At a time when America had no viable mines, mine policy, or mine doctrine England shared its mine research and combat experience furnishing samples of their own mines and captured superior German mines. In June 1940 the American magnetic mine was so inferior to the German sample mines furnished by the British that the Americans decided to copy the German mine and subsequently designated it as the Mark 12. When America entered the war the Navy's most immediate interest centered on rebuilding its Fleet that was virtually destroyed at Pearl Harbor. Minelaying simply did not play a significant role in such plans. The only American mining entity in September 1941 was the Mine Warfare Desk under the Office of the Chief of Naval Operations (CNO) that planned defensive mining and response to enemy laid mines. As late as 1942, the USN had no single bureau to plan and direct mine warfare which was still was not appreciated for its offensive potential. It was not

The first recorded aerial minelaying in combat occurred during the night of 20 November 1939, when nine Heinkel 59 floatplanes were dispatched to lay mines in the Thames Estuary. (AFHRC)

until January 1943 that the CNO made the Mine Warfare Desk an official section of his staff and gave it a role in plans and policy.

During 1942 there was some work was being done on developing mines but most of the US mining program centered on defending against mines, research and development, and training. The training of personnel from technicians to aircrews to commanding officers was to play an important role in future mining operations. Many AAF officers were included in the Naval training program and when large-scale AAF mining operations began in December 1944, many important members of the Wing and Group staffs and Command Headquarters had already been through mining training courses. In 1941 and 1942 laboratory scientists began developing mines that would not become available until 1944-45. By 1942, a small group in the Naval Ordnance Laboratory (NOL) and Navy Department began to envision a strategic mining campaign against Japan's "Outer Zone" and then against Japan itself, the "Inner Zone."

Classification of Mines
General Classification
There are two general classes of military mines: land mines, under Army control, and sea mines, under Navy control.

Classification by Use
There were three primary uses of mines: offensive, defensive, and psychological:

Offensive mines were sown in enemy waters, outside its harbors and along important shipping routes to sink its merchant and military ships.

Defensive minefields were laid to protect coastal and harbor areas from enemy ships and submarines and force them into areas that were easier to defend. Minefields designed for psychological effect were usually placed in shipping lanes and were used to stop maritime supply to the enemy.

Psychological mine fields were thinly spread to create an impression of random minefields laid over large areas. A single mine found along a shipping lane could stop shipping for days until the entire area was swept.

Classification by Position in the Water
Mines fell into three categories when classified to the position they occupied in the water: bottom mines, moored mines, and drifting mines.

Bottom Mines: These mines were influence activated and rested at the bottom of shallow water where they were most effective. A typical bottom mine consisted of an explosive case and a firing mechanism. A large negative buoyancy (i.e. tendency to sink) brought the bottom mine to rest on the ocean floor and held it there. In very deep waters, vessels on the surface could pass over the mine without activating its firing mechanisms or, if activated, without experiencing much damage but this mine would be effective against submarines.

Moored Mines: A typical moored mine used an anchor which was located on the front of the mine. Upon impact with the bottom, the anchor section broke away and the remainder of the mine rose upwards on a tether cable until it reached its predetermined depth. They were used for deep water embedding and were effective against both surface vessels and submarines. The moored mine's explosive charge and firing mechanism were contained in a positive-buoyancy case (i.e., one that tends to float). Influence-type mines contained a magnetometer, search coil, hydrophone, or pressure-sensitive device that was able to detect specific classes of ships.

Drifting Mines: This mine floated freely at or near the surface as their buoyancy was approximately neutral and thus had no anchoring devices. The depth at which this mine traveled was determined by one of three methods: by suspending the mine from a small float, by integrating a mechanical depth-control device, or by attaching a cable or chain that dragged on the bottom in shallow water. Drifting mines were banned under the Hague Convention of 1907 but were occasionally used in World War I and II. A moored mine that lost its tether cable became an unintentional drifting mine.

Method of Activation
Mines could be activated by contact, target influence, or remote control.

Contact Activation
Activation of a contact mine only occurred when the target ship actually touched the mine or one of its sensitive components. The contact point could be the mine case, a horn, an antenna, a snag line, or a protruding arm, depending on the particular type of mine. Contact firing mechanisms were then classified as electrochemical, galvanic, or mechanical:

Electrochemical contact mines possessed delicate protruding horns, each containing a glass vial of acid. The vial broke when any horn was forcibly struck with the acid then providing the electrolyte to the plates of a battery cell that generated sufficient current to fire the detonator.

Galvanic contact firing mechanisms used current drawn from a sea battery formed by the immersion of two dissimilar metals, usually copper and steel, in sea water which formed a weak electrolyte that was used to fire the mine. The copper was in the firing mechanism while the steel was either in the target's hull or in a mine component that required a blow from a target's hull to place it in a closed electrical system with the copper.

Mechanical contact firing mechanisms were normally triggered by the inertia of impact, or by the mechanical movement of a protruding horn, arm, or bridle. The contact area of this type of mechanism was sometimes increased by the use of snag lines.

Influence Activation
The nearby presence of a ship, rather than actual contact, was all that is necessary, under certain conditions, to activate an influence mine. The three classes of influence firing mechanisms were the magnetic, acoustic, and pressure types.

Magnetic Mines: The actuating influence in a magnetic firing mechanism was the magnetic effect of a cruising steel ship. Magnetic mines utilized a magnetic search coil or magnetometer to detect passing ships. The older, heavier search coils were used in bottom mines to detect changes in the earth's magnetic field caused by passing vessels. The later magnetometers were often used in moored mines and could detect ships or submarines in any direction.

Acoustic Mines used a hydrophone to detect the sounds originating from ships and submarines, including engine and propeller noises. Such sounds had to meet specific requirements, including frequency band and had to increase in volume at a prescribed rate or the mine would ignore them.

Pressure Mines: A ship in motion created an area of reduced or negative underwater pressure, to which the pressure mechanism responded. Pressure mines used electro-hydraulic pressure sensors to detect ships or submarines. The pressure sensor waited for the underwater pressure drop associated with the passing of a vessel and, if the targeted vessel was displacing enough water, the mine activated.

Note: In practice, influence mines could contain two of the three types of influence devices while others could contain an influence element and a contact one. If contact or influence elements were combined with a control element, the two could be independent of each other, or control could be exercised to render a given mine safe or dangerous at the will of the control station.

Remote Activation
These mine were operated by a cable or radio connected to the shore.

Method of Deployment
Mines could be deployed by surface vessels, submarines, or aircraft.

Surface Vessels
Any mine type could be deployed by a surface ship such as a destroyer or the purpose-built minelayer. It should be noted that by using appropriate modifications, aircraft-laid mines (less flight gear) and submarine-laid mines could be planted by surface craft.

Submarine
Specially configured submarine-laid mines were normally used in offensive operations and were launched from the torpedo tubes. Although submarines could transport mines long distances from their home ports, they carried limited numbers of them which was a tactical disadvantage. But a greater advantage of the submarine was that it could secretly operate at great distances to enter enemy waters normally denied to surface ships or aircraft because of the distance, enemy defensive forces, and weather or sea conditions. Submarines laying mines in shallow waters or enemy harbors were vulnerable to enemy detection and attack.

Aircraft
Mines weren't successfully sowed by aircraft until World War II at which time the many advantages of air release became evident. Almost any aircraft that carried bombs could also lay mines. Aircraft could lay mines suddenly and in great quantity and provided the means for replenishing minefields over an extended period of time without danger from previously laid mines. Also, planes could lay mines in shallow bodies of water, including rivers and harbors which could not be navigated by submarines or surface mine-laying vessels.

Specially constructed aircraft-laid mines were generally used in offensive operations and were dropped from aircraft like a bomb. To decrease water-impact velocity a parachute pack and release gear functioned was employed. As the mine struck the water, or submerged to a given depth, the release gear freed the mine case from the parachute, after which the parachute and mine then sunk individually from each other. Other impact-decreasing gear also included tail fins which provided stability during flight and free fall, while nose fairings could also be used to reduce drag.

Like bombs, air-laid mines were equipped with arming wires that maintained the mines in a safe condition until they were released from the aircraft. However, at the instant a mines was released from the aircraft's bomb rack, the arming wires were withdrawn, leaving the mine with the potential to arm. On the other hand, should it become necessary to jettison the mine in a safe condition, the pilot actuated solenoids that allowed the arming wires to fall intact with the mine.

Aerial Mines Described
Major Components
Case
The mine case provided a watertight compartment for the main charge and the firing mechanisms. The main charge was cast into the main compartment and in the case of bottom mines filled most of it. For moored or drifting mines, the case had to be large enough to provide air space for buoyancy. Smaller compartments within the case housed and secured the batteries, firing mechanism, and various accessories. Mine cases were usually made of steel, but a nonferrous metal was required when certain influence firing mechanisms were to be used. Some mines had attached fairings designed to improve the streamlining of the case and make the mine's trajectory easier to predict.

Most of the standard naval mine cases accommodated a choice of explosive fillers and a choice of various firing mechanisms and accessories. Because of this, the Mark designation of the mine usually applied only to the assembled case and anchor. On the other hand, a specific modification of a production mine usually designated its explosive filler, firing mechanism, accessories, and the special features which adapt this mine to surface, submarine, or aircraft planting.

Explosive Filler
US mines were filled with TNT, Torpex, or HBX. (See *US Aerial Armament of World War 2: Volume 2: Bombs. Bombsights, and Bombing* for a detailed discussion of explosive fillers.)

Anchors
Anchors for the various moored mines obviously differed in size, shape, and function. All anchors had to be able to moor the mine at a preset depth below the surface. For ease in handling, the anchor was assembled integrally with the case. Aircraft- and submarine-laid moored mines had the anchor secured firmly enough to the case to allow the mine to be lifted by either end or by a strap in the middle. Note that the surface-laid assembly had net positive buoyancy until the mine and case was separated, flooding the anchor. Conversely, aircraft-laid or submarine-laid assemblies, which are employed in offensive mining operations in enemy waters, had net negative buoyancy and never reached the surface after

An armorer prepares to insert the two hydrostatic (water pressure) devices that armed mines. Like bombs, aircraft mines had arming wires attached to the mine laying aircraft which were threaded through these hydrostatic devices to keep them in their unarmed condition. (AAF)

planting. The submarine-laid assemblies sank to a minimum depth of 65 feet and further incorporated a few seconds of delay before separation of case and anchor.

Arming Devices

Arming wires

Like bombs, aircraft mines had arming wires which were threaded through the delay devices to keep them in their unarmed condition. The "bitter ends" of the wires were attached to the mine-laying aircraft. The bombardier operated the bomb release controls which pulled the arming wires from the mine at the instant of release.

Hydrostatic (water pressure) Arming Devices

Mines were not armed by air travel as bombs were but by two hydrostatic (water pressure) devices similar to those used on depth bombs. The Extender, which was located in the deepest pocket of the mine, armed the explosive train of the mine by placing an electric detonator in the booster charge. An Extender was a hydrostatically operated device used to move the mine's detonator into the booster charge. Until the mine was planted, the extender held the detonator from the booster charge to prevent the premature firing of the detonator from exploding the booster or the mine. After the mine was planted and arrived at a certain depth, the extender moved the detonator into an envelope in the booster.

A Clock Delay Mechanism (CDM) was a device which delayed the arming of the mine for a preset time after planting. Basically it was a spring driven cam that operated electrical contacts or switches. The Clock Delay used at least two switches to arm a mine. Closing of the first switch connected the battery to the firing mechanism while the second switch closed three or more hours after the first, to complete the circuit from the firing mechanism to the detonator. There were two distinct types: a hand-wound clock which was started by the mechanical action of a hydrostatic clock starter and a motor-wound clock which was started by closure of one of the switches of the hand-wound clock that always had to be used

with it. Hand-wound clocks could be set to provide a delay in arming of a half day to 10 days, and motor-wound clocks could provide a delay of three to 100 days. In addition, motor-wound clocks had a "sterilizing switch," which could be used to end the armed life of the mine three to 210 days from the time of planting.

A Clock Starter Mechanism (CSM) was a hydrostatically operated device which could start or stop the operation of a clock delay mechanism. The clock starter, which was in the shallow pocket of the mine, started a clock which after 45 minutes connected the electric detonator to the firing mechanism and also armed the firing mechanism. This clock could only run while the clock starter was either manually depressed or when it was under water, so that the clock starter had to be operated for a total of 45 minutes before the electrical system could arm. Both the clock starter and extender had to be at least 16 feet under water to operate and would retract if pressure was removed.

Black wooden washers were always placed in the clock starters and extenders to prevent inexperienced personnel or impact from activating them. To keep the mine from arming even when underwater the washers were always kept in place until the mines were ready to be loaded. Immediately before hoisting the mines onto the bomb racks the wooden washers were replaced with white or brightly colored water soluble washers by the ordnance crews. These washers were made of a salt which dissolved within a few minutes when in water. It was necessary that the arming devices be dry when the washers were installed. If the mines were removed from the aircraft after loading the soluble washers had to be replaced by the wooden washers before transporting them back to the dump.

Parachute Equipment

Parachute Pack

To reduce the impact when aerial mines hit water they used a six foot diameter parachute. The parachute pack was folded inside a plastic dish that fit the contoured end of the mine case to which it was bolted. The

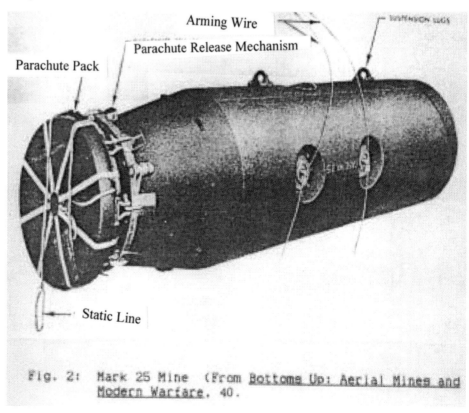

Parachute Pack The parachute pack was folded inside a plastic dish that fit the contoured of the end of the mine case to which it was bolted. The canvas cover had eight sectors or flaps and risers attached the parachute and the pack to the release mechanism. (AAF)

Fig. 2: Mark 25 Mine (From Bottoms Up: Aerial Mines and Modern Warfare. 40.

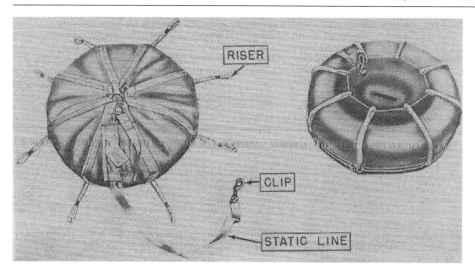

Parachute Pack Mk3 Mod0 with Parachute Mk3 Mod2 (AAF)

canvas cover had eight sectors or flaps and risers attached the parachute and the pack to the release mechanism.

Parachute Static Line

The static line prevented the parachute from opening dangerously close to the releasing aircraft. After the mines were loaded onto the bomb racks by the armament crews it was necessary for the ordnance crews to attach the parachute static lines to the aircraft. It was necessary to follow instructions in attaching static lines to prevent premature opening or failures of the parachutes. Most of the parachute static lines had a small clasp on the end which was to be fastened to the aircraft. On parachute static lines without clasps it was necessary to tie the end of the line to a part of the aircraft that was at least 1/4 inch in diameter or to a clasp of another static line. The length of the line was never to be shortened, and the end had to be attached to a smooth surface free of sharp edges. While one end of this line was securely attached to the releasing craft; the other end was attached by "break" cord to the parachute. When the mine was released from the aircraft the length of the static line pulled the parachute from the dish and immediately the break cord severed and freed the parachute from the static line.

Parachute Release Mechanism

If the parachute remained with the mine after water entry, it could foul the mine mechanisms and could possibly roll or drag the mine to cause a premature explosion. To prevent this from occurring a release mechanism was used which disconnected the parachute from the mine when it hit the water. The ordnance crews assembled the parachute and release to the mine. This release consisted of two semicircular straps which fit around the mine case and were held together by a bolt on one side and a lead weighted pin on the other side. The lead weight always had to be on the forward side of the release. When the mine hit the water the lead weight pulled the pin out of the release and the paddles on the two straps wiped the release off the mine. In order for the release to stay on the mine during descent and to come off after water impact it was absolutely necessary that the bands were tightened to the correct tension. The release mechanism could be oriented in any convenient position on the case as long as the paddles were placed directly over the lugs welded on the mine case.

The parachute was centered on the mine case by a small pin on the center of the tail plate and was held on to the release by several shackles. On some mines a small well was located in the center of the tail plate. On these mines a circular plate which fit into this well had to be screwed into the parachutes before installation. The parachute was opened upon

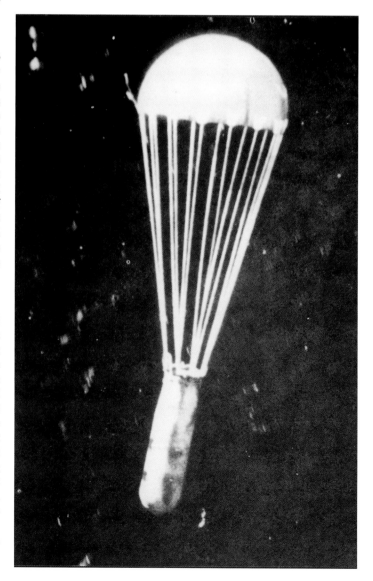

To reduce the impact when aerial mines hit water they used a six foot diameter parachute. The parachute was opened upon dropping by a static line which was attached to some fixed portion of the aircraft. (AAF)

dropping by a static line which was attached to some fixed portion of the aircraft. It was necessary that the parachute be oriented on the mine as instructed, so that the static cord would leave from the top of the pocket of the parachute. For correct operation the parachute and soluble washers had to be absolutely dry.

Later Parachute Release Mechanism
The later release mechanism secured the parachute to the mine until it entered the water. Upon striking the surface of the water the two impact plates pulled out the release pins that had been holding the two halves of the release mechanism together. Then the flat springs, located between the release mechanism and the mine case, forced the two halves of the mechanism apart and allowed the mine to sink free of the parachute.

Mine Accessories
The accessories of a mine included a number of units which assisted or modified the action of the actual firing mechanism. Some of the accessories were assembly and testing devices, safety devices, while others served to increase the efficiency of the planted mine.

Terminal Block (TB)
The terminal block was a device that significantly added to the ease of assembling a mine and testing its various circuits. The circuits, batteries, firing mechanisms, and various other electrical accessories were connected at this block. The block (or the main block, if the mine had more than one) was located immediately under the main cover leading to the firing mechanism so that it was quickly available for final electrical tests and for the connection of the detonator leads immediately prior to the sealing of the mine.

Batteries
Batteries used in a mine had to supply the voltages and power to operate the firing mechanism and set off the detonator. All naval mine batteries were dry-cells, comprised of several cells stored in a housing. The life of the mine was mainly determined by the life of the batteries.

Safety Mechanisms
Both clock starters and the extender mechanisms used some type of safety device to prevent them from operating prematurely. For safety in handling and stowage, safety nuts were always provided to keep extenders and clock starters in the unarmed condition and had to be removed before planting or the mine would not arm. Aircraft-laid mines used an arming wire that had to be pulled free of the mechanism (for surface-laid mines a soluble washer prevented a spindle attached to the hydrostatic piston from moving inward until the washer had been dissolved by the sea water while submarine-laid mines had a positive-locking safety bar which was released when the mine was ejected from a torpedo tube).

Anti-Countermining Device (AC)
An anti-countermining device was occasionally used to discontinue the mine's electrical circuits for a short time following a nearby shock or explosion.

Ship Counter (SED)
A Ship Counter formerly was termed as a Ship Eliminator Device (SED). It was used to delay firing of the detonator until a pre-set number of complete activations of the firing mechanism occurred. A number of ships passed over the mine before it became armed, reducing the effectiveness of the enemy's mine sweeping activities.

Sterilizer (SD mechanism)
A sterilizer self-destructive mechanism was used to limit the armed life of a mine to a predetermined period of time. Sterilization periods could vary over a wide span of time ranging from a few days or only after the mine's useful life has been spent. There were numerous methods of sterilizing a mine but it was usually done by shorting out the battery. This was the most decisive type of sterilizer and consisted of an electrolytic cell, a resistor, a spring-loaded plunger, and switches associated with the plunger. As current surged through the cell, the anode was electrolyzed away until it was amply weakened for the plunger to rupture the cell. The movement of the plunger closed two open switches which shorted out the battery. Other methods included: opening the detonator circuit; sterilizing switches also were occasionally incorporated in a clock delay mechanism; and in the case of a moored mine, it could function to fire a sinking detonator which blew out a plug that allowed water to enter the case. When a complete sterilization of a mine field had to be completed by a certain date (i.e. to allow the voyage of friendly vessels) two or more sterilizers were to be connected in parallel in each mine to be sure that each mine was destroyed.

Influence Firing Mechanisms
Influence firing mechanisms were the devices that were detonated by contact with a target ship or received a small impulse from the search coil, microphone, or pressure device; and sent a magnified firing impulse to the detonator. The mechanism had to obviously fire the mine only when a legitimate target passed by and then amplify the original signal to an impulse strong enough to trigger the firing circuit. The reason firing mechanisms were so complicated was that they were designed to avoid activation by enemy (i.e. mine sweeping). There were three classes of influence firing mechanisms: magnetic, acoustic, and pressure:

Magnetic Mechanisms
The magnetic proximity fuse that detected changes in the earth's magnetic field produced by the presence of ships was also developed at Bell Laboratories during World War II. Since magnetic alloys, particularly Permalloy, were important to the development of magnetic fuses Dr. G.W. Elmen, the retired Bell Laboratories' inventor of Permalloy, was engaged by the Naval Ordnance Laboratory to work jointly with the engineers at Bell Laboratories on magnetic mine fuses.

While the principal was simple, Bell Labs found its development and manufacture to be very difficult. The fundamental elements of the mine fuse were the Search Coil (SC) that detected feeble changes caused in the earth's magnetic field around the mine by the approaching magnetic field of a moving ship. The coil consisted of 15,000 to 30,000 turns of fine copper wire wound over a cylindrical core of high-permeability magnetic alloy, such as Permalloy. A search coil was always used with a steel mine case because the steel added to the effective size of the permeable core. The magnetic amplifier increased the strength of the detected feeble signal about a million times. Both the search coil and the magnetic amplifier required precise manufacture using a very high quality Permalloy.

After the mine was dropped from aircraft into enemy waters, its operation was very straightforward; it was armed by the usual arming devices and started its search. When a steel ship moved over it, the steady earth's magnetic field surrounding the mine was changed and generated a voltage in the search coil and the resulting signal current disturbed a delicate balance in the magnetic amplifier circuit. It first shifted slowly away from the normal steady condition as the ship approached and then moved slowly back to normal as the ship moved away. The fuse mechanism recognized the passing ship whenever it detected a magnetic disturbance with a slow flux change that caused an explosion when the ship was over the mine. The mine was provided with an innovative anti-sweep element, protection for counter-mining, and was equipped with a mechanical memory so that it could be set to blow up a particular numbered ship in a convoy, rather than to just destroy the first ship.

Every steel ship had definite magnetic characteristics produced by the permanent magnetism of the ship's hull and the induced magnetism resulting from passage through the earth's magnetic field. A ship's magnetic field could be significantly decreased by using degaussing coils, often in conjunction with the process of "deperming" (neutralizing the permanent magnetism of a ship). However, for practical and theoretical reasons it was impossible to eliminate these fields entirely even from ships of medium size.

Magnetic mine-firing mechanisms were of two general types: magnetic dip-needle and induction:

Dip-Needle Mechanisms

The activating unit of the needle-type mechanism was a magnetized needle assembly which reacted to changes produced in the vertical component of the magnetic field by the proximity of a vessel. Once the mine was laid, a very slight movement of the needle could fire the firing circuit.

Induction Mechanisms

The induction-type mechanisms used a search coil and a method of amplifying the signal from the search coil. Some induction mechanisms used a sensitive relay for amplification while others used an extremely complicated electronic or electronic-mechanical system. The needle-type mechanism basically functioned upon the magnitude of change in the magnetic field, whereas mechanisms of the induction type could require a magnitude of change and a rate of change, two or more activating pulses (called "looks") of opposite polarity, or other special conditions. This element gave the induction mechanism a distinct practical advantage by allowing a wider variety of selective firing. Induction firing mechanisms could be used in "minenonmags" with ferromagnetic cases while needle mechanisms required mine cases of "netic" material (usually aluminum). Induction mines could be made much more sensitive than needle mines.

Acoustic Mechanisms

Acoustic disturbances such as propeller noises, machinery noises, and hull vibration invariably accompanied the passage of a ship through the water. The sound output depended upon several aspects such as the size, type, and number of propellers, the type and speed of the engines, the condition of loading, the character of the bottom, and the depth of the water. A vessel's acoustic signal was therefore variable and acoustic mines had to be designed to prevent an intense signal from activating the firing mechanism at distances well beyond the effective explosive radius of the charge.

Acoustic mines also had to be unresponsive to certain types of underwater sounds that were likely to be non-target objects such as a school of dolphins. Another design requirement was that these mines were not easily activated by countermining noises. Therefore acoustic mines were usually fired by activating the mechanism when the sound intensity reached a predetermined value, after building up at a prescribed rate of change. If the incoming sound developed too quickly, as with an underwater explosion, the mine prevented itself from firing by the action of an auto-countermining device and would become passive for a short time. If the sound built up too slowly, the mine would not respond at all.

Microphones (MI) were used with acoustic firing mechanisms and needed to be particularly sensitive to sounds in the frequency range for which the associated firing mechanisms were designed. They were watertight and extremely rugged and usually of the crystal type.

Pressure Mechanisms

When a ship was moving there was a continuous flow of water from the bow to the stern. As the bow of the moving ship displaced water, an equal amount flowed to the stern of the ship to restore the displaced water after the ship had passed. This continuous water flow was measurable at considerable distances from the ship and created variations in the pressures which normally existed at various depths in the water. The pressure differential became more pronounced when the ship was moving in confined waters such as rivers and channels but continued to be substantial in the open sea, even at considerable depths. The pressure

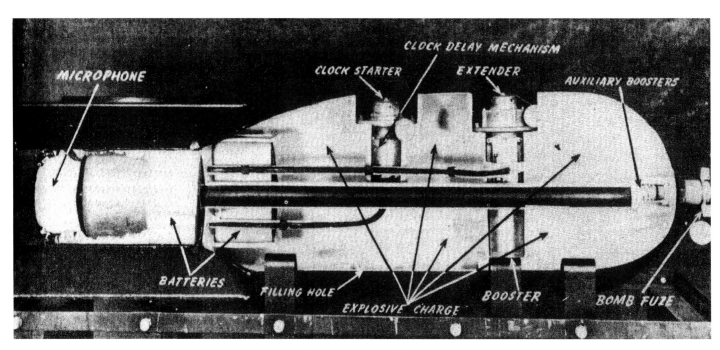

Mark 13 Model 5 Acoustic Mine (AAF)

Types of Aerial Mines

Aerial Mine Designation	Abbrev.	Actuating Mechanism	Availability %	Usage %
Mark 9, Model 1	M-9	Magnetic	--	48%
Mark 13, Model 5, A-3	M-13, A-3	Acoustic	03/45	17%
Mark 25, Model 1, A-5	M-25, A-5	Subsonic	03/45	10%
Mark 25, Model 2, A-6	M-25, A-6	Pressure- magnetic	04/45	25%

signature of a ship was a function of its speed and displacement and the water depth.

Ocean swells and surface waves also produced pressure variations of considerable magnitude; but in a much faster cycle than those of ships. Therefore, to avoid premature firing because of wave action, pressure firing mechanisms were designed to ignore rapid pressure fluctuations. Pressure firing mechanisms were seldom used alone but were generally combined with other influence firing devices.

Types of Aerial Mines

Mark 9 Model 1 Magnetic Mine
The Mark 9 magnetic mines were set off by the change in the earth's magnetic field produced by the iron in the hull of a passing vessel.

Mark 13 Model 5, A-3 Acoustic Mine
The Mark 13 the A-3 acoustic mine detected propeller noise in the acoustic region via a battery-supplied microphone in its tail section. It rested on the bottom at no more than 150 feet and was detonated by the noise of ship's propellers or engines that passed directly overhead. The microphone in the tail electrically influenced the mine's timing mechanism that then operated the firing relay. The only method of sweeping acoustic mines was to produce an artificial noise in the water ahead and all around the minesweeping ship.

Mark 13 Magnetic Mine
This mine was air-dropped with a magnetic pistol and did not use a parachute and could be used as a bomb. It weighed 1,048 pounds and carried a charge of 640 pounds of TNT or weighed 1,118 pounds when carrying a charge of 710 pounds of Torpex.

Mark 25, Models 1-3 Mines
The most adaptable and prolific aerial mine of World War II was the US Navy's Mark 25 magnetic mine that weighed 1,950 to 2,000 pounds including its 1,275 pounds of Torpex, HBX, or TNT explosive. The Mod1 had an A5 acoustic trigger the A-5 operated on ship hull vibration in the subsonic region. The Mod 2 had an A6 pressure trigger, and the Mod 3 also had an acoustic trigger. The A-6 contained a pressure mechanism operating on the reduced water pressure under a ship resulting from its motion. It began production late in the war and had limited operational availability. The A-6 was similar to a mine used with great success off the Normandy beachhead by the Germans. Depending on its flight gear this mine measured 22.4 inches x 87.2 inches. The Mark 25 looked much like a conventional bomb except for the half-slant to the nose that gave it improved underwater trajectory and the circular parachute pack at the tail. After the mine left the bomber a static line opened the parachute that decreased the impact when the mine entered the water. A pair of arming wires passed through small lugs that were recessed in two areas 90° from the two bomb suspension lugs. The smaller 1,000-1,072 pound Mark 26 carried 465 pounds of TNT or 520 pounds of Torpex explosive.

Mining B-29s were equipped with AN/APQ-13 navigational radar for night and bad weather minelaying over featureless waters. The B-29 required only minor modifications to carry the twelve 1,000 pound Mark 26 or seven Mark 25 mines or any combination of the two types. The Mark 25 could be dropped from any altitude above 200 feet at a maximum speed of 230 mph into waters of 16 to 150 feet deep. After the mine came to rest on the sea floor, it armed itself conforming to the preflight settings and then waited for an enemy vessel. The different Mark 25 models were distinguished by particular detonators for magnetic, acoustic or pressure actuation, by clock starters and delays, by ship counters and by redundant safety attributes. The minefield planner would select a Mark 25 model considering the water depth, types of ships and traffic frequency in the area and the enemy minesweeping capabilities. Aerial mines could be adjusted so that a number of ships, usually mine sweepers, were allowed to pass so that the mines could explode under the transports. All mines were equipped with "sterilizing" devices that disarmed them after a specific time.

Mark 15
The Mark 15 was a 19 x 80 inch air-dropped ground mine with an acoustic pistol that weighed 900 pounds and a 500 pound charge of TNT. Production stopped in 1944.

Anti-Sweep Mines
Entering service in 1944, Anti-Sweep mines were often scattered in a minefield along with normal moored mines. They were small 1,125 pound mines with a small two pound charge and moored to float. When the wire of a mine sweeping vessel snagged the mooring wire, the Anti-Sweep mine which had a very small positive buoyancy sunk until it hit the sweep wire; detonating and cutting the sweep wire, stopping the sweeping operation.

Mine Laying Aircraft
Many types of bombers were used for minelaying during the Pacific war in both the so-called Outer Zone and Inner Zone. The Outer Zone comprised of all Pacific areas outside the waters located adjacent to the Japanese Homeland (Inner Zone). Since accuracy was not of primary importance, aerial minelaying was usually carried out utilizing varying levels of darkness as it afforded greater safety to minelaying aircraft and more secrecy to the location of the planted mines. Occasionally, minelaying in the CBI was conducted in daylight during the monsoon season where heavy cloud cover gave the necessary safety and secrecy to the operations. There were several instances where minelaying was conducted in daylight to alert the Japanese that mines were being planted in the area and would be a danger to any ships or submarines attempting to resupply the garrison. Such was the case when aerial mines were employed the only time on a large scale by carrier-borne TBF Avengers during a fast carrier strike by Task Force 58 against the Palau Islands at the end of March 1944. The TBFs of Torpedo Squadrons 2, 8, and 16 laid their mines close to shore in order to suppress numerous Japanese ships plying the area and to prevent them from leaving the anchorage. The Avengers had to fly in low,

A Mk10 MOD5 mine being loaded onto a TBF-1 from the Lexington for mining operations off Palau, March 1944. (USN)

predictable patterns within range of shore-based AA guns and suffered heavy losses and subsequently, minelaying was carried out mainly by long range patrol aircraft or AAF B-24 or B-29 heavy bombers .

In the SWPA PBY-5 Catalinas were used extensively but because of the patrol bomber's low speed and vulnerability, the darkest, moonless nights of the month were usually chosen for operations. Mining approaches were made at less than 100 feet to avoid radar detection with visual drops usually made at 100 feet but up to 500 feet. In the CBI B-24 Liberators were commonly used with drops normally made visually during moonlit nights but some daylight operations were implemented along the Malay Coast during the monsoon season. Later a few radar drops were made along the China Coast. Mines were released at altitudes of 200 to 1,000 feet, mainly depending upon the surrounding terrain. B-29s were used in the CBI with mine drops made visually at altitudes of 2,000 to 8,000 feet

during moonlit periods, although provisions were made for dropping by radar if visibility was bad. The PB4Y-2 operated over Korean ports where they were well-suited to low and medium altitude minelaying.

TBFs and PV-1s operated in the Central and South Pacific and were able to carry a small number of mines for standard mining operations but the Avengers suffered a high proportion of losses for the number of mines they successfully laid. TBFs and PV-1s were used in both daylight and moonlight operations with drops made visually from altitudes of 200 to 1,000 feet. Formation minelaying was developed and found feasible in tactical mining operations. B-24s used visual tactics similar to those used in the CBI, except that formation tactics were used more often.

Early work in radar minelaying was done during the Bonin Island mining operations which led to establishing later B-29 tactics. Radar-equipped B-24Js and Ls of the 42BS/11BG/7AF dropped mines near Chichi Jima and Haha Jima in the Bonin Islands in 1944. The operation was part of *Project Mike*; which was to deny the Japanese anchorages there. The Liberators were equipped with SCR-717B search radar, AN/APQ-5 low altitude bombsight (LAB), and SCR-718 radar altimeter. The weight of the radar equipment was equalize by removing all armament but the tail guns which were supplied with only 200 rounds each which was considered sufficient as the threat from the Japanese fighters in the region was nil. All of *Project Mike's* radar missions carried the 2,000 pound AN Mk25 aerial mine with a six foot parachute. On some low altitude missions, 1,000 pound AN Mk26-1 mines were used, since these lighter mines could be dropped from altitudes as low as 200 feet. The AAF crews used Navy trajectory tables to determine the slant range release data for use with the radar bombsight. Night missions used radar pathfinders to illuminate the target with flares to enable visual mine-laying runs by other aircraft but in heavily defended areas individual radar-equipped B-24s laid mines. In daylight overcast conditions, radar-equipped Liberators were used instead of non-radar equipped aircraft.

The most successful minelaying aircraft was the B-29 Superfortress which was used in both Inner and Outer Zone Operations (in the CBI). In the Inner Zone mining campaign B-29s mined at night, preferably

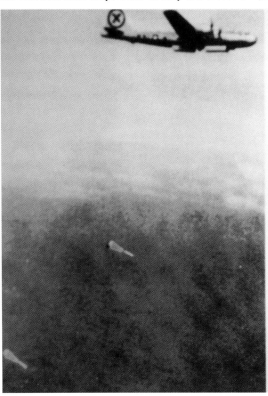

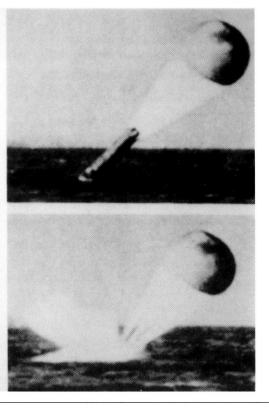

The most successful minelaying aircraft was the **B-29 Superfortress** which was used in both Inner and Outer Zone mining operations. (AAF)

A Mk13 mine being hoisted into the bomb bay of a B-29. The parachute pack is readily seen. (AAF)

on moonless nights and during cloudy or bad weather primarily, using navigation and dropping by radar at altitudes of usually 5,000 to 10,000 feet. If visibility was bad, drops were made by radar at an altitude at least 1,200 feet above surrounding terrain.

Outer Zone Aircraft Mining Performance

A/C Type	A/C Airborne	A/C Successful	A/C Lost	Mines on Target
B-24	1,230	1,077	14	4,981
B-25	46	43	0	101
B-29	176	162	0	987
PBY-5	1,242	1,153	11	2,548
PB2Y-3	5	4	0	12
PB4Y-1	46	31	1	101
PB4Y-2	94	88	0	186
PV-1	48	18	0	18
TBF	344	320	14	320
Totals	**3,231**	**2,896**	**40**	**9,254**

Inner Zone Aircraft Mining Performance

A/C Type	A/C Airborne	A/C Successful	A/C Lost	Mines on Target
B-29	1,529	1,427	15	12,135
Totals	**4,760**	**4,323**	**55**	**21,389**

Results

89.5% of Outer Zone missions were successful with 231 mines laid for a loss of 1.2% of participating aircraft

93.4% of Inner Zone missions were successful with 809 mines laid for a loss of 0.98% of participating aircraft

90.8% of all missions were successful with 407 mines laid for a loss of 1.16% of participating aircraft

Minefield Planning and Mine Laying

When a new weapon was introduced it was important to do so as a surprise and on a large scale before the enemy could develop countermeasures. In an apparent contravention of this principle, offensive minelaying began on a small attritional scale in the Outer Zone. Conditions dictated this situation but later experience confirmed the original hypothesis. In the Outer Zone the threat of a particular type of mine decreased after it had been used for a time. But this did not have the anticipated unfavorable effect on the overall mining campaign in other areas. The various

Japanese commands, particularly local commanders did not readily exchange information on mining and thus high echelons in Japan did not become aware of the increasing danger of mining attacks. When the large scale mining began in the Inner Zone in March 1945, the Japanese were not prepared and were unable to deal with the blockade. Once the final mining attack started and the Japanese finally seriously tried to develop countermeasures but the truth of the surprise/large scale maxim was borne out. The worth of the simple magnetic mine and the audio-frequency mine decreased after their introduction but was minimized by the widespread introduction of magnetic mines with specially adjusted mechanisms. The extensive use of pressure mines and low frequency acoustic mines soon followed and initially rendered Japanese magnetic sweep gear obsolete. The new mine mechanism was so complicated that the Japanese never developed countermeasures for the later types of mines.

Minefield planning depended on many details. All mining missions were radar-controlled with the radar IP and AP points to be selected taking into account the location of the minefield, the surrounding terrain, and any nearby AA opposition. The width of the channel determined the sensitivity of the mine's firing mechanism and the time between each mine release. The type and effectiveness of Japanese countermeasures determined the proper mix of detonators.

The minelaying procedure was for bombers to fly at low altitudes between 5,000 and 8,000 feet to drop mines at night. This scheme eliminated the need for large defensive formations, as bombers flying at night were less likely to be detected by enemy defenses and to be intercepted by enemy fighters. Also, more mines could be carried and could be dropped more accurately and the dropped mines were more likely to remain undetected. Another consideration for night drops was if a B-29 did not return to base, there was 12 hours of daylight for Search and Rescue (SAR) to find the downed crews. AN/APQ-13 radar made the identity of initial and aiming points easy and the bomber would drop its mines in a string. These individual strings of mines created a broad area of water that was dangerous to enemy shipping.

Mine Preparation, Handling, and Loading

There was no method of determining a mine's operational characteristics from its external appearance. All the adjustments controlling the sensitivity of magnetic, acoustic, subsonic, and pressure mechanisms were internal as were the ship-count selectors on magnetic mines and the arming delays and sterilizers on all types.

Identification of Mines

A five symbol code was developed in which the first three symbols specified the type of firing mechanism, its sensitivity adjustment, and the number of actuations required to fire it; the fourth symbol gave the delayed arming interval, and the fifth gave the sterilization period. After each mine was assembled, its code was stenciled in several conspicuous places. All mine assembly orders issued to the Mine Depot specified numbers of mines of each code type. Stowage in the ready ammunition areas was arranged in order of code type.

Duties of Ordnance and Armament Personnel

The duties of ordnance and armament personnel included the preparation of mines and loading. Training was given over only a three week period to all four XXI Bomb Groups. Mine training was necessarily short because at the same time the Wing was flying a maximum effort incendiary operation against the Japanese homeland. Instruction included methods of attaching parachutes to mines, orientation of parachutes in the bomb bay, protection of microphones in acoustic mines, installation of soluble washers and other

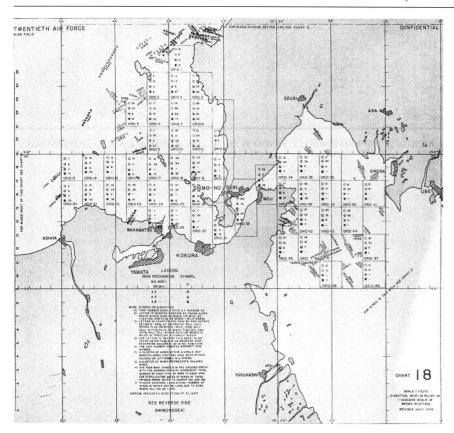

A **minefield map** of Shimonoseki Straits which is divided into sectors that have the number and type of mine laid in that sector entered. (AAF)

safety devices, and methods of securing parachute static cords. Because of the sensitive nature of the Torpex explosive filler careful handling was especially stressed.

Handling and Loading
Handling and loading was more complicated for mines than for bombs. Each mine, selected from among 200 different operational combinations, had to be loaded on a specific bomb station in a particular bomber, whereas bombs could be loaded in any station in any bomber. The first few mining missions were maximum Wing efforts and resulted in traffic backups at the ready-ammunition dumps caused by the simultaneous attempts of many crews to obtain specific types of mines from a small number of revetments. During maximum Wing efforts in a single day as many as 360 vehicles could be busy in transporting mines. This problem was alleviated somewhat by dispersing the mines over a large number of revetments and by scheduling crew trips. Because specific mine types were stored in specific revetments and the different code types were so complex a sufficient number of revetments was never achieved. Once the decision was made to lay mines at Group level, the traffic problem was practically eliminated and loading was greatly facilitated because closer supervision could be devoted to all phases of the activity.

A procedure was developed for hauling and loading mines for a B-29 Bomb Group flying approximately 30 minelaying sorties every two days. Careful planning and close liaison between the Wing Mining Section, Wing and Group Operations, Ordnance, Armament, and the Mine Assembly Depot were fundamental to successful operations. Early in the morning of the day before the scheduled mission, Group Operations, acting on the basis of a previously held planning meeting (described later), determined which sorties would be assigned to each of the several Squadrons, taking into account equal distribution of loads, rack changes for 1,000 or 2,000 pound mines, distance to be flown, risk involved, etc.

The Ordnance Section then consolidated the mines to be carried by each Squadron and obtained the number and code types from a Master Loading Plan furnished by the Mining Section. The Master Loading Plan determined which size mine types were to be loaded in sequence to be dropped. This consolidated list was also used as a basis for issuing parachutes, release mechanisms, soluble washers, and delayed arming cells.

The consolidated list of mines was then taken to the mine assembly depot which had already received the directive (described later) ordering the preparation of the mines. The issuing officer determined where each code type was stocked, made revetment assignments, and prepared issue

At a specified time during the day before the mission, each Squadron Ordnance Section drew in bulk all parachutes, release mechanisms, soluble washers, and delayed arming cells required for preparing mines for loading on the following day. (AAF)

cards. Each issue card contained the exact type and quantities of mines to be drawn by one ordnance crew (a load for one M-6 BST and two M-5 trailers, or one M-27 BST and one M-5 trailer). Each squadron was assigned a time schedule to report to the mine ready dump to draw mines. At the same time, the Squadron Ordnance Officer was given the issue cards for the mines his crews were to load. He in turn assigned one card (or load) to each of his Crew Chiefs who went to the assigned revetments and drew the mines. A triple check was kept on each load by requiring the Crew Chief, the crane operator, and the sentry at the exit gate to certify that the proper code numbers called for on the cards were actually drawn. The mines were then hauled to the squadron area on the flight line.

At a specified time during the day before the mission, each Squadron Ordnance Section drew in bulk all parachutes, release mechanisms, soluble washers, and delayed arming cells required for preparing mines for loading on the following day. With these were furnished special instructions for the size of parachute for each type of mine, color of the proper soluble washers to be used in each type, and information on delayed arming cells. Meanwhile, Group Operations had assigned aircraft and air crews to each sortie, and Armament had made any required changes in each aircraft's racks to carry the size of the mines specified in the assigned sorties. Therefore at the close of the day before the mission, all mines and accessories were on the line, aircraft were assigned to sorties, and aircraft were ready for mine loading.

Early on the day of the mission Individual Mine Loading Plans prepared by the Wing were given to each ordnance crew. This plan contained the size and code numbers of all mines for a particular sortie. The ordnance crew then obtained the necessary mines from the squadron area on the line and hauled them to the assigned aircraft for loading. The Armament Crew Chief of each aircraft checked the loading plan for the dropping sequence, chalking the rack number and location of the bomb station on the mine and entering this information on the mine loading plan. Following this the ordnance crew attached release mechanisms and parachutes, inserted soluble washers or delayed arming cells as necessary, and delivered the mines under the bomb bay. Armament crews hoisted the mines to the correct bomb stations; ordnance crews attached the static lines, and the aircraft was ready to take off. Occasional variations were made in this general procedure in order to suit the size of the operation and timing considerations.

Japanese Counter-Mining Measures

Throughout the war, the Japanese failed to anticipate Allied mining capability and were unprepared to counter the Allied mining campaign that increased in quantity and quality. Japanese deficiencies in minesweeping equipment and procedures remained far behind Allied mining efforts. Only when *Operation Starvation* began did the Japanese belatedly give

mining countermeasures a top priority but by then they had already lost a large portion of their merchant and naval shipping.

Cdr. Ellis Johnson and the Mine Modification Unit at Tinian constantly modified mines and each new minefield to disrupt Japanese countermeasures. The Johnson Unit used Intelligence from the observation of enemy sweeping techniques and the knowledge of the target areas so that the few basic mine types in the US inventory could be modified to give the Unit a great many possible mine combinations. The US mining campaign constantly experienced a shortage of the preferred mine and assemblies but the Japanese Navy was far from mounting a credible mine defense.

According to US Intelligence the Japanese relied principally on towed catenary (cable) magnetic sweeps which were easily capable of sweeping the US unmodified Mark 9 magnetic mines. These towed sweeps were wires supplied with an electric current that set up a magnetic field that fired the mines. The Japanese swept the Mark 13 Model 5 A-3 by sending artificial noise into the surrounding water which easily detonated a mine and one explosion could also cause the other nearby acoustic mines to detonate (acoustic mines often just detonated without reason). In areas where there was limited enemy mine sweeping the older type acoustic or magnetic mines were used while the more sophisticated pressure magnetic mines were used in the active Shimonoseki Straits.

In order to correct the defects and weaknesses in the standard Mk13 and Mk9 Mod1 magnetic and A-3 acoustic mechanisms, local modifications of these mechanisms were proposed to accomplish two objectives: first and most important was to defeat the known enemy sweeps; and the second requirement was to select the largest enemy ships for sinking so as to obtain maximum damage on a tonnage basis. The first of these goals required modification of mine mechanisms to meet specific enemy countermeasures for sweeping. The second required adjustment of the sensitivity of the mechanism to make them insensitive to small ships.

The Japanese had imprudently selected a rather crude sweep of towed magnets for mass production because it could be used easily with small boats and unskilled personnel. The USN had recovered examples of this sweep which were examined and analyzed. The Mk9 MOD1 mechanism, and less effectively the Mk13 mechanism, was modified by changing their timing which almost entirely overcame this type of enemy magnetic sweep. It was fortunate that the need for target ship selection required reduced sensitivity of these mechanisms, which further aided in reducing the effectiveness of the sweep. These changes were begun immediately.

The Japanese could sweep the original A-3 mechanism by explosive methods, so modifications of the mechanism were made by the Mine Modification Unit on Oahu, HI to alter the characteristics of the mechanism so it could no longer be cleared by simple explosive sweeps. So for a brief time US Intelligence believed that the magnetic mine could be made

Generally, the Japanese gave a low priority to minesweeping tactics, equipment, and vessels. Pictured is Minesweeper #26 which was a 648 ton **#19 Class Minesweeper**. Of the 17 ships of that class only two survived the war. (USN)

almost unsweepable with the proper modification prior to laying. As a result of these two modifications it was believed that the two magnetic and the A-3 mechanisms would be very effective for a limited period; possibly for two months before enemy countermeasures were developed to defeat it.

Another important alteration in the mine mechanisms was the adjustment of their sensitivities. All mines were designed for use in very deep water and most of the choice targets sailed in shallow water. An analysis of the accuracy which could be obtained in the mining operations and the probable width of enemy channels indicated that the logistic limitations of the mining effort would prevent enough mines from being laid to threaten all ships attempting to pass through the mined area. However, later analysis showed that the ratio of mines to ship passages was small. In order to make the maximum effectiveness of each mine, it was necessary to adjust the sensitivity so that the tendency would be sink the larger ships and to adjust the target width so that larger ships would be sunk or seriously damaged rather than slightly damaged, or the mines exploded without damage to the ships. These mine changes could not be ideally completed because of the complex consideration of sweeping, lack of exact information on the composition of enemy ship traffic, and the characteristics of the mines themselves. The effect of modifying the magnetic mines, however, might be such as to double or triple the amount of tonnage sunk or damaged, and at least some increase in damage would be achieved by modifying the A-3 acoustic mechanism. The Mine Modification Unit and adequate supplies were not available in the Marianas so that it was not possible to put all of these decisions fully into effect for Phase One of the mining campaign, but the mines were modified as much as possible for the first efforts.

The Mark 25 A-6 pressure mechanism and the subsonic A-5 mechanism were developed once the Mark 13 A-3 mines became sweepable. Even though these mechanisms were not available during early mining operations, planners believed that by laying large numbers of magnetic and acoustic mines; this early mining would produce a greater overall effect than could be achieved by waiting for several months for the A-5 and A-6 to initiate operations.

Aerial Mining in the Pacific

Outer Zone Mining

As early as 1942, American mining authority, Dr. Ellis Johnson then of the Naval Ordnance Laboratory suggested massive aerial mining operations first against Japan's "Outer Zone" (Korea and northern China) as well as the "Inner Zone," (Japanese home islands). First, effective aerial mines would have to be developed and then manufactured in great quantities. Once the mines were ready laying them would require sizeable numbers of large aircraft. The Navy lacked suitable mining aircraft but while the AAF had aircraft in size and numbers to carry the mines; it considered mining to be the Navy's province so it could carry out its strategic bombing responsibility on Japanese cities.

In February 1943 the Navy assigned mine warfare officers; Lt.Cdrs. S.L. Quimby, Kenneth Veth, and Ellis Johnson (now assigned to the USN), to the staffs of the Commanders in the SWPA (Gen. Douglas MacArthur), CBI (Adm. Louis Mountbatten), and Central (Adm. Chester Nimitz). These three officers would determine the emphasis and conduct of mining operations in the Pacific. The Navy's objectives for mining Japan's "Outer Zone" were: to disrupt Japan's maritime supply system, to deny enemy shipping of safe ports and shipping routes for the transport of essential war and economic materials, to sink and damage as many enemy ships as

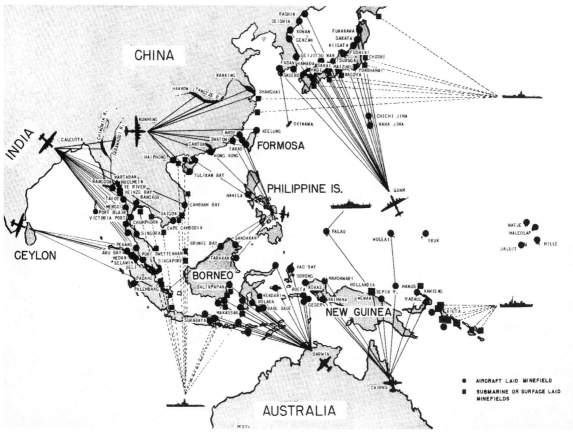

Offensive Minelaying Campaign Against Japan October 1942-August 1945 (USN)

possible, and to compel Japan to establish and maintain a mine defense which would entail a military and economic obligation. These early mining limited operations were to provide the indispensable experience for the Army and Navy for use in the final year of the war when both services undertook a concentrated mining campaign.

Mining by Naval Vessels of the Outer Zone
In August 1942 the Navy Department's Mine Warfare Operational Research Group identified the great vulnerability of Japanese shipping to "attrition mining" by USN submarines in Japanese controlled waters. During the war, 32 submarines laid 658 mines, creating 33 mine fields in shipping routes along coastal waters. Submarines were successful as minelayers, as they had range and freedom from detection but their crews universally favored carrying torpedoes which when fired gave immediate satisfaction of success. During the war submarine-laid mines sank 27 ships and damaged 27 others producing an enviable kill-ratio of one ship for every 12 mines sown. In addition to submarines, USN destroyers and mine layers laid 2,871 mines between August 1942 and May 1944 in 17 fields around the Solomon Islands sinking seven ships and hindering the Japanese reinforcement and evacuation of Guadalcanal.

Aerial Mining of the Outer Zone
Early aerial minelaying operations involved a coalition of British, Australian, and American aircrews. The RAF and RAAF (Royal Australian Air Force) carried out 22% and 38% of the sorties, respectively; while the AAF and USN conducted the remaining 40%. Using both British and American mines Japanese merchant shipping suffered huge losses and disrupted the resupply of Japanese garrisons and the flow of resources to the Home Islands. Meanwhile, Japanese mine sweeping forces were spread too thin trying to cover the oceans and extensive coastlines.

The RAAF was particularly successful in their Outer Zone mining operations as the 2,498 mines laid sank 90 enemy ships totalling 250,000 tons, approximately 40% percent of Japanese losses in the Netherlands East Indies, with a loss of only nine aircraft (0.8 % loss rate). Seventh Fleet Commander, Adm. Thomas Kinkaid, who had directed nearly all these RAF and RAAF mining operations whole-heartedly endorsed aerial mining, stating in July 1944 that "aerial mining operations were of the order of 100 times as destructive to the enemy as an equal number of bombing missions against land targets." However, during this period the Fifth Air Force flew only a single B-24 minelaying mission from Port Moresby in June 1943. Cdr. Quimby reported that 5AF CO, Lt.Gen. George Kenney felt that mining was unnecessary as his light and medium bombers were very successful in destroying enemy shipping and that the results of direct aerial attacks were easier to assess than the often unobserved results of mining.

Flying from bases in India and Ceylon, Tenth Air Force B-24s and B-25s and XX Bomber Command B-29s joined with Liberators of the RAF Nos. 222 and 231 Groups to conduct long range mining missions from Indochina to the Southwest Pacific. In this Theater mining was more workable than direct shipping attacks as the bombers operated at nearly the limit of their range, where it was not possible to spend time to search for individual targets. The first AAF minelaying mission of the war occurred on 22 February 1943, when ten B-24s laid 40 British-made mines in the Rangoon River which with further mining effectively prevented the reinforcement and resupply of Burma.

Lt.Cdr. Veth, the senior USN mining officer in the CBI, and Adm. Mountbatten and his Air Commander, Maj.Gen. George Stratemeyer, were wholehearted advocates of minelaying and in May the three persuaded AAF Commanding General "Hap" Arnold to allow 20th Air Force B-29s to begin mining. On 10 August 1944, 14 20AF B-29s laid their first mines

on a mission from China Bay, Ceylon to the refineries at Palembang, Sumatra. These mines sank or damaged seven ships and closed the Moesi River entrance to tankers for a month. However, the 20AF's next mining mission would not occur for five months when it completed the largest mining effort in the Pacific to date on the night of 25 January 1945 when 76 B-29s dropped mines around Singapore, Saigon, and Camranh Bay after which they reseeded those fields in February and March. Once the 20AF B-29s were assigned to join the XXI Bomber Command in the Marianas RAF Liberators continued their minelaying mission.

In the Central Pacific, the Navy conducted most of the limited minelaying, but 7th Air Force B-24s of the 42nd Bomb Squadron out of Guam and Saipan supplemented the mining effort. From 6 November through 18 December 1944; it flew 101 sorties laying 227 mines during Project Mike to blockade shipping in the Bonin Islands prior to the invasion of Iwo Jima. Although this was a limited mining campaign it did demonstrate that radar was superior to visual minelaying for accuracy, variety in axis of attack, and the benefit of night and all-weather capability which afforded protection from defenses and usually prevented the enemy from spotting the mines as they were laid.

The Navy used TBFs of Carrier Task Force 58 to conduct the first American carrier-based minelaying at Palau on March 30-31. TBF Avenger torpedo bombers dropped 78 mines to stop enemy shipping around Palau on 30 March 1944. Along with simultaneous conventional bombing and strafing attacks this intervention stopped 32 Japanese ships from escaping Koror Harbor; shutting down the port for 20 days. The combined operation sank or damaged 36 ships at the cost of two TBFs lost but with their crews saved. Further mine-laying in the area contributed to the Japanese abandoning Palau as a base. On the whole, however, US naval aviation contributed only 3% of the total of all air-laid mines in the Pacific. Naval aircraft operating primarily from carriers lacked the necessary range and payload for minelaying. But the probable reason for the Navy's limited mining participation was its distinct lack of enthusiasm for the minelaying and a preference to directly attack on ships.

Outer Zone Results
The Allied forces committed to mining the large area of the Outer Zone were usually inadequate, could not be concentrated, and did not have the support of the Allied High Command. While this mining campaign did not have any appreciable impact on the course of the war, its effects far surpassed in proportion to the effort expended. Of the approximately 13,000 mines laid in the Outer Zone, aircraft dropped 9,254 mines during 3,231 sorties to build 108 minefields. Aerial mining sank or damaged as many as 405 ships amounting to 776,260 tons at a cost of 40 Allied aircraft and delayed the movement of essential enemy shipping for periods of a day or two up to a month.

Inner Zone Mining
Planning Operation Starvation
When Dr. Ellis Johnson first advanced a plan for mining Japan's home waters at the Naval Ordnance Laboratory in May 1942, he failed to generate much support for it and the Navy decentralized responsibility for mining operations to its Area Commanders. In 1944, Johnson was assigned to Adm. Nimitz's staff and presented the first detailed plan for mining Japan's Inner Zone. Johnson's plan won Nimitz's support and developed into the model for the ensuing mining operation of the Inner Zone.

On 6 July 1944, Nimitz's staff, including Johnson, briefed the XXI Bomber Command advanced echelon on the mining plan when it arrived in Hawaii enroute to their new base at Saipan. After his briefing on the plan Brig.Gen. C.E. Thomas then proposed the mining plan to the Air Staff in Washington, DC where it met strong opposition from Maj.Gen. Lawrence

Kuter, the Assistant Chief of Air Staff for Plans and Brig.Gen. Haywood Hansell, the 20AF Chief of Staff. The two felt that the proposed mining program would cause a diversion from the strategic bombing which was to lead to the defeat of Japan.

The Committee of Operations Analysts (COA) studied target priorities in the impending bombing campaign against Japan from the Marianas. On 10 October 1944 the COA presented two separate plans; one based on defeating Japan by blockade and strategic bombing and the other based on the premise that an invasion of Japan had to follow a blockade. In the first plan, mining received top priority within a general anti-shipping program but the second plan, which assumed an invasion was necessary, gave mining somewhat less weight. The COA recommended an attack on the enemy aircraft industry and urban industrial areas with a concerted attack on shipping by all available means including mining by Very Long Range (VLR) B-29s. Important AAF planners construed the COA's recommendation to maintain the basic principles of strategic bombing of first gaining air superiority and then destroying the Japanese industrial capability and will to resist. In this context they considered minelaying to be a third priority and with the limited assets then available to the XXI Bomber Command mining would, necessarily, have to be delayed or even cancelled. But the COA report also strongly recommended B-29 mining from the Marianas and suggested a mining attack in November 1944 emphasizing that "It is possible that the Japanese islands can be blockaded by VLR aircraft through a comprehensive mining program." This mining recommendation by the COA was so strong that it could not be ignored by Air Staff planners.

Japan was very exposed to an air and sea blockade as its Merchant Marine imported 90% of its coking coal, 86% of its iron ore, 80-90% of its oil, 24% of all coal and 20% of its food. Particularly vulnerable was Japan's Inland Sea that carried 80% of the nation's commerce. In October 1944, the COA issued an ambitious three-phase plan that called for 14,800 mines to be laid between 1 December 1944 and 31 August 1945 that would sink an estimated 500 ships totaling two million tons. Adm. Chester Nimitz strongly "suggested" that an initial 150 monthly B-29 mining sorties laying 600 mines in the crucial Shimonoseki Straits and four major ports would be the minimum effort to secure an adequate blockade. Nimitz went on to ask for 250 monthly B-29 sorties to be conducted between April and September 1945. The XXIBC objected that the training for the mining missions and then the mining missions themselves would interfere with their primary strategic bombing mission. The AAF was between the proverbial rock and a hard place, as it did not want to divert its B-29s from their strategic bombing campaign but also did not want the Navy to ask for Long Range aircraft (i.e. B-29s needed to conduct the strategic bombing campaign) to conduct its own/Nimitz's mining campaign. However, there was some way out as the XXIBC could conduct radar directed mining sorties when bad weather prevented the strategic bombing of socked in primary targets.

On 20 January 1945, Gen. Curtiss LeMay replaced Hansell as Commander of the XXI Bomber Command and quickly supported the mining task. LeMay realized that he had no choice but to acquiesce to Nimitz's "suggestion" and drew up a mining plan. Instead of one group; he assigned the entire 313th Bombardment Wing (four groups, about 160 planes) to the undertaking, with orders to lay 2,000 mines beginning April 1945 involving 150-200 sorties per month for three months. The mining runs were to be made by individual aircraft at night at moderately low altitudes with radar providing mine release information. In February the newly arrived 313th Bombardment Wing arrived at Tinian and began preliminary training of its B-29 combat crews for the minelaying mission. Their aircraft were equipped with the AN/APQ-13 radar (for night and bad-weather mine drops over featureless waters) but needed only minor

modification to carry twelve 1,000 pound mines, seven 2,000 pound mines or a combination. Crews received ground training followed by four to eight practice flights, each with five radar approaches and a live mine drop on the last.

On 27 January LeMay approved the tactics for individual bombers flying at low altitude (between 5,000 and 8,000 feet) to drop mines at night. This approach eliminated the need for large defensive formations, improved accuracy, allowed more mines to be carried, complicated Japanese defensive measures, and provided 12 hours of daylight for search and rescue of bomber crews unable to reach home base. The RAF had been the first to drop mines using radar rather than by visual aiming and their technique had since been adopted for minelaying by AAF B-29s of the 58th Bomb Wing in India and by 11BG B-24s operating from the Marianas.

A Navy task force arrived on Tinian in mid-January 1945 and set up a mine depot. A detachment of aerial mining experts under Cdr. Ellis Johnson instructed the 313BW on the particulars of aerial mining and six trial missions were planned to test equipment and formulate mission tactics. The 504BG of the 313BW began the trial missions on 27 January over the bypassed Japanese Islands of Rota and Pagan. Minelaying tests were conducted at altitudes ranging from 1,500, 2,000, 3,000, 10,000 and 25,000 feet. The training of the 504BG was followed by training of four crews from each of the other three Bomb Wings of the 313BW that flew two test missions. These tests determined that low altitude solo mine drop sorties conducted at night with radar were optimal. Bombing altitudes of 5,000 to 8,000 feet were chosen for the same reasons as bombing Japanese cities; Japanese AA was ineffective at these altitudes, barrage balloons were moored below 4,000 feet, the majority of the Japanese hills were below 5,000 feet, and nearly double the mine load could be carried. The mines were dropped by parachute to decrease the effect of the impact on the water and these lower altitude parachute drops were more accurate than the high altitude drops as there was less drift. When dropped from 25,000 feet the mine floated for a minute and half and landed with an "accuracy" of one mile. The low level night missions with the increased mine loads were determined to be 20 times more effective as daylight high altitude mining sorties and 10 times more effective as nighttime high altitude mining sorties. The skill of the radar operator was paramount as all mines were aimed by radar. The 313BW became the "Mining Wing" and by the time its first mission was flown on 27 March it had 182 of its 205 crews trained for mining.

Operation Starvation

In Washington, the Joint Target Group, which replaced the COA, completed target prioritization for a five-phase mining campaign to begin on 27 March 1945. This mining campaign was appropriately code named *Operation Starvation* and was designed to play a part in the blockade of the Japanese Homeland with the objective of:

1) Blockading the Shimonoseki Straits through which 80% of the Japanese merchant fleet passed.
2) Blockading of the industrial and commercial ports in the Inland Sea and Tokyo and Nagoya.
3) Stopping shipping between Korea and Japan by mining Korean ports and those on the northwestern coast of Japan.

The five phases were:
Phase One targeted the Shimonoseki Strait, a narrow waterway between Kyushu and Honshu which was considered the single most vulnerable point in the enemy's shipping routes as it was vital to movement on the Inland Sea and along Japan's east coast. This phase also included mining

the naval bases at Kure, Sasebo, and Hiroshima's military port. Between 27 March and 12 April the wing flew 246 sorties and dropped 2,030 mines during seven separate missions. Mines closed the Shimonoseki Strait for almost two weeks and limited Japanese naval and merchant shipping through the Bungo Strait, the Inland Sea's southeastern exit. On 6 April a B-29 sighted a task force led by the battleship *Yamato* leaving the Inland Sea and was headed to attack the American invasion of Okinawa. The next day, carrier-based torpedo and dive bombers intercepted and sank *Yamato* and most of the task force. At the end of Phase One Ellis Johnson stated: "the continuation of this minelaying will achieve for the first time by strategic air power, a sea blockade, which previously has been possible only by sea power."

Phase Two was referred to as the "Industrial center blockade." It consisted of only two missions, on 3 and 5 May but sent almost 200 aircraft dropping mines against Japanese ports. Its purpose was to destroy maritime commerce between Japan's great industrial zones; the Shimonoseki Strait, Tokyo, Nagoya, Kobe-Osaka harbors, and shipping lanes of the Inland Sea. The majority of the 1,422 mines dropped were the 2,000 pound type of which half were the new, "unsweepable," pressure type. Aerial reconnaissance showed the number of ships and estimated tonnage passing through the Shimonoseki Strait was only about one-tenth what it had been before the mining campaign. Enemy shipping losses climbed and as the Japanese diverted shipping to western and northern harbors, the AAF mining campaign targeted these ports as well.

Phase Three began on 13 May and extended the minefields from Shimonoseki to northwest Honshu and Kyushu with the purpose being to blockade enemy shipping moving from the Asiatic mainland to Japan. During eight missions, 209 aircraft laid 1,313 mines of different types, including a small number of 'unsweepable' low frequency acoustic mines. The results of May 1945 showed, for the first time, that mines were sinking more ships per month (113 more) than submarines in the Shimonoseki Strait alone which amounted to 9% of Japan's shrinking merchant fleet.

Phase Four intensified the blockade of northwest Honshu and Kyushu, extended it to secondary harbors, and continued to target the Shimonoseki Strait. It began June 7th and consisted of missions flown on alternate nights for a month. During this phase, 404 aircraft, on 14 missions, dropped 3,542 mines.

Phase Five, the final phase, was a "total blockade," continuing from 9 July through 14 August and duplicated the previous month's operations. Sometimes B-29s returned to Iwo Jima rather than Tinian to extend their effective range to 3,675 miles placing all of Japan under a nearly complete blockade. The bombers maintained the minefields in the Shimonoseki Strait, the ports of northwest Honshu and Kyushu, and also Korean harbors at Pusan, Masan, Wonsan, Hungnam, and Chongjin. During this period the minelaying B-29s also dropped 4.5 million leaflets that called attention to the Japanese population that their deteriorating food situation was one effect of the mine blockade. In the last phase, 474 aircraft on 15 missions laid 3,746 mines.

Results of the Pacific Mining Campaign
Aerial Mining in the Pacific
A total of 21,389 aerial delivered mines were laid in the mining campaign against Japan of which the Navy laid only 3,000. There were a total of 4,323 aerial mining sorties of which 2,078 were flown by the AAF, 1,128 by the RAAF, 631 by the RAF, and 486 by the USN. The AAF B-29 carried 12 mines per aircraft and B-24 carried six mines per aircraft compared to a load of two to four for USN and RAAF PBYs. Thus the B-29s on 1,424 sorties accounted for 12,000 of the 21,000 mine laid or 34% of all sorties were flown by B-29s that accounted for 63% of the mines laid.

The result of the Outer and Inner mining campaign was 1,075 Japanese ships detonating mines totaling 2,027,516 tons damaged or sunk. Japanese losses included 147 warships consisting of two battleships, eight cruisers, two escort carriers, seven submarines, 46 destroyers and destroyer escorts, and 82 others. During the Outer mining campaign 405 enemy ships were sunk or damaged, totaling 776,260 tons by aircraft that laid 9,254 mines in 3,231 sorties to form 108 minefields. During the Inner Zone mining campaign conducted by the XXI Bomber Command, a total of 670 ships were sunk or damaged totaling 1,251,256 tons during 1,529 sorties laying 12,135 mines to form 26 minefields.

AAF Aerial Mining and Mining by USN Submarines Compared
The result of mining on the total blockade was difficult to separate from the other factors: submarine and direct aerial attacks on Japanese shipping. The *US Strategic Bombing Survey Summary Report* stated that during World War II in the Pacific 8.9 million tons of enemy merchant shipping had been sunk or damaged and credited 54.7% to submarines, 30.8% to direct air attack, 9.3% to mines and the remaining 5.2% to accidents and gunfire. Though the 9.3% attributed to mines seems small it was accomplished in the last four and a half months of the war as compared to the 44 month submarine campaign. During the Pacific War a total of 21,389 mines were laid and only 55 aircraft were lost in 4,760 sorties while the USN employed about 100 submarines and lost 52 along with approximately 4,000 crewmen during the entire war. The 20AF flew 40 minelaying B-29s and lost 15 aircraft with 103 crewmen. Mining comprised only 5.7% of the 20AF's missions as compared to the 94.3% for bombing and incendiary raids but this small percentage had a comparable economic impact. The destruction of 1.2 million tons of Japanese merchant shipping prevented food, raw materials and oil from reaching the Homeland. Thus it had a direct effect on civilian morale (food) and the war industry that had no fuel or raw materials for its factories that had been abandoned and were being fruitlessly bombed in the strategic bombing campaign. It was estimated that 10% of the 70 million Japanese civilians would have starved to death if the war had continued for another year. Not included in these figures are the millions of yen and the estimated 20,000 men and 350 vessels that the Japanese assigned to counter the mining campaign. Also not considered are the number of searchlights and AA guns that were drawn away from the Japanese cities that were beleaguered by B-29 bombing attacks.

The Aerial Inner Zone Mining Campaign vs. Economic Cost per Enemy Ton Casualty

	Inner Zone Mining	Submarine Campaign
Duration of Campaign	4.5 months	44.5 months
No. of Craft Employed	40	100
No. Crew per Craft	11	85
Total Craft Lost	15	52
Cost per One Craft	$500,000	$5 Million
Tons of Enemy Ships Lost	1.25 million	4.78 million

Relative Cost of Aerial and Submarine Campaigns

	Inner Zone Mining	Submarine Campaign
Enemy Loss (Tons/Month)	280,000	110,000
US Craft Cost/Enemy Ton Lost	$16	$100
Enemy Tons Lost/Craft Crew	3,500	560
Enemy Tons Lost/Craft Crew Lost	12,000	1,200
Cost US Loss/Enemy Ton Lost	$6	$55

Table 3–3. THE MINE OFFENSIVE AGAINST JAPAN

	Fields	Patrols/ Missions/ Sorties	Mines Laid in Target	Ships Sunk		Ships Damaged		Remarks
				No.	Tonnage	No.	Tonnage	
Outer Zone Operations	108	33 Sub. 49 Surf. 3231 A/C[1]	12,741[4]	201 (20)[2]	253,365 (24,000)	154 (30)	522,895 (90,000)	This includes 94 sorties by Fleet Air Wing One in July 1945 in support of Inner Zone Mining Operations.
Inner Zone Operations	26	1529 A/C[3]	12,135[3]	283 (11)	396,371 (15,400)	323 (53)	854,885 (132,500)	Damaged ships include 137 so seriously damaged that they were knocked out of the war.
Subtotal				484 (31)	649,736 (39,400)	477 (83)	1,377,780 (222,500)	Ship Casualties: 1075
Total	134	33 Sub. 49 Surf. 4760 A/C	24,876	515	689,136	560	1,600,280	Tonnage: 2,289,416

[1] *Mining aircraft airborne. Total includes 55 planes lost and 437 unsuccessful missions.*
[2] *( ) indicate ships of unknown tonnage. They are confirmed sinkings for which all data were not available from Japanese records.*
[3] *According to records in CNO. Twentieth Air Force records give 12,053 mines in target (Chapter 7), 1528 aircraft airborne, and 1424 successful sorties.*
[4] *Includes 1,791 British mines and 106 dummy mines.*

Table 3–5. AIRCRAFT MINES EXPENDED, BY TYPE AND THEATER

	Theater	Magnetic	Acoustic	Magnetic Acoustic	Pressure Magnetic	Low Frequency	Contact (Drifting)	Dummy	Total
Outer Zone	Central Pacific	575	34	—	33	20	—	—	662
	South Pacific	237	14	—	—	—	—	—	251
	Southwest Pacific	1933	465	124	—	—	—	—	2522
	India-Burma	4192	246	—	—	—	36	106	4580
	China	825	182	—	—	—	232	—	1239
	Total	7762	941	124	33	20	268	106	9254
	Percent	84.0	10.1	1.3	0.4	0.2	2.9	1.1	100
Inner Zone	Central Pacific	4291	3507	—	2959	748	—	—	12,135
	Percent	40.5	28.9	—	24.4	6.2	—	—	100

	Outer Zone	Inner Zone*	Mining Campaign
Successful Launchings	9254	12,135	21,389
Total Expended	9829	13,090	22,919
Percentage in Target	94.5	92.7	93.1

7

Guided Missiles

Early Development
Sperry Flying Bomb

In June 1914, brilliant inventor Elmer Sperry and his son, Lawrence Sperry, demonstrated an automatic gyrostabilizer that permitted a Curtiss flying boat provided by the Navy to fly straight and level without human intercession. Once the war began, Elmer Sperry in conjunction with the Royal Air Force linked the gyrostabilizer control system to a bombsight to keep an airplane on course while a bombardier lined up the target in his sights. In early 1915, the Sperrys were joined by Peter Hewitt, an American electrical engineer who had developed early radio-related devices which could be used to develop an "aerial torpedo."

Working at the Sperry facility at Amityville, NY, the Sperry team incorporated a steering gyro with a stabilizer gyro to create one of the world's first automatic pilot system. Their system was easily adapted to an aircraft that didn't require a human pilot and that year Lawrence Sperry filed a patent for an aerial torpedo, featuring the following:

1) A gyrostabilizer to keep the aircraft level.
2) An automatic steering gyro to keep the aircraft on a preset heading.
3) A barometer to indicate cruise altitude, causing the aircraft to level off.
4) A wind-driven electrical generator to provide power for the gyro motors and the servomotors that moved the aerial torpedo's flight control surfaces.
5) An engine revolution counter to determine when the aircraft was to cut power and dive into its target.
6) Ability to be installed in an aircraft which could be catapulted or flown from the water, and would climb to a predetermined altitude, fly a preset course, and after traveling a preset distance, drop its bombs or dive into the ground.

Elmer Sperry and Hewitt had served on the Naval Consulting Board where they were members of the Committee on Aeronautics and Aeronautical Motors. Because of these associations, they were able to persuade the Navy BuOrd to send a representative, Lt. T. S. Wilkinson, to examine the control equipment they assembled as the foundation of an aerial torpedo. Wilkinson reported that although the aerial torpedo was not yet accurate enough to hit a moving pin point target such as a warship; it warranted further development on the basis of its design and range of 50 miles.

After America declared war there was increased interest by the Naval Consulting Board in the aerial torpedo and on their recommendation

Josephus Daniels, the Secretary of Navy, granted an initial $50,000 to Sperry to work on two types of the weapon; one for wireless control and the other for completely automatic operation. Daniels gave the final approval for the project on 17 May 1917 and provided $200,000 to build the weapon in conjunction with Curtiss (the bomb was designated as the Curtiss-Sperry Flying Bomb). The Navy was to provide five (later six) Curtiss N-9 seaplanes and would purchase six sets of the Sperry automatic control gear. Sperry began to build hangars at Copiague, Long Island, NY to carry out the contract.

Sperry was working on developing a radio control system that could be controlled to the target by an observer in a nearby aircraft. Since Sperry was an international company it had several foreign scientists working on a radio control system prompting the Naval Consulting Board to have Westinghouse, a company without "enemy aliens" develop the system. Despite the lack of support Sperry continued its radio control development and on 18 December 1918 applied for the first patent.

Tests of an autopilot-equipped Curtiss N-9 biplane went well, though the aircraft still carried a pilot to handle takeoffs and to observe the flight. By November, the system successfully flew the aircraft with the "hands

In 1916 **Lawrence Sperry**, son of renown inventor Elmer Sperry, created one of the world's first automatic pilot systems that would be the basis of missile guidance. (AFHRC)

The **Sperry Flying Bomb** was built on a Navy N-9 Seaplane airframe. One of the launching configurations was on railway tracks from a sled equipped with rail wheels. (AFHRC)

off" pilot on board to its intended target where the distance-measuring gear dropped a bag of sand with an "accuracy" of within two miles of target.

Engineering a successful mechanism to launch the unmanned Flying Bomb proved to be difficult. The original concept was to launch it via a catapult mechanism or from the water (the N-9s originally were seaplanes). Sperry and Hewitt finally decided to try to launch it by sliding it down a long wire and during December 1917, they conducted three launching tests. On the first launch on 1 December, one wing was damaged as the Flying Bomb twisted on the wire. On the second test that day, it lifted from the wire but immediately plunged to the ground and the wire launch system was then discarded for a catapult. This was a conventional catapult with a track, with its power obtained by dropping a three ton weight. On the third trial, now using the catapult, the Flying Bomb was dragged behind the cart, damaging the propeller and flipping over on its nose. On 1 January 1918, they conducted a catapult test that saw it get briefly airborne but nose over and crash. Sperry and Hewitt then realized that the aircraft design could be at fault and began flight testing the basic design, especially the handling qualities.

In early February the team conducted three launches. On the first test on 1 February the aircraft was launched by a deadweight catapult where it stalled, side-slipped, and crashed during the launch. The next day Lawrence Sperry decided that he would be the test pilot, but the N-9 somersaulted during its taxiing; Sperry stepped away from the wreck unscathed. The next day Sperry again manned the N-9 which was rolled by the autopilot but Sperry was able to regain control.

Finally, an improved impulse-type catapult was developed, powered by a 2.5 ton concrete weight dropped 30 feet, which transferred teh resultant energy to the catapult via a system of pulleys. On 6 March 1918 the unmanned aircraft was launched cleanly from the deadweight catapult and was controlled in stable flight for the 1,000 yards the distance-measuring gear had been set for and the N-9 was landed safely on the water. This was the first time in history that an unmanned, heavier-than-air vehicle had been flown in a remotely controlled flight. On 7 April another test using the deadweight catapult was conducted. The Flying Bomb was unable to duplicate the 6 March accomplishment and the efficacy of the new catapult system and the aerodynamics of the N-9 again were questioned.

Sperry and Hewitt equipped one of the N-9s with sled-type runners as the landing gear and mounted the Flying Bomb to the top of a Marmon automobile to test its aerodynamics while speeding along the Long Island Motor Parkway. Using this outdoor wind tunnel Sperry adjusted the flight controls to their optimum settings and determined that the fuselage needed to be lengthened by two feet. Since the Marmon could not whiz down the crowded Parkway at 80 mph to launch the Flying Bomb it was fitted with steel railway wheels and placed on the vacant tracks of a spur of the Long Island Railway to act as a catapult. Once sufficient speed was built up the N-9s sled runners lifted off the Marmon but this N-9 crashed and Sperry had only two serviceable N-9 airframes remaining for testing.

Sperry and Hewitt hired a young and talented engineer named Carl Norden to design a new flywheel-powered catapult system that pulled the Flying Bomb along a 150 foot track at 100 mph and into the air. The new flywheel catapult system was first tested on 5 August 1918, and this launch also resulted in a minor, but repairable crash. In late September the final flywheel catapult tests were unsuccessful. On the 23rd the N-9 went into an erratic 100 yard flight and crashed. On the 26th the last Flying Bomb airframe was sent off the catapult, traveling 100 yards and spiraling into a crash.

Sperry and Hewitt decided to go back to basics and built a wind tunnel at the Washington Navy Yard and carried out a series of flight tests on the N-9 to check the stabilization system which was abandoned in favor of a four gyroscope unit. On 17 October with aerodynamics and stabilization improved an unmanned N-9 was launched and left the track cleanly, climbed steadily, and flew within 2° of the line of intended flight. The distance measuring gear had been set for a flight of eight miles but malfunctioned and the aircraft was last seen heading east over the Atlantic. By now numerous controlled flights had been flown in the N-9 with a safety pilot onboard and taking off from an airfield. During one of these piloted tests Sperry crashed and suffered a broken pelvis that immobilized him for three months. These tests caused the Navy concern and they asked Carl Norden to evaluate the Sperry components and recommend improvements. However, the war came to an end and the Navy assumed complete control of the program from Sperry which, in effect, meant the program was terminated. Lawrence Sperry then turned

Charles Kettering was solicited by the US Army Aircraft Board to design an unmanned flying bomb. Kettering's design was officially called the Kettering Aerial Torpedo but was later known as the Kettering *Bug*. (AFHRC)

to civilian activities and designed and built an inexpensive sport plane, the Sperry *Messenger*. On 23 December 1923, he took off in his *Messenger* from England for France over a fogged-in Channel and crashed and was killed. (Lawrence Sperry's invention of the autopilot is described in *U.S. Aerial Armament in World War 2: Volume 2*.)

Kettering Aerial Torpedo "*Bug*"

In 1917 Maj.Gen. George Squire, Chief of the Army Signal Corps, had observed a demonstration of the Sperry Flying Bomb to the Navy and ordered that a similar Army program be developed in secret. In January 1918, the Army awarded a contract to Charles Kettering and the Dayton Wright Airplane Company to develop and produce 25 *Liberty Eagle* aerial torpedoes which were to be less complicated and less expensive than the Sperry design.

In 1909, he and Edward Deeds formed the Dayton Engineering Laboratories Company (Delco). In 1916, Kettering and Deeds sold Delco to the United Motors Corporation for the then enormous sum of $9 million which they used to build a factory to manufacture Kettering's innovative farm lighting systems. Kettering then helped create the Dayton Airplane Company and retained Orville Wright as consulting engineer. The company intended to perfect Wright's automatic flight control system and to build private aircraft. But when the United States entered World War I the company became the Dayton-Wright Airplane Company and received contracts to build 5,000 DeHavilland warplanes using the new American *Liberty* engine.

Kettering's design, formally called the Kettering Aerial Torpedo but later known as the Kettering *Bug*, was built by the Dayton-Wright Airplane Company. Col. F.E. Harris was in charge of developmental work for the Army. A piloted developmental aircraft was built as the Dayton-Wright *Bug* in October 1918. Orville Wright acted as an aeronautical consultant on the project and contributed his expertise to the development of the airframe which was constructed of wood laminates and papier-mâché and actually looked like a torpedo that was fitted with dihedral biplane wings. The *Bug* was powered by a two-cycle, four cylinder V4, 41 hp Ford engine designed by C.H. Wills which ultimately cost only $40. The simple Kettering *Bug* launching system placed the airframe on a four wheel baby buggy-like launch vehicle that moved on two thin metal tracks. Lateral control was achieved by a dihedral angle tail and rudder developed by

The **Kettering *Bug*** was powered by a four cylinder 41 hp Ford engine. An inexpensive portable launch system consisting of a four-wheeled cradle riding on rails was developed. (AFHRC)

Orville Wright. The altitude of descent was automatically controlled by an aneroid barometer operating a pneumatic mechanism which controlled the elevator.

From April 1917 to March 1920 the Government funded about $275,000 on the Kettering *Bug*. Its specifications were:

Wingspan	15 feet
Length	12.5 feet
Height	7.7 feet
Total weight	530 pounds
Warhead weight	180 pounds
Speed	120 mph/105 knots
Range	75 miles/65 nautical miles

Unfortunately, Kettering was unable to build a workable autopilot and had to appeal to Elmer Sperry who agreed to assist. The *Bug* had no direct control. An altitude sensor and pneumatic

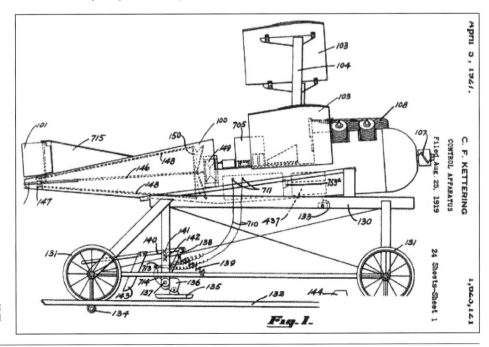

Charles Kettering's 25 August 1919 patent drawing of the control apparatus for the Kettering Aerial Torpedo. (Author)

Early manufacture of the **Kettering *Bug*** by the Dayton-Wright Airplane Company. Despite some successes during testing, the war ended before the 45 *Bugs* manufactured could be tried in combat. (AAF)

controls based on bellows from a player piano controlled its climb. To ensure the *Bug* hit its target, a mechanical system was devised that would track the aircraft's distance flown to its destination at an air speed of about 120 mph. Before takeoff technicians determined the distance to be traveled relative to the air, taking into account wind speed and direction along the flight path. This date was used to calculate the total number of engine revolutions needed for the *Bug* to reach its destination. When a total revolution counter reached this value a cam dropped down which shut off the engine and retracted the bolts attaching the wings. The wings fell off and the *Bug* began a ballistic trajectory into the target; the impact detonated the payload of 180 pounds of explosives.

The prototype *Bug* was completed and delivered to the Aviation Section of the Army Signal Corps in 1918, near the end of World I. The first flight on 2 October 1918 was a failure as the *Bug* climbed too steeply after takeoff, stalled and crashed. In a test several days later, a *Bug* was successfully launched and flew across the Ohio farmland before it crashed an hour later near Xenia. As an observer and cross country pursuer of the *Bug*, Col. H.H. Arnold became very enthusiastic and recommended the immediate manufacture of 100 torpedoes and future contracts for 10,000 to as many as 100,000 which in quantities of 50,000 would cost $400 each.

Subsequent flights were successful, and the aircraft was demonstrated to Army personnel at Dayton. During testing the Kettering *Bug* had two successes on six tests at Dayton, one of four at Amityville, and four of 14 at Carlstrom. Despite some successes during testing, the war ended before the 45 *Bugs* manufactured could be tried in combat. The aircraft and its technology remained a secret until World War II. A full-size reproduction of a *Bug* is on permanent display at the Air Force Museum in Dayton, OH.

After the war an attempt was made to incorporate Sperry automatic gyroscopic controls which had to be directed from a closely following aircraft by radio control developed by McCook Field Laboratory, OH. A large number of tests were conducted between October 1920 and July 1922 to develop the gyroscopic systems. While performance was an improvement over Kettering system; the gyroscopes of the time were not reliable enough and the Aerial Torpedo project was abandoned in November 1924. Work on radio control continued over the next five years but due to the lack of qualified engineers progress was slow.

Several years after the war, the Navy resurrected the Sperry N-9 project and tested it with safety pilots always on board. On 15 September 1924 the Navy launched an unmanned N-9, controlled it for 40 minutes during which it executed 50 commands, then landed it successfully, replicating a similar British flight the year before. This marked the first time than an American aircraft had been taken off, flown through a series of maneuvers, and landed, entirely under remote control. Work on radio control continued over the next five years but due to the lack of funds and qualified engineers progress was slow.

In 1928 P.T. Davison, Assistant Secretary of War, requested that the Aerial Torpedo be resurrected and in October the Acting Chief of the Engineering Division began to investigate the possibilities of adapting commercial aircraft of various sizes to carry bomb loads of 300, 600, 1,100, and 2,000 pounds which would facilitate the production of aerial torpedoes by commercial aircraft manufacturers in wartime on very short notice. One aircraft with the most suitable characteristics was to be chosen to carry each bomb weight and be fitted with controls for automatic flight. After testing the data on each successful aircraft was to be filed away for future use in case of war. The Curtiss Robin was the first aircraft equipped with a Sperry Automatic Pilot superimposed by radio control. The Robin was underpowered and evolved slowly, and was replaced by the Stinson Junior using the system whose throttle and landing required human control. Completely automatic takeoff and landing was thought to be economically unachievable in the near future and the project was closed in mid-May 1932.

General Motors A-1 (GMA-1, *Bug*)

During the inter-war years a handful of Army airmen maintained their interest in a pilotless aircraft. One of these was the influential Gen. H.H. Arnold who had been associated with the World War I Kettering *Bug* program and would be an influence for good and bad on America's pilotless bomb programs during World War II. During the 1930s Arnold struggled to keep interest alive in radio-control and "aerial torpedo" development, but it was not until August 1938, as America began to rearm that interest in the pilotless aircraft program resurfaced. On 8 August 1938, Chief of the Air Corps, Oscar Westover, ordered the Chief of the Materiel Division to develop ASAP a an "aerial torpedo" costing $300-$500 per unit in quantity production with a range of 20 to 30 miles to be controlled by radio. Westover authorized the then large sum of $100,000, of which $10,000 was set aside for a design competition. On 29 September, specifications for bids were authorized by Gen. Arnold who had replaced Westover as

The **General Motors A-1 (GMA-1) *Bug*** was a 1940 revival of the World War I Kettering *Bug* using a GM 200 hp, two-cycle engine with a 7.33 foot propeller mounted on a Cessna airframe built at the company's Wichita, KS factory. (AAF)

the Chief of the Air Corps who had died in the crash of an A-17 a week earlier. The specifications mandated a range of 20 to 50 miles, a payload of 200 pounds or a 300 pound bomb, and an accuracy (?) to hit a two square mile target from 20 miles. By late April 1939, the Vega Company, Burbank, CA was the only bidder and its dubious design was rejected by the Air Corps' Engineering Section.

The project was revived by Charles Kettering, who had been the motivating force behind the Army's World War I *Bug*. On 7 September 1939, Kettering, then the General Manager of the General Motors Research Labs, informed Arnold that GM had developed a low cost 150 hp engine and satisfactory instruments to build a practical "Aerial Torpedo" that would weigh 1,500 pounds and cost $1,500 in production quantities. Arnold countered that he desired a $700 weapon that could hit a one half mile diameter target from 100 miles while carrying 200 pounds of explosive. A short time later Kettering replied that an "appropriate missile could be built in quantities of 10,000 or so, and could be obtained at a satisfactory, although unstated, price."

In late February 1940, the Adjutant General approved the revised military requirements for the missile which now had to be able to hit a one half mile diameter target at 20 miles, be capable of having its range extended to 100 miles, and be immune to enemy misdirection and/or jamming. The minimum 20 mile range was set as it was the maximum range of existing ground artillery and the Army believed that this missile was essentially long range artillery. By September 1940, GM made a specific offer, proposing to use one of its tested GM X-250 200 hp, two-cycle engines with a 7.33 foot propeller mounted on a Cessna airframe built at the company's Wichita, KS factory. On 18 February 1941, the War Department approved a $500,000 contract with GM for the delivery of 15 "Aerial Torpedoes." In April 1941, the Army decided to install radio-control equipment in the missile. On 21 May 1941, the Army changed the weapon's designation from "Aerial Torpedo" to "Controlled Bomb, Power Driven" as a result of the recommendation of a joint Army/Navy Conference. In July, only six months later, GM unexpectedly delivered the completed missile, now designated as the "General Motors Type A-l" (GMA-1) and again nicknamed it the *Bug*.

The *Bug* was successfully tested in the full-scale wind tunnel at Langley Field and later that year, initial ground and air testing began at the Muroc Bombing Range, Muroc, CA. The *Bug* was to be launched from a dolly pulled by a tow car down a twin-rail track and when 175 pounds of excess lift was reached, a spring mechanism was to automatically release it. The first launch attempt on 15 November 1941 was a debacle as its 91 mph takeoff speed was insufficient and the aircraft immediately crashed. The second *Bug* was modified so that it was released at the end of a 1,500 foot run when it reached 100 mph. On the next launch attempt on 5 December, the *Bug* went into a sharp climbing turn which the radio-controls attempted to correct. But, because of inadequate elevator controls, the automatic controls were engaged which put the *Bug* into a sharp diving turn resulting in another crash after 2.5 minutes of flight. The third *Bug*, with limits placed on the controls, was tested on 7 December 1941 but despite this remedy it still demonstrated overcontrol characteristics and five minutes after its radio transmitter was accidentally disconnected, this *Bug* also crashed. On the fourth test the next day, with the controls further limited, the GMA-1 continued to show overcontrol on both radio and automatic controls. The GMA-1 did fly 95 minutes before crashing during its landing because it had neither landing gear nor skids.

The *Bug* continued to have serious control system problems and the altitude and preset controls were sent back to Detroit for further development in late January 1942. Two-axis gyroscopes and spoilers were installed and a new launching system developed. Another *Bug* was sent to Detroit for the installation of television control equipment in February.

The modified *Bug* was tested at Eglin Field, FL in March and April 1942. Since automatic controls had not yet been perfected, they were not installed and all further testing was with radio-control equipment. The *Bug* was mounted atop a Cadillac chassis powered by two engines, geared through a Chevrolet transmission giving the vehicle four-wheel drive. When the driver reached 100 mph, he was to release the GMA-1. On 10 March the initial launch from a car failed because of a crosswind and a defective control connection. On 19 March, another GMA-1 took off and flew for 115 minutes before the operator purposely dove it into the ground after it experienced more control problems. The next test on 2 April showed better pitch control but difficulties with directional control continued to be encountered. After flying 110 minutes, the *Bug's* radio-control system failed, probably because of a bad generator, and 10 minutes later it crashed. The fifth, sixth, and seventh were equipped with two axis gyro stabilization units, but during tests in April directional stability remained poor, the crashes were uncontrolled and headwinds easily threw the bombs off course. At this point, there were three GMA-1s remaining at Eglin from the original ten, with five more being built.

On 16 April 1942, General Motors reported on the state of its A-1 project with its greatest concerns being its limitations of range, payload, and control. To increase range and inadequate payload GM suggested a twin-engine vehicle with a range of 900 to 1,200 miles, a speed of 150 mph, and a 2,000 pound payload. The cost was $9,900 for each bomb, $20,000 for the monorail launching gear, $2,000 for the tricycle launching gear, and $1,500 for each tricycle landing gear. A catapult launch was considered impractical and the report recommended a rocket assist along a short track and a GMA-1 with tricycle landing gear for conventional takeoffs.

However, only a week later the Chief of the Engineering Section raised a number of serious questions. Since the General Motors Lab Division had no manufacturing capacity; it would require a year to get a plant into production to build the GMA-1. The existing 500 pound payload was simply too small; but a larger payload would dictate a twin-engine vehicle and a new design; starting with an entirely new airframe. The report stated that launching the GMA-1 remained a critical problem. The means for controlling the GMA-1 directly to the target were not perfected and although in tests the GMA-1 had been easily controlled to the target by radio from a control aircraft which limited the number of *Bugs* controlled to five or ten due to radio interference. The training of radio-control equipment operators had not been addressed. However, the Chief felt that if the GMA-1 could be made operational by late 1943 or early 1944 the project should be continued and the range and payload problems could be addressed. In any case, a conference in late April recommended purchasing five more GMA-1s with a tricycle landing gear for landing after testing, as well as installing TV guidance, and three-axis gyros. As for launching the conference recommended launch tests with automobiles, monorails, and tricycle landing gear. In order to facilitate testing the 500 pound payload was standardized.

During testing at Eglin in the summer of 1942, modified GMA-ls with TV and three-axis gyros proved to be disappointing. On 17 July, the eighth GMA-1, equipped with TV and three axis control, took off in a steep climb from an automobile top but was non-responsive to the radio-controls and crashed after being airborne for two minutes due to moisture from the humid Florida air that permeated the control equipment. On 6 September, the ninth GMA-1 went out of control while it was taxiing, destroying its wings. On the 25th the same GMA-1, with new wings, was destroyed on its final taxi test prior to launch, possibly because one brake seized. Then five days later, the tenth A-1 went out of control and was destroyed on a takeoff attempt. Despite the lackluster results Gen, Arnold approved further development and training of personnel.

Tests were transferred to the drier climate at Muroc Bombing Range, CA but test continued to be unsuccessful. On 16 June 1942, GM proposed air launching, "pick-a-back," the GMA-1 in order to carry a 500 pound bomb and radio and TV control equipment for 15 minutes at a speed of 185 mph. After more unsuccessful tests in July and September, a conference held on 26 October 1942 decided that the air launching scheme was the A-1's only practical application. The "targets against which it can be economically used, the bomb will be useful only as an air-launched weapon due to its short range and low weight carrying capacity...." Landing gear testing was stopped because of the new emphasis on air launching and because the original A-1 design precluded takeoffs with landing gear. However, a wind tunnel test in 1943 at Wright Field of a GMA-1 mounted on top of a B-25 wooden model was as far as this air launching scheme ever progressed. In December 1942, Arnold approved a new A-1 development program and authorized the purchase of 100 A-1s with a planned range of 1,000 miles and a payload of 2,000 pounds.

The final tests of the GMA-l using automobile launching occurred on 24 and 27 May 1943 at Muroc. The GMA-1s were equipped with TV and three axis gyro stabilization. A control aircraft flew about a mile behind the *Bug*. On the first test the eleventh GMA-l made an erratic takeoff from a car top and showed instability in turns and sluggish control but flew for 95 minutes and then, with the aid of TV, the operator purposely crashed the missile within 75 feet of its target. Three days later, the last missile was launched from an automobile and also showed instability in turns and rolled out of control during a turn and crashed after 80 minutes flying time. Because of these basic problems and the cost of correcting them, it was recommended that further development be limited to operations with safety pilots aboard.

At this time the negative GMA-l test results caused Col. T.A. Sims, AMC Deputy Chief of Staff to recommend that the project be cancelled. On 24 August 1943, a scathing 14 page AAF report estimated that it would take 100 tests, $700,000, and 18 months to successfully develop the GMA-1's control system and the weapon would remain of limited value. An alternate plan was to redesign the *Bug* to accommodate a safety pilot; this would require $200,000 and two years. The question remained that even if the GMA-1 could be modified; it was judged to be of "questionable value" because of its limited payload of 500 pounds and range of 200 miles. On 6 September 1943, Maj.Gen. O.P. Echols, Assistant Chief of the Air Staff for Materiel, Maintenance, and Distribution, also recommended discontinuing the program. Following the successful October Muroc demonstration of controllable XBQ series weapons; it was determined that this new series promised greater success than the GMA-l and the program was cancelled on 23 December 1943. Due to the shortage of storage space, the remaining GMA-l airframes and wings were destroyed, the engines salvaged, and the control equipment and launch car returned to Wright Field.

The GMA-1 program, despite the large amount of time, effort, and money spent was a failure; not only because it did not see any combat but because its development and testing did not offer any new information for future developments. It only confirmed that that there were continued problems to be solved in just getting the weapon airborne. The GMA-1 verified the problems of testing an aircraft without a safety pilot onboard as without him the loss of the missile was much more probable. Also, testing without telemetry collected a reduced amount of information from each test.

GB Series Glide Bombs
GB-1 Glide Bomb
Brig.Gen. O.P. Echols initiated the Glide Bomb Project on 19 February 1941 with a request to the Intelligence Division to obtain information from the British about their glide bombs and torpedoes. The British Air

Commission in Washington sent W/C J.D. Brace to Wright Field on 13 February 1941 to discuss the glide bomb. A report on this conference prepared by the Experimental Engineering Section at Wright Field concluded with the statement that "effort should be directed to television and/or other equipment which would permit the changing of direction of the missile while in flight." Since America was not a belligerent at the time no further contact with the British on their glide bomb project was made.

The initial general specification issued by Wright Field for a glide bomb stated that the weapon was to be a simple winged glider airframe having control surfaces and housing gyro and servo mechanisms for stabilization. The airframe was to be interchangeable for use with a naval torpedo or 2,000 pound M34 bomb. Three aircraft manufacturers were requested to design a suitable GB airframe while the Experimental Engineering Section at Wright Field under Col. B.W. Chidlaw was to concurrently develop radio-controlled and seeking devices to be installed on the completed airframe.

The Aeronca Aircraft Company of Middleton, OH, incorporated glide bomb concepts of the Experimental Engineering Section into a radio controlled glider design that was more complicated than the origin specification. The weapon was tested on 8 and 9 December 1941 at Muroc Bombing Range, CA and the tests were successful resulting in a flight of 6.5 miles using radio control. On 18 April 1942, Echols reiterated that there was no directive eliminating radio control and further emphasized the need to develop all types of control, including radio, television, heat, light, and sound. The day before Gen. Arnold, eager for the weapon to reach combat readiness, personally reviewed work already completed on the project at Eglin Field. He recommended that development of complicated radio-control and seeking mechanisms be terminated until a simple glide bomb with wings and automatic pilot had been built and perfected. Chidlaw objected that the glider needed to be controlled and stabilized if it was to be as accurate as conventional bombs. Arnold was adamant and on 20 April 1942 sent an immediate and succinct response to Wright Field:

"There appears to be a misunderstanding as to the priorities on development and production of glide bombs. In order that all concerned may work to these same objectives I am again listing the order of priorities on these projects:

First priority: A simple glide bomb with stabilization only. This type of bomb will, of course, not have the accuracy of a more complicated type but when used in quantity will accomplish the result desired against vertical area targets. These bombs will be either attached to airplanes for release or be towed by airplanes and released. These will depend upon quantity of projectiles released for effect.

Second Priority: A glide bomb with stabilization plus control, either radio-television, heat, light or what have you. This type of bomb will have the accuracy required for semi-precision work against a particular target.

While work would continue on the radio-controlled versions, clearly the unguided, preset, gyro-stabilized glide bombs would receive the bulk of the Air Force's R&D resources at least for the time being."

On 24 June 1942, Arnold's gyro-stabilized glide bomb was officially designated as the GB-1 by the Production Engineering Section at Wright Field. The weapon was a 12 foot long, high-wing monoplane airframe of simple wooden construction with a 12 foot wing span including two ailerons for turning. Twin, P-38-type booms extended back from under the main wing and carried B-25-type tail assembly. This tail unit consisted of a horizontal stabilizer with a movable elevator and had two, square,

On 24 June 1942, Arnold's gyro-stabilized glide bomb was officially designated as the **GB-1 (MX-108)** by the Wright Field Production Engineering Section. This is a photo of an early mockup of the weapon which was a 12 foot long, high-wing monoplane airframe of simple wooden construction with a 12 foot wing span including two ailerons for turning. Twin booms extended back from under the main wing to the tail unit consisting of a horizontal stabilizer with a movable elevator and had two, square, rudderless, vertical fins attaching to its ends. (AAF)

Close up of the bomb shackle attachment to the slings retaining the Glide Bomb. (AAF)

rudderless, vertical fins attaching to its ends. The weapon weighed 2,338 pounds including the 2,000 M34 pound bomb warhead. The guidance system was located on a platform just behind the wing between the two booms. This system was a rudimentary, preset, automatic pilot-type system; gyro-stabilized in azimuth. It was adjusted on the mother aircraft just before release by the bombardier who could, after making his calculations for altitude, airspeed, and wind, adjust the bomb's ailerons, rudder, and stabilizer correspondingly before releasing the bomb. After release the bomb would then continue on its course without any further input possible from the bombardier. At 15,000 feet the theoretical accuracy was 700 feet in azimuth and 2,800 feet in range with a glide ratio of six to one (i.e. for every foot of altitude, it could glide six feet in distance). Because of their long flight time glide bombs were subject to the effect of winds which significantly influenced their accuracy.

At Gen. Arnold's request Gen. Grandison Gardner investigated the project's status at Air Material Command. Gardner was told by AMC Colonels Williams and Holloman that a simple gyro-stabilized glide bomb could probably be design frozen and mass produced by late summer 1942. Thus, it appears that Arnold was led to believe that the GB-1 was only weeks or a few months away from combat readiness. But when the late summer arrived the Aeronca-built airframe was in the test stages at

Muroc, CA. Of 12 tests (one with radio-control), seven were successful. Gen. Echols recommended to Gen. Arnold that "We might profitably put the glide bomb to immediate use" and a directive was issued in October for the necessary procurement to get the GB-1 into combat as soon as possible. The Aeronca design was selected and frozen for production as "a controllable glide bomb essentially consisting of a high-wing type of aerodynamic structure with two booms and tail surfaces, equipped with a servo control assembly and attached to a 2,000 pound demolition bomb. The course was to be preset and no control was to be exercised after launch." Designated as project MX-108, Aeronca was scheduled to provide 4,300 GB-1 airframes at 800 per month by December 1942 and the Hammond Instrument Company was to manufacture the more intricate gyroscopic stabilizers at the same rate by March 1943. The Hammond Instrument Company was founded by Lauren Hammond of the electronic organ fame. By December GB-1 production was reduced to 250 per month as Hammond was unable to maintain the required production rate but somehow 2,225 GB-1 assemblies were scheduled to be delivered by no later than the end of February 1943.

In late 1941 initial tests using a Douglas B-23 bomber were conducted to demonstrate it was suited for the project. The B-23 flew at 200 mph carrying the Glide Bomb below its fuselage between the engine nacelles

In late 1941 initial tests using a **Douglas B-23** bomber were conducted to demonstrate it was suited for the project. The B-23 flew at 200 mph carrying the Glide Bomb below its fuselage between the engine nacelles on specially fabricated carrying mechanisms. The photo shows a B-23 testing its carrying capabilities by dropping a 1,000 pound bomb which was the payload of the GB-1. (AAF)

on specially fabricated carrying mechanisms. Three B-23 Glide Bomb Squadrons were to be formed in Seattle, San Francisco, and Los Angeles by May 1942. However, there were not enough B-23s available in tactical quantities. Upon further consideration Wright Field suggested to Gen. Gardner that the B-17E was the most suitable aircraft and in July 1942, the necessary technical instructions were issued for B-17E modification kits. The GB-1 could not be carried internally so special wing racks and shackles were devised which could be installed in a half hour. The underwing hard points had to be retrofitted to provide adequate structural strength to mount a wing rack unit able to suspend a 2,500 pound glide bomb assembly. The wing rack's mechanical and electrical connections to had to be installed to permit the bombardier to activate the GB's stabilizing gyroscopes and set its flight controls before releasing it. Originally it was thought that the B-17s could be modified by installing the hard points and wiring for the wing racks and shackles while the bombers were still on the assembly lines. But this would not be possible until early February 1943 and until then all GB-carrying B-17s would have to be modified by the Materiel Command.

B-17E	Max. Speed		
Payload	25,000 ft	Ceiling	Range
Internal Bombs	310 mph	28,000 ft	2,300 mi
Glide Bombs	280 mph	26,500 ft	2,150 mi

There was a delay in procuring a B-17E for testing as officers under Arnold had no interest in the GB and in July Arnold finally had to let his subordinates know that they had better develop an interest in "his" project. Col. F.O. Carroll, the new Chief of the Experimental Engineering Section, immediately ordered the delivery of ten B-17Fs to the Middletown Air Depot for GB modification by 18 August in time to meet Arnold's order for large scale B-17/GB-1 tests. Ten modified B-17Fs were to drop a total of 60 GB-1s, 20 from each of three altitudes and although the records of the results of the tests are incomplete, it seems that they were successfully carried on external wing shackles and dropped singly and en masse by B-17s. About 70% of those released flew straight courses and struck the ground in formation with reasonably reliable results; placing them in an equilateral triangle, one mile on each side, but from only 5,000 feet which was an altitude which would make the dropping aircraft vulnerable to AA fire. Amazingly, the report stated that 100% "accuracy" could be achieved "hitting" a medium sized city, similar to nearby Dayton Ohio, from 30,000 feet! The report went on to state that a smaller target could be accurately hit but from decreased altitude and range, which, of course, again meant more vulnerability to AA fire, which negated the point of the project. The Project Officers reported that inaccuracy was the nature of this design configuration and that it should not be intended for precision bombing but for bombs dropped en masse. The tests showed that the externally mounted wing racks caused aerodynamic drag which reduced cruising speed, maximum altitude, and range. Therefore it was decided that the B-17Fs were to be internally wired before leaving for Britain and GB bomb shackles and wing racks were to be forwarded separately to be installed only when a glide bomb mission was scheduled.

On 8 October 1942 the Assistant Chief of Air Staff Plans directed that the use of stabilized glide bombs be initiated in the UK at the earliest possible time. He directed the procurement of 1,000 glide bombs per month by March 1943. It was established that a minimum of 20 glide bomb mechanics would be required for each bomb group equipped with the glide bombs. These mechanics were to maintain the bombs and make certain they were correctly mounted and if not dropped during a mission, dismounted. The Plans Division directed the Individual Training Division to train 20 glide bomb mechanics by 15 December 1942 and

150 by on 1 March 1943 but first a preliminary training curriculum would have to be developed by the Materiel Command's Special Weapon Unit. Pilots, bombardiers, and aircraft instrument technicians would also need extensive specialized training. In December 1942 there was a shortage of modified B-17Fs to fulfill all the training and testing requirements. A single B-17F was sent to Eglin (and later transferred to Muroc Field, CA) to be shared by the instrument technicians and glide bomb bombardier students with the Wright Field engineers who were performing high altitude glide bombing tests.

Between 20 and 29 November 1942 the Equipment Laboratory conducted tests to collect glide bomb ballistic data at Eglin during which time 13 drops were made with only two of the bombs stalling or tumbling and failing to glide. Tests number one through eleven were single bombs dropped by a B-23 while in tests number twelve and thirteen two bombs were dropped simultaneously from a B-17F. The Hammond gyroscopic stabilizers functioned effectively if the bomb was released smoothly and in level flight and were adopted as standard for the pre-set glide bomb. The stabilizers kept the GB's wings level and corrected for wind gusts and turbulence as required. However, small discrepancies in construction would cause variations in the center of gravity; causing a few bombs to wobble when they were released. If the movement was too great, the stabilizing gyroscopes were unable to compensate and the bomb would tumble. The average miss during these tests was a non-precision quarter mile in azimuth and a half mile in range. The T-4 detonator/destructor with 0.1 second delay fusing for 2.5 pounds of Tetrytol was standardized.

The Equipment Laboratory conducted a second series of tests from 6 through 24 December 1942 which basically had the same results as the November tests. The GB-1 was found to be a stable glider but was comparatively inaccurate and susceptible to stalling and tumbling if the bombardier did not set the rudder and aileron controls correctly before release. The accuracy of the bomb was subject to the bombardier knowing the bomber's exact heading and altitude; the accurate distance to the target before release; and his ability to precisely factor in the effect of the winds.

As was the case with any new weapon the GB-1 was prone to developmental bugs and then the inevitable demands for further testing which frequently led to the need for modifications which then hindered mass production. Reliable ballistic data was essential for design concerns and was fundamental for training bombardiers. Each new test threatened to invalidate previous test data so on 4 January 1943, the Equipment Laboratory at Wright Field recommended that the design of the GB-1 be frozen.

By January 1943 the GB-1 specifications were workable and frozen; the B-17F could effectively carry and deliver the weapon; and there were ample trained personnel: pilots, bombardiers, mechanics, and technicians to maintain and deploy these bombs in combat. Aeronca was manufacturing enough GB-1s for combat use. But the bottom line continued to be that the GBs were Gen. Arnold's pet project and he wanted them tested and used in combat so 1 March 1943 was set for the GB-1's operational debut.

However, delays continued to hinder the weapon's progress toward combat. Among the most important issues was the need to complete testing to determine operational limitations and to develop an operational doctrine. In testing not one GB-1 had been dropped from the combat altitudes of 15,000 feet or more. The Hammond electric gyro continued to have problems and the new GB-1 B-17 modification kits would not be ready until mid-March. Also, there not enough bomb racks and shackles available to equip the four bomber groups scheduled to carry the GB and then they could not be shipped until 1 March at the earliest.

In test drops at Tonopah, NV the bombs had an extreme net deflection error (i.e. the distance the bomb landed left or right of the target) of

Eglin GB-1 Test

Between 20 and 29 November 1942 the Equipment Laboratory conducted tests to collect glide bomb ballistic data at Eglin during which time 13 drops were made with only two of the bombs stalling or tumbling and failing to glide. The Equipment Laboratory conducted a second series of tests from 6 through 24 December 1942 which basically had the same results as the November tests. (AAF)

Reliable testing data was essential for training bombardiers and to begin mass production so on 4 January 1943, the Equipment Laboratory at Wright Field recommended that the design of the GB-1 be frozen. (AAF)

Tests number 1 through 11 were single bombs dropped by a B-23 while in tests number 12 and 13 two bombs were dropped simultaneously from a B-17F. (AAF)

between 4,023 and 6,084 feet when the bomb was dropped from an altitude of 9,700 feet (i.e. the error was one-half to two-thirds the altitude of the bomber at the time of release). This deflection error would only increase in combat due to the lack of accurate information on the winds over enemy territory. With a six to one glide ratio; a 10,000 foot release would mean the GB would glide 11.5 miles before hitting the target and at 25,000 feet the glide distance would 28+ miles which would require perfect visibility (rare in the ETO) and preclude the use of the existing Norden Bombsight. When dropping a GB from 25,000 feet, an error of only one degree in the dropping angle would cause a range error of approximately three miles, while a one degree heading error would result in a deflection error of a half mile. The externally mounted glide bombs slowed the B-17's cruising speed at high altitudes by as much as 30 mph, reduced its maximum combat ceiling by at least 1,500 feet, and adversely affected the bomber's combat range by as much as 150 miles.

By the end of January 1943, Aeronca had over 1,500 GB-1 completed assemblies in storage but was provided with no shipping destinations during the first quarter of 1943 because the GB-1 had not yet been approved for combat use from either a technical or a tactical perspective. The Air Materiel Command reduced Aeronca's production requirements from 2,000 to 1,000 per month.

Concerning the proposed 1 March operational date of the GB-1 there still were no tactical requirements for their combat employment in the ETO, nor had the Operational Plans Division determined the operational need for glide bombs except that Gen. Arnold wanted them. So on 2 March the Air Materiel Command released a memorandum proposing the termination of GB-1 production but on the same day the Operational Plans Division asked that GB-1 manufacture be continued until its worth had been determined by not less than 100 operational missions in the ETO. These operational planning problems resulted in the delay of the combat debut of the GB-1 until at least 1 May 1943. On 15 March Aeronca advised Wright Field that it was reducing its production to 500 units per month and at this reduced rate the contract for 4,300 units would not be completed until 10 May.

On 2 April, the Air Plans Division issued a comprehensive report on the status of the GB-1 to Gen. Arnold. The report stated that due to their large average range and deflection errors, 100 or more glide bombs should be dropped as "area bombs" from 16,000 feet in clear weather when there was little or no wind over the target area. Because Aeronca had been ordered to reduce its production to 1,000 units per month until an evaluation was made, the report asked that the evaluation be made ASAP so that unnecessary production could be halted in case the GB glide bomb was unsuccessful. The report also recommended that future glide bomb development concentrate on "precision guided variants." Finally the report requested that the 8th Air Force "promptly evaluate" the glide bombs and either reject them or be obligated to use them. The report caused Arnold to visit Eglin to personally investigate his pet project's lack of development. Once there the General saw the inattention and apathy surrounding "his" project and launched a tirade and ordered that the unguided GB-1 project be allocated the majority of available funds and personnel. Arnold's dictum would have dire consequences on America's research and development of guided weapons during World War II. The GB-1 was a "concept" weapon that should ideally have been immediately replaced once the basic concept had been proven viable. It could then be adapted to any of the many other guided variations glide bombs could take. Arnold's insistence on developing and testing the GB-1 and then proving it in combat removed funds and researchers from the more promising and nearly completed guided GB-4 and GB-8 radio-controlled GB-1 versions; delaying their introduction by many months.

On 13 May 1943, the Eighth Air Force found that it had been issued no operational requirements for glide bombs so the GB project was neglected in favor of precision bombing. Gen. Ira Eaker, Commander of the 8AF, stated that American bombing doctrine stressed "precision bombing of point objectives" rather than the inaccurate area bombing demonstrated by the GB. Eaker also knew that the GB-1 would decrease the speed and payload of the carrying aircraft and increase its vulnerability beyond that of conventional bombing methods and would require fighter escort. When the GB-carrying B-17s flew in formations with conventional bomb-carrying B-17s the loss of airspeed would open up the tight protective formations as the maximum cruising speed of a B-17F carrying glide bombs was 280 mph which was 30 mph less than when carrying conventional bombs internally. The decrease in air speed meant that the bomber formations equipped with only GBs were over enemy territory 10% longer and increased the relative speed advantage of *Luftwaffe* fighters and made it easier for them to catch and attack the slower GB bomber formation.

Maj.Gen. Barney Giles, Chief of the Air Staff Operations, Commitments, and Requirements Division (OC&R) then recommended that glide bomb and components procurement to be concluded as soon as possible and that permanent storage be arranged for completed units. On 3 June Aeronca was notified that after the initial 4,000 on order were produced and delivered production was to cease. Nonetheless, on 16 May the Materiel Command sent a glide bomb contingent of four pilots and four bombardiers who had received limited glide bomb training; a control technician, an ordnance engineer, and a Boeing factory representative to England to demonstrate the GB-1. The unimpressive demonstrations were completed on 22 May and concluded that all future GB units be equipped and trained in the US

After the costly 17 August 1943 Regensburg-Schweinfurt bombing raids Gen. Arnold personally flew to Britain to visit Gen. Eaker at 8th Air Force headquarters to reassess the Eighth's operational status and also to check on his GB-1 project. Arnold ordered the Glide Bomb Program to be immediately instituted in the ETO in early October 1943. On 11 September Arnold directed Eaker to prepare 36 B-17s for testing the GB and that 1,000 sets were to be sent to the UK. Meanwhile, the AAF School of Applied Tactics (AAFSAT) in Orlando, FL was to conduct tests to determine detailed operational and tactical factors for employing GB-1s in combat particularly: the range of the GB, the effect of reduced airspeed of the mother aircraft, evasive actions of the mother aircraft, the effect of GB use on bomber formations (i.e. the best defensive, mutually supporting formation that allowed for the simultaneous release of bombs from this formation), and to determine the types of targets that were suitable for the deployment of glide bombs. Again these testing requirements clearly revealed that the operational need for glide bombs still had not been officially determined and that the GB-1 existed only because Arnold wanted to use it in combat.

On 14 September Air Staff directed Air Materiel Command to ship 500 GB-1s to the 8AF in England ASAP for use in the first glide bomb missions scheduled to be flown in October. On 20 October 1943, 40 US trained crews along with their aircraft arrived in England and were assigned to the 41st Combat Bomb Wing with Capt. James Tillman assigned as the 8AF Project Officer. Once assigned the GB crews learned that the supposedly ASAP-shipped GB-1 sets were still in the US and would arrive in about two months but this delay was beneficial as it would permit the necessary training of the more than 80 ordnance technicians assigned to the project. Also, Brig.Gen. Robert Travis, CG of the 41st Combat Wing, wanted additional aircrew training with these weapons before the first mission was flown.

On 19 October 1943 Gen. Arnold wrote Gen. Spaatz:

"At present some doubt is felt that these bombs (GB-1s) in their standardized mass glide version will have sufficient accuracy to attain great effectiveness against specific buildings in submarine pen attacks. From 5,000 feet these bombs can consistently be placed in a one mile square and it is possible that improvements will cut this to a one half mile square. Even this may not be sufficiently accurate for anti-submarine purposes.

Meanwhile we are exerting every effort to make possible the precision version of this glide bomb (GB-4s). It now appears possible that this version will be available in the spring and should be a much more valuable weapon than the mass glide type."

Grapefruit Practice Missions
By 19 November, 115 aircraft and crews were trained and by 2 December an additional 28 crews in three bomb groups were fully trained to fly operational missions, code named "*Grapefruit*." The Grapefruit designation was thought to have been from its Florida tests in June 1941. For these practice missions Col. Maurice Preston of the 379BG delegated pilot Maj. Robert Kittle, navigator Capt. James Edwards, and bombardier Capt. Joseph Glaser to investigate and develop GB bombing tactics. They determined that the minimum speed at bomb release was to be at least 180 IAS to put the GB into glide attitude. To get the B-17 to 185 to 200 IAS the bomber had to climb to 2,000 feet above the intended GB release altitude and enter a gentle two minute descent and release the GBs at the prescribed altitude. After releasing their burden the lighter bombers accelerated to 250 mph to leave the flak in the target area.

The first *Grapefruit* mission was scheduled to be flown on 12 December but was inexplicably cancelled. However, 25 individual practice missions were flown along with one mass-formation drop into the North Sea. The test drops, often in the poor visibility, made it apparent that at least one bomber in each formation would have to be equipped with H2X radar and six navigators were sent to receive training on this equipment. Also, special bombardment charts had to be developed to provide data to bombardiers to ensure that they could quickly perform the calculations necessary to accurately predict the glide bomb trajectory which was much longer than conventional bombs and could continue for up to six minutes after release.

Belated Debut
The first documented GB-1 operational mission was not flown until 28 May 1944, five and a half months later. Searching the incomplete records of the 41ˢᵗ Combat Bomb Wing and its three Bomb Groups, the 303ʳᵈ, 379ᵗʰ, and 384ᵗʰ from December 1943 to late May 1944 there is no specific explanation given for the GB-1's belated debut but it appears that the dismal European weather, operational priorities, and logistical delays were probable causes.

The GB-1 operational missions required perfect weather conditions which were not prevalent in the winter of 1943-44. The English winter weather arrived early and was so bad that the 8AF was seldom able to assemble formations large enough to takeoff in the early mornings when there was rare good weather and then return to base before the weather closed in. From mid-December 1943 to the end of January 1944 the 8AF flew only 10 missions that reached their targets in Germany and the majority of these required H2X blind bombing radar to bomb through the cloud cover. When the weather finally improved on 20 February, the newly formed (29 December 1943) US Strategic Air Forces (USSTAF)

under Gen. Spaatz was committed to the *Big Week*, a major concerted air campaign against German aircraft and oil production. On every day that there was clear weather the USSTAF put up as many as 1,000 heavy bombers against aircraft and oil targets deep inside Germany and to lure *Luftwaffe* interceptors which were intended to be shot down by escorting P-51 Mustangs. These large missions increased in March with the better Spring weather and by the end of April German oil production had been severely curtailed and the *Luftwaffe* had lost many veteran pilots and faced a shortage of gasoline. The GBs were not suited to *Big Week* operations as aircraft factories, airfields, and oil facilities were pinpoint targets which were not conducive to glide bomb attack. Also, obviously the slower B-17s carrying the GB-1s could not be incorporated into the faster conventional bomber formations without being shot down by *Luftwaffe* fighters.

Another reason for the GB-1's delayed operational introduction was that the glide bombs had been stored for so long that a number of the batteries that powered the gyroscope were unable to hold a charge. The Exide Battery Company was contacted to send 100 more but the company had stopped production of that type of battery. To secure the battery Exide would have to set up a new production line that would have to turn out at least several thousand for Exide to agree to accept a contract. Once the contract was signed the new batteries could not be shipped until late spring.

First Glide Bomb Mission
The first glide bomb mission was scheduled for 26 April 1944 but was recalled because of bad weather. It was not until 28 May 1944, that weather, logistical, and other snafus were remedied so the first glide bomb mission could be dispatched. Three Bomb Groups of the 41ˢᵗ Combat Wing were to drop their GB-1s on Koln Eifeltor (Cologne) marshalling yards. Fifty nine aircraft each carrying two glide bombs took off with one 379BG B-17 aborting. After assembly the lead 303BG (under Col. Kermit Stevens) flew at 19,500 feet, the low 379BG (Col. Maurice Preston) at 19,000 feet, and the high 384BG (Col. Dale Smith) at 21,000 feet. The groups cruised at 140 mph indicated airspeed (IAS) in excellent mission weather with 20 mile downward visibility, encountering no enemy flak or fighters. As the initial point (IP) was reached (about 20 miles from the dropping point, using a north-south road as a reference) each group went into a predetermined dive sequence of 1,000 to 1,500 feet per minute for 90 to 120 seconds to pick up the necessary 195 mph release speed. At 1306 hours, 108 bombs were released, first by the low 379BG at 17,000 feet, followed by the lead 303BG at 17,600 feet and finally by the high 384BG at 19,300 feet. After release the three Groups made a climbing turn; reassembling with the lead group at 19,000 feet. The B-17 ball turret gunners had a quite a show as 28 of the bombs went into either nose down spins or flat spins, while others did acrobatics. As they continued to watch they saw explosions occur over a large area with the P-38 recon aircraft recording the debacle. The results were very poor and were described as comparable to the worst kind of indiscriminate area bombing:

GB Bomb Data	303BG (Lead)	379BG (Low)	384BG (High)
Bombs on Target	28	22	31
Bombs Spun In	10	14	4
Late Release	0	2	2
Accidental Release	0	0	2

Of the 81 "on target" bombs 44 bursts were counted within the city as defined by a radius of 3.5 miles from the central cathedral with seven hitting factories and railroad yards; six hitting residential areas throughout

First Glide Bomb Mission

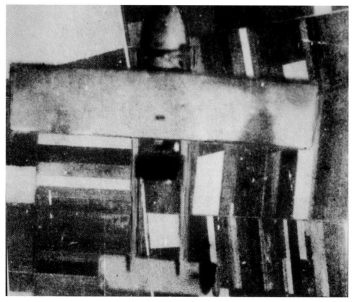

On 28 May 1944 the **first glide bomb mission** occurred when three Bomb Groups of the 41st Combat Wing, 59 B-17s each carrying two glide bombs, were assigned to drop their GB-1s on Cologne. At the Initial Point each group went into a predetermined dive sequence of 1,000 to 1,500 feet per minute for 90 to 120 seconds to pick up the necessary 195 mph release speed at which time 108 bombs were released. After release the three Groups made a climbing turn and reassembled at 19,000 feet. The results were very poor and were compared to the worst kind of indiscriminate area bombing with only 44 of the 108 GB-1s hitting within 3.5 miles of the aiming point. (All AAF)

the city; six hitting previously bombed out areas in the central city; and at least 25 hit parks, rivers, and other open areas within the city. But 15 bursts were seen in open fields located 17 miles to the southwest of the city center while another hit an open field 15 miles to the west of the city. There were three "effective" hits which were probably accidental: one hit was recorded on the Shagen-Hagen submarine battery factory, another on a siding of a railroad marshalling yard, and a third hit on a small warehouse on the at the river wharf northeast of the city. The bombs arrived before German air raid sirens sounded and the Germans reported that 82 civilians were killed and at least 1,500 injured in what German radio propagandist, William Joyce, "Lord Haw Haw" described as a "terror raid' which perhaps it was considering the gross inaccuracy and lack of warning.

On 28 May, a post mission investigation concluded that the Mutual Furniture Co., an Aeronca subcontractor, was found to be responsible for faulty workmanship in airframe fabrication particularly in the gluing of joints and skins. The preset automatic pilot data was extremely sensitive to inaccuracies in construction especially on the forward ends of the booms. Also, it was concluded that the large number of times the bombs were loaded and unloaded waiting for good weather also affected settings. Prop wash and "imperfect adjustment" were determined to be the cause of the 28 bombs which "spun-in."

A memorandum from Brig.Gen. Robert Williams of the 1BG assessed the mission and made the following recommendations:

"This type of bombing while it avoids flak, subjects the airplanes to greater fighter hazard, and results in the worst type of area bombing. It is the opinion of this headquarters that for an enemy installation in this theatre much better results can be accomplished at very little extra cost by utilization of conventional type high altitude precision bombing. It therefore recommended that a review be rendered on this project and its use be discontinued in this theater."

Another, later report weighed the operational advantages and disadvantage of GB-1 deployment:

Advantages
1) Safety of release away from anti-aircraft defenses
2) The weapon's flat trajectory increased the percentage of hits on built up areas as compared to conventionally dropped bombs.
3) The glide bomb had a very large skip on impact, up to one mile on land and one third mile on water with a 40 to 50 foot high bounce. This gave the glide bomb a good chance to hit some obstacle in its path.

Disadvantages
1) The wind affected ballistics.
2) The 6 to l glide angle required a release of 20 to 25 miles from the target and therefore the visibility needed to be excellent.
3) At 25,000 feet a 1° error in the drop angle caused a three mile range error. A 1° error in heading caused a half mile deflection error.

4) The external mounting of the GB-1 precluded its use in any weather condition where icing threatened; as ice would coat the missiles fuselage and wings and often clog the release mechanism.
5) Also the external mounting of two GB-1's slowed the B-17 mother aircraft by 30 mph at high altitudes, decreased the service ceiling by 1,500 feet, and decreased its range. The bomber's lift was decreased and its stalling speed decreased by nine mph.
6) Since the release speed was 195 mph the maximum formation altitude was only 20,000 feet.
7) GB-1 release speed was critical. If the release speed exceeded that for the control settings on the missile, the GB-1 could fly up into the mother aircraft and if the release speed was too low then the GB-1 would go into a spin.
8) The GB-1 when used as an area bombardment weapon had a better chance of hitting vertical targets such as buildings than a conventional bomb. The glide bomb however was not as destructive, as it would hit the upper one third of a building on its glide-in or bounce rather than hit the building's base which often destroyed the entire structure. Also, the destruction of utilities and blockage of streets was not as great.
9) The conduct of a major glide bomb offensive would require a large amount of precious shipping space transiting from America to England. At this time the Allied invasion of France required vast amounts of supplies and cargo space was at a premium

After the bomb's 28 May debut fiasco, interest in the GB-1 program quickly subsided. On 23 June the Production Engineering Section notified the Equipment Section that all GB-1 parts and subassemblies were to be examined and those that were considered to be of poor quality were to be written off. On 4 August the Air Materiel Command was directed to inventory all GB-1s stored in the continental US so that a plan could be instituted to dispose of them. On 15 September 1944 the GB-1 program was officially terminated by finance report #405710 which stated that the program had cost $2,223,261 and the cost of termination was $275,112.

Despite Gen. Arnold's support; the GB-1 program never had the backing of operational commanders in the ETO, which slowed not only the development of this potentially valuable weapon but also its radio-controlled successors. To be effective glide bombs had to be accurate but it was only Gen. Arnold's insistence that the designers and scientists working on the guided glide bomb programs were to concentrate on the simple unguided GB-1 which delayed work on the more promising television-guided GB-4 and GB-8 glide bombs being developed concurrently. While the GB-1 was no longer considered a viable weapon, its airframe would be used for GT-1, air-dropped Mark 13 naval torpedo.

GB-2 and GB-3 Glide Bombs
The GB-2 and GB-3 both used a 2,000 pound AN-M66 bomb. The Bellanca GB-2 was 11.75 feet long, had a span of 12 feet, glided at a speed 309 mph and used the same preset glide path principle as the GB-1. However, compared to the latter, the GB-2 had more adverse effects when carried by the bomber and the control equipment was more difficult to

GB-2 (AAF)

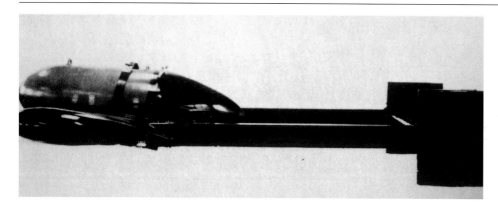

GB-3 (AAF)

install. The Timm GB-3 was 14.1 feet long, had a span of 12 feet, glided at 168 mph and had similar disadvantages as the GB-2. Therefore, the GB-2 and GB-3 were cancelled after the initial test flight phases in early 1942 and the GB-1 was selected for mass production.

GB-4 Television Controlled Bomb

The GB-4 program (MX-108) used a modified GB-1 Aeronca airframe designated as the Pomykata glider named after Maj. J.M. Pomykata of the Technical Service Command. The Pomykata version, built by the Klassen Company of Los Angeles, had the same general dimensions as the Aeronca type (12 foot wingspan and length including the bomb) but the twin tail boom assembly was replaced by a cylinder which was bolted to the bomb itself. Design changes were made to make the GB-4 more aerodynamic and thus more expensive.

The GB-4 had an 8:1 glide ratio and traveled at 230-240 mph with this speed increased by putting the mother aircraft into a dive before release. Two GB-4s were to be carried on external wing racks on the B-17 cutting its speed by only eight mph due to the better aerodynamics of the missile and carrying racks. With an eye towards use in the Pacific, design provisions were made to carry one GB-4 on a B-25 twin engine medium bomber.

The 8AF brass objected to the area bombing characteristics of the GB-1 because it opposed 8AF precision bombing doctrine but accepted the GB-4 because it employed a guidance system intended to provide precision bombing. The GB-4 had a remote radio that controlled range and azimuth with a television transmitter for position determination placed in a faired "bathtub" container under its airframe fuselage.

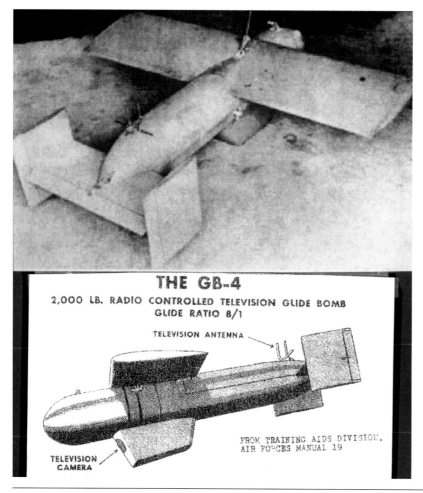

GB-4 (AAF)

Production
There were 2,000 on order from the Klassen Company with an initial experimental order for 200 for delivery on 15 April 1944, 300 in May and June and 300 per month until the contracted 2,000 was completed. However, there were no Hammond control boxes available in April with 100 due on 8 May, 250 to 300 in June and 350 to 400 per month until the contract with Hammond was completed. The Aircraft Radio Laboratory had only 300 television sets immediately available with no more available until August.

Television Equipment for Guided Bombs
In 1927, Philo Farnsworth, the first inventor to transmit a television image, developed the dissector tube which was the basis of all current electronic televisions. NBC began regularly scheduled broadcasts in New York on 30 April 1939 with a broadcast from the 1939 World's Fair. Pre-war television transmission and receiving equipment being dependent upon vacuum tube technology was very heavy and bulky and also very fragile.

New TV standards had to be established for military use after considering the size, weight, power demand, circuit complexity, resolution, and linearity interrelationships. Military television transmitting systems for guided missiles needed to be smaller, lighter, and more durable but where possible broadcast TV standards and equipment was to be used.

In December 1940, RCA proposed radio and television control for glide bombs and Wright Field which had previously been working

The **ARE/F/G/H receivers** (Signal Corps SCR-550-T1) were fixed frequency complements to the ATE/F/G/H camera/transmitters. The 7 inch green phosphor CRT (Cathode Ray Tube) is seen on front of the set. (Author's Collection)

on television control for target aircraft accepted the proposal and drew up military specifications for the unit. Consideration was given to the transmitter unit: size, weight, and power demand along with picture quality, sensitivity, and reliability. In early 1941, the Hazeltine Corp. of Little Neck, NY, submitted an independently conceived television system for testing. Meanwhile, the radio-controlled (only) tests using the glide airframe were successful leading personnel at Wright Field's Aircraft Radio Laboratory (ARL) to predict that in four months a gyro-stabilized, radio/TV system could be developed once a suitable TV unit became available. A.V. Loughren and D.E. Hartnett of Hazeltine and Section D-3 of the NDRC pursued development in this area. The design of the first small television system, known as SCR-549-T1, was the result of their investigation.

Television Systems Used During World War 2
Three basic television systems were developed for the military during the war: BLOCK, RING, and MIMO.

BLOCK 1
The ATE, ATF, ATG, ATH television camera/transmitters series (contracted in 1942) was known as BLOCK 1 and were housed in a single case. The sets consisted of four fixed frequencies, 78, 90, 102 and 114 MHz with the channels 9 mc wide due to the use of double sideband transmission. The pickup tube was an iconoscope and the output tube was an 829. The input voltage is 12.5 VDC and the RF power was 15 watts. The components to the system were the CRV-59AAA to AAD camera transmitter, CRV-21ABY dynamotor, CRV-66ACS to ACV antenna, and CRV-60AAR monitor.

The ARE, ARF, ARG, ARH sets were the matching receiver/displays for the accompanying camera/transmitters. The receivers were fixed frequency, complements to the transmitter, with a self-contained dynamotor and 7 inch green phosphor CRT (Cathode Ray Tube). The input voltage was 25 VDC. The components to the set were the CRV-46ABP to ABS receiver, CRV-23ACR voltage control unit, CRV-66ACO to ACR, and ADV to ADY antenna.

Early RCA television camera being installed in a Beech AT-11 Kansan for testing. (AAF)

The Signal Corps version of the camera/transmitter was the SCR-549-T1, T2. The receiver was the SCR-550-T1, T2. The AAF sets were similar to the Navy sets except for slight modifications of design. BLOCK I was flight tested in a B-18 in April 1941 at Wright Field.

BLOCK 3-A
The ATJ set was known as BLOCK 3, the first in a series contracted in 1943 that was refined during and after the war. The improved camera and transmitter were separate units. The transmitter could be tuned to five different frequencies from 264 to 312 MHz, each 9 mc wide. The pickup tube was an iconoscope and the output tubes were 8025's. The RF output power was 15-watts and the input voltage was 27.5 VDC. The set components were the CRV-59AAE (BC-1211) camera; CRV-52ACA, ABW, ABX, ABY and ABZ (BC-1212) transmitters; remote start switch (SW-219); CEK-21981 (DM-56) dynamotor; CRV-53AAB (JB-101) junction box; CRV-66AED to AEH (AN-142 to AN-146) antenna; CRV-60ABK (BC-1214) monitor; and CRV-60058 (I-206) test meter. Each of the five transmitters was preset to channels 1 to 5.

The ARJ set was the matching receiver to the ATJ transmitting set. The receiver was tunable to five channels in the 300 mc band. The set had a self-contained dynamotor and 7 inch green phosphor CRT. Input voltage was 28.6 VDC. The components to the set were the CRV-46ACC (BC-1213) receiver, CRV-66ADT (AN-133) antenna, and CRV-60ABK (BC-1214) monitor.

The Signal Corps version of the transmitting set was SCR-549-T3 and SCR-549-T3-A while the receiver was the SCR-550-T3 and SCR-550-T3-A.

BLOCK 3-B
The ATK set (contracted in late 1943) was known as BLOCK 3B. The major changes from the ATJ BLOCK 3-B included improved sweep oscillators in the camera and stability improvements to the transmitter. The transmitter was tunable to 10 channels from 264 to 372 MHz. The input voltage was 28.6 VDC. The components to the system were the CRV-59AAE camera; CRV-52ACB transmitter; CEK-21981 or CC-21981 dynamotor; CRV-53AAB junction box; and CRV-66AFX to AGB, AEJ to AEN antenna.

The ARK set was the matching receiver to both the ATJ and ATK transmitting sets. The major changes from the ARK were the improved RF and IF stages. The receiver could be tuned ten 8 megacycle channels, separated by 12 megacycles in the 300 mc band. The set had a self-contained dynamotor and 7 inch green phosphor CRT. The input voltage was 28.6 VDC. The components to the system were the CRV-46ACD receiver; CRV-66ADT, AFW and ADU antenna; CRV-60ABK monitor; CRV-10175 monitor light shield; and CRV-10173 receiver light shield.

RCA subcontracted part of the production run to Farnsworth Television (CFN), which also produced the ATK and ARK sets.

BLOCK 3-B Second Contract
Under the new contract, the nomenclature was changed to the AN nomenclature system and further improvements were made. The AN/AXT-2 was the transmitting set. The PH-522/AXT-2 camera was an improved CRV-59AAE with a solenoid-controlled haze filter. The transmitter was the T-61/AXT-2, which was the same as CRV-52ACB. The J-60/AXT-2 junction box was the same as CRV-53AAB. The dynamotor was the DY-25/AXT-2. The antennas are the same as the ATK and the remote switch box was the SA-34/AXT-2.

AN/AXR-1 was the receiving set while the receiver was the R-68/AXR-1 which was the same as the CRV-46ACD except for the addition of 11 enemy destructors. The antennas were the same as the ARK. The ID-66/AXR-1 monitor was the same as CRV-60ABK except for the addition of four enemy destructors.

This set was built by RCA and Farnsworth Radio & Television and was contracted in 1944.

BLOCK 3-B Third Contract
This contract (1945) was to take advantage of the new image orthicon technology for the cameras. Two models were built. The first model, the CRV-59AAG, incorporated the first LM-15 production image orthicon tube, contracted in 1944. The next generation camera, the PH-548/AXT-2A, used the improved 2P21 image orthicon. Both of these cameras were interchangeable with ATJ and ATK equipment. The AN/AXT-2A used the same transmitter, dynamotor, junction box, and antennas as the AN/AXT-2 with the addition of the PH-548/AXT-2A camera.

BLOCK 3-B Modified
After the war, the AXT-2 camera was modified for use in observation and telemetry applications; such as on the jet-propelled Bell YP-59B. Two cameras were connected to a relay unit feeding a single transmitter. The guidance aircraft could remotely switch from a display of the instrument panel to the horizon.

The set was designated as the AN/AXT-3 and consisted of the PH-565/AXT-3 camera with flood light package, PH-569/AXT-3 camera, T-61A/AXT-2 transmitter, AT-126/AP stub antenna, AS-425/U & AS-426/U Yagi antenna, and RE-26/AXT-3 relay unit. The remainder of the components was those of the AXT-2.

CRV-59 TV Camera
The expendable BLOCK equipment was used by both the Army (radio-controlled GB-4 and B-17 "war-wearies") and Navy (TDR drones and radio-controlled *GLOMB*s). BLOCK used a new lightweight, compact (the camera weighed 33 pounds and the transmitter 26 pounds) "New Image Orthicon" Iconoscope which operated at 350 lines and 40 frames per second, sequential scanning. The GB-4 used a Signal Corps radio transmitter and TV receiver operating at 300 MHz operating at 625 lines, 20 frames, 40 fields interlaced scans. It used either an 1848 or 1846 iconoscope tube.

CRV-59 cameras were used in the BLOCK series and were part of the ATJ/ATK (transmitter) ARK (receiver) system. The CRV-59 embodied some of the finest in miniaturized technology of the time weighing 33 pounds and measuring 20 inches long, 9 inches wide, and 10 inches high and contained 17 vacuum tubes, including the iconoscope tube.

RING System
The RING system, contracted in 1944, was a joint development between NBC and RCA, was a more sophisticated high resolution system developed for long range, high-altitude, reconnaissance. This equipment was designed for operation by personnel, with weight and complexity considerations secondary to the production of high definition television pictures. Cameramen operated two or more cameras installed in the nose and waist positions and were not considered expendable. It operated at 567 lines interlaced at 20 frames per seconds at 8 MHz bandwidth. Two cameras were developed using image orthicons, PH-536/AXS-1 and PH-537/AXS-1, the AN/AXT-5 transmitter, R-90/UXR-2 receiver, and ID-86/UXR-2 monitor. The transmitter operated on 90 to 102 mc with

TV Camera (CRV-59)

With case (Author's Collection)

Left interior (Author's Collection)

Right interior (Author's Collection)

Installed in a B-23 (AAF)

Flight tests in early 1942 using 100 megacycle equipment in a **Douglas B-23** bomber with showed that lightweight television equipment was feasible but had a number of inherent limitations for military use and new performance and operational standards needed to be formulated. The photo shows a TV camera installed in the side fuselage door. (AAF)

a peak power of 1400-watts. Range was 200 miles at 22,500 feet. The transmitting set was the AN/AXS-1 and the receiving set, the AN/UXR-2.

MIMO System

During the war, advances in tube miniaturization made MIMO system possible and was similar to the BLOCK system but lighter and more compact and weighing only 50 pounds; using the new MIMO (Miniature Image Orthicon). The MIMO system, contracted in early 1945, was to consist of a small cylindrical camera unit placed in the nose of the missile, a small transmitter, power supply and a dipole antenna. The transmitter was a 325 line, 40 frames per second sequential type that sent a TV picture back to the controller. The pick up tube in the transmitter was stabilized and the lens iris was controlled by the video signal to give constant average signal intensity. The complete system weighed 50 pounds, and had a power of 8-watts in the 264 to 372 mc range. The designation was the AN/AXT-7. The MIMO system was to be installed into the AAF Douglas-built ROC medium-angle guided bomb for which it was specifically designed.

Testing and Use

BLOCK 1 100 Megacycle Equipment

The design of the first small SCR-549-T1 television system to new military standards created a 60 pound transmitting set with a power output of 15 watts at 100 megacycles. The monitor weighed an additional 20 pounds while the 14-volt seven cell storage battery (that delivered 32 amps at 13-volts) weighed 37 pounds. The SCR-550-T-2 (BLOCK 1) receiver could not be simplified because the maximum possible sensitivity was required in order to complement the relatively low power output of the transmitter. A 40 pound small receiver, delivering nine amps at 25-volts, was designed by ingeniously placing the components, including the dynamotor power supply in one case. A monitor unit was designed for adjusting the performance of the camera/transmitter and for providing an additional picture at the receiving point.

However, flight tests in early 1942 using this 100 megacycle equipment in a Douglas B-23 bomber showed that lightweight television equipment was feasible but had a number of inherent limitations for military use. New performance and operational standards needed to be formulated. Among the new requirements were:

1) Change the input voltage requirements from 12.5-volts to 28-volts DC.

2) The necessity for simultaneous operation of several television channels.

3) The benefit of separating the camera and transmitter into two units.

4) The necessity of a smaller antenna.

5) Need for the equipment to operate at low temperatures and high altitudes.

In May 1943 the 100 megacycle transmitting unit and camera were placed in a small General Motors PQ-8 target aircraft at Muroc Dry Lake, CA. The PQ-8 carried the television camera/transmitter guidance unit housed in a streamlined ventral nacelle while the dorsally mounted antenna and radio-control and flight servo equipment was placed inside its fuselage. The receiving equipment was installed in a B-23 bomber. While the 120 line picture resolution was considered satisfactory by AAF personnel, the NDRC was disappointed as it was not possible to identify a small building from 9,000 feet. Continued testing and failures and modifications finally led to a successful TV guidance and radio-control system.

BLOCK 3 300 Megacycle Equipment

The new 300 megacycle SCR-549-T3 and SCR-550-T3 equipment circumvented the limitations of the 100 megacycle equipment and a number of improvements were incorporated. The operation of the 300 megacycle set was similar to the 100 mc set and differed only in details. The camera/transmitter was separated into two units and the total weight was increased to 90 pounds. Because of the lower efficiency of the 300 megacycle system operation the input power was raised to 29-amps at 26-volts. The monitor was of the direct driven (slave sweep) type and could be used either for observing the output of the camera and to provide an additional picture at the receiving location when driven from the output of the receiver.

In August 1943 the 100 megacycle radio-control and television guidance systems had been sufficiently developed that the demonstration of their military potential was scheduled at Muroc. For the demonstration a SCR-549-T2 transmitter was installed under the right wing of an unmanned YPG-12A single engine target aircraft that had a 500 pound bomb placed in the former pilot's cockpit for the final test. During the trials the television picture was adequate so that the YPG-12A was under radio-control at all times and was controlled to crash into the target on its final self-destructive run.

In June 1943 a small number of GB-4 Glide Bombs became available to test the 300 megacycle equipment. The flight servo equipment, the radio-control equipment, and television transmitting equipment were housed in the body of the airframe while the camera was located in a streamlined nacelle under the bomb. For a number of reasons very unsatisfactory TV pictures were received from the first five GB-4s tested at Eglin in August 1943. The TV pictures had fine horizontal lines caused by the camera's acoustic pickup which was solved by placing the camera in a sound-proof box. Heavy horizontal lines were produced by the acoustic pickup of the transmitter and were generated by the plywood body of the airframe. These were resolved by sound-proofing the inside of the airframe. The loose bonding of the airframe caused heavy streaking in the picture and was solved by better bonding. A change in the picture shading was caused by the influence of the earth's magnetic field on the iconoscope and was solved by shielding the entire iconoscope. Interference was caused by improper selection of RF channels of the radio-control system. The iconoscope was saturated by high light levels and low contrast caused by haze and was dealt with by placing a yellow filter in front of the camera lens. It was found that the 12 to 20 mile range of the equipment would have to be increased. A directional antenna in the receiving aircraft coupled to a gyro-stabilized antenna mount resulted in an increase in range to 50 to 80 miles. After these problems were solved the 300 megacycle equipment was used in the GB-4 and *Castor* war-weary guided missiles.

Cost of Expendable Weapons

During their development the philosophy of missiles was argued in various circles. Since the expendable guided weapon and its components were expendable and could not be reused; the reliability and accuracy of the controlling and carrying equipment were to be the overriding consideration and needed to meet Signal Corps requirements. Therefore there were no low budget developmental programs to produce low cost equipment as any savings were not warranted if they caused the glide bomb mission to be unsuccessful. The cost of the TV equipment was considered to be high at $2,000 but was only a fraction of the total cost of the entire missile; particularly in regard to the war-weary B-17s.

CTI-811

On 19 October 1942, Air Materiel Command circulated CTI-811, which permitted the procurement of radio-controlled and television guided glide bombs. CTI-811 did not cite any specifications for the GB-4's components or capabilities which would be fundamental for design engineers. These glide bomb specifications were supposed to be provided to the AMC by Air Staff's Directorate of Operations, Commitments, and Requirements (OC&R) which was to obtain the general specifications from the end users. The OC&R did not or could not furnish them; either because of Gen. Arnold's focus on the GB-1, or because the OC&R was simply too busy organizing the early, immense expansion of the AAF after 7 December 1941. Nonetheless, AMC design engineers at the Air Radio Laboratory (ARL) had to develop the new weapon without suitable end user specifications and then were to let design contracts to civilian manufacturers to construct a prototype.

On 9 February 1943, four months after CTI-811 was issued, the ARL still did not have any approved specifications and was unable to delineate requirements, recommend modifications, or elucidate performance parameters for the civilian companies which were hoping to build television equipment for the GB-4 project. To expedite matters the ARL drew up and submitted a list of minimum requirements that the AMC's Engineering Division should supply: detailed drawings, allowable weights, service range, the desired operating life with fully charged batteries, and that the designed equipment was to be compatible with an SCR-550-T3 receiver. In the meantime, the NDRC and industry researchers would continue to improvise; designing the GB-4 in relation to their views of what form the weapon should eventually take.

In early 1942, RCA received developmental contracts for a large order for 1,000 (500 each for the AAF and USN) of the new 300 megacycle BLOCK 3 system television sets for glide bomb installation. The BLOCK 3 sets were not standardized and were relatively untested and because of the lack of specifications were found to be too large and heavy for use

in glide bombs. By March 1943 it became evident that the entire glide bomb program totally lacked centralized leadership, management, and coordination and importantly, it just did not have the priority of other programs. Because of the delays in the GB-1 program and Arnold's insistence on its priority, the advanced glide bomb program was again pushed to the back burner, and it would remain there for the balance of the year. In an investigation done immediately after the war, the AMC stressed that from June until September 1943, the bulk of its research and design emphasis had been focused on the preset, gyro-stabilized GB-1 glide bomb. Notwithstanding, a modicum of research and development on the GB-4 continued.

GB-4 Television Installation

While the SCR-549-T2 version was in the process of being tested in small pilotless target aircraft at Muroc, CA in June 1943, a small number of GB-4 airframes became available to test the performance of the improved SCR-549-T3 TV system. The T2 and T3 versions were essentially similar except the T3 operated, for technical reasons, at 300 megacycles instead of 100 megacycles, and, in the T3, the camera and transmitter were separate units which increased the unit weight to 90 pounds. The servo control mechanism, radio-control equipment and television transmitter were located in the airframe body while the camera was housed in a faired nacelle under the bomb. Early tests were conducted to determine the satisfactory installation and function of the equipment.

Five GB-4s were launched at Eglin Field, during August 1943 with very poor TV picture resolution. Analysis of these tests showed that most of the difficulty could be traced to acoustic problems which were solved by sound proofing and to vibration problems were solved by better bonding of the glued wooden airframe. To solve lens problems a yellow filter was placed and a heater was installed to reduce fogging. Tests and initial tactical hypotheticals showed that range would have to be increased to make full combat use of the system. A directional antenna in the mother aircraft was linked to a gyro-stabilized antenna mount on the GB-4 to increase the missile's range.

RCA, the ARL, and the NDRC continued the development of the BLOCK 3 television system that could be used with a GB-4 airframe. By early September they had built a BLOCK 3 transmitter and camera unit that was small enough to fit in the nose of a GB-4 and powerful enough to transmit images over 80 miles. So GB-4 technical testing, delayed for

GB-4 TV controller looking into a BLOCK 7 inch CRV-60AAR monitor during GB-4 tests during August 1943. (AAF still from training film) (Note: Downsize photo due to poor quality)

GB-4 gliding into a target at Eglin in the August 1943 tests. (AAF still from training film)

half a year, started again at Eglin Field from 23 October to 11 November 1943.

Before being mounted in a GB-4 the BLOCK 3 transmitter was tested successfully in a United Airlines research aircraft and then in a B-25. At the outset the TV screens had excessive "noise" (i.e. "streaks and bars") that was ultimately removed by enclosing the transmitter and the camera in acoustically treated boxes using an automobile body sound-proofing material.

When Eglin testing concluded, the GB-4 had been successfully released and controlled from both B-17 and B-25 bombers with satisfactory reception of television images at ranges up to 80 miles and with the bomber flying 180° away from the bomb as it was being guided. Although the Engineering Division recommended that further testing was needed, they accelerated the schedule for GB-4 standardization and production to 15 January 1944 and recommended that aircrew training begin as soon as possible. But the decision to build the radio-controlled GB-8 rather than the GB-4 diverted funds and personnel from the GB-4 and this new goal could not be met.

But the success of the GB-4's TV system left little doubt that it would once more be the primary radio-controlled version of the glide bomb. By late December 1943, the AMC redirected the Hammond Corporation to stop the manufacture of GB-8 radio transmitters and restart the manufacture of the GB-4 compatible sets beginning with 50 GB-4 radio transmitters to be available within two weeks so that accelerated testing could begin. Also, if the January GB-4 tests were successful, the AMC, foreseeing the possibility of an early combat debut, contracted Hammond and RCA for an initial production run of 250 television and radio units. GB-4 compatible B-17s would be needed and the B-17Fs that were wired for the GB-1 were found to be most easily modified for GB-4 deployment. To expedite these modifications they were to be performed in England. Operationally, the GB-4 unit would require nine B-17s, plus six spares to cover maintenance requirements and combat attrition.

The operation of the GB-4 required two bombardiers. One located in the bombardier's usual position in the bomber's nose to preset the GB-4's controls and conduct the bomb run up until release and the other using the television screen and control equipment in the navigator's position to guide the bomb after release. The television bombardier guided the GB-4 with a joystick while watching its flight on a five inch cathode ray television screen. The complexity of the unit required the bombardier to take an additional 12 to 15 weeks to learn to use it correctly which meant

taking vital bombardiers already proficient in conventional bombing away from their combat units

After the GB-4 was standardized, the tests beginning on 17 January 1944 were the first to try to hit a precision target using television guidance. Two of the first six tests did not use television guidance as they only tested the radio-control from the B-17F test bomber. All of the other four bomb tests did not hit the target either due to television or radio malfunctions or because, in one case, the test was flown in the late afternoon and there was insufficient daylight to make out the target on the small television screen.

Additional tests were required and between 18 March and 13 April these tests revealed more problems with the GB-4 particularly concerning the malfunctioning of the glide bomb's radio receiver, television transmitter, and the gyroscope. Poor quality vacuum tubes were the biggest cause of the failures but the control boxes needed to be built under better quality control and standardized before operational use. The bombardiers often had significant difficulties in distinguishing the target on the small television screen due to the lack of ambient light, too little contrast between the target and its surroundings, or simply poor picture quality that was too grainy or distorted. The test results were inconsistent with encouraging successes and discouraging failures due to bombardier blunders which could be prevented with additional and better training while further testing would uncover and resolve technical problems.

By May 1944, 500 television transmitters and radio-control receivers had been ordered for mounting on GB-4 airframes most of which had been built before the March/April tests and had been found to have serious problems that had to be resolved. By July, all 60 of the remaining GB-4 television transmitters at the ARL required modifications before they could become operational. Also, the RCA BLOCK 3 production runs until September 1944 did not include the required modifications identified in the March/April tests, which meant that ARL engineers would have modify every BLOCK 3 set produced before then. By spring 1944 BLOCK 3 television equipment was in increasingly high demand for use in other priority projects, such as the Navy's *Campbell Project* (radio-controlled, television-guided boats) and the AAF's *Project Castor* involving war-weary B-17 guided drones.

On 5 August 1944, after further testing, the AAF Board released a report that determined that the GB-4 was not ready to be deployed for combat "except in special circumstances," but that technical and tactical development was to be continued. The Board identified the most suitable targets as those that could be easily penetrated by large bombs at low terminal velocity; those easily identified by distinguishing characteristics and landmarks; and those that were small in area. However, only two weeks after the Air Force Board had recommended these weapons not be employed in combat, GB-4s were being used in operational testing in the ETO (as will be described with the GB-8 Radio-controlled Bomb).

The GB-4 in Combat: *Batty* Missions
Eventually GB-1 development progressed, freeing funds and personnel for the GB-4 and GB-8 programs. Slowly GB-4 problems were eliminated and satisfactory television pictures were finally transmitted allowing a procurement order for 2,000 GB-4s equipped with SCR-549-T3 BLOCK transmitting units to be manufactured. In January 1944, letters of intent to contractors were issued for airframes and controls and the Signal Corps was instructed to procure the television guidance system. By spring 1944, Wright Field received the first units and stated that "while the bomb itself functioned with excellent reliability; the degree of skill required to hit a target with desired accuracy was evidently more than anticipated." Additional training of personnel was required and conducted and by June 1944, development had progressed to a point to merit limited operational testing.

Once the glitches in the BLOCK TV system were corrected the tactical deployment of the GB-4, codenamed *Batty*, was initiated. Pictured is a ***Batty* control B-17** of the 388th Bombardment Group based at Fersfield, England. (AAF)

On 15 July 1944 a glide bomb unit of specialists from the Air Technical Service Command was sent to the 388th Bombardment Group based at Fersfield, England to begin the tactical deployment of the GB-4 and GB-8. The program was codenamed *Batty* which was regarded as a subsidiary program of the 8th Air Force's *Aphrodite* project that included television guided bombs and drone aircraft (which will be discussed in detail later). The unit was headed by Major J.M. Pomykata, who directed the modifications to the B-17s and assisted in the training for the test combat sorties using the GB-4. During the combat tests only one GB-4-equipped B-17 was to be flown per mission rather than the nine bombers recommended by the AAFSAT.

The 388th Bomb Group History published in 1946 had this to say about "the strange things going on at the Fersfield Base (UK).....Two or three complete crews were transferred to Fersfield and such transfers were made orally as no paper was kept.....Not too much was told of the activity at Fersfield but that was the proving ground for robot planes or radio-controlled planes ...."

Seven GB-4s and seven GB-8s were shipped to Fersfield, at the end of June 1944 along with two B-17Gs (42-97518 and 42-40043) and *Batty* personnel. All GB-4 and GB-8s were assembled and ready for use in one week. Both aging B-17s were in very poor mechanical condition and 42-97518 required two weeks to arrive due to mechanical problems during the entire flight from the US. On its arrival 42-40043 was assigned to the *Aphrodite/Castor* expendable, "war-weary," drone project. Once 42-97518 arrived it was repaired but unfortunately this B-17 crashed and burned on 29 July, leaving *Batty* without a mother aircraft. At the time Third Division HQ decided that the GB-4 (Radio/Television) glide bomb would be used first and the GB-8 (Radio/Flare) glide bomb afterwards. This decision came at a time when targets had not been selected for the GB-4. On 6 August the original B-17 (42-40043), was returned by the *Aphrodite/Castor* project and was put into serviceable condition and everything was finally ready for GB-4 deployment. Five crewmen were used on all the missions flown:

Maj. J.N. Hall: Pilot
Maj. J.M. Pomykata: Radio/TV control operator
1Lt. L. Kata: TV operator
1Lt. R.J. Norris: bombardier
T/Sgt. F.L. Wallis: radio operator

Initially *No-Ball* V-weapon sites were scheduled to be attacked by the GB-4s but the compactness of the target and the nature of the surrounding area made TV picture resolution poor for identifying these targets. It was then decided that the GB-4s were to be used on the first mission scheduled on 7 August against E-Boat pens at Le Havre on the northern coast of France. However, due to poor weather conditions no missions were flown until 13 August. On that date the reconditioned B-17G mothership, a photo-reconnaissance Mosquito, an observer/pathfinder P-38, and B-17 observer carrying another TV receiver took off for Le Havre. The observer B-17 remained over the English Channel about 20 miles northeast of the target. The bomb run was made from south to north in good visibility with scattered clouds. The first GB-4 was released at 1643 from 15,000 feet at 170 mph at the standard 80° bombing angle, 13 miles from the target. After the release the mothership followed the normal procedure of turning 180°, flying in the opposite direction. The second bomb was released at 1708 from 14,700 feet and 175 mph. The TV picture in the mother B-17 on both drops was of poor quality and unusable for control. Consequently, the first bomb landed in the Seine River Estuary, one mile short of the target while the second exploded on a beach one mile east. Both bombs were found to respond to radio-control from the other observer B-17. Since the observer B-17 had good reception from the GB-4's TV camera, it was determined that the glide bomb's TV unit functioned satisfactorily. After the mission the poor quality of the TV picture was found to be due

On 13 August 1944 a B-17G mothership, a photo-reconnaissance Mosquito, an observer/pathfinder P-38, and B-17 observer carrying another TV receiver took off to attack E-Boat pens at Le Havre, France. The TV reception from the GB-4s camera was poor and the two GB-4s released crashed far from the intended target. The photo recon Mosquito followed too close behind the second GB-4 and was struck by fragments from its explosion and crashed. (AAF still from film)

The second GB-4 mission took place on 17 August 1944 when two B-17s loaded with one GB-4 each took off on to attack the U-Boat pens at **La Pallice**. Again, the TV reception was poor for both bombs and after this mission the mother's TV unit was intensively tested. (AAF)

to interference from the bomber's radio equipment. Sadly, the photo recon Mosquito followed too close behind the second GB-4 and was struck by fragments from its explosion and crashed.

On 17 August the second GB-4 mission took off at 1445 to attack the U-Boat pens at La Pallice. The formation consisted of 12 escort P-51s, one P-38 photo recon aircraft, the B-17 observer/TV aircraft, and the mother B-17 equipped with two GB-4s. Due to the mechanical condition of the mother B-17 it was not possible to climb above 17,000 feet while carrying two GB-4s. In excellent weather and visibility, the first bomb run was made over water at 1759, at 17,000 feet, 165 mph, and initiated at 25 miles from the target. The shutter on the bomb's TV camera failed to open and the bomb was quickly lost from the screen and was not seen to hit. However, visual observation confirmed that the bomb responded to radio control. Seven minutes later the second bomb was released at 17,000 feet and 175 mph. TV reception was again unusable due to sunlight reflections off the water but this bomb responded to radio-control during its five and a half minute flight. It exploded in the city to the right of the target and was out of control for the last few seconds of its flight. Despite extensive preflight checks the mother's TV unit malfunctioned but the observer B-17 again had good reception. After this mission the mother's TV unit was again intensively tested. The original receiver with a gyro-stabilized antenna was adjusted and a second receiver with a fixed antenna installed on the B-17's left horizontal stabilizer was added. The original TV receiver with its gyro-stabilized antenna remained on the B-17. This new arrangement provided a better picture and in future operations both receivers were to be used simultaneously. In order to achieve the desired 20,000 foot altitude, only one glide bomb was to be carried. Also, due to the reflection of sunlight on the water it was recommended that future attacks against coastal targets be made from an overland approach.

On 26 August the third *Batty* mission consisting of seven P-47 escorts, one P-38 photo recon aircraft, the B-17 observer, and the mother B-17 carrying only one GB-4 tookoff to attack a railroad bridge at Ravenstein, Holland. As the pilot approached the target, it was shrouded by clouds and the mission was aborted and the glide bomb was brought back to base.

No missions were flown between 27 August and 10 September due to poor weather conditions. On 10 September, nine P-38 escorts, one P-38 photo recon aircraft, and the mother B-17 carrying one GB-4 attacked a steel factory transformer switching station at Duren, Germany. It had been decided to carry only one missile so the mother B-17 could climb to

20,000 feet. At 1614, the bomb run was made from 20,000 feet, 25 miles from the target in six to eight tenths cloud cover which obscured the glide bomb until it broke out of the clouds at 3,000 feet which by that time had passed over the target. Since no suitable alternative target could be located, the bomb was directed toward a tree in an open space about three miles from the target. The TV picture on the new fixed antenna installation was very good while the old unit again produced a useless picture.

The next day the *Batty* mission took off to attack a railroad bridge and locks at Munster. Upon climbing to altitude a short circuit developed in the glide bomb's TV unit making it necessary to abort the mission. The mission scheduled for 12 September was cancelled due to lack of escort fighter cover.

On 13 September, the fifth and final *Batty* mission was flown against an oil refinery at Salzbergen, Germany. The mission consisted of the B-17 mother equipped with one glide bomb escorted by 18 P-47 fighters, and a Mosquito photo ship. There were no clouds over the target but a ground haze made target identification difficult. After two bombing runs the bombardier made an error in locating the target due to the haze and at 1709 the GB-4 was released at 20,200 feet towards Ensburen instead of Salzbergen. Maj. Pomykata, the TV operator chose the largest building in Ensburen as a target of opportunity and directed the bomb towards it. After the bomb passed through the haze, the TV picture became clearer and it appeared the target might be a church. The operator attempted to change the missile's course but it was too close to miss. Post-mission strike photos confirmed a direct hit, totally demolishing the building which no longer was identifiable as a church or not. Again the radio control and the new fixed antenna functioned "very satisfactorily" and the original TV unit was useless.

From 14 to 30 September there were no GB-4 missions as fighter escort could not be provided due to other unspecified obligations. So after six GB-4s were dropped in five missions, resulting in the destruction of an enemy tree, a church (?), and one Allied Mosquito photo reconnaissance aircraft; orders were cut to give the British the remaining GB-4 and the seven GB-8s. All Wright Field personnel were returned to the US on 2 October. These unsatisfactory results led to the cancellation of GB-4 production after 1,200 were manufactured.

On 15 February 1945 the GB-4 program was re-evaluated and found unsatisfactory in its present state. The following conclusions were made:

1) Carrying the GB-4 externally limited the aircraft's speed, range, altitude, and maneuverability.

2) The adverse weather conditions prevalent in the ETO precluded the missile's use throughout most of the year.

3) The GB-4 could only be used effectively on targets which could be easily distinguished from their surroundings on the TV monitor.

4) No GB-4 unit was to be sent into operations unless it could operate independently without depending on other organizations (obviously the 8AF was less than cooperative with the GB-4 mission as shown by their reluctance to provide fighter escort.)

5) Only new and fully equipped mother aircraft were to be used in future operations.

On 19 February Gen. Arnold notified the Air Technical Section that all future production of the GB-4 glide bomb was to be cancelled but additional work on the GB-4 and GB-8 was to be continued despite the poor operational results. Further development for use against Japanese caves and fortresses was continued, but on a very low, 3A, priority basis as part of the *Hermit, Willie/Abusive* TV controlled drone, project. It was decided that these war-wearies equipped with GB-4 TV and control equipment could more effectively perform the GB-4 function. Thus, the

GB-4 Glide bomb project was abandoned. A resurrected glide bomb project, designated as the GB-15, that used APW-5 radar and TV control will be discussed later.

Conclusions

Generally, the radio-controlled glide bomb was as ineffective as the gyro-stabilized, unguided GB-1. When the radio-control was supplemented by television guidance the GB-4 bombs weren't any more accurate than conventional bombs. A major reason for their use was to decrease the carrying aircraft's vulnerability by being used as a stand off weapon but, in fact, these drag-inducing weapons increased the vulnerability of the bombing aircraft to enemy fighters without a concomitant increase in offensive capabilities. The television guidance did not increase accuracy as expected. The images transmitted from the bomb should have allowed the bombardier to direct the path of the bomb into the target. In reality, the television images were so poor from the long range launching ranges and the speed of the bomb was so fast that the bombardier was unable to pick up the target to guide the bomb into it.

The bottom line does not seem to point to a deficiency in GB-4/-8 technology but to the AAF's intractable airpower doctrine of high altitude, daylight strategic precision bombardment from heavy bombers flying above 20,000 feet. When using the GB-4 or -8 as a standoff weapon the AAF should have followed the *Luftwaffe*'s *Fritz X* PC1400 example and deployed these weapons against more appropriate (easier to distinguish) targets using a smaller mother aircraft (medium bombers) at much lower altitudes (below 8,000 feet) and at shorter attack ranges (two miles).

SD-1400X Fritz-X

The Germans were far advanced in their research and development of guided bombs compared to any American project. Dr. Max Kramer of the German Aviation Research Institute (DVL) began the development of the SD-1400X guided bomb in 1939. Early experiments with annular tail surfaces were satisfactory and a contract was let for the adaptation of the PC 1400 Fritz, a 3,000 pound armor and concrete piercing bomb for radio control. The new SD-1400X built by Ruhrstahl AG featured a cruciform wing, angled at 28° and a segmented annular tail, with electromagnetically activated spoilers for pitch and yaw control. The annular tail arrangement was intended to cause drag at high speeds and thus limit the bomb's transonic terminal velocity to increase accuracy.

The PC 1400X used the FuG-203 Kehl III/FuG-230b Strassburg guidance package with the bombardier then using a joystick to steer the

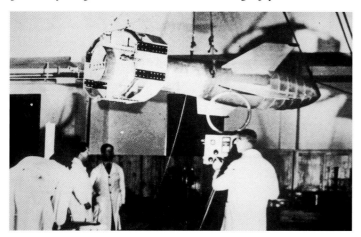

The German **SD-1400X "Fritz X"** guided bomb was far advanced in research and development compared to any American project. The joy stick-controlled radio guidance system was successful in sinking the Italian battleship *Roma* and the Royal Navy battleship *Warspite*. (AHFRC)

bomb until impact. An attempt to adapt the Duran/Detmold FuG 208/238 wire guidance system was abandoned. It had a unique gyro package for roll stabilization. The spoiler arrangement was situated between boundary layer fences, and six pairs were used, two pairs in the guidance control loop for pitch/yaw steering, and one pair for roll stabilization, controlled by the rate gyro. The machined steel penetrating casing contained three internal tubes with 750 pounds of Amatol explosive, impact fused.

The guidance package included the command link receiver, roll stabilization loop, and actuators. The guidance package was externally heated by air from the launch aircraft's deicing system prior to launch. Part of the tail was electrically insulated to act as a conformal antenna for the radio link. The operator tracked the weapon through the standard Lofte 7 bombsight, using a smokeless white or blue tail mounted flare or lamp.

Instead of using the *Fritz X* PC1400 to penetrate deep into enemy territory to attack heavily defended strategic targets the Germans used it at much lower altitudes and at much shorter distances against tactical objectives; particularly maritime targets. The Fritz X was intended to be used against armoured ships such as heavy cruisers and battleships. The Germans used the *Fritz X* to maximize the potential for a hit, sneaking in at short ranges, attacking at medium altitudes, below 8,000 feet, and launching the bomb within two miles of its target. The mothership had to decelerate upon bomb release so momentum would carry the bomb in front of the aircraft where the bombardier could see and guide it. This deceleration was achieved by making a steep climb and then level out. The bombardier could make a maximum correction of 1,600 feet in range and 1,100 feet in bearing.

The *Fritz X* was successful in sinking the Italian battleship *Roma* and damaging the battleship *Italia*. During the Allied landings at Salerno in September 1943, *Fritz Xs* sank the Royal Navy battleship *Warspite*, damaged USN cruisers *Philadelphia* and *Savannah*, the RN cruiser *Uganda*, and a destroyer, as well as several merchant cargo vessels. Perhaps, the AAF glide bomb program outcome could have been different had the GB-4 and GB-8 been carried by B-25 or B-26 medium bombers against tactical targets at lower altitudes and shorter ranges.

GB-5 and GB-12/GB-13 Light Contrast Seeking Bombs

The photosensitive light seeking sensors used on guided bombs during World War II were among the most successful employed. They were deployed on variants of the GB-5 and GB-13 glide bombs with the two most important seekers being the maritime light-contrast seeker and the flare seeker. All used the Aeronca Target Seeker 2,000 pound vehicle.

GB-5 Series

On 17 September 1942 the Joint New Weapons Committee (JNWC) issued a summary report stating that the photoelectric cell developed by Hammond Electric Company, was the best of the contemporary guidance seekers for use in the proposed GB-5 series maritime glide bomb. But the Hammond unit was superceded by the development of the simple light seeking guidance system designed by the Fairchild Corporation which could be manufactured quickly compared to the more complex Hammond seekers. While testing determined this seeker to be dependable under the suitable conditions it had not been installed in a glide bomb and at the time there was no demand for the system. The Navy showed some interest in the GB-5A but was more attracted to a radar guidance system that could used in any light and nearly all weather conditions and was more suited to attacking maritime targets. The AAF was not interested in a weapon that was mainly designed for use against maritime targets and was seeking a weapon to be used against land-based targets.

The GB-5A was a 2,000 pound GB-1 Aeronca airframe fitted with a Fairchild photo-electric marine target seeker which homed on the

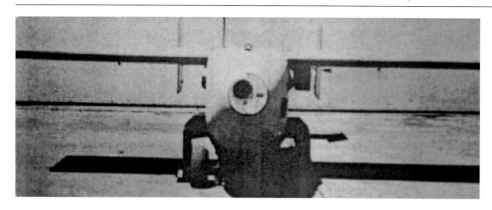

The **GB-5A** was a 2,000 pound GB-1 Aeronca airframe fitted with a Fairchild photo-electric marine target seeker which homed on the light contrast between a ship and the water surrounding it. (AAF)

light contrast between a ship and the water surrounding it. The Fairchild homing unit was a small 10.5 inch diameter by 11 inch long cylinder with an 18x12x2 inch relay box connected to a 12-volt battery. The tests began in November and December 1943 and met with many weather delays. In testing in good weather it realized sensor acquisition of the target at ranges of five to 25 miles, depending upon the light conditions and position of the sun. The GB-5A lost 1,000 feet of altitude in 15 seconds over a three to five mile range. The system required too much time to acquire control of the bomb after release as the falling bomb oscillated for over 4,000 feet before the internal guidance stabilized it. Many times during testing the oscillations were so large that the seeker lost the target and would guide on any contrasting structure that came into its range. Redesign and more testing became necessary but proceeded slowly and nine months later the GB-5A development priority had been reduced to a lowly 3A. At the time the LAB low altitude bombsight was successfully integrated into a number of combat units and the additional training and problems that would be met in introducing the GB-5A into combat could not be justified.

The GB-5B equipped with a Hammond flare seeker was considered obsolete in design stages and was abandoned. While work on light contrast seekers continued until the end of the war, it was apparent the development was for research only rather than to develop a tactical weapon. Glide bombs that briefly were given a much higher priority were the GB-5C light seeker and the flare-seeking GB-5D which were redesignated as the GB-12 and GB-13 respectively and will be discussed as such.

GB-12 Photoelectric Light-Seeking Bomb

The GB-12 was a renamed GB-5C, using the standard GB airframe housing a photoelectric light-seeker in its false nose. The Hammond (developer)/ Crosley (manufacturer) unit was a marine-type photocell contrast light seeker. The amplifier and control system directed the missile on a collision course against shipping offering a contrast against the water. Seven to 10 miles was considered the operational range due to target identification difficulties but the missile could be dropped at longer ranges as the preset photocell eyes opened automatically at the operational range. The Air Material Command considered the design the most promising marine seeker. This GB was also tested as an air-to-air missile to detect aircraft up to two miles away. The seeker needed to be pointed upward, away from the distracting horizon and the background needed to be uniform; either all cloudy or entirely clear. Initially 25 were procured with five used in preliminary tests in May 1944 at Tonopah.

GB-13 Photocell Flare-Seeking Bomb

The GB-13 was originally developed from the GB-5D as a weapon to be used against enemy searchlights and pinpoint land targets. The GB-13 used a standard GB airframe with a 2,000 pound bomb and a faired nose containing a Fairchild photocell flare seeker. The Fairchild unit fit into an eight inch diameter by 10 inch long cylinder and had a homing cone of 70°. It was adapted for use against burning targets or flare-illuminated targets. Flares were three feet long, seven inches in diameter and weighed 80 pounds and burned at a million candlepower for three minutes, and were dropped by parachute by low-flying target marking aircraft. The mother aircraft would release the GB-13 at six miles on a preset automatic pilot course which was overridden when reaching the Fairchild's operational range. The bombs were to be used against specific point targets such as blockhouses, power plants, etc. The flare could be planted in front of the target by fast, low-flying aircraft or by ground-based mortars or rockets. Because of its flat trajectory the bomb would skid into the target.

Twelve GB-13s were produced for testing. GB-13 testing was conducted between 13 December 1944 and 9 January 1945. During these tests three of six GB-13s missed the target by only 10 feet and on 21 December one hit the flare directly. Tests proved the seeker to be very reliable and 50 GB-13s were ordered for the next stage of testing. However, these 50 GB-13s were never delivered and the next tests were conducted with the remaining five GB-13s. The results of these tests were undocumented and testing of the GB-13 ended in the late spring of 1945 but research and development on the light-contrast and flare-seeking systems continued until the end of the war

An interesting plan to use the GB-13 against enemy dams was proposed. These targets were usually heavily defended by anti-aircraft fire and were resistant to conventional bombing tactics and ordnance. The scheme was to drop flares at night into the dam's reservoir and have them

The **GB-12** was a renamed GB-5C, using the standard GB airframe housing a photoelectric light-seeker in its false nose. (AAF)

The **GB-6A** Aeronca Target Seeker Vehicle was essentially a GB airframe fitted with the usual 2,000 pound bomb using the heat-seeking Infra Red (IR). (AAF)

float with the current to the lip of the dam where they would remain. The light-seeking homing device on the glide bomb would guide it to strike the face of the dam at a preset level below the flare to explode. The Special Operations section of the OSS also proposed using the GB-13 in China against high priority targets which were identified with flares or beacons set out by units on the ground. On 10 April 1945 a memorandum directed that no additional GB-13 missiles were to be manufactured for the OSS or made available for their tests unless and until a specific requirement was obtained from the theater commander.

GB-6 Infra Red-Seeking Bombs
Using the Aeronca Target Seeker Vehicle, the Infra Red (IR) carrying glide bomb was designated as the GB-6 and its development was directed by the NDRC and conducted by the Offner Electronics Corporation of New York City in the spring of 1942. The GB-6 was essentially a GB airframe fitted with the usual 2,000 pound bomb and the standard Hammond Corporation gyroscopic stabilization equipment; and when assembled with its seeker it resembled the GB-13 flare seeker.

There were 120 GB-6s on order due by 1 August 1944 with 115 available to the AAF and five to the Navy. The GB-6 utilized the basic Aeronca airframe with a faired nose housing containing an Offner thermopile heat seeker and amplifier unit. The missile was to be used against marine targets, refineries, steel mills, blast furnaces, power plants and other targets which radiated more heat than surroundings. The GB-6 traveled on a pre-set course with the thermopile seeker taking over control when in range which was four to five miles.

Initial IR seeker unit tests were conducted by Offner at its New York offices. The IR seeker was installed on a tripod on the 35th floor of the Offner building where it was to detect and track ships moving on the Hudson River. The IR seeker was effective as long as the sun or its reflection off the water did not enter the IR detector. The Experimental Engineering Section approved air testing which showed that the IR seeker was much more effective against isolated heat sources such as shipping than against ground targets that had radiant heat surrounding them. Although the Bemis Corporation developed a more effective IR seeker it was allocated for use on the VB-6 *Felix* bomb so the GB-6 retained the Offner system. Some 200 Offner seekers were ordered and most were used during operational testing by January 1945.

Offner-equipped GB-6 tests were conducted with the main objective to improve its ability to recognize ground targets. The Offner seeker had an effective detection range of seven to 10 miles under perfect conditions and was considered to be a "promising heat seeker if the target is sufficiently isolated." During a test at Eglin, Florida late in the afternoon on 27 February 1944, a GB-6 was directed to a beacon fire but the bomb quickly lost the target and crashed into the ground. Investigation found that humidity and ambient background heat radiation was the cause and the GB-6 project was moved to less humid Wendover Field in Utah.

During the summer and early fall of 1944 tests at Wendover showed that the optimum detection range over land was three miles when the test drops were made in the very early morning when background IR interference was minimal. Testing against industrial targets was impractical as these targets could not be easily duplicated for test purposes. A scheme using 3,000 square feet of metal sheeting, warmed by orchard heaters, was tried with some success but could not duplicate the variations and gradations of IR radiation that surrounded the actual large industrial target. Humidity and haze could affect both detection ranges and the ability of the bomb to stay on target once released. During tests when the relative humidity reached 70% percent at Wendover Field it was virtually impossible to continue the tests against large land targets. By late September 1944 only three of the 14 bombs dropped on the 3,000 square foot sheet metal target struck or missed it by a few feet as weather, haze, dust, humidity, and ambient IR energy continued to interfere with GB-6 accuracy. A relay malfunction was determined to be the cause of two poor results. It was also found that the slower speed of the B-17 at release made the glide bomb much more difficult to control during descent than when it was released from the faster B-25 Mitchell medium bomber.

The project remained on a very low priority throughout its existence and never progressed beyond the testing stage. Once the VB-6 *Felix* IR system which could be carried internally by a B-17 was proven to be a better and more reliable weapon the GB-6 quickly lost what little support it had in the AAF and in February 1945 the GB-6 project was cancelled.

GB-7A, -7B (GB-14), and -7C Radar Controlled Bombs
Radar was deemed to be better target-seeker than light, Infra Red, or television as it could function in darkness or bad weather. In April 1942 Col. B.W. Chidlaw requested that the NDRC develop a radar system and

Radar was deemed to be better target-seeker than light, Infra Red, or television as it could function in darkness or bad weather. In April 1942 the NDRC developed a radar system and equipment for controlling glide bombs which resulted in three radar-directed glide bomb projects being developed concurrently; the GB-7A, -7B, and -7C. The **GB-7A** (shown) was designated as a Radar Homing Bomb (RHB) because its seeker homed in on the radar energy that bounced off of the target. (AAF)

equipment for controlling glide bombs which resulted in three radar-directed glide bomb projects being developed concurrently; the GB-7A, -7B, and -7C. The Dryden 2,000 pound vehicle with a 12 foot wing span was to be the vehicle but the Aeronca 2,000 pound Target Seeking Vehicle was considered. The Navy *Moth* was a radar homing glider bomb developed at the same time but was cancelled.

Both the GB-7A and -7B (later redesignated the GB-14) versions attained flight testing status. The GB-7A was designated as Radar Homing Bomb (RHB) because its seeker homed in on the radar energy that bounced off of the target. This Glide Bomb used Hammond gyro control and an accelerometer for pitch control. Two rates of turn control were employed; a slow rate during the early portion of the flight and a much higher rate during the final portion. The unit was built around a 2,000 pound Aeronca Target Seeker vehicle which had a similar airframe to the GB-8 but used special plywood nose and a different control box. The nose section was mounted forward of the bomb and a metal plate anchored in place by the flange of the nose fuse. The radar receiver which was sensitive to signals in four quadrants was mounted in the nose while the batteries, stabilizing equipment, servo mechanisms for the operation of the control surfaces,

the control relays that were connected to radar receiver were located in the mechanism housing. The radar homing device homed on radar pulses transmitted by a radar transmitter in the control aircraft and reflected from the target. In operation the target was radar illuminated from the GB-7 and the return signal differentials between the target and the background were received by the radar receiver to give up, down, right, left signals in accordance with the target's location. These signals were used to operate the control relays in order to transmit the correct control through the stabilizing equipment to the servo mechanisms and then to the airframe control surfaces so that the glide bomb would be guided to the target. The target had to be sufficiently isolated (at least by 500 feet) to prevent distraction from other sources of reflection that would be within the range of the bomb's receiver. The GB-7A was planned for use against marine targets or isolated large buildings.

The more complicated GB-7B (GB-14) system was designated as a Send-Receive-Bomb (SRB) as its radar transmitter and receiver were contained in the bomb itself. It carried its own AN/APG7 radar transmitter (500 ordered from the Navy) to illuminate the target. Using its RC 171 radar receiver it rode the returned echo to its source; making it independent and self-contained; not requiring the mother aircraft for control. Production was scheduled to begin in September 1943 with 200 units to be finished by 1 January 1944 and then at 50 per month afterward.

The GB-7C, called the "*Hairy Butterfly*," was an end of the war design employing an AN/APQ-14 radar seeker for homing on enemy early warning and fire control radar signals. It was adjusted to enemy frequencies so that it would home on their transmitting antennas. The Aircraft Radio Laboratory ordered 25 for experimental use and the NDRC hand-built five which were test-dropped but the developmental problems were too overwhelming and it would not be until the 1960s before the AAF developed the *Wild Weasel* against enemy radars during the Vietnam War.

RHB and SRB Radar Development

The AMC decided to develop the simpler RHB and more tactically desirable SRB simultaneously. After launching, the SRB bomb was self-guiding; allowing the mothership to turn immediately away from the target to safety. The simpler RHB was a semi-active system that required the mother aircraft to illuminate the target with radar energy, which the RHB then guided on. This procedure required the illuminating aircraft to continue to fly towards the target until the bomb struck which greatly increased its vulnerability.

On 7 October 1942, after some encouraging preliminary laboratory tests conducted at MIT's Radiation Laboratory; the AAF requested aerial

The more complicated **GB-7B** system was designated as a Send-Receive-Bomb (SRB) as its radar transmitter and receiver were contained in the bomb itself. It carried its own radar transmitter to illuminate the target and using its radar receiver it rode the returned echo to its source; making it independent and self-contained; not requiring the mother aircraft for control. (AAF)

A later GB-7B which was redesignated as the **GB-14**. The GB-14 was similar to the Navy's SWOD-series *Pelican* and *Bat* and GB-14 tests were held in abeyance until *Bat* tests were completed. (AAF)

testing of the RHB. Due to the size and weight of the radar-homing device, initial testing was performed using a twin-engine Beech AT-11. On 28 October testing was concluded when the AT-11 successfully homed on an anchored 125 foot lightship that was illuminated by ground-based radar positioned on a nearby island.

Although the test results were generally inconclusive, they were encouraging enough that further testing was ordered to begin at once. These new tests were conducted from 9 to 12 November 1943 to establish the maximum and minimum operational range; to determine if the RHB equipment functioned when the radar energy was provided by an airborne set operating from another aircraft; and to determine the RHB's ability to pick out the largest target when it was surrounded by smaller vessels (it could not, but headed for the center of the largest amount of returned radar energy). The results of these tests were disappointing because of frequent equipment malfunctions but again the AMC requested that the testing continue.

On 1 January 1943, Col. Chidlaw requested that NDRC Division 14 begin development on the SRB system (Project AC-51) installed on both powered and glide bombs. Tests continued on the RHB by the Radiation Laboratory and SRB by Division 14 and were relatively successful and on 12 June 1943 both projects were standardized with both systems to be installed on a "controllable missile," with the radar receiver functioning as the controlling method to guide the bomb. The RHB was to use energy from a distant source while the SRB was to supply its own radar signal that was to be powerful enough to illuminate the target and receive reflections from it.

At this time the Navy BuOrd and the MIT Radiation Laboratory had been working on a larger semi-active RHB system for an anti-shipping adaptation which was to guide either towed gliders or powered bombs equipped with a warhead large enough to sink a capital warship The larger Navy RHB and the smaller AAF RHB (the GB-7A) had shown that there was a basic duplication of effort in the two programs which was slowing the development of radar seekers. On 14 June, Dr. Louis Ridenour, Director of the Radiation Laboratories, suggested that the AAF's GB-7A which was also being developed by the Radiation Laboratories should be transferred to the NDRC's Division 5 due to its small size. Ridenour also suggested that to avoid unnecessary duplication that all SRB development be transferred from MIT to Bell Telephone Laboratories which had been contracted to develop SRB components for the AAF. Only Dr. Ridenour's suggestion to move the development of the GB-7A airframe, its automatic controls, and the radar to NDRC's over-worked and unqualified Division 5 was taken.

In spring 1943, MIT's Radiation Laboratory, the Bell Telephone Laboratory, NDRC's Division 14, AMC's Engineering Division, and the Navy's BuOrd were all involved in SRB development and the resultant bureaucracy threatened the entire radar-guided glide bomb program. In May 1943, after the first SRB unit had been proven satisfactory by the NDRC it did not have the facilities to develop the service test models so the Aircraft Radio Laboratory (ARL) was assigned to place contracts with companies in the field; a process that dragged on into September. As a result, despite some attempts to rectify the SRB situation, months passed without any concrete results in bringing the program to fruition. Because the RHB system was deemed to be provisional until the SRB was finalized; on 17 November 1943, the Radiation Laboratory gradually withdrew from all RHB research to allow its research engineers to work on more critical projects. Meanwhile the SRB program continued to decline as it was 26th on the joint Army-Navy Radar Research and Development Precedence List. So duplication of effort and bureaucracy caused the SRB and RHB programs to stagnate. On 11 May 1944, Maj. Gen. R.B. Colton, Chief of Engineering and Technical Service, suggested the cancellation of the AAF's SRB program in favor of the Navy's *Bat* project which was considered to have more potential. (The Navy used the *Bat* against Japanese late in the war which is discussed later.) On 6 June 1944, the NDRC ended its SRB research and its initial basic results would eventually be applied to the GB-7A, but essentially the AAF's SRB project was postponed until after the war.

GB-7A tests were performed along with the Navy's tests on their *Pelican* system. While the GB-7A had a 2,000 pound bomb attached to a GB-8 airframe, the *Pelican* initially used a 500 pound bomb, which was later increased to 1,000 pound bomb when carried by Dryden glider airframe. During tests in the summer of 1944, the *Pelican* was shown to be very accurate as out of 16 test drops from 6,000 feet and six miles distance, six direct hits were recorded on a stationary Liberty ship. (The *Pelican* is discussed later.)

Because it was so similar to the Navy's *Bat* project, GB-7A/GB-14 tests were held in abeyance until *Bat* tests were completed. The technical problems with the GB-7A were basically the same as with the IR-guided GB-6 as the radar was able to detect isolated marine targets but had almost no capability to distinguish point targets on land, particularly in built up areas; so would be ineffective against strategic targets such as factories, oil refineries, and like targets. Thus, the AAF lost interest in the GB-7A for the same reasons it lost interest in the GB-6. When there was little demonstrable progress made in the GB-7A by November 1944, the GB-7A was reduced to a 3-A priority and development was stopped in August 1945 as the *Bat* was found to be inaccurate and in need of further development.

In late 1943 the AAF decided to eliminate television guidance and to concentrate on the **GB-8** radio-controlled glide bomb using a modified GB-1 airframe. The GB-8 used the same radio-controls for azimuth and range as the GB-4 but instead of TV control a smoke flare was fitted to the airframe which was guided visually by the bombardier. (AAF)

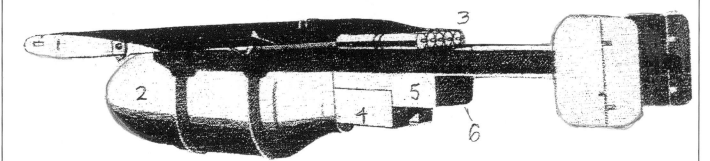

GB-8 (Radio Controlled)
2,000 Pound 6:1 Glide Bomb

1) **Antenna in Wing**
2) **2000# Bomb**
3) **Flares**
4) **Batteries**
5) **Detonator**
6) **Remote Receiver & Remote Control Box**

GB-8 Radio-Controlled Bomb

During the development of the GB-4, the television transmitters and receivers continued to cause numerous technical problems and in late 1943 it was decided to eliminate television guidance and to concentrate on a radio-controlled glide bomb. The bomb was designated as the GB-8 and resembled the radio-controlled German FX-1400 *Fritz X* winged bomb which had sunk the Italian battleship *Roma*. The GB-8 used the same radio-controls for azimuth and range as the GB-4, but instead of TV control a smoke flare was fitted to the airframe which was guided visually by the bombardier. This GB weapon, like other GB projects, used leftover GB-1 airframes modified to the GB-4 non-twin tail boom design. Because the GB-8 used a modified GB-1 airframe, which was somewhat smaller than the one designed for the more complex GB-4, the GB-8 radio equipment component which was designed for use with the GB-4 had to be redesigned to fit the GB-8 Aeronca airframe. There were 2,000 GB-8s on the production order with 130 scheduled to be delivered in April 1944 (with 100 Hammond control units) and then 500 per month thereafter (with 300-400 Hammond control units).

The GB-8 had a glide ratio ranging from 5 to 2 to 6 to 1 and its speed on this glide path was approximately 250 mph which could be increased by diving. The GB-8 was guided by the bombardier who operated a small joystick located on top of the radio-control box. As the bombardier had to observe the GB-8 the entire way to the target, the mother B-17s had to fly a curved path after releasing the bomb and could not immediately turn away from the target, as could be done upon releasing the GB-1. The bombardier had the difficult task estimating angles, distances, relative movement, and rates of closure from long distances and at difficult perspectives. The average release point from the target was eight miles so to hit the target the bombardier had to "eclipse" or visually cover the target with the moving bomb which was only 15° below the horizon and flying at about 300 mph just before impact. The bomb could only be corrected at a rate of 3° per second but there was a sizeable time lag between applying controls and the bomb responding. The bomb's wing span was only 12 feet and when viewed against surface objects surrounding the target at such long distances it was impossible for the human eye to distinguish the bomb's rate of descent or whether the wings were level. Bombardiers were given an additional 10 weeks of training but nonetheless they could not make the GB-8 into a precision weapon.

A problem which affected not only the GB-8 but all other radio-controlled guided bombs; glide, vertical, or powered, was the limited number that could be deployed at one time. Each bomb required up to five separate radio channels to control it: one each for commands to climb, dive, turn left, turn right, and for powered bombs to increase or decrease the throttle. Radio frequency could be partially modulated allowing more bombs to be controlled simultaneously in the same band width. However, it became obvious that there were too few available radio channels to allow more than a few bombs to be controlled in flight and those available channels could be easily jammed. The maximum number of bombs that could be controlled simultaneously was determined to be nine and since each bombardier could control only one bomb at a time, the AAF School of Applied Tactics recommended that the optimal formation for GB-4, GB-8, and all other radio-controlled bombs was to be nine B-17s in elements of three aircraft each.

In early 1943 the 8AF considered the 63 bomber combat box to be the smallest bomber formation to have satisfactory defensive armament for operations over Germany. B-17s carrying externally mounted glide bombs did not have the sufficient speed, range, or ceiling to be added into conventional bombing formations and needed to fly independently. The nine B-17s in glide bomb formations could deploy only one weapon at a time and were very vulnerable to enemy fighters which just did not fit in the scheme of AAF strategic bombing tactics.

In May 1944 because GB-4 development was lagging; a higher priority was given to the GB-8 and recommendations were made to have it become operational as soon as possible. Seven were sent to England as part of the *Batty* GB-4 operational testing program in which none were employed and after which the GB-8 project was halted and GB-8 airframes were transferred for testing for further development and to other glide bomb programs. The very optimistic procurement order for 10,000 GB-8s was cancelled.

Nonetheless, there were some positive outcomes and lessons learned while testing the GB-8 that could be employed to improve the GB-4 and later glide bombs. First, all of the radio technicians trained for the GB-8 program could be rapidly employed to support any other radio-controlled glide-bomb project. Also GB-8 testing had established the basic flight characteristics, glide ratios, and airspeeds for all similar radio-controlled glide bombs. Finally, the GB-8 experimentation permitted at least the radio-control aspect of the GB-4 design and development to proceed until problems with television guidance were resolved.

During its development several new operational uses were suggested for the GB-8. The Flare Carrying Glide Bomb was intended for tactical use to lead conventional night bombing missions to illuminate the target area. The standard glider frame and GB-8 control box were used but instead of carrying a bomb it was equipped with a streamlined wooden box containing 90 parachute flares with a mechanism to release the flares at one second intervals by radio control. The first bomber in a large formation would drop its gliders over the target area and steer it by observing an electric light mounted on the glider which could only be seen from above. When the glider reached a low altitude over the target the glider controller would hold down a release button that would drop flares 200 feet apart with the 90 flares lighting an area about three miles long. Several gliders launched in parallel simultaneously could light up a large section of the target. Since American bombing strategy was geared toward daylight bombing this flare-carrying GB-8 never saw fruition.

The anti-personnel glide bomb used the standard glider, control box, and flare panel unit but in place of the bomb a streamlined wooden box similar to the Flare Carrying GB-8 box was employed. Instead of flares, eighteen 100 pound anti-personnel bombs (or a larger number of smaller bombs) were carried and released individually or in train during attacks on roads.

In order to determine if the GB-8 could be used as a close support weapon for ground troops a series of tests were set up to determine whether reliable control could be obtained with a ground control transmitter which was to allow azimuth control of the GB from one station and elevation or range control from another. During tests 15 GB-8s of various types were tested; consisting of 11 standard GB-8s (with rudder only/azimuth control) with Hammond radio control, two with ARL radio control, and two GB-6 airframes (with rudder and aileron control) with Hammond radio control to be used to compare control surface responses to radio control signals. In the tests the Hammond radio control system was found to be satisfactory but the rudder and aileron controls of the GB-6 airframe responded better to radio control. The accuracy of the ground control was dependant on the ability of the controller to judge the amount of turn required to bring the bomb on course and to give the correct amount of control to make this turn. The relatively slow and variable response of the standard GB-8 to azimuth control signals made accurate control very difficult for even the most experienced operator. It was essential that the azimuth operator get the GB on course early in the flight or the flight path as observed from the range station would be distorted and accurate range control would then

GB-15 Radar/TV Seeking Bomb (AAF)

be impossible. Development and testing continued until September 1945 when this facet of development was terminated.

GB-9 Barometric Seeking Bomb
The GB-9 or "Ground-Skimming Bomb" was similar to the GB-8 design again using surplus Aeronca GB-1 airframes. The GB-9 used pull-out stabilizers and radio altimeter control or aneroid (barometric) control. The radio altimeter unit maintained the bomb at a constant level above the ground irrespective of altitude above sea level but the unit was easily jammed. The aneroid (barometric) unit could not be jammed and was simpler and cheaper. It maintained the missile at a constant pressure (altitude above sea level) but, of course; this method met problems when flying over mountainous terrain.

The GB-9 was released at a steep dive of 45° and was leveled out at 1,000 feet and 400 mph by the APN-1 radio altimeter or aneroid unit controlling the pullout stabilizers. The missile proceeded at this constant altitude for three to five miles using a flare or emitting a smoke trail to enable the operator to guide the missile to azimuth and range accuracy. Over the target the operator would dive the GB-9 abruptly onto the target. The project was not fully developed at V-J Day but later versions were to be projected to be jet propelled to extend the range of level flight to ten miles.

GB-10 Television Glide Bomb
The GB-10 was a GB-4 outfitted with television equipment in a plywood nose instead of being suspended under the fuselage as in the GB-4. The TV was a Farnsworth or modified BLOCK 3 with image orthicon. The TV incorporated a built in attitude adjustment to compensate for variable angles of attack. It was to be flown on a glide path or on the GB-9 leveling out system, until the operator could take over control. The GB-10 project was put on low priority and cancelled at the war's end.

GB-11 Smoke/Chemical Carrying Guided Bomb
Again, using the basic GB airframe with a 12 foot wingspan this weapon was to carry a standard 33A smoke tank for dispensing smoke or chemical spray. Release was to be at 10,000 feet at four miles range. The controls were preset for course, with the GB-11 diving at 350 mph and pulling out of its dive using GB-9 units to fly at a predetermined altitude. It would then fly level for two miles while it dispensed smoke or chemical spray.

GB-15 Radar/TV Seeking Bomb
In June 1945, Air Technical Service Command directed the Engineering Division to continue with its efforts to find a method to use the APW-5 radar to track a glide bomb as the radar/TV-controlled GB-15 project. The initial radar tracking permitted the bombardier to establish the location of the bomb relative to the target through most of its flight. Once the bomb was close to the target the television image could provide the final guidance to the target. However, when the final Air Technical Service report on the ETO operations concluded that the present TV control was "too primitive to reach effective operational development in the near future" the TV control phase of the GB-15 project was cancelled in February 1945. The radar only glide bomb project was presented to Gen. Curtis LeMay, Commander of the XXI Bomber Command, for use against Japanese targets. LeMay responded, "The present shortage of combat crews in this Theater does not permit allotting the additional time for training in the use of this bomb. The bomb load which could be carried in terms of GB-4 Glide Bombs and the probability of damage expectation of such 2,000 pound bombs is not commensurate with the total bombing capacity of the B-29 aircraft."

So the lack of interest by LeMay and technical problems with the APW-5 radar system, the GB-15 (aka GB-4) was effectively, but not officially, cancelled when Air Technical Service Command recommended no further development on the GB-4 be pursued until the radar could

GB-11 Smoke/Chemical Carrying Guided Bomb (AAF)

be perfected which was projected to be March 1946. These delays in the development of the radar equipment until caused the project to be cancelled by the Wright Aircraft Projects Section and further work on radar control was transferred to other projects.

XBG Series

The last of the AAF's glide bomb series was not of the GB series designation but was designated as the XBG. It was a towed bomb similar in design to the GB series and is discussed with the *GLOMB*, glider bombs as the BG gliders were more similar in concept to the Navy's *GLOMB*.

War Weary Bombers and Fighters as Towed Gliders

The AMC also investigated the possibility of stripping down "large worn out" aircraft removing their engines and armament and using them as remotely controlled towed gliders. The pilot would takeoff and then bail out while the "glider" was towed toward the target and then remotely controlled into the target. The initial studies singled out the B-24D (less engines, fuel, and armament) which could carry a 25,000 pound payload and the C-66 (less engines and fuel) which could carry 20,000 pounds. There are brief mentions of a study that was made to determine the performance characteristics of "war weary" and/or obsolete P-39 fighters when towed as a glider by a P-38 or B-25.

Conclusions

Generally, it seems that the Air Force was uninterested in the glide bomb as a tactical weapon providing the program with low priorities and few funds. It was the enthusiastic personnel at Wright Field looking for advanced ideas from the NDRC and private industry which pushed these projects as far as possible under the circumstances. Also, when a project, such as the GB-1 and GB-4, caught the fancy of Gen. Arnold they were given top priorities in order to reach combat as soon as possible, but this was done so in a hurried and haphazard manner which ultimately was deleterious to the project. Little cooperation was given by upper echelon operational officers who were steeped in conventional tactics which had been only recently proven at high cost. The developmental history and poor operational results of the GB-1 and GB-4 demonstrated these points. Later, other promising homing systems which basically, through not intentionally, used glide bomb airframes as test beds, received the same treatment resulting in deliberate development and slow, often incomplete, testing. These early systems had merit as many were resurrected in the post-war missile-oriented environment that led to seeking systems that were effective in combat.

VB-1 AZON

During September 1940, a group of scientists visited Wright Field to study target-seeking controls for Army Air Corps glide bombs. Among their considerations was the possibility of correcting errors during high-angle bombing. It was the group's general consensus that the conventional high angle bomb fell so rapidly that manual guidance would be inadequate to improve accuracy.

The NDRC originally designated the remotely-controlled bomb as the "AZ-1," but the AAC designated it as Project AC-1, with the purpose of determining the "means and methods of precision bombing while flying above or in overcast." This designation was changed to AC-36 on 30 December 1941 when Lt.Col. B.W. Chidlaw the AAC representative to the National Defense Research Committee asked them to undertake development of "controlled trajectory bombs." The specification asked that the "bomb be controlled in flight by a bombardier. Azimuth control was essential and azimuth and range control highly desirable." Section 5.2 of NDRC at MIT under Dr. L.O. Grondahl began work on the project (MX-225) only to see it receive low priority in favor of weapons with built-in homing devices. Before February 1944, it was usually referred to by the VB-1 designation and after the 1,000 pound VB-1 prototype went into production, the 2,000 pound *AZON* became known as the VB-2. In press releases the VB-1 was usually referred to by its acronym *AZON* for **AZ**imuth **ON**ly.

In early design stages, the models were directed with rudders to control azimuth and elevators to control range. It was obvious that this means of control required that the bomb could not rotate as the rudders always had to remain vertical and the elevators horizontal in order to achieve the correct control response. It was decided that radio-control was the only practical link between the controlling mother aircraft and the bomb. Three control systems were proposed for the project:

1) Installation of a television camera and transmitter to show the operator the deviation from the true course of the bomb and the application of course corrections by the radio link.

2) A target seeking device which would independently and automatically direct the bomb.

3) Direct sighting of the bomb from the controlling aircraft by the operator who would manually steer the bomb via radio link.

The first step in the project was to solve the aerodynamic problems associated with high angle controlled bombing. A series of wind tunnel tests at MIT and model bomb drops at the Aberdeen Proving Ground concluded that control by rudders was feasible, that gyro-stabilization was absolutely necessary, and that a tail flare was required to adequately see the falling bombs in order to control them.

Flight testing was conducted at Eglin Field, FL between 19 and 23 April 1942 where it was verified that the normal trajectory of a bomb could be controlled after its release. Projectiles tended to rotate when they fell which was desirable and even enhanced by tail fins in conventional bombs. Like the rifling in a gun barrel, spin made bombs more accurate and caused less dispersion. However, this spin made remote control of a bomb difficult. Early attempts to reduce or eliminate this rotation were to add an aerodynamic structure to the bomb casing which made the bomb so large as to be impracticable. The addition of a small tab or rudder on the tail fin controlled by radio signal caused the tail to oscillate in a wider circle than the nose; lessening, but not eliminating, the spin. During design and testing at Aberdeen, Dr. Grondahl's NDRC unit concluded that gyro-stabilization was the solution to the rotation issue. Like glide bombs, two gyroscopes were installed; one to control roll and the other to prevent yaw.

Further aerodynamic testing was conducted using high angle bombs which could be controlled in azimuth (e.g. side to side vs. range: long or short) only. Earlier tests had concluded that range control development should be temporarily lowered in priority because of technical difficulties. During tests these azimuth bomb research vehicles showed good accuracy on films of test drops on long, narrow, targets. One particularly good film showed an *AZON* falling 15,000 feet following a 12 foot wide road and finally hitting it after an estimated 2,500 foot side-to-side correction by the controller. The NDRC brought these results to the attention of the Special Weapons Branch of the Air Technical Service Command (ATSC) under Project Officer, Maj. J.H. Evans. Further comparison testing by the ATSC showed that 16 test *AZON*s had an average error of 42 feet compared to the average error of 1,215 feet by eight uncontrolled conventional comparison bombs. The result of these tests was the restoration to top priority of direct sighted *AZON* bombs followed by the *RAZON* (**R**ange and **AZ**imuth **ON**ly) bombs while television guidance and target seeker development was deferred.

Because Gen. Arnold's memorandum of April 1942 gave the GB-1 priority for guided bombs and because the VB-1 still required the basic level of research; the AMC transferred its personnel from vertical bomb research and design to the GB program for the remainder of 1942. At about the same time the prototypes were nearing completion to conduct field trials, the NDRC contracted Gulf Research and Development Company of Pittsburgh to enter the project directed by R.D. Wyckoff to solve the rotation problem and to establish methods of control. Dr. Grondahl, the Project Chief, recommended that control by direct visual sighting was the most feasible method and could be introduced into combat in the shortest time. However, it was the position of many aerodynamics experts working on homing devices that target-seeking units and a television-guidance system were the most practical. Their premise was accepted when NDRC researchers moved VB-1 testing to the Aberdeen Proving Grounds where they worked with Gulf Research and Development. At Aberdeen the NDRC and Gulf designers wasted time and funding developing a unit very similar to the one that would be used on the GB-4. When their efforts failed to perform satisfactorily in tests in August 1942, their television guidance scheme was discarded and the control of the bomb reverted to Grondahl's direct visual sighting proposal.

As in the GB-8 project direct visual line-of-sight control of the VB-1 required bombardiers to rely upon visual acuity and eye-to-hand coordination to manually use a joy stick to guide the bomb. Initially bombardiers collectively rejected the system. The majority reported that it was almost impossible to judge where the bomb was headed and many times the bomb appeared to be accurately aimed on the target and then miss or vice versa. However, gradually, with practice, bombardiers were able to accurately guide the VB-1 from a distance of one or two miles vs. the eight miles for the GB-8.

The VB-1 was easier to guide not only because of the shorter distance to the target, but also because the bombardier did not have to "fly" vertical bombs as he did the radio-controlled glide bombs which were small gliders that had to maintain a specific speed and relatively level wings or else they would stall and spin out of control. The bombardier had to "fly" glide bombs on three simultaneous axes; yaw (using the rudder to point the nose on the horizontal plane), roll (using ailerons to keep the wings level), and pitch (using the elevator to point the nose up or down on the vertical plane). The bombardier did not "fly" the vertical bomb, but only changed its trajectory as it fell, and it was found to be virtually impossible to produce a stall large enough to make the bomb go out of control. To control VB trajectory, the bombardier was required to only use rudder

control as *AZON* bombs moved only in azimuth, requiring a left or right correction; which was relatively easy to judge, when viewing the bomb from above as it moved toward the target.

By February 1943, NDRC designers were set to exhibit 10 VB-1s to the AMC at Eglin Field. There was only one test with "excellent control" but the other nine bombs were failures with five of the bombs becoming uncontrollable and spinning in; one had a flare failure and was quickly lost from sight; two had obvious radio-control problems; and one bomb was lost due to a miscommunication between the bombardier and radio-control operator. However, the success of the one test bomb gave hope that the *AZON* project was headed in the right direction and further design and testing was authorized. On 1 June 1943, to facilitate further design, Brig.Gen. B.W. Chidlaw, Chief of Materiel Division of the Air Staff's Materiel, Maintenance, and Distribution (MM&D) Directorate, circulated the military requirements for the VB-1: control in azimuth; good ballistic characteristics; suitable radio-control apparatus; a means to visually follow the bomb in flight; and it should consist of the simplest and most durable components possible. While looking forward to future requirements, the request went on to emphasize that VB-1 design and testing should in no way interfere with the further development of radar- or television-controlled versions having control on two axes. On 5 June 1943, the design and procurement of the VB-1 was officially requested by the Air Materiel Command.

The second key series of VB-1 tests were conducted at Eglin Field from 23 June to 7 July 1943. The purpose of these tests was not to determine the accuracy of the bomb but only to determine if the roll stabilization problem had been solved which it had. In August 1943, *AZON* bombs were included as part of a guided missile demonstration for VIPs at Muroc Lake, CA. During these tests, bombardiers were directed to aim at a cross-shaped target with the long arm being 4,000 feet in length to aid in determining azimuth control. A B-25 flew all test drops using two bombardiers, one to complete the bomb run emphasizing range, and the second, located in the rear of the aircraft, to radio-control the bomb in flight, with an emphasis on azimuth. Of the 24 test drops, 12 were released and accurately controlled; but nine had radio malfunctions, and three had inoperative tail guidance flares. Two of the flare failures occurred in the only two drops from 22,000 feet; all other drops were made from 17,000 feet. Of the 12 VB-ls that were accurately controlled, the mean deflection error was 35 feet, while mean range error was 427 feet. Despite the 50% failure rate and large range errors; the *AZON* concept was beginning to show outstanding potential for the degree of accuracy necessary for pinpoint bombing and were considered successful enough to be put into production.

Production, Tactical Testing, and Teething Problems
On 24 August 1943 Col. R.C. Wilson, Chief of the Development Engineering Branch of the AMC, was named to expedite the *AZON* Project. The promising August tests warranted the procurement of a pre-production lot of 200 *AZON*s and on 13 October Gen. F.O. Carroll released the bomb for final ballistic and evaluation testing and for possible training purposes to a tactical group. In early September 1943, the NDRC, in collaboration with the Union Switch and Signal Company of Swissdale, PA, had standardized components for the mass production of VB-1 tail assemblies. Union Switch subcontracted Schwien Engineering, Los Angeles for gyros, Willard Battery, Cleveland for six volt batteries, and White Rogers Motor Company, St. Louis for servo motors.

On 23 October 1943, Gen. Wilson directed the AMC to contract Union Switch and Signal for an initial production run of 10,600 VB-1 tail and flare assemblies for $10,600,000 or $1,000 per unit: 10,000 for the AAF, 600 for the USN, (and a possible 50 for the RAF). The first lot of

600 was scheduled for January 1944 production, then 1,200 for February, 1,800 for March, and followed by 2,200 in May and 2,400 in June. This production schedule was modified to 500 for March delivery, at least a 1,000 for April, 2,000 to 2,500 in May, and 3,000 per month thereafter to a total of 20,600 *AZON*s but radio shortages could prove to be a bottleneck. In June 1944 the production schedule was again amended to greatly increase *AZON* production from 20,600 to 50,600 in 1944 and 60,000 for 1945, again with the admonition that radios and other subassemblies availability could be a problem. Another yet to be named manufacturer was to supply 15,000 units (1,000 in September, 4,000 in October, and 5,000 each in November and December) for 1944. Union Switch was to supply 3,000 in June, 4,500 in July, and 5,000 per month for the rest of the year. A "realistic estimate" dated 25 August 1944 decreased the 1944 total form 50,600 to 37,967 but with 110,600 planned to be completed by August 1945 with a production of 10,000 per month to begin in December 1944.

Once technical testing was completed and production contracts awarded, Gen. Arnold increased his demands to deploy the VB-1 operationally. To provide for training the AAF Board Project 13 (T-1) was created. Technical training was to be carried out at Ft. Dix, NJ, while practical bombing was conducted at Eglin Field. Brig.Gen. H.M. McClelland was selected as the Air Communications Officer (ACO) of the Development Engineering Branch of the AMC. The position of ACO was the most important in the guided bomb program as this senior officer had the authority to prepare design plans and policies for all guided bomb development. Like Gen. Arnold, the ACO needed to have a dominant and influential personality; be a staunch advocate of the program; to understand its complexities; and be able to drive it through its development, from research, to design, to procurement, and finally to AAF acceptance for testing and deployment in combat. However, McClelland was to prove a poor choice for ACO as his understanding of guided bombs and their development was inadequate, his personal influence in the AAF hierarchy was limited, and he was also burdened with other responsibilities which precluded his full attention to the new and complex guided bomb programs.

The Special Projects Section was pressed to begin tactical VB-1 testing as soon as possible. Six B-17Gs and aircrews were provided by the OC&R to begin VB-1 training at the School of Applied Tactics in Orlando by 7 February 1944 with the goal of deploying to 8th Air Force for combat trials not later than 1 March 1944.

During tactical tests at Eglin Field in February 1944, teething problems appeared with these first *AZON*s which delayed the production schedule. It was found that the amount of azimuth control applied to the bomb significantly decreased the bomb's range as every azimuth correction increased the aerodynamic drag when the bomb changed directions. A VB-1 with no azimuth corrections had a range of 10,573 feet when dropped from an altitude of 15,000 feet with the bomber flying at 250 mph ground speed. When the same bomb under the same parameters was adjusted by the bombardier to the "average" azimuth correction, the range only decreased 32 feet. But, if the bombardier made nearly continuous azimuth corrections, the generated drag reduced the range by 607 feet to 9,966 feet. Also, range differences increased as the bomber's airspeed and altitudes increased. In addition to the experience they received during testing, the bombardiers were assigned to receive further extensive training in target recognition and *AZON* technique. The tactical use of the *AZON* for precision bombing was now being questioned and it was suggested that perhaps the *AZON* was better suited to "strip target bombing."

This opinion was not changed during continued tactical testing at Eglin, when problems occurred when the VB-1 used the standard 1,000 pound bomb nose and tail fuses. Most standard 1,000 pound bombs included nose and tail fuses to increase the chance of the bomb exploding. Bombs were designed to hit the target nose first but nose fuses could be easily damaged on impact and not ignite the bomb's explosive charge; while the better protected tail fuse was more likely to detonate the bomb. Due to lack of space, the AMC decided to delete the tail fuse despite the dependence only on a nose fuse would increase the probability of duds.

It was also found that the RC-186 radio transmitter was satisfactory but the poor quality of construction and workmanship surfaced with the VB-1 tail assemblies, particularly concerning the superheterodyne radio-control receivers and flares. While the radio receiver was sufficient for

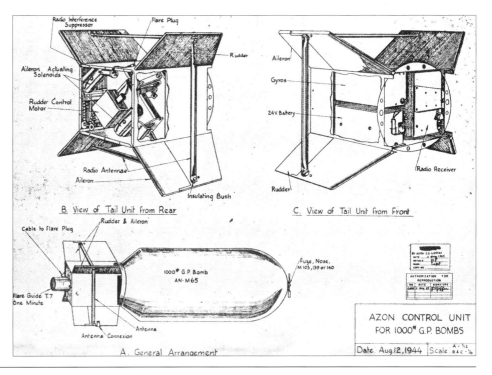

AZON Control Unit (AAF)

The **exterior of the AZON tail unit** contained the guiding flare (A), radio antenna (B), and rudders (C) and ailerons (D). (AAF)

the original testing program, it was found to be wanting in selectivity and stability for operational use. During pre-flight preparations, 30% of these receivers were rejected for testing and of those accepted an astonishing 71% failed during flight testing. MIT, in cooperation with Harvey Radio Laboratories, developed a more sensitive, stable, and selective crystal-control super-heterodyne receiver. The precise tuning of this unit allowed more control frequencies within the operating band which permitted more individual bombs to be controlled simultaneously.

Enemy jamming was a concern. It was assumed that the enemy could not acquire complete control of the *AZON* because it would be too difficult for him to determine the modulation and frequency combination used for control. However, by transmitting enough energy over a broad band, the enemy could interfere with the bombardier's control signal. The superheterodyne unit made jamming much more difficult due to its fine tuning feature. However, once the radio receiver problems were remedied there was a bottle neck in their production.

Problems continued when the Picatinny Arsenal and Wesleyan University investigated troubles with the tail flare and found that the flares were not suitably sealed against humidity and would fail to light or stay burning if they did light at all. The flare situation did improve but flare malfunctions continued throughout the war. Other testing problems occurred. The *AZON*s rolled and the ailerons had to be connected mechanically and the storage battery had to be redesigned by the Willard Battery Company.

The Operational *AZON*

The problems with the *AZON* were finally remedied and the VB-1 was declared as operational. The VB-1 *AZON* bomb consisted of remote controlled movable fins attached to the special tail attached to a standard AN-M-65 1,000 pound high explosive GP bomb adapted for guidance in azimuth (right or left control), but not for range, by the bombardier who altered the bomb's trajectory in flight with radio signals which moved the fins. Also, a collar was added to its mid section for additional control by attached elevators which were similar to preset trim tabs on control surfaces of an aircraft. The elevators created a stabilizing effect on the falling bomb, allowing the *AZON* to be more easily controlled in azimuth.

The weight of the *AZON* tail unit was approximately 75 pounds and consisted of the following:

RC 106 Transmitter: (9x19x17) 32 pounds (with batteries)
Dynamotor: (8x7x9.5) 16.25 pounds
Control Box: (7x5.75x5) 2.125 pounds
Wiring and Antenna: 25 pounds

Preparing the *AZON* for Operations

On average it required about five hours for an *AZON* to be readied for operations. During the unpacking of the *AZON* tail units from their shipping crates; the tail units in each crate had to be separated to those with the Emerson and those with the Government Issue (GI) CRW-7 receivers. Due the differences in function, maintenance, and adjustment the GI assemblies were favored and the Emerson receivers were placed in reserve. Once the tail was unpacked the collar, gyro, and receiver was removed from the tail. The fins, controls, and general framework of the tail were examined with particular attention paid to the wiring, the servo mechanism, and mechanical coupling of the moving parts. The receivers were tuned to the bands transmitted by the equipment mounted in the various bombers. If the Emerson receiver was to be used all sets required major maintenance of the wiring to increase their sensitivity. Once the receiver had been checked and any necessary adjustments made it was mounted in the tail assembly and rechecked. It was found that in about two thirds of the time the sets lost sensitivity after being mounted and required a change in grounding of the tail antenna. After unpacking each gyro was tested for balance, precession, and uncaging and that it would rotate properly through a 45° rotation of axis of the bomb after it fell free of the bomb racks. After testing the gyro was installed in the tail. Once the flare was unpacked its socket contacts were scraped clean of the shipping wax which was used to prevent corrosion during shipment and storage. The flare was then installed in the tail assembly. The batteries were filled and charged to the proper potential a few hours before their installation in the tail.

In the *AZON*-carrying bombers there a number of routine checks of the transmitting equipment usually requiring an hour. The transmitter frequencies were measured by a signal generator and the values were used to tune the receivers. The warm up circuit wiring on each bomb station was checked and the antenna was cleaned to achieve optimal control.

The **interior of the AZON tail unit** was comprised of the rudder control motor (A), aileron actuating solenoid (B), and radio interference suppressor (C), the radio receiver (D), 24-volt battery (E), and gyros (not visible). (AAF)

Adding the *AZON* Unit to the M-65 Bomb
The normal fixed tail of the AN-M-65 was removed and replaced with a special tail assembly or "shroud." The shroud was cruciform and had movable flaps on each side of the four fins. Two of these flaps were installed on opposing fins to function as ailerons. The other pair of opposing fins functioned together as rudders to steer the *AZON* to the right or left of the plane of its trajectory. The rudders were powered by an electric motor, responding to simple ON/OFF radio signals received from the remote controller. If there were no commands, the rudders returned to their center position. Full 15° deflection of the rudders was reached in 0.7 seconds and caused the bomb to yaw to a steady angle of about 12°. If there was no commands the rudders returned to center.

The *AZON* tail contained a central compartment housing the gyroscopes/solenoid, radio receiver, battery, and servos. The gyroscope and solenoid changed the pitch of the ailerons to prevent rolling as the

bomb fell as various corrections were made. The gyros were kept spinning by compressed air during the time of fall. The radio system was powered by a dry cell battery whose life was about three minutes which was more than enough to exceed time for a the *AZON* to strike a target. To mark the bomb's flight path a 600,000 candle power pyrotechnic flare which burned for 50 seconds was positioned centrally and behind the shroud. It produced a streamer of red, white or green smoke (yellow was added later) to distinguish between individual bombs being controlled.

Due to the lack of space tail fusing was omitted but the impact nose fuse remained. Settings for the fuse were instantaneous. Difficulty had been encountered early in the development stages using as little as one second delay, accounting for almost as many duds as explosive bombs. This created disadvantages in some types of targets where a delay fuse would have more destructive force as in the armor-like surface of bridge spans or concrete construction. But it did add a security factor, deemed

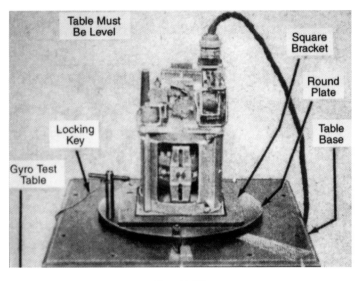

Gyro (AAF)

Radio Receiver (AAF)

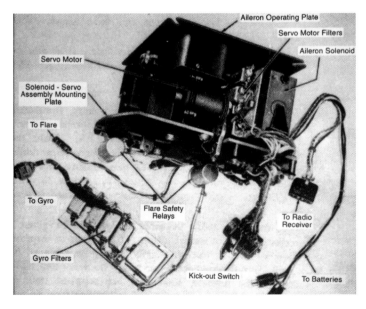

Servo Assembly (AAF)

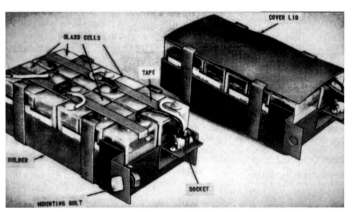

Batteries (AAF)

VB-Series Controlling Units This photo shows the standard Signal Corps radio transmitter box controller (left) and a television receiver/monitor controller (right) with the operator using a joy stick. (AAF)

necessary, in that the secret weapon would more likely be destroyed on contact rather than fall into enemy hands intact.

The standard Signal Corps radio transmitter box in the mother aircraft used a simple three position (left-center-right) joy stick arrangement for signaling commands to aircraft, ships, tanks, and drones. It had a power output of 25-watts and could send out six different frequencies. The standard transmitter weighed 33 pounds but the modification to the B-24, added an additional 25 pounds. Each aircraft had three antennas mounted beneath its tail section for control purposes. One transmitted a signal on 475 cycles for left deflection, one on 3,000 cycles for right deflection and the third at 30-40 cycles to activate the flare. All three frequencies were

A simple three position (left-center-right) **joy stick** unit was used to signal commands to aircraft, ships, tanks, and drones. (AAF still from training movie)

changed periodically to prevent jamming by enemy radio monitoring crews.

Loading the *AZON* into the Bomber
Initially it required about an hour per bomb to load the aircraft, but after a while the total time was an hour for all bombs. The bomb without the tail assembly and without fusing was hung on the rack by the armorers. The tail collar was mounted on each bomb after it was slung from the racks and then trued so that the two studs used in aligning of the tail assembly were vertically one above the other. The tail assembly was mounted on the collar so that it was level. The armorers then rechecked that all parts were in place and then rechecked after the bomb was mounted.

Checking the *AZON* after Loading
The *AZON* bombs that were checked on the ground were checked after loading into the aircraft as follows. The Main Line switch, battery switches, *AZON* warm up switch, and filament switch on the control transmitter were turned ON. If no engines, generators or auxiliary power units (APU) were operating then the control transmitter was to be switched to "High Power" but if the generators were charging the bomber's batteries and the APU was running then the control transmitter was to be switched to "Low Power." The *AZON* kick out plug on one bomb was plugged in and after sufficient warm up time (30 to 60 seconds) the bombardier was to turn ON the carrier switch and give right, center, and left signals of at least five seconds during each. The radio operator or another crewman was to observe the action of the *AZON* rudder for proper functioning. The first bomb was then to be unplugged and the kick out plug was placed into the second *AZON* and the procedure repeated for all bombs loaded onto the aircraft. When the check was completed on all loaded bombs the kick out plugs were placed into each bomb. The arming wire was to be inserted through the kick out plug, passing through the bomb lugs, and it was to extend no more than four inches without too much slack and was to be secured by a Fahnstock clip. The bombs were to be checked for correct fusing, correct delay, and that the arming wire and Fahnstock were properly installed. Once all units were thoroughly checked the bombardier turned all switches OFF and reported to the Project Officer or his Assistant.

Checking the *AZON* in Flight
The *AZON* bombs were checked in flight by the following procedure. The bombardier was to turn ON the *AZON* warm up switch immediately after take off which caused the batteries in each *AZON* to be charged by the bomber's generators. The bombardier then entered the bomb bay to plug in the flare plug on each *AZON*, remove the kick out plug pin (after inspecting the arming wire), and remove the safety cotter pin on the nose fuse.

Dropping the *AZON*
When each *AZON* was checked and ready to be dropped the bomb bay doors were opened and the bombardier turned ON the Flare Arm Switch and the carrier switch on his control-stick box. After all the *AZON*s were dropped; all of the above switches were turned OFF. Control of the *AZON*s was not to be applied until two thirds of the time of fall had elapsed. If the aircraft returned with bombs the bombardier was to insert safety pins in the nose fuse and kick out plug and pull out the flare plug.

Initially, the bombardier in the mother aircraft aimed the bomb using the conventional Norden bombsight procedure. The only change from normal bombing was the setting of a larger trail angle to compensate for drag due to use of the *AZON* shroud. Prior to release the bomb's gyros were run up using electrical power from the mother aircraft. Upon release power was transferred to the *AZON*'s battery. Six to nine seconds after release the flare automatically ignited at 8,000 to 10,000 feet. The bombardier tracked the falling *AZON* flare visually without an optical aid. He saw the AZON's flare as a bright circle of light against the ground and guided it right, zero, or left to keep it on line. It was not necessary for the controlling aircraft to maintain straight and level flight or constant speed within the limits of not impairing the bombardier's view. Accuracy was wholly the consequence of the bombardier's individual skill in using the joy stick much like playing today's computer games. The transmitter had six frequencies to permit simultaneous drop of six *AZON*s. At 1,500 feet it was possible for the bombardier to detect azimuth errors on the order of five to 10 feet as the bomb reached a speed of 850 feet per second. An experienced bombardier could master *AZON* technique within a week after six to eight practice drops.

Advantages of the *AZON* over Glide Bombs

The major advantage vertical bombs had over the externally mounted glide bombs was that, having no wings, they were smaller and could be carried inside the bomb bay of both heavy and medium bombers which would consequently experience no loss of range, altitude, or speed. Also, because the VBs were carried internally, they were not exposed to the weather enroute to the target, which permitted pilots to fly through icing conditions.

AZON Aircraft

Typically an *AZON* could be carried by any aircraft with a 1,000 pound bomb bay station and therefore any aircraft could carry more *AZON* bombs than glide bombs. Aircraft scheduled to carry the *AZON* were the B-17 (6), B-24 (8), B-25 (2-3), B-26 (4), B-29 (16) and P-38 (2). Additionally, a bomber could carry a mixture of VB and conventional bombs. These bombers required very few modifications to carry and deploy vertical bombs. The major structural change to the bomber was the installation of a bomb rack inside the bomb bay that could accommodate the somewhat larger tail assembly of the vertical bomb. Also required were minor structural and electrical system changes such as installing the

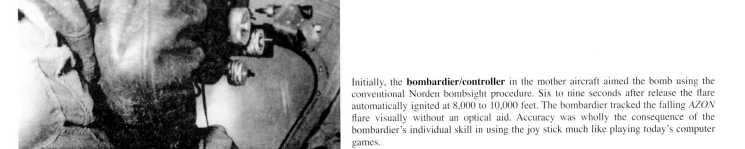

Initially, the **bombardier/controller** in the mother aircraft aimed the bomb using the conventional Norden bombsight procedure. Six to nine seconds after release the flare automatically ignited at 8,000 to 10,000 feet. The bombardier tracked the falling *AZON* flare visually without an optical aid. Accuracy was wholly the consequence of the bombardier's individual skill in using the joy stick much like playing today's computer games.

Each controlling aircraft (B-24 shown) had three **antennas** mounted beneath its tail section for control purposes. One transmitted a signal on 475 cycles for left deflection, one on 3,000 cycles for right deflection and the third at 30-40 cycles to activate the flare. All three frequencies were changed periodically to prevent jamming by enemy radio monitoring crews. (AAF)

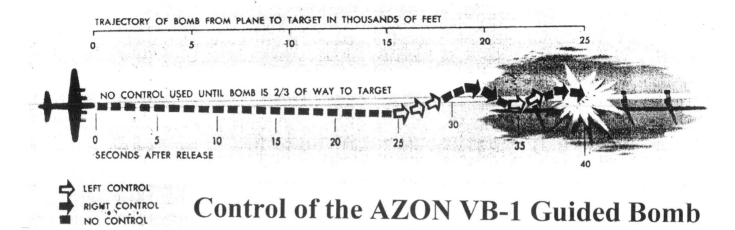

TRAJECTORY OF BOMB FROM PLANE TO TARGET IN THOUSANDS OF FEET

NO CONTROL USED UNTIL BOMB IS 2/3 OF WAY TO TARGET

SECONDS AFTER RELEASE

LEFT CONTROL
RIGHT CONTROL
NO CONTROL

Control of the AZON VB-1 Guided Bomb

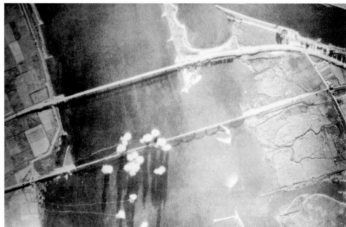

These stills are from an AZON mission film during an attack on the rail bridge at Moerdijk, Holland on 25 August 1944. The flares of eight AZONs are seen as bright circles of light trailing smoke against the ground. By using the joy stick the controller guided the AZON right, zero, or left to keep it on line to the target. (AAF)

proper radio-control gear or cutting observation ports in the nose or side of the bomber.

The only practical *AZON* targets were long, straight, and narrow, such as rail lines, highways, long bridges, and railway marshalling yards which were classified as interdiction targets which were the province of low altitude medium bombers such as the B-25 or B-26 rather than the B-17 or B-24. However, this seemingly good concept of dropping the *AZON* from medium bomber was never embraced until testing at the end of the war. The initial combat tests were implemented by B-17s and the majority of VB-1 combat missions were flown by heavy bombers .

AZON Operational Use in the MTO
In early 1944 a brief informational film introducing the *AZON* was shown to 8AF brass in England. Having just learned of threatening German V-1 launching sites in France, an order for 100 *AZON* units was made to attack them. However, the small size of these sites prohibited *AZON* use and the 15AF in Italy inherited the bombs.

On 25 March 1944, four weeks behind schedule, the first experimental *AZON* Squadron equipped with six *AZON*-equipped B-17Gs was sent to conduct operations with the 419BS of the 301st Heavy Bomb Group of the 15AF. Lt.Col. Helmick was the *AZON* project officer and Abner Wollan served as Technical Observer. The unit was preceded by 100 VB-1 tail assemblies airlifted to Caserta, near Foggia, with 400 more being shipped

by sea. Special storage facilities and workshops were constructed next to the bomber's hardstands where the VB-1 tail and flare assemblies could be stored, maintained, and assembled. By 9 April the aircrews and aircraft had arrived from North Africa and during the week of 10-16 April the 100 airlifted VB-1 tail assemblies arrived.

Wollan administered the unpacking, assembly, and testing of each VB-1 before it was ready for combat. Each of the six B-17s was allocated a separate flare color, and all assembled individual VB-ls and their radio equipment were marked with that color. Once assembled and loaded into a bomb bay the VB-1 control mechanisms deteriorated quickly. The flare/moisture problem continued but the most serious problem was the inability of the batteries in each VB-1 tail assembly to hold an adequate charge to be able to control the bomb. After five days stored in the bomb bay the battery charge often fell below the minimum optimal 20-volt level. The onboard generators on the B-17s could recharge these batteries but often the tail assemblies of bombs containing weak batteries had to be removed and new batteries had to be re-installed. Depending on the location of the *AZON* in the bomb bay this could be a very time-consuming procedure.

On 17 April 1944, the 419BS flew the first *AZON* mission against railway lines between Rimini and Ancona but soon after takeoff heavier than expected cloud cover caused the three bombers to become lost and to be unable to rendezvous with the 16 P-38s of their fighter escort. The three lost B-17s were intercepted by 20-35 *Luftwaffe* FW-190 and

Aircraft scheduled to carry the *AZON* were the B-17 which could carry six, **B-24** (8), B-25 (2-3), B-26 (4), B-29 (16) and P-38 (2). Additionally, a bomber could carry a mixture of VB and conventional bombs. (AAF)

Me-110 fighters that badly damaged one B-17 whose *AZON* transmitter was heavily damaged and the operator was slightly wounded. A second suffered minor damage but all the bombers and their valuable *AZON*s were able to return to their base.

On 24 April, 30 *AZON*s were released by five 301BG B-l7s, escorted by 18 P-38s against lines of track and four railway bridges between Rimini and Ancona in central Italy. Nineteen *AZON*s were dropped from 19,000 feet and followed to their targets on strike photographs. No bridges were hit but the rail line was reported to have been cut in three places. One bomb made an "incidental hit" on a warehouse in the vicinity of the Cesano River Bridge. Three *AZON*s suffered flare failures and two were "accidentally" dropped, falling into the Adriatic Sea north of Rimini. The average deflection error (right/left of target) was 700 feet which compared very favorably to the 1,250-1,500 feet deflection of conventional bombs. However, range errors tended to be greater averaging 1,900 feet which was approximately equal in magnitude to conventional bombing results. At the debriefing the bombardiers reported that they seemed to lack control of the remaining 14 VB-ls in the last part of their flight which was thought to be due to low battery charges.

On 29 April the third *AZON* mission was flown by five B-17Gs that dropped 24 VB-ls on three railroad bridges on the Rimini-Ancona rail line from 5,000 feet. One *AZON* was reported to strike the Fano Bridge over the Metauro River, one of three dropped apparently hit the Senegalila RR Bridge, and one hit the highway at Pasaro. But the success of the mission could not be analyzed due to poor strike photography and bad weather. Four bombs could not be controlled due to the failure of their flares.

The next *AZON* mission was flown on 30 April once more against the same railway bridges as the previous missions. Five B-24s attacked in column, stacked down, with each bomber carrying two bombs. Experienced Group bombardiers made the drops and *AZON* bombardiers controlled. Despite only one bomb having reported control problems; only one bomb of 30 hit its target which happened to be the Fano Bridge which was being repaired from the previous day's damage.

After four missions that could claim only two hits scored out of 73 bombs dropped; there was a hiatus in the program while the test team evaluated the *AZON*'s huge decline in accuracy compared to its Eglin test results. The test team's report noted that these missions, assigned to attack rail bridges, were by flown in heavy clouds and poor weather by no more than five *AZON* bombers rather than large formations. Technical failures such as weak batteries, radio receivers with bad vacuum tubes, gyros damaged by rough field takeoffs, and nose fuse damage on impact

were blamed as contributing factors in bomb failures. The most important finding of the report was that the bombardier had problems accurately dropping the bomb and then controlling it, particularly when the bombers arrived over targets in rapid succession in order to minimize susceptibility to enemy AA fire and fighter interception. The use of the radioman, navigator, or other regular crew members to be trained to control the bomb was judged as unwise as these crewmen were needed to man machine guns against enemy fighters that usually appeared over the target area. The report suggested that one bombardier drop the bombs and then have a specially trained *AZON* bombardier control it.

After another two *AZON* missions had been flown, the AAF Board prepared another evaluation on 8 May 1944. The new report now ambiguously stated that the VB-1 had "performed well" with 58 of the 108 bombs dropped "operating successfully" but that the *AZON* required "better weather than ordinary bombs." The low success rate was attributed to the use of the last of an "experimental lot of bombs," and that the new standardized operational *AZON*s would function much better. The report went on to specify that the control of the bomb was "positive, adequate, and satisfactory" and that while the cost of the *AZON* was about four times more than a conventional bomb "its accuracy warrants this additional cost."

The report recommended that the bombardier was not to control the bomb until it had fallen two-thirds of elapsed fall time which would positively effect range calculations since the induced drag due to changing the trajectory would be minimized. As the bomb neared the end of its fall it approached terminal velocity which made it more responsive to its controls making shorter commands necessary to initiate trajectory changes; also saving battery power until the most critical, last stage of the guidance sequence.

The report also noted *AZON*-carrying bombers could not take evasive action against enemy AA fire and fighters until the bombardiers completed control and the bombs impacted. The *AZON*s could not be used against the well-defended targets specified by the AAF daylight, precision, strategic bombardment policy. Since the number of existing radio channels restricted the number of *AZON* bombers that could be employed at any given time, the report suggested that *AZON* bombers be added to formations carrying conventional bombs. Of course, in order to maintain formation integrity this procedure would expose the ordinary bombers to AA fire for an additional length of time while the *AZON* operators controlled their bombs.

On 13 May, the Avisio Viaduct on the Brenner Pass railway about 10 miles north of Trento in northern Italy was attacked using *AZON* bombers "seeded" into conventional formations. This significant raid was the first to successfully evaluate an operational sortie by the *AZON* group thanks to the outstanding effort of the 1st Combat Camera Unit. The viaduct was located on the left bank of the Adige River and crossed 3,500 feet of rough gorge at the confluence of the Adige and Avisio Rivers. The Germans had large numbers of 88mm AA guns sited along the gorge and fighter defenses were considered as moderate. The viaduct was curved making it a poor *AZON* target with the most suitable bombing approach being from the south, following along the railway tracks to give the *AZON*s full right deflection to follow the curve of the viaduct. Since the four *AZON* bombers were only a small part of the 301BG mission, the attack was made from the north giving the *AZON* bombardiers no guide line to lead them into the viaduct's long axis. The initial reports of this mission highly commended the *AZON*'s bombardiers, crediting them with scoring four direct hits (of 21 bombs released) on the viaduct which blocked the pass to all rail traffic and made repairs very difficult. This misleading report influenced senior AAF leaders to the effectiveness and, thus continued use of the *AZON*s.

It was not until five months later, on 2 October 1944, that 15AF's Operational Analysis Section thoroughly examined the strike and post-mission photos. They found that the *AZON* bomb dispersion had been too great, and that "All indications pointed to the fact that the damaging hits were that of a regular bomb." The initial report had indicated four hits, but the Analysis Section found that some *AZON*s missed the target by so much that they could not be accounted for on the post-strike photos and the others had impacted a "considerable distance" from the viaduct.

The raid was a technical failure for the *AZON*s as the strike photography showed very little evidence of control and no indication of any last second corrections to bring the bombs on the target. Only one of the four *AZON* bombardiers had a good view of his bombs. Therefore, the *AZON* bombardiers were unable to gain effective control of their bombs until they could see them in the proximity of the curving railway lines during the last eight or nine seconds of fall. The *AZON*s were dropped in clusters of six, with each controller transmitting the same command to all bombs in the cluster which invariably led to a wide dispersion of all the bombs in the cluster except the one selected as the guide bomb.

Several possibilities were suggested for this lack of control but probably the most likely reason was the danger of the mission itself which encountered heavy anti-aircraft fire and fighter interception. Confronting a heavily defended target, the *AZON* crews did not relish continuing a less than a choice bomb run controlling bombs until they impacted. Strike photos indicated that the bombardiers chose their best bombs from the cluster and gave them one or two long controlling maneuvers to line them up during the early part of the bomb's fall. The bombardiers would then abandon control of the bombs to allow the pilot to take evasive action before the *AZON*S impacted.

The report concluded that the ideal "entire bomb load" for an *AZON* bomber should be one, accurately aimed 1,000 pound VB-1. With six *AZON* bombers seeded in each formation, only 6,000 total pounds of guided bombs, albeit each having a much greater probability of attaining a hit on the target, was pitted against a conventional B-17 that could drop strings of six 1,000 pound bombs at once but with much less accuracy on the standard single bomb run. However, controlling a single VB-1 would require that the entire formation, conventional and VB bombers remain together for the repeated runs over the target until every VB-1 was released; repeatedly (for five or six runs) exposing the conventional bomber crews to AA fire after they had dropped their own bombs.

This one (*AZON*) bomb per heavy bomber bomb run did not comply with AAF operational thinking and it was decided that each *AZON* bomber was to release strings of three to six *AZON*s simultaneously on the formation's conventional bomb drop. Each *AZON* bomber was directed to drop multiple VB-1s in rapid succession and then control all of them by guiding the center bomb only. Six *AZON* bombers were then able to release up to 36 VB-ls in a single bombing run, ideally responding as a single, compactly controlled cluster while being carefully guided to the target by six bombardiers. The logical progression of this idea was to have one bombardier control all *AZON*s, up to 36 bombs, simultaneously by six *AZON* B-17s.

During the 2 June raid on the marshalling yards at Oradea, Rumania, a solitary *AZON* bombardier attempted to control 12 VB-ls dropped by six B-17s in a single bombing run. Because the target was a large area, the radio receivers of the 12 *AZON* bombs were tuned to the same frequency and all were controlled by the lead aircraft from 22,400 feet. The bombardier directly guided one bomb but the other 11 bombs were dispersed over a very wide area. The cause for this extreme dispersion of the indirectly guided bombs was that the casing of each bomb had small exterior flaws and when the bomb was spinning the effect of these flaws was nominal. But because the *AZON* bomb did not spin, a flaw on one side

could draw the bomb in that direction. If the bombardier was guiding a bomb with a casing flaw, he could appreciably offset its effect. But when the bombardier was guiding several bombs at once, a signal to turn the guide bomb would move it in the correct direction but the same signal to the other bombs with casing flaws would cause them to deviate from their original trajectories. Also, each bomb had slightly different control characteristics. The result was widely scattered bombs that had a much greater dispersion error than conventional bombs. After the Oradea dispersion setback it was decided that only one *AZON* was to be controlled at a time from the mother B-17.

In June, the 301BG flew two missions against locks on the Danube River near the Iron Gate and although the unofficial news release stated the locks were "successfully attacked," the *AZON* results were inconclusive due to the raid seeding only a few "one bomb at a time" *AZON* bombers with many conventional bomb-carrying B-17s in the same formation which could claim credit for any damage. The 301st suffered the loss of its first *AZON* bomber in an attack against a railroad bridge in Szolnok, Hungary, on 2 July 1944. But the decision to drop one controlled *AZON* at a time ended the *AZON*'s possible role as a strategic bombardment weapon and the 15AF had had enough of the *AZON* experiments which it considered a nuisance and superfluous in the context of its overall mission. On 13 July, the 15AF notified the CG of the Mediterranean Allied Air Forces (MAAF) that the five remaining *AZON* bombers were to be restored to their regular heavy bombardment duties because:

"These five heavy bombers fly an average of only one sortie every 21 days and, because of the lower weight of the bombs carried, accomplish little. They have served their purpose as a successful experiment. The final conclusion is that *AZON* is not a heavy bombardment weapon but should be used by tactical air forces. Recommend consideration be given to possible installation of present *AZON* equipment in B-25 aircraft of 12th Air Force."

The following is a summary of 15AF *AZON*s sent by Gen. Ira Eaker to Gen. Carl Spaatz (Message M27820 August 11, 1944: Eaker to Spaatz):

"*AZON* project discontinued by 15TAF and is now in hands of MATAF (B-25s)
1) Total combat missions flown: 14
2) Total *AZON* bombs released: 316 (three missions were ineffective)
3) Release of bombs was first done with each aircraft releasing independently (three missions) with bombs individually controlled.
4) On two missions bombs were released in salvo and each aircraft controlled its own pattern.
5) On six missions bombs were salvoed from a three ship element with center bomb as guide. The entire pattern was controlled.
6) Average altitude of release was 15,000.
7) On the earlier missions the aircraft attacked the target singly in line astern. For pattern release and control the aircraft flew in a three ship element and in two element line astern.
8) Under individual release and control a deflection correction of 1,340 feet was obtained. Average deflection error for 63 bombs was 605 feet and average range error was 1,600 feet. These figures compare with average errors for normal bombing (15,000 feet altitude) of 780 feet deflection and 950 feet range.
9) In salvo release and control the average deflection error was 702 feet and average range error was 1,400 feet."

Thus the *AZON* was abandoned by the 15AF.

AZON Operational Use by Medium Bombers in the MTO

Several weeks after the 301BG gave up on the *AZON* it transferred the equipment, six specially-trained *AZON* crews, and VB-1 tail assemblies to the 446th Bomb Squadron of the 321st Bomb Group based on Corsica which began training during the first week of August. The Squadron flew the North American B-25 Mitchell medium bomber which could carry two VB-ls. By the end of September the Squadron had flown only two unsuccessful *AZON* missions against steel bridges and trestles as the bombs missed or passed through the steel structure before detonating. At the time Gen. Alexander Patch's Seventh Army had invaded Southern France on 15 August 1944 and was quickly driving north to link up with Patton's Third Army. Both Patton and Patch wanted bridges to remain undamaged so advancing Allied forces could use them and for most of August and September *AZON* missions against bridges in South France were prohibited. The Group suffered from a shortage of crews and found it impossible to run *AZON* and conventional missions. There were 183 *AZON*s on hand in Corsica and another 1,112 ready for shipment in Naples, which amounted to a three months supply with missions flown every day. The crews of the 321st continued to fly their conventional missions and became more disinterested in flying *AZON* missions at all. Finally, with the coming of the poor winter weather conditions and the Group's request for an additional six specially-trained *AZON* crews was ignored and the 321st would fly no further *AZON* missions during the war.

The Martin B-26 Marauder medium bomber equipped to carry four VB-ls was assigned to the 397th Bomb Group of the 9AF. On 4 August 1944, the unit flew its first and only *AZON* mission of the war when five B-26s equipped with 10 VB-ls attacked bridges near Chartres, France to prevent the Germans from counter attacking Patton's breakthrough at Avranches. The B-26s attacked a series of three bridges in quick succession from 11,500 feet but the lead bomber flew too close to the concentrated German AA batteries and three B-26s were hit. One Marauder immediately burst into flames and crashed but most of the crew bailed out; the second B-26 was so damaged that it could not continue on its bombing run; while the third returned to base so badly damaged that it was written off. The two undamaged B-26s failed to hit the bridges although one VB-1 cut the rail tracks just short of the first bridge. The 397th's operational report concluded:

"There can be no question concerning the effectiveness of enemy flak at the operational altitude of medium bombardment aircraft, 10,000 to 12,000 feet, and it must be admitted that against defended targets the 30 seconds longer bombing run necessary to control the *AZON* bomb to the target will be a deterring factor with *AZON* unless some method can be devised which will offset it."

Tethered VB-1s

In June 1944, it was thought that the "one bomb at a time" and dispersion problem could be minimized by fastening two bombs together. The tethered VB-1 method was tried in a practice mission on 10 June 1944 against a target on Pianosa Island in the Adriatic Sea. In the test, two VB-ls were tethered with a 25 foot length of wire with only one of the bombs controlled. The tests showed that the bombs could be tethered without parting and tethering did not interfere with guidance or negatively affect ballistics and would ensure that the two bombs would land within 25 feet of each other. However, the basic *AZON* ballistics problem remained and to drop and control three or four pairs of tethered *AZON*s on a single bombing run; every controlled bomb would have to respond exactly the same way; every time.

AZON Operational Use in the ETO

The second group of US *AZON* trainees were assigned to the 753rd Bombardment Squadron under Maj. Robert Holbrook and his assistant, Lt. David Baltics with Maj. J. Henry Rand, *AZON* designer, serving as the technical liaison. On 2 May, this group left Florida's Pine Castle Field for bridge-busting in Burma. With the invasion of France imminent, Gen. Carl Spaatz, Commander of the US Strategic Air Forces, felt the *AZON*s could be useful against bridges in Northern France to prevent German armor and supplies from reaching the beachhead. On 8 May 1944, a request for *AZON* crews and bombers to sent to the ETO was issued and the 753rd was crossing Africa enroute to Burma when orders they were diverted to the 8AF to conduct *AZON* sorties under the project code 90653-R. The 10 specially modified 753rd B-24 Liberators loaded with *AZON* tail (guidance) units arrived at the 458th Bombardment Group station at Horsham St. Faith, Norfolk on 16 May.

These 10 B-24J-155-COs were modified in the US and had the *AZON* transmitter unit AN/ARW-9 installed on the flight deck and linked to the

Movie film still of two **tethered AZONs** that were connected by a 25 foot length of wire with only one of the bombs controlled. The tests showed that the bombs could be tethered without interfering with guidance or negatively affecting ballistics and would ensure that the two bombs would land within 25 feet of each other. However, the basic *AZON* controller guidance and individual bomb ballistic inaccuracies remained and affected two bombs. (AAF)

three mast aerials under the rear fuselage. The control unit situated at the bombardier's position was operated by a simple left-right toggle joystick. An observation port was cut in the fuselage floor aft of the bombsight to aid the bombardier in observing the missile during its descent.

The original *AZON* B-24Js and their pilots assigned to the 753BS were:

44-40264	*Kiss Me Baby* (2Lt. John Lansing)
44-40273	*Howling Banshee* (F/O Arnold Piskin)
44-40275	*Shack Time* (1Lt. John Jones)
44-40277	*Miss Used* (1Lt. Gerald Matze)
44-40281	*A Dog's Life* (2Lt. John Lamed)
44-40283	*Lassie Come Home* (F/O John Tracy)
44-40285	*Table Stuff* (Capt. Maurice Speer)
44-40287	*Bachelor's Bedlam* (2Lt. Patrick McCormick)
44-40288	*Bad Girl* (2Lt. Frank Fuson)
44-40291	*Royal Flush* (1Lt. Robert Morford)

(Note 1: Other pilots were Lt.Col. F.M. O'Neill, Lieutenants Shaw, DeNeffe, Griffith, Lansing, Larned, and Tooman)
(Note 2: Between the two operational periods for *AZON*, 31 May to 22 June and 17 August to 13 September, three aircraft - 44-40066, 44-40277 and 44-40283 - were detached to work with the *Aphrodite* Double-*AZON* guided drones. The aircraft returned to the 753rd in August but the crews transferred to the *Aphrodite* project. Following the cancellation of *AZON* operations in September, the equipment was removed from all aircraft which were then used on normal daylight bombing operations.)
(Note 3: Nine additional B-24H and Js of the squadron were to be eventually modified in England.

By 26 May, nearly 3,000 *AZON*s were ready for combat use in the ETO. As the 458th was eager to combat test the *AZON*s and because the 753rd had not completed its move to Horsham St. Faith, it was decided to use a single B-24 (41-29300), the *Lorelei*, which was not among the original 10 *AZON*-trained crews. An unofficial trial mission on 23 May was escorted by eight P-51 Mustangs and was led by Lt.Col. F.M. O'Neill, the 753rd Squadron's CO and Capt. Fred DeNeffe over Northern France where four bridges were "claimed" to be damaged or destroyed by four *AZON*s. A total of 13 *AZON*s missions were flown between 31 May and 13 September 1944 in the ETO.

Howling Banshee piloted by F/O Arnold Piskin was one of the original ten B-24Js assigned to the 753BS of the 458th Bombardment Group for the initial operational use of AZONs. A total of 13 *AZON*s missions were flown between 31 May and 13 September 1944 in the ETO against bridges in northern France before the ETO was found "not to be conducive to *AZON* operations." (AAF)

Mission #1: 31 May 1944
The first "official" and large scale *AZON* mission took place on 31 May with five B-24s, carrying five AZONs each. The mission was escorted by five Mustang squadrons (48 aircraft); eight assigned to each bomber with eight to fly general support. 2Lt. John Lansing was the lead pilot with Lt.Col. Frederick O'Neill as the Command Pilot for the mission. The bombing was to be by individual bombers in trail, stepped up 200 feet each from an altitude of 17,000 to 17,500 feet. Only four of the five bombers attacked their target as one aborted due to mechanical problems. Five bridges in the Paris area were attacked in 5/10 to total cloud around all target and 10 miles visibility above. A summary of the attack on these bridges was as follows (in the order they were made):

#1 Melun Bridge embankment (5,300 feet long)
Four bombs dropped by three aircraft:
1 fell in the river near the bridge
1 fell near the entrance to the bridge
1 hit 100 feet from the bridge
1 hit the far side tracks
#2 Verberie Bridge (300 feet long)
The mission was scrubbed prior to briefing as clouds obscured the three assigned targets.
#3 Precy Suspension Bridge (350 feet long)
Two bombs dropped by two aircraft:
1 fell 300 feet from the target
1 fell short
#4 Beaumont-sur-Aire Bridge (300 feet long)
Four bombs dropped by four aircraft:
1 hit the end of the bridge
1 hit just over the end
1 hit 100 feet over the end
1 hit 300 feet over the end
#5 Mantes-Gassicourt Paris RR Bridge (250 feet long)
Three bombs dropped by three aircraft
1 hit an island in middle of river
1 hit the RR tracks just short of the bridge
1 hit the RR tracks at end of bridge
A target of opportunity, the bridge at Meuhlan was attacked by one bomber with poor results.

A total of 13 bombs were dropped with each being controlled individually and the seven unused bombs were returned to base. The group reported light inaccurate flak and no enemy aircraft.

Mission #2 1 June 1944
The mission was scrubbed prior to briefing as the three targets were reported by reconnaissance as obscured.

Mission #3: 4 June 1944
On 4 June, the Melun line junction and the 5,300 foot long Melun Bridge and embankment over the Seine River were attacked with 13 *AZON*s carried by five B-24s led by Lt.Col. Frederick O'Neill. Fifteen miles inside enemy territory one B-24 returned to base when a hydraulic line was cut by flak and five B-24s continued to their targets. Just before reaching the target another B-24 had a bomb rack malfunction causing three bombs to be released over the French countryside. The remaining four aircraft attacked the Melun line junction, dropping one bomb each, all falling within 200 to 1,000 feet from the target. The four bombers continued on to the Melun Bridge; three of them dropping one bomb each and the fourth dropping three bombs. The visibility was 10 miles/hazy.

with a 2/10ᵗʰs cloud cover. Near misses were reported but most bombs were off in azimuth but no conclusive results were assessed as there were no SAV (Strike Attack Vertical) photos taken.

Mission #4: 8 June 1944
Fifteen aircraft 458BG flew with to the Melun Bridge embankment twice without being able to drop their bombs as the target was covered by undercast.

Mission #5: 14 June 1944
Fifteen bombers in sections of five each took off to attack six French bridges: Corbie Bridge (180 feet), Perrone Bridge (150 feet), Hon-sur-Somme Bridge (170 feet), Estaples Bridge (1,004 feet), Frevent Bridge (2,460), and Doullens Bridge (150 feet). All bridges except Target #2 (Perrone Bridge) were obscured by cloud and sections No.1 and No.2 remained together to attack that clear target while section No.3 flew alone to a target of opportunity. Ten bombers approached Target #2 but two had *AZON* equipment malfunctions and one was too far off course to bomb effectively. The five bombers of Section No.3 became lost and attacked an unidentified target before returning to base. There were no results recorded of this unsuccessful mission.

Mission #6: 15 June 1944
The RR bridges at Etaples (by 11 bombers), Perrone (by seven bombers), and Doullens (by six bombers) were attacked by 14 bombers with 27 bombs, 20 controlled in 4/10 cloud and five miles, hazy visibility. The results were good with Perrone being destroyed by direct hits, and Targets #1 and #3 severely damaged by near misses. Generally flak over the targets was light and inaccurate but that over Caen was very accurate and six aircraft received minor damage and one received major damage. (Note: some bombers attacked more than one bridge.)

Mission #7: 22 June 1944
Railway bridges over the Loire River were attacked by nine B-24s in 2/10 cloud and unlimited visibility. The Saumur RR Bridge (3,600 feet) was attacked with 18 *AZON*s of which nine were controlled with three hitting within 500 feet of the target. Another 18 *AZON*s, nine controlled, were

On 22 June 1944 the 3,600 foot **Saumur Railway Bridge** over the Loire River was attacked by nine B-24s dropping 18 *AZON*s of which nine were controlled in 2/10 cloud and unlimited visibility. (AAF)

25 August 1944 the 1,100 foot **Tours le Riche Bridge** was attacked with 16 *AZON*s, 10 controlled, with at least one hit seen on post mission recon photos. The photo shows three *AZON*s as bright circles (arrows) heading for the target. (AAF)

dropped on the Tours le Riche RR Bridge spanning 1,120 feet without recorded results.

Mission #8: 17 August 1944
A mission on an unidentified RR bridge near Les Fallons was aborted as clouds obscured the target.

Mission #9: 25 August 1944
The 340 foot Moerdijk RR Bridge in Holland was attacked by 16 *AZON*s dropped in clusters with all bombs under one set of commands. This method was used to increase the mission's effectiveness in a single run over the target rather than expose the bombers to anti-aircraft fire and enemy fighters during the repeated runs for individually controlled drops. The dispersion of the *AZON*s was very large except for the control bombs near the center of the cluster one of which scored an apparent direct hit on the bridge. That same day the Tours le Riche Bridge (1,100 feet) was attacked with 16 *AZON*s, 10 controlled, with at least one hit seen on post

mission recon photos. The visibility was 20 miles with no clouds on both attacks.

Mission #10: 26 August 1944
On this mission the Moerdijk bridge mission was scrubbed due to heavy cloud cover obscuring the target. However, AA fire caused slight damage to six aircraft and major damage to one.

Mission #11: 1 September 1944
The Ravenstein RR Bridge and a secondary target, an ammunition depot near Kropp, Germany were the scheduled targets. Six *AZON* bombers dropped 12 *AZON*s in clusters, 10 controlled, on Kropp, with a few near misses and fires recorded. The cloud was 7/10th and the visibility unlimited.

Mission #12: 5 September 1944
A mission to an unidentified RR bridge near Mulheim, Germany, was recalled near the English coast due to bad weather.

Mission #13: 13 September 1944
An oil refinery at Flensberg, Germany was attacked by 11 aircraft with 25 *AZON*s dropped and no results were recorded. The cloud was 4/10 and the visibility was unlimited.

Notes on missions:
Missions #1 and #2: Aircraft flown in trail with bombardier sighting and controlling individually.
Missions #3, #4, and #5: Lead aircraft made a regular sighting, the wing aircraft sighting for range only and each controlling individually.
Missions #6 through #13: All aircraft dropped on lead aircraft and controlled individually.

After 13 missions the ETO was found not to be conducive to *AZON* operations for the following reasons:

Poor weather conditions were prevalent in this theater; especially during the time the 458th was to fly its first missions. For example, on D-Day alone, the group was alerted three times but flew no missions. During this time a constant state of alert was necessary to take advantage of any break in the weather but this alert with few resulting missions caused a morale problem. As seen from the mission summary five missions were recalled over the target. Any cloud conditions over 3/10 interfered or precluded *AZON* use.

Targets had to be limited to objectives not heavily defended by AA guns or interceptors. To fly at a higher altitude gave the bombers more protection against flak however guiding the bomb from 20,000 feet was much more difficult than from 10,000 feet. This was because high altitude drops made visual tracking of the tail flare difficult due to the chronic smoke and haze over the targets. It was found that flak turbulence, evasive action, or even simple weaving upset the bombardier's aim and perhaps composure.

The threat of enemy fighter interception made the use of small groups of *AZON* bombers hazardous and Allied fighter escort was in short supply and could not be delegated to small *AZON* raids. Thus the *AZON*s were carried by bombers which were only a small fraction of a larger formation of conventional bombers and consequently operational plans were formulated to suit the larger formation. At that time Air Force bombing evaluation was based on tonnage of bombs dropped (quantitative) rather

than damage done (qualitative) and directed their resources and tactics in that direction.

If the *AZON*s were utilized as recommended, one dropped and controlled per aircraft per bombing run, the total tonnage decreased. Only one bombing run could be made as the conventional bombers would be jeopardized by waiting for *AZON* bombers to make individual attacks in the face of enemy AA fire and interceptors. Therefore, all *AZON*s were dropped at once in salvo with the one bomb being used as a control. This method resulted in a wide dispersion of hits even though all bombs from each aircraft were under single-simultaneous control. As previously discussed, the reason for this dispersion was that each *AZON* had slightly different aerodynamics due to manufacturing inaccuracies and each also had slightly different control characteristics.

A "Report on *AZON* Operations" dated 31 October 1944, from HQ 8AF: Office of the Commanding General for the Commanding General concluded:

"It is believed that the weather expectancies in this theatre and bombing results obtained on these experimental missions justify the following recommendations:
1) The *AZON* bombing project be discontinued in this theatre.
2) *AZON* equipment now assigned to the group conducting these experiments be released to that unit to be utilized as radio bomb release equipment."

AZON Operational Use in the CBI
On 5 April 1944, 10 B-24J bombers , which were destined for service with 10AF in the CBI, arrived at the School of Applied Tactics in Florida to begin their transitional VB-1 training. Soon all 10 bombers were equipped with new radio transmitters and antennae were installed. Also, further modifications were necessary to give the bombardiers adequate visibility to acquire and track the bomb as it fell so a small, six inch diameter hole was cut in the forward right corner of the floor in the bombardier's compartment and covered with a Plexiglas window.

Training began at once as 10 B-24 bombardiers controlled 103 test VB-ls but of the first 40 drops; 19 failed. These malfunctions were due to problems with the bomb rack, gyros, radio transmitter or radio-control box, and, as usual, with the flares. The *AZON* technical representative quickly determined that the radio-transmitter problems were caused by "frequency drift" in the radio tuners. In contrast to today's aviation radios, which can lock onto and track a specific frequency, those of the World War II era had to be constantly monitored to make certain reception and transmission remained the same as originally dialed in. These radios could drift off frequency and the signal to become garbled or lost altogether due to vibration, changing antenna angles as the aircraft or bomb maneuvered, and atmospheric conditions. After technicians set up new radio-tuning procedures; not one radio failure occurred during the following 60 VB-1 practice drops. By the time bombardiers had dropped four or five VB-ls each, azimuth errors of zero feet were the norm for any bomb not having a malfunction. Of the last 53 VB-ls dropped, 43 had a zero azimuth error and 12 also had a zero range error. The B-24 crews completed their US training and departed for 10AF on 29 April 1944 as part of the 7th Bomb Group (H); hoping that the *AZON* accuracy achievable over practice ranges in the US were as easily to reproduce under combat conditions

In late September, the B-24s and crews of the 493rd Bomb Squadron reported to the 7th Bombardment Group of the 10AF under Col. Harvey Alness stationed at Pandaveswar, India. Because the negative reports of the *AZON* experience of 15AF and 8AF in the ETO had preceded them, these recently trained crews were greeted unenthusiastically upon their arrival from Ft. Dix. Since the CBI was a low priority theatre of operations, there was a chronic shortage of aircraft and therefore, the *AZON* tails and transmitters were unloaded from their B-24s and stored in warehouses and the valuable B-24s were allotted to the four squadrons of the 7BG for conventional operations. Also, vital *AZON* testing equipment was not shipped from Ft. Dix and had to be reissued from there. Meanwhile, two of the B-24s were lost in conventional bombing raids and five were consigned to the "Hump Airline," ferrying gasoline to the B-29s then based in China.

Administratively the 7BG was part of the 10AF but it was under the operational control of the Strategic Air Force within the theater. At the time, with no ordinary strategic targets to attack such as industry and cities; the Strategic Air Force attacked supply lines as high priority targets in order to cut Burma off from supplies from Thailand and Malaya. Railways and particularly bridges and trestles were the priority targets assigned to the *AZON* bombers. All *AZON* bombers were kept in the 493rd Squadron that would function as a normal Squadron with the other three Bomb Group Squadrons except when assigned to *AZON* missions. By keeping the *AZON*s in one Squadron all the special equipment and maintenance men and equipment was concentrated at one field. Operational briefings and procedures and training were greatly simplified in one Squadron.

On 10 December, NDRC official, Maj. William Denies and technical advisor, Dr. T.J. O'Donnell, arrived in India to act as *AZON* liaison to HQ 10AF. The data and films they brought with them demonstrated the bomb's merits sufficiently to regain five gasoline hauling B-24s for *AZON* operations. The necessary instruments and equipment were installed in the B-24s, so that three were ready for the first *AZON* sortie in the CBI.

On 27 December 1944 the three Liberators tookoff carrying eight bombs; four *AZON*s and four standard 1,000 pound M65 bombs to attack the Pyinmana railroad bridge located between Rangoon and Mandalay. The bridge had withstood aerial attack for nearly two years and was a perfect *AZON* target having a straight bombing approach and was long enough at 380 feet in three spans to permit the predicted range errors to destroy the target. Each bombardier was given one practice bomb run on railway lines on the way to the target. Two bombardiers were used with the first bombardier positioned in the standard nose station to initially aim the *AZON* using the Norden Bombsight. He was to aim the *AZON* as close to the target as possible, thus reducing range errors. The second bombardier was located in the tail of the dropping aircraft giving him an unobstructed downward view of the falling bomb which he was to guide towards the target. Three passes were made by each Liberator with one *AZON* and one standard bomb dropped on each pass, all from 9,300 feet. Anti-aircraft fire and enemy fighters were not present. Three hits were made on the bridge with the center span destroyed and another span damaged by *AZON*s as all standard bombs missed.

On 30 December 1944 he 225 foot steel road bridge on the **Prometaugup Road** (right) and 400 foot concrete bridge at **Tausgup** (left) were destroyed with 16 *AZON*s. (Both AAF)

On 30 December, with another B-24 *AZON*-equipped, four B-24s armed with 28 *AZON*s were to attack one bridge with two alternatives from 10,000 feet; all bridges supplied the Japanese offensive on the Arakan Front. The 225 foot steel road bridge on the Prometaugup Road and 400 foot concrete bridge at Tausgup were destroyed with 16 bombs. Having 12 unused bombs, the B-24s attacked the 200 foot Okshitpin Bridge destroying it with eight bombs, leaving four. An unscheduled 75 foot wooden bridge was located and destroyed by three of the four bombs.

Four B-24s, each carrying four *AZON*s flew the third mission on 1 January 1945, attacking three bridges at 10,500 feet. The weather was bad with 4/10 to 10/10 cloud cover. One bridge was confirmed destroyed but two others were rated as "possible but doubtful."

The fourth mission on 3 January dispatched three bombers carrying six *AZON*s each at 8,000 feet. Two bridges and a section of track were attacked with one bridge destroyed, two probably damaged, and three direct hits were made on the tracks.

On the fifth mission, 8 January, six bombers carrying six *AZON*s each attacked four bridges from 10,000 feet with three bridges destroyed but the fourth was undamaged.

On the sixth mission on 9 January, three bridges were attacked from 10,500 feet by three bombers carrying four *AZON*s each resulting in two bridges destroyed and the third undamaged.

The seventh mission on 11 January had two bridges attacked by five bombers carrying five *AZON*s each at 10,500 feet. Both bridges were destroyed and for the first time some AA fire was encountered, doing no damage.

The 493BS squadron flew seven missions in 15 days before expending their supply of *AZON* bombs. A total of 154 bombs were released with 34 hits being scored to destroy 14 bridges and damaging three more. Of the 154 bombs about 35 were considered to be "wasted" for various reasons with the majority being salvoed because of engine problems, a few being released late because of rack malfunctions, and a few because of "personnel failure." A Memorandum of 1 March 1945 from Division HQ stated:

"The overall economy of *AZON* bombing on those seven missions is somewhat startling. At least 35 of the *AZON*s were either direct hits or close enough to damage the targets…. Conservatively we can say that one out of five *AZON*s gave a damaging hit…. (when) one damaging hit of 50 bombs would be an over-optimistic guess….On this basis *AZON* is ten times as effective against bridges as standard bombing or one *AZON* Squadron is equivalent to two and a half standard bomb Groups."

During these seven missions the most efficient *AZON* bombing technique was determined. The best bombing altitudes were to be at 8,000 to 10,000 feet which allowed sufficient time for the bombardiers to determine and enter corrections but was not too high that the range error would be too great due to human error and ballistic error due to bombs not spinning. Individual *AZON* release rather than train release was employed as each *AZON* bomb required a different amount of control and the bombardier had to concentrate on controlling one at a time to the target as narrow as a bridge. It was particularly important that experienced lead bombardiers were to be used as it was necessary that the bomber be correctly lined up on the bridge.

On missions where there was little chance of enemy fighter interception the first IP (Initial Point) was chosen and upon arrival there, each bomber flew into trail at 30 second intervals. At the second IP, each bomber turned in on its bombing run. A pattern was made around the target, with each bomber sighting for its own range and deflection, dropping one bomb on each run.

On missions where enemy fighter interception was probable, a formation of six bombers in two three aircraft elements was flown javelin down. The bomber formation made a pattern around the target, each bomber dropping one *AZON* on each run. Aircraft from other Squadrons were sometimes assigned to attack the gun emplacements with 20 pound cluster fragmentation bombs to neutralize the gun positions at least long enough for the *AZON* bombers to complete their bombing runs.

Most mission failures were caused by undercast of 3/10 or more in which the path of *AZON*s could not be followed closely enough for proper control. Missions under these overcast conditions were either cancelled or aborted over the target. Equipment failure occurred about 3% of the time with half due to flare failure and the remainder due to control failure right or left.

On missions where AA fire could interfere with the completion of six *AZON* bombing runs; the bombers were loaded with three *AZON* and three standard 1,000 pound bombs. Each bomber made three runs, dropping one *AZON* and one standard bomb on each run.

Maintenance was considered the most significant factor for effective operational *AZON* use. In the 493BS there were ten enlisted men and one officer in charge of *AZON* maintenance and testing who did an exceptional job, in view of 25 men being considered optimal.

The Group considered themselves so successful that they put up a sign stating; "Dentist's Office: Bridgework: Our Specialty." The missions were so successful that Hugh Spencer, Chief of Division 5/NDRC and Maj. Donics requested the expedited shipment of kits to modify 50 more B-24s for *AZON* use before the Monsoon season that was expected to begin in May. They also requested a monthly shipment of 700 VB-1s and 300 VB-2s to the CBI.

Once the new supplies of the bomb arrived, the good results continued as the Group's official report for 27 December 1944 to 5 March 1945 stated:

"The group (7BG) expended 459 *AZON* bombs, resulting in the destruction of 27 bridges. During this period an average range error of 201 feet and an average deflection error of 131 feet have been maintained. Ten to 15% of the bombs dropped have been direct hits, the bridges averaging approximately 250 feet in length. These accuracy figures do not include those dropped as standard bombs, nor malfunctions or gross errors from heavy overcast."

The following table demonstrates the effectiveness of the *AZON* compared to the conventional 1,000 pound General Purpose Bomb:

Bomb Type	Effectiveness Ratio
6-1,000lb. GP bombs	1.0 (as a standard)
1-*AZON*	4.0 to 8.0
1-*AZON* plus 5-1,000lb. GP bombs	4.7 to 8.7
6-*AZON*s (in salvo)	5.2 to 9.2

As can be seen one *AZON* dropped on the same target was four to eight times more effective than six 1,000 pound GP bombs. Any use of the *AZON* was more effective than conventional bombing techniques.

The following table is a summary of operations by the 493BS squadron between 27 December 1944 and 5 March 1945. This table denotes a variance in *AZON*/conventional bomb effectiveness from the preceding table. The unguided bomb figures in the table are outstanding. This was due to two factors. The success of the *AZON* crews caused a rivalry between their squadron and the other three conventional squadrons in the 7BG. The second factor was the lack of Japanese anti-aircraft and fighter defenses at that time allowing the conventional bombers to carry out very accurate low level glide attacks (as low as 1,000 feet on some missions).

AZON was used effectively in the CBI. The Japanese were dependent on the railways from Siam (now Thailand) and Malaya to Rangoon and northwards to Mandalay. The 10AF carried out continual attacks against railway bridges mainly with *AZON* bombs but also with ordinary GP bombs. Because the river bridges were destroyed the Japanese throughout Burma were forced into many railway car unloadings on one side of the river into ferry and barge transport and then reloading back into railroad cars on the other side. By 5 March, Japanese resistance in Burma was limited into pockets without outside supplies.

The superb results in 10th Air Force, as opposed to those in Europe, can be attributed to the much lighter AA defenses in the CBI which permitted repeated passes by *AZON*-equipped B-24s, allowing them the

Summary of Operations by 493rd *AZON* Squadron/7th Bomb Group
November 1944-March 1945

Date	Target	Size (ft)	No. of Bombs GP	AZON	Hits GP	AZON	Bombs per hit GP	AZON
1 Nov	RR Br.	780 x 18	6	-	1 poss.	-	6	-
5 Nov	Tunnels		10	-	0	-	10	-
23 Nov	RR Br.	500	72	-	0	-	72	-
25 Nov	RR Br.	320	35	-	1	-	35	-
26 Nov	RR Br.	770	54	-	0	-	54	-
27 Dec	RR Br.	380 x 14	21	9	0	3	3	3
30 Dec	Road Br.	75 - 400		28		4		7
1 Jan	2 RR Br.	200 x 15 / 210 x 14	10	16	0	0	10 above 16	
3 Jan	RR Br.	1400 x 14	6	11	0	1 ?	64	11 ?
3 Jan	2 RR Br.	-	2	5	0	0	2 above 5	
8 Jan	RR Br.	-	0	17	-	2	-	8.5
8 Jan	RR Br.	-	0	9	-	3	-	3
8 Jan	RR Br.	-	0	3	-	0	- above 3	
8 Jan	RR Br.	-	0	1	-	0	- "	1
9 Jan	RR Br.	-	6	6	2	2	3	3
9 Jan	RR Br.	-	4	5	1	2	4	2.5
9 Jan	RR Br.	-	2	1	0	0	3	(salvo)
11 Jan	RR Br.	450	1	9	1	8	1	1.12
11 Jan	RR Br.	-	13	15	2	8	7.5	1.19
13 Jan	Jetty	1350 x 450	0	15	-	1	-	15
27 Jan	RR Br.	430	0	18	-	6	-	3
27 Jan	RR Br.		0	18	-	3	-	6
3 Feb	RR Br.	360 x 15	0	16	-	3	-	5.3
5 Feb	RR Br.	360 x 15	0	12	-	1	-	12
7 Feb	RR Br.	740 x 16	24	24	Multiple		Few	Few
9 Feb	RR Viaduct	1230	24	18	2 Gaps		Indeterminate	
11 Feb	RR Br.	500	0	18	-	4	-	4.5
11 Feb	RR Br.	150	6	9	0	-	6	-
15 Feb	RR Br.	260 x 15	12	24	0	2	12	12
21 Feb	RR Br.	500 x 16	11	21	0	3	11	7
23 Feb	RR Br.	300 x 15	0	6	-	2	-	3
25 Feb	RR Br.	400	48	0	6 or 8	-	7	-
27 Feb	RR Br.	430	0	18	-	4	-	4.5
3 Mar	RR Br.	600 x 16	0	24	-	1	-	24
3 Mar	RR Br.	740 x 16	48	0	2	-	24	-
5 Mar	RR Br.	280	36	36	Damage	7	36	5.1
Totals	30 Bridges	-	226	361	18	50	12.5 approx.	7.2 approx.

luxury of dropping one guided bomb per bomb run. To deal with targets having heavier than normal AA defenses, however, 10AF routinely flew bombers loaded with 20 fragmentation cluster bombs to deliberately attack AA batteries a few minutes before the B-24s carrying VB-1s arrived. Still, 10AF operational planners clearly acknowledged that in theaters having heavier air defenses, repeated passes with the VB-1 would have been out of the question. The advent of the summer monsoon season sidelined the VB-1 in the 10AF once again. By the time the weather had cleared in August 1945, the war was over.

On 21 April 1945, *AZON* equipment was standardized and design frozen and by 5 May the project was closed except for manufacture. A total of 15,271 *AZON*s were built and an additional order for 10,000 was cancelled after V-J Day.

VB-2 *SPAZON* Bombs
Basically the VB-2 was a 2,000 pound version of the VB-1 using identical gyros, radio, and battery as the VB-1. It differed in that it was larger, required a shorter flare and stronger solenoids. It could be carried by any bomber equipped with 2,000 pound bomb racks.

The only way to finally solve the *AZON* ballistics problem was to allow the bomb to spin but still have some control over it. VB-1s that were permitted to spin were referred to as *SPAZON* bombs (**SP**in **AZ**imuth **ON**ly) or "Spinning *AZON*s." Work on anti-dispersion modifications by the Development Engineering Branch at Wright Field and Gulf Research and Development permitted the VB-1 to rotate for the first half of its fall, then become stabilized, and guided as before. There was an initial 15 second pre-set period of spin through 15,000 feet after which there was a three second interval for stabilization with 1,200-1,500 feet left for azimuth control by the bombardier toward the target. As a result of this spinning the innate dispersion introduced by the asymmetric properties of the bomb were partially cancelled and the dispersion pattern was substantially reduced.

Twenty VB-2s were sent to Tonopah, NV for tests during June 1944 with 12 being dropped from external racks on a B-17 as the short flares were not available and the bombs with long flares were too long to be carried internally. The bombs were dropped together because a better estimate of control could be obtained by observing and photographing the parallel flight paths of the two bombs. Of the 12 bombs dropped in the test eight performed satisfactorily for full flight. The VB-2 anti-dispersion method was considered successful but in need of a time switch and linkage within the gyro case. At the end of the month the Development Engineering Branch requested increased funding and that the project to be accelerated.

Tests continued at Pinecastle AAB between 6-16 February 1945 with 12 VB-2s dropped. These tests also showed promise and it was suggested that the anti-dispersion modification be incorporated into the VB design. However, making modifications after the bombs left the assembly lines would require additional time and resources while retooling and retraining workers to add the new components on the assembly line would cause delays in beginning production. Both solutions were unsatisfactory to the AMC and the next 30,000 tail assemblies were to be produced without the anti-dispersion modification and the bomb remained an *AZON* type. A total of only 132 SP*AZON*s were produced and although research continued through the end of the war, none were deployed in combat trials. Finally and again, the best solution to the dispersion problem was to guide each bomb separately.

RAZON
VB-3 and VB-4 *RAZON*
When the Air Corps requested that the NDRC undertake the development

of controlled trajectory bombs at the end of December 1941 the specification requested that the "bomb be controlled in flight by a bombardier. Azimuth control was essential and....range control highly desirable." In April 1942, the "*RAAZ*" (*RA*nge and *AZ*imuth) bomb project was initiated but several considerations caused the de-emphasis of the *RAAZ* two co-ordinate control in favor of the one co-ordinate control *AZON*. R.D. Wyckoff, Project Director, felt that the problem of roll stabilization by ailerons was insurmountable when simultaneous pitch (range) and yaw (azimuth) control was utilized. Gulf Research & Development, the project development contractor, found roll could easily be prevented if only range or azimuth control were used. If there was a choice to be made, officials felt that azimuth (*AZON*) control was to be used as its design and development was simpler and it could be of more use tactically than a range only bomb. A last consideration was that the *AZON* was easier to steer than the *RAAZ*, as the problem of parallax plagued the *RAZON*. This problem meant the bombardier could not look along the bomb's trajectory and decide the probable point of impact. This occurred because the *RAAZ* fell virtually in the same forward motion as the aircraft so the bombardier viewed the *RAAZ* as moving at an increasing distance almost directly below him. As the bombardier did not know the remaining distance the *RAAZ* had to fall at any given time in its trajectory he had no direct way of determining the projected point of impact in the range co-ordinate. However, to move the bomb from right to left (azimuth) was relatively simple so the *AZON* project was given priority until June 1943, when the Air Materiel Command decided that the *AZON* project had progressed sufficiently so that the *RAZON* design could be resurrected and assigned to Gulf Research & Development.

The *RAAZ* bomb was to be controlled on the vertical and horizontal axes simultaneously. Preliminary experiments utilizing the square/cruciform *AZON*-type tail assembly which had controls on both axes was shown to be not viable. Continued *RAAZ* control tests by Gulf in February 1943 and again in June and July failed badly as not one bomb responded correctly on either axis to radio-control. Whenever either range or azimuth control was used; the falling bomb went into a spin, losing control. To solve this problem Gulf attached two VB-1s together by their tail assemblies at 90° angles by which a left correction signal on the horizontal tail assembly would register as a LEFT whereas it would register as an UP on the tail assembly turned on its side. Between 23 June and 7 July 1943, six bombs, controllable in both range and azimuth were tested with unsatisfactory results due to radio failure. At this time the *RAAZ* bombs assumed the *RAZON* or *R*ange and *AZ*imuth *ON*ly designation.

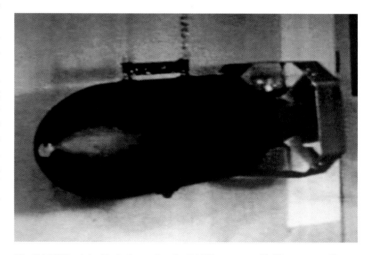

The ***RAZON***, originally designated as the *RAAZ*, was controlled in two co-ordinates (range and azimuth) as opposed to the one co-ordinate (azimuth) control of *AZON*. (AAF)

Feasibility tests at Eglin Field in February 1944 proved the *RAZON* idea to be too complicated as the system required separate frequencies for each tail assembly and the control surfaces were found to respond much differently in the vertical plane as opposed to the horizontal plane. Significantly, the center of gravity of two bombs attached to each other varied so greatly between each different pair that no two responded the same way to radio control and bombardiers consistently over-controlled these bombs, causing them to spin or tumble.

MIT submitted several anti-roll fin designs to Gulf R&D to eliminate roll during simultaneous range and azimuth control. These new fin designs removed the square/cruciform *AZON* tail and added structures that had circular symmetry which was almost free of roll torque and could be steered by an auxiliary tiltable cylinder. These circular structures afforded much larger and far more responsive control surfaces than was available with the *AZON*. While the design was aerodynamically superior it was larger and the tiltable control cylinder used excessive power for control. Gulf modified the design by surrounding the bomb at its center of gravity with a cylindrical lifting shroud and installed an octagonal tail for steering and stabilization. Movable flaps serving alternately as elevators and rudders were placed on the tail surfaces. The downside to this change to the tail assembly was that it made the VB-3 considerably larger than the VB-1, resulting in fewer VB-3s that could be loaded inside a bomb bay. The B-17 could carry up to six VB-1s but could carry only two VB-3s; the B-24 was able to carry eight VB-1s but only four VB-3s; while the large B-29 could only carry eight VB-3s versus 12 VB-1s. But the fewer VB-3s carried would be acceptable if the VB-3 was found to be more accurate than the VB-1.

Gulf built six VB-3s for the AAF for demonstration at Muroc in the summer 1943; during which time these bombs were controlled as *AZON*s and had fixed range control which paradoxically showed that the *AZON* was a viable weapon. But nonetheless, neither guided weapon received much attention until the *Luftwaffe* successfully deployed the Hs-293 glider bomb and the FX-1400 "*Fritz X*" vertical bomb in combat. The *Fritz X* had overcame the chronic parallax problem that plagued guided weapon systems by having the bombardier first sail and then dive the

bomb while the controlling medium bomber went into a steep climb to its decrease speed. By using these maneuvers the bombardier could direct the bomb so that it could eclipse the target during the last several seconds of its fall. Gulf tried several adaptations of the *Luftwaffe* method but decided that AAF heavy bombers could not climb steeply enough to reduce speed without stalling.

The parallax problem made it exceedingly difficult for the bombardier to distinguish the bomb's height above the ground when looking down on it from the mother aircraft. It was almost impossible for the bombardier to determine if the VB-3 was going to travel too long or too short and to necessitate the proper control downward or upward. During February 1944 testing was conducted to remedy the parallax problem by using a second bomber positioned to the side of the dropped bomb to better observe its height and control the vertical axis. This method was quickly rejected by operational commanders, who already had to tolerate having one of their heavy bombers deliver only one 1,000 pound VB-1 during a bomb run and would now have another bomber used to observe the delivery of that single *RAZON*.

At the time, renowned bombsight designer, Carl Norden, had discovered the solution to the parallax problem which was then developed into the "*Crab I Bombsight*" by H.A. Van Dyke at the Franklin Institute and later at L.N. Schwein Engineering Company when he transferred there. The *Crab I* Norden Bombsight consisted of a small stationary silvered mirror that was inserted between the telescope objective lens and the target mirror so as to intercept a portion of the light from the target normally entering the telescope and to substitute for this portion, light coming from the flare of the controllable bomb. The *Crab I* allowed the bombardier to see and track both the target and the falling bomb simultaneously. The simultaneous tracking was essential since the bomb's horizontal speed fell off quickly after it was released from bomber, causing the bomb's trajectory to "trail" behind the bomber. The amount of trail was a dynamic of the bomber's groundspeed and altitude when the bomb was released and how long the bomb had been falling (i.e. the higher and faster the bomber flew, the more distance behind the bombers the bombs were when they struck the target). As a result, when the target was in front of the bomber, the falling bomb

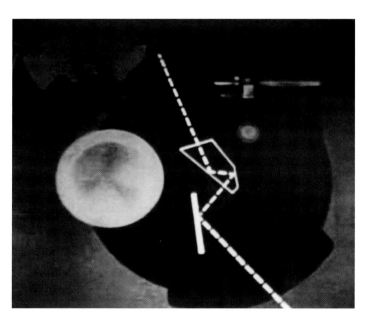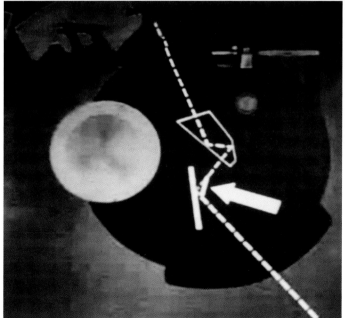

The *Crab I* Norden Bombsight (right) the solved parallax problem in sighting the moving *RAZON*. It consisted of a second small stationary mirror that was inserted between the telescope objective lens and the target mirror (see the left standard Norden drawing) so as to intercept a portion of the light from the target normally entering the telescope and to substitute for this portion, light coming from the flare of the *RAZON*.

would be slightly behind. When dropping conventional bombs, once the bombardier had considered lateral drift due to winds, he could then more easily drop the bombs based upon time of fall calculations but once the bombs were dropped, he could do nothing further. When guiding the VB-3 the bombardier had to continuously measure the difference between the target's position and the relative position of the falling *RAZON* and make corrections accordingly which only could be achieved if the bombardier could see both at the same time.

When using the *Crab* attachment, the bombsight lens was calibrated to move to keep the crosshairs on the target as the bomber passed over it and the *Crab* mirror was fixed on the proper ballistic trajectory of the falling VB-3. Initially, the bombardier would see two widely separated images; which would gradually converge as the bomb fell and the bomber flew over the target. When the VB-3 struck the target, the bombsight lens would have rotated so that both the target and bomb images were one. If the bombardier kept the falling bomb in the center of the mirrored reflection, the VB-3 would hypothetically hit the target.

Studies by Gulf demonstrated that time of bomb fall (and range error) varied by as much as three seconds due to the amount of control required during the fall. To inform the bombardier of this error a device known as "*Jag*" ("*J*ust *a*nother *g*adget") was designed and attached to the *Crab I*. *Jag* was a small silvered mirror which projected the image of the falling *RAZON*'s tail flare onto the bombsight's field of view. The operator would control the *RAZON* keeping it lined up in the sight at the point where the bomb should strike and no further control would be necessary. Later the control mechanism was integrated into a one operator unit.

Until June 1944, the NDRC had directed most of the experimental work on guided missiles but at that time the Materiel Command, Wright Field was authorized to assist the NDRC in conducting tests. Capt. J.H. Evans was appointed the Project Engineer for VB-3 and VB-4. In tests at Wendover in July 1944, two of six VB-3s landed within 45 feet of the target using the *Crab* attachment and during tests between 4 August and 9 September the *Crab* further improved VB-3 accuracy. Although, during these tests eight of 19 VB-3s failed to guide due to radio and other malfunctions, the other 11 had a impressive mean impact of three feet to the right and 17 feet over in range when dropped from 15,000 feet. The VB-3 showed "promise of becoming an invaluable weapon against special targets but was not yet ready for combat use." Evans recommended that changes necessary for mass production should be made so that sufficient units could be on hand for final acceptance tests.

At the end of October 1944 the NDRC, at the urging of the Air Technical Service Command and the Navy BuOrd, placed a tooling contract for 150 *RAZON* assemblies with Union Switch and Signal for delivery by the end of January 1945 with 50 each to the AAF and Navy and the remaining 50 would be used by NDRC for continued testing. Twenty VB-3s would be supplied by Gulf Research and Development for tests in November 1944. On 28 October Brig.Gen. H.M. McClelland, Air Communications Officer authorized Maj.Gen. O.P. Echols Chief of Air Staff, Materiels and Services to procure 3,000 *RAZON*s for the 20AF "to ensure sufficient numbers were on hand for both future testing and initial operational needs." However, no quantity production had yet been authorized although the ATSC had been directed to fund no more than $1,000,000 for the first 1,000 *RAZON* tails and to procure 2,000 more. Although service tests were scheduled for November 1944 *RAZON* development was incomplete as the optimal position of the shroud, fusing, arming devices and antennae had not been determined and modified designs were prepared. However, tests at Wendover indicated that the former *RAZON* design was more stable than the modified versions.

Two unforeseen issues caused critical delays in bringing this guided weapon to combat. The first delay was a recommended design change

while the other was the sudden lack of operational need for guided weapons. The design change was to add a second shroud to increase the maneuverability of the VB-3. By adding a second octagonal shroud to the tail, the maximum azimuth correction range increased from 1,600 feet to 2,660 feet when dropped from 15,000 feet. This was a significant improvement in guidance performance, offering the bombardier a 60% increase in azimuth correction capability. Unfortunately, this design change required redesign of many of the VB-3's other components, including the radio receiver and replacement of the gyros which would require time. While all these changes did increase range correction, they also made the VB-3 much less stable aerodynamically and more difficult to steer. This instability became so obvious in test drops from 6 November to 8 December 1944 that the AMC recommended that the NDRC return to the original, single-shroud design.

RAZON Models
Given a high priority, Gulf continued to develop its *RAZON* into a number of separate models:

Mark I: Single rear mounted shroud with an 11.5 inch diameter central cylinder that contained the radio, gyro, and battery mounted in the forward half of the cylinder. The rudder and elevator surfaces were 2.5 x 12 inches and had a travel of 20° in 0.5 seconds. There was an individual linkage to the ailerons from the solenoids. The servo motors moved at six rpm. It had no tail fuse cavity.

Mark Ia: Single rear mounted shroud with a 12 inch diameter central cylinder that contained the radio, gyro, and battery mounted in the forward half of the cylinder. The rudder and elevator surfaces were 3 x 12 inches and had a travel of 15° in 0.5 seconds. There was a disc linkage common to all four ailerons. The servo motors moved at four rpm. It had a T-75 tail fuse cavity.

Mark II: Single shroud mounted near the front with a 12 inch diameter central cylinder that contained the radio, gyro, and battery mounted in the rear half of the cylinder. The rudder and elevator surfaces were 3 x 12 inches and had a travel of 20° in 0.7 seconds. The servo motors moved at four rpm. It had a tail fuse cavity.

Mark IIa: Same as the Mark II except that the shroud was moved aft 2.125 inches. This model was tested and found to have low stability.

Mark III: Double shroud with the leading edge of the forward shroud extending beyond the forward end of the 12 inch central cylinder and with the trailing edge of the rear shroud extending beyond the rear end of the

The **single shroud tail** appeared on the Mark I, II, and IIa *RAZON* models. (AAF)

The **double shroud tail** appeared on the Mark III and IV *RAZON* models. (AAF)

central cylinder. The rudder and elevator surfaces were 3 x 12 inches and had a travel of 20° in 0.7 seconds. The radio, gyro, and battery mounted in the forward half of the central cylinder. The servo motors moved at four rpm. It had a tail fuse cavity. This design never went beyond the design stage.

Mark IV: Double shroud with the trailing edge of the rear shroud flush with the rear end of the central cylinder and with an octagonal forward lift shroud and a 12 inch central cylinder. The radio, gyro, and battery mounted in the forward half of the central cylinder. The rudder and elevator surfaces were 3 x 12 inches and had a travel of 15° in 0.5 seconds. The servo motors moved at four rpm. It had a tail fuse cavity.

The models with a central lift cylinder and an octagonal tail shroud prevented the loading of the *RAZON* onto standard 1,000 pound bomb bay racks. Gulf then redesigned the VB-3, making the central lift cylinder part of the tail while continuing to maintain adequate stability and maneuverability. This redesigned tail shroud consisted of three sections; the tail section or "control shroud" had flaps in the horizontal and vertical surfaces of the octagon itself which acted as elevators and rudders, respectively to steer the bomb. Ailerons, called the "lift shroud," were located on the 45° struts attaching the octagon to the bomb and were gyro-controlled to prevent rolling. The third component was the cylindrical section.

On 19 January 1945 a military and civilian conference discussed the *RAZON* program after *AZON* production had been discontinued. The surplus *AZON* components were anticipated to be used for the *RAZON* program but the radio receivers from the Signal Corps were delayed and the *RAZON* tails would not be ready before April 1945. Union Switch began retooling but the final design would not be available before mid-February with an anticipated monthly total of 2,000 to 3,000 thereafter. However, Union Switch soon modified that optimistic estimate to 150 in July, 500 in August, and 1,000 per month thereafter.

Tests of the Mark Ia and Mark IV *RAZON*s at Wendover proved both types to be satisfactory although the Mark IV with the double octagonal shroud was preferred because of its greater maneuverability. Additional tests of 18 VB-3s in April were "very satisfactory" and it was determined that one *RAZON*-equipped bomber had the same effect as two bombers dropping conventional bombs. The *RAZON*'s mean error was 150 feet in range and only 16 feet in azimuth which was considerably less than the 580 and 384 foot errors when using standard 1,000 pound bombs dropped at the same time.

In May 1945 the Physical Vulnerability Section of the Joint Targeting Group listed targets considered most appropriate for the *RAZON*. Since

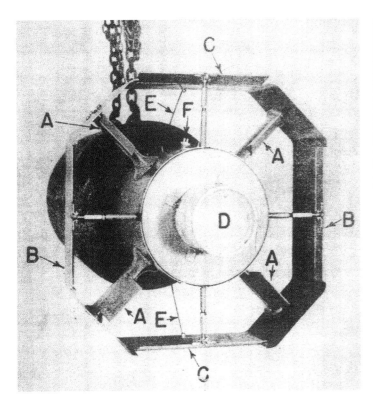

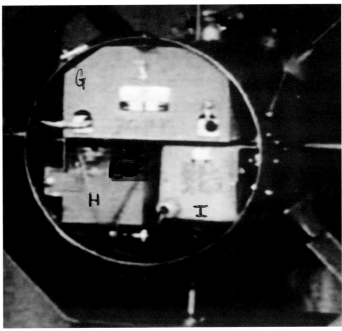

RAZON VB-3 Tail Assembly Legend:

A)	Ailerons	F) Arming Plug
B)	Rudders	G) Radio Receiver
C)	Elevators	H) 24-volt Battery
D)	Flare	I) Gyroscope
E)	Antenna	

only one *RAZON* could be guided per bombing run certain targets were suited to *RAZON* attacks. Generally they were any targets that could be delineated by a square 200 feet on each side:

1) Any *AZON* target (e.g. bridges, causeways, roads, railway lines). Improvement over *AZON* was minimal except for short bridges or overpasses
2) Power plants
3) Steel mills, Coke ovens, blower houses, boiler houses, aluminum industry rectifier buildings.
4) Ships
5) Gun positions

Interestingly, the Joint Targeting Group study pointed out that if a bomber could carry eight 1,000 pound conventional bombs "the accuracy of *RAZON* against a given target must be at least eight times that of standard bombs before there is any advantage on the part of *RAZON* before it can be recommended…the *RAZON* should be used only against those targets on which the percentage of *RAZON* hits is expected to be 15-20 times the percentage of hits with standard bombs."

By early 1945 Union Switch and Signal was unable to reach quantity production because of all the design changes. While these technical design issues were being resolved, the need for and interest in VB-3 guided weapons began to diminish particularly in the ETO as after March 1945 bombing operations against Germany began to decrease. In the Pacific the Tactical Air Forces showed little interest as their operations were quite successful using more conventional weapons. In the CBI both the 10AF in Burma and the 14AF in China were definitely interested but summer monsoon season would be in progress before the VB-3 would be ready for combat testing. The strategic 20AF using B-29s found that the previously unknown jet stream over Japan precluded the use of the VB-3 as it was virtually impossible for the bombardiers to calculate the effects of these winds on the trajectory of the bombs as they fell. Also, the nature of Japanese targets which unlike the large, concentrated European industrial targets were smaller and interspersed throughout built up areas in major cities and were very susceptible to the low altitude incendiary bombs.

Technical testing of the VB-3 continued through May 1945, when the development of the prototype was sufficient to freeze the design for standardization for tooling and production. In tests the VB-3 production model had realized consistent impact errors of 150 feet in range and 16 feet in azimuth from combat altitudes of 22,000 feet which were projected to improve as bombardiers became more experienced. On 10 May 1945 the NDRC recommended that the AAF Board begin tactical evaluations of the VB-3 and, if successful, an initial order of 3,000 was to be made and due in July. At V-J Day, 3,150 VB-3s were completed for shipment to the Pacific for tactical testing.

In autumn 1950, an Air Proving Ground Command technical team worked with the B-29-equipped 19BG in testing 1,000 pound *RAZON* bombs against bridges during the Korean War. Early malfunctions resulted in only 331 of the first 487 *RAZON*s (67%) responding to control commands. However, the last 150 *RAZON* bombs dropped had 97% reliability and 15 bridges were destroyed with four bombs required to destroy an "average" bridge.

Advanced *RAZON* Bombs

The VB-5 through VB-8 VB-series were true *RAZON* vertical bombs while the VB-9 through VB-12 were medium-angle ROC system bombs. Of these, only the Infra Red-seeking VB-6 reached the prototype stage before the war ended.

VB-5

The VB-5 was essentially a VB-3 equipped with a light-seeking homing device which was small was enough to be installed in the nose of a VB-5 and could direct the bomb to a flare previously dropped on the intended target by a pathfinding aircraft. The VB-5 used the same simple, rugged, easily-produced light-contrast seeker that was used on the GB-5 glide bomb. Like the GB-5, the VB-5 was ineffective against strategic targets but under specific circumstances it could have been used against dams, large bridges, and other targets that were in complete contrast with their background such as maritime targets against the surrounding sea. Since the VB-5 was only marginally effective against industrial targets, it did not interest AAF operational commanders. Difficulties with the light-seeking device and low priorities kept its development in the experimental stage and the VB-5 project was cancelled in June 1944, at the same time as the VB-7 and VB-8 projects.

In October 1944 the VB-5 project was briefly re-evaluated when the possibility of using light-seeking VB-5s to track and follow the flare of radio-controlled VB-1s or VB-3s was considered. This would allow a bomber to drop one radio-controlled VB-1 or VB-3 bomb which would be followed by a string of 1,000 pound, self-guiding VB-5s. However, this technique was impracticable at the time due to the ballistics of falling bombs. If the VB-5 was to track the flare of the radio-controlled bomb released earlier its light-seeker would have had to look down and aft which was beyond contemporary technology and the project was shelved.

VB-6 *"Felix"*

The idea of fitting a bomb with an automatic homing device which could distinguish the target from its background was contemplated and experimented with during the war principally with glide bombs and torpedoes. Soon after the establishment of the NDRC in late June 1940, Dr. Alan Bemis of MIT was appointed chairman of NDRC Section D-4 to investigate target detecting devices. In December 1940 there was discussion of fitting a homing device in the high angle bomb. John Strong at the California Institute of Technology and later Harvard, had studied target discrimination and guided Bemis and his colleagues in the basic precepts of high angle bomb homing guidance that had been established for the *Felix* high angle bomb. Because *Felix* relied on infrared to detect and home on targets at night, it was this cat-like ability to see in the dark which gave the weapon its name, after the popular *Felix the Cat* cartoon character.

The *Felix* consisted of a standard 1,000 pound AN-M65 bomb with a metallic bolometer (an instrument for detecting and measuring radiation such as visible light, and infrared and ultraviolet radiation) heat-seeker

"Felix" VB-6 Heat Seeking Bomb (AAF)

located in the nose compartment and a gyro stabilization control servo mechanism operating the control surfaces in both range and azimuth located in the tail compartment.

Nose Assembly Component: Manufacturer
Commutator and Speed Regulator: Harvey Radio Laboratory.
Six Volt Battery: Willard Storage Battery
Bolometer and Tubes: Cambridge Thermionic and Eppley Laboratories
Mirrors: Polaroid
Scanning Motors: Electric Motor Corp.

Tail Assembly Component: Manufacturer
Servo Motors: White-Rodgers
Gyroscopes: Schwein Engineering
24-volt Batteries: Willard Storage Battery
Kickoff Switches and Plugs: Union Switch and Signal

Of the two types of tails developed for the VB-6 the cruciform was preferred although tests seemed to indicate the octagonal shroud could be controlled most successfully. The accuracy of aim and the short interval of fall compensated for the missile's lack of maneuverability due to its small aerodynamic surfaces. *Felix* had an estimated range of 10,000 to 15,000 feet with a minimum extent of control of 2,000 feet in a 15,000 foot drop.

By May 1943 *Felix* showed promise and the NDRC decided to issue contracts to develop and build 240 preproduction bomb bodies by mid-May 1944 with 40 to be experimental models to be used in field tests in mid-May 1944. The NDRC awarded prime contracts to the Remington Rand Company of Bridgeport, CT for 100 complete shroud units; to the Norton Company of Worchester, MA for 100 cruciform tail units; to the Fairchild Camera and Instrument Company of New York for 140 more assemblies of which 100 would be used in Norton's tail assemblies, and 40 with tail assemblies made by Gulf Research; and to General Instrument of Elizabeth, NJ for 100 amplifiers for use only with the Remington units. Fairchild and Remington were responsible for final assembly of the units manufactured by them. Gulf Research which had previous experience in developing the *RAZON* bomb and Heat Research Laboratory of MIT were to serve as advisors during manufacture and set up testing.

In January 1944, the six completed VB-6s were sent to Eglin Field for flight tests. The six were test dropped from 15,000 feet using a large fire as the target. One bomb homed satisfactorily, three did not engage the intended target, and two went out of control in a spin. However, filmed records showed the results to be not as dismal as first indicated. One bomb guided perfectly in range and landed only 60 feet to the right of the target. The three bombs which did not home on the intended targets only homed on other targets because at launching the human controller allowed other targets to come into the eye of the seeker which was unable to distinguish the specific desired target. The two spin failures were easily correctable as they were due to a gyro malfunction that caused the bombs to oscillate and spin. The B-23 control bomber was limited in space and during the bombing run a crew member inadvertently stepped on the rubber tubing connecting the bomber's air supply to *Felix's* gyros causing them not to spin. Soon after these tests the Brig.Gen. H.M. McClelland, Air Communications Officer (ACO), granted the NDRC funding and personnel for 240 VB-6 prototypes for continued testing.

At this time Allied intelligence had discovered the German V-1 "Buzz Bomb" fixed launching ramps in northern France. McClelland felt *Felix* would be well-suited to attack these sites and ordered a crash procurement program to be completed in early May. Contracts were let to Fairchild Camera and Instrument for bomb head manufacture, General Instrument

for electrical component manufacture, and Remington-Rand and Norton for tail production.

Because the oscillation problem was causing some concern, Gulf was still undecided about the relative merits of the cruciform VB-1 *AZON* tail vs. the VB-3 octagonal tail for the *RAZON* bomb. In a series of tests at Tonopah, NV, in October 1944 using 40 of the first *Felix* prototype bombs fitted both tail types, cruciform and octagonal, results showed that the *Felix* bombs with the cruciform-type tail dropped from between 10,000 and 25,000 feet went into a severe spin and were less controllable. As a result the 100 cruciform tails ordered from Norton were cancelled while Remington-Rand's 100 octagonal units continued to be scheduled for combat use. The external design was quickly completed by Gulf and was somewhat larger than the test models in order to accommodate the 1,000 pound GP bomb between the head and tail.

The homing devices continued to encounter successive problems which delayed the *Felix* project. Originally, MIT had individually built the seekers used in testing but their facility was limited in capacity and standardization was necessary. General Electric Company Laboratories, under Saul Dushman and A.J. Kling, undertook the study of the seeker problem and designed a photo electric seeker vacuum tube which was reliable and suitable for mass production. However, tests at Tonopah were unsatisfactory principally due to lack of manufacturing quality control on *Felix* components which was the natural outcome of any accelerated, high priority developmental program.

The original Eglin tests were exhaustively re-examined and found to be wanting. To prevent large bomb oscillations it was deemed necessary to introduce some time lag method which unfortunately meant further extensive development. The *Felix* scientists realized that the accelerated developmental program should be slowed down and the project should be returned to the laboratory for a systematic study of the problems and their resolution before placement in the production model. By late 1944, development of a seemingly reliable redesigned weapon had progressed once more to the pre-production testing stage and tests at Tonopah had 12 of 16 test VB-6s fall within 200 feet of the target.

By the end of October, the VB-6 design had been standardized so that aircraft installation testing was begun to determine how many could be carried and what modifications to each bomber would be required. These tests determined the B-24 could carry a maximum of four VB-6s and four standard 1,000 pound bombs, the B-29 eight but no standard bombs, the B-17 two and two 1,000 pound bombs, the B-25 one and one 1,000 pound bomb, and the A-26 none. Finally, tactical testing was ordered by

The **Bemis Infra Red Heat-Seeking Bolometer** head manufactured by Cambridge Thermionic and Eppley Laboratories was installed in the VB-6 nose. (AAF)

the Army at Eglin Field and Remington-Rand was contracted to produce 1,000 units

Meanwhile, MIT and Wright Field studied target suitability for assorted *Felix* seekers and the Navy BuOrd also conducted an elaborate study of the sensitivity of various seeking devices towards land and marine targets. Additional target analysis was also carried out in October 1944 using the improved Bemis Infra Red seeker. These tests demonstrated this IR could be best used at night against landlocked, heat-emitting targets, such as steel mills and factories; as at night the heat of the sun would not be radiating off the surrounding land and adjacent buildings that would interfere with target acquisition. Targets located in coastal areas, particularly navy vessels and docks, could be attacked during daytime because the cooler surrounding water usually caused these targets to be obvious.

The NDRC anticipated getting the first 125 prototype VB-6s into their first production run by early January 1945 at an estimated average per unit cost of $2,500 which would in reality increase to $4,000 per unit due to cost overruns and delays before the first production run. In order to keep the VB-6 Project viable the NDRC requested that an additional $200,000 be provided to pay for the design costs. To begin production the AAF had to complete VB-6 tactical testing and obtain approval. The NDRC recommended that the VB-6 to be sent to Eglin Field for tactical evaluation as soon as possible and that an initial production run of at least 1,000 units be started. This recommendation had to be completed by 15 December to avoid a five or six month delay and to prevent Fairchild, Offner, Remington, and other subcontractors from moving on to other projects and releasing trained workers.

It was not until the last week of December 1944, that the AAF Tactical Center at Eglin received 27 upgraded VB-6 prototypes for tactical evaluation testing. Each of their components was thoroughly checked by NDRC engineers and AAF technicians before testing. From 27 December to 13 January the 23 sand-filled dummy bombs were dropped from a B-17 at 20,000 feet and four more from 15,000 feet along with standard 1,000 or 100 pound bombs dropped in trail (to prevent it from getting in front of the *Felix* and becoming a target) to act as spotters for each *Felix*. But after testing only nine of the 27 bombs were considered to have passed the testing standards. The failures were attributed to seeker head guidance problems, flare non-lighting problems, battery charge problems, and excessive Florida humidity.

The VB-6 batteries had to power the seeker-head, the stabilizing gyroscopes, and the servomotor flight-control apparatus. Battery charge had been a problem with the two batteries in the VB-1 tests and now it occurred with some of the 10 in the VB-6 which held only a low charge or were completely dead. The low batteries caused the Bemis seeker-head to malfunction, caused poor aileron and rudder responses to seeker-head inputs, and underpowered stabilizing gyros. The automatic-guidance system in the VB-6 was unable to recognize and compensate for weak control inputs from the drained batteries.

The transfer of testing from arid Tonopah to semi-tropical Eglin led to target identification problems due to dampness. Due to the high Florida humidity, the thermal guidance varied so much at a range of altitudes and on different days that it was almost impossible for the testers to determine whether the VB-6 homed on the intended target. At Eglin because, unlike Tonopah, where a target was set out in the middle of the desert, the intended Eglin target was surrounded by vegetation which tempted the homing eye of the seeker to stray from its target. But actually, the movement of testing to Florida was beneficial in that these moisture problems were discovered then rather than in operational use in the damp Pacific.

The erratic original handmade VB-6 tail assemblies were replaced by the more precise apparatus before the next trials in February 1945. During

these tests a small island in the Florida Keys was selected as it was isolated and provided good contrast in the surrounding water. Although the results were marginally better it was not until after six were tested in March and 18 more in April that AAFSAT determined that the main cause of VB-6 acquisition and guidance failures was not due to the bomb but rather to the poorly conceived heat radiating target which could bewilder the VB-6 seeker as to which source of energy was the actual target. By April 1945 the VB-6s that were totally machine-made produced good enough results that both the NDRC and the AAF Board declared the VB-6 as ready for acceptance trials, with the NDRC recommending that the VB-6 be slowly introduced into combat. The first VB-6 shipments were ready from Remington in May and by June a schedule for the first 1,000 units was set up: 875 to the AAF for storage at the 829th Specialized Depot, Gadsden, AL; 100 to the Navy; 15 to the AAF Board; and 10 for training.

On 9 August 1945, the day of the Nagasaki A-Bomb mission, the 20AF requested that 300 VB-6s of the 1,000 on order be shipped to Guam for experimental combat testing. By late August the VB-6 contract was 95% completed but the war ended with the VB-6 still officially considered an experimental prototype but the teething problems encountered by the VB-6 project had been eliminated and the project became the only one of its type to reach the status of a combat requisition. At the end of October 1945 the Engineering Division requested that the 739 completed VB-6 units that were stored and 82 spare tail units be "held for experimental purposes." The NDRC assigned any records, test results, and equipment to the Special Weapons Units for further research. Post-war interest soon waned as the military became preoccupied with the atomic bomb tests at Bikini and other potentially more destructive projects than the placing of a mere 1,000 pound bomb on target.

There was, however, one last flurry of testing on the VB-6 In October 1945 the Equipment Branch of the Air Technical Service Command assumed control of the incomplete VB-6 service tests at Eglin. ATSC personnel again descended upon the test facilities at Eglin to help assemble the remaining VB-6 units but there are no records of any testing. The engineering characteristics and specifications of the equipment were (only) reviewed in 1948 by the recently independent USAAF which was seeking more effective methods to guide air-to-surface missiles carried by strategic bombers .

VB-7 and VB-8
The VB-7 with a 1,000 pound warhead and VB-8 with a 2,000 pound warhead were early TV seekers with wind stream-operated vanes or "ears" to aim the TV camera into the direction the bomb was aimed. The project experienced major technical problems in the experimental stage and was discontinued by the NDRC on 1 June 1944. The main problem was that, unlike glide bombs, these vertical bombs dove very steeply on the target at near transonic speeds which greatly reduced the time the bombardier had to make the necessary course corrections. The orthicon television transmitter and camera system provided a poor quality image that made it difficult for the bombardier to distinguish the fast-moving target against its background, especially when transmitted at the steep closing angle

VB-9
The VB-9 was a radar-directed, specialized 1,100 pound Armor Piercing bomb fitted with four symmetrical wings and a tail with four fins spaced midway between the wings in a cruciform array. This low priority project was cancelled after the radar seeker was found to be unusable in experimental testing. The VB-9 was a medium angle bomb of 30° to 60° glide angle from horizontal but even a minimal 30° angle was considered too great for the radar to acquire the target. The radar energy from this active homing (SRB) type system could not discern the target from the

The body of the **original *ROC*** was similar to that of the VB-9 having four large wings were set in a cruciform pattern with the four smaller tail fins also forming a cross and set to bisect the angle formed by the two wings in that quadrant. (AAF)

surrounding ground clutter, making it impossible to discriminate the target against the background interference called "noise."

VB-10 "*ROC*"

The VB-10s were purportedly named "*ROC*" after the large mythical bird which destroyed Sinbad's ship in the <u>Arabian Nights</u> by dropping boulders on it. An initial paltry $30,000 was granted to begin the project which was would eventually consume $2.5 million from late 1941 and on through the next four years. During the preliminary design stage five different means of guidance were considered: direct sighting, radar, heat-seeking, light-seeking, and television (MIMO). MIT's Radiation Laboratory had developed the AGL radar beam following system was to be modified for use on these missiles under the direction of L.N. Ridenour and David Griggs. NDRC commissioned Douglas Aircraft, Los Angeles, CA for the research and development of the airframe under the direction of Frank Collbohm and was thus was initially designated as the *Los Angeles Project* and then the *Douglas Project*. W.B. Klemperer of the Douglas Santa Monica Engineering Laboratory designed and developed the airframe which was designated as the *X-ROC*.

The *X-ROC* possessed two unique features; it could turn without banking and it flew at a zero angle of attack (e.g. the missile always pointed at the target). The body of the *ROC* was similar to that of the VB-9 having four large wings that were set in a cruciform pattern with the four smaller tail fins also forming a cross and set to bisect the angle formed by the two wings in that quadrant. The need for a 45° glide angle and the requirement that lift be generated in any direction normal to the bomb axis without the need to bank was achieved in wind tunnel tests using this cruciform arrangement. Flight and roll control was accomplished by gyroscopically regulated wing flaps (ailerons) activated by individual servo motors.

The originally proposed radar beam following system was soon substituted with a radar-homing system to give the mother aircraft more freedom of action. When the first flight test drops were scheduled the radar equipment was in short supply and was not be used to be expended in tests. A photo-electric homing device was to be used but this original photo cell was found wanting and a new photo cell had to be developed by the Farnsworth Company for use in the first nine *X-ROCs*.

The nine *X-ROCs* were tested in June 1943, with four homing satisfactorily and five malfunctioning. Farnsworth could not spare time

from their television research to build additional cells for the *X-ROC* project and the Fairchild Camera and Instrument Company was contracted to build six cells to be used in further testing. For more extensive testing to accommodate the photo electric eyes (and later radar homing devices and radio-controls) the Pacific Division of Bendix Aviation was contracted to develop an intermediate amplifier and decoder to translate information from the target-seeking eye into commands to the control surfaces.

ROC X-1000

In December 1943, Douglas Aircraft was charged with the redesign of the *X-ROC* to carry a 1,000 pound GP bomb or 1,100 pound SAP bomb and a Zenith RHS radar receiver. The missile, codenamed *X-1000*, was to fly with a zero angle of attack suitable for control either in line of sight or by the installation of television equipment, or by a suitable homing device. Bendix Aviation, North Hollywood, CA was given a contract to develop the radio control equipment. Polaroid, Cambridge, MA, was to develop and build a heat scanner for of the *ROC* heat seeker. The Radio Corporation of America, Princeton, NJ, was to develop the MIMO television equipment. MIT worked on the task of modifying the Zenith RHS which had been developed for glide bombs using a lower angle of approach than the *X-1000*'s 45° angle. In April 1944 the Navy decided it would terminate its interest in the *ROC* project unless its carrier-based aircraft could carry it. The 11.42 foot long X-1000 had wings measuring 6.83 feet which could be carried only by large bombers .

ROC 00

Under the direction of Project Engineer Kingdon Kerr and Douglas Research Director W.B. Klemperer a unique new ROC model, the *ROC 00-1000*, called the "00" was developed.

Description of the VB-10: *00-1000*:
The *00* had the cruciform wings and tail of the original *ROC* replaced by a set of two ingenious circular lifting shrouds that had the advantage of a smaller cross-sectional width. The two shrouds gave this new model its nickname, "The Double Cookie Cutter." The smaller, perforated, fixed tail shroud had no control surfaces and was used to decelerate the *ROC* to make guidance easier for the remote control operator. The larger mid-fuselage mounted shroud was movable being mounted on a universal joint to create lift in any direction. Aerodynamic deflection in range and azimuth was controlled by two electrically-operated actuators whose servo motors were energized by remotely controlled radio-link equipment. One actuator in the fuselage moved the shroud in yaw (azimuth) while the other located in the shroud itself moved the shroud in pitch (range). The power to drive the actuators was obtained from an electronically-controlled amplifier developed by Bendix. This amplifier received its signals from the radio-link receiver mounted in the tail shroud. The *00* was roll stabilized by gyros which controlled the four ailerons in the empennage. At maximum aileron movement a 7,500 foot turning radius could be achieved. Like the *X-ROC* this "00" configuration also flew at a zero angle of attack and did not have to bank to turn. Since the shroud was mounted on gimbals, the *00* was steered by tilting the shroud in two orientations at right angles to each other, corresponding to azimuth and elevation. The design permitted symmetrical and interchangeable function of azimuth and range control allowing a minimum of time delay in response.

The fuselage and wings were both of hollow cast magnesium and the structure was designed to contain either a 12 inch 1,100 pound, or a 14 inch 1,600 pound Armor Piercing bomb. The forward compartment contained the homing device and the aft for the power supply. Servo motors actuated by the homing device were mounted in the wings and moved the controlling surfaces. The tail had no elevators or rudders but flaps attached to the fins acted as a brake to keep the maximum velocity to 800 feet per second.

Weight:	1,593 pounds
Payload:	1,000 pounds
Wing (shroud) areas	8.9 feet
Length	12.3 feet
Fuselage diameter	1.5 feet
Control shroud diameter	2.5 feet
Braking shroud diameter	4.0 Feet

The *ROC* was a hybrid between the large glide bomb structure and the much smaller vertical bomb tail assembly. While it was smaller than a glide bomb, only the B-29 could actually carry the weapon internally and when employed by any other AAF bomber the *ROC* displayed all of the negative qualities externally mounted weapons; aerodynamic drag, small numbers carried per bomber per sortie, and the exposure of the weapon to the weather while on the way to the target.

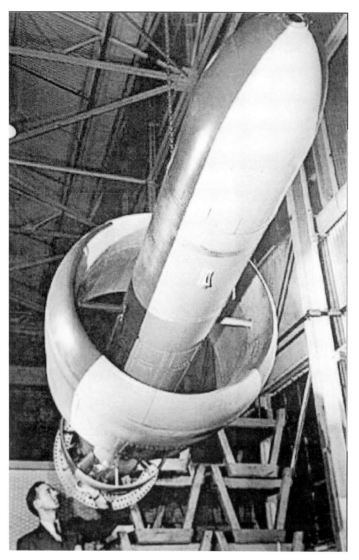

The **ROC 00** had the cruciform wings and tail of the original *ROC* replaced by a set of ingenious circular lifting shrouds. The payload of the *00* was 1,100 pound or a 1,600 pound Armor Piercing bomb. The forward compartment contained the homing device and the aft for the power supply. (AAF)

Unlike the other Vertical Bombs of the VB series the *ROC* was a medium angle bomb of 30° to 60° glide angle from horizontal. Although bombs equipped with the *ROC* system could approach the target at an angle as shallow as 30°, this was still too steep to effectively use television, except under the most ideal lighting conditions. The problems encountered were the same as those encountered with the VB-7 and VB-8. Efforts to enable the VB-10 to "sail" at shallower angles began to pay off in the summer of 1945, giving the *ROC* television-guidance system a new lease on life and tests on the VB-10 continued throughout the war. The maximum speed to allow maneuvering turns was 400 mph. Also the target could move up to 60 mph making *ROC* suitable as an anti-shipping weapon.

The initial lot of 20 *00*-models was built by Douglas on small scale production with the final three being expended by 25 April 1945. A second lot of 100 *00*-models was contracted of which the first 35 were completed by June. The cost break downs for the *ROC 00-1000* were $20,000 each for the first batch of 20 while the next 100 were to cost $13,000 ($7,500 for the airframe, $5,000 for the TV guidance, and $500 for the radio equipment) with an estimated cost of $8,000 per unit projected for the mass produced version.

Soon after the *00-1000* airframe was available for testing MIT determined during its modification of the Zenith RHS radar that reliable homing signals could not be obtained from the *ROC*'s 45° glide to target angle. Thus, the *ROC* airframe which had been specifically developed to house this "nearly perfected" radar now had to find another target seeking system.

The first consideration was a direct-sighting *RAZON*-type system. Schwein Engineering Company was contracted to adapt the *Crab* bombsight attachments to provide preliminary control by adhering to an established regimen; after which the remote control operator was to follow a pre-calculated plan to "line up" the *ROC* with the target. First, the remote operator sailed the bomb towards the target, followed by a diving maneuver, and then in the last few moments the operator would attempt to continuously superimpose the *ROC* over the target until it was hit. This method was planned for the *RAZON* but was discontinued as the *RAZON* lacked suitable maneuverability. The *ROC*, being carried externally and not in confining bomb bays had much larger control surfaces and therefore greater mobility. Although this method appeared theoretically feasible, in practice the results were mediocre at best as the remote control operator was unable to cope with the complicated new sighting mechanism and the maneuverable *ROC*.

The Far Infra-Red Receiver (FIR) was developed by Dr. Marcel Golay of the Signal Corps Engineering Laboratory but its sensitivity was limited and Golay continued with its development. The next guidance system proposed for *ROC* was the installation of a television camera in the nose and then controlling the missile from a mother aircraft or a ground station. For the *ROC* TV installation Section 5.3 of the NDRC coordinated TV research and development under director, O.E. Buckley of Bell Telephone Laboratories. Previously RCA (and to a lesser extent Hazeltine, Farnsworth, and Remington-Rand) had received numerous contracts calling for the improvement of the picture and reduction of equipment size. By late 1943 TV systems were available from three manufacturers, each having individual advantages and disadvantages. The Columbia Broadcasting System's Engineering Research Laboratory was requested to conduct comparative tests of the three units. The BLOCK 3 TV unit with a Hammond radio-control was tried first as this unit was at the time being installed in the GB-4 series. When placed in the *ROC 00-1000*, the nose of the missile needed to be extended making the system unsuitable for the proposed internal stowage in a B-29 and the increased length also affected *ROC* inflight stability. The RCA image orthicon was then selected and the company was contracted to further develop the unit and have test models ready by the end of 1944 with full production ready at the end of 1945. The unit designated MIMO (Miniature IMage Orthicon) weighed only 59 pounds and used electro-magnetic deflection and focusing. The TV receiver in the mother aircraft had 350 lines and flashed 40 frames per second.

To control *ROC* the simple radio link used in the *AZON/RAZON* series was proposed. Tests demonstrated that while the ON/OFF control was satisfactory, the *ROC* with its larger, more responsive, control surfaces required a proportional control system in which the setting of the missile's control surfaces was to correspond to the position of the remote operator's control stick. Bendix Aviation undertook the modification of existing standardized units and Proportional Modulation (PM) was developed. It was not until March 1945, that the first MIMO-equipped *ROC*s were ready for testing. Scientists felt that now that control and a good TV picture had arrived that flying the *ROC* would be much the same as flying an airplane. Tests proved this not to be the case as many remote operators reported that they missed the "seat-of-the-pants" feeling associated with flying an aircraft. The initial results were unsatisfactory with the smallest miss being 70 feet. Due to the need for further training and the expense and shortage of *ROC* models, Columbia University and Douglas Aircraft began to develop simulators to train operators, but these simulators would not be ready until the early autumn of 1945.

Since the television/*ROC* phase was progressing so slowly in late 1944, concurrent tests were made using the direct-sight/radio-link method with 20 direct sight tests conducted with "encouraging" results. MIMO testing continued into the summer of 1945 without simulator training and the next six MIMO tests were regarded as "promising failures" and extensive tests were scheduled by the AAF at Wendover. By early summer 1945 the VB-10 which had been developed under 2A priority, had achieved results in tests extending from 21 September 1944 to 24 May 1945 that did not justify its cost and complicated system and further development and on 30 November 1945 Douglas closed out the *ROC* project. The unused *ROC* and equipment was divided into laboratory equipment to be transferred to Wright Field and field test equipment to Wendover Field.

In late 1944 there were continual tests to resolve 00 problems, particularly in the various seeking systems. The television phase was progressing slowly and concurrent tests were made using the direct-sight/radio-link while MIMO continued into the summer 1945. The photo shows a B-17 conducting load tests with a *ROC* mounted on the fuselage centerline aft of the chin turret and another under the starboard wing between the inboard engine nacelle and fuselage. (AAF)

VB-11 *"Dove"*

In April 1944, a USN version of AAF's VB-6 *Felix* was approved and named *Dove*. The project was assigned to the Bureau of Ordnance and Polaroid which was to employ the VB-10 *ROC* advanced IR heat-seeking unit. This homing device and all controls were located in a special nose attached to a standard bomb and consisted of an optical system, a IR heat detector, a scanning system, and an amplifier. The Polaroid scanner-detector responded to the angular velocity of the optical axis relative to the direction of the heat target area. Steering was by yawing the bomb by the action of seeker directed lift-spoilers protruding from the nose. The nose was roll-stabilized by an internal reaction against the remainder of the bomb

The *Dove* was basically a standard 1,000 pound AN-M65 GP bomb which was fitted with a simple heat-seeking device in the nose and control fins in the tail. The *Dove* was 8.25 feet long, 1.7 feet in diameter. and weighed 1,350 pounds. The *Dove* was to be able to be dropped from unusually high altitudes of up to 30,000 feet because the seeker could correct aiming errors of up to 1,500 feet. The bomb was to be used against targets with a clear IR signature, such as ships in the open sea or isolated industrial plants. Development was transferred from Polaroid to Eastman Kodak in July 1946 and the *Dove* was subsequently designated as Air-to-Surface Missile ASM-4 in September 1947 and finally as the ASM-N-4 in early 1948. Due to the slow development of the *Dove's* IR guidance system, it was not until a year later that a contract for 20 XASM-N-4 prototypes was let. "Moderately satisfactory" testing of the XASM-N-4 prototypes by the Bureau of Ordnance was completed in October 1952 but no production orders were placed.

VB-12 and 13 *"TARZON"*

The last of the VB series, VB-12 and 13, was designated *"TARZON"* is discussed as a Very Heavy Conventional Bomb.

War-weary drones
Aphrodite

In its search for a powered bomb the AAF considered using unmanned, remote controlled training aircraft as a relatively inexpensive delivery vehicle but these aircraft had a limited range and were too small to carry an effective bomb load. In January 1944, the Development Engineering Branch recommended the modification of the obsolete twin engine Douglas B-18 bomber, its B-23 variant, and Douglas C-47 transports into powered bombs. These aircraft not only could carry a heavy bomb load under remote control but could accommodate the extra radio and ordnance specialists who would be necessary to arm the bombs and check that the radio-control equipment was working properly before bailing out and relinquishing control to operators in the controlling aircraft. However, the B-18 and B-23 were no longer being manufactured by Douglas and their limited numbers could jeopardize the continuation of the program if it were successful. The C-47 transport was still in production and in 1944 was the workhorse transport in every combat theater and was in short supply so the AAF was reluctant to expend them as bombs.

In March 1944 a Development Engineering Branch study determined that battle damaged B-17s or B-24s, so-called "war-weary" combat aircraft were an alternative and constant source of large aircraft that could be used as powered bombs. "War-weary' or Category "E" aircraft were damaged BER (Beyond Economical Repair) and were to be salvaged for parts only. However, while emphasis was placed on the fact that the aircraft were worn out; their engines, landing gear, and AFCE had to be in at least very good condition. These war-weary aircraft were soon being dubbed as "*Weary Willies*" and by the summer of 1944, any program involving war-weary aircraft, such as *Aphrodite* or *Castor*, was called a "*Willie*" project. In the

"War Weary" B-17F ("Mugwump") discarded by the 96BG was stripped of armament and modified to the "Double *AZON*" configuration at Fersfield. This Drone was used to attack Heligoland on 30 October 1944. (AAF)

spring of 1944, the largest concentration of war-weary bombers meeting these requirements were battle-damaged B-17s and B-24s parked in 8th Air Force maintenance and repair depots throughout Britain. While these aircraft would serve as the guided powered bombs, new and undamaged bombers were required for conversion into control mother aircraft. On 24 June 1944, the Special Weapons Branch began modifying six B-17Fs and six B-24Hs at an Air Service Command Maintenance Depot at Woodbridge, England. On 1 June, Gen. James Doolittle had informed Gen. Carl Spaatz that he had two B-17s, two B-24s, and two Droopsnoot P-38s available to be converted into control aircraft in time to participate in the upcoming *Castor* program tests at the Proving Ground Command scheduled for later in the month.

Shortly after D-Day, the V-1 "Buzz Bomb," the first of Germany's secret V-weapons struck London. It was apparent to Gen. Eisenhower that for political and military reasons these weapons had to be quickly neutralized and on 18 June Eisenhower met with British Prime Minister Churchill and directed that the V-1 "targets are to take first priority over everything except urgent requirements of the ground battle." Eisenhower's urgent V-1 target directive to his staff would include the 19 June authorization to the AAF Engineering Division at Wright Field to expedite development of all *Castor* aircraft and equipment. This authorization was provided through Technical Instruction No. CTI-1747, which stated that "the project . . . was to have highest priority in order that shipments of the equipment for the control plane to combat theaters would be possible prior to 1 August 1944" CTI-1747 went on to provide preliminary military requirements, which included the following:

1) The range of missile planes, after pilot bail out, was to be 600 miles;

2) The aircraft were to be able to operate at 25,000 feet altitude;

3) The drone aircraft were to have necessary servo mechanism to dive the plane from a 15-45° angle;

4) Each drone aircraft was to be equipped with BLOCK 3 television equipment;

5) The controls to be designed to permit radio-controlled direction of drone aircraft to point targets;

6) The combat load was to be about 20,000 pounds.

By March 1944 an astounding 1,250,000 aerial photos of nearly 100 suspected V-1 sites under construction in northern France and the Low

Countries had been taken. So targeting the V-1 "*Noball*" launch sites was not the problem but destroying them was. With hundreds of Buzz Bombs being launched against England even the most concerted efforts to speed the *Castor* program would take too long to provide operational American powered bombs. If V-1 launching sites were to be neutralized quickly, more immediate action was necessary and *Operation Aphrodite* was born. Had the Germans not started launching their V-1 guided missiles against London on 13 June 1944, the *Aphrodite* program would certainly have taken the normal three to six months to complete technical testing and another month or more for acceptance and tactical trials at the AAFTAC at Eglin.

"*Project A*" or *Aphrodite*, the Air Force's use of war-weary B-l7s was initiated on 23 June, l944 with the following message from Lt.Gen. Carl Spaatz to Gen. H.H. Arnold:

"*Aphrodite* is the code name which this headquarters will use to refer to the overall project of attacking targets 'by special techniques.' Our first flight test with modified *AZON* units in war-weary airplanes demonstrated the practicability of this makeshift and we are going ahead immediately with four more war-wearies."

Unlike *Castor*, which was tested at the Eglin Proving Ground Command test facilities and received technical support from the Air Materiel Command, *Aphrodite* was an improvised program that utilized any available equipment and technical support available to the 8AF in England.

On 20 June 1944, Gen. Spaatz sent a priority report to Gen. Arnold stating that he considered that success was possible against rocket sites "if large enough loads of explosives can be placed with extreme precision, namely within 10 to 20 feet of the aiming point." Spaatz informed Arnold that he had directed that surplus VB-1 *AZON* guidance equipment be used to convert war-weary B-17s into powered bombs. Spaatz further stated that he had directed that the "urgency of this project is paramount and therefore only those equipments and crews which are immediately, repeat, immediately available should be selected." Gen. Doolittle, commander of 8AF, responded on 24 June by directing the Third Bombardment Division to initiate a project to prove the tactical soundness of remotely controlled B-17 "robot aircraft" as weapons, to develop methods for their employment, and test them in actual combat operations. Of course, Arnold, long a proponent of guided weapons, supported Spaatz and the resurgence of *Aphrodite* Program.

As early as 8 May Gen. Doolittle had requested that 12 sets of equipment, including BLOCK 3 television apparatus for the drones; five sets of equipment for the controlling aircraft, and technical support personnel be dispatched to the 8AF as soon as practicable. On 1 June, nearly two weeks before the start of the V-1 attacks; Doolittle had informed Spaatz that he had two B-17s, two B-24s, and two Droopsnoot P-38s available to be converted into *Castor* control aircraft and had designated six B-17G and six B-24J war-wearies to be used as powered bombs. Consequently, when General Spaatz directed Doolittle to expedite the *Aphrodite* program, much of the *Castor* equipment and personnel were already available.

The tests were to be conducted by the Third Bomb Division with the 388th Bomb Group stationed at Khettishall was to staff the operation and to provide base facilities at remote RAF Fersfield an airfield specially selected for security reasons as it was located in a sparsely populated area of Norfolk. Initially RAF Woodbridge had been selected because of its long runway but damaged conventional aircraft returning from combat were diverted to Woodbridge for landings and colliding with a drone loaded with 20,000 pounds of explosive caused some anxiety for planners.

Aphrodite was under the overall command of Maj.Gen. Earle Partridge with Lt.Col. Roy Forrest acting as CO and Maj. Henry James Rand, son of the President of Remington-Rand, heading the developmental team.

Maj. Rand was able to prepare the first *Aphrodite* powered bomb for testing in less than two days and by 1 July both aircrew and technical personnel had started training. Four controller aircrews received 25 hours of training on controlling the drones along with comprehensive training in target study and route navigation. Ten safety pilots and 10 C-1 autopilot technicians received training on setting automatic flight controls in the drones and arming the explosives.

To control the B-17s and B-24s, Rand's team had modified the same control system used to control *AZON* free-falling guided bombs. The *Aphrodite* system used two *AZON* units, one to control azimuth and one to control range. This *RAZON*, range and azimuth system was dubbed "Double *AZON*." The first test of this control system occurred in late June, when Rand in the mother or controlling B-17 climbed to 20,000 feet while the drone circled at 2,000 feet waiting to be taken under control. However, the unpredictable English weather closed in and Rand lost the drone! There were several anxious minutes until Rand's mother B-17 descended to 6,000 feet to make visual contact with the drone and was able to take control. Despite, this initial setback, the succeeding tests were generally successful with Rand controlling the test drones for two hours or more; putting them through various maneuvers. Rand did find that the mother aircraft had a tendency to over run the drone and Rand determined the solution was the use of flaps, prop pitch, Essing maneuvers, etc. by the mothership.

Two major concerns were that the Germans could jam the *AZON* radio frequencies and the possibility of Allied FM radio signals causing interference with control frequencies. Intelligence verified that *AZON* radio frequencies did not fall into the bands normally jammed by the Germans but determined that "great care would have to be exercised to ensure no friendly spurious radio signals interrupted control over the unmanned guided aircraft, especially when loaded with explosives and still over friendly territory."

At first it was decided that the mother and drone should cross the Channel at a high altitude in order to stay out of AA range. But, tests with sand-loaded B-17s demonstrated that the bomber could not be put into a 30,000 foot dive. The faster the bomber fell the more pronounced was its natural inclination to level off. The servo-motors of the Double *AZON* unit were not powerful enough to overcome the anti-dive tendency the Boeing Company prided itself on building into the aircraft design.

Low level trials were tried using an ACE (Automatic Control Equipment) radio altimeter which held the drone at 300 feet while the mother aircraft transmitted left or right steering signals to the automatic pilot. Over the target a radio signal was transmitted to overpower the ACE unit sending the drone diving into the target. To aid in the visual tracking of the drone, its upper wing surfaces were painted white or yellow. To improve the visibility of the drone from the mothership smoke tanks on the wing tips or under the rear fuselage of the drone were also tried. The smoke tank was a modified 75 gallon auxiliary fuel tank used by fighter aircraft equipped with twin nozzled smoke generators attached underneath. The smoke tank was activated by the mothership.

War-weary B-17's, designated as BQ-7s, were withdrawn from combat and stripped of all unnecessary equipment, armament, and armor plate and had the special Double *AZON* equipment installed. The first motherships were to be B-34 (ex-RAF Lockheed Ventura) bombers but were replaced before trials by B-17s designated as CQ-17s but later a B-24 (CQB-5) was also used. In operational sorties another B-17 was used for navigation and observation. Because of the vulnerability of the drone

and mother a fighter escort was required for each drone with one fighter assigned to shoot down any errant drone.

The combat technique evolved for *Aphrodite* was to have a pilot assisted by an autopilot technician, takeoff in the drone. After takeoff the drone would fly a rectangular course so that the autopilot could be tuned after which the autopilot technician would bail out. The pilot would cut the drone's speed to 175 mph and put it into a gentle dive which would eventually take it down to 300 feet where the ACE would take control as it crossed the Channel. As the drone was diving, the pilot set a 10 minute clock on the instrument panel, checked the safety lights on the electrical fusing device and then completed the fusing circuit by plugging in two jacks. The pilot pulled a lanyard to arm the 14 impact fuses leading to the 20,000 pounds of explosives crammed throughout the bomber. After his responsibilities were completed, the pilot strapped on his parachute and dropped through the navigator's hatch. A static line was rigged to the main backpack parachute and a reserve chest pack was also worn. Early trials resulted in the loss of several pilots when they had struck a radio antenna (subsequently relocated) upon bailing out of the drone. At first nitrostarch

Two flanking B-17 motherships take control of the war-weary B-17 drone heading for its target. The drone pilot had gone through his check list and armed 20,000 pounds of explosives crammed throughout the bomber and can be seen in his parachute (lower right) after bailing out. (AAF)

After his responsibilities were completed, the pilot strapped on his parachute and dropped through the navigator's hatch. A static line was rigged to the main backpack parachute and a reserve chest pack was also worn. (AAF)

was used as the explosive but later 50 pound boxes of Torpex were stowed in every available space in the bomber. Half of the drones were scheduled to carry a load of jellied gas but since a cargo of loosely-packed jerry cans filled with jell-gas was not relished by pilots, further development of carrying methods were required. After the pilot bailed out the operator in the mothership at 20,000 feet took over control of the drone. The AAF crew vernacular for the controlling aircraft was "Mother" while the drones were referred to as "Babies."

First Aphrodite Mission
On 27 August 1943, the 8AF attacked a large underground concrete V-weapon facility under construction at Watten, a few miles inland from the Pas de Calais, with 2,000 pound conventional bombs. Most of the bombs missed the target but those that did hit the target did not penetrate the thick reinforced concrete structure. The second 8AF mission against this site on 7 September was just as futile. By March 1944 three more large concrete underground V-weapon sites in northern France were completed or near completion at Mimoyecques, Siracourt, and Wizernes.

The possible use of these four "giant sites" caused great consternation among the AAF high command.

On 8 July 1944, Gen. Spaatz estimated that a total of 65 drones would be required to knock out the V-weapon sites. Forty-four drones were to carry nitrostarch while the remainder was to carry jellied gasoline whose oxygen-consuming fires would suffocate the occupants of the underground sites. Because of a shortage of equipment, only one drone was equipped with BLOCK 3 television while all others would be guided by the radio controlled GB-8 glide bomb method.

The operational plan called for 250 RAF bombers to carry out a diversionary raid north of Paris just before the *Aphrodite* raid which was scheduled for 1500. The four drones were each to have a primary and backup mother aircraft with 16 P-38s were to fly cover for the mothers. There were to be observation and navigational B-17's with escorting fighters for each. Also accompanying the mission were four photo-recon P-38's to take movies and stills, two Mosquitoes to photograph the drone pilots parachuting, and several light liaison aircraft to follow the parachuting pilots. The entire operation was to be covered by two Spitfire squadrons. British AA defenses, which had become trigger happy since the Buzz Bomb siege on England, were alerted. All mother aircraft were instructed to crash any malfunctioning drones into the North Sea and to call in fighters to destroy drones which could not be controlled.

On 4 August, the first Aphrodite mission commenced when four drones tookoff from Fersfield toward northern France to attack the giant sites at Mimoyecques, Siracourt, Watten, and Wizernes. Lt.Gen. Jimmy Doolittle and Maj. Gen. Earl Partridge followed the progress of the mission while flying in P-38s. The first drone, #835, carrying the only BLOCK 3 television equipment available to the *Aphrodite* program, flew its specified rectangular course after takeoff to allow the autopilot technician to check out instrumentation and prepare the autopilot and ACE before bailing out. The pilot, Lt. John Fisher, finished his assignments and sent the code word, "taxi-soldier" for James Rand in the mother aircraft to take control. As Fisher tried to leave the drone, there was a malfunction and it went into a steep climb, stalled, and spun to earth carrying Fisher to his death along with it. The drone crashed into a wooded area near Suffolk, the tremendous explosion being marked by a 25x35 foot crater which was five feet deep; demolishing the trunks of large, grown oaks for 200 feet around.

The second drone, #342 was assigned to attack the giant site near Watten which was protected by its massive ferro-concrete dome. The autopilot technician and the pilot vacated the drone by parachute without incident and it was guided by experienced *AZON* bomb controller, Glen Hargis. After takeoff and upon descending to 300 feet the drone encountered an Allied balloon barrage over the coast which had been forgotten to be removed! Somehow Hargis guided the drone through the maze of cables and chains without mishap using only slowly responding servo-controlled to the left or right maneuvers. The drone continued to respond to Hargis' signals on route to the target but when he toggled the switch to overpower ACE to apply full down elevator there was no response to dive the drone into the target. Despite the loss of surprise and the resulting heavy flak Hargis turned #342 drone around for another run at the target again with the same no response by the elevators to the dive command. The alternate mother was summoned to try a different set of controls but these also did not did trigger the defective elevators. Hargis was instructed to destroy the faulty drone so he flew it over a particularly harassing German flak battery. On the first fly past the drone escaped unscathed and Hargis again flew it directly over the flak battery whose accuracy was much better this time. There was a great ball of fire and explosion and a battered and surprised flak battery!

The third drone, #461, tookoff piloted by 2Lt. Frank Houston and at the co-pilot's control by autopilot was Tech. Willard Smith who parachuted to safety after completing his duties. The mothership with Rand aboard as controller headed toward the Wizernes V-site. The approach to the target was not hindered by the 400 flak guns reported to be protecting the site. However, just at the moment for full down elevator dive on the target; #461 passed into a small cloud causing Rand to lose sight of the target. Nonetheless, he toggled the dive switch by guesstimate but the drone had over flown the target and it exploded about a quarter mile away without causing any damage.

The fourth drone, piloted by 1Lt. Cornelius Engles with Tech./Sgt. Clifford Parsons, took off at 1600 for Mimoyecques and both parachuted from the drone without incident but both were injured during their parachute landings; Engles seriously. Control of the drone was passed to the B-24 mother with Hargis on board and it was guided and lined up perfectly on the target. The drone instead of remaining at 300 feet climbed to 600 feet and Hargis tried to dive the drone back to the pre-set ACE 300 foot altitude. The B-17 descended to 300 feet but would not level out and crashed about 500 yards short of the aiming point in a spectacular but ineffective explosion.

The first *Aphrodite* mission was, at best, inauspicious with three drones missing their V-site targets and one blowing a huge crater into the Suffolk countryside, Lt. Fisher was killed, five parachutists were injured, two hospitalized, and to add insult to injury, Hargis' mothership was nearly shot down by British anti-aircraft gunners. The rendezvous, control handoff, and arming procedures functioned reliably but several changes in the drone crew bailout procedures were needed. The use of two motherships for each drone was a safeguard against losing control over the drone in case of malfunction of the mothership's control equipment. It also provided a second aircraft to visually keep track of the drone, especially if the lead mothership, flying at 20,000 feet, was separated by clouds from the lower-flying drone. The second mother could then descend and monitor the drone until the lead mothership regained visual contact. Conventional bombing missions included many bombers striking one target while an Aphrodite mission had one or two drones strike one target. The *Aphrodite* missions required large amounts of intelligence on each of its targets which further overloaded Allied intelligence resources and it was recommended that future *Aphrodite* missions have only one assigned target.

Second Aphrodite Mission
On 6 August, after 48 hours of round-the-clock adjustments, two drones were readied to attack Watten on the second *Aphrodite* mission. At 1050 the first drone, *Franklin Yellow*, was to takeoff followed 10 minutes later by *Franklin White*. Each was to be controlled by its own mother and alternate mother. The first drone, well over manufacturer's maximum gross weight carrying 18,000 pounds of Torpex, rather than the standard 20,000 pounds of nitrostarch, was to crash into the Watten's dome causing the cement casement to crack and fissure and then *Franklin White* carrying combustibles would follow it to crash the site and would then push burning jelled gasoline and incendiaries through the newly created fissures.

A diversionary raid of 100 RAF bombers was sent over the target to occupy the heavy German AA defenses. Almost immediately *Franklin Yellow* ran into a group of Liberators which were rendezvousing for an unrelated bombing mission. Pilot 1Lt. Joseph Andrecheck, aided by Tech./Sgt. Ray Healy, managed to bank the heavily overloaded B-17, piled high with boxes of Torpex, from the rendezvous area and then miraculously got it back to level flight. Although it wasn't uncommon for B-17's to carry a few pounds over "max gross" that weight was positioned in the bomb

bays therefore at the bottom of the fuselage where this weight acted to stabilize the aircraft much like a sailboat's keel. But the explosives in the drone were piled four to five feet above the center of gravity and a tight turn could throw the aircraft out of control.

During the hectic maneuvering the motherships lost sight of *Franklin Yellow* but after a few anxious minutes it was spotted again with the crew still onboard not wanting to bail out leaving the drone without control. Mother found the Baby circling and once positive control had been established by the mothership the crew bailed out without incident. The drone was successfully controlled over the North Sea as briefed but then abruptly began a sharp turn to its port and rolled over, with neither mother able to correct the course before the drone crashed into the sea

The second drone *Franklin White*, piloted by 2Lt. Frank Houston, carried nine incendiary bombs in the nose, 35 in the pilot's compartment, 116 in the radio operator's compartment, and 20 in the ball turret. All this fireworks was augmented by 830 gallons of inflammable jellied gasoline in the bomb bay tanks. Tests conducted at Eglin Field showed that occupants of the site would suffocate if the exits were blocked by flames. After an uneventful takeoff, rendezvous, but early bailout the drone came under Hargis' control. Hargis found that the drone drifted toward the right because the autopilot had been seemingly incorrectly set, possibly because the pilot and Tech./Sgt. had bailed out prematurely. Hargis passed control to the alternate mother and the drone made a 360° turn, causing Hargis to think the new controller was trying a different heading in an attempt to unlock the autopilot. But the drone then turned again and headed toward London! Hargis tried to contact the alternate mother but received no answer indicating that control had not been passed. Meanwhile, *Franklin White* disappeared into the haze and the escorting fighters were quickly radioed to find and destroy the missing bomber. Finally, the tail gunner in the observer B-24 spotted the drone circling the suburbs of Ipswich and Hargis again tried hard left controlling maneuvers which were only slightly successful but on each circuit the drone moved slightly farther away from Ipswich. A cloud bank moved in from the North Sea and again *Franklin White* disappeared and another frantic search began. Hargis briefly spotted the errant drone over the sea and decided to risk diving the drone to its destruction and fortunately, the tail gunner was able to report a huge flaming explosion in the sea below him.

In a stormy post-mission debriefing Gen. Doolittle angrily returned the group to training status. However a few hours later Third Bomb Division HQ ordered the group to abandon the Double *AZON* system as it was considered too dangerous, especially since it was not designed for this use. Thus the Air Force's drone project was cancelled and the fate of America's first drone program, *Aphrodite* was passed to the Navy's Special Attack Unit #1 (SAU1), under the codename *Anvil* which was a parallel project.

US Navy *Anvil* Drone Project
Doolittle's grounding order for the AAF *Aphrodite* program did not pertain to the USN component attached to *Aphrodite*. On six July 1944, 11 officers and 16 enlisted men had began an expedited drone program at the Naval Aircraft Factory (NAF) in Philadelphia as US Navy Special Attack Unit (SAU-1) under ComAirLant, with Cdr. James Smith as the CO. They were to adapt the results of the Navy's experimental drone program, which had begun seven years previously, using the PB4Y-1, Privateer (the Navy's version of the B-24) as the Assault Drone. Within a week a factory-fresh PB4Y was divested of all non-essentials and a control and arming panel was installed to attack German V-1 and V-2 launching sites.

The PB4Y and a R4D transport (Navy version of the C-47) were ferried to the AAF *Aphrodite* drone base at Fersfield without incident

Aphrodite/Castor

This **drone,** formerly of the 95BG, has undergone *Castor* modification at Fersfield and has had its nose armament removed, the forward crew hatch removed and an anterior wind spoiler installed, a TV antenna installed under the nose, and a smoke tank installed on the centerline under the wings. (AAF)

The drone **smoke tank** was a modified 75 gallon auxiliary fighter fuel tank equipped with a **smoke generator** attached below the smoke tank. The tank was activated from the mothership. (AAF)

Double *AZON* **servo motor linkage** to the throttle of the drone controlled to increase or decrease engine power settings. (AAF)

Ventral receiving antenna on drone. (AAF)

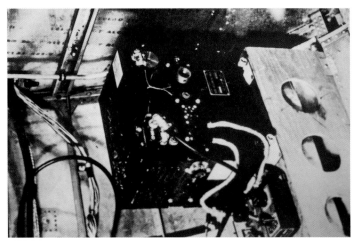

Dorsal receiving antenna on drone. (AAF)

Eureka **AN/TPN-1 airborne radio beacon transponder** installed in drone. (AAF)

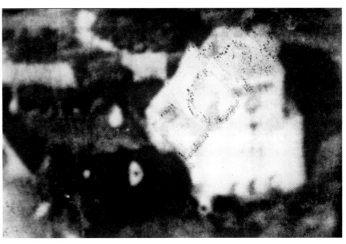

View on mothership's 7 inch TV monitor of drone TV camera transmission of the target. The photo has "SECRET" stamped on it which "ECR" can be seen superimposed on white building. (AAF)

Rebecca **AN/TPN-2 airborne interrogator antenna** installed on the side of the mothership's fuselage to track the *Eureka* AN/TPN-1 airborne radio beacon transmissions. (AAF)

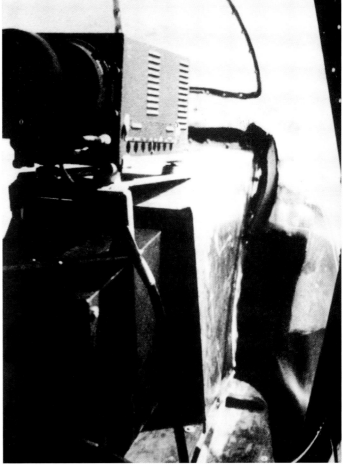

Rebecca **AN/TPN-2 airborne interrogator** was a precursor of Identification Friend or Foe (IFF) designed to keep track of the drone. (AAF)

Drone **BLOCK 1 CRV-59 TV Camera** installed on starboard side of the nose. (AAF)

but the two PV Ventura motherships became stranded by storms in Greenland for three weeks. Meanwhile Cdr. James Smith and AAF base CO Lt.Col. Roy Forrest were trying to resolve Army-Navy differences and jealousies at various levels at the base. The Navy's control system used television control and was much more sophisticated than the AAF Double *AZON* system. A RC-487 television transmitter and a *Eureka* AN/TPN-1 airborne radio beacon were installed in the drone. A *Rebecca* AN/TPN-2 airborne interrogator was installed on the motherships to track the *Eureka* transmissions. In addition to being controllable on the vertical and horizontal axes like the Double *AZON*; *Anvil* controlled an increase or decrease in engine power settings. The *Anvil* drones could automatically assume straight and level flight when control contact was interrupted or on the controller's command. They could transmit a radio beacon signal, code-named *Rebecca*, which provided controllers a relative bearing to the drone from the mother. The control equipment was able to direct 10 drone functions including steering, diving and climbing, varying speed, and activating the ACE from the PB4Y. The controller not only had a televised image from the nose of the drone but also a second televised image was provided of the compass in the drone which allowed the controller to quickly determine the exact heading of the drone which was essential during final guidance to the target. The drones also could trail colored smoke on command to help the controller in visually acquiring them in hazy conditions.

The arming of the explosives would be done remotely from the mothership after the crew bailed out. A FM radio signal would cause a solenoid to release the safety pins from the inertial switches to arm the system. The chance of a stray FM signal activating the system was a possibility though a remote one. In tests at the NAF back in Philadelphia, this remote possibility had occurred and since a safety pin had been installed which was to be removed by the pilot prior to bailing out. Also, in another check against accidental arming, frequency searching recon aircraft flew over both English and Nazi-occupied territory in search of FM signals on the drone's intended FM channel but none were found. Also, unlike the Air Force drones, the Navy pilots flew their drones fully loaded in test flights, enabling the pilots to become accustomed to the heavy flying characteristics of the loaded drone. The explosive loading of the *Anvil* drone was the same 20,000 pounds of Torpex loaded but into 335 boxes: 210 in the bomb bay, 100 in the radio room, and 25 next to the pilot in the co-pilot's seat position.

First Navy *Anvil* Mission
The first Navy mission was scheduled for 11 August, but was scrubbed due to bad weather and reset for the next day. The PB4Y drone (#32271) dubbed *"Zootsuit Black"* was loaded with Torpex while technicians checked the two PV-1 Ventura motherships: *"Zootsuit Pink"* and *"Zootsuit Red."* The mission was to include a B-17 radio relay ship, four P-51 Mustangs to fly cover, two P-38s, and two Mosquito weather and observer aircraft along with several liaison planes to spot parachutists jumping from *Zootsuit Black*. An AAF B-17 navigation ship would lead the drone to the rendezvous point where it would be acquired by lead mother.

The mission plan was uncomplicated with the PV-1s scheduled to takeoff after learning that the weather over the target was clear. Upon reaching the rendezvous point at 2,000 feet, the mothers were to clear the drone for takeoff from Fersfield. *Zootsuit Black,* piloted by Joseph Kennedy, the future president's older brother, and crewed by Lt. Bud Willy, the executive technical officer, was to fly a check out course under the control of Lt. John Anderson in Lt. Hugh Lyons mothership *Zootsuit Red*. The drone crew was to bail out and drone control was then given to Lt. Harry Wherry's mother, *Zootsuit Pink,* whose controller Lt. John Demlein was to guide the drone over the Channel to an area six miles from

the French Coast. In order to avoid anti-aircraft fire Wherry was to return control to Lyons/Anderson flying 10 miles behind. Controller Anderson was then to guide the drone into the Mimoyecques site via TV control.

Due to morning fog and haze over the target the mission was postponed until early evening. The takeoff and initial control went well but as Anderson was to turn control over to Demlein in preparation for the bailout leg of the mission, a huge double explosion disintegrated the drone, Kennedy, Willy, and seven years of Navy experimentation. The final irony in the mission's failure was when Allied troops overran these four hard V-sites soon afterward; making their destruction by the *Anvil* drones unnecessary.

A comprehensive post-mission investigation suggested 13 possible causes for the explosion, and some, such as the possibility of friendly fire from British AA batteries or friction caused by the shifting of the explosive load, were quickly and easily discounted while others, such as the possibility of an onboard fire or static electricity, required more time to eliminate as a cause. Finally, three possibilities were culled out: radio jamming or interference, a possible short circuit in the arming panel, and the inherent instability of the Torpex explosive which was the next discounted cause. The investigation concluded that the most likely cause was the overheating of the arming circuit holding relay which was designed to prevent the accidental tripping of the detonators. The holding relays had been hastily developed by the NAF and designed to be activated as the mother transmitted the arming signal to the drone. In this way, the relays would permit the electronic detonators to arm but protected them from being accidentally fired by spurious FM radio signals. Once the holding relays were activated, only the physical G-forces caused by impact with the target or the ground would cause the detonators to fire and explode the 20,000 pound of Torpex.

Second *Anvil* Mission
After the breakout from the Normandy beachhead beginning on 25 July; by September ground forces had overrun V-weapon *Noball* launching sites in northern France and the four hard sites previously targeted by *Aphrodite*. With these targets no longer available the *Anvil* team felt they could prove their worth in future missions against dams, canals, locks, viaducts, marshaling yards, and submarine pens. The next attack was scheduled in early September against the U-Boat pens cut into the cliffs of Heligoland, some 300 miles away across the North Sea.

The *Anvil* mission of 3 September was aimed at the U-Boat pens cut into the cliffs of **Heligoland** 300 miles away across the North Sea. The mission's TV system went dead and the drone was dumped and exploded on a coal pile. (AAF)

Another Navy PB4Y arrived, not factory-new, like the first, but war-weary and refurbishing began immediately. The first order of business was to replace the disastrous defective electronic arming panel which was to be replaced by the manual lanyard system used in the Air Force's early *Aphrodite* B-l7s and consequently the drone pilot's last action before bailing out would be to physically pull a bundle of lanyards to arm the firing mechanism. The drone was also thoroughly checked, engines changed, all control surface cables replaced, new tires installed, and the arming wires encased in aluminum conduit.

The mission was postponed several times due to bad weather but in the morning of 3 September the drone piloted by Lt. Ralph Spalding, flying alone with no technician, made a perfect takeoff. Sixteen P-51 escorts, a photo recon Mosquito, a weather Mosquito, two P-38 photo ships, a P-38 radio signal search aircraft, and three B-17s for observation, radio message relay, and navigation joined the mother which was flying 200 feet over the drone flying at 2,000 feet. There was no diversionary bombing raid. The usual hour of instrument checking had been deleted to eliminate the flying time of the drone over heavily populated eastern England and to minimize the radio signals which could be picked up by Nazi jamming stations. Spalding turned over control to the mother PV piloted by Wherry and controlled by Demlein and bailed out successfully over England. The 300 mile flight across the North Sea to Heligoland encountered a squall which caused the second mothership, piloted by Lyon and crewed by controller Anderson, to lose their VHF radio which was to be used to transfer control of the drone from Demlein to Anderson five miles from the target. Unable to contact Demlein of the situation Anderson blinked an Aldis Lamp message "N-O/V-H-F" at the Wherry/Demlein mother aircraft but the message wasn't understood. As the Heligoland cliffs came into view, Demlein tried to raise Anderson on the VHF to transfer control but was unsuccessful. Demlein instructed pilot Wherry to stay on course as he watched through his TV monitor to see the

The first Navy *Anvil* mission on 11 August 1944 to attack the Mimoyecques V-weapon site via TV control was piloted by **Lt. Joseph Kennedy**. There was a malfunction that caused a huge explosion of the drone's ten tons of explosive and the future president's older brother and son of the influential US Ambassador to England was killed. (USN)

drone fly through flak puffs. The sub pens came into view but the drone was off course to the right and did not respond to Demlein's correction probably due to flak damage. Unfortunately, the TV picture was of poor quality and the controller mistook the breakwater on nearby Dune Island for the breakwater on Heligoland and within seconds the television picture went black, probably due to a hit by anti-aircraft fire. As the TV picture went dead and Demlein toggled the dump control and ordered Wherry to climb away. Simultaneously, Anderson, not knowing Demlein was controlling the drone, also continued to follow the drone's course through his TV monitor controlling it too! As the picture faded from his screen, he also toggled the dump control. Both mothers turned from the target, Wherry/Demlein climbing through flak a few hundred feet above the Heligoland cliffs and Lyon/Anderson fleeing some 20 miles behind. A large mushroom cloud was observed but the outcome of the attack would have to wait for the P-38 Droopsnoot photo recon aircraft to bring back their photos. The next morning SAU1's second *Anvil* mission found it had destroyed a large coal pile, scattering coal dust over the island and had added a 60 foot wide, 12 foot deep crater to the much-attacked island's collection of bomb craters.

The expense of the program and the resulting failures gave the anti-drone contingent in the Navy Department cause to cancel the program. Besides, if the true nature of the death of Joseph Kennedy Jr. was ever revealed, his father, the very influential and irascible Joseph Kennedy Sr. would raise holy hell and heads would roll throughout the Navy Department. To placate "old man Kennedy," a Medal of Honor was requested for Joe Jr's. "heroic" exploit but a Navy Cross for he and Willy were approved instead. A destroyer (DD 850) which later stopped Russian ships during the Cuban missile crisis was also named after Joe Jr. Future President, John Kennedy, was also recommended for the Medal of Honor for his PT-109 exploits but also was awarded the Navy Cross instead.

The New AAF *Castor* drone Contingent
After the Navy left Fersfield five mothership crews of the departed James Rand remained behind along with a new group of technicians from Wright Field. This group used a TV guidance system designated as *Castor* which was almost identical to the Navy's system. Lt.Col. Dale Anderson was the brilliant new technical head of the new *Castor* contingent and was aided by Peter Murray, a civilian electronics genius. These two men added several innovative concepts, using the lessons learned from the previous *Anvil* failures to secure success for *Castor*. The controller was able to see the drone's own compass through the TV monitor to determine its exact bearing. The drones were equipped with all-weather electronic navigation gear to prevent the loss of control. Also a P-47 drop tank was fashioned into a smoke-emitting device with radio-controlled ON/OFF switches to allow the drone to be followed more easily.

Roy Forrest, CO at Fersfield had expected the Air Force program to be cancelled after its failures and especially after the Navy's failures and cancellation. But scuttlebutt had it that *Aphrodite* was Hap Arnold's pet project and no one was going to take his toy away from him! Arnold had approved 500 *Castor* "M" ("Missile") and 100 *Castor* "C" ("Control") B-17s and B-24s and modification kits all to be ready by 1 November 1944. The *Castor* "M" B-17Gs code was BQ7 and the B-24Js was BQ8 while the *Castor* "C" B-17 code was CQB4, the B-24 was CQB5, and the P-38 was CQB6. The *Castor* "C" aircraft, 50 B-17Gs and 50 B-24Js, were to be modified in the US at the Birmingham, AL Modification Center at 200 man-hours for the first several aircraft and then decreasing with subsequent modifications.

The presence of the German battleship *Tirpitz* holed up in Norway's Alten Fjord intrigued Roy Forrest. To placate Arnold a plan was concocted using British hydrostatic bombs packed in a B-17 drone which was to

"Roadster" was a one-of-a-kind B-17 which had the cockpit and upper fuselage removed to have 26,000 pounds of hydrobombs were lowered into the aircraft to attack on the German Battleship *Tirpitz*. The aircraft was never used as the British refused permission for it to takeoff with huge and lethal load which could endanger surrounding English countryside. (USN)

crash land next to the battleship. The *Hydrobomb*s were set to explode simultaneously underwater from the sunken B-17 and rupture the battleship's hull. The large *Hydrobomb*s did not fit into the bomb bays of a B-17 even if there was equipment available to load them. After consulting Boeing Company representatives the top of the B-17 fuselage was removed and the bombs were lifted by a cherry picker-type crane and 26,000 pounds of *Hydrobomb*s were lowered into the aircraft. As the cockpit top was also removed Forrest dubbed the chopped top B-17 as the "Roadster." The bomber was gingerly loaded with the hydrostatic bombs but the British hearing of this huge and lethal load refused permission for the aircraft to takeoff. At least this was the official explanation as shortly afterward the British announced that their bombers using the huge 12,000 pound *Tallboy* bombs had sunk not only the *Tirpitz* but also this *Aphrodite* scheme.

The immediate problem facing *Castor* was the lack of suitable targets. The first mission on 11 September repeated the three September attacks on the submarine pens at Heligoland. The mission was marred when the pilot of the drone was killed when his parachute failed to open. A postmortem determined he had broken his back when the parachute static line wrapped around him as he fell through the escape hatch. The second drone crewman landed without mishap. The drone flew perfectly to the initial point of the bomb run and, on cue, descended to 300 feet and bore in on the aiming point. The controller had perfect television images of the target and the drone's compass all the way until impact. Unfortunately, the drone was hit by very intense and accurate AA fire, which caused the right wing to catch fire, causing the mother to lose control of the drone at the last moment, resulting in a miss of some 200 yards to the right of the submarine pen doors. Post-mission reporting suggested that had the drone continued on course a mere fifteen seconds longer, it would have squarely hit the target. As was the result of the mission of 3 September, the bomb destroyed some barracks and yet another large pile of coal but this time, at least, it did hit Heligoland Island!

On 11 September, the *Castor* group was briefed for another mission to the Heligoland U-Boat pens. The drone piloted by Richard Lindahl and co-piloted by Donald Salles took off at 1800 with Salles parachuting without difficulty but Lindahl's chute failed to open and he was killed. The primary mothership, this time a B-17, had Wilfred Tooman piloting and John Anderson controlling. Both drone and the primary mother flew

at 2,500 feet with the second mother two miles astern. Heavy AA fire caused Tooman to violently dive his mother aircraft to wave top level but lost the drone in the process. Anderson activated the smoke release on the drone and was able to pick up it up five miles ahead. However, by then it was the time for the drone to turn on its course toward the submarine pens but Anderson was too far behind to execute the turn visually. He turned the TV monitor on and the drone's compass appeared. The experienced Anderson deftly maneuvered the drone to the desired heading via the TV monitor and control box. The ACE was activated and held the drone at a steady 250 feet. The drone's TV cameras focused on Heligoland's cliffs and soon Anderson was able to view the various target identifying landmarks on his monitor. As the U-Boat pens came into view he turned ACE off and readied the dive controls which would crash the Torpex-laden B-17 into the pens. But the U-Boat pens began to disappear out of the side of his TV screen and when he tried to correct they disappeared altogether and then the picture went dark. Tooman had seen the drone's right wing hit by flak setting it on fire, causing it to veer off course only a quarter mile from the target. The drone crashed putting a large indentation in the cliffs about 150 feet from the mouth of the pens. Roy Forrest had had enough and transferred back to America.

In mid-September the *Castor* targets were changed to attack vital German oil production and storage facilities which had become an 8AF priority. It was thought that the large blast of the 20,000 pounds of Torpex would cause the oil storage tanks to rupture causing enormous fires. On 14 September two formations with two mothers controlling one drone in each formation attacked a large oil refinery in Hemmingstedt, Germany. Both mothers rendezvoused with and were able to gain control of the drones after the safety pilot and technical sergeant bailed out. But then one controller lost the television image and tried to guide the drone to the target visually but, having little practice with this method, the controller released the drone at the target too late and it overflew it by over a mile. The second drone was guided by the low mothership to the coast and was passed to the control of the high mothership at 16,000 feet. The drone's *Rebecca* radio-beacon system malfunctioned and the drone was unable to transmit a radio direction signal; making it necessary to keep the drone in visual contact to guide it to the target. The high mother's pilot was about to overfly the drone and made a 360° turn during which the controller lost sight of the drone in his television monitor due haze and sun. The drone's smoke generator failed to ignite and the escorting fighters began a search, worried that drone loaded with fuel could wander back over friendly territory. The controller had no choice but to dive the drone into the North Sea.

With three abject failures, the *Castor* operations were postponed for a month to make necessary modifications in equipment and technique; particularly in view of the upcoming bad weather of fall and winter. The danger of bail out by the drone crews was a problem that needed addressing. The solution was to pad and increase the size of the escape hatch and to use a static line to automatically pull the parachute from the pack as the drone crew jumped. A bizarre suggestion to have the drone crew slide down a rope from the drone to board the mothership in midair was quickly rejected! A television image of not only the drone's compass but also of the airspeed and altimeter was recommended as was the installation of the new "*Black Maria*" radar beacon on the drone that would allow it to be controlled in any weather.

The submarine pens at Heligoland were attacked again on 15 October. Since the island was heavily defended by German AA batteries 20 B-17s of the 452nd Bomb Group were to bomb them 15 minutes before the first drone arrived. The B-17s and two drones tookoff in weather that was quickly deteriorating. The 452nd B-17s had to bomb using radar through a solid undercast cloud. As the first drone approached the target below the cloud deck, the weather there began to worsen even more. Without warning, this drone began to lose airspeed and altitude and drifted to the port and the controller was unable to correct the problem remotely. Just as the drone turned on its final descent toward the sub pens, the television monitors went blank and the controller had to guide the drone visually. About a half mile from the target the undamaged flak batteries hit the drone causing it to slew and hit about 500 yards from the aiming point, leaving the target intact. The second drone was also hit by flak, exploding it at 500 feet altitude and a mile ad half from the target.

On 30 October another mission to Heligoland was undertaken with even worse results. The flak batteries were again bombed by B-17s but their effectiveness would remain unknown as both drones were lost before reaching the target. One drone managed to fly to Sweden putting a large hole into that country's southern region and neutral Sweden which had also been subjected to the attack of errant German V-2 rockets issued a protest. The second drone could not be made to turn or dive and headed along the Danish coast at 10 feet and crashed with an enormous explosion into the sea.

The next *Castor* mission was flown on 5 December against railroad marshalling yards at Herford, Germany. The first drone was destroyed by AA fire but the second never reached the target area as it went onto a protracted, uncontrollable descent over Holland through thick clouds. Incredibly, the fully loaded drone made a perfect belly landing in soft, wet ground, and failed to explode. So that *Aphrodite's* secrets would not be compromised the Air Force sent sorties to find and destroy the aircraft on the ground but their extensive search failed to find the drone. After the war it was found that German soldiers investigating the crash shot at the aircraft getting a very, very momentary surprise as the bomb load detonated.

On 1 January 1945, a *Castor* mission was sent to attack the thermal power station in Oldenburg, Germany. Both drones escaped AA fire but missed target due control malfunctions.

With the onset of winter weather and only one fully equipped *Castor* drone on hand, the *Castor* program was cancelled. The scorecard for *Aphrodite/Castor* tallied a perfect record of B-17 drone 19 sorties and 19 failures. Since the drones could not hit strategic targets Gen. Arnold, its major booster, instructed Gen. Spaatz to use 25 war-wearies a month over Germany "as an irritant and possibly a means of breaking down the morale of the people of interior Germany." The British Chiefs of Staff refused approval of this proposed mass use of war-wearies called *Willie Orphans* as they felt the Nazis also could retaliate and London certainly presented a large target that could not be missed. (*Willie Orphans* are discussed in detail next). Roosevelt consulted Churchill at Yalta in early February, 1945 on the subject and Churchill indicated he would reconsider. Roosevelt died on 12 April and Truman took over the Presidency and Churchill wrote Truman reluctantly again approved *Aphrodite's* use hoping it would not backfire endangering beleaguered London which had suffered V-1 and V-2 terror weapon attacks. Truman, knowing the atomic bomb was a reality and would render schemes such as *Aphrodite* obsolete, cancelled the project.

The reason that *Aphrodite* was not transferred to the Pacific was chiefly one of geography. The longest distance from England to the most distant *Aphrodite* target in Germany was less than 400 miles but it was 1,600 miles from the Marianas airbases to strategic targets in Japan. These long distances required the B-29 to be used as the controlling mothership since neither the B-17 nor B-24 had the range to guide a drone to Japan and then return. If the controlling two mother configuration was to be retained then two B-29s would be delivering only 20,000 pounds of explosive which was 12,000 pounds less than both bombers could carry

as a bomb load in a conventional mission over the same distance. Also, the difference between the most efficient cruising speeds for the B-29 and a fully loaded B-17 drone was as much as 200 mph which meant the B-29 had to fly slower which meant lengthening an already very long mission. Using a B-29 as a drone was considered as it could carry up to 50,000 pounds of explosive which soon seemed ludicrous when B-29s could deliver Atomic Bombs with an explosive power rated in kilotons.

A summary of the Final Report on the *Aphrodite Project* (and *Anvil/ Castor*) from the CO, USSTAF appeared in a memorandum to the Assistant Chief of Air Staff dated 7 February 1945. The basic conclusions were:

"The results of the missions flown were not satisfactory as far as damage to enemy installations. However, these missions were in the nature of experimental missions and have proved the value and serviceability of the weapon and equipment. The failures can be chiefly attributed to weather, with personnel failure, and in the possibility of equipment failure. Since the equipment was designed for a limited number of flying hours and since none of the equipment had had nearly 100 hours of actual flying time on training missions, any equipment failure does not reflect on the serviceability of these installations…."

"….This weapon is not satisfactory as a strategic weapon in this theater due to extremely adverse weather conditions and very concentrated flak defenses on all important targets…."

"….This weapon does not constitute a worthwhile striking force when limited to only two missiles per mission, as with this project, due to limited radio frequencies…."

"….It is felt that his weapon is of less value against small installations as against heavily built up areas, since its effectiveness is due to blast alone…."

"….The equipment has been dangerously compromised in the theater, due to the fact that on the mission of 5 December 1944, one Robot aircraft, flying through severe icing conditions, landed in an open field in enemy territory from a power stall without exploding. This means that a full set of equipment has fallen into enemy hands…."

The Report recommended:

"If this weapon is to be continued in use in this theater, it should be used as a tactical rather than a strategic weapon with its launching base well forward….because of the extremely adverse weather conditions greatly limit the frequency with which long range flights can be carried out under visual conditions. It is further suggested that this weapon would prove of more value in a different theater where weather conditions are more favorable…."

"It is strongly recommended that sufficient radio frequencies be assigned for both control equipment and television to allow a minimum of ten missiles to be dispatched simultaneously without interference from each other…."

"Targets should be selected which are susceptible to blast effect and should not have too concentrated an anti-aircraft defense…."

"Steps should be taken to obtain new frequency ranges and make necessary changes in the equipment to minimize the danger arising from the compromise of the equipment on the 5 December 1944 mission....A radio detonator should be installed enabling the load to be detonated at the will of the controller...."

Willie Orphans

Even though the major emphasis was placed on *Aphrodite* and *Castor* guided powered bombs by the AAF; Brig.Gen. Grandison Gardner, Commander of Eglin Proving Ground, suggested to Gen. Arnold in September 1944, that these unmanned powered bombs could be used for area bombing deep inside Germany in the winter months which limited normal bombing operations. Once the *Aphrodite/Castor* program began to fail; Arnold decided that the *Castor* technology could be employed to convert hundreds of readily available war-weary bombers into very potent ground-launched and ground-controlled cruise missiles designated as *Willie Orphans* to bombard industrial and other strategic targets located deep inside Germany and, eventually, bomb the Japanese home islands. By the summer of 1944, any program relating to war-weary aircraft became a *Weary Willie* project, which was frequently abridged in most official communication to simply a *Willie* project with the controlling aircraft remaining as "*Mothers*," the missiles air controlled by *Mothers* were called "*Babies*" and ground-controlled missiles were called "*Orphan's*." These rather obvious codenames were later, 28 November 1944, changed as *Willie* became *Abusive*, *Mother* became "*Bluefish*," the *Baby* became "*Corticated*," and *Orphan* became "*Cottongrass*."

A plan was made to develop A-5 Autopilots for remote use in *Willie Orphans* in B-17s and B-24s already equipped with A-5s and install obsolete A-4s and A-5s in A-20s, B-25s, and B-26s for use as drones. B-17 and B-24 *Willie Orphans* with C-1 autopilots were considered for use with radar tracking and plotting of approach resulting in dead reckoning course with preset flight after the pilot had bailed out, or tracking and plotting the entire flight after the pilot had bailed out, or tracking and plotting the entire flight with remote radar after the pilot had bailed out. The operational plans for *Mother* and *Baby* were: visual tracking of *Baby* by remote radio control, altitude control, TV and smoke dispenser (i.e. the same as *Castor*); continual determination of relative position of *Baby* and *Mother* by visual control and radar; long range operation by visual control, radar, telemetering of *Baby* instruments, and remote control of other *Baby* instruments. The ATSC directed the procurement of 550 drone and 110 control kits for *Willie* and to cancel the installation of control equipment for all *Castor* aircraft which was to then be used in *Willie Orphans*. The cost for automatic pilots for remote control was C-1: $4,700 without or $6,000 with bomb stabilizer; A-5: $5,000, and A-4: $800. Only a few *Willies* were required for testing at Eglin so there was no need to store them in the US and about 100 were available in the UK and MTO and Gen. Spaatz planned to use 25 per month in operations. The lack of targets in the MTO made their use in that theater doubtful. Fifty of the 550 were scheduled to be sent to the ETO by 15 January 1945 but the Germans had captured a Baby intact and the deployment could possibly be reduced until radar control development was ready in about four months. The 20AF also had expressed interest in the *Orphan Program*.

A major factor in the failure of the *Aphrodite/Castor* project was their susceptibility to enemy AA fire. To circumvent this, the *Orphans* were to be deployed at night or in bad weather by dead reckoning or ground-based radar control without the need for visual ground references to guide the weapon. The *Orphan's* location in the air was to be provided by a *Black Maria* radar beacon signal transmitting from the *Orphan*. In early October 1944, the ground controlled radar stage of the project was given a top priority in the American guided missile program while the NDRC was to adapt the SCR 584 radar unit for control. The ground based controllers would control the *Orphan* by directing its beacon over the target and,

when it was in the correct location, give it a final command, causing the heavily loaded bomber to dive onto the objective.

Willie Orphans controlled by a ground radar control station did not have any where near the range or the accuracy of their air controlled counterparts. Initially, the *Willie Orphans* were anticipated only to be able to hit a 1,200 by 200 foot rectangle and only from 100 miles from the ground control station but later even this unfavorable estimate was found to be too optimistic. The *Orphan* B-17s and B-24s, carrying 20,000 pounds of explosives, had a one way range of 1,600 miles, adequate to hit targets in Japan from bases in the Marianas. But once the *Orphans* flew beyond 100 miles they were out of range of the ground controllers and became unguided and flew to their targets by dead reckoning, a method which used in 1918 by the Kettering *Bug*! The dead reckoning procedure was to be as follows:

The drone was to be flown by a pilot in a direct line towards the target 50 or 60 miles away. The drone was tracked over friendly territory by a tracking station several miles inside friendly territory using modified SCR-584 radar, automatic plotting board, and a UPN-2 beacon in the drone. The drone pilot was then informed of his corrected course and time from the target; and would then make the necessary corrections and set the air log or time mechanism after which he bailed out over friendly territory. The drone was then flown by preset automatic pilot and altitude control equipment to the target where the air log or time mechanism flew it onto the target.

The ground control of the drone was through "continual control" using a modulator added to the SCR-584 ground radar equipment and a CRN-3 selector added to the UPN-2 equipment in the drone. Ground control could also be accomplished by the use of FM radio control link with a 250-watt amplifier in conjunction with the previous equipment described above.

Even veteran navigators had problems using dead reckoning and often experienced navigation errors in the order of seven miles in every 100 miles flown. Despite their rather lackluster promised performance, on 12 October 1944, Gen. Arnold gave the *Willie* program the highest priority of all the AAF guided weapon programs and within the *Willie* program the *Orphans* received the highest priority.

With the poor weather of the 1944 fall and winter approaching it appears that Arnold would rather continue his attacks on targets in Germany with inaccurate weapons than not attacking at all. An extraordinary letter to Gen. Spaatz in November 1944 demonstrates that Arnold would readily forego his precision daylight bombing doctrine to break the will of the enemy population to continue to fight by turning the *Willie Orphans*:

"....loose to land all over Germany so that the Germans would be just as much afraid of our war-weary planes on account of not knowing just where they were going to hit, as are the people in England from buzz bombs and rockets. I think the psychological effect on the morale of the German people would be much greater this way, not knowing where they were going to fall, and they would have to be constantly on the alert with fighters and anti-aircraft to knock them down."

Shades of RAF Bomber Command CG "Bomber" Harris and his indiscriminate policy of area terror bombing!

Spaatz answered Arnold:

"We are making a study as to the requirements for an organization to launch war-weary airplanes at a maximum rate of 25 per month. The rate of operation will be limited by the extensive amount of training and technical preparation, and the supply of war-weary airplanes. For this reason, I do not believe that we will achieve significant effect if we "turn them loose to land all over Germany." We must perfect our equipment and control technique so that we can be reasonably sure of hitting the target. The Germans' V-2 lands all over eastern England, but only those which land where they cause damage and casualties have any significant effect on morale. Even that effect is localized."

The British Chiefs of Staff refused approval of this proposed mass use of *Willie Orphan*s from UK bases as they felt the Nazis also could retaliate and London certainly presented a large target that could not be missed. On 31 January 1945, General Marshall sent a priority, top secret message to General Eisenhower, informing him the British had withdrawn their agreement to use the US *Willie Orphan* project and that "all launching of aircraft in connection with this project be suspended."

Nonetheless, Arnold continued the *Willie Orphan*'s 1-A priority and its extensive testing at Eglin because it was the most promising, numerous, and otherwise expendable AAF missile. By March 1945, the Eglin tests reestablished that the *Orphans* could only be ground radio-controlled out to 96 miles and only if the drone was above 7,000 feet and if the *Orphan* descended below that altitude, all radar contact and radio-control was lost. Tests continued but found the *Orphans* just were not precision weapons being unable to to hit a target the size of an average size industrial factory. To position the radio-control station with the 96 mile limit near a major strategic enemy target in the ETO was difficult and was impossible against the Japanese homeland. *Orphan's* accuracy against a tactical target was significantly less than that regularly achieved by medium or fighter bomber attacks.

Further tests concentrated on deploying *Orphans* against targets on the Japanese home islands but due to the long distances the idea of using a modified *Aphrodite* system was resurrected. The safety pilot would fly the *Orphan* from a distant base to a predetermined point where he would bail out to be picked up by a submarine or ASR picket ship used for B-29 raids. The *Orphan* would continue to fly itself to a point off the Japanese coast where a B-29 mother would rendezvous with it and gain radio-control. The *Orphan* would then be guided to the target, not by the mother following the drone as with the *Aphrodite* system, but by using the B-29's H2X radar to locate the target and an onboard receiver to track emissions from the *Orphan's Black Maria* radar beacon. When the *Orphan's* beacon signal appeared to be at the correct distance from the target; it would be given the final command to dive into the target. Tests showed the greatest accuracy achievable using this method was a circular error of one to two miles which was about the same as if the *Orphan* had been controlled by a ground station. The time and effort in training and employing specially trained aircrew and ground technicians precluded XXIBC interest in the project. Another suggestion was to use Babies controlled by B-24s or B-29s as decoys to draw Japanese fighters from targets areas attacked by B-29 formations; however, B-29s dispensing Rope/Window could be an effective alternative.

In tests during May 1945, to determine if the Offner Infra Red heat seeker, which had been used with moderate success in the GB-6 glide bomb, could be employed to provide terminal guidance in the *Orphan* B-17 with it large nose which allowed the Offner seeker to pivot 10° vertically or horizontally to keep the target in its sight as the aircraft banked and turned. But in practice it was much more difficult to remotely control a multi-engine bomber carrying 20,000 ponds of explosive than a 3,000 pound glide bomb.

As the *Orphan* approached the target the Offner seeker was unable to anticipate or make the rapid fine adjustments a human controller was able to make and would attempt to force the nose of the bomber onto the target with increasingly large corrections. These corrections would ultimately cause increasing oscillations in the *Orphan's* final approach to the target and often resulted in the loss of the control of the drone.

In 62 test dives using the Offner Infra Red seeker there was an 80% miss rate of between one quarter to four miles but the 20% hit rate was considered to have been able to cause some damage to a large industrial site. These tests did not actually expend an *Orphan* on each test but the test drone had a safety pilot on board who would intercede just before the *Orphan* was to hit the target and fly back to base. Engineers onboard the *Orphan* would evaluate where the drone would have hit if it was allowed to proceed to the target. The Offner's continued poor showing resulted in its cancellation in May 1945.

Due to the accuracy, guidance, and control problems encountered during testing, the *Willie Orphan* was never deployed in combat. By September 1945, with the war over and the number of available war-weary aircraft quickly decreasing, the Air Force Board suggested the cancellation of the *Willie* project.

Fighter *Baby Project*
In late April 1945 Col. V.R. Haugen, Chief of the Aircraft Project Section issued a directive to the Special Weapons Branch for the modification and testing of P-38, P-39, P-40, P-47, and P-51 fighters for use as "*Babies*" (drones). The Special Weapons Branch was to estimate the suitability and the amount of modifications required for each fighter with a possible range of 130 miles from either a control aircraft or from a ground station (launched from a ramp) and to incorporate controls to permit low level operations (minimum 25 feet) over land or water targets. The instruments and controls were to be designed for all weather operation and maximum security against jamming. Investigation showed that the P-38 and P-39 were most suitable as *Babies* but the war ended in the ETO where these fighters would be useful and the fighter *Baby Project* was cancelled.

Cottongrass
Cottongrass later became another scheme using fighter and bomber *Babies* under shipboard control stations located at close range to bombard targets on the Japanese Mainland. The close proximity to the target made the controlling ships vulnerable and also only five or six sorties could be flown per day and therefore would harass the Japanese less than conventional multi-aircraft bombing methods and the *Cottongrass* scheme was discontinued.

Hermit
Hermit was a *Cottongrass* ground-controlled, rather than shipboard-controlled, scheme flying drone aircraft into Japanese cave entrenchments in order to minimize American infantry casualties. Because of the unimpressive ETO operations aircraft in better condition than "war-weary" was a requirement and procurement was only to go to a point necessary to complete the development program and the master kits for the *Cottongrass* phase of the project. The project was initiated by the Air Technical Service Command while NDRC was to develop a ground-control system not utilizing radar due to a prolonged development time. Testing, using ground controlled B-l7s was generally successful, but prolonged, as the war ended before operational use could be effected.

Postwar Use of the B-17 drones
After the war the surplus bomber drone project was again revived for use in the May 1946 A-bomb tests at Bikini (*Operation Crossroads*). War surplus B-17 drones were to carry scientific equipment and instruments to take various readings of the atomic mushroom cloud at different altitudes. The radio-control technique was mastered and improved upon in the postwar years. These drones were entirely pilotless throughout the flight

The final role of the B-17 drones in the AAF was the dual role of the **QB-17** radio-controlled target drone (pictured) and the DB-17 controlling mother aircraft in anti-aircraft missile testing. (AAF)

During the summer 1946 US postwar A-Bomb tests at the Bikini Atoll, *Operation Crossroads*, five motherships were to control four B-17 drones into the atomic explosions. Pictured is a **"Drone Control Ship III"** taking off from Stickell Field, Eniwetok. (AAF)

and takeoff and landing was carried out by technicians stationed in two jeeps equipped with radio-control boxes stationed near the runway. Jeep #1 was located at the very end of the runway and controlled direction through rudder control and also applied the brakes on landing. Jeep #2 positioned to one side of the runway controlled throttles and elevators on takeoffs and landings. The control boxes were small weighing four pounds and had 10 radio channels. Once the Jeep controllers got the B-17 into the air, control was transferred to a mother aircraft circling above and equipped with an identical control box in the nose and guided the drone to the target at a long distance. Upon landing the drone; the mother switched control back to the Jeep controllers at about 400 feet altitude. The final role of the B-17 drones in the USAAF was the dual role of radio-controlled Target Drone (QB-17) and the controlling mother aircraft (DB-17) in anti-aircraft missile testing. As the control devices and missile monitoring instruments were expensive, the QB-17 drones were not destroyed on each missile test mission. The missiles being tested were usually programmed for near misses rather than direct hits to conserve the drone. The last B-17 Target Drone was expended in June 1960 and with it both the B-17 in any role and war-weary drone era closed.

XBQ-1/2/3/4 Series and PQ Series
Fleetwings XBQ-1/XBQ-2
XBQ-1
In March 1942, the AAF initiated a program to develop radio-controlled Assault Drones, frequently called "aerial torpedoes" at that time. These aerial torpedoes were to be unmanned expendable aircraft (either purpose-built or converted from existing types), fitted with a large payload of high

explosive, remote-control equipment, and a forward-looking TV camera. The drones were to be directed to the target by radio commands from a control aircraft, where the operator would control the drone by watching the image transmitted by the camera.

In July 1942, Fleetwings of Garden City, NY was awarded a contract for $1.34 million to develop the XBQ-1 Assault Drone with a scheduled delivery date of February 1944. The sleek aircraft, with a fixed tricycle landing gear covered by faired wheel spats, was powered by two 225 hp Franklin O-405-7 piston engines that gave it a speed of 225 mph and a range of 1,700 miles. The XBQ-1 had a high wing with a span of 48.6 feet and weighed 7,700 pounds without the proposed 2,000 HE pound warhead. The XBQ-1 was provided with a cockpit so that it could be flown by a pilot during test and ferry flights while for unmanned flights the cockpit was to be replaced by a flush fairing. It was not until October 1943 that Fleetwings was able to successfully develop a guidance system in an YPQ-12A Target Drone that was converted to a radio-controlled bomb with a TV camera. The BQ-1 program was cancelled in July 1944, when the only XBQ-1 prototype crashed on its first flight.

XBQ-2 and -2A
Along with the XBQ-1, the AAF also ordered one XBQ-2 which was to be identical to the XBQ-1 except for using Lycoming XO-435-3 engines and a jettisonable landing gear. The XBQ-2 had a scheduled delivery date of December 1943 but was not built and was replaced by a contract for a single XBQ-2A. The XBQ-2A design replaced the XO-435-3 engines with two Lycoming R-680-13s. After the -2A was built the project was terminated in December 1943 because of high costs and the aircraft was subsequently redesignated as ZXBQ-2A to denote its obsolescence.

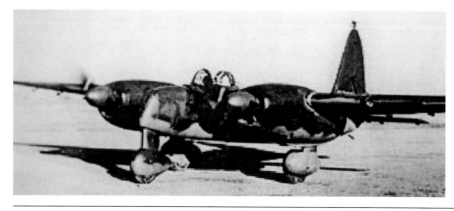

Fleetwings XBQ-1 (AAF)

Fleetwings XBQ-2A (AAF)

Fairchild XBQ-3

In October 1942, Fairchild Aircraft of Farmingdale, NY was granted a $1.4 million contract to build two XBQ-3 prototype unmanned Assault Drones based on the Fairchild AT-21 *Gunner* twin-engined trainer design. These drones, also called "aerial torpedoes" at that time, were to be fitted with a large pay load of HE and directed to the target by radio commands from a control aircraft. The first flight of an XBQ-3 occurred in July 1944, but the XBQ-3 program was cancelled later that year.

The XBQ-3 was 52.7 foot long, had a 37 foot wingspan, was 13.1 foot high, and weighed 15,300 pounds. The XBQ-3 was powered by two Ranger V-770 piston engines, which propelled it to 220 mph over a range of 1,500 miles, and ceiling of 17,000 feet. It had a retractable tricycle landing gear and carried 4,000 pounds of high explosive (two 2,000 pound bombs or two torpedoes) which was twice as much as the purpose-designed, but smaller, Fleetwings XBQ-1/XBQ-2 drones. For test flights,

Fleetwings XBQ-2A-1 (AAF)

Fairchild XBQ-3 (AAF)

Interstate XQB-4 (USN)

it was flown with onboard pilots. Like the other XBQ-series drones, the XBQ-3 was equipped with a TV camera, whose image would be used by the remote control operator to control the drone. Two XBQ-3s were procured with a delivery date of February 1944.

XBQ-4 and XBQ-5
The Interstate XQB-4 was designated as the Navy Assault Drone XTDR-1 and the Interstate XQB-5 was designated as the Navy Assault Drone XTD2R-1 and is next described as TDR drones.

XBQ-7 and XBQ-8
The XBQ-7 was a Boeing B-17 associated with the operational *Aphrodite* and *Castor* programs. The XBQ-8 was a Consolidated B-24 D/J that was not used operationally by the AAF while the other XBQ-8 was a Consolidated PB4Y-1 that was used operationally by the USN in the *Anvil* program. The XBQ-7 and -8 are discussed elsewhere in detail.

The BQ program was cancelled because it was slow in developing and expensive, requiring almost as much time and money as would the development of a full-fledged combat aircraft without sufficient tactical return. The power-driven XBQs required clear visibility, extensive fighter protection, and highly trained crews.

PQ Series
As a surrogate for the BQ series the PQ series was used in initial television tests. The PQs were commercial monoplanes used as targets for AA practice, equipped with servo assemblies, three axis gyros, and radio control equipment. In October 1943 a PQ-12A radio target aircraft was fitted with a television camera transmitter mounted on a wing and a 500 pound bomb in the fuselage to become a power driven controllable bomb. A television receiver was installed in a mothership in which the radio control operator controlled the PQ-12A using the TV picture as a reference for the attitude of the PQ-12A to the target. On 10 October 1943 the Materiel Command conducted a test at Muroc to demonstrate an air-to-air explosion. Using different radio frequencies, a radio controlled PQ-9 was intended as the target and the PQ-12A as the controlled missile. A UC-78 control aircraft controlled the PQ-8 visually and the PQ-12A by reference on a TV screen toward the PQ-9. The control aircraft flew about a mile off the right wing of the two PQs. The bomb on the PQ-12A was armed remotely while in the air. After 25 minutes the PQ-9 was centered on the TV screen of the control aircraft and appeared to be of a size to indicate a reasonably close range and the detonator circuit was remotely actuated (later this range was estimated to be 75 feet). The PQ-12A completely disintegrated and the PQ-9 spiraled steeply into the ground.

The second demonstration had a PQ-12A fly into a target by using a TV camera that transmitted a picture to a screen in the control aircraft flying three to five miles away. The takeoff and climb to 1,000 feet was controlled visually after which control was established using the TV screen as reference. Once the target was located on the screen the PQ-12A

On 15 September 1924 the **N-9 seaplane** training aircraft was the first aircraft to be flown by radio-control. The flight was carried out by the Navy's BuOrd at the Naval Proving Ground at Dahlgren, VA. (USN)

was put into a shallow dive at full throttle with the target being held on the screen for a minute appearing to grow larger and larger as the distance decreased between the target and the PQ-12A. At the last instance the target filled the whole screen but off to the left center as the increasing speed of the dive caused a deviation in the directional trim.

USN TDR drones
The US Navy drone Program Development
The Navy successfully launched its first "NOLO" (**NO L**ive **O**perator) aircraft as Target Drones in 1924. The first attempt to fly an airplane by radio-control was put under the auspices of the Navy's BuOrd and BuEng at the Naval Proving Ground at Dahlgren, VA. Talented radio engineer, C.B. Mirick had developed a radio control system for the N-9 which was tested 33 times in 1924 with a control (safety) pilot and on 15 September 1924, the aircraft was readied for a flight without a safety pilot. The N-9 was equipped with a Norden automatic pilot and a keyboard teletype controller that controlled the aircraft in set values of turn, climb, or glide. The N-9 was taken off smoothly by radio control and maneuvered through a long series of 50 maneuvering radio signals and after 40 minutes the aircraft was brought down for a hard landing that damaged the float causing it to sink. The next aircraft equipped with automatic pilot and radio-control gear was a Vought VE-7H seaplane and was flown without a safety pilot on 11 December 1925. During takeoff the plane porpoised four times with each jump more violent than the last causing the float struts to fracture and the plane crashed and sank. Further NOLO drone development was curtailed in the low budget inter-war years.

Navy interest in radio controlled aircraft was revived in 1935 when orders organizing a new radio-controlled aircraft project resulted from the necessity to supply realistic aerial targets for the training of Fleet anti-aircraft gunners and to improve AA fire control equipment. Anti-aircraft gunners fired on practice sleeves towed by aircraft at set altitudes and speeds which were found to be stereotyped and artificial and did not

PQ-12A (AAF)

duplicate combat situations. The Chief of Naval Operations (CNO), Adm. William Standley, while on an official trip to England early in 1936, witnessed firing tests on the radio-controlled aircraft target called the *Queen Bee*. Standley was impressed with the *Queen Bee* test results and on his return to Washington, DC, conferred with the Chief of BuAer, R.Adm. Ernest King; who he found was in full agreement with his view that it was necessary to develop a realistic target for anti-aircraft firing practice. On 23 March 1936, the CNO sent a letter on the subject to the BuOrd, Aeronautics and Engineering calling their attention to the urgent need for radio-controlled aircraft targets for realistic training of shipboard gunners and he outlined the characteristics of the plane and the performance that was desired. He received prompt and enthusiastic replies from BuAer and BuEng. But BuOrd regretted that the services of Carl Norden and his staff were not available as they were totally involved in the development of the Norden Bomb Sight and further, the crowded condition at the Dahlgren Proving Ground precluded work there on such a project as radio-control of aircraft. The BuOrd letter also observed that "the cost of provision and operation of such targets for routine training of anti-aircraft batteries would be out of all proportions to the benefits obtainable thereby. It will be interesting to see that the BuAer carried on the successful development with a small expenditure of funds."

On 1 May 1936, the CNO authorized the BuAer and BuEng for the development of radio-controlled aircraft targets and gave BuAer primary control over the project, which was to be pursued at high priority. On 20 July 1936, Capt. Delmer Fahrney became the Officer-in-Charge of the project and was given three to five years to fulfill its objectives. Fahrney's orders stated that a study of all previous work in the field of radio-control should be made and then a plan submitted for the implementation of the project.

On 6 August 1936, Fahrney submitted a plan which requested development of unmanned remotely-controlled aircraft for combat use as "Assault Drones." Fahrney is often credited with coining the term "drones" for unmanned aircraft to acknowledge the British *Queen Bee* project. The projected budget of $77,500 was include the purchase of two JH-1 Stearman Hammond aircraft the development of special mechanical gear for the target planes; installation of radio-control gear in the target planes and in the control stations (two field control carts and two control planes); and the salaries of an engineer and a draftsman. This budget was exceeded by $11,625 because the delay in receiving the Stearman Hammond aircraft necessitated the prototyping of two Curtiss N2C-2s training planes by adding a tricycle landing gear.

On 9 September 1936, the CNO approved the plans of the Officer-in-Charge and the project got underway. In addition to the O-in-C's primary base of operations at the Naval Aircraft Factory (NAF) in Philadelphia, PA, he was given a desk in the BuAer designated as the Special Designs Desk. This dual responsibility did much to pursue the project at a high priority.

The Officer-in-Charge at the NAF was Lt.Cdr. Delmar Fahrney assisted by civilians, William Wait, Aero Engineer and George Spangenberg, Assistant Aero Engineer. At the Naval Research Laboratory (NRL) at Anacostia, the director was Dr. J. Hoyt Taylor with C.B. Mirick as a consultant.

The standard radio equipment had greatly improved over the last decade with the introduction of the GP-2 transmitter and RV-3 receiver. The development of the radio equipment mainly involved the establishment of an oscillating circuit which when activated would send out a note or tone of modulated frequency over the selected carrier wave via the transmitter. This tone would be picked up by the receiver and filtered out by another oscillating circuit which was similar to the one at the transmitter and would respond only that exact tone. These oscillating circuits were created by the use of a vibrating steel reed which gave off a tone when forced to vibrate between the magnetic poles of two standard headphones. The transmitting end of the tonal production was called the modulator and the receiving end was called the selector. There were 12 distinct oscillating circuits which allowed the assignment of two circuits for up and down aileron, two for up and down elevators, two for on and off throttle, two for on and off control of any desired instrument or control device (as flap controls or steering control on the ground), and a circuit to disengage the radio-control gear instantly by the safety pilot. The rudder and ailerons were operated together so there was no direct rudder control. With this circuit assignment; four circuits were available for future control applications. Standard stick or wheel control and foot rudder controls were used to activate electrical contacts which caused the radio-control signals to be sent out. The necessary hydraulic servos with control valves and electric solenoids were developed by the Radio-Control Unit at NAF and installed in various test aircraft; first in an NT plane and later in two Curtiss N2C-2 training planes and two JH-1 Stearman-Hammond aircraft both fitted with tricycle landing gear.

There was a delay in the delivery of the JH-1s and to attempt landing a controlled drone without a tricycle landing gear was judged hazardous. So in August 1937 the N2C-2 was equipped with a makeshift nose gear and the required radio-control equipment. The development and fabrication of the essential equipment progressed so well at the NAF and the NRL that tests of an N2C-2 drone under radio-control with a safety pilot were started on 7 October 1937. Fahrney controlled the first takeoff and landing using a field radio unit cart and three others followed. The next tests used a radio-control pilot in a TG-2 torpedo plane. The TG-2 was a tandem, open cockpit seaplane built by the New Standard Aircraft Corporation and modified by the Naval Aircraft Factory. The first tests were ground tests in which the drone's throttles and control surfaces were controlled by an airborne TG-2 from as far 25 miles away. The field control pilot would take the drone off, turn over control at around 200 feet to the control pilot in the front seat of the TG-2 plane. After maneuvering the drone, the TG-2 control pilot would line the drone up for the landing approach and turn control over to the field cart control pilot, who would make the landing.

On 7 October 1937 the Navy began tests on radio newly developed radio control equipment using an **N2C-2 drone** under radio-control with a safety pilot. The nose wheel added to aid take offs and landings can be seen in the photo. (USN)

The **TG-2** was a tandem, open cockpit torpedo plane/seaplane built by the New Standard Aircraft Corporation and modified by the Naval Aircraft Factory used as a control plane for the N2C-2. (USN)

In early November 1937, testing was moved to the Coast Guard Air Station at Cape May, NJ, which had better overall facilities and weather conditions and was not located in a highly populated area and no commercial or military air operations were conducted in the area. By the 13 November, many tests simulating a flight of the drone without a safety pilot were carried out with each of the four pilots (Fahrney, S.E. Herbst, Fred Wallace, and W.M. Bowlin) becoming proficient in each of the required operating posts: as radio-control pilot on the field cart or in the control plane; pilot of the TG-2 control aircraft; or safety pilot in the drone.

Fahrney scheduled the first NOLO drone flight for 15 November. In the morning four flawless takeoffs and landings were made by the N2C-2 under radio-control with a safety pilot. At 1330 a N2C-2 drone without a safety pilot was taken off under the control of Fahrney with the ground control cart. The N2C-2 climbed to 200 feet where TG-2 control pilot F. Wallace controlled it in basic maneuvers for about 10 minutes before he lined it up for the landing. Fahrney, in the field cart control, took over control at around 100 feet and made a hard landing that damaged the nose wheel causing the plane to skid along on its nose but causing only slight damage that put the aircraft out of service only briefly. Slight accident, aside, this was the first successful flight of a full-scale American aircraft under radio-control and without a safety pilot.

The next NOLO attempt was carried out on 23 December using a JH-1 Stearman-1 drone which had finally arrived and had been equipped. Fahrney used the same method as used on the 15 November NOLO flight, except the troublesome hard landing was to be modified by using a slightly stalled landing that was to be controlled close to the field control cart. Also a Sperry directional gyro had been modified so that it could be connected by radio to hold the drone on an accurate heading.

For the test the TG-2 control aircraft took off first and flew to 300 foot altitude and in down wind position from the drone. The Stearman-Hammond JH-1 drone then began its takeoff run under control from the field cart and when it reached an altitude of about 200 feet control was transferred to the control aircraft. The control pilot put the drone into simple maneuvers for about 10 minutes and then maneuvered the drone down to a landing approach. When the drone had descended to about 50 feet on the glide approach, control was transferred to the field cart to end the first wholly successful flight.

After the 23 December flight all test flying was suspended for the winter and these months were used to improve existing equipment and develop new equipment. The NAF designed and manufactured an invaluable automatic pilot with greater input that would be used as a radio-controlled wing-leveling instrument bringing the drone into level flight under any flight condition. All instrument modifications and fabrication of needed parts were carried out in the Instrument Laboratory under the direction of Lt.(jg) Robert Jones and his assistant George Shaefer.

On 1 June 1938, after a several demonstration NOLO flights at Cape May for the Chief of BuAer and other high-ranking officers, the project began its move to the West Coast for anti-aircraft tests by the Fleet. Fahrney selected a section of flat land on the Otay Mesa south of San Diego which offered the requirements of safety and remoteness from a populated area and from other aircraft operations. The move was completed by early July while two TG-2 control planes were ferried across the US and the four drones (two N2C-2s and two JH-1s) were shipped by rail as well as the two field control trucks and necessary gear and spare parts. Fahrney and his four enlisted pilots alternated at the radio-control stations; two in the field control carts and two in the control planes. Each became proficient at controlling the drone from the field cart for takeoffs and landings and from the control plane for maneuvers in the air. Each rotated as a safety pilot in the drone, the pilot of the TG-2 control plane, control pilot on the field cart, and control pilot in the TG-2 plane.

By 10 August Fahrney reported to the C-on-C that the unit was ready to conduct the first firing tests. The aircraft carrier *Ranger* was selected by the C-in-C to conduct two firing runs which were to simulate the firing by a screening vessel on a bomber passing over the ship. Firing was to commence when the slant range was 4,000 yards and to cease when the slant range reached 6,000 yards. The Radio-control Unit made practice runs over the *Ranger* on 15 and 16 August using a safety pilot positioned in the drone. The procedure was for the No. 1 control aircraft to take station at 10,000 feet, one mile abeam of the drone. The No. 2 standby control aircraft trailed the drone at a two mile interval. All control for the run was placed in the No. 1 control plane while No. two would take over control if there were a malfunction in No. 1. On 24 August 1938, the *Ranger* fired on the drone with its starboard AA battery on the first run and the port battery on the second run. No AA bursts came near the drone and the unit was ordered to return it to Otay Mesa. Unfortunately, the *Ranger* requested that the No.1 control plane to increase its distance abeam of the drone during the second and last runs. The increased distance and the

The **JH-1 Stearman-1 drone** was successfully tested during the November 1937 NOLO test flights. (USN)

In 1932 the old Battleship the **USS Utah** was converted into a target ship which could be radio-controlled from another ship without onboard human intervention. The *Utah* was used during the September 1938 radio-controlled diving attack tests by Curtiss N2C-2 drone controlled by a TG-2. (USN)

smoke of the bursts of the shells, together with the failure of the wing-leveling device on the drone during its climb to 10,000 feet, caused the control pilot to lose control and the drone was lost on the return to base. The poor results of the Fleet's AA effectiveness during the drone tests caused more demanding tests to be conducted at Guantanamo Bay, Cuba, during the following winter. Again the drone maneuvered much more like an attacking aircraft than the stereotyped towed target sleeve and results were again poor.

The World's First Guided Missile Attack

Fahrney's next test was the dive bombing of the old Battleship USS Utah (BB-31) which was launched in 1909. In 1932 the *Utah* was converted into a target ship which could be radio-controlled from another ship without onboard human intervention. She would serve for the next nine years as mobile target and gunnery training ship until she was sunk at Pearl Harbor. In preparation for the *Utah* tests the unit completed dive tests on selected land targets on Otay Mesa from 10,000 feet. It was found that at that altitude the control pilot was able, with visual guidance, to direct the drone accurately into near collision with the target. The runs were made with a safety pilot riding in the drone. Meanwhile the NAF installed radio-control equipment in 12 more N2C-2s to convert them to drones.

On 14 September 1938, a Curtiss N2C-2 drone without a pilot was taken off under radio-control and flown to the *USS Utah's* firing area. A field control cart was placed on the deck of the *Utah* to control the last part of the dive to keep the drone from actually crashing into the ship. The control pilot in the TG-2 control aircraft put the drone in a dive from an altitude of 8,700 feet to a position angle of about 38° after which the drone settled in the dive toward the ship at a final dive angle of 45°. The *Utah* had a newly installed battery of 75 caliber guns operating in a single mount. Two bursts of gunfire were fired and during the second burst, the drone was hit and went out of control and crashed into the sea. This hit apparently was by chance because in later identical tests at Guantanamo Bay, Cuba, many dives were made on the *Utah* by the Target Drone and no hits were made by the poor shooting by Navy deck gunners. This attack by a Target Drone on the *Utah* was the world's first by a guided missile in that the drone was a full-scale powered aircraft capable of carrying a bomb, was controlled remotely by radio, and was visually guided to the target by a control pilot at a safe altitude. The first German guided missile was successfully tested on 18 December 1940. This missile, developed by Prof. Herbert Wagner, was an unpowered glide bomb, remotely controlled by radio and visually guided from an altitude of 7,000 feet which has been previously discussed as the SD 1400 Fritz X.

After the completion of tests on the *Utah* Fahrney and the drone target unit returned to the Naval Aircraft Factory and turned the equipment over to the Commander of the Utility Wing US Fleet at San Diego, who placed it under VJ-1 Squadron with Lt.(jg) Robert Jones in command. While he was in charge of the Instrument Laboratory at the NAF Jones had played a

large part in the modification of instruments for the Radio-control Project. When the experimental drone unit was transferred to a US Fleet Service Unit it was given the new designation of *Project Dog* and returned to Cuba for more drone AA practice.

From 1 February through 30 March 1939, AA positions on 17 US Fleet warships practice fired on drone targets off Guantanamo Bay. For the *Project Dog* personnel the firing tests were a success as there were no equipment malfunctions or control problems. The drones suffered no hits in about half of the practice tests and a few of the drones carried on with hits in their wings or fuselages and only two drones were brought down by gunfire. This second round of poor shooting by Navy warships against the Target Drones caused a reappraisal of Fleet anti-aircraft defenses and caused important changes in the defenses against bombing aircraft and the redesign of both fire control and gun systems.

Capt. George Holloman and Capt. Gilbert Hayden of the AAC, and a Mr. Hendricks of Wright Field observed and took part in radio-controlled flights at the NAF on four February 1938. As the control pilot in the TG-2, Capt. Holloman easily controlled the JH-1 Stearman Hammond drone (with a safety pilot). Holloman reported positively on the sensitive and instantaneous responsiveness of the drone to the control signals. His report commented on the manner the drone responded when the lateral stabilizing instrument (a modified Sperry Horizon) leveled the wings when it was activated on radio signal.

Capt. Holloman and Lt. Rudolph Fink attended the next Navy firing tests at Guantanamo Bay to advise AAC Chief H.H. Arnold as to the adaptability of the radio-control gear for AAC service. The two officers observed the ground control operations for the *USS Idaho* firing on 16 March 1939 and made flights in the control planes for the *USS Patterson* practices the next day. Holloman and Fink's report recommended that the AAC begin programs for the development of radio-controlled aircraft targets and weapons. In April 1939 Gen. Arnold requested a TG-2 control

In November 1935 RCA's **Dr. Vladimir Zworykin**, who is considered to be a co-inventor of television, proposed a 50 pound "electric eye" but the BuOrd had no interest in the proposal at the time. Zworykin would soon play a more important in the US TV control program. (Author)

plane, an N2C-2 drone, and a field control cart from the Navy which the Navy delivered in the summer of 1939.

The success of the *Project Dog* drones led Fahrney and the NAF to consider the concept of a flying missile that could be guided to its target beyond visual ranges. In the drones the NAF had the vehicle and was able to control it by radio and only a guidance system was needed. In November 1935 RCA's Dr. Vladimir Zworykin, who is considered to be a co-inventor of television, had proposed a 50 pound "electric eye" but the BuOrd had no interest in the proposal at the time. In 1937 Zworykin again presented the Navy Department with the possibilities of guided missiles and after some consideration the Chief of Naval Operations concluded that he was satisfied with the status quo for the present and didn't want to fund experimental work on guided missiles. Meanwhile, RCA continued to develop television and in 1939 it was the NAF that approached the company to ascertain the possibility of developing a small TV transmitter to be carried on a drone and a small TV receiver to be carried in a control plane. On 14 October 1939 the BuAer authorized the purchase and test of a small TV set which was contracted on 24 February 1940 and was shop tested by the NAF with good results during 1940. In January 1941, the TV equipment was tested satisfactorily in a two-seat, twin-float Berliner-Joyce XOJ observation aircraft. By 4 June 1941, the TV transmitter in a plane was producing pictures of such good quality on the TV receiver in a second plane that the operator in the second plane could direct the first plane to pass directly over a designated target. The 325 line picture at 40 frames transmitter weighed 35 pounds with dimensions of 7.5 x 7.5 x 23 inches and the power supply also weighed 35 pounds.

In the early summer of 1940 Fahrney was designated as Commanding Officer of the Naval Air Modification Unit (NAMU) which had control over all Target Drone and guided missile design and development as well as all modifications to combat aircraft. At the time there were several projects under way that held promise in the development of a guided missile:

In August 1940, **Lt. Robert Jones,** CO of VJ-3 Squadron, conducted tests that demonstrated that a drone could be visually directed toward a target from a control plane operating at a safe distance. In September 1944 Jones would head the Navy's TDR drone program (Jones is seen in photo inspecting TDR/SATFOR personnel). (USN)

for torpedo release. When the tests of the TV guidance and the radio altimeter were satisfactorily completed, the design of a service weapon was the next stage which would become the *Assault Drone* program.

In August 1940, Lt. Robert Jones, CO of VJ-3 Squadron, conducted tests at Cape May, NJ, to demonstrate the viability of visually directing a drone toward a target from a control plane operating at a safe distance. The tests showed that a drone could be consistently directed through small puffs of smoke and C-in-C Adm. James Richardson's report on the tests to the CNO stated "that the radio-controlled attack offers promise." In a letter to the NAF Adm. John Towers, the Chief of BuAer, stated that "The Bureau is particularly desirous that the technique of operating offensive torpedo-carrying, radio-controlled aircraft in quantity be pushed on to a conclusion and that sufficient flight tests of aircraft television be carried out to permit recommendations of useful application for naval purposes." Adm. William Blandy, the Chief of BuOrd sent a letter to the CNO dated 15 April 1941, suggesting that all efforts for development of radio-controlled offensive weapons be concentrated on the development of a torpedo plane drone.

The radio altimeter was an essential piece of equipment for a successful torpedo attack by a drone aircraft as it would hold the drone at a set low altitude for the torpedo release. In late 1938, RCA hired young electronics engineer, R.C. Sanders, to assist Dr. Irving Wolff to work on the radio altimeter. On 29 January 1941, the radio altimeter was demonstrated in a flight for naval personnel and the equipment gave a very successful performance. It was concluded that the radio altimeter would fulfill the rigid specifications required of a torpedo Assault Drone. Once the television guidance equipment, the radio-controlled automatic pilot and, the radio altimeter were convincingly proven, the next step was to incorporate them in a TG-2 Assault Drone.

In 1941 Navy *Project Ram* attempted to adapt obsolete conventional manned aircraft into drones that could be remotely controlled to fly into enemy bombers by an operator in the control plane who no longer needed to keep visual contact with the drone but could instead watch a TV screen with an image from a drone-mounted camera. The ill-starred and deservedly much maligned Brewster F2A Buffalo fighter was chosen as the controlled drone but crashed during testing. When a second F2A was assigned to testing, the BuOrd rejected it as unsafe to fly and *Project Ram* was terminated.

In March 1941, the CNO ordered that a Target Drone squadron was to be organized on the Atlantic Coast for use by the Atlantic Fleet as part of the newly conceived NAF *Project Fox* guided missile program. On 3 May 1941, this squadron was designated VJ-5 commanded by Lt. Robert Jones who brought key pilots and technicians with him from VJ-3. On 9 July 1941, Jones presented a proposal for the development of a radio-controlled fighter aircraft, dubbed as an "aerial ram," which could be aimed into a large enemy bomber formation and exploded. On 8 October 1941, the CNO issued a broad directive to VJ-5 to develop, test, and operate radio-controlled offensive weapons and to train personnel in their use. Besides being a duplication of the research and development projects at the NAF and NRL; this assignment was too much for VJ-5 as it was too involved as an operating unit and in supplying services to the Fleet and lacked adequate laboratory and shop facilities, and test equipment facilities to carry out such a complicated experimental program. Two Brewster F2A-3 Buffalo fighter planes and one pilot were lost in the tests but some of the equipment developed was later used in the Assault Drone program.

Under the direction of Cdr. W.P. Cogswell, Officer-in-Chief of Radio-Controlled Aircraft, the NAF's development and tests using the TG-2 torpedo aircraft plane had advanced so satisfactorily that by 8 October 1941, the NAF felt that service trials could be initiated. The Chief of BuOrd agreed to torpedo dropping tests to be carried out off Newport-

As the Director of the Plans Division in the office of the CNO, **Capt. Oscar Smith**, was instrumental in developing the Navy's drone equipped TV guidance programs. (USN)

Quonset when the drone was ready. At a BuAer and BuOrd conference on 24 October 1941 the service tests were planned and it was further suggested that 100 obsolete TBD torpedo bombers be assigned for modification to Assault Drones and when SBD bombers became obsolete they should be also be allocated to the drone program. On 29 November 1941, BuAer completed the preliminary design of a special Assault Drone that could be manufactured outside the regular aircraft industry that was fully occupied in producing aircraft, engines, and aircraft equipment for Great Britain as well as manufacturing that equipment for the Army and Navy air arms. After Pearl Harbor the plans to use obsolete aircraft for Assault Drones were cancelled, as every available aircraft was now needed for combat and the specially designed Assault Drone was consequently given high priority for earliest development with tentative plans to build 5,000 Assault Drones for deployment in 18 drone squadrons.

In mid-December 1941 Capt. Oscar Smith, proposed that a simple type of radio-control be placed on a "robot plane" that would be flown to a distance of not less than 50 miles from the target where the pilots in the robot planes would put them under radio-control and parachute to the sea for a prearranged pickup. The robot aircraft would then be directed by a controlling aircraft to fly within 100 yards of the enemy ship before dropping a torpedo. It would not be until mid-February 1942, that Smith was finally assigned as Director of the Plans Division in the office of the CNO. Immediately Smith investigated the previous *Projects Dog* and *Fox* and determined that the *Project Fox* tests using a drone equipped with TV guidance showed the greatest promise for operational use. In a report on 9 March 1942, to the CNO, Smith urged that "the possibilities of this weapon are such as to make it essential that regular peacetime developments be shortened and the TV guided drone be hurried along for combat use." After reading Smith's impressive report, the Vice Chief of Naval Operations, Adm. F.J. Home authorized Smith to prepare tests which would prove the drone's ability to accurately hit moving targets. On 14 March, on the advice of his Vice Chief, the Chief of Naval Operations signed off on Assault Drone attack tests.

On 1 April 1942, NAF *Project Fox* was transferred to Quonset Point, RI to conduct a test of a torpedo attack by a TG-2 torpedo drone

guided by television. On 9 April, the *Project Fox* unit was ready for the important trial with Smith's associate, Lt.(jg) M.B. Taylor manning the drone control station located in the Beech JRB (AAF/AT-11 Kansan) control plane piloted by Ens. S.E. Herbst. The destroyer, *USS Aaron Ward* was the target vessel which navigated parallel to the torpedo range off Narragansett Bay. The unmanned TG-2 torpedo bomber Assault Drone takeoff by radio-control at 1113 hours with its torpedo set to depth of 38 feet so it would pass under the destroyer. The TV camera in the drone picked up the target at four miles with the drone flying at 85 knots speed at an altitude of 130 feet. On the approach of the drone the destroyer turned north from an easterly course and increased speed to 15 knots. The control plane was eight miles from the target when Taylor, the drone control pilot, directed the drone to the torpedo release point about 300 yards astern of the destroyer. Taylor released the torpedo by radio and it passed directly under the full length of the *Aaron Ward* for another historic first successful air-to-surface guided missile attack.

On 19 April 1942, the NAF *Project Fox* unit conducted yet another successful historic test which confirmed the viability of crashing an Assault Drone into a moving target for the first time. A BG-1 drone equipped with a sensitive radio altimeter, radio-control, and television guidance was chosen to crash into a "battleraft" moving at eight knots. The drone tookoff by radio from Liveley, VA, by a field cart control pilot and was turned over to the control pilot, Lt.(jg.) Taylor, in the JRB. At five miles the drone picked up and relayed a good television picture of the target and the control plane turned away and Taylor was able to maneuver the drone by watching the television screen and directing it into a collision course by radio. Taylor was 11 miles away when the drone crashed the target raft.

In early May, films and oral presentations by Captains Smith and Fahrney on the notable 9 and 19 April tests were offered to Commander-in-Chief (COMCNCH) Adm. Ernest King and other chiefs of Navy Department Bureaus. Immediately after the presentation, Adm. King ordered his senior naval aviator and chief of BuAer, R.Adm. John Towers, to direct the design, development and procurement of an unmanned guided missile. King appointed Capt. Smith as O-in-C of the new *Project Option* (which absorbed *Project Dog*) which was under COMINCH Aide for Readiness, R.Adm. Willis Lee. Smith's basic duty was to develop an operational weapon from the experimental guided missile Assault Drone and to get the weapon ready for quantity combat deployment at the earliest possible date.

On 22 May 1942 the initial directive from CNO requested the BuAer to provide and train personnel for 18 Assault Drone squadrons, supply 162 control planes and 500 Assault Drones with 500 more in reserve. BuAer planners analyzed that a program of this large scale would require 1,300 naval aviators and 8,700 men; and to realize a production rate of 300 to 500 drones per month, an initial contract for 5,000 would be required at a cost of $235 million. Disagreement soon developed between Smith and BuAer Chief Adm. Towers due to the large scale of the program outlined by Smith and his staff and from CNO orders to carry them out. Towers was very opposed to a plan that would put a new weapon into mass production before it had been proven on a small scale in combat which would prove its effectiveness as well as to determine its performance and logistic requirements. More traditional high ranking naval officers also criticized the program as being a waste of critical material and manpower resources at the time US production and manpower capacity were already at their limits. On 29 June 1942, Towers requested that no more than 500 drones be manufactured and the CNO approved this request and suggested that the 500 drone program be comprised of the following: 100 TDNs, 200 TDRs, 100 TD2Rs, 100 TD3Rs with the TDNs designed and manufactured by NAF and the TDRs by Interstate Aircraft Co.

Plans for early combat trials were then prepared by Fahrney and Capt. C.L. Stevens, the Assistant Director of the Engineering Division in BuAer, and were approved by Adm. Towers. The combat tests were to be conducted as soon as the Assault Drones were completed. The tests were to be held in England were the drone could be flown into German submarine pens along the French coast and in the South Pacific where the weapon could be directed at the Japanese stronghold at Rabaul. However, when Capt. Smith became the Director of the Plans Division in the CNO, the early combat tests lost their sponsor and the BuAer's plans were abandoned.

In the in the meantime Radio Corp. of America made great strides in vastly improving radar-control, target-seeking, and target-homing equipment. The development of a sensitive radio reflection altimeter was assigned to Dr. Irving Wolff with electronic engineer R.C. Sanders, his project engineer. Once Sanders perfected the altimeter, dubbed a "*Sniffer*," he proposed its use to determine the presence of a target directly ahead by operating in the horizontal instead of the vertical plane. As well determining the presence of a target ahead, it could be adapted to launch a torpedo or drop a bomb at a selected distance from a target. Lt.(jg.) M.B. Taylor, suggested that right and left switching be added to make it a target-seeking apparatus. Taylor's suggestion was incorporated in the *Sniffer* and in the summer of 1942 was tested and performed effectively for ranges up to 4,000 yards.

Following these tests, RCA developed the RL 101 *Sniffers* and produced 10 which would, after detecting a target, lock on it and launch a torpedo or drop a bomb automatically at a preset distance from it. Concurrently, RCA established a parallel project developing the RL 102 *Supersniffer* that had all the features of the RL 101 but had the added ability of searching an arc and then locking upon a target. In November 1942, specifications for this device requiring range of two miles (later increased to six miles) were drafted and approved by the Bureau of Aeronautics.

By April 1943 the RL 101 satisfactorily released bombs at speeds between 130 and 180 knots and by May the minimum speed was decreased to 90 knots. Meanwhile, testing of the RL 102 showed it could hit ships and lighthouses at ranges of four to five miles when released at an altitude of 50 feet and hit a target at ranges of six to eight miles when released at 200 to 300 feet. However, the power and frequency of the *Supersniffer* equipment had to be changed to have it function at the six mile range from the shorter range. During tests a drone was flown into an area and searched for and locked upon a moving tanker at a distance of two miles for the first successful radar homing test on a moving target. At late Spring 1943 conference Wolff reported these RL 102's success and Fahrney emphasized its significance and that it should be used as a air-to-ground glide bomb and also as a surface air-to-air missile.

In December 1943, the first 12 Assault Drones were delivered to the Board of Inspection and Survey for tests. On 19 January, following these initial tests, the Board presented its report with the recommendation that an adequate control system should be developed immediately to be made available for future drone development. During the next five months, the 12 drones underwent further testing and Smith submitted a progress report on the developmental and service testing of the weapon including details of the guidance and control systems. Smith specified that the drone was superior to a gun, bomb, or torpedo in accuracy and was able to make an accurate horizontal approach against targets that were out of the range of other weapons. He recommended that this "airborne remote-control bomb be brought into action by trained crews and that it be used during periods of low visibility, boldly, and in sufficient force to gain full benefit of its power and surprise characteristics." USN C-in-C Adm. Ernest King was inclined to approve Smith's recommendations but first wanted information relative to organizational planning which was submitted to him in a plan which called for three combat units of 99 control planes, 891 drones, 441 officers, and 3,210 enlisted personnel, plus a training force of 12 control planes, 45 drones, 259 officers, and 2,238 enlisted personnel. On 23 March, King approved the plan with the admonishment that the secrecy of the weapon would be maintained and information concerning it limited to those who must know. On the same day, Adm. Home directed that the program be increased to a total of 3,000 Assault Drones at a delivery rate of 250 per month by June 1944. However, the Chief of the BuAer was concerned about the requirements of the program and the ability to provide the 3,000 drones, necessary pilots, and other personnel, without significant interference with the production of conventional aircraft. During subsequent discussion the requirement was reduced to 1,500 drones in addition to the 500 already under contract.

For combat these 2,000 drones had to be configured for and fitted with radio control equipment, radio altimeter, television, automatic bomb release device, radar beacon, and radar equipment. Contracts were let to the F.M. Fink Co., NY, to produce the frequency modulated radio control equipment and to RCA for the altimeter, television, automatic bomb release, and homing equipment. The RCA television equipment used frequencies of about 100 mc and later the company developed equipment in the band between 264 and 312 mc. Development of experimental television systems at about 1,000 mc was conducted by the Philco Corp., Philadelphia and at about 1800 mc by the General Electric Co., Schenectady, NY.

On 22 September 1943, Admiral King directed the Vice Chief of Naval Operations to coordinate and expedite all guided missile development and research projects and get them into operations ASAP. Adm. Home sent Smith to Pacific Fleet Headquarters to discuss the combat deployment of drone missiles in the PTO. At the time the war in the Pacific was moving forward with the use conventional weapons and Adm. Nimitz was advised against the experimental use of an unproven weapon that could interfere with normal operations. Nimitz did not want to commit personnel, materiel, or equipment, especially aircraft carriers, to the drone project. Furthermore, Nimitz' decision was based on the low speed and maneuverability of the Assault Drones and he specifically recommended that SBD Dauntless dive bombers , if suitable and available, be converted into drone missiles.

On 15 February 1944, Navy Capt. H.B. Temple was named the head of the guided missile program as part of the Office of the Chief of Naval Operations. Temple immediately reviewed program and in a memorandum to Adm. King he advised that, because "of the time and space requirements of the Pacific war, target availability, and because of the fast movement of our forces, a declining requirement for a weapon such as the Assault Drone was indicated." He recommended that the program be reduced considerably and changed to a "combat test" which was in agreement with the opinions of the Head of the Research and Development Branch of the Bureau of Aeronautics. Temple's recommendations were approved and in March 1944, a planning directive was issued reducing the number of Assault Drones to a total of 388. No reduction was made in the orders for electronic equipment because it was considered that these devices could be used in obsolete planes. On 10 March, the operating force for delivering the Assault Drone attacks was reduced to four operating and one headquarters squadron.

TDNs and TDRs Described

In April 1942, the Navy ordered two XTDR-1 Assault Drone prototypes and 100 TDR-1 Assault Drones designed to carry torpedoes from Interstate. Shortly before, the Naval Aircraft Factory in had also received an order for 100 production examples of the TDN-1. Despite the fact that the drones were designed as Assault Drones, the "TD" signified Target Drone, with

Naval Aircraft Factory TDN-1

the "N" identifying the Naval Aircraft Factory as its manufacturer while the "R" denoted Interstate Aircraft and Engineering Corporation of El Segundo, CA.

TDN-1

The 36 foot long TDN-1 was similar to the TDR-1 except for its high wing layout which spanned 50 feet. The drone had conventional vertical and horizontal stabilizers but had an unconventional fixed tricycle landing gear that was considered somewhat avant-garde for the time. It was a relatively simple, low-performance twin-engined aircraft with a TV

camera, radio-control equipment, and a 2,000 pound bomb load carried under its fuselage. The XTDN-1 originally was powered by Franklin O-300 engines but they were changed to the Lycoming O-435s on the production aircraft and would power the TDN at a cruising speed of 175 mph. In addition to the TV control system a standard cockpit was included for the tests or ferrying.

Delivery of only 114 total TDNs began in December 1942 and dragged on through 1943. The design was not well suited for mass production and the TDNs were used for evaluation and targets. Information on the testing and operational career of the TDN-1 is meager but the drone was most likely never used in combat.

TDR-1

The 5,900 pound TDR-1 closely resembled the TDN, except its 48 foot wing was low mounted. The TDR-1 used low-performance engines and relatively few strategic materials, so it didn't interfere with other wartime aircraft production. Two horizontal six cylinder 150 hp, Franklin engines or the flat, air-cooled 220 hp Lycoming 0-435-2s provided power. The latter version cruised at about 150 knots (173 mph) with a payload of a 2,000 pound bomb or torpedo over a range of 425 miles. For testing and ferrying, several TDR-1s had very simple standard open cockpits. The cockpit included an instrument panel with an air speed indicator, a ball and turn indicator, an altimeter, and a compass. However, to cut costs the engine gauges (oil pressure, cylinder head temperature, etc.) were located on the engine cowling, causing the pilot to look out four feet forward to read them. The pilot would only take over the controls if the remote control equipment failed or when the aircraft was to be landed. For unmanned operational missions, the cockpit canopy was replaced by a flush fairing and the landing gear was jettisoned after takeoff to increase the TDR's terminal velocity (150 knots) when crashing the target.

Piloted TDR-1 For testing and ferrying, several TDR-1s had very simple standard open cockpits. The pilot would only take over the controls when the remote control equipment failed or when the aircraft was to be landed. (USN)

TDR-1

Unmanned TDR-1 For unmanned operational missions, the cockpit canopy was replaced by a flush fairing and the landing gear was jettisoned after takeoff. The TDR-1 was to carry a 2,000 pound bomb. (USN)

Operational TDR-1 This a is a well-known PR photo issued by manufacturer Interstate to promote its formidable drone carrying a torpedo with the port for a TV camera located above the port engine. (USN)

The Navy wished to deploy the **TDN-1 drone** off carriers and conducted tests from the *USS Sable*, a converted Great Lakes paddle-wheel steamship in 1943. (USN)

The Navy awarded Interstate a contract to build 500 TDR-1 drones, the version that would see combat. The TDR was practical to manufacture with a steel tubing frame covered by molded wood. The steel tubing frame was built by the Schwinn Bicycle Company and musical instrument manufacturer Wurlitzer was the subcontractor for the wood framework. Brunswick-Balko-Collondor Company and the American Aviation Corporation were associate contractors in the assembly with P.M. Link, RCA, Philco, and GE supplying the electronic equipment. A total of 189 TDRs were built by the Interstate, Dekalb, IL plant and only one exists today and is displayed at the Naval Aviation Museum at Pensacola.

In April 1943 the USN consigned a single TDR-1 to the AAF which tested it as the XBQ-4 but did not continue the program after the initial tests in December. The TD2R was a proposed TDR variant mounting two 450 hp Franklin 0-805-2 engines. The two XTD2R-1 prototypes were cancelled by the Navy and completed as the XTD3R-1. The AAF was interested in the XTD2R-1 as the XBQ-5 but did not purchase any. The TD3R was the last of the TDR variants and was powered by two 450 hp Wright R-975-13 radial engines. Three XTD3R-1s and one XTD3R-2 were built but a batch of 40 TD3R-1 production drones was cancelled. The AAF allocated the designations XBQ-6 for the prototypes and BQ-6A for production models but did not obtain any BQ-6 aircraft before the program was cancelled in 1944.

TDR-1 Deployment

Training took place at Clinton, OK, using Twin Beech SNBs (AT-7 and AT-11precursor) as the control aircraft and the Vultee BT-17 training aircraft as the radio-controlled drones. One the TDRs began to come off Interstate's DeKalb assembly line they were ferried to Oklahoma. The AT-11s were replaced by TBM-1Cs which carried the radio controls in the forward cockpit while these controls were duplicated in the rear cockpit along with the BLOCK TV monitor and radar scope. A retractable radome under the rear fuselage held the receiver for all three.

The Special Air Task Force (SATFOR) was officially established in the summer of 1943, was comprised of Special Task Air Groups called STAGs with each STAG comprised of two to three squadrons. Three STAGs were established initially under the command of Cdr. Oscar Smith. STAG-1 was organized under Cdr. Thomas South for carrier-based missions. STAG-2 was intended for service in the ETO. STAG-3 was established later, and records are vague concerning its mission. It joined STAGs -1 and -2 at the newly built Naval Air Station at Clinton, OK. STAG-2 and -3 were intended to use the next generation 200 knot TD2R-1s which were to be guided by controllers in medium bombers . This intended use was never realized and in March 1944, two months before the Normandy invasion, STAGs -2 and -3 were disbanded.

Only STAG-1 was to see action. From Clinton, OK the unit was transferred to Traverse City, MI. Grand Traverse Bay served as the training site for deck and catapult launchings of TDRs from the training carrier *Sable*, a converted side-wheel passenger steamer sailing on Lake Michigan. On 10 August 1943, STAG-1 executed the first carrier launch of a radio-controlled drone which was a TDR-1. STAG-1's subsequent training catapult launches included fully loaded drones carrying 2,000 pound bombs. The training phase also involved launching six fully loaded TDR-1s from an escort carrier in the Chesapeake Bay.

Meanwhile, in 1943, new orders trimmed Smith's *Project Option* originally sought after 5,000 drones to 2,500 drones, and then to only 500, plus 162 control aircraft. On 10 November 1943, a conference was held at the headquarters of Commander in Chief (C-in-C) US Fleet, Adm. Chester Nimitz, in Hawaii to discuss the future deployment of Assault Drones in the Pacific. At the meeting was: Adm. Nimitz, V.Adm. Towers (newly appointed as the Commander Air Forces Pacific), V.Adm. John

Newton, R.Adm. Charles McMorris, Capt. Forrest Sherman, and Lt.Cdr. Oscar Smith. Smith fervently outlined and defended his drone program but openly clashed with Towers who again questioned the worth of consigning indispensable resources to Smith's unproven project. This meeting, perhaps influenced by the piqued Towers, determined that before the drones (TDR-1s) went into combat the following recommendations were to be fulfilled:

1) The drone had to demonstrate advantages over weapons in use.
2) The method of deployment had to be established.
3) The speed and maneuverability of the drones had to be increased as slow speeds reduced it effectiveness.
4) Combat drones of high speed and maneuverability were to be developed.
5) SBD dive bombers , if suitable and available, were to be converted to drones.

Additionally, Adm. Towers called attention to the fact that the already heavy responsibility on every air facility in the Pacific to furnish conventional weapons to fulfill its normal combat tasks made it imprudent to provide any shipping space or any support for operational testing of the unproven TDR-1. Furthermore, as part of a 25 November 1943 report to Adm. King, Adm. Nimitz stated, "While deeply interested in the development of new weapons of this type, we lack carriers, landing fields, and other facilities to try out unproven weapons." Thus, Tower's recommendations seemingly effectively blocked the deployment of the TDR-1s in combat even though Smith backed their use during low visibility or in association with conventional bombing and torpedo attacks. Smith pointed out that targets could be attacked with greater accuracy and with less exposure to the attacking force and at a lesser cost than any other weapon currently available.

During the Tower/Smith debate, STAG-1, including a headquarters squadron and two combat squadrons, had been transferred to Monterey, CA, in November 1943 for training in anticipation of being deployed to the Pacific. In February 1944, Adm. King (COMINCH) and Admiral Home (CNO) reviewed the objections to the deployment of STAG-1 to the Pacific and on 24 February King directed C-in-C Pac that "experience with the STAG-1 drones must be gained methodically but without delay" in order that when Germany was defeated; large numbers of long range B-17s and B-24s would become available for use as drones, using B-29s as control planes in the Pacific. King ordered STAG-1 to provide tests of this weapon in Central or South Pacific ASAP and ordered Cdr. Smith as the CO of the newly organized SATFOR to report to C-in-C Pac and organize a combat trial of the Special Task Air Group 1 using TDR drones and TBM control planes. While Admirals King and Home had recommended the deployment of Assault Drones and Nimitz reluctantly agreed. However, Towers as the Chief of BuAer was opposed to any further prototyping of the SBD Dauntless as a drone until operational experience with the TDR-1 was successful and confirmed that there was a justification for it.

V.Adm. Raymond Spruance, Commander of the 5th Fleet, was in Pearl Harbor planning the attack on the Marshall Islands and became acquainted with SATFOR and the TDR drone project. Spruance expressly requested that the drones be deployed during the planned invasion on Eniwetok and his suggestion was approved by Nimitz and King. STAG-1 with the SATFOR staff was to be moved to one of the airfields in the Gilbert Islands and be staged forward to Majaro to assist in the attack on Eniwetok in late May 1944. Unfortunately, for STAG-1, the initial Marshall Islands' campaign was so successful that the date of the attack on Eniwetok was moved forward making it impossible to transfer STAG-1 in time to join in the campaign.

For the next five months, STAG-1 remained in Monterey while their future deployment was continually being deliberated. Adm. King supported their immediate and extensive use while Adm. Towers maintained that they should be further tested under controlled conditions and then utilized on a limited basis only after Cdr. Oscar Smith went to Pearl Harbor to personally request the transfer of an escort carrier for the project. To make the situation more difficult for Smith the ComAirPac recommended that the SATFOR project be disbanded.

STAG-1 Combat Operations
Smith's request for a valuable carrier was denied and he was ordered to report to Adm. William Halsey, CO of the South Pacific area. Halsey then sent Smith to R.Adm. E.L. Gunther, CO of the Air Forces, South Pacific, to discuss the fate of STAG-1. On March 18, Gunther approved the Russell Islands as a SATFOR base for STAG-1 operations. By mid-May 1944 most of STAG-1's personnel and materiel, plus personnel of two squadrons from the disbanded STAG-2 and STAG-3 left Alameda, CA aboard the carrier *Marcus Island*. Several days later, the remainder of the unit's personnel, materiel, and a dozen crated TDRs followed on two transport ships.

Drone Preparation
The drone and its components were packed in several crates and were unpacked and reassembled after which the electronics were installed, calibrated, and checked. The drone was ground checked as an aircraft and then its radio control and other electronics were checked by equipment in a command car. The command car was a panel truck which could communicate with the control aircraft in the air and also was outfitted to control the drone for ground check out or prior to handing off the airborne drone. After the ground checks the drone was flight checked by the check pilot as a conventional aircraft. Then the check pilot served as passenger while the mothership controlled it as a drone. The check pilot had to be constantly alert to take over control as the new electronics and control mechanisms were unreliable. An important electronics check was of the Radio Altimeter (ACE) which was important in controlling the drone's plunge toward the target. ACE was a shoe-box sized container mounted inside the fuselage that contained the altimeter scaled from 0 to 1,000 feet and worked off two antennas (one forward facing and the other aft on the aircraft's ventral centerline). The altimeter control box allowed the check pilot testing the drone to set his altitude in 100 foot intervals from 600 down to 100 feet to check the accuracy of a drone being radio-controlled into a target.

TBM/TDR Control
Preliminary tests on the Russell Islands were conducted using Douglas SBD Dauntless dive bombers as the motherships with an ungainly control box suspended under the port wing. Soon, STAG-1's motherships were modified Grumman and General Motors (built under license) TBM Avenger torpedo bombers. A large radome which protruded about a foot out of the fuselage when retracted and extended several feet in flight was installed in the Avenger's radio position. The radome contained the radio and TV receiver/transmitter and did not appreciably affect the Avenger's speed or performance. The radio controls were carried in both the forward and rear cockpit but the rear cockpit also had the BLOCK television receiver (scope) and radar installed. Besides the radioman and gunner, the TBM crew included two carrier qualified pilots: the normal or Control Plane Pilot (CPP) who sat in the front cockpit and the drone Control Pilot (DCP) who sat next to the radioman cramped in the rear cockpit with the TV control equipment. The CPP gained control of the drone after takeoff after the command car guided the drone into the air. The CPP jettisoned

its landing (really a takeoff) gear and then guided it until it was within television range of the target where the DCP would take control. Once the DCP gained control the CPP Avenger pilot could turn away to a safe distance from the target area while the DCP continued to guide the drone's attack via television. The DCP was entirely dependent upon the picture on his seven inch CPV-59 television screen that was transmitted by the TV camera and transmitter located in the drone's nose. To operate his TV and radar set the DCP would lower his head under a black drape to block out the sun and turn the sets on. The only input to the target the DCP had were the TV image, the position indicated on the radar scope, and instrument repeaters on the control panel. Once the DCP acquired control of the drone using a joy stick, he was able to control its attitude. This control was supplemented by the automatic control system based in the electronic "telephone box" that was distinguished by a telephone dial which controlled a number of pre-programmed commands. These commands included left and right rudder, up and down elevator, left and right bank, increase and decrease throttle, ACE on and off, BLOCK on and off, step altitude (e.g. if the operator dialed "1" the drone would fly at 50 feet, "2" at 100 feet, etc.), and four irreversible functions; drop landing gear, arm bomb, drop bomb, and detonation. Each TV transmitter and receiver operated on one fixed channel and the transmitter had only four pre-channels which allowed only four drones to be operated at once without interference. Several types of smoke tanks and generators were tried to more easily follow the TDR drone to the target.

STAG-1 Operations
STAG-1, divided into two squadrons (VK-11 and VK-12), was based at Sunlight Field, a 4,400 x 150 foot coral strip, on Banika Island, which was a small island in the Russell Islands group in the Solomons, 25 nautical miles off the northwest tip of Guadalcanal. Though STAG-1 had been designated and trained for carrier operations, it was now land-based. By mid-1944 the Pacific war was being fought far to the north but STAG-1 needed to demonstrate that their drones could be tactically effective. Drone test flights began on 20 June, and six days later the technical staff successfully achieved the first radio-controlled TDR-1 takeoff from the airfield. Through the last few days of June and much of July, numerous test and practice flights were flown from Sunlight airfield under the codename *"Affirm."* After four weeks of training, eight TBMs were ready as control aircraft and 12 TDRs as drones. Eighty three of the 92 controlled takeoffs were successful and on the others the safety pilot had to take over. During testing two Avenger control aircraft were lost as were several TDRs. Weather occasionally was a factor in canceling flights as tropical rain squalls would suddenly appearing while winds of over 16 knots made unmanned takeoff very hazardous. On the 92 total test flights 45.3% were judged to be successful, 77.3% of the altimeter controlled flights were successful; followed closely by 76.3% of the radio-controlled flights; and then by 63.9% of the television controlled flights. Cdr. Oscar Smith reported that the radio-control equipment, although successful due to the constant efforts of STAG-1 engineers, was "fragile, cheap, and should be entirely redesigned in order to make them more rugged, more reliable, and less liable to interference with and from other equipment."

Smith concluded that although the TDR was limited by the specifications to which it was built performed "with few minor exceptions….has established a good record for reliability. It carries its full load without apparent effort. The manufacturer has done an excellent job in producing the TDR-1 as a drone, considering the many restrictions imposed on him as to the quality of parts and non-interference with the regular airplane programs."

In their log, July 30 was officially termed STAG-1's "D-Day," as it was the date of a scheduled demonstration for Adm. Gunther and

Control Aircraft

The **Douglas SBD** was used as an early control aircraft. The crude box installed on the Devastator's port wing contained a TV camera and a radio transmitter. (USN)

In addition to the standard pilot, radioman, and gunner crew; for TDR missions the **Grumman TBM-1C** carried a Drone Controller who shared the rear cockpit with the radioman. The photo shows the radio and TV receiver/transmitter deployed in a retractable radar dome from the rear fuselage. (USN)

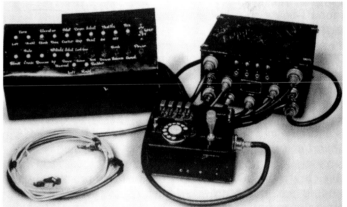

Control apparatus in the TBM cockpit. The joystick/telephone box (center), the telephone box command control box (left), and radio control box (right). (USN)

The **cockpit of the TBM** contained the "state-of-the-art" control equipment which included the BLOCK TV monitor (mid-right) and a central joystick controller located on the so-called "telephone box." (USN)

TBR Drone

STAG-1TDR Drone Edna III being prepared for operations. A fairing was placed over the cockpit while a 2,000 pound bomb was loaded under the fuselage. (USN)

Since the bomb was not dropped it was strapped to a special cradle under the TDR's fuselage. (USN)

Several types of **smoke dispensers** were tried to more easily follow the TDR drone to the target. (USN)

The small **CVR television camera** is being installed in the TDR nose while the other BLOCK equipment is tested. (USN)

A TBM control aircraft follows the TDR drone just after takeoff. Soon the CCP would jettison the drone's landing gear and guide it until it was within television range of the target. (USN)

USMC Maj.Gen. Ralph Mitchell, CO Solomon Island Air Forces. Four control Avengers and a standby for each and four drones carrying 2,000 pound bombs with a standby for each were scheduled to attack the hulk of the Japanese merchant ship *Yamazuki Maru* which was beached near Guadalcanal's northwestern tip, Cape Esperance, 34 miles away.

Five drones were controlled in their takeoff in early afternoon but the nose wheel of one drone collapsed on takeoff. The four drones arrived over the target area with their control TBMs following six to eight miles away. At 1359 the first TDR-1 dove toward the target vessel and hit the port side ripping open a 25x8 foot hole. Three minutes later, the second drone just missed the ship's superstructure by five feet and crashed into a coconut grove beyond. At 1405 the third drone dove in and hit the ship a glancing blow but its demolition bomb did not explode. Ten minutes later the fourth drone which was the standby, slammed into the port side and exploded at the deck line causing another large hole that was similar to the first.

Encouraged by the success of the 30 July test, Smith left for Pearl Harbor with film footage of the test and the endorsement of Adm. Gunther to promote the SATFOR project. He wished to expand the project and to propose the carrier flight deck testing of a SBD scout bomber modified

The Japanese freighter *Yamazuki Maru* beached off Cape Esperance, Guadalcanal was used for the 30 July 1944 TDR demonstration during which two of four hit the target tearing open large holes in the hull. (USN)

The view of the *Yamazuki Maru* that the DCP in the TBM saw in his television monitor as the TDR closed to crash into it. (USN)

Still photo from movie film of the first TDR drone as it dove toward the target vessel which it would soon crash on its port side ripping open a large hole. (USN)

into a drone. Once back at Pearl Harbor Smith not only met strong resistance to his proposals but was transferred back to America when he objected, perhaps too strongly! Cdr. Robert Jones became SATFOR's acting Commander on 5 September 1944 and also was determined to use STAG-1's Assault Drones in combat operations. Films and reports of the July 30 test had impressed USMC Brig.Gen. Claude Larkin Commander of Air Forces in the Northern Solomons and Jones gained approval for a 30 day combat trial.

On 19 September STAG-1 left Banika to mount combat operations from Stirling Island, located 300 miles to the northeast and only 50 miles south of Bougainville. On 27 September, STAG-1 launched the first TDR-1 attack on an active enemy target which was a Japanese anti-aircraft battery located onboard a 460 foot merchant vessel beached in the shallows off the southern tip of Bougainville near Kahili. Each of the four TDR-1s carried a 2,000 pound GP bomb. One drone was lost on the way but the remaining three reached the target. One crashed into the ship's port quarter and detonated; one hit the water 30 yards astern but its bomb failed to detonate; and the last made a direct hit amidships at the main deck and destroyed the AA battery.

Four days later, STAG-1's control planes successfully guided four TDRs to AA installations on Ballale and Poporang Islands off the south Bougainville coast. The first drone dove through heavy AA fire and exploded among three heavy AA positions. The second exploded within 100 feet of heavy and automatic gun positions at the southwest end of Ballale's runway. The third and fourth exploded among heavy gun positions located on a ridge on the northern portion of Poporang Island.

That afternoon STAG-1 launched four additional TDR-ls into Japanese AA positions on Kanga Hill on South Bougainville. This mission was not quite as successful as the first. In the midst of AA fire, the first drone exploded below the Kanga Hill gun emplacements. The second drone hit within 50 feet of the guns but failed to detonate. The third struck near a town but failed to detonate while the fourth exploded four miles north of the hill.

STAG-1 moved to Green Island, about 100 miles north of Bougainville which placed the unit within range of the major Japanese base at Rabaul on the eastern end of New Britain. On 5 October STAG-1 launched four drones against the Karavia supply caves overlooking Rabaul Harbor. Because of radio frequency control problems, two drones were lost on route to Rabaul. The third drone flew through anti-aircraft fire and exploded in the area of cave entrances. The final drone overflew the target area and hit near Japanese barge dockage.

Four days later, four TDR-1s were launched against the Matupi Island Bridge that connected the island in Rabaul Harbor to the mainland. Two drones were shot down by heavy anti-aircraft fire; one exploding 1,000 feet from the bridge and the other exploding near a cluster of AA emplacements. The third was thought to have been shot down while the fourth crashed in St. George Channel between Rabaul and neighboring New Ireland Island.

On October 15, four more TDR-ls were guided to Rabaul for another attack on the unscathed Matupi Bridge. One crashed en route due to equipment failure. Another went down on land south of the target when the television signal to its control plane failed. The two remaining drones crashed off-target, due to problems that were traced to TV signal failures.

Two Days later, four STAG-1 drones attacked a target area near East Rabaul Town. On route, equipment failure caused one drone to crash off Cape St. George on the southern tip of New Ireland. A second hit its target, a building in East Rabaul Town. The third blew up in the junction of Rabaul Town's two main thoroughfares, setting off a huge secondary explosion. The final TDR-1 crashed into buildings on a ridge west of town.

The next day, three control plane/drone elements attacked the lighthouse on New Ireland's Cape St. George which was 30 feet high and about 10 feet wide at its base. One drone crashed on route and the other two hit the target area but only one of their bombs exploded, leaving the lighthouse still standing.

On 19 October, STAG-1 again attacked the gun positions on Ballale, using a variation in the usual method of attack. A single TDR-1 drone was dispatched, armed with two 500 pound bombs in the fuselage and four 100 pound bombs under each wing for a total payload of 1,800 pounds. But before reaching its target, the drone was lost because of mechanical problems. An identically loaded TDR-1 made a more successful solo attack that same afternoon. The drone control pilot remotely dropped the two 500 pound bombs that landed just short of the gun positions and then hit them with eight 100 pound bombs, dropped in two clusters. For the first time the drone was used not as a self-destroying guided bomb, but as a pilotless bomber. The drone's left engine was hit by AA fire and 20 minutes later it crashed.

The following day STAG-1 further refined their attack method with an ambitious plan by using three TDR-1s which would act as guided bombers dropping their two 500 pound bombs on the Ballale Island gun positions but then would fly on to crash into the derelict Japanese cargo ship *Kahili Maru*. One drone crashed on route. The second made an accurate bomb run over the gun emplacements but before it could be directed to attack the ship remote control was lost and that drone crashed on South Bougainville. The third TDR-1 straddled the gun positions on its bomb run and then accurately struck the cargo ship at the deck line amidships.

On 23 October, three drones carrying 2,000 pound bombs attacked the beached *Kahili Maru*. Control of one drone failed on the way and it exploded just west of the Shortland Islands just south of Bougainville. The second drone hit the target at its deck line while the third overshot and detonated in the sea. That afternoon three more drones attacked beached ships in the area. Two made direct hits while the third overshot its target.

Four more drones were expended on 26 October. One crashed into the lighthouse at Cape St. George on New Ireland and destroyed it. Two of the other three hit their targets in Rabaul Town. When the fourth TDR-1 had signal trouble over Rabaul Harbor, it was redirected to its secondary target, AA positions on Duke of York Island outside Rabaul Harbor.

On 27 October 1944, the Navy suddenly and unexpectedly cancelled the SATFOR Project. Part of the Stirling Island and Green Island detachments were returned to the main base at Banika to complete their temporary duty. On the next day two TDR-ls from Stirling were guided along Bougainville's southwest coast as target drones for Army AA gunners on the shore. The Army gunners were finally able to shoot down the first TDR-1 on its fifth run and managed to blast the second out of the air on its third pass.

A Summary of STAG-1's Operations

All controlled takeoffs were successful. Of the 46 drones lunched, two were lost on the way to the target due to interference believed to be from friendly communications in the area whose frequencies overlapped with those employed by the drones. Seven drones were lost on the way to the target due to equipment failure. The remaining 37 drones reached the target area and were launched into attacks. A large number of the 37 encountered medium to intense AA fire and three were shot down before reaching their targets. Despite their low speed the drones were not easy targets for AA fire as many passed through AA barrages to hit their targets. Five suffered TV failures and could not locate their targets. The remaining 35 completed their attacks. So by most standards, the SATFOR program had been a success as 46% of the drones launched by STAG-1 made hits or damaging near-hits. And not a single American had been killed or even injured on any of the drone attacks, many of them against heavily defended areas.

In a report to Adm. Halsey on 30 October 1944, Brig.Gen. Claude Larkin, Commander of Air Forces in the Northern Solomons concluded:

"During the period of concentrated operations against enemy targets, the STAG-1 Detachment was confronted with many difficult technical and operational problems. Operating from forward fields from which heavy routine combat missions were being flown involved a high degree of coordination with other units. Due to the uncertainty of weather, availability of diversion aircraft, limited periods of radio silence on control frequencies and similar features directly involving these operations, it was often necessary to plan attacks hastily and to change pre-arranged details at the last minute. The STAG-1 Detachment, with no previous actual combat experience with drones, carried out its difficult operational and highly technical missions in an admiral manner. It is considered that valuable practical experience was gained during the one month period of combat operations and that the knowledge gained by this unit may well serve to advance the development of this specialty."

The Navy's attention became focused on the *Bat* radio-controlled glide bomb and all the useful technology the SATFOR project had collected was assigned a top-secret classification which essentially consigned it to be buried but to have profound effects on US post-war guided missile development. The SATFOR project was not publicly mentioned until 1952 and was not officially declassified until 1966. On 5 July 1990, SATFOR was finally officially recognized by Secretary of the Navy Henry Garrett who stated, "The vision, determination, and dedication with which you performed your secret duties during World War II laid the groundwork for today's modern cruise missile." The SATFOR project's only remaining TDR-1 was found in Oklahoma long after the end of the war and is on display at the National Museum of Naval Aviation in Pensacola, FL.

SWOD (Special Weapons Ordnance Device) Series
Visual Tracking and Radio Control
Dragon
The first of these visual tracking and radio control gliders was the *Dragon* (also known as the "Dryden Bomb") which was 14 feet long, had a 12 foot wingspan, and could carry a 2,000 pound bomb against shipping. Only a few were built or tested as the project was terminated as the controlling aircraft had to follow too closely to the *Dragon* to guide it accurately and was thus vulnerable to enemy AA fire.

Television Controlled Systems
Once America entered the war, David Sarnoff, President of RCA, pointed out that his company had been engaged in airborne television and guided missile research since 1935 when Ray Kell began work on

an "aerial torpedo with an electric eye" based on a design proposal that Dr. Vladimir Zworykin submitted to RCA on 25 April 1934. Zworykin's proposal essentially outlined a program for the control of a guided missile by television. Sarnoff set up a meeting for Zworykin with Navy Admirals Ernest King and Harold Stark and Army Generals Oscar Westover and W.H. Tschappat who would pledge financial support for the development of the project.

In 1935 Kell and assistants, Waldamar Poch and Henry Kasanowski, began work on a lightweight aerial reconnaissance television unit that would be first demonstrated in 1937 using a Model 1850 Iconoscope mounted in a Ford Tri-motor. Work continued on the development of a smaller and lighter television unit for use in the smaller aircraft that would be used as guided missiles. The work culminated on 6 March 1940 when the unit received public attention during a demonstration by RCA and NBC. The small camera and transmitter were mounted in an American Airlines' Boeing Mainliner which took off from LaGuardia Field and circled New York City for 45 minutes at 2,000 feet. The TV camera transmitted very clear pictures to the ground. The success of the demonstration suggested the possible future adaptation of the "tele-plane" in wartime, for reconnaissance flights, bombing operations, and map-making and the Zworykin design was approved for advanced development.

In August 1940 RCA, confident in its television/radio control, discussed the development of the aerodynamic aspects of the aerial torpedo with Richard Tolman of the NDRC. In January 1941 RCA began to develop television control with the Dr. Hugh Dryden team at the Aerodynamics Section of the National Bureau of Standards (NBS). Between August 1941 and September 1942, the RCA Research Laboratories were consolidated into the world's largest radio laboratory at Princeton, NJ with Otto Schairer as its General Manager and Vice-President; Ralph Beal as its Director of all Research and Development; C.B. Jolliffe as Chief Engineer of the Frequency Bureau; and Elmer Engstrom as overall Director assisted by Browder Thompson and Zworykin.

Robin
The summer of 1942 saw the nadir of German U-Boat successes with reports of ships sunk just off the American coast being a daily occurrence. In the previous year, the NDRC and NBS with BuOrd sponsorship was contracted to develop a glide bomb for use against enemy shipping and submarines using television guidance.

The first television-guided Dryden Glide Bomb test project, called *Robin*, began in January 1941 under the NBS and RCA. Preliminary tests of both 7/10 scale and full scale models of the *Robin* were conducted but Dryden and the NDRC were under funded and the development of the final airframe portion of the project proceeded very slowly. Meanwhile, due to Dryden's slow progress, RCA contracted an outside manufacturer to complete the airframe which subsequently was a failure. The Bureau of Standards took offense and because it was providing project funding took complete control of the project and contracted Vidal Research to build the airframes.

Dragon **Radio-Controlled Dryden Glide Bomb** (USN)   *Robin* **Television-Controlled Dryden Glide Bomb** (USN)

On 18 October 1943 the NDRC tested an early *Pelican* carried by an AAF B-17 against a barge on Chesapeake Bay. The *Pelican* (arrow) in the film still overflew the barge and crashed into the Bay. (AAF)

Early **Pelican** ground tests (Dr. Hugh Dryden standing on left). (USN)

Although the RCA television system functioned properly; it did have an average error of 600 feet with some of this error due to the method of attack. At the 11° glide attack angle the target appeared to be foreshortened to the TV operator and a small compensating steering error in range caused a larger error at the target. RCA was able to produce a smaller iconoscope using electron multiplication which gave an eight fold increase in sensitivity but this set was still was below RCA's goals and further development would be needed. The Radar Homing System (RHS) developed by the MIT Radiation Laboratory had shown it was able to perform better than the *Robin's* RCA TV/manual guidance system so the TV research for the *Robin* was suspended and transferred to the more promising *ROC* guided vertical bomb series. Meanwhile, the *Robin's* airframe was used to continue testing Radar Homing System (RHS) systems.

After the reorganization of the NDRC in December 1942, radar development continued at the MIT Radiation Laboratory and a closer coordination with the Navy was established. The BuOrd formed an Experimental Unit at the Bureau of Standards and a Field Test Unit at Warren Grove, NJ. The experimental design and testing role of the RHS radar was assigned to Dr. Dryden's group and their *Robin* airframe while assembly and mechanical support were furnished by the Navy.

Following the *Robin's* initial tests and transfer of the RCA television unit to the *ROC* project, Capt. Dundas Tucker and Lt.Cdr. Dan Jurias of BuOrd proposed using the *Robin* glider equipped with a Radar Homing System being developed by MIT and carrying a payload of a 325 pound depth charge to be used against vulnerable surfaced U-Boats at night. The RHS weapon had three possible methods of operation: a transmitter

located on a mother aircraft could guide the weapon (e.g. *Pelican*), an enemy radar transmitter could be the target (e.g. *Moth*), or it could carry its own transmitter (e.g. *Bat*).

SWOD Mk7 *Pelican*

In 1942 the NDRC began the development of radar-guided anti-shipping glide bombs carrying a 325 pound depth charge payload for the Navy to be used against submarines and small surface vessels by Navy TBFs, PBYs, or PBMs. A 600 pound depth charge could be carried by the larger PBY or PBM. The project, called *Pelican* (originally designated as the *Bomb Mk55*), consisted of an airframe developed by the National Bureau of Standards. *Pelican* used a semi-active RHS radar seeker that homed on radar reflections from the target which was illuminated by the AN/APS-2 radar.

The *Pelican* glide bomb had a 10 foot wing span carrying a 325 pound depth charge or 500 pound bomb. The *Pelican* used elevon controls which were merely ailerons operating as flaps or spoilers as well as conventional ailerons. It had a proportional control system which allowed high rates of turn correction with large course deviation and conversely low rates with small course deviations. The glide ratio was 3.5 to 5.5 to 1.

Components included:

Airframe	SWOD (air stabilized) MkI2
RHS	SWOD (radio receiver) MkI carried on board
Gyros	SWOD (gyro panel) Mk6
Demolition Unit	MkI17
Fuses	Mk235-236
Bomb	500 pound GP

SWOD MK7 *Pelican* Radar-Guided Missile (USN)

Two 1,000 pound Pelican MkIIs carried under outboard the engine nacelles of a **PV-1** Lockheed Ventura (B-34). (USN)

In 25 radar test flights in early 1943 good results were obtained, initially against a target beacon and later against a reflector hung from a barrage balloon. By that autumn 35 more tests, using improved techniques and refined instrumentation, were conducted with increasingly better results. On 18 October 1943 the NDRC tested an early *Pelican* carried by an AAF B-17 against a barge anchored in Chesapeake Bay. The B-17's radar search set illuminated the target and the *Pelican* was released at about 5,000 feet at 3.5 to 4 miles range. The missile passed 15 to 20 feet over the barge and crashed into the Bay about 100 yards beyond. The near miss was attributed to the *Pelican* being too close to the target for the search radar to illuminate it properly during the end of the attack run as the set could only be depressed 50° to 60°. Despite this failure the Radiation Laboratory then terminated the tests as it considered the development of the radar homing device to be fully evolved.

By 1943 BuOrd wished to extend the *Pelican's* use against surface vessels of all sizes by increasing the warhead size to 1,000 pounds using the AN M-65 bomb and a larger glider body. The Bureau of Standards' Ralph Lamm was named project engineer, assisted by Perry Stout, at the MIT Field Experimental Station. Lamm's group was to continue pure research and conduct the project engineering phase to build standardized enlarged production models. With any design change concomitant teething problems arose which were finally resolved and the airframe, radar system, and controls were all put into production. The NDRC placed an order with Timm Aircraft Corp. for tooling and 20 enlarged *Pelican* glider bodies to be completed by the end of January 1944 at a cost of $800 to $1,000 per unit.

The enlarged *Pelican* was to be air-launched at 205 to 230 mph by a Lockheed PV-1P (P for *Pelican*) and later by a North American PBJ (Navy version of the B-25) each equipped with search radar, shackles, and control equipment as the carrier aircraft. The carrying aircraft were to be ready for tests beginning in April or May 1944. The PV-1P (also known as the B-34 or Lockheed Ventura) could carry either two 1,000 pound *Pelican* Mk IIs or a single 1,500 pound *Pelican* Mk III. The *Pelican* Mk II was originally designated as the *Bomb Mk55*, but the 1,500 pound Mk III version was later redesignated as SWOD Mk7. This is the only known SWOD designation for *Pelican* but possibly the 1,000 pound Mk II type received one of the earlier SWOD numbers.

The first tests of the Mk II and III *Pelicans* in June 1944, using the old Liberty ship *James Longstreet* as a target, were dismal failures, as all

six production models failed to home on the target. Lamm and Stout were able to determine and correct the relatively minor problems and the first successful *Pelican* tests were conducted at the end of July. Two of four missiles hit the *Longstreet* and subsequent tests demonstrated a 30 to 40% success ratio.

Meanwhile, the Navy had planned to send two squadrons of PV-1Ps to the Pacific in mid-1944. Crews were trained and the PV-ls modified to carry three *Pelicans* but work was stopped when it was found that the PV-1 had insufficient range to reach its target when loaded with two or three externally mounted Pelicans. Soon the Navy Brass decided that the *Bat* SWOD project was more promising and terminated the *Pelican* program.

Both the *Bat* and *Pelican* used the same type airframe, controls, and radar receiver. The *Bat's* advantages were that it carried a 1,000 pound warhead and contained its RHS on board requiring no maneuvering of the mother aircraft after release to radar illuminate the target for precise control by the radar operator. However, the *Bat's* combat readiness would later be delayed by its untried, self-contained, radar transmitter. The advantages of the *Pelican* over the *Bat* were that it had twice the effective range, was lighter, carried less expensive expendable equipment, and was not hindered by increased signal strength as it approached the target. The major factor in the Navy's decision to use the *Bat* was its inflexible requirement that targets be positively identified before attack and two advantages of the *Pelican*, its ability to attack from 20 miles out and through cloud or overcast, were voided by this restriction. Although the defects in the *Pelican* project were minor and it was near operational status, BuOrd decided to concentrate on the *Bat* project.

On 18 September 1944, the production program (3,000 at 300 per month) specified in October 1943 was terminated. The project was returned to developmental status and sent to the Special Weapons Test and Tactical Evaluation Unit at Traverse City, MI, for further testing. *Pelican* was utilized as a test vehicle there but this phase was also soon terminated. Many experts considered that if equivalent time and effort were expended on the *Pelican* project it could have been a better weapon than the favored *Bat* project.

Once the *Pelican* program was cancelled, a number of airframes remained and a few were used in the *Moth* missile program and several hundred others were converted to anti-aircraft targets, designated as *Vultures* in late 1944. These sand-filled targets were dropped in a high angle dive from patrol bombers which orbited above the fleet and provided a simulation of Kamikaze attacks for shipboard gunnery practice.

An interesting aside to *Pelican* project is the pigeon-guided missile. In early 1942, renowned behavioral scientist B.F. Skinner studied the use of trained pigeons to guide the *Pelican* (described in Chapter 17).

Falcon

The *Falcon* was a *Bat* or *Pelican* airframe powered by jet or rocket motors to increase its range but little else is known about this weapon which probably did not progress beyond the drawing board or scale model stage.

Moth

The *Moth* was 650 pound, bomb with a 10.2 foot wingspan developed from leftover *Pelican* airframes when that program was cancelled. The airframe was fitted with radar receivers and antennae that could be tuned to home on enemy radar frequencies and crash into it; much like a moth drawn to a flame; hence the name. The first test flights of the radar homing glider were conducted against a beacon target. Although operational reasons precluded the *Moth* from reaching combat status, work continued

Moth **Radar-Controlled Guided Missile** (USN)

PMB (Poor Man's Bat) (USN)

utilizing the beacon homing apparatus as a testing device. The Navy canceled its *Moth* program but the AAF did successfully develop its own version as the GB-15.

PMB

The so-called *PMB*, "*Poor Man's Bat*," was a 325 pound depth bomb with an 8.4 foot wingspan. It was a very inexpensive and practical modification of the *Pelican* radar system as it contained its own radar sender located in a tube under nose cone and was dependent on the accuracy of the initial approach onto the target by the mother aircraft. This radar system was both earlier and superior to the *Bat's* system but the fixated Navy top echelons thought the *Bat* system to be more desirable and quietly allowed the *PMB* fade into oblivion.

SWOD Mk 9 *Bat*

Bat was an air-to-surface missile developed by the National Defense Research Committee and Bell Telephone Laboratories to BuOrd specifications originally as the Bomb Mk 57 which was soon changed to the SWOD Mk 9. The prime mover in *Bat's* development was Dr. Hugh Dryden, now the head of the NBS Mechanics and Sound Division, who was awarded a Presidential Certificate of Merit for his work on this project.

The airframe was basically a small monoplane glide bomb with shoulder mounted wings spanning 10 feet. The tail assembly resembled

that of the B-24 Liberator bomber with the horizontal tail plane attached under the rear of the fuselage and supporting two small round vertical fins at each end. Like the *Pelican*, the *Bat's* elevons acted as ailerons or spoilers, functioning on each wing to give a proportional system of control. *Bat* weighed 1,660 pounds, was 11.5 feet long, and measured 2.5 feet in maximum diameter. The designed glide ratio was between 3.5 and 5.5 to 1. The equipment was designed to operate at temperatures between -40°F and 131°F, in humidly up to 95%, and at attitudes up to 30,000 feet. A dehydrating silica gel was placed in the radar compartment which was found to be ineffective in rainy weather. The missile was named the "*Bat*" after the mammal which emits a series of ultrasounds (echolocation) which when reflected are received by its auditory system to distinguish, locate, and then capture the prey.

The *Bat* warhead was a 1,000 pound GP bomb which was attached to the airframe by straps and was entirely enclosed by removable plywood sections to give an aerodynamically clean fuselage. Two special fuses were used which armed from the side by means of a connection to spinners on the underside of the airframe. Arming wires were attached to the carrying rack. A Mk122 self-demolition system was installed to prevent the secret RHS from falling into Japanese hands.

A Mk51 Model 7 missile carrying rack was mounted outboard of each outboard engine. The *Bat* was lifted onto the rack by two standard Mk9 bomb hoists operated from the top of the wing with their lifting cables extending down through holes in the wing. The *Bat* hoisting equipment was stored on the flight deck behind the pilot.

SWOD Development Team (Left to Right) R.C. Newhouse (Bell), H.K. Skramstead (NBS), O. McCracken (BuAer), D.P. Tucker (BuOrd), L.P. Tabor (BuOrd), H.L. Dryden (NBS). (USN)

The ***Bat*** was an air-to-surface missile developed by the National Defense Research Committee and Bell Telephone Laboratories to BuOrd specifications originally as the Bomb Mk57 which was soon changed to the SWOD Mk 9. (USN)

SWOD Mk 9 *Bat*

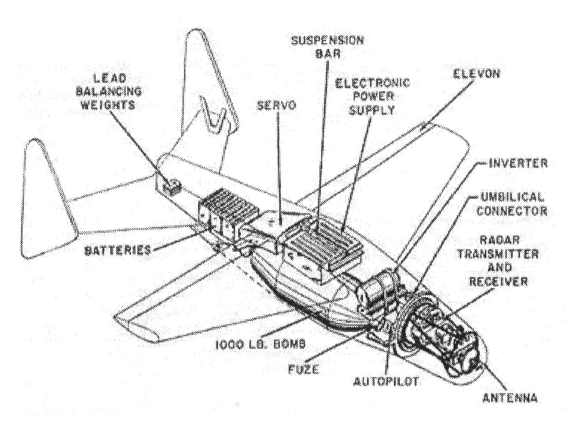

(USN)

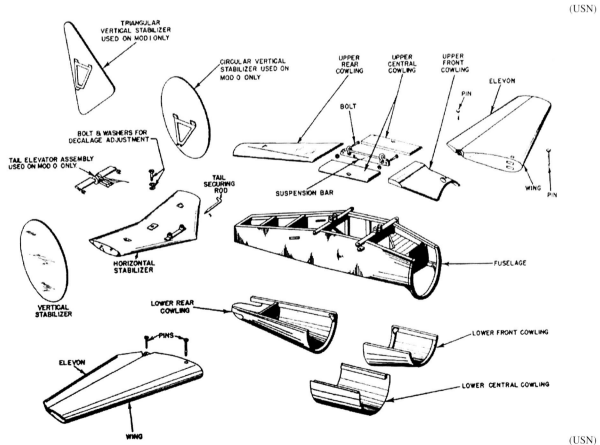

(USN)

SWOD Mk 9 *Bat*

***Bat* Nose Section** (USN)

***Bat* Body Section** (USN)

The *Bat* was lifted onto the rack by two standard **Mk9 bomb hoists** operated from the top of the wing with their lifting cables extending down through holes in the wing. (USN)

The SWOD Mk2 Radar Homing System (RHS) was developed by Bell Telephone Laboratory and manufactured by Western Electric and was functionally complete with its own transmitter and receiver. The Mk2 radar seeking components were mounted in a circular faired bulkhead in the forward end of the airframe. The Mk2 was to automatically track the pre-selected target and to furnish directional control signals to the *Bat* to home it on the target. The RHS was a self-sufficient complete S-Band system with a frequency of 3,000 mc. A strong pulse transmitted from a rapidly revolving spinner (reflector) and antenna located in the *Bat's* nose threw out a conical beam which illuminated the target on the screen. The target reflected a small part of this transmission back to the spinner and antenna which directed it into the radar receiver circuits. The result was a display of video signals on a Type A oscilloscope which had horizontal sweeps of 10 and 25 miles. In combat the target was first selected by the AN/APS-2 search radar in the mother aircraft. The search radar operator helped the *Bat* operator identify the target on his auxiliary Type A "*Bat* Scope" on the mother aircraft. Once the target was identified the SWOD Mk2 was adjusted to automatic tracking. A video signal was used to activate the directional control units and also to energize a directional indicator that disclosed whether the target was above or below and/or to the right or left of the axis of the radar antenna system. This system was an adaptation of the indicator used for blind landing systems on aircraft which determined course and glide angle. The *Bat* operator and mother aircraft pilot each used this indicator so that the *Bat* could be carried into target range which had a theoretical maximum distance of 25 miles but under test and operational conditions was found to be more on the order of 12 to 13 miles. The *Bat* was not released until specific range, glide ratio, altitude, and release speed (205 mph) limits were met along with the positive locking of the target into the radar system. After release, the radar set and surface controls were powered by three storage batteries. The Mk2 radar then completely controlled the *Bat* causing it to home on the target. An Automatic Volume Control (AVC) system controlled the receiver sensitivity of the target echo "pip" on the *Bat's* locked in radar. As the missile closed on the target the "pip" echo strength increased. To prevent these ever stronger "pips" from saturating the receiver, the receiver sensitivity was automatically decreased. The AVC therefore,

concentrated the receiver on the target "pip" on which the *Bat* locked and was prevented from changing targets. Two 14-volt, batteries powered the radar while a third 14-volt battery operated the servo motors. Upon tracking a target early *Bats* "hunted" moving back and forth through a true straight line course to the target. The reduction of hunting oscillations had previously been studied at MIT's Servomechanisms Laboratory as part of the *Pelican* project and was continued for the *Bat* under the direction of Dr. A.C. Hill. When the missile moved off its proper heading in one direction, the course was altered by the radar in the other direction along the true heading. Accuracy then depended on what stage in the hunting cycle the *Bat* happened to be when it reached the target. Because of the time and expense of manufacturing such intricate and sophisticated (for 1945) equipment all idiosyncrasies needed to be eliminated before operational use. A gyroscopic automatic pilot was adapted to stabilize the weapon while an intricate system of servo motors controlling external steering surfaces (elevons) were developed to reduce deviations in the hunting cycle. Throughout *Bat's* development, the *Bat* scope operator had difficulties in identifying a target on which the *Bat's* RHS could lock. A Range Coordinator was developed to help the *Bat* operator to pick out the correct target "pip" on his *Bat* scope. By pressing a button, a downward moving "pip" on the scope indicated the target "pip" by moving adjacent to it. Only one Range Coordinator was ever used in combat which was installed in an aircraft of VOB-124 that was lost on its first mission.

In November and December 1944 45 test drops were made against reflectors on land and sea and ten drops against target ships; the 416 foot long ex-liberty ship, *James Longstreet* (1 test drop) and 189 foot target ship, *Carisee* (9). After 30 to 40% accurate test drops the *Bat* was ordered to become operational. The PB4Y-2 Privateer was modified for *Bat* operations with a simple kit which allowed modification to be completed in less than two days (300 man hours). During testing the *Bat* was test mounted on the F6F Hellcat, F4U Corsair, and SB2C Helldiver but little is known about these the results of these tests.

On 6 February 1945, the Chief of Naval Operations ordered VPB Squadrons 109, 123, and 124 of Fleet Air Wing Two into operational training at the Kaneohe Naval Air Station, HI. On 17 March, Lt.Cdr. Ortho McCrackin was named the head of the operational *Bat* training program and 22 trained personnel and the *Bat* equipment arrived on 2 April. Five days later the first three PB4Y-2s of VBP-109 were outfitted to carry the *Bat* and their crews were briefly instructed in its use before practice drops were made.

A Mk51 Model 7 missile carrying rack was mounted outboard of each outboard engine. (USN)

SWOD Mk2 Radar Homing System (RHS)

The **SWOD Mk2 Radar Homing System** (RHS) was developed by Bell Telephone Laboratory and manufactured by Western Electric and was functionally complete with its own transmitter and receiver The Mk2 radar seeking components were mounted in a circular faired bulkhead in the forward end of the airframe. (USN)

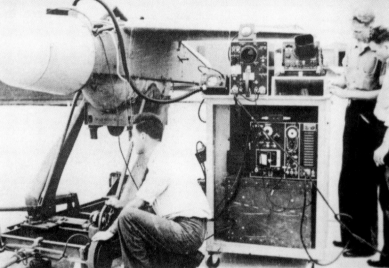

Ground check of the Mk2 RHS system. (USN)

AN/APS-2 search radar antenna on the mother aircraft. (USN)

In November and December 1944 forty five test drops were made against reflectors on land and sea and ten drops against target ships: the 189 foot target ship, *Carisee* (9 test drops) and the 416 foot long ex-liberty ship, *James Longstreet* (1 test drop) shown in photograph. (USN)

On 23 April 1945, two PB4Y-2Bs (B for *Bat*) of VPB-109 based at Palawan launched the first *Bats* in combat against Japanese shipping 700 miles away in Balikpapan Harbor, Borneo. Led by Squadron CO, Lt.Cdr. George Hicks and Lt. Leo Kennedy in the second aircraft, the two bombers approached the harbor containing a large transport, a freighter, and five smaller merchant vessels. The two *Bats* were launched from six miles at 10,000 feet but behaved erratically, each falling short of their intended target. Thus the first employment of World War II's only automatic homing missile was a failure.

On 28 April two Privateers, each carrying two *Bats*, and flown by Lt.Cdr. Hicks and Lt. Chay again attacked Balikpapan Harbor. Hicks released the first *Bat* from nine miles and 10,500 feet at a large transport but the *Bat* locked on a small freighter and destroyed it and a wharf at the Pandanseri Oil Refinery instead. Lt. Chay aimed at the same large transport but his *Bat's* radar again locked on another small freighter which happened to lie in line with the intended target causing the unfortunate vessel to sink. Chay released his second *Bat* from seven miles but it veered off target at 45°, flying inland, and only by luck destroyed a large oil

storage tank of the refinery; three miles short of the transport. So chance, rather than technology, made the raid a great success. In these attacks the *Bat* had difficulties detecting the selected target from long range or where multiple targets were located along the same range. Further operational use of the *Bat* was suspended as no worthwhile shipping targets were available and the Squadron would have to wait until it reached its new base at Naha, Okinawa in May to see further action.

The potential of the *Bat* was spectacularly demonstrated on 27 May 1945, when a two Privateers piloted by Lt.Cdr. George Hicks and Lt. Leo Kennedy took off carrying a *Bat* under one wing and a load of conventional bombs in the bomb bay. On the way to the target a large Japanese coastal freighter was encountered and strafed and then sunk by conventional bombs. A quarter hour later four small vessels were sighted a strafed and sunk by gunfire alone. About an hour later two destroyers were sighted and the *Bats* were readied for an attack. Kennedy's Privateer closed to make a head on attack from the optimum launch distance of five miles so that the targeted destroyer could not make evasive turns once the *Bat* was launched. The bomber's radar was locked on the target but was not transferred to the *Bat's* homing device until just before launch. The *Bat* hit the destroyer's bow and it was sinking as the Privateers returned to base. In the same attack Kennedy also sunk a 2,000 ton freighter, four small freighters, and damaged two smaller vessels by more conventional means for which he was awarded the Navy Cross. However, the award was posthumous as Kennedy was killed in action by AA fire three days later.

On 29 May Lts. May and Warren of VBP-109, checking intelligence reports, searched for large concentrations of shipping in the mouth of the Yangtze River off Shanghai. They spotted two ton and a three ton freighter which were attacked but the *Bats* were defective and did not track the target.

VBP-124, based on Okinawa, deployed their *Bats* on 23 and 25 June 1945 patrolling over the Tsushima Straits between Japan and Korea. On the second mission Lts. Pries and Griffin were on patrol when Pries launched a *Bat* at 8,000 feet and eight miles out toward three Japanese patrol boats and although the missile flew true it's homing radar became come confused by the multiple targets and exploded between them. VBP-124 soon discontinued its patrols carrying *Bats*.

Of the 33 *Bats* used in combat between 23 April to 15 July 1945 the following results were recorded: Hits-4 (12.1%), Near misses-4, Misses-7, Mechanical failure-3, Jettisoned by mothership-14 and Unobserved-1. Only 15 *Bats* were launched successfully with four hits but three of four of these were dubious successes due to chance. Three suffered mechanical

Curtiss SB2C Helldiver (USN)

Vought F4U Corsair (USN)

Of the 33 *Bats* used in combat between 23 April to 15 July, 1945 the following results were recorded: Hits-4 (12.1%), Near misses-4, Misses-7, Mechanical failure-3, Jettisoned by mothership-14 and Unobserved-1. (USN)

failure but 14 were jettisoned due to carrying aircraft engine trouble or gasoline shortage. The failure to identify the target initially on search radar or later on the *Bat* scope caused the cumbersome drag-inducing *Bats* to be jettisoned by the mother aircraft rather than be carried back to base for a hair-raising landing with a over-sized 1,000 pound bomb slung under the wing. Tropical temperatures, humidity, mud, dust, and fungus did not agree with the sophisticated and delicate nature of the weapon. Some *Bats* were damaged while being flown to forward areas (if not flown they would not have been available before the war ended). Rough ground handling and lack of spare parts affected the *Bat's* performance in combat.

By V-J Day 3,000 Bats were manufactured and combat ready and in March 1946, amid numerous post-war cut backs, the Chief of Naval Operations ordered the project to be completed which meant curtailment and oblivion.

SWOD Mk 10

The SWOD Mk 10 was a guided bomb originally designated as Bomb Mk69 but no further information can be found in the literature.

SWOD Mk 11 *Kingfisher A*

In August 1944, BuOrd defined the *Kingfisher* series of radar-guided torpedo-carrying weapons. The SWOD Mk 11 *Kingfisher A* was a glide bomb equipped with a Mk21 torpedo. It was to be an interim weapon for use against ships not defended by fighter aircraft but apparently no *Kingfisher A* missiles were built.

***GLOMB* (Glider Bomb) Series**
US Navy *GLOMBS*

In December 1940 Lt.Cdr. Delmar Fahrney who had been working on the Navy's powered drone project since 1936 suggested the use of an explosive-filled remotely controlled glider to attack pin-point targets. Fahrney's glider would weigh up to 15,000 pounds and was to be towed under automatic stabilization to within its glide range of a target by a fighter or transport aircraft. A television camera in the nose of the glider would provide a picture of the target to the remote control pilot located in a nearby mothership who would guide the glider by radio control. The gliders were inexpensive airframes and could be towed by an aircraft that also contained the remote controller. Plans were also made for the glider to provide supplemental fuel to its towing aircraft. In March 1941 Fahrney was appointed to direct the glider bomb project at the Naval Aircraft Factory, Philadelphia, under the direction of Cdr. Ralph Bamaby, Assistant Chief Engineer at the NAF. Bamaby was a skillful glider pilot who supervised the Navy's entire transport glider developmental program. On 19 April 1941 the Navy ordered the start of the program under the official designation of *Project George* but Bamaby originated the term "*GLOMBS*" (**GL**ider b**OMBS**) for the project.

XLNT-1

In early 1942 two Schweizer LNS-1 (Army TG-2) two-place training gliders were obtained to test the radio control but were found to be

On 23 April 1945, two **PB4Y-2Bs** (B for *Bat*) of **VPB-109** based at Palawan launched the first *Bats* in combat against Japanese shipping 700 miles away in Balikpapan Harbor; Borneo. (USN)

Schweizer LNS-1 (Army TG-2) (AAF)

inadequate. Three 7,320 pound Taylorcraft XLNT-1 (Army TG-6) three-place training gliders, based on light aircraft designs were obtained from the Army in September 1942. Changes were made including a modified main landing gear, a new nose gear, and electronics gear with external antennae installed in the cockpit. The conventional landing gear was replaced as it proved to be too unstable for towing off the ground under automatic control and also made radio-controlled landings too difficult.

Automatically stabilizing the glider on takeoff and tow was a problem and the NAF attempted to develop an auto-tow system using its previous experience using drone autopilots. On 20 May 1942, a Great Lakes BG-1 drone was towed by a Douglas TBD-1 Devastator using an in-flight radio connection. This drone was designated as the XLNT-1, but progress on *GLOMB*s was slowed by parallel auto-tow work on other gliders. Although a safety pilot was in the glider until a final successful test on 4 April 1943, the XLNT-1 appeared most suitable for conversion to a *GLOMB*. Some 31 additional XLNT-ls and LNT-ls were obtained in the last half of 1943, from a cancelled USMC training program and from the AAF which had them in storage. These LNT-1s would be used in more thorough testing while the production design was completed. The tests included towing by a F4F-3 (#3990) and a catapult of the combination at NAS Patuxent River. The land-based fighter was shot off the catapult with the glider in tow. Because the XLNT-1 (TQ-6 #42-58561) did not have the nose gear modification, its tail was placed on a ramp and the tail wheel held back with a frangible restraint. Small revisions to reinforce the glider's structure were required to withstand launch loads while the towline release mechanism was also modified. The towline was 100 feet of 0.44 inch steel cable, a small drogue parachute attached to the glider end (taped to the nose) to keep the line from whipping after release. A solo XLNT-1 was also test-catapulted using a hook on the end of an extended truss protruding from the nose.

The auto-tow system was ultimately finalized, allowing the glider to takeoff and follow behind the tug. The XLNT-1 had a maximum weight of

The **RCA radio remote control and TV transmit/receive systems** for targeting used on the XLNT-1 was finally developed into the BLOCK I. The photo shows the unit on the ground powered by a generator used on ground-directed tests. (AAF)

5,000 pounds; could be towed up to 240 mph, and descended at 2,400 fpm with dive tests up to 260 mph and with 5G pull-outs performed. The RCA radio remote control and TV transmit/receive systems for targeting finally developed into the BLOCK 1 design that fit into both the XLNT-1 and a control aircraft as small as a trainer. The system permitted controlled flight all the way to the target or on locking into a stabilized flight path. The TV image was only available after release. By fall 1943, further alterations were made to the XLNT-ls and three were selected for expenditure in destructive trials of the experimental *GLOMB* design.

The first *GLOMB* test was conducted at "Pax" (Patuxent) River on 17 September 1943. The XLNT-1 (#36429) carried a live 325 pound depth charge armed by remote signal and was towed by a Vultee SNV-1 Valiant (#12963) whose pilot also controlled the XLNT-1 after release. The takeoff

Taylorcraft XLNT-1 (Army TG-6) (AAF)

The 25 February 1944 second and final **XLNT-1 test** was conducted at NAS Lakehurst, NJ, with a 30x50 foot sand pit acting as the target. After a three minute flight, the *GLOMB* struck within 23 feet of the center of the target as seen in the photo. (AAF)

of the first unmanned *GLOMB* auto-tow, which Bamaby had nicknamed "NOLO" (**NO**-pilot So**LO**) was faultless and while the 35 mile flight met turbulence; there were no problems on the way to the target located off Bloodsworth Island in the Chesapeake Bay. Release was at 3,000 feet and three miles from the target; but disappointingly, there was no TV image and the target could not be located. The control pilot was obligated to put the *GLOMB* into a spiral descent into the Bay, well short of the target, where the depth charge exploded on impact. It was determined that the *GLOMB*'s magnetic field disrupted the delicate TV equipment which could have been corrected if the final system adjustments had been made in the final flight configuration.

On 25 February 1944, the second and final test was conducted at NAS Lakehurst, NJ, with a 30x50 foot sand pit acting as the target. The weight of the XLNT-1 (#67803) and the radio and television equipment left only 228 pounds of sand bags to represent the explosives. The test was termed an "expeditionary operation," with the aircraft and all equipment and personnel flown to Lakehurst, the mission completed, and leaving in only six hours. After a practice run, release was at 4,500 feet and four miles upwind of the target. After a three minute flight, the *GLOMB* struck within 23 feet of the center of the target and with enough force to trip an arming circuit. Despite the limitations of the early TV systems the tests were promising and demonstrated that a tow pilot could direct the *GLOMB* after release.

XLRN

The production *GLOMB*s were also to serve as Marine Corps cargo gliders supporting amphibious glider operations and on 29 June 1942 BuAer requested a glider that could carry fuel, freight, or explosives which was expanded to three types on 29 September. The smallest glider was to be developed from one of two 24-place transport gliders then being developed for the USMC. It was to carry 1,000 gallons of fuel or 6,000 to 8,000 pounds of explosives but due to the lack of interest in this project it was never completed. The intermediate size glider was to carry 2,000 gallons of fuel or a 12,000 to 14,000 pound load of explosives. This glider was to be developed by enlarging a 12-place glider under development by Bristol Aeronautical Corporation as the XLR2N-1. This project also lagged and was sent to the NAF where it never was developed. The largest glider was to carry 3,000 gallons or 18,000 to 20,000 pounds of explosives. This project was developed by the NAF as the XLRN-1 which first flew in November 1944 but never underwent *GLOMB* testing when it underwent flight testing under pilot control.

XLBE, XLBP, and XLBT

In August 1943 the requirements for a production *GLOMB* were issued specifying a 3,000 pound empty weight glider with a 4,000 pound explosive payload and a 400 mile radius of action when deployed by a Grumman F6F. These gliders could be towed at 150 mph while the LNT-1 was limited to 100 mph which would have been rather slow for the proposed mothership fighters. Auto-tow, remote control, and television systems were to be installed along with a warhead. Six companies submitted proposals in September 1943 and contracts were negotiated with three companies.

XLBE

The Pratt Read and Company, Deep River, CT, (later the Gould Aeronautical Division) built three XLBE-1s (#85290 to #85292). These aircraft resembled a modified Culver TD2C-1 Target Drone with split dive flaps and with the engine replaced by an enclosed nose. A ram air turbine under the nose, with variable speed fan, generated electrical power. The prototype had a cockpit for a safety pilot but in the combat configuration the pilot compartment would be replaced with mounts for a 4,000 pound bomb case without fins.

XLBP

Piper, Lock Haven, PA, built the XLBP-1 glider that resembled a light aircraft with all surfaces fully cantilevered and its lines aerodynamic configured for high speed tow. The fixed tricycle gear included main gear posts under the wing with spring shock absorbers. The forward fuselage was low set for ease of loading a 4,000 pound bomb into the nose. The prototype XLBP-1 (#85165) had an anti-spin parachute pack installed in the tail.

XLBT

Taylorcraft, Alliance, OH built the LBT-1 designed for a 2,000 pound bomb. The LBT-1 resembled a modified LNT-1 except for a stronger structure, cleaner lines, and simplified canopy. The perforated dive brakes located on the aft fuselage were aligned with the airflow but could be

Bristol Aeronautical Corporation as the XLR2N-1 (AAF)

Pratt Read and Company XLBE-1 (AAF)

Taylorcraft LBT-1 (AAF)

rotated 90°. The LBT-1 used spoilers like the LNT-1 but had no flaps. Takeoff weight was increased to 5,000 pounds, tow speed to 240 mph, and landing speed 120 mph. The sink rate was 2,200 fpm with a 260 mph dive speed. The first XLBT-1 was ready for testing in April 1944 to be towed and controlled by a Grumman F4F or a Lockheed PV-1.

Conclusion of the *GLOMB* Program
As was usual with many wartime projects, production orders were placed for all three *GLOMB* designs before the system had passed testing. An order for 100 Taylorcraft LBT-ls was reduced to 85 in November 1944 and then 35 in February 1945 and the contract was canceled in October 1944 after 25 were eventually produced (#85265 to #85289). One hundred Pratt Reed LBE-1s were ordered initially (96 were #85293 to #85389), but reduced to 85 in November 1944 then 35 in February 1945. The contract was finally terminated in August 1945, with only four delivered. Admiral Ernest King, Chief of Naval Operations, requested that three be modified for homing radar but time constraints prevented this. An order for 100 (#85165 to #85264) was reduced to 85 in November 1944 then to 35 in February 1945. The contract was cancelled in June 1945.

Continuing problems, particularly with auto-tow system delayed *GLOMB* system and an LBT-1 accident at Traverse City, MI, in July 1945 caused a review the following month resulting in the cancellation of the entire *GLOMB* project before testing.

Gargoyle
In November 1943, the LBD-1 *Gargoyle* (RTV-N-2), the last of the LB series was developed by the Navy as part of their glider bomb series as an answer to the successful German HS-293 and *Fritz-X* guided anti-

shipping glide bombs. Operationally it was to be used by carrier dive and torpedo bombers against shipping. The 1,500 pound low wing monoplane missile was characterized by a short (10.1 foot), thick fuselage, stubby (8.5 foot) wings, and a broad V-shaped butterfly tail assembly. In March 1944, an Aerojet 8AS100 solid fuel rocket booster motor was added to the final design to give it a higher diving speed. The speed was projected to be 600 mph over a range of five miles when released from 15,000 feet. It was remotely radio-controlled using a bright flare in the tail to aid control via simultaneous or separate operation of the elevators or rudders in the tail. It was to carry a 1,000 pound M65 General Purpose or M59 Semi-armor piercing warhead. In September 1944, McDonnell Aircraft was awarded the prototype contract and successful glide tests began in March 1945 after which McDonnell was awarded a full production contract. The first powered tests in began in July with only five of l4 tests considered successful. It was redesignated as the KSD-1 anti-shipping missile just as the war ended and then was redesignated as the KUD-1 test and research vehicle which first flew in July 1946. McDonnell produced 250 *Gargoyles* before ending production in mid-1947. The remaining missiles were again redesignated as the RTV-2 in September 1947 and the RTV-N-2 in early 1948 and were used to test components for other missile programs. The *Gargoyle* program was officially terminated in December 1950 and the remaining missiles were scrapped.

Interstate BDR
In 1944, the Interstate Aircraft and Engineering Corp. designed a little known tailless jet-powered Assault Drone, under the USN designation BDR. This missile probably only reached the scale model wind tunnel testing stage before the program vanished.

7Piper XLBP-1 (AAF)

The forward fuselage of the **XLBE-1** was low set for ease of loading a 4,000 pound bomb into the nose. (AAF)

McDonnell Aircraft LBD-1 *Gargoyle* **(RTV-N-2)** (USN)

Interstate BDR (AAF)

AAF *GLOMB*S

The USAAF investigated a guided weapons program to reduce the losses that mass bomber raids were sustaining while attacking individual targets. The AAF focused on manually or autonomously directed free-fall bombs from only one bomber or bombs with minimal glides so that the releasing aircraft could remain outside AA range of a heavily defended target. However, projects MX-166 and MX-197 did explore gliders carrying bombs.

The last of the AAF's glide bomb series was not of the GB series designation but was designated as the XBG. It was a towed bomb similar in design to the GB series. After being towed to the vicinity of the target, the XBG-1 was released to glide toward the target being radio-controlled from the towing aircraft. The XBG-2 was a standard troop glider filled with explosives. It was equipped with radio-controls and was guided after release by the towing aircraft. The BG gliders were similar in concept to the Navy's *GLOMB*.

Fletcher XBG-1

After the AAF had cancelled the order for the Fletcher PQ-11A radio-controlled Target Drone it contracted Fletcher Aviation Corporation, Pasadena, CA, for ten XBG-1s (42-46892 to -46901) for $87,000. Ten PQ-11As under construction at Fletcher were completed and were delivered in May 1942 as XBG-1 bomb gliders by removing the P&W R-985 engine and installing remote control systems and a 2,000 pound bomb. The XBG-1 was to be towed to the target area by a larger aircraft and upon release was to be guided to target impact by radio-commands using imagery transmitted from a TV camera in the glider's nose. The

BG-1 was to be released as far as 11 miles from the target; the operator aboard the towing bomber guiding the glider into the target by using TV. No information on the XBG-1 test program is available but the model was never used operationally

Fletcher XBG-2

Fletcher was also contracted for $16,546 for the development of three XBG-2s (42-46902 to -46904). The XBG-2 was converted from Fletcher's CQ-1A drone control aircraft. After flight testing the contract was terminated in September 1942 with no XBG-2s delivered.

There were two alternate designs for the XBG-2. When the Frankfort eight seat XCG-1 troop-carrying glider was cancelled in 1941, the three XCG-1s under construction were completed by Fletcher as XBG-2 bomb gliders. The other configuration was two Frankfort XCG-2 (a larger 15-seat derivative of the XCG-1) fuselages joined by common center wing and tail sections and could carry two 2,000 pound bombs. There is no information available either configuration was built before the XBG-2 program was cancelled in 1942.

Cornelius XBG-3

In 1942 Cornelius Aircraft, Dayton, OH, was contracted for one XBG-3 (42-46911) but that order was cancelled the same year before delivery. The XBG-3 was to be a tailless design that was to be 28.8 feet long with a 53 foot forward-swept wing, with nose-mounted horizontal stabilizers, and forward-swept wings which was similar to Cornelius' XFG-1 fuel glider.

XCG-4A/-13A/15A

The Cargo Glider was designated as the CG and the first model, the CG-4A was designed and built by the Waco Aircraft Company of Troy, OH, upon AAC specifications. The CG-4 was designed by Francis Arcier, a Waco Vice-President and Chief Designer. The CG-4A was 48.31 feet long, 12.62 feet high, with a wing span of 83.67 feet, and a gross weight of 7,500 pounds. A total of 13,909 CG-4A gliders were constructed during the period 1942-1945. The ACG-15, although outwardly similar to the earlier CG-4, and carrying the same number of passengers, a number of

Fletcher XBG-2 (AAF)

Waco XCG-15 (AAF)

Naval Aircraft Modification Unit (NAMU) *Gorgon* (USN)

changes in the design, including shortened wings and a more streamlined nose enabled it to travel faster.

Like the Navy, the AAF also worked to perfect a glider auto-tow system and an autopilot, as part of project MX-296. The angle of the tow rope segment just ahead of the nose was provided by a feeler attached to the nose and resting on the tow rope a few feet forward by a mechanical input to a cockpit instrument called the Tow Rope Position Indicator. The pilot attempted to maintain vertical and horizontal bars centered in the instrument. This, in combination with an attitude gyro (artificial horizon), allowed a pilot to hold the proper tow position on the tug and a wings-level attitude. It was inadequate for sustained instrument flight due to vertigo and pilot fatigue but worked adequately for intermittent flying into clouds. By mid-1943 it was evaluated by operational units and plans were made to deploy it. The system was improved by adding an instrument that would place the angle input to zero via electric servos; providing the calculation of auto-tow capability relieving the pilot workload but again requiring adjustment with trim changes and so was unsuitable for extended instrument flight.

The D-l, a modified aircraft A-3 autopilot, using gimbals and hydraulic actuators to move the flight controls, and powered by a ram air-driven pump was introduced; although it still required pilot trimming with changes in flight conditions. Flight tests by CCAAF were conducted with CG-4A, CG-13A, and CG-15A gliders, and were very promising. Ultimately, the expense and time of introducing auto-tow and autopilot equipment in the glider fleet appeared impractical as at this point of the war there was not much of a future for the military transport glider.

Gorgon Series
Newly developed US liquid-fueled rocket and turbojet propulsion systems led to the approval of the *Gorgon* developmental program on 19 July 1943, to be designed and built by the Naval Aircraft Modification Unit (NAMU), Johnstown, PA. In late 1943, 25 missiles each of *Gorgon* II and *Gorgon* III type were ordered to be used as test and evaluation vehicles. This order was later amended and changed, and by April 1945 had arrived at 21 *Gorgon* IIA, 4 *Gorgon* IIB, 34 *Gorgon* IIIA, 16 *Gorgon* IIIB and 20 *Gorgon* IIIC.

Gorgon Models:
The original *Gorgon* design was to be a light 660 pound air-launched missile using a small 9.5 inch Westinghouse turbojet which would give it a maximum speed of 510 mph. The *Gorgon*'s principal mission was to be the interception of bombers or transports with a secondary ground-

attack capability. The proposed guidance options included TV command guidance, radar homing, or a simple infrared heat seeker with an 18 mile range. For the air-to-air mission, the missile would be equipped with both proximity and contact fuses. At the time air-to-air missile guidance meet technological problems and initial *Gorgon* development focused on airframe and propulsion. In late 1943 two alternative airframe configurations were proposed, the *Gorgon* II with canards, and the *Gorgon* III with conventional layout. Both configurations were to be tested with rocket, turbojet, and pulsejet propulsion, indicated by suffix letters A, B, and C; respectively

Gorgon IIA
This missile was an air-to-air missile powered by an acid-aniline rocket motor and was guided by radio from a mothership using television transmission from the missile. The *Gorgon* IIA was to have a range of ten miles.

Gorgon IIB and IIIB
These missiles were turbojet propelled with the former unconventional and the latter of conventional design. These models were considered to be obsolete by the end of the war.

Gorgon IIC
This program was initiated in May 1945. It was powered by a Reso pulse jet motor, was radar tracked, radio controlled, launched by catapult from ship-to-shore. It had only reached testing stage at the end of the war.

Gorgon IIIA
This *Gorgon* was a rocket propelled missile guided by visual radio direction and used radar homing. None had been completed by the end of the war.

No turbojet variants (*Gorgon* IIB and *Gorgon* IIIB) were built because there was no suitable flight-rated engine was available at that time. The other *Gorgon* II/III variants were built, although the *Gorgon* IIIC would be equipped with a rocket instead of a pulsejet propulsion system. In March 1945 a live test of a TV command-guided air-to-air *Gorgon* IIA failed badly because the controller could not manually steer the slow reacting missile to an interception point when closing speeds reached 800 mph. In mid-1946 continued problems with the guidance systems caused the *Gorgon* program to become a research and development program and all existing *Gorgon* variants were redesignated as test vehicles.

The Reaction Motors CML2N liquid-propellant rocket engine

Northrop JB-1 Jet Bomb

powered the 21 *Gorgon* IIAs which were built. Unpowered flight tests began in early 1945 and were followed by the first powered launches in March that year. While launching and flying characteristics were generally satisfactory, the radio command guidance system with a TV camera in the nose was unsuitable for air-to-air applications or air-to-ground. Initially designated as KA2N-1 anti-aircraft missile in October 1945, *Gorgon* IIA was redesignated as KU2N-1 control test vehicle in 1946. In September 1947 and early 1948, the KU2N-1 was redesignated as CTV-4 and CTV-N-4, respectively.

JB: Jet Bomb Series
In 1939 Gen. H.H. Arnold, an avowed advocate of advanced technology, failed to appreciate the potential of jet engine technology and by 1944 America was not close to matching that of the Germans or English. When the Germans launched their first pulse jet powered V-1 in mid-1944, America's attempt to duplicate the Buzz Bomb with their Jet Bomb followed the same improvisation and lack of direction in research, design, and procurement as did many other AAF guided bomb programs. Nonetheless, Gen. Arnold had earmarked the Jet Bomb program for production runs as high as 75,000 costing $1.5 billion; and thereby would have jeopardized existing guided bomb programs and even conventional weapon programs by redirecting funding, highly skilled personnel, materials, and production space. It was estimated that the deployment of operational Jet Bombs would require a quarter of all future Allied shipping space to transport them overseas in the large numbers required to be effective. The American designs were so mediocre that the only Jet Bomb to approach being tested in combat by the AAF during the war was the JB-2 that was copied directly from the captured German V-1 Buzz Bomb!

Northrop JB-1
The AAF's most highly developed Jet Bomb project (MX-543) in 1944 was the large delta-winged JB-1 developed by Northrop Aircraft of Hawthorne, CA which was contracted to produce 13. The JB-1s weighed 7,084 pounds fully loaded, measured 10.5 feet long, 4.5 feet high, and had a 28.25 foot wingspan and total 155 square foot wing area.

Northrop was aided in its redesign of the jet engines when a damaged V-1 was shipped to the US for study. The captured German pulse jet design impressed Northrop engineers to the extent that they wished to adapt it to the JB-1 using a single centerline pulse jet engine while streamlining its airframe and reducing its weight. The new JB-1 design, equipped with a single pulse jet, was hypothetically capable of producing 500 pounds of thrust to a maximum speed of 400 mph over 220 miles. The redesign would reduce the bomb load from 4,000 to 3,400 pounds which was carried in enclosed bomb containers located in the wing roots.

The center section of the wing was constructed of welded magnesium alloy, stressed skin construction while the outer wings were of a combined riveted and spot welded aluminum alloy, stressed skin, multi-cellular construction incorporating integral fuel tanks and magnesium wing tips. The wing access panel covers were found to be held in place by too many self-threading screws which were difficult to remove. Also, the integral fuel tanks leaked and needed to be sealed. The elevons were constructed of welded magnesium alloy and measured 5.5 square feet. Their angular movement as an elevator was 13° Up and 8° Down and as an aileron 10° Up and 10° Down. The tail fin was constructed of magnesium alloy and measured 3.7 square feet.

The all-electric automatic control equipment manufactured by the Hammond Instrument Company, Chicago, was mounted in the outer wing panels and consisted of a roll gyro servo, a pitch gyro and servo and an aneroid altitude control device; all powered by Delco-Remy 14-volt AC

batteries. The JB-1 carried an early version of the "Black Box" which contained a movie camera set to record air speed, elevon position, jet velocity, and altitude. This unit did not function properly during the only test of the JB-1.

The launching sled was designed to launch both the JB-1 and JB-2 within a distance of 1,000 feet and a provision was made to stop the sled's movement in an additional 1,000 feet. The sled engaged the double rail (56.5 inch gauge) track on two pairs of "slippers" (one pair fore and the other aft) which had rail shaped grooves that fit over the rail. The sled was powered by two Monsanto Mark I, 11.75 inch rocket motors incorporated into the rear of the sled. There was an alternative provision to use five 10 inch Monsanto rocket motors. The airframe was mounted on sled at 9° from horizontal and both elevons were carefully adjusted to 9° Up from their streamlined position.

While Northrop was actively pursuing the single pulse jet, the company also decided to continue with its original twin-engine design using redesigned General Electric turbo-supercharged Type B-1 200 hp engines able to produce the required 400 pounds of thrust which were to propel the missile over 670 miles at 452 mph while carrying two 2,000 pound GP bombs internally. While the proposed 800 pound combined thrust of the two GE B1 400 hp engines was 300 pounds more than produced by the single pulse jet engine of the German V-1 Buzz Bomb; they had to propel the JB-1 which weighed nearly 2,000 pounds more. However, in June 1944 static tests showed that each JB-1 engine was only capable of producing 200 of the anticipated 400 pounds of thrust which meant that combined they produced 100 pounds less thrust than a single V-1 engine. This reduction of power was supposed to be compensated by the lighter weight aluminum and magnesium construction of the body and wings.

The September 1944, manned aerodynamic glide trials using a towed unpowered glider proved the airframe to be aerodynamically stable but somewhat difficult to land. Northrop decided to test its only prototype, not with the single pulse jet engine which was still unavailable, but with the original two 200 pound thrust GE engines. Northrop had to postpone the tests while the airframe was modified to reduce its weight to slightly over 3,000 pounds so that these less powerful engines could keep the missile airborne. This model encountered numerous leaks in its integral fuel tanks and from the inaccessibility of the engines and the control equipment (which required the removal of 270 screws in each wing panel for maintenance). The engine was started by turning the turbines with compressed air and at the same time applying a spark via spark plugs

The sled was powered by two Monsanto Mark I, 11.75 inch rocket motors incorporated into the rear of the sled which rode on "slippers" which had rail shaped grooves that fit over the 56 gauge rails. (AAF)

Still from a movie of the 7 December 1944 JB-1A test showing the steep 45° liftoff angle which was too steep to be compensated for by the JB-1's 9° elevon setting and the insufficient thrust of the GE jet engines. (AAF)

Only weeks after the first German V-1 Buzz Bombs were launched against England on 12 June 1944, engineers at Wright Field were able to examine a captured and reverse engineer a copy. The photo shows a 393rd Fighter Squadron Bomb Service crew carting off a captured V-1. (AAF)

charged by a high voltage transformer. This difficult starting procedure postponed the first test at Eglin on 6 December 1944 until the next day. This first powered test was conducted on with the JB-1 propelled by two Monsanto rockets mounted on a modified JB-2 sled at 0° (level) and launched along a 500 foot ramp which was similar in construction (not elevation) to the German V-1 "Ski Ramps." Thirty seconds before launching with both engines running at full power substantial sparking was observed in the tail pipe of the right engine. The JB-1's underpowered

Wind tunnel tests of scale models helped in the quick reverse engineering of the JB-2. (AAF)

jet engines did get it airborne but only for 400 yards of flight from the end of the launch ramp after which the continued thrust of the engines was insufficient and the JB-1 went into a stall and crashed. An investigation of the salvaged wreck showed that there was incorrect setting of the elevons and that the GE jet engines "were not suitable power plants for the JB-1" as half the buckets of the right turbo were damaged and missing at speeds great enough to provide only half the required thrust.

The mid-January 1945 delivery date was met and the reworked GE jet engines were tested that month in a JB-1 airframe. However, the improvement in performance was so insignificant that the twin-engine design was abandoned in favor of a single pulse engined airframe that differed enough to be designated as the JB-10 (to be described in detail later). But even before the final JB-1 twin-engine tests were completed; the AAF had tentatively decided on the JB-2 as its primary Jet Bomb project.

JB-2

Only three weeks after the first German V-1 Buzz Bombs (Fiesler Fi-103) were launched against England on 12 June 1944, engineers at Wright Field were able to examine the remains of a crashed V-1. Within weeks they reverse engineered a copy of the V-1's 900 pound thrust Argus-Schmidt pulse-jet engine and contracts for 25 experimental engines were signed with Ford, Dearborn, MI which was able to complete the first example three weeks later. The first JB-2 test vehicles were built directly by the AAF at Wright Field, with the program initiated as Project MX-544 and as JB-2 by the AAF with the nickname "*Thunderbug*." Later the Navy began its Jet Bomb program as the KUW-1 "*Loon*."

As late as early October 1944 the Engineering Division of the AMC still had not been provided with the military requirements or been informed as to the purpose of the JB-2 so it was unable to establish its final configuration. At that date there also was no official authorization for developmental work on the JB-2 and so the Engineering Division of the AMC was unable to coordinate with industry or to request personnel or other resources from other sectors of the AAF. This was typical of the AAF attitude toward its guided missile program. However, Gen. Arnold boosted the JB-2's production priority to 1-A which was that of the *Willie Orphan* and the JB-2 project was definitely underway.

Within weeks after receiving the first German example Wright engineers reverse engineered a copy of the V-1's 900 pound thrust **Argus-Schmidt pulse-jet engine** and contracts for 25 experimental engines were signed with Ford which was able to complete the first example three weeks later. (AAF)

Bell Aircraft, Buffalo, NY and Republic Aviation, Farmingdale, LI were the manufacturers considered for the first quantity production of the JB-2 in October 1944 but Bell soon withdrew leaving Republic with the contract for the first 1,000. Republic plant floor space was limited and much of the work was subcontracted to Willys-Overland, Toledo, OH. After their initial contract for 25 experimental engines, Ford Motor, Detroit was contracted for the manufacture of the production Argus pulse jet motor copies. RCA was contracted for remote guidance and Jack and Heintz, Cleveland for the automatic controls. Alloy Products, Waukesha, WI was to supply the pressure vessels and Air Reduction Sales, the pressure regulators. The AN/ART-19 radio transmitters were contracted to Jack Mack, Plymouth, IN. Monsanto Chemical, Dayton, was contracted for the manufacture of the launching rockets, the launching carts were

to be built by Northrop, and the concrete launching ramps were to be constructed by the Army Corps of Engineers.

JB-2 Described
The JB-2 with a 17.67 foot wingspan and 5,025 pound weight was almost identical to the German V-l, except for the launching method and in later missiles the guidance system was modified. The simple impulse duct Ford jet engine on top of the main body was a copy of the German Argus version being 11.63 feet long (vs. 12.13 for the German); with an identical diameter of 1.89 feet in its forward end and 1.28 feet in its rear end.

	V-1/Fi-103	JB-2/LTV-N-2
Wing Span	17.52ft	17.67ft
Length	27.25ft	27.09ft
Height	4.67ft	4.67
Max. Fuselage Diameter	3.75ft	3.81ft
Engine	Argus 109	Ford PJ-31
Engine Length	12.13ft	11.63ft
Max. Engine Diameter	1.89ft	1.89ft
Engine Orifice Diameter	1.28ft	1.28ft
Thrust	807lbs	900lbs
Fuel	176gal	180gal
Engine wt.	337lbs	-----
Empty wt.	1,864lbs	-----
Warhead wt.	1,830lbs	2,100lbs
Warhead	Amatol	T-8 LC Bomb
Launch wt.	4,796lbs	5,025lbs
Optimum Range	150mi	150mi
Service Ceiling	8,840ft	6,000ft
Optimum Cruise Speed	360mph	400mph
Maximum Speed	400mph	440mph
Speed at Launch	250mph	220mph
Launch Time	1sec	1sec
Duration of Flight	25min	25min

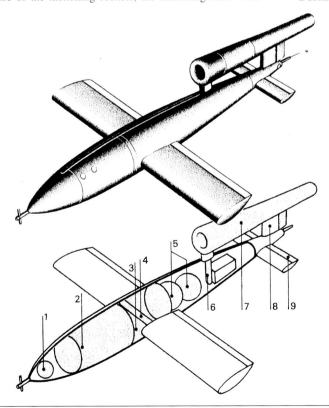

Republic JB-2
1) **Compass**
2) **HE Warhead**
3) **Fuel Tank**
4) **Main Spar**
5) **Compressed Air Bottles**
6) **Fuel Pump**
7) **Ford Pulse Jet Engine**
8) **Rudder**
9) **Elevator**

JB-2 Components

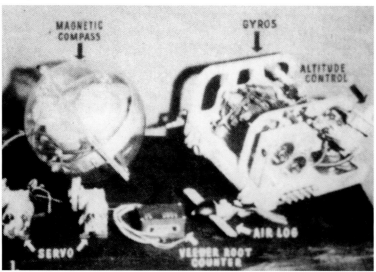

(These photos were taken from an AAF training movie)

JB-2 Launching Apparatus

Republic Aircraft Corp. static test of a Ford pulse jet copy of the German Argus-Schmidt at Farmingdale, NY. (AAF)

Pulse Jet Engine Cutaway

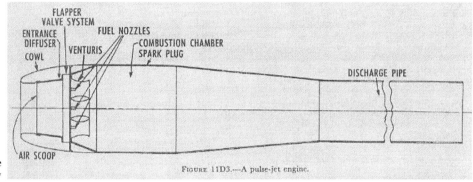

FIGURE 11D3.—A pulse-jet engine.

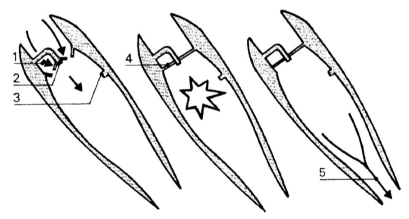

The pulse-jet (above) operates by a two-part cycle. To begin its operation there must be enough air pressure against the air intake valves to force them to open. This is achieved by catapult or rocket booster launch.
1 Air pressure opens valves.
2 Fuel is mixed with air as it enters combustion chamber.
3 Spark plug ignites fuel/air mixture.

4 Pressure of explosion closes valves.
5 Burning exhaust gases exit at high velocity to rear because of their high pressure. This causes the valves to re-open, air rushes in, and the process is repeated. After the first few cycles spark ignition is not needed as a residue of burning gases ignites the incoming mixture.

Pulse Jet Engine Function

Pulse Jet Engine

All pulsejet engines operated by alternately accelerating a contained mass of air rearward and then taking in a fresh mass of air to replace it. The energy to accelerate the air mass was provided by the burning at a very high heat (deflagration) of fuel mixed thoroughly into the newly acquired fresh air mass with this cycle repeated many times per second.

There were two basic types of pulsejets; the valve and valveless designs. The valve-type was the traditional pulsejet combustion chamber and an acoustically resonant exhaust pipe. Starting the engine usually required forcing air through the spring-loaded flapper valves and an ignition method in which the fuel was either mixed with the air in the intake or injected into the combustion chamber plug for the fuel-air mixture which had a set of one-way reed-type valves through which the incoming air passed. When the fuel-air mixture was ignited, these valves slammed shut so that the hot gases could only exit through the engine's tailpipe causing a forward thrust. Part of the exhaust gases flowed back up the discharge pipe and met the new air coming through the valves, compressing the new air slightly. This compression, plus residual burning fuel, plus the heat of the walls of the combustion chamber, ignited the new fuel-air mixture at about 250 pulses per second. The frequency of the cycle was mainly dependent on the length of the engine. A small engine would have a low frequency of about 40-50 pulses per second. The advantages of the pulse jet were that it was cheap and easy to manufacture, used ordinary, low-grade aviation fuels and atmospheric oxygen, and didn't need an oxidizer. Its disadvantages were its low subsonic speed (450 mph), low operating altitude, and high fuel consumption which made it vulnerable to AA fire and interception by aircraft.

Launching

Because the pulsejet engine only functioned efficiently in forward flight, the missile had to be boosted into the air to a speed of about 240 mph. The Germans achieved this speed by using a 155 foot ramp with rails containing a long hollow tube with a piston inside. A slot on top of the tube allowed the piston to be attached to a dolly to which the V-1 was attached and the dolly would slide up on rails to the top of the tube. The launching explosive charge had to give a fast but steady rise in pressure inside the tube to move the Buzz Bomb smoothly along the ramp but have enough power to push the bomb to flying speed at the end of the ramp after one second. Analysis of the German launching propellants found that a high concentration (89%) of hydrogen peroxide and potassium permanganate was required for launching. That high peroxide concentration could not easily be duplicated by American facilities which generally produced 30% concentrations and production of that percentage was already fully utilized and new facilities would have to be built. Also, the storage of hydrogen peroxide concentrations of over 50% was an unknown factor at the time in America.

With the German peroxide launching method unavailable several alternative methods of launching the JB-2 were suggested:

1)   Air turbine
2)   Large motor operated flywheel connected to a cable that would pull the bomb along the ramp.
3)   A cart with either tricycle wheel or operating on a rail; pulled by a cable winding around a motor operated windlass along a runway or long track.
4)   A launching cart operating along a long rail (2,000 to 5,000 feet) powered by sufficient aircraft engines to attain the required launching speed and then braked to a halt.

5)   A flash boiler system to generate the steam for the German-type ramp instead of using peroxide or explosives.

Impact, the official AAF publication, issued this propaganda statement in its January 1945 issue about the very successful German peroxide/permanganate launching propellant: "Since we felt that this was not as good as some others, we have been experimenting with steam and have found this to be a satisfactory substitute for use with the German-type ramp. But this requires a steam generator and much equipment." Steam propulsion would not be the solution because it did require a steam generator and much complex equipment which was unavailable and would require a long developmental timeline.

The final propulsion solution was to drive the JB-2 along a 500 foot/6° ramp with the help of a solid fuel rocket booster which required two seconds to take it off the ramp. The August 1945, *Impact* later stated that the extra one second launch time with rocket launching system had "important advantages, now secret." This complicated and dangerous rocket assisted takeoff method was called *RATO*. The method had been successfully used to assist overloaded aircraft in taking off from short airfields and appeared to be a feasible method to get the JB-2 airborne. Test firing revealed that when used with JB-2 that four small solid-fuel *RATO* rockets were needed for each launching. However, these rockets were inherently dangerous using a very volatile fuel. The *RATO* rockets had to be jettisoned promptly after the Jet Bomb had reached flying speed, or their induced drag would cause it to go into a stall and crash. To assist in the jettisoning of the *RATO* rockets they were attached to a sled, to which the Jet Bomb was fastened. The rocket sled was intended to fall away when the Jet Bomb left the end of the ramp but on several occasions JB-2s were destroyed when they collided with bouncing rocket sleds during or immediately after the sled-release sequence. Other JB-2s were lost when the *RATO* rockets exploded during the ignition cycle, causing sympathetic detonations of the Jet Bomb's fuel. It was determined that 100 operational launches per day would require approximately 2.5 million pounds of propellant powder per month which would hamper conventional weapon production. Four ramps using rocket launch were completed by September 1945 and the JB-2 was ready for flight testing.

Initial JB-2 Testing

Initial JB-2 test flights began at Eglin Field on 12 October 1944 on a 400 foot 6° concrete and steel launching ramp facing the Gulf of Mexico built

Initial JB-2 test flights began at Eglin Field on 12 October 1944 using a 400 foot 6° concrete and steel launching ramp facing the Gulf of Mexico. The photo shows a JB-2 in a cradle ready to be transported to the test ramp. (AAF)

JB-2 Launching

A JB-2 is readied for launch along a **500 foot, 6° ramp** with the help of a solid fuel rocket booster which required two seconds to take it off the ramp. (AAF)

JB-2 used four small solid-fuel **RATO rockets** for launching which were jettisoned promptly after the Jet Bomb had reached flying speed. (AAF)

To assist in the jettisoning of the RATO rockets they were attached to a **sled**, to which the Jet Bomb was fastened. The rocket sled was intended to fall away when the Jet Bomb left the end of the ski ramp. (AAF)

A sequence of stills from a test film showing a JB-2 launch. The last two photos show the rocket sled separating from the JB-2. (AAF)

on Range 64 at Eglin. Range 64 was a self-contained JB-2 facility with barracks, a mess hall, assembly shop, engine shop, rocket shop, ordnance/explosive storage building, and two bomb-proof range equipment shelters.

On its first flight on 18 October the JB-2 climbed away from the ramp but then went into a shallow dive and crashed into the Gulf after flying 40 seconds and two miles. Between 18 October and 11 November eight more test launches were conducted to establish a feasible launching system. The first two launches were failures with the JB-2s crashing off the ramp or several miles away. Photographic studies determined that the takeoff speed was too low and future launches were to be made with five or six rockets instead of four and with an 8.5° ramp incline instead of 6.5°. The next two JB-2s launched unsatisfactorily and crashed as different combinations of five or six launching rockets and ramp inclines were tried. Investigation of the wrecks showed that the elevator control surfaces had been burned off causing the JB-2s to crash just offshore. When the JB-2 was placed on the launching car at 8° or more the tail dropped four inches and the rocket blast from the six rockets burned the elevators. The fifth test was a disaster as the gasoline shutoff valve malfunctioned and gasoline flowed onto the ground and began to burn as two rockets exploded and the remaining three ignited and launched the burning wreck into the Gulf.

Finally during the sixth test the JB-2 was launched by five rockets at a 6° ramp incline and became airborne successfully and flew at 400 mph, losing the P-63 chase plane before crashing nine miles out into the Gulf. The altitude control had been set for 1,500 feet but radar tracking indicated only 800 feet during the flight. The next day the seventh unit was launched and reached its 6,500 foot altitude pre-set and finally was shot down as it passed its allotted 50 mile distance. The eighth JB-2 left the launch ramp successfully and leveled off at the pre-set 3,500 foot altitude at 400 mph but lost its tracking fighters which were assigned to shoot it down and where this JB-2 landed was not determined.

Tests continued between 12 November and 21 December 1944 and despite the successes of tests seven and eight; six of the next nine test flights ended in crashes and by 20 January 1945, 15 of 24 JB-2 launches resulted in crashes during or immediately after launch. In January 1945 the NDRC investigated alternatives to the inadequate rocket-propelled

ramp launches. Also, at the time there was doubt that American launching rocket propellant production would not be sufficient if the JB-2 did become operational and if it did it would be at the expense of other vital ammunition production. The flywheel inertial system, in particular, was thought to have merit, and was tested as a scale model but never developed any further.

Because of these launching problems, real and potential; the AAF considered launching the JB-2 from a B-17 in flight. The *Luftwaffe* had successfully air-launched 1,176 V-1s from He-111s from July 1944 to January 1945 after the land-based launch sites were over run. The JB-2's 17.67 foot wingspan and 5,000 pound weight and consequent aerodynamic drag required it to be carried externally under the wing of the B-17. A second JB-2 had to be carried under the opposite wing for balance and symmetry to prevent the mother from going into a stall. In December 1944 tests determined that a B-17 could carry two JB-2s over a combat radius of 1,000 miles but it wasn't until 2 March 1945 that the first successful air launch of JB-2s from a B-17 took place.

Until the end of 1944 the salient fact remained that the majority of JB-2 launch attempts failed but by early 1945 the launch problems were essentially solved. In May 1945, with the introduction of a zero length launch system 97 consecutive launches were successful.

By 1945, the JB-2 still did not have a guidance system except for a fixed compass heading flown for a predetermined time after which the engine was shut off optimistically over the intended target which was necessarily a large city. This system basically was the same as used by the 1918 Kettering *Bug* and by the German V-1 which the Allies maligned as an indiscriminate terror weapon. Again, this problem was due to the slip shod research, design, and procurement practices that the AAF and ultimately, Gen. Arnold allowed to continue. The Engineering Division's answer to the guidance problem was to redevelop a guidance system similar to the system used by the *Willie Orphan* program. In order to know the exact location of the Jet Bomb relative to the target at all times, the Engineering Division used the AN/APW-1 control equipment with modified SCR-584 gun-laying radar that was originally developed to aim anti-aircraft gun batteries. This system was similar to the *Cottongrass* phase of the *Abusive Project*. The controller was able to track and guide the JB-2 anywhere

JB-2 Air-Launched Tests

The JB-2's 17.67 foot wingspan and 5,000 pound weight and consequent aerodynamic drag required it to be carried externally under the wing of the B-17. A second JB-2 had to be carried under the opposite wing for balance and symmetry to prevent the mother from going into a stall. (AAF)

Close up of the wing rack carrying the JB-2. (AAF)

On 2 March 1945 the first successful air launch of JB-2s from a B-17 took place. The JBs were launched on at a time in quick succession so as not to cause aerodynamic balance problems. (AAF)

within the range of the radar with a theoretical accuracy of 15 yards in range and 250 yards in azimuth out to a distance of 60 miles. With the installation of a low frequency radio transponder on the Jet Bomb, it was thought that the range and same accuracy could be increased to 200 miles. However, tests showed that with the transponder the maximum range was only 85 miles with a large average error of six miles.

Gen. Arnold Authorizes JB-2 Manufacture and Deployment
On 12 January 1945, with ground launching tests becoming more successful, Gen. Arnold directed that a astonishing 75,000 JB-2s be produced with a delivery schedule of 100 per day not later than 1 September 1945 and then increasing by 100 more per day for each month until 500 per day were produced in January 1946. Arnold also ordered that remote control be "added as soon as practicable but ….not delay the delivery or launching programs." As discussed previously the amount of explosive propellant and presses to grain the explosive into rocket propellant to launch 100 JB-2s per day was worrisome but to launch 500 per day was an exorbitant demand on America's munitions production. Launching ramps were another problem as Arnold ordered 100 ramps to be constructed by the Corps of Engineers; 20 immediately for training and 80 ramps at 16 per month beginning July 1945.

A then colossal total of $950 million was to be expended to produce 150,000 JB-2s:

Airframe Prime Contactors*	$390 million @ $2,600 each
GFC Contractors	
Control Units	$300 million @$2,000 each
Pressure Regulators	$15 million @ $100 each
Air Containers (2 per unit)	$25.5 Million @ $170 per set
Shutoff Valves (2 per unit)	$7.5 million @$50 per set
Jet Engine and Metering Units	$150 million @$1,000 each
Warheads	$90 million @$600 each
Radio Sets	
(1,500/1 for each 10 airframes)	$2.25 million @ $150 each

Launching Requirements for 150,000 JB-2s would add $458,500 million for a staggering total of $1,408,750,000 billion**:

Propellant Fuel***	$36 million for 75 million pounds @ $45 per 100 pounds
New Propellant Facilities	$130 million
Rocket Motor Cases	$125 million (750,000 @ 5 rockets per Launch) @ $250 each or $1250 per launch
Launching Carts	$75million @ $500 each

*Airframe prime contractors were Willys producing 3,275 and Higgins, Murray, Budd, Firestone, and Nash Kelvinator each contracted for 30,260 by July 1946. The monthly total production was to reach 15,200 by December 1945 and the grand total by July 1946 was to be 154,575.
** The cost to develop and produce 3,943 B-29s was $3.7 billion, the 9,817 B-25s cost just over $1 billion, while the Atomic Bomb cost over $2 billion so the $1,4 billion for JB-2 project would not have been insignificant if the war had continued.
***The Ordnance Department was to contract for one million pounds of rocket fuel per month which was to be sufficient for 1,500 launchings at 500 pounds of fuel per launch. A new $5 million plant to produce propellant for 1,000 launchings per month was recommended to be built at the New York Ordnance Works by Monsanto which was then to be in charge of production beginning in April 1945. To provide for 15,000 launchings per month (500 per day) was estimated to require a facility ten times as large.

Questions arose as to the reason for Gen. Arnold's extremely large request for 75,000 JB-2s to be produced by 1 October 1945. It appears that Generals Marshall and Eisenhower demanded that Arnold provide large numbers of JB-2s to the ETO as a large "all-weather" weapon that could have been used during the recent Battle of the Bulge when the Germans attacked the Allies under cover of poor weather and low cloud ceiling. More importantly, the small scale deployment of the bomb was thought to be purely as terror weapon but it was considered that launching at a rate of between 500 and 1,000 per day against a target such as the industrial Ruhr could achieve significant strategic results. To manufacture 75,000 JB-2s would require 60,000 aircraft workers and five million square feet of production floor space and would jeopardize other AAF guided bomb programs as well as conventional bomb production and production of medium and heavy artillery ammunition for the Army Ground Forces. The filling of warheads for the JB-2s would reduce by over 4% the amount of TNT available for artillery ammunition and aircraft bombs would be similarly affected. Also, 10 cargo ships would have to arrive safely at European ports each month to maintain the required JB-2 daily firing rate. An interesting suggestion to meet the JB-2 production quota was to manufacture the propulsion units, gyros, and other components in the US and then ship these components to France where the airframe would be fabricated and the final assembly completed. The Germans had several V-1 assembly and manufacturing plants in France one of which (at Thil) was captured intact and there were adequate French laborers available in the area. Also there was factory floor space and labor available in the Paris area that could be converted to JB-2 manufacture and assembly.

On 12 January 1945, despite these objections, Arnold, instead of reducing the requirement, increased them to 3,000 per month and 100 launches per day by September 1945 and which was to be further increased to 6,000 per month and 200 per day by October; which were followed by incremental increases until reaching a launch rate of 300 per day and an overall production of a staggering 15,000 per month by January 1946. This rate of JB-2 production would require the priority transfer of factory space, machinery, the use of critical materials, along with the diversion of over 13,000 skilled airframe and instrument personnel from conventional aircraft production. Once the JB-2 was in full production it would require seven to nine months to transfer units operating in the ETO back to the US to train them and afterward deploy them to the Pacific. After two weeks, it appears that rationality prevailed as on 25 January Gen. Arnold cancelled the 12 January requirement, and reset the launch rate at 100 per day which would require a production rate of 3,000 JB-2s per month which was nonetheless a very large requirement.

Instead of the standard procurement system that was used to research, design, and acquire conventional aircraft; the JB-2 and other AAF guided missile programs suffered from the haphazard way they were handled. The JB-2, particular, being a ground launched missile that threatened to compete with manned aircraft, had many more adversaries than advocates. In October 1943, Brig.Gen. H.M. McClelland, the Air Communications Officer (ACO) had been assigned inclusive responsibility for guided aerial weapons research and development. However, the ACO had little expertise outside the field of communications and had no authority within the AAF and was ineffectual and in December 1944 was relieved and no replacement was named. So by early spring 1945, only Gen. Arnold remained as the JB-2's major supporter. Arnold, who had suffered multiple heart attacks due the stress of commanding the entire AAF for seven years, named himself the CG of the new 20th Air Force and had little time to vigorously defend the JB-2 against influential factions in the AAF.

It was not until 6 February 1945; that Gen. Barney Giles finally issued a memorandum to justify not only the control of guided aerial weapons by the AAF, but specifically the JB-2 ground launched missile which was being validated by the AAF based upon strategic as well as tactical requirements. Giles' intent was to continue future control over ground launched missiles of any type or range or capability for the AAF. The Joint New Weapons Guided Missile Committee was formed on 16 January 1945 with its authorized intention being to "study the influence of guided missiles on future trends in warfare and to recommend a national program for their development." In response to Giles' memorandum the Committee concluded that ground launched missiles would be controlled by the AAF "when they supported tactical aerial bombardment or had a strategic target" and that control of ground launched missiles would be granted to the Army Ground Forces "when they complemented artillery fire and to the AAF." The bottom line was that the JB-2 was considered both an air and a ground weapon and the service, AGF or AAF, that would be the most effective in utilizing it in combat would most likely gain possession of it.

The Army Ground Forces (AGF) decided that the JB-2 could be launched from the beach during an amphibious operation and that they would be used as very long range artillery to strike an area rather than a precise target and consequently would not require complicated guidance and control equipment. The AGF wished to deploy the JB-2 in large numbers as early as 1 September 1945 as part of *Operation Olympic*, the invasion of Kyushu, Japan but the Atomic Bombs ended the war before that could happen.

The competition between the Army's Air Forces and Army Ground Forces for control of the JB-2 had begun with the salvage of a damaged German V-1 by the AGF in July 1944. The V-1 engine was soon duplicated and tested and the AGF requested 25,000 and not to be outdone Gen. Arnold counteracted with his request for an eventual 75,000 to be launched at a rate of 100 per day by October 1945. This AAF/AGF skirmish for JB-2 control led to the *McNarney Directive* on guided missiles which gave the AAF responsibility for all guided missiles launched from aircraft as well as ground launched guided missiles that "flew using aerodynamic forces." It gave the AGF responsibility for missiles that flew by way of momentum (e.g. ballistic missiles such as the V-2). Arnold did not realize the potential of the German V-2 rocket and that in the post-war the V-2 would be under AGF control.

To gain the initiative on the AGF, the AAF authorized the formation of the first operational JB-2 unit which was to be able to launch four missiles per hour, 24/7 which would be only four missiles less than the 100 per day Arnold had set as his goal. When the war in Europe ended in May 1945, the squadron was to be deployed to the Pacific where it was to be deployed from captured territory in the Japanese home islands. However, by June 1945, with AAF conventional bombing decimating Japanese cities, interest in combat testing the JB-2 diminished and production requirements were reduced from the 10,000 that were then on order to 7,000 which included the JB-2s already delivered.

The inter-service rivalry between the AAF and the AGF for the control of guided missiles continued during the summer of 1945; but the combat testing the JB-2 ended with the Hiroshima and Nagasaki Atomic Bombs which not only ended the war but also questioned the need for any other weapon systems; including Jet Bombs. Production of the JB-2 continued until 15 September 1945, when all contracts were cancelled after the AAF had taken delivery of only 1,391 which was less than half the number Arnold had wanted to be available for operations by 1 September. Each JB-2 required about 400 man hours to manufacture and cost around 20 times as much as each German V-1 which was partially due to its much smaller production run but still amounted to $30 million of the authorized $90 million.

Once Germany surrendered in May 1945, the JB-2's range was far too short for deployment in the Pacific. Using the B-29 to air launch the JB-2 was considered but was not possible as the bomber would require extensive modification and besides, was unavailable because the XXI Bomber Command was unwilling to divert any from its bombing of Japan.

Although it was never used in combat, the JB-2 played a significant role in the development of more advanced surface-to-surface missile systems after World War II. Nearly every one of these 1,391 JB-2s were expended in testing until the program was officially closed out on 1 March 1946. The development of the JB-2 was continued and was redesignated as the LTV-1 in late 1947 and then as the LTV-A-1 in early 1948 which was cancelled in early 1949. There were two versions: one with preset internal guidance and another with radar control. Several launch platforms

The **LTV-N-2** *Loon* (USN JB-2 designation) made the first successful submarine launch from the *Cusk* on 12 February 1947. The photo shows the large watertight cylinder and launching ramp located aft of the conning tower. (USN)

Spectacular test launch of a Loon from the *Carbonero*. (USN)

were developed, including permanent and portable ramps, and mobile launching from under the wings of the B-17 and B-29 bombers .

Loon: The US Navy Buzz Bomb Project

The Navy's Buzz Bomb project was initiated by the Bureau of Aeronautics in April 1945 and designated the KGW-1 *Loon*. In late 1945, tests of the XM-1 launching system (using a slotted tube powder catapult) using dummy *Loons* were conducted at the newly opened Naval Air Missile Test Center, Point Mugu Naval Base, CA. In January 1946, the USN completed several operational test launches of a *Loon*, now redesignated as the KUW-1. Directives were issued to develop a launching capability from submarines with the designation LTV-N-2 and the first successful submarine launch was from the *Cusk* on 12 February 1947. The missile was carried behind the conning tower in a large, water-tight cylinder. Once the submarine surfaced, the tank was opened and the *Loon* moved to the rear of the boat and positioned on its aft-facing ramp where it was assembled, the wings attached, and a guidance check was run. The *Loon* was then placed on a launching sled on rails and a booster rocket launched it. The entire operation took nearly an hour to complete the launch and submerge. The LTV-N-2 was redesignated as LTV-2 in September 1947 and finally as LTV-N-2 in early 1948.

Several months after the first *Loon* launch, a second Balao class submarine, the *USS Carbonero* (SS-337), joined the tests to launch the *Loon* and act as the control and tracking station. In August 1947 with the successful results of these tests, the Navy continued the *Loon* submarine launchings continue through 1949 to develop terminal guidance procedures and tactical concepts for the *Regulus*, a submarine-launched guided missile with a range of 500 miles that was then under development. Also modified was the heavy seaplane tender *USS Norton Sound* (AV-11, later AVN-1), becoming the USN's first guided missile ship, and was also adapted to fire the *Lark*, the first sea-to-air missile, designed primarily to intercept Kamikaze attacks

Hughes JB-3 *Tiamat*

The JB-3 *Tiamat* subsonic air-to-air missile program began in January 1944 under project MX-570. The prime contractor was Hughes which was to develop 25 *Tiamats* with the assistance of the NACA; four of which were to be ready for testing by 3 July 1945. The 14.33 foot long, 600 pound JB-3 was propelled by a Monsanto dual-thrust (7,200 pound boost/200 pound sustain) solid-fueled rocket motor and had three comparatively large wings with control surfaces for stability and control. The initial ten units were to be auto-pilot controlled by modified Jack & Heintz units that were used on the JB-2. The *Tiamat* used a semi-active radar seeker mounted on gimbals that acted as a gyro. Control was a pendulous gyroscopic radar seeker which operated pneumatic servos to the three wings. It was to carry a 500 pound HE warhead was triggered

Hughes JB-3 *Tiamat* (USN)

JB-4 (AAF)

by a proximity fuse. The projected cost was to be $363 million at $13,721 each with an additional $56 million allocated for a wind tunnel test model. A Northrop P-61 Back Widow was to be the control aircraft but prototypes were initially launched from the ground with the aid of a booster and then from A-26 Invader aircraft.

Testing and development of the JB-3 continued until after World War II but the program was eventually terminated in late 1946 or early 1947 at which time the more promising air-to-air missile projects had been started, notably the AAM-A-1 *Firebird* and AAM-A-2/F-98/GAR-1 *Falcon*.

JB-4

The 3,000 pound, 12 foot wingspan JB-4, developed under project MX-607, was a basically a GB-1 guided glide bomb fitted with a Ford PJ31 pulsejet engine, the same type as used in the JB-2/LTV-N-2 *Loon*. This pulsejet was to extend the standoff range to 75 miles at 445 mph. Like the GB-4, it was equipped with an AN/AXT-2 television transmitter, sending its TV camera image to an operator in the launching aircraft, which could send radio commands to change the course of the missile. The JB-4 was reported as a surface-to-surface missile in some official records but it seems that is was also intended for air launch. The missile was tested in 1945 but the program was cancelled at the end of World War II.

JB-5, JB-6, JB-7, JB-9, and JB-9

The JB-5, 6, 7, and 9 were all cancelled in the design or concept phase before being built. The JB-5 (project MX-595) was designed to be a wingless unguided air-to-surface rocket with a 3.7 mile range, while the JB-6 (project MX-600) was planned as a spin-stabilized supersonic air-to-surface guided missile. The JB-7 (project MX-605) was to be a 9,700 pound turbojet-powered surface-to-surface cruise missile with a range of 400 miles. It was cancelled when no suitable design was tendered. The Boeing JB-8 designation was briefly assigned to the MX-606 project for a surface-to-air guided missile.

Northrop JB-10

The JB-10 was the successor to the JB-1 Project using a single pulse engined airframe that was 12 feet long, 4.8 feet high, had a wingspan of 29.2 feet, and weighed 7,210 pounds. A single Ford PJ31 pulsejet engine rated at 900 pounds thrust was mounted in a centerline shroud which was of a larger diameter than the pulsejet to allow the flow of cooling air around the engine. The pulsejets were to drive the JB-10 at 425 mph over a range of 200 miles at an operating altitude of 2,500 feet. The prominent cast magnesium bomb containers of the JB-1 were also removed and replaced by two integral 1,825 pound HE warhead sections in the wing

Northrop JB-10 (AAF)

roots. The Hammond control equipment was the same as used on the JB-1 with slight modification in the rigging of the control surfaces for elevon control in both pitch and roll. The JB-10 was equipped with a telemetering transmitter which was to send data in flight to the test center for six minutes from the firing of the rockets. During tests this unit functioned "very successfully" during tests.

The JB-10 testing program was delayed for long periods due to problems due to the loading of the inert warheads. During weight and balance measurements it was found that the weight of plaster and lead added to the warhead at the factory was 750 pounds too heavy. The correct weight and balance for each bomb had to obtained by the removal of a portion of the warhead and adding approximately 100 pounds of lead to the airframe rear section.

Like the original JB-2 the JB-10 was to be a low-precision standoff weapon for the planned invasion of Japan. The missile used a simple preset guidance system, where it would fly a predetermined distance into the direction of launch and then dive to the ground. Eleven JB-10s were built and ten were expended in testing. The first flight of a JB-10 occurred in April 1945 at Range 64, Eglin Field using a level ramp with 370 feet of track with modified launching sleds equipped with five Monsanto rockets having a burning time of 1.8 seconds but was not successful. In fact, of the ten test-launches of JB-10s the first eight were failures caused by the mechanical malfunctions at launching or during takeoff. JB-10 #9 climbed to 1,300 feet and then flew level for 90 seconds at 225 mph. It then began a pitch oscillation flying for another three minutes ten seconds and 16 miles before crashing into the Gulf. For the next test (JB-10 #10) slight modifications to the altitude control were made to improve pitch control. When this JB separated from the sled, it moved up sharply and went into a spin to the right apparently due to the malfunction of the control equipment. JB-10 #11 was prepared for testing but since this was the last available bomb it was decided to save it as a museum piece and sent to Freeman Field, Seymore, IN. So, because of system component developmental problems, its expensive construction, and finally because the need for such a weapon had disappeared, the JB-10 program was terminated in March 1946.

Guided Air-to-Air Fragmentation Bomb
In November 1944, after preliminary wind tunnel tests, the NDRC issued specifications on Project MX-570 which was for a "Special Fragmentation Bomb." The weapon was to have a maximum weight of 150 pounds and dimensions of 15 inches in diameter and 15 inches long so that "the most

efficient fragmentation can be had against aircraft structures within a 25 foot radius." It was to have a proximity fuse, an electric detonator with a safety switch operated by an external electric circuit, and an air travel safety device. The Development Engineering Branch AMC was assigned to furnish the Air Service Technical Command with a prototype by 1 January 1945 and ten inert units by 1 March for flight tests. This project seems to have had very low priority and nothing more is known about it.

Conclusions on the American World War II Guided Missile Program
Before 1939 only a few innovative men in American industry and in the military were engaging in research in missile systems and design albeit with limited funds and authority. It would not be until September, 1939, only weeks before Germany invaded Poland to start World War II that the AAC received the then very sizeable Congressional allocation of $300 million to begin a program to expand its insufficient forces. But of this amount only $3.5 million was allotted for research and development which was then pursued with limited and undirected vigor. Throughout the war America, despite its superior resources, production capacity, and production proficiency, continued to neglect technological research with an indifference to its vast potential. America was fortunate that at the beginning of the war it had under development and manufacture, or at least on the drawing boards, every combat aircraft which it had in operational service at the end of the war. From 1939 to 1945, with vast funding, these weapons were improved and relied on to win the war without resorting to "exotic" technological weapons.

During its 12 short years in power the Nazi government encouraged scientific research with no consideration for its monetary or moral cost. Its research scientists were indulged and basic research was encouraged for the sake of science without the immediate assurance of possible practical or technological application. But had Germany advanced in technological development and manufacture as she had in fundamental research, had she waited a few years to begin the war, or had she not made initial and costly mistakes in conducting it, the Allies could possibly have lost the war, or certainly not have won it as soon as they did. Had Germany not committed these miscalculations and had been able to develop and manufacture these possibly decisive advanced weapons in mass quantities; the prewar American military machine had nothing on its drawing boards to counter them. At the end of the war America and Russia both discovered how far they lagged behind the Germans in guided missile research, development, and production and made it a priority to capture German scientists and equipment to rapidly advance their postwar missile agenda.

8

GT-1 Glide Pattern Torpedo

In March 1941, while the British were working on their glide torpedo project, Gen. Hap Arnold ordered Gen. Oliver Echols CO of Wright Field's Air Materiel Division to assemble the necessary personnel to develop an American glide bomb and glide torpedo, the latter to be patterned after a British design.

Before work could be initiated on the glide torpedo, several Army-Navy conferences became necessary in the spring of 1941 as the Navy felt that the torpedo was in their sphere of influence. Working in cooperation with the Joint Air Advisory Committee the Army and Navy had to establish the difference between the terms *torpedo* and *glide bomb*. On 16 April it was agreed that a torpedo was a weapon that was "intended to travel horizontally under water to affect its final contact with its target" while the glide bomb, on the other hand, was any explosive delivered from an aircraft "intended to be controllable in flight beyond the usual gravity or parachute types." It was further established that the Navy would develop the glide torpedo and the Army the glide bomb.

The AAC did not concur with this definition and continued to lobby and finally, after much interservice bickering, was allowed to continue both projects. Some sources state that the AAC, in deference to the Navy changed the glide torpedo designation to *Hydrobomb* but the *Hydrobomb* was a distinct project utilizing a bomb which was propelled underwater by a solid fuel. (The "real" *Hydrobomb* will be discussed next.)

One of the basic problems with conventional aerial torpedo attacks was that the aircraft had to approach the target in a low straight and level run before releasing the torpedo that made it vulnerable to defensive AA fire. In experimentation with what later became known as "stand off" weapons, the B-25 was used to test a number of these weapons which attempted to overcome the lack of an internal guidance system. The solution was to attach small vertical, and horizontal aerodynamic surfaces to stabilize a body section that contained the warhead, such as the GB-13 which was developed both as a glide bomb and a glide torpedo, the latter being designated as the GT-1 for training purposes.

After Pearl Harbor, there was a renewed Air Corps interest in air-dropped torpedoes by medium bombers . The problem in developing an aerial torpedo was to slow them down when they were released from medium altitudes at high speeds. In January 1942 the AAC requisitioned 5,000 standard naval Mark 13 torpedoes but the Navy was able to transfer only 114 torpedoes due to their own combat requirements and due to production problems and shortages. Despite the prospect of not receiving any more torpedoes from the Navy during the next year, in February 1942, the AAC set specifications for the GT-1 Glide Torpedo. The GT-1 was to

attach a standard Mk13 Naval aerial torpedo to a slightly modified Air Force GB-1 Glide Bomb twin boom airframe. However, any effort by the AAC to design its own torpedo breached the earlier agreement and the Air Corps quickly yielded following persistent Navy objections in March 1943.

The fundamental problem in developing the GT-1 was that it was a modification of the GB-1 glide bomb which was being developed concurrently. The release of the torpedo from the glider was much more complicated than merely releasing a glider holding a bomb as it had to be at the correct angle to ensure a clean entry into the water. Also, once the torpedo entered the water a simple device was needed for changing the straight run of the torpedo to a large spiraling pattern that would cover a large area to increase the probability of a hit. The weapon was intended for use in crowded harbors or against large convoys and the Japanese bastions

GT-1 Glide Torpedo was a modification of the GB-1 designed to carry the standard Mk13 torpedo. The booms of the GT-1 were somewhat longer than the GB-1 to correctly position the tail for the longer torpedo. (USN)

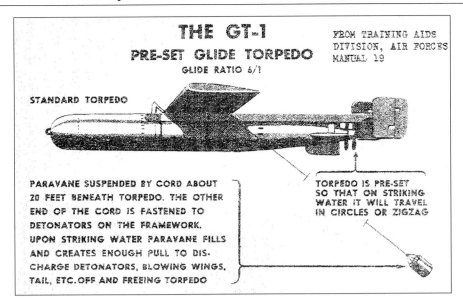

at Truk and Rabaul where 40 to 50 ships were often concentrated. Also, the glide torpedo in running in a spiraling underwater pattern was considered to be a choice weapon for night attacks as the conventional torpedo had to be carefully aimed which would be difficult at night and the conventional torpedo had to be dropped at a close-in low altitude attack that would expose the torpedo bombers to search lights and AA fire. In the face of these problems it was fortunate that the glide torpedo had some zealous supporters; Gen. Hap Arnold, in particular, and Gen. Barney Giles and Col. George Younger who were Arnold's movers and shakers.

The GT-1 weighed 2,455 pounds of which 2,120 pounds was the standard Mk13 torpedo that measured 13 feet long and was 22.4 inches in diameter. The booms of the GT-1 were somewhat longer than those of the GB-1 to correctly position the tail for the longer torpedo. The GT-1 had a glide ratio of 6:1 and was dropped from 5,000 to 6,000 feet that would make the dropping aircraft safe from light caliber AA. The proposed accuracy of the glide torpedo was comparable to placing a dropped bomb into a 1,000 foot circle from 5,000 feet. The range of the standard torpedo was 19,500 feet and could be used with any run pattern. The controls were preset and a paravane fired explosive bolts which released the airframe when the torpedo was at the correct altitude above the water for normal launch.

The Office of the Assistant Chief of Air Staff, Operations, Commitments, and Requirements (OC&R) of the Special Weapons Branch at Wright Field directed that facilities and personnel be made available to develop an airborne glider torpedo. After both the British and US Navy had abandoned the weapon in tests against moving targets, Wright engineers felt that the GT-1 would be only effective against stationary targets. There was an initial order for 700 units followed by 250 more with a production rate of about 75 per week. On 6 April 1944 290 were available with 90 delivered to Eglin for testing and the remaining 200 for delivery to the Pacific for combat use in a priority project.

Col. Hollaman, Chief of Special Weapons, set up the tests at Eglin under Maj. Maryrath, Capt. Pierce, and Lt. Moorman of the Special Weapons Branch who all had extensive experience with the glide bomb. At Eglin, Maj. James Muri, CO of the First Proving Ground Torpedo Squadron was assigned to the project. The group was given GB-1 glide bomb airframes, a B-17 equipped with standard glide bomb wing racks and the associated electrical release mechanisms, and 10 Mark 13 torpedoes were procured from the Navy. From 25 August to 12 September 1943, 19 of 22 GT-1 glide bombs using the GB-1 airframe and dropped from B-17s

at the Eglin were successfully guided to their targets. However, these drop tests revealed several basic problems that needed to be overcome before the GT-1 could become operational. First, the torpedo needed to separate from the glider airframe before it entered the water and then the torpedoes needed to enter the water at the proper angle to be able to dive to the correct depth and remain on course. If the angle of entry were too steep, the torpedo tumbled damaging the control surfaces and could even cause it to fracture. If the torpedo entered the water at too flat an angle, the control surfaces were also damaged; the propeller shafts fractured; and the internal machinery including the main turbine bearings damaged; all rendering the torpedo inoperable. For aircraft drops of conventional torpedoes the Navy had previously determined the correct angle of entry to be 18° and 33° but for glider drops the proper angle was not yet determined. A conventional torpedo dropped from an aircraft was from about 300 feet whereas a torpedo was released from the glider when it and the airframe hit the water. To achieve the proper angle the torpedo was mounted on the glide bomb airframe at 10° nose down attitude when it hit the water on the glider. Tests showed that at this setting the torpedo/glide bomb airframe would not continue to glide into the water but immediately spun and crashed into the water. The next attempt to achieve the correct diving characteristics was to mount the torpedo on the glider with its longitudinal axis parallel with the glider's twin booms. In this configuration the torpedo/glide bomb airframe hit the water flat and skipped off the surface.

The solution was to have the glider released from the mother aircraft and while in the glide, a small paravane was released from the glider which permitted the torpedo to fall free, allowing it to attain the proper entrance angle during its free fall. The paravane resembled a bucket suspended below and behind the torpedo on the end of a 20 to 30 foot cord. When the paravane bucket struck the water it filled, the weight of the water exerting enough pressure to close an electric circuit that actuated an electric firing mechanism that detonated the retaining pins containing an explosive charge that released retaining bands that held the torpedo to the glider.

When the torpedo was released from the airframe at 25 feet, however, the torpedo had a tendency to hit flat on the water and skip, often several times, before it began to sink. This skipping could damage the torpedo's steering mechanism or deflect it off its course. During drop tests in November 1943, it was observed that the released GT-1 airframe would climb suddenly as the torpedo fell away. Engineering Division designers thought that this upward movement of the GT-1 assembly could be controlled to pull the tail of the torpedo up and cause its nose to hit

Previously the B-25 was designed to carry a conventional torpedo externally (*see* chapter 4), but engineering trials established that the GT-1 could most readily be attached to the underside of the B-25J medium bomber, although only one GT-1 could be carried at a time. (AAF)

the water first. When a cable was attached to the tail of the torpedo and clipped to the GT-1 assembly, the torpedoes began to release nose first from the glide assembly making the GT-1 a viable weapon.

The AAF next had to determine which bomber was to carry it. Engineering trials established that the GT-1 could most readily be attached to the underside of the B-25J medium bomber, although only one GT-1 could be carried at a time. Operational testing using the B-25/GT-1 combination began in February 1944 and the B-25J demonstrated it could carry and successfully drop the GT-1, but with some accuracy problems. As was seen in the conversion of B-17Fs to carry the GB-1, modifying large numbers of B-25Js to carry the GT-1 was much more difficult than making modifications to a single B-25J for test purposes. Then in March 1944, the Hammond Instrument Company reported that it would be unable to meet mass production requirements until Spring 1944, at the earliest, for the specified electrical switching equipment necessary to permit the B-25J to carry the GT-1.

The Eglin tests were concluded on 11 October 1943 and the results were satisfactory enough to prompt the Air Materiel Command to immediately order 500 and to place further orders in November with more in February and March 1944. Operational testing of the GT-1 carried by B-25s began in February 1944 and proved to be more successful than the earlier B-17 tests. In early April 1944, 18 B-25J-1s (43-3905, 3906, 3907, 3955, 3957, 3959, 3963, 3971, 3973, 3975, 3976, 3977, 3978, 3979, 3980, 3981, 3982, and 3983) were modified by Hammond Instrument and equipped to carry the GT-1. Crews were trained in GT-1 use at Hunter Field, GA and during December 1943 final drop test were made with both dummy and live torpedoes. It was found that the Norden bombsight was less accurate than the pilot's standard NC-3 gunsight for delivering the GT-1 but neither was accurate enough to hit the water within a circular error of 1,600 feet while 75% launched at 5,000 feet would hit within a half mile of the aiming point. The Joint New Weapons Committee

concluded that the GT-1 proved to be an "Area" weapon that would have to be released in "large quantities to be effective." The carrying B-25s experienced such loss in speed and range performance when carrying the GT-1 that the Air Staff Requirements Committee was about to abandon the project in January 1945.

Not willing abandon the GT-1 Project the Air Technical Service aided by the 594th Air Materiel Squadron Command traveled to Pacific to prepare the weapon for combat in May 1945. The reason for this continuation of the GT-1 Program has not been documented but appears to be Gen. Arnold's reluctance to abandon it without an operational test, just as he had done with the GB-1 Program. The First Provisional Glide Torpedo Squadron (1PGTS) was formed and trained for a month on deployment tactics. The aircraft and crews then departed for McClellan Field at Sacramento and then to Fairfield-Suisun (Travis AFB today). They departed 1 May for Hickam Field, HI for assignment with the Seventh Bomber Command Training Detachment.

To make the GT-1 more effective, once the torpedo was in the water a tail mounted mechanism was pre-set to enable the torpedo to travel in spirals that threatened a large circular area and helped it to avoid detection. The spiral pattern automatically put the torpedo into an ever increasing circular pattern that would reach a limit of about 2,000 feet in diameter and then go into an ever decreasing circular pattern that would be reversed when the rudder reached its original position.

To test the concept in actual combat the First Provisional Glide Torpedo Squadron was assigned to the 41st Bombardment Group, 47BS of the VII Bomber Command of the 7AF. This unit, consisting of 18 crews, was issued 14 B-25J-ls that were equipped with specially modified bomb racks to carry the glide torpedo underneath the fuselage. The initial testing was done in Hawaii when the 1PGTS arrived with four officers: Lt.Col. George Younger of the Bombardment Office of the Chief of the Air Force; Capt. Atwood, Operations Officer of the Torpedo Training Command at Eglin; Lt. Moorman, a torpedo engineer from Wright and Lt.(jg)

Two views of a GT-1 loaded on a **B-25 of the 47BS**. (AAF)

Hoover, the USN Torpedo Ordnance Representative. In Hawaii the crews completed not only their torpedo training but also their combat training as they also flew missions other than torpedo missions. In a demonstration off Molokai Island the crews put on an impressive show making perfect drops with torpedoes that entered the water successfully and then functioned perfectly in their spiral patterns. After about 20 hours of training the crews returned back to the mainland and would later join the 41BG.

The First Glide Torpedo Squadron rejoined the 41BG stationed at Okinawa and the glide torpedo saw action for the first time on 28 July 1945 but the mission was scrubbed when fighter escort failed to rendezvous. The following day nine B-25Js took off to attack two Japanese fleet carrier (CV) and one light (CVL) carrier which were discovered by aerial reconnaissance in Sasebo Harbor, Kyushu, Japan. The fighter escort arrived late and the carriers could not be attacked as the fighters would have run out of fuel continuing the escort. Instead, secondary targets were attacked. Six Mitchells hit merchant shipping in Makurazaki Harbor while the other three attacked Kagoshima. The results of the attack were difficult to determine as many torpedoes were dropped far from the target and the paths of the torpedoes could not be followed to their circling termination

On 31 July 1945 13 47BS B-25s attacked two Japanese carriers based at Sasebo Harbor. All 13 GT-1s were dropped and 11 made their entrance into the water normally and then circled around the harbor. The results were difficult to determine but post-strike recon indicated that the two carriers may have been hit. (AAF)

due to the evasive action and break away of the carrying aircraft soon after the drop to evade the moderately heavy AA fire in the area. Another mission on the 30th was again aborted when the fighter escort did not appear.

On the 31st, 13 B-25s attacked the enemy carriers at Sasebo and all 13 GT-1s were dropped from 7,500 feet. One failed to glide and spun in and another suffered a direct AA hit after leaving the aircraft and exploded in midair. The remaining 11 torpedoes made their entrance into the water normally and then circled around the harbor. Two GT-1s hit the shore; two were lost during observation while the remaining seven entered the area where the carriers were moored. Again the results of the attack were difficult to determine as many torpedoes were dropped far from the target and the paths of the torpedoes could not be followed to their circling termination due to the evasive action and break away of the carrying B-25s soon after the drop to evade the moderately heavy AA fire in the area. Post strike photos did indicate that hits could have been made on the enemy carriers, *Haystake* and *Kasegi*, or their surrounding torpedo nets. Two B-25s returned to base with AA damage.

The final attack was made on 1 August by nine B-25s against shipping targets in Nagasaki harbor. Upon arriving a haze was encountered that restricted vision to four to seven miles near the harbor while a portion of the city was on fire from an attack on the previous day by Task Force 38 and further obscured the harbor targets. Nine GT-1s were dropped with one spinning in on the drop. Three were seen to hit the water but five just disappeared into the haze heading toward the targets. The results were not observed due to the narrowness of the harbor, the evasive action of the retreating bombers , and heavy AA fire.

These operational tests concluded that in the future it would be necessary for reconnaissance aircraft to accompany the B-25s on these missions to determine their effectiveness. However, the war in the Pacific ended before any further glide torpedo missions could be carried out but these tests eventually led to an entirely new family of postwar anti-shipping weapons. Both the GB-1 and the GT-1 was abruptly removed from AAF inventory although the Navy continued to show some interest in glide torpedoes after the war. In the atomic bomb, the AAF had the ultimate weapon and glide torpedoes were, at best, only an option to strategic bombing and soon the AAF lost interest.

To test the GT-1 concept combat the First Provisional Glide Torpedo Squadron was assigned to the 47BS of the 7AF. The 18 crews were issued 14 B-25J-ls that were equipped with specially modified bomb racks to carry the glide torpedo underneath the fuselage.

9

Speedee Bombs

The *Upkeep* Dambuster's Bouncing Bomb
In early 1942, Barnes Wallis, the brilliant British aeronautical engineer and inventor, conceived the idea of the famous "bouncing bomb" which could be dropped upstream of a dam, ricochet over the water in a succession of bounces over anti-torpedo nets, and hit the dam wall and sink and explode at the vulnerable underwater face of the dam.

After some initial tests Wallis decided on a barrel-shaped bomb given a back spin to keep it gyroscopically on an identical axis on every bounce. The barrel shape was chosen as the rounded sides of the barrel would hit the water's surface on every bounce and after the bomb hit; the residual back spin would cause the bomb to "crawl" underwater flat against the dam wall. Once the barrel-shape was chosen, Wallis and his staff worked on developing a number of stout, barrel-shaped models, each with differing weight-size-shape ratios that were small enough in diameter to be carried by a Lancaster four engine bomber. Wallis repeatedly tested models in test tanks with varying combinations of back spin, catapult velocity,

and release height. By trial and error and by simple elimination he was able to choose the model with the widest range of reliable performance. Wallis chose a 10,000 pound barrel which could safely spin 450-500 rpms backwards before release from an aircraft and achieve enough gyroscopic stability to bounce for half a mile or more.

Full-scale test drops of this design began at Chesil Beach in September 1942 using a modified Wellington bomber. These tests were successful and Wallis was able to convince officials to approve further tests which led to the development of two separate variants of the bouncing bomb idea; a large cylindrical mine codenamed *Upkeep* to be carried by the newly introduced Lancaster for use against dams and a smaller spherical mine codenamed *Highball* to be carried by Mosquitoes for use against capital ships, such as the German battleship *Tirpitz*. During tests *Upkeep* proved satisfactory, while *Highball* was found to be less accurate after release. Informally referred to as "bombs," *Upkeep* and *Highball* were officially described as "mines' as they were to detonate in water, but technically they were depth charges as they were to explode at a set depth.

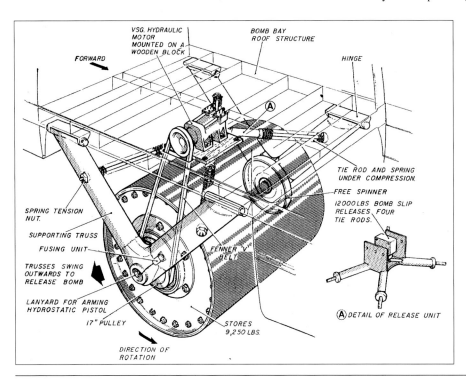

British *Upkeep* Bouncing Dambuster's Bomb

The 10,000 pound **Upkeep Bomb** was not stored in the Lancaster's bomb bay but was slung horizontally below the bomber on a cradle. (AFHRC)

The top secret *Upkeep* mission was flown on the night of 16/17 May 1943, under the code name *Operation Chastise* but will forever be immortalized as the "Dambusters Raid." The **Möhne Dam** (shown) and Eder Dams were breached with great loss of life down river but very little actual damage occurred to Ruhr industrial capacity as all damage was quickly repaired. The more vital Sorpe Dam was not damaged. (AFHRC)

The *Upkeep* bomb was not stored in the bomb bay but was slung horizontally below the bomber. On the approach to the target the bomb was spun up to 500 rpm. The bombs had to be dropped from an exact height of 60 feet and as barometric altimeters were not sufficiently accurate; spotlights were aimed at an angle at the ground. When the two spots of light on the water merged into one, the pilot knew he was at an exact height of 60 feet. A hydrostatic fuse was set for 30 feet and if it malfunctioned, a delayed detonation fuse was included. Details of the bouncing bomb and its release mechanism were kept secret until 1962.

Wallis presented his concept to the Chief of the Air Staff and was ordered to prepare the bombs for an attack on the Möhne, Eder, and Sorpe dams in the important German industrial region of the Ruhr. The specially formed 617 Squadron, with hand-picked crews commanded by celebrated Wing Commander Guy Gibson, was chosen for the mission and practiced their bombing raids on Derwent Water.

The top secret mission, carried out on the night of 16/17 May 1943, was code named *Operation Chastise*, but will forever be immortalized as the "Dambusters Raid," made famous in Paul Brickhill's bestseller and the 1955 movie. The attack had huge propaganda and morale-raising value and made Gibson a national hero who was awarded the Victoria Cross. Of the 19 Lancasters and 133 crewmen that took part in the attacks; eight bombers and 56 men were lost. Both the Möhne Dam and Eder Dams were breached with great loss of life down river but very little actual damage

occurred to Ruhr industrial capacity as all damage was quickly repaired. The more vital Sorpe Dam was not damaged.

The RAF *Highball* Bouncing Bomb
The *Highball* came in two spherical versions. The larger was 48 inches in diameter and weighed 1,200 pounds, of which 750 pounds was explosive charge. The bomb was dimpled to give it better aerodynamics in the fashion of a golf ball. Four were intended to be carried by the Wellington and six by the Warwick. However, the elderly Wellington was near the end of its operational career while the Warwick was experiencing developmental problems and would not be ready for two years. The smaller smooth case *Highballs* were carried in tandem by the Mosquito and weighed 1,000 pounds of which was 545 pounds of Torpex exploded by a Mk14 depth charge pistol. The *Highball* could be bounced 4,500 feet to the target.

The 618 Squadron was specially formed at RAF Skitten on 1 April 1943, as part of Coastal Command No. 18 Group from crews of No. 105 RAF Squadron and No. 109 RAF Squadron. The unit was initially equipped with the Beaufighter II but soon converted to the Mosquito IV and was equipped with the *Highball* bomb. It was designed to attack the Kriegsmarine Battleship *Tirpitz* which was anchored Norwegian Fjords. The squadron trained in Scotland with the bomb but encountered chronic problems with their release mechanisms and the bombs had accuracy problems. Since the Ruhr dams needed to be attacked on a moonlit night

The barrel-shaped bomb was carried on a special cradle that would spin it backwards 450-500 rpms before release in order to achieve enough gyroscopic stability to bounce for half a mile or more. (AFHRC)

The British *Highball* came in two spherical versions. The larger **dimpled** version was weighed 1,200 pounds while the **smooth** case smaller *Highballs* weighed 1,000 pounds. (AFHRC)

The *Highball* was designed to be carried in tandem by 618 Squadron **Mosquito IVs** to attack the German Battleship *Tirpitz* but the Germans protected their battleship with net systems to foil the bouncing bombs. The Squadron was dispatched to the Pacific with hopes to use it against the Japanese Battleship *Yamato* but the huge ship was sunk by conventional weapons before the Squadron arrived. (AFHRC)

in May the *Tirpitz* attack was postponed and after the *Operation Chastise* attack the Germans surrounded the *Tirpitz* with multiple net systems to foil the bouncing bombs which precluded a *Highball* attack.

The Squadron then waited in Scotland for the German surface fleet led by the *Tirpitz* to sortie into the North Sea. In August 1944 the Squadron was deployed to RAF Beccles in Suffolk and continued training while converting to different Mosquito Marks at different bases. The *Tirpitz* was sunk by *Tallboy* bombs of the 617 Squadron on 12 November 1944 and the 618 Squadron was then deployed to Australia in January 1945. It was hoped that the Pacific would present more Japanese shipping targets for their *Highball* bombs; possibly the immense 72,200 ton Battleship *Yamato* and three other Japanese capital ships that remained as threats.

The *Highball* detachment was sent to British Pacific Fleet base at Manus in March 1945 with three months supplies and enough *Highball* bombs for three missions. But difficulties arose from the use of an RAF unit in areas under the control of the US Navy. The USN felt that there was no place for the 618th or the *Highball* in their plans and the squadron was posted to India in July and disbanded with *Highball* kept in reserve under a secret classification where it remained until 1962. In April 1945, the *Yamato* was sunk by conventional American air power and in July the other three were sunk, again by conventional US airpower.

Highball always seemed to be a toy for the Chiefs of Staff for which they could not find a use. While *Chastise* and *Upkeep* were a success and provided an impetus for *Highball's* development; *Highball* and its potential targets were never brought together.

AAF *Speedee*

After the success of *Chastise* the AAF became interested in the British *Highball* bomb because it promised increased release range (i.e. out of AA range) without losing accuracy when compared with conventional low level maritime bombing tactics. The AAF also was attracted by *Highball's* ability to remain in contact with the target's hull as it submerged after hitting the ship where the proximity to the bottom of armored hulls when it exploded caused considerable damage. In December 1944 a Douglas A-26 Invader was sent to the UK modifications center at Brooklands for conversion to *Highball* configuration.

Speedee was basically a copy of the British *Highball* bomb being spherical with flattened sides, weighing 1,000 pounds of which 600 pounds were the Torpex explosive charge. The bomb was revolved in the bomb bay by a ram air turbine at a speed of 800-900 rpm in a direction of rotation opposite to the aircraft's wheel rotation. The spin transmitted gyroscopic stability to the bomb for long period after its release.

The time from release at about 1,600 yards until *Speedee* reached the target was normally between 10 and 16 seconds. It was recommended that the bomber was to continue on course after releasing *Speedee* and not turn sharply away which would give enemy gunners a good shot at the A-26's large bottom profile. Like the *Upkeep* bomb the *Highball* was designed for minimum altitude high speed release on water where a long series of ricochets occurred with the gyroscopic effect of the rotary movement acting to keep the bomb on a true course. Upon striking the shipping target,

The **American *Speedee*** was basically a copy of the British bomb being spherical with flattened sides, weighing 1,000 pounds of which 600 pounds was the Torpex explosive charge.

Eglin Field *Speedee* bombs lined up for testing in the nearby waters of the Gulf of Mexico in early 1945. (AAF)

the bomb would either penetrate the hull or sink down beside the hull, maintaining contact while sinking. *Speedee* was fused with a hydrostatic as well as a 60 second self-destruct fuse.

The A-26 was considered to be the only existing AAF medium bomber that combined the speed, maneuverability, and load-carrying characteristics required for a successful adaptation to the *Speedee*. A glass-nosed C-model A-26 was selected for the Eglin tests of *Speedee* because it provided a place for an observer to sit but testers acknowledged that the A-26B with the solid nose armed with six to eight machine guns would be preferred as it's heavy forward gunfire would distract enemy AA gunners during the attack.

For the *Speedee* tests the AAF modified an A-26C by cutting holes in the flat-bottomed bomb bay doors; allowing the round bombs to be carried and released without opening the bomb bay doors. During tests the cutout bomb bay doors and the gyroscopic action of the external spinning bombs had no obvious effect on the bomber's flight characteristics. With two *Speedee*s revolving at full speed in the bomb bay the test aircraft tolerated steep climbs, turns, and dives normally.

The bomb contacted the water with brief and shallow impacts with the travel between successive impacts decreasing as speed decreased. At the end of the bomb's travel it plowed along the water's surface with its speed decreasing to about 70 to 90 mph. The loss of rpm was gradual and

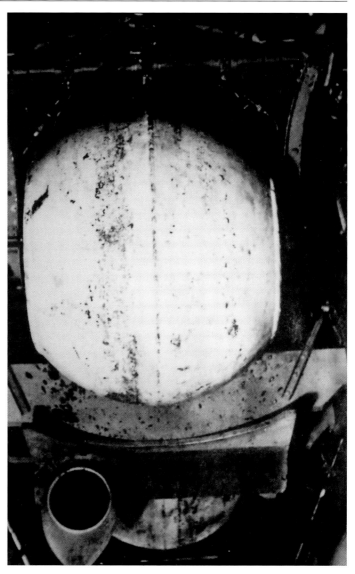

A view looking up into the cut out bomb bay to see the tandem two *Speedee*s with the air turbine duct between them at the left. (AAF)

A glass-nosed C-model A-26 was selected for the Eglin tests of *Speedee* because it provided a place for an observer to sit but testers acknowledged that the A-26B (pictured) with the solid gun nose would be preferred as it's heavy forward gunfire would distract enemy AA gunners during the attack. (AAF)

Another view of the two *Speedee* protruding from the bomb bay openings with the air turbine between . (AAF)

the residual rpm, the time of impact and sinking usually exceeded 50% of the initial rpm. The distance *Speedee* traveled, the height of each bounce into the air, and the number of bounces were all interrelated and were affected by the condition of the water over which the *Speedee* bomb was released. When dropped on calm water, low bounces, a high number of bounces, and a long run resulted. As the water got rougher the altitude of the bounces also increased while range and number of impacts decreased. The increased severity of impact on the surface of rough water caused a higher bounce with greater loss of forward speed and a harder succeeding

impact. The tests showed that rough water releases had a larger variation in results, since the angle of a wave as it was hit by the *Speedee* affected the bomb's bounce and subsequent travel. If the first impact was severe; the first bounce was unusually high and resulted in a short, quick end of the bomb's run. Release at lower altitudes, particularly over calm water, extended the range that the bomb traveled before sinking. The optimum bomb release was to take place in level flight following a dive to build up airspeed. If the bomb was released while the A-26 was still descending in its dive; the downward movement of the bomber had the effect of increasing *Speedee*'s downward velocity, which had the same effect as dropping from a higher altitude.

Between 4 March and 8 May 1945, as war in Europe was ending, *Speedee* was tested and evaluated at Eglin Field, FL. The objective of the tests was to ascertain the general operational effectiveness and the best tactics for using the *Speedee*, while determining the operational suitability of the bomb's installation in the A-26C Invader.

For the tests over Gulf of Mexico waters, the A-26C was flown at a calculated indicated airspeed ranging from 360 to 400 miles per hour during the bomb's release and at altitudes above the water that did not exceed 35 feet (but were often intentionally lower). The majority of 36 *Speedee* releases during testing showed that the bomb's true course throughout its run remained along the track of the aircraft at release.

As in the British tests clearance between the bouncing bomb and the aircraft was a concern. Testers set a minimum safety margin of 26 feet between the bomber and the bomb after first impact when released

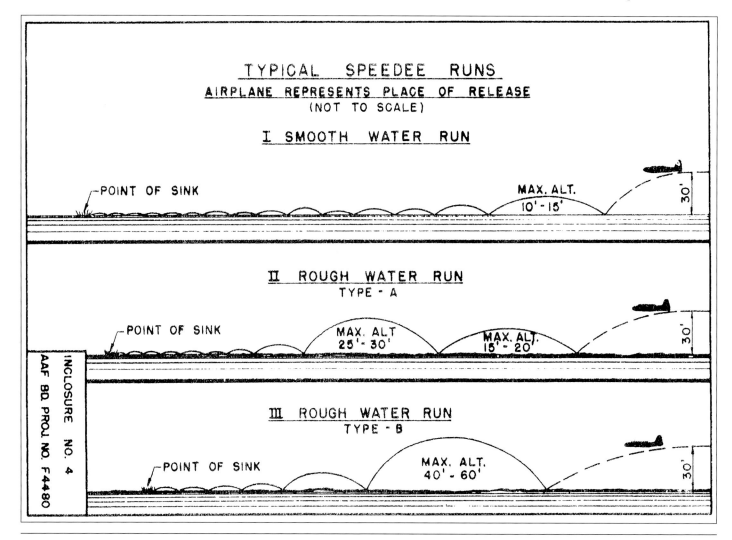

During the 24 April 1944 tests last bomb hit hard into a wave, causing a geyser of water to smash hard into the bottom of the A-26, denting the fuselage and damaging the modified bomb bay doors. (AAF)

at about 30-35 feet above the water. This clearance diminished as the A-26 released at lower heights, until at a release height of only 11 to 15 feet above the water, *Speedee* came within four feet of the bottom of the bomber on its first rebound. On 24 April three releases were made at six to 10 feet which were considerably lower than any previous releases. One release cleared the bottom of the aircraft by three feet, one by 10 feet, and the last appeared to pass within only one half foot of the bomber. This last bomb hit hard into a wave, causing a geyser of water to smash hard into the bottom of the A-26, denting the fuselage and damaging the modified bomb bay doors. From then on minimum release was set at 15 feet.

On 28 April a pilot mistakenly released a *Speedee* at nine to 10 feet on rough water with three to four foot waves. The bomb impacted heavily on a wave and quickly ricocheted up and struck the bomber aft of the ventral turret; breaking the tail structure off causing the A-26 to disintegrate upon hitting the water. During future testing release altitudes were never to be lower than 30 feet as the first bounce could possibly strike the aircraft in

rough seas and future installations were to have an automatic altitude limit warning device.

After the crash of this *Speedee*-equipped A-26 the program fell behind schedule and the project was reevaluated at Eglin. Results to that date showed that *Speedee* could "be expected to fall short of low level bombing, since the probable increase in deflection error will more than counterbalance the greater ease of solving the range problem." When compared to torpedo bombing, the overall aiming problem on moving targets was simplified with *Speedee* by the reduction in elapsed time from release to target, "but on stationary targets in harbors, the problem is substantially the same" with torpedoes or *Speedee* bombs.

The war was ending as Eglin issued this evaluation of *Speedee*: "It is doubtful whether there are in the Pacific enough appropriate targets ... which cannot be handled with already available weapons to make the use of *Speedee* an urgent requirement. In this connection, *Speedee*'s lack of adaptability to other loads and other types of attack also carries weight."

10

Hydrobomb

The *Hydrobomb* project was another example of Army-Navy interservice rivalry as each of the services wished to maintain control over weapons particular to their needs (e.g. the Navy for torpedoes and the Army Air Corps for bombs). In April 1941 the Joint Air Advisory Committee recommended that the Navy would control the development and acquisition of torpedoes while the AAC would deal with bombs. But this supposed agreement only led to further debates concerning the characteristics and deployment of the two weapons, especially when the AAC decided to arm some aircraft with torpedoes immediately after Pearl Harbor. There was little interest or enthusiasm among either Navy or AAC officers to acquire torpedoes from the Navy as mandated by the 1941 Joint Service Agreement.

In early December 1942, Gen. Arnold issued a directive requesting the Air Force to investigate an air-launched weapon that would be propelled underwater to strike a vessel under its waterline. Arnold pointed out that the Navy could not produce enough torpedoes to supply both itself and the AAF and that the current Navy torpedoes; besides being defective and inadequate, subjected the launching aircraft to enemy AA and fighter defenses as was discussed in chapter 4 (Torpedoes). Most significantly, Arnold and his staff maintained that their independent and unrestricted development of an anti-shipping weapon would result in one which would more meet their requirements for an "aerial torpedo" to be dropped at not less than 250 mph with a range of more than 2,000 yards by B-25 or B-26 medium bombers.

The AAF Materiel Command evaluated the Army-Navy torpedo situation and on 30 December 1942 it stated that the Navy had the most experience with "these types of weapons" and decided that it was the Navy's province to produce torpedoes. On 14 January 1943, Brig.Gen. T.J. Hanley, the Deputy Chief of the Air Staff, asked for a "requirement for a missile which can be dropped from an airplane moving at high speed and which can be directed toward a vessel." Eight days later, Hanley issued an in depth statement in which he blamed the Navy for not meeting Air Force needs for a weapon that could be released from high-performance aircraft and urged the design and development of an "aerial torpedo" (MX-363).

According to the 1941 Joint Service Agreement the Navy was to administer all torpedo projects and Hanley's use of the word "torpedo" rankled Navy BuOrd so much so that he almost immediately backpedaled and proposed that the AAF "torpedo" would need a new name. In early February 1943, Maj.Gen. O.P. Nichols of the Materiel Command's Engineering Division ordered that the word "torpedo" not be used and suggested the word "*Hydrobomb*" be used instead.

Name change aside, the Navy went to Assistant Secretary of War for Air, Robert Lovett, declaring the AAF *Hydrobomb* proposal infringed on and duplicated their work on torpedoes. In response, on 22 February, the AAF tendered design data for the *Hydrobomb* which was to be a much more imposing weapon than conventional air-launched torpedoes. According to the design proposal the *Hydrobomb* was to be released at not less than 250 mph at an altitude of 100 and up to 600 feet. The faster speed of the carrying aircraft was proportional to the faster average speed of the *Hydrobomb* and this factor and an increased releasing range would protect the carrying aircraft from enemy AA fire and fighter aircraft. The *Hydrobomb* was to have a minimum of 2,000 yards underwater travel with an underwater speed of more than 70 mph to decrease the effect of enemy evasive action. However, increased releasing distance also decreased the chances of hitting the target. The initial entering depth of the *Hydrobomb* was not to be more than 50 feet which would preclude its use in shallow water and harbors. The *Hydrobomb* was to be able to travel at any depth from 0 to 30 feet at an accuracy of +/- 2 feet with the depth setting to be made "conveniently " from outside the bomb and within the aircraft by either direct or remote control. The *Hydrobomb* was to carry 800 pounds (but not less than 600 pounds) of TNT high explosive equipped with a safety device that would allow it to impact the water without exploding and then arm after traveling a minimum of 200 feet so that it would explode upon impact with the target. The *Hydrobomb* was to be provided with carrying lugs, spaced at the established 14 or 30 inches, so that it could be carried like a conventional bomb on standard bomb shackles. The AAF design proposal made no mention of the propulsion system which was to be selected by the manufacturer chosen to design and produce the *Hydrobomb*. The *Hydrobomb* project would draw the attention of three manufacturers: Westinghouse Transformer Division at Sharon, PA, United Shoe Machinery Corporation (USMC) of Boston, and the A.O. Smith Company of Milwaukee, WI.

As the AAF *Hydrobomb* project gathered momentum the Navy again challenged its existence to Assistant Secretary of War, Robert Lovett, on the grounds "that this development was duplicating their efforts along the line of torpedo development." In a letter of 1 April 1943, Brig.Gen. B.W. Chidlaw, Assistant Chief of Staff AMC, stated:

"…very emphatically it is General Arnold's desire that all Army Air Forces personnel be again advised that we are not specifically working on a torpedo development paralleling that of the Navy but are developing

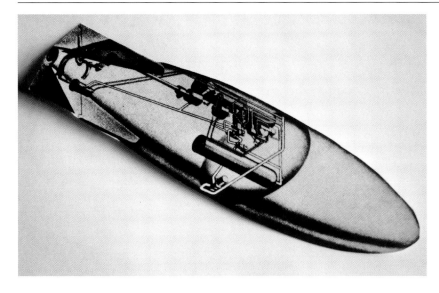

The **Hydrobomb** was a 14 foot long, 2,200 pound weapon using the proposed Westinghouse the "hydroduct" system in which a large amount of water would be drawn into a tapered duct and channeled out a restricted tube called a venturi which was located at the tail of the weapon. (AFHRC)

a *Hydrobomb* or self-propelled bomb which may be used in any manner seen fit when the development is complete.

In view of the controversial jurisdiction over the development of this nature, all personnel connected with the project should be advised that exceptional caution should be used when discussing this development with anyone...."

Westinghouse which had been developing an electric torpedo for the Navy expressed an interest in the *Hydrobomb* project and in mid-April, the Materiel Command and representatives from Westinghouse's Sharon research laboratories met to discuss specifications for the *Hydrobomb*. Westinghouse agreed to quickly complete a small scale model to demonstrate a proposed means of propulsion. On 19 April Westinghouse submitted an innovative and promising propulsion system proposal for the 14 foot long, 2,200 pound weapon. Because of the proposed high speeds at which the *Hydrobomb* would enter the water, a conventional screw propeller would be destroyed on impact. But more to the point, the conventional screw propeller would be unable to provide the high underwater speeds required by the design specifications. Instead, Westinghouse proposed the "hydroduct" system in which a large amount of water would be drawn into a tapered duct and channeled out a restricted tube called a venturi which was located at the tail of the weapon. Here a gas produced either by a chemical reaction or released from a storage tank inside the bomb was to be injected under high pressure into the stream of water. The principle of the hydroduct was uncomplicated; using no pumps, turbines, or other moving parts, and is used in contemporary turbofan jet engines. Newton's Second Law of Motion states that "a higher level of thrust can be achieved most economically by the addition of a small increment of velocity to the flow of any large mass (e.g. water)." For safety and design purposes; the propellant gas was to be in the form of a liquid constrained within a suitable pressurized container, rather than be generated chemically.

While using some innovative design facets Westinghouse engineers also incorporated a number of elements already found in torpedo design. Because of the high underwater speeds required, specific consideration was given to aerodynamic and hydrodynamic principles in determining the optimum shape for the *Hydrobomb*. An in-flight stabilizer was developed to slow the *Hydrobomb* before it struck the water and the control surfaces were to be retracted to prevent damage on impact. Directional control

was provided by a gyroscopic mechanism and depth was controlled by an electric system that Westinghouse had used in its production of Navy torpedoes. Although the Westinghouse proposal reduced the *Hydrobomb*'s submerged range to 1,000 yards; the AAF approved the project because this 1,000 yard range would increase its accuracy. On 11 May 1943 Westinghouse and the AAF signed a letter of intent which allowed the company to start work to construct several scale models, followed by a full-scale model for water tests, eight full-scale devices for launch tests, and then 10 prototypes for $465,300.

Meanwhile, on 8 May, the A.O. Smith Company of Milwaukee, WI was contracted to produce ten *Hydrobomb* shells (bodies) at an estimated cost of $3,000 each plus another $30,000 for engineering, administration, and tools. The General Electric Company was contracted to develop controls and the AMC Armament Laboratory was to engineer the project. The A.O. Smith *Hydrobomb* would progress very slowly, particularly after GE withdrew from the project due to design and developmental problems with its controls and also because of the lack of available personnel at the Armament Laboratory to work on the project.

By September 1943, it became evident that the hydroduct system would not be completed in time to be installed in Westinghouse's prototype. Tests of the scale models discovered that although the duct design was viable, sustaining the propellant gas in liquid form caused critical handling and storage problems in the field. In a memorandum of 20 August, Capt. J.F. Healey reported that Westinghouse had "discovered certain impracticalities" in the hydroduct and had requested that the AAF assist in developing a conventional rocket propulsion system. Materiel Command Armament Laboratory and Westinghouse engineers met and the company was authorized to initiate establishing a research facility to study the use of solid rocket motors to be supplied by the Aerojet Engineering Corporation of Pasadena, CA.

Qualitative experiments were conducted with solid fuel rocket motors fired underwater beginning in the fall of 1942 by the Guggenheim Aeronautical Laboratory, California Institute of Technology (GALCIT) at Pasadena, CA, (GALCIT was the predecessor for the JPL, the Jet Propulsion Laboratory). The results demonstrated that these engines could be used for JATO (Jet Assisted Takeoff) for flying boats and for the propulsion of underwater weapons. Upon reading of these tests the Armament Laboratory of the AAF Air Technical Service Command at Wright Field realized the potential for the development of a *Hydrobomb* that could fulfill Arnold's requirements.

In a memorandum dated 20 February 1943, Drs. Frank Malina and Theodore von Karman proposed an underwater rocket propulsion research tunnel (similar to a wind tunnel) which was to include research on the AAF's *Hydrobomb*. Preliminary tests were done on half-scale models without rocket motors to determine their hydrodynamic characteristics, the effect of rocket propulsion on stability and performance, and the effect of cavitation. GALCIT developed a special solid propellant and motor for the full-scale *Hydrobomb* that would be able to withstand water impact at speeds up to 400 mph. The launching tests were conducted at the Cal Tech's Torpedo Launching Range at Morris Dam, CA. The rocket units were to be built by Aerojet which was formed in March 1942 by Cal Tech faculty members, von Karman (President and Director) and Malina (Treasurer and Director). Von Karman and Malina formed the new company as Cal Tech was an institution of education and research and it was deemed inappropriate for it to engage in engineering development and production. Aerojet developed a solid propellant jet unit producing 2,200 pound thrust of 30 seconds duration. The unit had initial problems with a limited safe operating temperature range of 40°F to 110°F. The use of liquid fuels was investigated and abandoned as it would necessitate pressure vessels, regulating valves, the considerable use of tubing, the use of strategic materials to withstand corrosion, and its explosiveness rendered the *Hydrobomb* vulnerable in combat situations.

The United Shoe Machinery Corporation (USMC) of Boston originally undertook the entire development of their own version of the *Hydrobomb* (less the control system as the company wanted to avoid any conflicts as it was working on controls for the Navy Mk13 torpedo). USMC had been investigating the use of various propellants and concluded that pressed or cast solid type fuel was the most promising, Initially, USMC contacted Aerojet but that company's price was too high and its propellant operating temperature range was too limited. The AMC Armament Laboratory began to design and build a solid fuel motor using large hydraulic presses for powder pressing.

While investigating propellants and control mechanisms relating to the *Hydrobomb* United Shoe Machinery requested the torpedo depth and directional controls for use with the *Hydrobomb* from the Navy. BuOrd complained that the *Hydrobomb* was actually a furtive torpedo and the AAF countered declaring that the Navy's supremacy of guided missile

The 500 foot **GALCIT hydrodynamic tow tank** referred to as the "Channel" in June 1945 with the rocket carriage raised and the Hydrobomb suspended above the tow tank. (AFHRC)

research and development was proof that the Navy did conform to the 1941 Joint Service Agreement. Since control was a major problem in the project's development, the Navy tried to use its expertise in the field to coerce its way into the project and by September 1943, the impasse threatened the *Hydrobomb*'s cancellation. On 9 November Army Air Force and Navy representatives met with representatives from the National Defense Research Committee to try to forge a compromise. As it had previously done with a similar project (the Mk13 air-launched torpedo); the Navy wanted the AAF to turn the project over to the NDRC which was a civilian agency responsible for coordinating weapons research. The AAF unequivocally refused but since it had let many contracts, and since a large amount of money was at stake, it allowed the NDRC to monitor the project starting January, 1944.

After wind tunnel tests using a quarter-scale model the USMC prepared the first of several full scale concrete dummy bombs to be ready for air launch tests from a B-25 at Eglin Field. Additional tests were to be conducted by the NDRC at the CIT high speed water tunnel using two inch models to determine drag, pitch and yaw, and cavitation characteristics. The correlated data from these tests was to be used in a full scale tow tank tests made at the GALCIT facility. The tow tank, referred to as the "Channel" was a 500 foot hydrodynamic tank with a rocket towing carriage and test instruments to measure hydrodynamic forces on scale models and full size *Hydrobomb* versions. Various nose shapes were tried to reduce cavitation and enhance water entry and fins ranging from 26 to 34 inches were added to increase stability.

Westinghouse accomplished little in its independent *Hydrobomb* proposal as it ran into problems with its duct system of propulsion. On 13 November 1943, Westinghouse submitted a new *Hydrobomb* proposal for AAF approval; reducing its original contract price from $465,300 to $100,605, which included the design and engineering of a full-scale operating model powered by a 1,000 pound thrust solid fuel Aerojet rocket motor. The model was not to be air-droppable, and it was intended only to test the propulsion and control systems at speeds up to 40 knots. Subsequent versions were powered by 2,500 pound thrust motors intended to attain the initially required 70 mph speed. Westinghouse assured the Air Force that its Pittsburgh research laboratories would continue to be fully occupied with the hydroduct and in the future expected to have developed models using the hydroduct system.

Meanwhile, pending approval of its revised proposal, Westinghouse (Sharon) proceeded with the design and construction of the *Hydrobomb*. By early February 1944, the full-size model was nearly three-quarters completed when the company realized that it would be necessary to reinforce the outer casing to accommodate the loads of the rocket motor and to elongate the exhaust nozzle to make room for the new propulsion unit. By 17 March, the test model was ready.

The AAF had insisted that the *Hydrobomb* had to reach the required performance during air tests before Westinghouse would receive a contract. Conversely Westinghouse maintained that due to the experimental character of the *Hydrobomb*, issuance of a contract should not be conditional on test results. After protracted negotiations the two parties agreed to terms on 22 March 1944 which only specified that the AAF was to inspect and approve the design and workmanship of the test model but the contract did not require that the *Hydrobomb* meet the specified performance conditions.

As soon as the Northeast's Spring weather permitted, trials began at the Westinghouse experimental torpedo range at Lake Pymatuning, a manmade reservoir located on the Pennsylvania-Ohio border north of Pittsburgh; near the Sharon factory. The first test run from a launching raft was scheduled for 13 April with a large contingent of AAF and company officials present but bomb balance problems caused the test to be cancelled. Company engineers redistributed the ballast and another test the following day failed when the igniter fired prematurely, allowing water to enter the rocket casing. A third attempt was cancelled when cracks in the rocket motor casing allowed water to flow in while the *Hydrobomb* was suspended under the launching raft. The *Hydrobomb* did not run under power until 19 April but continued to experience problems with its directional control mechanism.

After further revisions Westinghouse scheduled more tests at Pymatuning in late May. On the first test the *Hydrobomb* was released from the launching raft and quickly dove to the bottom of the reservoir, buried itself in the mud until a small explosive charge detonated which separated the dummy warhead from the body. The *Hydrobomb* was recovered and the next test was more successful as the weapon traveled about 1,500 feet. But in an ensuing test the *Hydrobomb* was described as "running completely wild" due to a malfunction that prevented electrical current from reaching the directional control mechanisms. There were eight trial runs at Pymatuning in this first series of tests, of which five were considered as "very promising," with speeds up to 45 mph and running times of 20 seconds. On 6 June Capt. Healey concluded that: "It now appears very certain that rocket propulsion for this application is entirely feasible and appears to add little or no problems to the proper control of such a weapon." Although these tests showed that substantial development work needed to be done before the *Hydrobomb* was ready for production and Westinghouse began a second series of tests of the *Hydrobomb* at Pymatuning on 13 July. The results of these tests were better but the Aerojet rocket motor igniter caused problems. However, there were no fundamental problems in the propulsion system and Westinghouse was approved to manufacture the *Hydrobomb*. The AAF wanted to order 10 but Westinghouse wanted to manufacture at least 25. The Navy decided that it wanted as many as the AAF prompting Brig.Gen. F. O. Carroll, the Chief of the Materiel Command's Engineering Division to recommend to Gen. Arnold on 12 July that Westinghouse should be awarded a contract to manufacture 50 *Hydrobomb*s for $1,522,750 at its Sharon plant. The contracted *Hydrobomb*s were to use the new, more powerful 2,500 pound thrust Aerojet rocket motors which were expected to have higher underwater speed and greater range. The company was to deliver this first batch of *Hydrobomb*s in January 1945 and 10 per month thereafter. The first 10 were to be tested by Air Material Command and then deliveries were to be alternated with the Navy.

The scheduled January 1945 *Hydrobomb* deliveries had to be continually set back while Westinghouse personnel labored to solve the numerous design and production problems. A special igniter circuit had to be developed to prevent any possibility that the *Hydrobomb* would fire before being released from the aircraft. The rocker motor had to run efficiently after its high speed entry into the water, so Westinghouse engineers developed a mounting that cushioned the shock of impact. Once the design was frozen, preparations began for production and contracts were completed with the various subcontractors to supply parts and components

Westinghouse subcontracted bodies manufactured by A.O. Smith and the sled and wing assemblies by Robert Irwin Co. The Westinghouse model weighed 1,300 pounds of which 600 pounds were explosive. The wing and tail units were combined roughly resembling a sled and was mounted on top the shell body. This air-launched anti-shipping weapon was to be released at a high speed (up to 350 mph) and relatively low altitude (400 to 2,000 feet). The bomb fell freely through the air, entering the water, shedding its sled-like dorsally mounted wing/tail unit. It proceeded at a set depth along the heading of the launching aircraft, propelled underwater at speeds up to 45 mph by the solid fuel rocket motor that delivered 2,500 pounds thrust for 30 seconds.

Production and testing proceeded concurrently in 1945 with Westinghouse delivering the first five *Hydrobomb*s on 11 April after which the company manufactured the weapons at a rate of 10 per month. The first powered trials with the 2,500 pound thrust rocket motor were conducted at Lake Pymatuning on 17 April but revealed further control and igniter problems. In May live drop tests released from a Navy B-25 PBJ twin-engine, medium bomber at the USN torpedo test range at Newport showed similar results. The war came to an end before Westinghouse could demonstrate the effectiveness or the reliability of the rocket-propelled *Hydrobomb*.

It appears that the United Shoe Machinery placed a lower priority on the *Hydrobomb* project and lagged far behind in building its prototypes which appeared to be superior on paper. Its pneumatic (vs. electric) controlled version was larger at about 10 feet long and 28 inches in maximum diameter and weighed 3,200 pounds with a warhead weight of 1,250 pounds. This air-launched anti-shipping weapon was to be released at a high speed (up to 350 mph) and relatively low altitude (400 to 2,000 feet). Its mechanism was similar to the Westinghouse version with the bomb falling freely through the air, entering the water, releasing its dorsally mounted wing/tail unit. It proceeded at a set depth along the heading of the launching aircraft, propelled underwater by a solid fuelled rocket at speeds up to 70 mph by the same solid fuel Aerojet rocket motor. The war ended the USMC *Hydrobomb* project which appears to have only reached the initial prototype stage.

Conclusions

In 1942 the *Hydrobomb* seemed to have significant tactical advantages over the Navy's air-launched torpedoes and allowed the AAF to develop the weapon without niggling procurement restrictions. But the *Hydrobomb* would exacerbate interservice rivalries because it closely resembled the Navy's torpedoes under development and in the procurement pipeline. The *Hydrobomb* was certainly desirable as a powerful anti-ship weapon concept but the developed conventional torpedo was sufficient to meet projected requirements. Late war technology that was sufficient for the slower running conventional torpedoes in service; was too slow and unsophisticated to meet the advanced requirements of the *Hydrobomb* and Westinghouse's attempt to combine the old and the new technologies was unsuccessful. When the war ended, neither service could afford to give much priority to the *Hydrobomb*, although the program did linger with minimal funding until 1947. Postwar anti-submarine rockets were developed that ignited and burned underwater.

11

Disney Rocket-Assissted Bomb

Dr. Patrick Blackett of British Operations Research (OR) worked with the Royal Navy on a new method to deploy depth charges against submerging U-Boats and developed 100 pound shaped depth charges to be dropped from an aircraft or as the *Hedgehog* to be fired from warships. The first trial of the airborne depth charge resulted in an explosion that blew up the dropping aircraft, killing the pilot. Blackett left the project and RN Captain Edward Terrell, a former barrister who had been working for the Royal Navy on armor protection, and Willis Jefferis, an eccentric inventor, took over the project. Terrell developed airborne and shipborne 35 pound bombs with hollow shaped-charge projectiles that had been used for ore mining before the war. The hollow charges had explosives placed behind a steel cone, so that when fired, the heat and directionality of the explosive propelled the cone at 7,000 feet per second penetrating both the outer hull of a U-Boat and the ballast water and oil tanks that protected its inner hull.

Terrell was then joined by Lt.Cdr. John Murray and the team designed the 14 foot long, 4,500 pound rocket bomb which was attached to a set of rocket motors in the tail for use in the penetration and destruction of U-Boat and E-Boat pens. The weapons were dubbed *Disney* bombs for some unrecorded reason. The streamlined hardened case cylindrical bomb had a sharply pointed nose which contained 500 pounds of Shellite (similar to Composition D). Two suspension lugs were bolted to the bomb casing

which attached to suspension from under the bomb bay. The 900 pound rocket tail unit had six tail fins attached to an adapter plate mounted to the base of the bomb. The tail unit contained three rocket motors bundled together and containing 12.5 pounds of cruciform-shaped flashless cordite rocket propellant. An M111 mechanical time fuse activated a switch allowing electrical ignition of the rocket motors that was powered by a wind-driven generator mounted on a conical fairing at the tail. Individual pullout wires were used to arm the M111 time fuse, the pistol fuses, and to allow free spinning of the wind generator. Two British No. 58 Pistol fuses were mounted in the base of the bomb.

The bomb was dropped from 20,000 feet and then allowed to free fall until the rocket motors ignited at 5,000 feet. A barometric fuse fired the rockets installed in the tail, propelling the missile to a speed of 2,400 feet per second at impact causing a penetration of 20 feet before detonation of the explosive charge.

Because the bomb was 14 feet long there were no Lancaster bombers available to deliver them. In 1944 trials were conducted by Operational Engineering at Bovington using a B-17G carrying two *Disney* bombs on racks on each wing. With this 9,000 pound load the B-17 grossed out at 66,000 pounds so only its main fuel tanks were filled. The takeoff run required 4,200 feet and the climb to 20,000 feet took 40 minutes at 150 mph IAS. To prevent the bombs from swinging on their racks sensible maneuvering was essential.

The *Disney* **Rocket-Assisted Bomb** was a 14 foot long, 4,500 pound rocket bomb which was attached to a set of rocket motors in the tail for use in the penetration and destruction of U-Boat and E-Boat pens. (AAF)

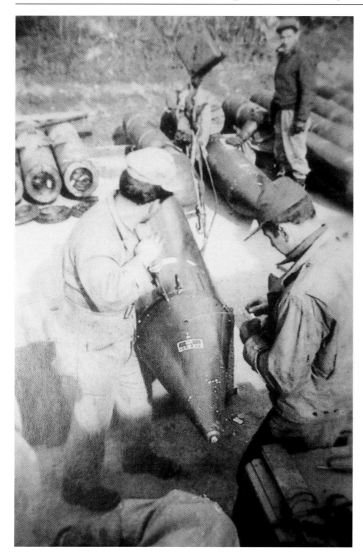

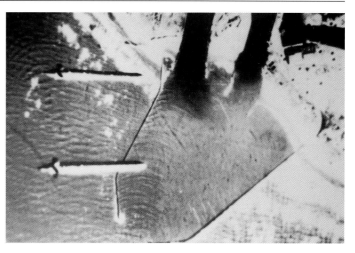

The *Disney* bomb was dropped from 20,000 feet and then allowed to free fall until the rocket motors ignited at 5,000 feet. A barometric fuse fired the rockets installed in the tail, propelling the missile to a speed of 2,400 feet per second at impact causing a penetration of 20 feet before detonation of the explosive charge. Pictured are two *Disney* bombs falling on the E-Boat pens at Ijmuiden, Holland on 10 February 1945. (AAF)

Due to the secret nature of the weapon operational records are sketchy with only brief descriptions in the microfilm records. On 10 February 1945, the *Disney* Bomb was first used by nine B-17s of the 92nd Bomb Group led by Group CO, Col. James Wilson, to attack E-Boat pens at Ijmuiden, Holland. Strike photos were examined by Col. Anthony Mustoe, CO of the 40th Combat Wing, and by Terrell and Murray and revealed several bursts on the target and several near misses. Oblique reconnaissance photos several days later showed a direct hit at the north end of the pens where a portion of the roof did not have its final concrete pour and destroyed the roof structure over three pens and damaging a large supporting wall. The near misses did no damage to the pens.

On 30 March the *Disney* bombs were dropped on the Valentin U-Boat pens at Farge near Bremen with one scoring a direct hit and penetrating the thick concrete roof. Later *Disney* missions were conducted on 4 April 1945 by the 92nd Group when it flew another mission to the Fink II U-Boat pens Hamburg on the Elbe River exit to the Baltic. There is brief mention

The *Disney*'s streamlined cylindrical hardened case had a sharply pointed nose which contained 500 pounds of explosive. In the background of the photo is the 900 pound rocket tail unit which would have six tail fins attached to an adapter plate mounted to the base of the bomb. (AAF)

Post strike photo of the 4 April 1945 *Disney* mission by the 92nd Group to the Fink II U-Boat pens in Hamburg on the Elbe River exit to the Baltic. The photo shows large bomb craters which were probable caused by RAF 12,000 pound Tallboy bombs. (AAF)

Henschel HS-293 Rocket-Propelled Guided Missile (AFHRC)

of its limited use by the 305th and 306th Bomb Groups while the 94BG was also preparing to carry *Disney* Bombs during the final weeks of the war. A total of 158 *Disney* Bombs were deployed during the war. After the war, in August 1945, the *Disney* bomb was further tested as part of *Project Ruby* against the ex-German U-Boat facilities at Farge.

Henshel Hs-293

The German research and development and the operational use of guided missiles in World War II was far in advance to that of America and warrants mention. Although the German radio-controlled, rocket-powered Hs-293 is often compared to the Navy's unpowered, radar-controlled *Bat* missile it also resembles the free-fall, rocket-powered *Disney* bomb. However, unlike the *Fritz X*, the other operational German controlled missile, in order to give it greater control over its fall, it was fitted with wings, an aerodynamic tail unit carrying control surfaces, and a rocket motor to boost the speed of the missile for greater penetration and to prevent interception during the flight.

The forward portion of the Hs-293 fuselage was a modified standard 500 kg SZ bomb casing with an aluminum covering or fairing. A vertical plastic beam, fastened to the rear of the bomb, attached it to the aft section of the fuselage. The radio and the associated bomb-controlling equipment were mounted on either side of this plastic beam. The aft portion of the fuselage was a stressed-skin, semi-monocoque structure while the wing and tail were the usual aluminum type. The 18-channel E-230 radio receiving set received signals from a *Kehl* transmitting set. The missile was controlled in roll by normal type ailerons on the trailing edge of the outer portion of the wing. The ailerons also controlled the yaw effect. The He-293 was controlled in pitch by the normal type of control surfaces on the trailing edge of the horizontal tail surface. The Walter HWK 109-507 liquid-fuelled rocket provided for only about ten seconds power giving it a short burst of speed making range dependent on the height of launch (from a height of 5,000 feet the Hs 293 had a range of about two miles). The Hs-293 was very successful, sinking seven vessels and causing damage of varied degree to 17 others.

The Hs 293 was carried by Heinkel He 111, Heinkel He 177, Focke-Wulf Fw 200, and Dornier Do 217 bombers . Unlike the *Fritz X* that was intended for use against armored ships; the Hs 293 was intended to destroy unarmored ships. The operator controlled the radio-guided missile with a joystick by watching colored flares attached to the rear of the weapon to make it visible at a distance to the operator. During nighttime operations flashing lights instead of flares were used. The Hs-293B was a proposed wire-guided version while the Hs-293D was television-guided model which was put into production, but never used operationally because of its unreliable TV equipment.

12

Very Heavy Conventional Bombs

British Concept and Development

After the Germans had conquered France and then abandoned their plans of invading England in the summer of 1940 they began to build submarine pens along the French coast to protect their U-Boats which were ravaging Allied shipping. These heavy concrete U-Boat pens were thought to be impregnable against the existing RAF 1,000 and 2,000 pound bombs.

In the Fall of 1940 Dr. Barnes Wallace, an engineer at Vickers Armstrong Ltd., published a paper entitled "A Note on a Method of Attacking the Axis Powers" in which he proposed a 10 ton *Earthquake* bomb. Wallis' 10 ton bomb would be dropped from 40,000 feet; impacting the earth at supersonic speed, penetrating as deep as 100 feet underground. Wallis calculated that a very large bomb exploding deep underground next to a target would form a cavern called a camouflet rather than a crater. The bomb's entire explosive energy would be contained within the ground and the shockwave would be transmitted into the foundations of the target which would then collapse into the camouflet. These shockwaves transmitted though a non-compressible medium such as the earth were less affected by distance than those transmitted through a compressible medium such as the air. Early in the war bomb aiming was very inaccurate

Dr. Barnes Wallace is not only the father of the Upkeep Dambuster's bouncing bomb but he also devised Britain's 12,000 pound *Tallboy* and 22,000 pound *Grand Slam* Very Heavy Conventional Bomb program. (AFHRC)

Comparison of the 12,000 pound *Tallboy* and 22,000 pound *Grand Slam* bombs. (AFHRC)

and the major advantage of the *Earthquake* bomb was that it could miss by hundreds of feet and still achieve the desired result via these shockwaves. Wallis' bouncing *Upkeep* bombs that destroyed Ruhr dams during the Dambuster's Raid used this principle by using water as the non-compressible medium. Also, if this large bomb were exploded closer to the surface it would form a huge solitary crater which would require many man hours and heavy equipment to refill and would be particularly effective against such targets as railway marshalling yards and airdromes. However, at the time there were no bombers available which were capable of carrying this large 10 ton weapon and although Wallis suggested that a 50 ton, six-engine high-altitude bomber called "*Victory*" be developed to fly at 320 mph at 45,000 feet, the *Earthquake* bomb concept was shelved. Wallis became engaged in the research for a second paper in 1942 entitled "Spherical Bomb-Surface Torpedo" which led to the successful Dambuster bouncing bombs and *Operation Chastise* on the night of 16-17 May 1943, after which there was renewed interest in the *Earthquake* bombs.

Though there still was no RAF bomber that could carry a 22,000 pound bomb to the desired 40,000 foot release height, the RAF requested that Wallis use a penetrating bomb at an altitude (20,000 feet) that existing bombers could reach. Wallis' report suggested the down scaling of the 10 ton bomb to one weighing six tons and dropped from at least 8,000 feet which would cause a measurable earthquake. Wallis refined the design through late 1943, until the scaled down 12,000 pound bomb, called *Tallboy*, was ready for testing.

The British *Tallboy*: Bomb, HE, Aircraft, MC 12,000 Pound
On 18 July, 1943, using the code designation *Tallboy* Small, Medium, and Large, the Ministry of Aircraft Production let contracts for 12 *Tallboy* Small scaled down 4,000 pound ballistic test bombs, 100 *Tallboy* Medium 12,000 pound bombs, and 100 *Tallboy* Large 22,000 pound bombs. The

The light alloy tail cone of the ***Tallboy*** was about half the overall length of the entire bomb with the bomb casing comprising 10.67 feet of the overall 21 foot length, measured 3.17 feet at its maximum diameter, and 3.5 feet across its four fins. (AFHRC)

bombs were to be manufactured by the English Steel Corp. foundry at Sheffield. Due to the British lack of industrial capacity to manufacture steel casings for both the 12,000 and 22,000 pound bombs, the production contract for the 22,000 pound version was terminated on 30 September, 1943 after only nine were completed. With no 22,000 pound bombs contracted its 100 casings were transferred to the order for 100 12,000 pound bombs which was in turn increased to 325, with the additional 125 casings to be manufactured under license in America. To manufacture the steel casings, precision molded concrete cores were produced then lowered into a sand mould. After the steel was poured and cooled, the concrete core was carefully chipped out. The casing was precision machined inside and out to the prescribed dimensions then shipped to one of several Royal Ordnance Factories for filling.

After less than a year from the drawing board, manufacture, aircraft modification, and testing, the *Tallboy* was ready for combat. The 12,000 pound bomb was first deployed on the night of 8-9 June, 1944 against the Saumur Railway Tunnel, which the Germans were using to send reinforcements to the Normandy invasion beaches. The RAF dropped 19 bombs and the tunnel was blocked for weeks before it was usable. The success at Saumur led to the increase of *Tallboy* bomb production to 2,000 with the English Steel Corporation in the UK and A.O. Smith Corporation of Milwaukee, WI each manufacturing 1,000 bombs.

Most very large Allied bombs had very thin skins (Light Case) in order to maximize the weight of explosive. To be able to penetrate the earth or hardened targets without the *Tallboy* casing breaking apart; the casing had to be strong and was cast in a single piece of high tensile steel that enabled it to endure the impact before detonation. To attain the required penetration the *Tallboy* was very aerodynamic so that when it was released from a great height it would reach a velocity higher than conventional bomb designs. During initial trials the bomb was inclined to tumble, so Wallis modified the tail by giving the fins a slight 5° twist to the axis of the tail cone imparting a right hand spin as it fell providing the bomb a gyroscopic effect that ended the pitching and yawing and improved the aerodynamics and accuracy. When dropped from 20,000 feet *Tallboy* created an 80 foot crater that was 100 feet in diameter and could penetrate 16 feet of concrete.

The long aluminum tail cone was attached by bolts to 12 half inch studs positioned around the circumference of the rear of the bomb casing. Three hand-holes in the tail covered by circular plates gave access to the three fuse pockets and studs that held the tail cone to the casing. Fuse pullout wires were threaded through a small hole in the tail cone to the carrier aircraft for arming the bomb at the time of release. Upon release from the Lancaster bomber flying at 18,000 feet and 200 mph, the tail fins which were canted 5° to the right caused the bomb to spin stabilize at 300 rpms with an impact velocity of 1,097 feet per second. The bomb casing was painted an olive drab green with the tail assembly in bare metal. Identification markings included a red band painted just behind the nose plug and a green band with "Torpex D1" stenciled just behind the red.

The operational version of the English *Tallboy* was 21 feet long including the tail assembly, 3.17 feet at its maximum diameter, measured 3.5 feet across its four fins, and had a hardened steel case thickness of more than four inches in the nose and then tapering to 1.25 inches near the rear of the casing. A special hardened steel plug was installed into the nose of the casing. The bomb was loaded with 5,200 pounds of Torpex explosive which comprised 41% of the 12,622 pounds total weight. After filling the casing with Torpex; a one inch layer of TNT was added followed by four inches of woodmeal/wax which was then sealed with a 0.25 inch plywood plug with three holes cut to allow the booster assemblies to penetrate the explosive filler. The primary boosters consisted of two ring and two solid Tetryl pellets that abutted four solid RDX/Beeswax pellets. These were

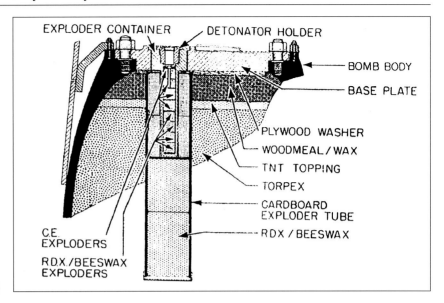

Tallboy **Exploder** (AFHRC)

inserted into the secondary boosters which consisted of two ring and two solid large RDX/Beeswax pellets surrounded by a cardboard tube. The bombs were shipped with the exploders in place but sealed with plugs.

Three No. 47 fuses with delays up to 60 minutes or three No. 58 MK I fuses with delays from instantaneous to 11 seconds were screwed into pockets offset 120° forming a triangle in the base plate that was secured to the casing by 20 bolts.

The explosive train for a No. 47 fuse developed as follows: Upon release, the retracted pullout wires broke a vial of Acetone that began dissolving a celluloid disk that kept a spring-loaded striker from moving. Depending on the thickness of the disk, a predetermined length of time elapsed before the weakened disk allowed the striker to punch through to the primer. The primer contained a small quantity of contact sensitive high explosive that would detonate a booster explosive contained in a small (2x3 inch) container. The booster contained enough explosive force to detonate the main charge of the bomb.

The No. 58 Mk I fuse was a No. 30 Pistol body that had the head cup filled with a brass plug which had hole to insert a heavy striker. The top end of the striker had a brass cross held by a screw was fitted into it

to prevent the striker from moving. Two arming wire holes were drilled through the assembled pistol body at 90° to each other to provide a choice of optimum angle for the pullout wire. A transit safety pin was inserted through a third hole parallel to one of the arming wire holes.

The explosive train for a No. 58 Mk I fuse progressed as follows: The single pullout wire for each fuse was released which removed any restraint to the movement of the heavy striker pin except for a small brass cross that held the pin until the inertia of impact drove the pin into the primer. The primer held a small pellet of contact sensitive chemical that burned at a predetermined rate (as much as several seconds) before detonating. The primary exploders then detonated the secondary exploders that finally detonated the main charge of the bomb.

After the tail assembly had been attached to the casing, the armorer began to fuse the bomb by working through access holes in the tail. He obtained the arming supplies from a storage box that contained 20 pistols, 20 safety wires, and 40 clips. He removed the fuse pocket plugs and then determined the depth of the cavity with a Cavity Detonator Gauge. The correct detonator was then inserted in the cavity and the pistol bodies were screwed tight. A single safety wire was inserted into the pistol

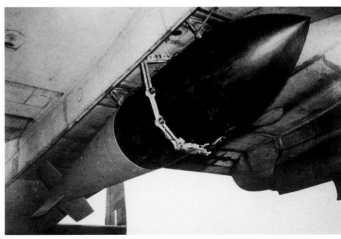

The heavy 12,000 pound weight of the *Tallboy* required a heavy crane to lift it onto a special bomb carrier to be transported under a Lancaster bomber. The bomb was attached to the bomber by two chains connected by a Vickers electrical or manual release mechanism located under the bomb casing at the center of gravity. (AFHRC)

safety wire hole that was optimal for pullout. Two safety clips held each pullout wire with approximately three inches protruding beyond the clips. Once loaded into the aircraft, the armorer attached the pullout wires to the aircraft, pulled the transit safety pins and secured the covers over the access holes.

Avro Lancaster Mk Is were assigned to the *Tallboy* test program that had been striped of unnecessary equipment and most defensive armament, and equipped with a strengthened bomb rack and more powerful Merlin 24 engines. These Lancasters, operated by No. 9 and 617 Squadrons, had specially bulged bomb bay doors so that the *Tallboy* could be carried internally. These enlarged doors were originally used to carry the 8,000 pound and 12,000 pound High Capacity Blockbusters. Specialized support equipment was required to load the Lancaster with the *Tallboy* and later the *Grand Slam*. The bomb was attached to the bomber by two chains connected to a Vickers electrical or manual release mechanism located under the bomb casing at the center of gravity. The five point electrical connection was located fore (*Tallboy*) or aft (*Grand Slam*) of the spring-loaded center of gravity pin depending on which weapon was carried. Two cables were attached to the chain ends to prevent the chains from hitting the aircraft after the bomb was released and were used to pull the chains into the aircraft through a hole in the bomb bay ceiling. When loaded with a *Tallboy*, the Lancaster carried 1,650 imperial gallons of fuel and had a 250 gallon reserve giving an operational range of 700 miles radius.

The RAF deployed the *Tallboy* to penetrate heavily reinforced V-weapon assembly and launching sites, U-Boat and E-Boat pens, viaducts, tunnels, canals, bridges, oil refining and storage facilities. From June 1944 through April 1945, 854 *Tallboy*s were dropped by the RAF.

The American *Tallboy*: Bomb, GP, 12,000 Pound, M109 (T10)
Except for external markings, the American and UK versions were virtually identical. The American version of the *Tallboy* was 21 feet long (including a casing of 10.33 feet and 11 foot tail), 3.17 feet in diameter and weighed 12,488 pounds. The Ml 20 tail assembly was 11 feet long and 3.71 feet in diameter and weighed 134 pounds. Twenty bolts held the Ml 20 to the bomb casing bringing the overall length to 21 feet and weighed 12,622 pounds when fully assembled. A circular metal band held in place by the joining of the bomb body and tail assembly, streamlined the bomb.

While the earliest versions were loaded with 5,200 pounds of Torpex with a one inch layer of TNT at the rear; beginning in the first quarter of 1945, the bombs were loaded with 5,500 pounds of Tritonal (80% of TNT and 20% of Aluminum) which was 43.8% of total weight. An armor piercing plug was fitted to the nose of the cast casings. Due to wartime manufacturing limitations in steel casting most of the American T-10 bomb casings were assembled from rolled plate steel, with five plates welded together using techniques adapted from the manufacture of large pressure vessels. The nose and tail rings were made of forged steel and the sidewalls were assembled from three pieces of rolled plate welded along the longitudinal axis.

The casing was painted olive drab green with a yellow band at the nose and tail. Stenciled in black on the casing was data on the Type of weapon (GP), weight, model, explosive filler, ammunition lot number, AIC symbol, ICC shipping designation, Inspector's stamp, the letters "US", displacement, and may have carried the shipping address and shipping ticket number. Inert training rounds carried minimal markings or were painted a high visibility black and white to aid tracking cameras. Some inert training examples displayed for the public were painted silver or olive drab green overall.

Like the UK versions, three fuses were installed into pockets on the base plate offset 120° forming a triangle. Access to the fuse pockets was

facilitated by three holes in the tail assembly. For reliability, three four inch long Ml 69 (T708) impact tail fuses with the long end of the M40 primer-detonator extending into the four inch M118 adapter booster were screwed into a fuse seat. The time delays ranged from .025 to 30 seconds with the selection of the delay time being that which would give the bomb time to penetrate to optimal depth before detonation based on the target construction and geology of the target area.

B-29 *Tallboy* Modifications
A B-29 (42-63577) was modified by Bell Aircraft (Marietta, GA) to be employed in suitability tests of the *Tallboy* hoisting, carrying, and releasing equipment and mechanisms. Modifications to the B-29 included the shortening and strengthening the forward and aft bomb bay doors providing a cut out for clearance for the bomb that was carried partially externally due to its large size. The two bomb bays were separated by a fixed bulkhead located under the wing spar. This bulkhead was modified into two longitudinal bulkheads with a cut out area allowing clearance for the top half of the bomb, which extended into the second bomb bay. The oxygen bottles, tubing and other equipment that was located there were moved elsewhere. During flight the cutout bomb bay doors provided adequate streamlining around the bomb casing that extended half outside the aircraft. However, once the *Tallboy* was dropped, the large hole in the bomb bay doors caused enormous drag.

A H-frame, which was removable by four bolts to a fitting near the front wing spar, consisted of sway bracing, a fore and aft load centering pin, and an attachment point for an A-4 bomb release with a D-7 shackle. Four removable pendant-type manually operated hoists attached to the corners of the H-frame were used to hoist the weapon. Special metal

In March 1945 a B-29 arrived at Eglin for testing by personnel from Wright Field. Modifications to the B-29 included the shortening and strengthening the forward and aft bomb bay doors providing a cut out for clearance for the bomb that was carried partially externally due to its large size. (AAF)

During flight the cutout bomb bay doors provided adequate streamlining around the bomb casing that extended half outside the aircraft. However, once the *Tallboy* was dropped, the large hole in the bomb bay doors caused enormous drag. The curved cut out bomb bay doors can be seen on the photo. (AAF)

caused by the large opening in the bomb bay doors after release prevented joint operations with standard B-29s. This drag caused a 4% reduction in true air miles per fuel gallon at high altitudes with the bomb and 10.5% reduction without. During practical tests of this configuration, 14 *Tallboy* casings were loaded to the proper 12,000 pound weight and dropped from various altitudes with good accuracy. The final testing report of 11 June 1945 recommended that a B-29 group equipped to carry the *Tallboy* be formed as quickly as practical and only be used against specialized targets selected by the Joint Target Group.

In early 1945 the Army Ordnance Department continued to work on Americanized versions of the *Tallboy* with the deficient aspects of the British *Tallboy* corrected. Wind tunnel tests of reduced-scale model *Tallboys* were conducted to evaluate how ballistic performance was affected by varying the length of the tail. The long tail of the *Earthquake* bombs, which provided stability, made internal stowage in bomber aircraft impossible until the Consolidated B-36 Peacemaker entered service. The AAF also considered a number of other mammoth earth penetration bombs that could be used as multi-use bombs. The prototypes of these American very large bombs were still in development when the war ended.

hoisting slings with chocks were used to support and position the bomb on the ground prior to loading. The bomb was correctly positioned under the rack by a pair of triple width chains when a shallow 2.125 inch hole in the bomb casing which denoted the bomb's center of gravity was aligned directly under a plumb-bob suspended from the carrying pin on the H-frame. A small windlass in the navigator's station was attached to a cable threaded through the chain links to provide retraction. A turnbuckle was attached at the end of each chain to the H-frame to be certain that the loaded bomb was tightly attached. The bomb loading process required nine men: two to operate each of the four chain hoists and one additional man to oversee the hoisting process and keep the bomb centered in the rack.

The B-29 arrived at Eglin on 23 March 1945, for Phase One and Phase Two testing by personnel from Wright Field; with each Phase scheduled to take two weeks. Phase One tests were to determine the B-29's performance with the bomb while Phase Two tests were functional tests with the procedures of hoisting, carrying, and releasing the *Tallboy*. At the same time the AAF Proving Ground Command tested a B-29 that had been modified at Boeing's Wichita factory. This B-29 was capable of carrying either a *Tallboy* or a *Grand Slam* bomb but only the *Tallboy* configuration was used until *Grand Slam* engineering and testing was successful. Another test program, involving the addition of two underwing racks capable of holding two *Tallboys* or *Grand Slams* per aircraft, was in progress during the summer of 1945 at Boeing Wichita.

During testing several problems were discovered that requiring a solution before the *Tallboy* could become operational. More powerful chain hoists were required to reduce the time and number of men required for bomb loading. The fixed ends of the chain support apparatus were to be moved from the right to left side of the H-frame. The tail fins on the *Tallboy* were offset 5° to spin stabilize the bomb in a clockwise direction and the small counter clockwise rotation that was conveyed as the bomb rolled off the support chains at the time of release needed to be counteracted. Since there was sufficient room to carry several 500 pound GP bombs on the rear bomb bay racks; a release circuit was incorporated in the *Tallboy* release circuit to allow these GP bombs to be released after the *Tallboy* was dropped.

The degradation in performance due to the drag from the partially external attachment of the bomb combined with the even higher drag

The **British *Grand Slam*** bomb including the tail was 25.42 feet in length (the body was 12.5 feet long) and 3.83 feet in diameter. The *Grand Slam* tail was 13.33 feet long, 4.33 feet across the fins. (AFHRC)

22,000 Pound Grand Slam Bomb
British *Grand Slam*: HE, Aircraft, MC 22,000 Pound

On July 18, 1943 production contracts were issued for 100 *Tallboy* Large bombs but immediately the capacity of the English Steel Corporation foundry could not provide for both the *Tallboy* Medium and the *Tallboy* Large so production of the *Tallboy* Large was terminated on 30 September 1943 after only nine casings were produced. Manufacture of the *Tallboy* Large was resumed in July 1944 under the designation *Grand Slam*. The name *Grand Slam* comes from the bridge card game where it is a term that means winning all the tricks in a dealt hand. Manufacture of the large casings was slow and expensive so additional contracts were let with an American company, A.O. Smith of Milwaukee, WI. The filling and fusing of the *Grand Slam* was identical to the *Tallboy* as previously described except for scale. The UK-manufactured bombs were initially referred to as *Grand Slam* MkI while the American manufactured bombs were designated as *Grand Slam* MkII. The *Grand Slam* and the *Tallboy* were identical in all respects except dimensions.

The *Grand Slam* bomb including the tail was 25.42 feet in length (the body was 12.5 feet long) and 3.83 feet in diameter. The *Grand Slam* tail was 13.33 feet long, 4.33 feet across the fins and was attached to the bomb end plate by 12 half inch studs with nuts. There was a cylindrical metal cowling place between the bomb body and tail cone to enhance streamlining. The casing thickness around the hardened steel nose plug was 7.75 inches but tapered to only 1.75 inches at the base. The color of the bomb was dark green or gray while the tail assembly remained as bare metal. Markings on the casing were minimal with the nose of the casing having a thin red stripe followed by a wider green stripe with a stenciled "Torpex D1." The bomb explosive charge of Torpex comprised about 43% of the bomb's weight. There was a one inch layer of TNT topping added to the aft end of the charge. Four inches of wood meal/wax composition filler was then added and this filler was sealed with a half inch plywood washer. Three exploders passed through holes in this washer and were held in place by a heavy base plate secured by bolts to the bomb body.

The bomb was ballistically perfect and had a very high terminal velocity. When it was dropped from 16,000 feet at a 200 mph airspeed, the bomb would develop a terminal velocity of 1,097 feet per second and be rotating at 60 rpm (by the 5° cant of the tail fins). When dropped from 35,000 feet it had a terminal velocity of 3,600 to 3,700 feet per second (or

The effects of a direct hit by a 22,000 pound ***Grand Slam*** bomb on a 16 inch poured concrete roof of the Farge U-Boat pen complex on 27 March 1945. (AFHRC)

about 2,500 mph), and because it was so much faster than the speed of sound the noise of its fall would be heard after that of the explosion (like the German V-2 Rocket).

During the winter of 1944, the British War Cabinet, predicting a quick end to the war, conducted an indiscriminate cancellation of new bomb production contracts including those for the *Grand Slam*. The modification of Lancaster bombers to carry *Grand Slams* was also terminated. Once it was apparent that the war would continue well into 1945, production was resumed but the delay prevented the deployment of the *Grand Slam* until the spring of 1945.

Even though *Grand Slam* production had been held up, testing continued and by October, development work on the original nine casings manufactured in 1943 was complete. Modification to the MkI Lancaster Special *Grand Slam* bomber included removal and fairing over of the nose and dorsal gun turrets, and removal of the H2S radar blister. The bomb bay doors were removed and the more durable tires and wheels of the Avro Lincoln bomber were installed. The front and rear ends of the bomb bay were contoured to improve airflow around the bomb.

Three *Tallboy* craters can be seen in this photo of the Hamburg Fink III U-Boat pens. (AFHRC)

Operational Testing
The first operational test of a *Grand Slam* was carried out by the RAF on 13 March, 1945. The next day, a single *Grand Slam* was dropped from 16,000 feet during a *Tallboy* raid carried out by 617 Squadron against the Bielefield Viaduct which had been frequently bombed previously with smaller conventional bombs without destroying its supporting spans. During this attack a very near miss by the *Grand Slam* and several *Tallboys* produced the predicted earthquake effect that destroyed several spans and shut down rail traffic for the rest of the war. The raid showed that upon hitting the ground the *Tallboy* was capable of displacing a million cubic feet of earth and made a crater which would have taken 5,000 tons of earth to fill.

Further operational testing was required with the purpose being to determine the strength of the casings; the sensitivity of the detonation and fusing system; the reliability of fuses, primers, and boosters; and the sensitivity of the explosive filling of several penetration bomb designs. The target for these tests was the U-Boat assembly pens at Farge that were protected by a 16 foot thick steel reinforced concrete roof. The RAF dropped 13 *Grand Slams* and four *Tallboys* on the Farge complex on 27 March 1945 and a total of 41 *Grand Slams* were dropped during the war.

American *Grand Slam*: Bomb, GP, 22,000 MHO (T-14)
The American *Grand Slam* was 25.83 feet in length including the 13.83 foot tail unit, 3.83 feet in diameter, and weighed 22,850 pounds. For use in AAF bombers the American Grand Slam was to be 18 inches shorter than the British design (287 inches) by substituting a two inch rounded tail cap for the 20 inch tail cone which was located aft of the stabilizing fins. There were to be no dimensional changes between the UK and US bombs forward of the trailing edges of the stabilizing fins. The explosive filler was 9,600 pounds of Tritonal (41.6% of total weight) but early production models were filled with 9,200 pounds of Torpex (41% of total weight of 22,113 pounds in these models) with a one inch layer of TNT over the rear of the casing. An armor piercing plug was fitted to the nose of the cast casings.

The 924 pound M121 tail assembly was 13.33 feet long and 1.44 feet wide at its greatest diameter and was attached by 20 bolts to the casing. With the tail assembly the total weight of the T-14 was to 23,037 pounds and the overall length of the weapon was 25.42 feet. To accommodate the

Grand Slam the B-29 bomb bay doors (like the *Tallboy*) needed to have an oval cut out that encompassed the bomb when closed which gave better aerodynamics and performance. The cone at the farthest end of the tail assembly could be removed so that the *Grand Slam* could be loaded semi-submerged into the joined bomb bays of a modified B-29. (The *Grand Slam* or *Tallboy* was investigated for use with the Northrop XB-35 Flying Wing and the Convair B-36 which was under development at the end of the war and could easily accommodate either large bomb.)

Like the British *Tallboy*, the American version of the *Grand Slam* was produced in cast and welded versions. Welded versions were assembled from five pieces: a forged nose piece approximately 26 inches long, three cylindrical sections of rolled plate with a longitudinal axis weld and a forged end ring held to the assembly with a stainless autinentic weld not heat treated for stress relief. The casing was taper-bored internally then placed in a die and hammered to form the proper exterior shape. Wax was poured into the nose of the casing to act as a desensitizing agent before the pouring of the explosive filler.

Except for painting and markings, the American and UK versions appeared identical. The entire casing was painted olive drab green with a yellow band at the nose and tail. Stenciled in black on the casing was the following information: Type of weapon (GP), weight, model, explosive filler, ammunition lot number, AIC symbol, ICC shipping designation, Inspector's stamp, the letters "US," displacement, and perhaps the shipping address and shipping ticket number. The inert training bombs carried minimal markings or were painted a high visibility black and white to aid tracking cameras but some of these models for public exhibit were painted silver or olive drab green.

The three fuse pockets set in the base plate were arranged in a straight line unlike the triangular arrangement found on the British *Grand Slam*s. For increased reliability, three, four inch long Ml 69 (T708) fuses with M40 Primer-detonators and the Ml 18 adapter booster were screwed into a fuse seat. Access to the fuses was through circular holes in the tail assembly.

B-29 *Grand Slam* Modifications
In early summer 1945, three Wichita-built Boeing B-29-75-BWs were modified to carry *Grand Slam* or *Tallboy* bombs on external bomb racks under each wing between the inboard engine and fuselage (44-70060 in

To accommodate the *Grand Slam* the B-29 bomb bay doors (like the *Tallboy*) needed to have an oval cut out that encompassed the bomb when closed which gave better aerodynamics and performance. The cone at the farthest end of the tail assembly could be removed so that the *Grand Slam* could be loaded semi-submerged into the joined bomb bays of a modified B-29. (AAF)

In early summer 1945, three Wichita-built Boeing B-29-75-BWs were modified to carry *Grand Slam* or *Tallboy* bombs on **external bomb racks** under each wing between the inboard engine and fuselage (44-70060 in photo). (AAF)

photo). After experiments at Eglin, an order was placed for 50 B-29s to be fitted with underwing racks for *Grand Slam* and *Tallboy* Bombs and the conversion was initiated at the Boeing Wichita factory. These racks were also designed to carry alternate loads of four 1,000 pound, four 2,000 pound, or four 4,000 pound bombs. This modification did not alter the existing bomb bay and allowed the carrying of additional fuel tanks in both bomb bays when the wing racks were in use. Preliminary flight testing at Wichita revealed no unexpected buffeting or vibration even when provoked with misleading power settings and deliberate stalls. These aircraft were to be equipped with the latest improvements: APQ-13 or BTO (Bombing Through Overcast) Radar, Curtiss electric propellers, and fuel injected engines. If the war hadn't ended with the dropping of the Atomic Bombs, the twin *Grand Slam* B-29s might have been available to see action over Japan. Fifteen B-29s assigned to the 886th Squadron of the Twentieth Air Force were to be based at North Field, Tinian in the Marianas and to be tactically available by mid-September 1945. An interesting proposed use of the *Grand Slams* was to be against the Japanese coastal city Yokohama which was located on a well-defined earthquake fault.

Since the range of the B-29 with two underwing 22,000 pound *Grand Slam*s was only about 300 miles, it could not fly along with B-29 missions using twin 12,000 pound *Tallboys* where the range was upwards of 2,100 miles. It was also determined that the number of Japanese targets suitable for the *Grand Slam* was considerably less than those for *Tallboys*, with an estimated monthly requirement of only 125 *Grand Slam*s versus 600 *Tallboy*s. Because of these differing requirements, it was decided that the 886th would carry only *Grand Slam*s and a second unit of 15 B-29s, attached to the 450th Group would carry the *Tallboys*

B-32 in the *Tallboy* and *Grand Slam* Programs
The Consolidated B-32 design was a hedge bet in case the Boeing B-29 failed to meet expectations. Testing and production problems delayed the B-32 program to the extent that only 115 were built by the end of World War II and only a single squadron of 15 actually saw combat in the Philippines and Okinawa. On 21 April 1945, Order No. B4-5-1, coded as the "*Albert Project*," for the use of *Tallboy* and *Grand Slam* bombs recommended that the Armament Laboratory prepare experimental tests for these bombs using a factory modified B-32 (42-108535) to be attached to the Army Air Forces Proving Ground Command, Very Heavy Bombing Unit (Squadron E, 611th AAFBU) at Eglin, Once modified, the B-32 would

The American World War II *Tallboy*s were converted to **TARZONs** which were basically a *Tallboy* with a new tail assembly that provided limited azimuth and range control via an command radio transmitter in the launch aircraft and an radio guidance receiver radio link with the mother aircraft installed in the bomb. (USAF)

have been able to carry two *Tallboy*s, or one *Tallboy* and one *Grand Slam* side by side within its large bomb bay.

The B-32 modifications were to include replacement of the sliding bomb bay covers (that had caused a nine mph drop in speed during the bomb run) with snap opening hinged doors similar to the type found on the B-29; the relocation of numerous antennas that were mounted along the keel-like partition that divided the large bomb bay into side by side parts. This keel structure, which provided a catwalk connecting the front and rear of the aircraft, was to be extensively modified or removed altogether. Quick changeover suspension arrangements were to use two stainless steel straps with each strap being fixed to one end of a removable beam with the other end attached to a bomb shackle hook. The bomb shackle was to be suspended vertically and operated by a Type A-4 bomb release unit.

The *Tallboy* was to be released horizontally while the *Grand Slam* would have exited the aircraft at a 17.5° angle due to bomb bay space limitations. The length of the 305 inch *Grand Slam* (with tail) was too long to fit the 297 inch long B-32 bomb bay so the bomb's tail was shortened by 18 inches. This shortened tail design delayed the engineering of the semi-external bomb bay installation for both the B-32 and B-29 as the ballistic data had been developed for the full length bomb. The engineering challenges of loading and releasing a *Grand Slam* at such an angle had not been overcome prior to the cancellation of the project. By late July, the B-32 test program was progressing so slowly it was apparent to planners that it would not be ready for very heavy bomb sorties for the foreseeable future and the short tail bomb was cancelled. Since the 305 inch *Grand Slam* was going to be the only version to go to war, work on the B-29 bomb bay conversion got back on track without having to worry about ordnance optimized for the B-32's limitations. The B-32 program was officially terminated in October 1945.

12,000 Pound, Bell V-13/ASM-A-1 *TARZON*
In January 1945, the Air Force proposed the development of remote controlled very high tonnage bombs to be designed and manufactured by Gulf Research and Development. The project was entitled "Development of a Control for the British 12,000 lb. *Tallboy* Bomb" with the code name *TARZON*. At the time there were very few targets available for the smaller remote controlled 1,000 pound VB-3 or 2,000 pound VB-4 *RAZON* bombs and those available could be destroyed with a full load of the less expensive and more easily deployed conventional M-65 1,000 pound bombs. However, it was thought that if the *RAZON* guidance system could be combined with substantially larger bombs a use could be found for that system such as targets requiring destruction by deep penetration and very heavy explosives such as battleships, concrete fortifications and structures, caves and other underground installations, dams and dikes, and causing landslides. Use of the *TARZON* was limited to daytime with excellent visibility and the launching bomber had to remain on the bomb run to guide the *TARZON* to the target.

The American World War II *Tallboys* were converted to *TARZONs* which were basically a *Tallboy* with a new tail assembly that provided limited azimuth and range control via an AN/ARW-38 command radio transmitter in the launch aircraft and an AN/URW-2 radio guidance receiver radio link with the mother aircraft installed in the *TARZON* bomb. The M-series bombsight was modified so that it was possible to see a superimposed image of both the flare and the target. Roll stabilization was accomplished by ailerons mounted in the tail of the bomb. Range and azimuth were control led by a set of elevators in the bomb tail. An electrical servo system in the bomb actuated the elevators and ailerons in response to radio signals from the launch aircraft. After release, a flare in the tail assembly aided the bombardier in guiding the weapon to the target.

Several modifications were made on the B-29s in order to accommodate the *TARZON* bomb. The fuselage section between the bomb bay doors was removed, and the bomb bay doors were cut to conform to the cross section of the bomb. Modifications were made to the bomb racks in order to support the weight at the individual shackles. (USAF)

The projected impact velocity was to be 1,000 feet per second compared to the 1,250-1,300 feet per second impact of the British uncontrolled *Tallboy*. Because of its large size the controllability of the *RAZON Tallboy* was to be about only one third of the VB-1. NACA was assigned to provide the *RAZON Tallboy* with increased controllability to +/- 1,000 feet from 15,000 feet after a fall of 15 seconds with no control and to increase impact speed.

Several modifications were made on the B-29s in order to accommodate the *TARZON* bomb. The fuselage section between the bomb bay doors was removed, and the bomb bay doors were cut to conform to the cross section of the bomb. Modifications were made to the bomb racks in order to support the weight at the individual shackles. In June 1945 it was projected that only one B-29 squadron, 15 aircraft, was scheduled to carry the *TARZON* as its developmental time for combat was to be late in the war which was projected to end in September 1946. It was recommended that funds and personnel could be better used to deploy the standard *RAZON* to the Pacific.

This project was initiated on 26 February 1945 and soon the Air Force, NDRC, and Gulf Research and Development obtained several standard 12,000 pound *Tallboy* bombs for development into the guided *TARZON*. NACA was to aid in solving the supersonic aerodynamic problems with entirely new bomb shapes with new control surfaces. A fixed shroud of 20 inch chord and five inch diameter was placed about the center of gravity. A *RAZON* octagonal tail unit also of 20 inch chord and 54 inch diameter was placed 11.58 inches from the center of gravity. Tests demonstrated the control forces and speed to be too great for *RAZON*-type controls. None were ready in time to be used in World War II and only 13 prototypes were completed by January 1946.

After resurrecting the *RAZON* bomb for testing several months earlier, the 19BG switched to developing the *TARZON* bomb in December 1950. Three B-29s, similar to those modified to carry *Tallboy*s in World War II were tested to attack heavily defended bridges during the Korean War. During the first tests of the first ten bombs dropped, only one scored a hit. But by March 1951, the 19BG became reasonably skilled in the use of the *TARZON*s but technical problems continued. By this time FEAF bombers in Korea had destroyed all of their bridge targets but the enemy quickly built bypass spans and repaired the damaged bridges. On March 29, three *TARZON*-equipped B-29s were assigned to bomb Korean Sinuiju

bridges. One aircraft returned to base with mechanical problems, a second aircraft with Col. Payne Jennings, 19BG CO, ditched at sea and exploded, and the third aircraft continued on to the target only to have the *TARZON* miss the bridge and as a result of this debacle the *TARZON* program was cancelled.

During the Vietnam War, before the light case, 15,000 pound parachute BLU-82 *Daisy Cutter* Bomb was introduced, the left over *Tallboy*s were considered for use in clearing helicopter landing zones in the jungle.

Post-war *Projects Ruby* and *Harken*

Analysis of *Tallboy* and *Grand Slam* attacks made during the war revealed that their effectiveness against reinforced concrete structures was debatable as these bombs failed to penetrate hardened targets as they were designed to do. The problems were linked to bomb casing break up and explosive sensitivity which required further testing under similar combat conditions. *Projects Ruby* and *Harken* were joint Anglo-American bomb tests undertaken to furnish ballistic data and performance records of very heavy bombs piercing reinforced concrete targets. The tests began in late 1945 using heavy bombs developed and used during World War II and were continued into 1946 testing newly designed bombs.

Project Ruby

During the war the US Army Ordinance Corps was allotted $380,000 to develop large penetration bombs capable of puncturing 32 feet of reinforced concrete but no controlled tests had taken place. Post-war analysis of *Tallboy* and *Grand Slam* attacks revealed that their effectiveness against reinforced concrete structures was questionable. Problems associated with casing break up and explosive sensitivity required testing under conditions similar to those on the battlefield in order to better understand why these specially designed bombs failed to penetrate hardened targets. *Project Ruby* was created to this end as a joint Anglo-American endeavor and the bomb trials were conducted from 28 March through 19 July 1946 in Europe by the Air Proving Ground Command. RAF Bomber Command organized and coordinated the program and each country provided suitable aircraft, bombs, and personnel.

The American bombs tested included the fabricated (welded plate) *Tallboy* (T-10) and fabricated *Grand Slam* (T-14) from World War II; the 2,000 Pound SAP (M103); and a new 22,000 Pound SAP design called

During **Project Ruby** the British bomb carriage was not adequate to load *Grand Slam* bombs into a B-29 so another loading method had to be devised. A trough was dug to give a Boeing bomb trailer carrying a *Grand Slam* enough room and the bomber was then backed over the trench until the bomb bay was directly over the bomb which was then raised into the bomb bay by using the internal hoists. (USAF)

Amazon (T28). The British bombs included the cast *Tallboy* and *Grand Slam*, the *Disney*, and the 1,650 pound decreased-scaled version of a proposed 12,000 pound rocket assisted concrete penetrating bomb.

The post-war American demobilization had caused the mass transfer of personnel and numerous base closures in Britain. To conduct heavy bomb tests a permanent AAF detachment of three B-17s, three C-54 transports, and support personnel was established at RAF Mildenhall on 10 January 1946. In March 1946, three B-29s and four B-17s were added to the Mildenhall detachment which was moved to the RAF Central Bomber Establishment Marham for the *Project Ruby* (UK: *Operation Front Line*) test program. All US bombs supplied by the Director of Armament Research and Development were marked as "PROC Q.3304 and a serial number. The Marham complement included 160 officers and enlisted men commanded by Col. D.G. Hawes of 15 Squadron, RAF, equipped with specially modified Lancasters.

The British designed H-Trolley was too high to fit under a B-29 so to load bombs larger than a *Tallboy* another loading method had to be devised. The method was similar to that developed for loading the Atomic Bombs. A trough, one foot deep, was dug to give a Boeing bomb trailer carrying a *Grand Slam* enough room under the bomber's tail skid after it was moved down into the trough. The bomber was then backed over the trench until the bomb bay was directly over the bomb which was then raised into the bomb bay by using the internal hoists.

Once the US tests were completed the testing was transferred to Europe with the former U-Boat assembly factory at Farge, Germany used as a test target. Previously the RAF had used the V-weapon site at Watten for penetration tests but the French people in the area protested as by that time they had received their quota of bombs. Regardless, the structure at Watten was scarcely thick enough to offer the required resistance. The Farge facility was never used during the war and was of a particularly modern type of construction. The construction material was concrete, with massive steel reinforcing frames and the only damage resulting from RAF attacks during the war was two small holes in the roof made by 22,000 pound *Grand Slams*. The Farge structure was 1,400 feet long and measured between 318 feet and 220 feet in width. The huge concrete footings extended to a depth of 55 feet in some places with the outer walls poured in layers 67 feet long and 14.75 feet thick. The roof thickness ranged from 14.75 feet to 24 feet with four different types of roof construction employed but the primary one consisted of pre-stressed reinforced concrete arch trusses. Because of the Farge target's proximity to inhabited areas planners decided that since the tests were to determine depth of penetration, not blast effect, the bomb casings were filled with sand for inert loaded/penetration trials and were to take place at Farge. Live bomb trials were moved to the isolated uninhabited U-Boat pens on the Heligoland, an island in the North Sea in the British Occupation Sector. The structure was 506 feet long and 310 feet wide with a roof thickness of approximately 10 feet.

The *Ruby* tests were conducted over five months using various combinations of dropping height, fusing, and explosive filling. After each test drop, ordnance experts immediately inspected the Farge or Heligoland facilities recording the results. During the test the seven B-17s flew 57 sorties over Heligoland dropping 225 tons of bombs and 37 sorties over Farge dropping 116.5 tons. The three B-29s flew 27 sorties over Farge dropping 281.9 tons. During the tests there were bombs that actually bounced off the concrete roof and were recovered bent and twisted out of shape. There were bombs that shattered upon impact, that left only pockmarks on the roof surface but there also were a few bombs that smashed through the concrete and exploded on the structure's floor leaving a large hole and a tangle of reinforcing steel bars dangling from the ceiling.

The German standard for a bomb proof structure was a 23 foot thick steel reinforced concrete structure which they calculated would require a 27,000 pound bomb striking at Mach One at a precise angle to penetrate. However, the German calculations did not consider that it was not essential to completely penetrate a structure to cause damage inside. The shock waves produced by a large explosion could displace the reinforcement bars causing a scab to separate from the face opposite the one impacted. The *Tallboy* bomb could penetrate concrete to almost 10 feet and scab to a depth over 18 feet. If the target roof was only 16 feet thick, then a large scab could be separated from the inside face of the structure and come crashing down on anything underneath it. The heaviest weapon used during the war was the 22,000 pound *Grand Slam* bomb which could penetrate concrete to 12 feet and scab to a depth of almost 23 feet. The exposure to falling scabs was more than that from penetration so the Germans added a layer of steel beams to the underside of many structures to give additional strength and catch the concrete scabs that were detached from the ceiling. (See *Volume 2: Bombs, Bombsights and Bombing* for the effects of bombs on concrete.)

Although the welded American bomb casings were stronger than the cast British casings, when they were dropped from high altitudes none of the welds in the casings could endure the impact for penetration of the target. However, the explosive fillers were shown to be insensitive enough to survive the impact from high altitude drops. Both the American welded *Tallboy* and *Grand Slams* could survive more than 50% of concrete impacts at velocities of 610 feet/second but broke up at impacts of 850 feet/second or greater. As the tests progressed, unsuccessful attempts were made to strengthen the welds. The tests showed that the *Tallboy* and *Grand Slam* shapes did not have suitable dimensions for penetration of concrete. Though the bombing accuracy from low altitudes was a success, the changeable European weather and the necessary accuracy to hit the relatively small target roofs from the planned 25,000-30,000 foot altitudes produced poor results. Generally, the outcomes of the Ruby tests were disappointing as the *Tallboy* or *Grand Slam* bombs failed to meet their design criteria.

Project Harken

Project Harken was initiated on 1 April 1947 as a follow up to *Project Ruby* to continue testing weapons from *Ruby* as well as new designs. An airbase in England was to be secured that could operate three modified B-29s and approximately 200 personnel. A port facility was also to be acquired to receive the 25,000 pound bombs along with transportation facilities to move them to the airbase. The RAF would be allowed to observe the tests in exchange for participation and logistical support. The Farge U-Boat pens were again to be the test target. The testing of two new penetration designs were to be conducted simultaneously and 35 large inert bombs of two types, each weighing about 25,000 pounds, code named *Amazon* (T28E1) and *Samson* (T28E2) were tested during a program that was to take approximately four to six months to complete.

Amazon, Bomb, 22,000 Pound, SAP, T28

The *Amazon* T28 was designed to give better penetration while being carried by *Project Ruby* aircraft. The T28E1 *Amazon* bomb was 3.17 inches in diameter, 12.83 feet long, and had a main wall thickness of 4.5 inches with a maximum 20 inch nose thickness. The charge weight was 4,200 pounds, a total weight of 25,000 pounds, corresponding to 16.8% explosive. *Amazon*s were supplied in both cast and welded versions. The welded *Amazon* was comprised of six sections: a forged steel nose, four 3.17 foot diameter cylindrical sections with three inch thick walls which formed the body, and a forged base ring. All sections were welded together in six circumferential welds with a stainless austenitic weld holding the base ring to the body. The casing had an endplate bolted to it which contained three welded fuse pockets forming a triangle. T723 fuses with adapters and auxiliary boosters were screwed into these fuse pockets. Though similar in length to the *Grand Slam* with the tail assembly attached, the casing of the *Amazon* was considerably longer. This extra length placed the center of gravity farther aft than on the *Grand Slam*. With the release and shackle assemblies fixed in the B-29s forward bomb bay and optimized for the *Grand Slam/Tallboy*, the *Amazon* tended to hang unbalanced and slightly tail down. This unbalanced loading caused two malfunctions in the release that resulted in lost casings over the North Sea.

The 22,000 pound *Amazon* T-28 was dropped on Farge and its performance compared with that of the 22,000 pound GP *Grand Slam* and 12,000 pound GP *Tallboy*. But the tests indicated the need for redesigning the bomb to give greater case strength without materially reducing the explosive charge to weight ratio. Although the bomb was capable of perforating the 14.75 inch section of the target's concrete roof, it broke up either upon perforation of the roof or upon secondary impact within the structure. A weakness of the rear weld which joined the base ring to the bomb body was a contributing factor for the bomb casing breaking-up.

Sampson, Bomb, 25,000 Pound SAP, T28E1 and T28E2

The *Samson* bomb, designed for greater penetration than the *Amazon*, had approximately the same weight at 25,200 pounds as the *Amazon* but it was longer at 16.33 feet and had a smaller maximum outside diameter at 2.67 feet. The main wall thickness was 4.125 inches and the nose section had a maximum 20 inch thickness. The charge weight was 3,900 pounds giving 15.5% of bomb weight as explosive. Both the T28E1 and T28E2 bombs had the *Tallboy* type fin assembly consisting of a tail cone carrying four radial vanes which were set at an angle of 5° to the axis of the bomb to produce rotation in flight.

Project Harken Results

During initial US tests high speed motion pictures were taken of the *Amazon* and *Samson* test bombs as they struck the target. This film was sent to the Aberdeen Proving Ground, where the Measurements Analysis Branch, Computing Laboratory of the Ballistic Research Laboratories analyzed the results which showed that actual range errors were less than one mil from provisional bombing tables.

The welded American *Amazon* was designed for concrete penetration and was able to survive initial impact on concrete at a velocity of 1,100 feet/second but sidewall breakdown occurred due to failure of the rear stainless austenitic welds upon secondary impact after passing through a 14.75 foot concrete roof (all other welds held). The T723 fuses installed in the end plate did withstand all impacts but could not survive a breakup of the casing. If dropped from 35,000 feet, the *Amazon* was calculated to be able penetrate up to 22 feet of concrete if the casing could withstand the much higher impact velocities and would impact at a near vertical angle.

The test results led to recommendations for a new design with a similar weight/charge as the *Amazon* but with a more pointed nose, smaller diameter, and a casing resistant to bending by use of multiple layered walls, internal ribs, corrugations, or the use of special alloys. A method was to be devised to drop the bomb so that it was perpendicular to the surface of the target at the moment of impact to maximize penetration and reduce sidewall stress.

Bomb, SAP 25,000 Pound T28E4

Project Ruby had determined several limitations in the *Grand Slam* design which had failed to penetrate the massive concrete roof of the Farge target during several tests. Development work on the 25,000 pound SAP bomb began sometime in 1946 with testing beginning during 1947 as part of the

Project Harken. Little information is available on the T28E4. The overall length of the bomb was about the same as the *Grand Slam* at 16.625 feet (or 18.17 feet?) in length with a diameter of 2.67 feet. The tail assembly was attached to the casing by 16 bolts in the base plate. The tail section was measured 7.25 feet long and weighed about 800 pounds. Unlike the *Grand Slam*, the nose was a solid piece without an armor piercing plug. The last information on the T28E4 had it still in development in 1950.

42,000 Pound Bomb T-12 *Cloudmaker*

In 1942 design of the massive 42,000 pound T-12 general purpose bomb began based to some extent on the *Tallboy* and *Grand Slam* designs and was dubbed the *Cloudmaker*. The final production version saw the weight increase to 43,600 with 17,600 pounds (41%) comprising high explosives. The T-12 was 16.67 feet long, 4.5 feet in diameter, and assembled from six welded sections of steel. The bomb's total length was 26.83 feet including the 10.17 foot tail assembly with the large tail fins offset at 5° to provide rotation. Several improvements were made by the Ordnance Corps engineers at the Aberdeen Proving Ground to correct features that had been copied by war time practicality directly from the *Tallboy*. By the end of the war, the T-12 was purely American, and the largest bomb ever designed with ultimate configuration projected as a 100,000 pound bomb!

It was not possible to carry the T-12 completely inside the carrying bomber during the war because of its length and it produced enormous drag and ballistic problems when carried externally. The long tail could not be shortened as it provided the stability essential for precision bombing of the target. The original British design had aluminum tail fin assemblies which were replaced by steel assemblies. The tail was attached to the base plate of the bomb by 24 bolts. A collapsible fin assembly was considered but rejected as being too complicated and susceptible to delay or failure while opening causing range and deflection errors. As an expediency British fuses and detonators were used but these fuses could not be armed in flight and were replaced with American fuses by the Ordnance Corps engineers.

During the summer of 1945, Boeing Wichita converted the Renton-built B-29A-70-BA (44-62263) to carry the T-12. The fuselage center section between the bomb bays was removed, making a cutout in the forward and rear bomb bay doors to fit the contours of the bomb. Instruments to record dynamic forces on the airframe during release and recording cameras were installed. A low-slung 50,000 pound hydraulic bomb lift trailer-type vehicle was developed to lift bombs from ground clearance blocks to be transported over short distances for loading into aircraft.

During the war the Army Ordnance Department had placed an order of 100 T-12s with the A. O. Smith Corporation but when the contract was cancelled only 57 casings had been manufactured; 50 forged steel and seven cast steel bombs. All seven of the cast bombs and a few of the forged bombs were inert loaded to test ballistics and mating with the carrying aircraft. Tritonal was loaded into 20 of the forged casings

Flight testing continued through 1946 with testing continued at Muroc AFB, CA with six inert casing drops from an altitude of 25,000 feet made from 5 March 1948. A Convair B-36 was assigned to the program and its huge bomb bays could easily accommodate two T-12s or an alternate load of one T-12 and two *Tallboys* or two *Grand Slams*. On 29 January 1949, B-36B-5CF, (44-92043) flew 1,450 miles from Ft. Worth, TX to the Muroc bombing range dropping two T-12s from 35,000 feet and 40,000 feet and then returning to Texas. Further development and testing continued until the program was terminated on 11 August 1954 when earth penetrating nuclear weapons that weighed a fraction of the T-12 and finally made large conventional bombs obsolete.

10,000 Pound *Pumpkin* Bomb

Origin and Development

The *Pumpkin* bomb concept was originated by Navy Capt. William "Deak" Parsons of the Los Alamos Ordnance Division and AAF Col. Paul Tibbetts, CO of the 509th Composite Group on 13 December 1944. *Pumpkin* provided a means of combat development and testing of the *Fat Boy* Atomic Bomb by the Los Alamos Laboratory and realistic training for the B-29 crews assigned to drop the Atomic Bomb.

The California Institute of Technology (CIT) under the direction of Dr. Charles Lauritsen was responsible for the delivery system of the *Fat Man* Atomic Bomb and contracted 486 of these 10,000 pound conventional bombs that had casings and ballistic and handling characteristics similar to the *Fat Man* Bombs. The bomb casings were manufactured by two Los Angeles companies, the Consolidated Steel Corporation and Western Pipe and Steel Company, while the tail assembly was produced by the Centerline Company of Detroit; all under contract to the CIT. The bombs were supposedly called the *Pumpkin* because of their orange color and ellipsoidal shape but there is no evidence that the bombs were ever painted other than the standard olive drab used by the AAF on all live ordnance. Some Los Alamos correspondence between Parsons and Dr. Lauritsen used the term *Pumpkin* when describing the bombs.

After initial development the management of the US atomic program was assigned to the USN BuOrd in May 1945, using the same manufacturers. The USN became responsible for the high explosives research and non-nuclear engineering (i.e. *Pumpkin* testing) for the *Fat Man* bomb at their Inyokern rocket range under the codename *Project Camel.*

Description

The *Pumpkin* bombs were externally similar to the *Fat Man* bomb in size and shape, and both had the same 52 inch square tail assembly and single-point attachment lug. The *Pumpkin* bombs were 12.67 feet long and five feet in maximum diameter. The weight was 10,520 pounds, consisting of 3,800 pounds for the casing, 425 pounds for the tail assembly, and 6,300 pounds of explosive filler or concrete test filler (59.9% of total weight). The shells were fabricated by welding together four ellipsoidal segments made of .0375 inch mild steel plate and the tail assemblies from 0.20 inch aluminum plate. The estimated cost of the *Pumpkin* shells in May 1945 was $1,500 to $2,000 each. The *Pumpkin* bomb had three prominent contact fuses arranged in an equilateral triangle around the nose of the

The **Pumpkin** bombs were externally similar to the *Fat Man* bomb in size and shape. The 10,520 pound *Pumpkin* bombs were 12.67 feet long and 5 feet in maximum diameter. (AAF)

bomb while the Atomic Bomb had four fuse housings. The *Fat Man* had its front and rear sections bolted together with eight fairing-covered bolts to the outer lugs of the inner sphere. Most, if not all, of the *Pumpkin* bombs had their front and rear ellipsoidal outer casings welded around the major circumference with a four inch hole used for filling the casing. The *Fat Man* also had four external mounting points for radar antennae around the circumference of the forward ellipsoidal casing as part of the arming and firing system while the *Pumpkin* bombs had none. *Pumpkin* and the *Fat Man* bombs both used the same tail assembly which was bolted in eight places to the rear section.

Pumpkin bombs were produced in both inert and high explosive models. The inert models were filled with a cement-plaster-sand mixture combined with water to the density of the Composition B which filled the high explosive versions. The filler of both variants had the same weight, weight distribution (center of gravity) and moment of inertia as the inner sphere used in the plutonium bomb. The inert concrete mixture was one bag of Plaster of Paris, 240 pounds of sand, and enough water to give a final concrete density of 1.67 to 1.68 which the same density of the Composition B high explosive with which the live *Pumpkins* were loaded.

Training and On to Combat

All of the inert versions were shipped by rail from Consolidated Steel and Western Pipe directly to Wendover Army Air Field, UT, where they were flight tested by the 216th AAF Base Unit (BU) Special. The 216th was a special ordinance test unit formed and designated to work on *Project W-47* which was a key part of the *Manhattan Project.* The 216th initially assembled inert bombs which were dropped by B-29s to furnish information on ballistics, electrical fusing and detonators, release mechanisms, and flying characteristics of the aircraft. While most inert bombs were dropped by the 216th some drop test missions were flown by 509th crews in training exercises in specially modified *Silverplate* B-29s (see next chapter). A few live bombs were used during tests at Wendover.

The live bomb casings and tails were shipped to the Naval Ammunition Depot, McAlester, OK for filling with explosives. The shells had a 4 inch diameter filling hole at a point on the maximum diameter and were placed on a cradle in a horizontal position and the Composition B mixture poured into the shell in a slurry form and then solidified in a drying facility for 36 hours. The filler hold was sealed, the attachment lug added, and the *Pumpkin* assembly was completed with the addition of the tail assembly. The nose contact fuses were not installed until the bombs were ready for missions on Tinian in the Marianas.

After the testing phase was completed each live *Pumpkin* was placed into a specially designed shipping container and was transported by rail to the USN Magazine at Port Chicago in the San Francisco Bay area (code named *Three Igloo Job* by Los Alamos). The combat *Pumpkins* were transported from Port Chicago to Tinian by ship where they were uncrated, offloaded, and then transferred to a bomb storage area to be used in "Air Force Special Missions" by the 509th Composite Group of the 313BW.

Combat Missions

When a combat mission was scheduled, the *Pumpkins* were transferred from the storage area to the 509th bomb loading pits which had been dug for loading the Atomic Bomb. The *Pumpkin* bomb was then loaded into the front bomb bay of each *Silverplate* B-29 and the three contact fuses were installed and safety pullout wires from the fuse arming vanes connected to attach points in the bomb bay structure. The purpose of the high explosive *Pumpkin* bombs was to continue the training and improve the efficiency of 509th crews after their arrival on Tinian. The *Pumpkin* mission parameters were to be similar to those of the actual Atomic Bomb missions and all targets were to be located in the vicinity of the cities designated for atomic attack. The flying procedure for *Pumpkin* missions from Tinian was purposely similar to the atomic missions flying at 30,000 feet and especially when the *Pumpkin* bomb was released and cleared the bomb bay doors. The pilot then put the B-29 into the sharp turn for the escape maneuver from the future powerful atomic blast.

The 509th *Pumpkin* missions included 16 missions on six days consisting of 51 sorties (two aborts) dropping 51 bombs. There were 15 crews with three flying five missions and seven flying four. Thirteen *Silverplate* bombers participated with two other arriving on 2 August 1945 flew no missions. The *Pumpkin Silverplate* B-29s included: 44-27296 (*Some Punkins*), 44-27297 (*Bockscar*), 44-27298 (*Full House*), 44-27299 (*Next Objective*), 44-272300 (*Strange Cargo*), 44-272301 (*Straight Flush*), 44-272302 (*Top Secret*), 44-272303 (*Jabit III*), 44-272304 (*Up an' Atom*), 44-272353 (*The Great Artiste*), 44-272354 (*Big Stink*), 44-86291 (*Necessary Evil*), and 44-86292 (*Enola Gay*). The two non-flying B-29s were: 44-346 (*Luke the Spook*) and 44-86347 (*Laggin' Dragon*). The 16 *Pumpkin* missions were:

Date	# A/C	Target
20 July	3	Koriyama
20 July	2	Fukushima
20 July	2	Nagaoka
20 July	3	Toyama
24 July	4	Kobe
24 July	3	Sumitomo
24 July	3	Yokkaichi
26 July	6	Toyama
26 July	4	Nagaoka
29 July	3	Ube
29 July	3	Koriyama
29 July	2	Yokkaichi
8 Aug.	3	Osaka
8 Aug.	3	Yokkaichi
14 Aug.	4	Nagoya
14 Aug.	3	Koroma

Mission Notes:
1) Radar bombing was used on 13 sorties and visual on 36 sorties
2) Only B-29 #44-272302 *Top Secret* flew all six *Pumpkin* missions
3) The 14 August missions were part of the largest bombing raid of the Pacific War with 1,014 bombers and fighter escorts taking part.
4) At the end of August 1945, out of a total order of 1,000 *Pumpkins*; 261 *Pumpkin* bombs had been produced and 225 additional units were in the production process; and 51 had been dropped.

A *Pumpkin* bomb (middle right) dropped from 29,000 feet on Nagoya on 14 August 1945 on the last mission of the war. (AAF)

Immediately after the end of the war, the US Strategic Bombing Survey (USSBS) Unit conducted an analysis of the effectiveness of the US bombing campaign against Japan, including the Atomic and *Pumpkin* missions. A special report was issued by the USSBS on the effect of the *Pumpkin* bomb dropped on nine selected targets. The report concluded that it "was a reasonably effective weapon against Japanese plants when direct hits were scored on vital areas, or when the near miss hit was sufficiently close to important buildings to cause severe structural damage." The report went on to state that blast was the primary cause of damage with secondary fires occasionally contributing to the total effect of the bombs.

13

Atomic Bomb

Historical Background
Brief History of Nuclear Physics

The study of radioactivity began with the discovery of uranium ores by Henri Becquerel in 1896. Two years later, Pierre and Marie Curie's research with radium showed that atoms that were previously thought to be ultimately stable and indivisible, actually had the potential of containing and releasing enormous quantities of energy. In 1903, Becquerel and the Curies were awarded the Nobel Prize for their work. In 1919, a New Zealand physicist Ernest Rutherford achieved the first artificial nuclear disintegrations by bombarding nitrogen with alpha particles emitted from a radioactive source, thus becoming the first person in history to intentionally "split the atom." In 1921, while working with Niels Bohr (who postulated that electrons moved in specific orbits), Rutherford theorized about the existence of neutrons, which could somehow compensate for the repelling effect of the positive charges of protons by causing an attractive nuclear force and thus keeping the nuclei from breaking apart. Rutherford was to become known as the Father of Nuclear Physics for his work.

Probably the most well-known figure in nuclear physics is **Albert Einstein** (right) who in addition to his theoretical work was instrumental in alerting FDR to the importance of developing the Atomic Bomb before the Germans. Pictured with Einstein is Dr. **H.C. Urey** who devised a system of separating two isotopes based upon gaseous diffusion. (AFHRC)

Even such celebrated physicists as Rutherford and Einstein could not find a method of artificially releasing the atom's massive energy any faster than natural emission. However, in the 1930s progress in controlling and understanding nuclear fission accelerated when the manipulation of the nuclei of atoms became possible. By 1932 the atom was thought to consist of a small, dense nucleus containing most of the atom's mass in the form of protons and neutrons and surrounded by a shell of electrons. In 1932 Sir John Cockcroft and Ernest Walton were first to "split the atom" (cause a nuclear reaction) by using artificially accelerated particles. In 1934 Irene and Frederic Joliot-Curie discovered that artificial radioactivity could be induced in stable elements by bombarding them with alpha particles. That same year Enrico Fermi reported similar results when bombarding uranium with neutrons but he did not immediately appreciate the consequences of his results.

In December 1938, Germans, Otto Hahn and Fritz Strassmann published experimental results about bombarding uranium with neutrons producing an isotope of barium. Shortly after, their Austrian co-worker Lise Meitner and her nephew Otto Robert Frisch correctly interpreted these results as the splitting of the uranium nucleus after the absorption of a neutron as nuclear fission which released a large amount of energy and additional neutrons. Frisch then performed direct experimental evidence of the nuclear fission.

In 1933 Hungarian physicist Leo Szilard had proposed that if any neutron-driven process released more neutrons than those required to start it; an expanding nuclear chain reaction could result. Chain reactions were familiar from chemistry where they typically caused explosions and other runaway reactions but for the first time Szilard was proposing them for a nuclear reaction. Shortly after the uranium fission discovery by Frisch, Szilard found that the fission of uranium released two or more neutrons on average, and immediately realized that a nuclear chain reaction by this mechanism was possible in theory. Initially, Szilard kept this a secret because he feared that the Nazis would develop it into a weapon, considering the work of Hahn et al. However, the Joliot-Curie group soon published identical results. Hitler's anti-Semitic ideology caused German Jewish physicists who later would make key contributions to go into exile in England and America. After Germany invaded Poland in 1939 many scientists in the United States and the United Kingdom, Albert Einstein in particular, wrote several letters to President Roosevelt urging him to develop nuclear capability before the Germans. These letters were also factors in the prioritizing the nuclear developmental project.

Establishment of the US Nuclear Program

University of California, Berkeley theoretical physicist J. Robert Oppenheimer was named to head the fast neutron research project and summoned a conference on the topic of nuclear weapon design. Once the OSRD gained control of the atomic bomb project from the National Bureau of Standards, the project leaders began to accelerate the program. Arthur Compton organized the University of Chicago Metallurgical Laboratory in early 1942 to study plutonium and fission piles which were primitive nuclear reactors. Compton then asked Oppenheimer to replace Gregory Breit, an early designer of the Atomic Bomb who had resigned his position feeling that the work was going too slowly. Oppenheimer was to head the research on fast neutron calculations which were vital to calculations about critical mass and weapon detonation. John Manley, a physicist at the Metallurgical Laboratory, was assigned to aid Oppenheimer by coordinating and contacting several experimental physics groups.

During the spring of 1942 Oppenheimer and Robert Serber of the University of Illinois worked on the problems of neutron diffusion (how neutrons moved in the chain reaction) and hydrodynamics (how the explosion produced by the chain reaction behaves). In June 1942, Oppenheimer summoned a conference at the University of California, Berkeley to review this work and the general theory of fission reactions. Theoretical physicists Hans Bethe, John Van Vleck, Edward Teller, Felix Bloch, Emil Konopinski, Robert Serber, Stanley Frankel, and Eldred Nelson (the latter three former students of Oppenheimer) confirmed that a fission bomb was feasible although there were still many unknown factors in the development of a nuclear bomb. The properties of pure Uranium-235 were relatively unknown, as were the properties of Plutonium, a new element which had only been discovered in February 1941 by Glenn Seaborg. Plutonium was the product of Uranium-238 absorbing a neutron which had been emitted from a fissioning Uranium-235 atom and could be produced in a nuclear reactor. But at the time no reactor had been constructed and Plutonium as an additional fissile substance (capable of undergoing nuclear fission, capable of being split) was not available.

During the summer 1942 Berkeley Conference a number of different fission bomb assembly methods were examined and only the "gun" method and a more complicated variation of the "implosion" design were to be used. It was determined that there were many possible ways of arranging the fissile material into a critical mass, the simplest being the shooting of a cylindrical plug into a sphere of active material

Oak Ridge, TN (Site X) engaged in enriched uranium production and plutonium production research. (AFHRC)

Hanford, WA (Site W) was the largest a plutonium production facility. (AFHRC)

with a tamper (a dense material which would focus neutrons inward and keep the reacting mass together to increase its efficiency). They also explored designs involving spheroids, a primitive form of implosion and explored the speculative possibility of autocatalytic methods which would increase the efficiency of the bomb as it exploded. The conference considered the idea of the fission bomb as theoretically established until more experimental data was available. Hungarian physicist Edward Teller advanced the idea of an even more powerful bomb he called the "Super," which would use the explosive force of a detonating fission bomb to ignite a fusion reaction in deuterium and tritium. But the idea of what is now the Hydrogen Bomb was set aside to concentrate on actually producing fission bombs. During the Conference Oppenheimer became convinced of the advantages of a single centralized laboratory to direct the research for the bomb project, rather than having specialists working from different locations across America.

Manhattan Project Initiated

In June 1942 The Army Corps of Engineers established the Manhattan Engineering District (MED), most commonly referred to as the *Manhattan Project*, to manage the design and production of Atomic Bombs. The project originally was headquartered at 270 Broadway in Manhattan and thus the name. The *Manhattan Project* would eventually employ more than 130,000 people and cost nearly $2 billion (about $24 billion in 2008 dollars). The project had three primary research and production sites: the weapons research and design laboratory at Los Alamos; the uranium-enrichment facilities at Oak Ridge, TN; and the plutonium-production facility at Hanford, WA. There were an additional 30 sites located in the US, Canada, and the UK. The MED continued to control US atomic weapons production until the formation of the Atomic Energy Commission in January 1947.

Although the *Manhattan Project* involved over thirty different research and production sites, it was mainly conducted at three secret sites: Los Alamos, NM; Oak Ridge, TN; and Richland, WA. All the sites were distant from coastlines and therefore less vulnerable to a possible enemy attack.

The Oak Ridge facilities included more than 60,000 acres appropriated from several farm communities in the Tennessee Valley area. The site was chosen for the vast quantities of cheap hydroelectric power available from the Tennessee Valley Authority which was necessary to produce Uranium-235 in massive ion separation magnets. At one stage the Oak Ridge facilities were consuming one sixth of the electrical power produced in the US which was more than New York City. The site was so secret that the Tennessee Governor was unaware that Oak Ridge (which was to become the fifth largest city in the state) existed.

After the US government annexed thousands of acres of farm land and fruit orchards and the towns of Hanford and White Bluffs; the

Hanford Site would encompass nearly 1,000 square miles. The Hanford Site near Richland, WA, was chosen for its location near a river that could supply water to cool the reactors which would produce the Plutonium. in a sparsely populated area adjacent to the Columbia River.

Major Manhattan Project sites and subdivisions included:
Site W (Hanford, WA): a plutonium production facility (now Hanford Site)
Site X (Oak Ridge, TN): enriched uranium production and plutonium production research (now Oak Ridge National Laboratory)
Site X also included:
X-10 Graphite Reactor: graphite reactor research pilot plant (on the site of what is now Oak Ridge National Laboratory)
Y-12: electromagnetic separation uranium enrichment plant
K-25: gaseous diffusion uranium enrichment plant
S-50: thermal diffusion uranium enrichment plant
Site Y (Los Alamos, NM): a bomb research laboratory (now Los Alamos National Laboratory)
Radiation Laboratory (Berkeley, CA): electromagnetic separation enrichment research (now Lawrence Berkeley National Laboratory)
Metallurgical Laboratory (Chicago, IL): reactor development (now Argonne National Laboratory)
Project Alberta (Wendover, UT and Tinian): preparations for the combat delivery of the bombs
Project Camel (Inyokern, CA): high explosives research and non-nuclear engineering for the *Fat Man* bomb
Project Trinity (Alamogordo, NM): preparations for the testing of the first atomic bomb
Project Ames (Ames, IA): production of raw uranium metal (now Ames Laboratory)
Dayton Project (Dayton, OH): research and development of polonium refinement and industrial production of polonium for atomic bomb triggers
Project "9" (Trail, British Columbia): Heavy Water (deuterium) production.

The Army Takes Control of the *Manhattan Project*

By September 1942, the need for improved coordination of the program was apparent. Studies on nuclear weapons were conducted at universities scattered throughout the country and the need for a laboratory dedicated solely to that purpose was essential. During the winter of 1942-43 the Los Alamos School for Boys located on a secluded mesa in the mountains of northern New Mexico was selected for the super-secret atomic research site.

Vannevar Bush, the head of the civilian Office of Scientific Research and Development (OSRD), requested President Roosevelt to consign the emergent nuclear weapons project to the military. Roosevelt selected the Army Corps of Engineers to collaborate with the OSRD in constructing the production plants that would separate uranium isotopes and manufacture plutonium for the bomb. Col. James Marshall and his deputy, Col. Kenneth Nichols, were to direct the project, but as laymen they did not understand nuclear physics, nor the brilliant but often eccentric scientists with whom they had to work. The nuclear weapons program was experimental and did not receive priority as America was desperately trying to hold off the global advances of Germany and Japan. The scientific research and production plant construction often were delayed by Marshall's inability to obtain critical materials required by other military projects.

Bush informed Secretary of War Stimson and Army Chief of Staff Marshall of his dissatisfaction with Col. Marshall's failure and asked Brig. Gen. Brehon Somervell, Chief of Engineers, to replace Marshall with a more energetic officer. Somervell chose Col. Leslie Groves who was the Deputy to the Chief of Construction for the Army Corps of Engineers and had overseen the construction of the immense Pentagon office project. Groves was an intelligent, motivated, though often brusque officer who was an excellent choice to move the project forward. Groves wanted a combat command and strongly objected when Somervell appointed him to the weapons project. Despite Oppenheimer's radical political views and possible security risk, Groves appointed him as the project's scientific director, as he was convinced Oppenheimer was the genius required for this unique project. Groves was promoted to Brigadier General, giving him the rank necessary to deal with senior people whose cooperation was required, or whose own projects would be delayed by Groves' now top-

The intelligent, often brusque **Brig.Gen. Leslie Groves** (left) was appointed to head the *Manhattan Project* and he named the controversial genius, **Robert Oppenheimer** (right) as the Project's Scientific Director. (AFHRC)

priority project. Soon, Groves had begun to solve the *Manhattan Project's* most urgent problems with his dynamic and effective approach.

On 2 December 1942, Enrico Fermi and his team initiated the first artificial self-sustaining nuclear chain reaction in an experimental nuclear reactor (Chicago Pile-1) located under the bleachers of Stagg Field at the University of Chicago. By spring 1943, the theoretical scientists at Los Alamos began to transform their paper calculations into a truly awesome weapon. The scientists had determined that there were two active elements that were particularly well-suited for making atomic bombs; an isotope of Uranium (U-235) and Plutonium, which was an artificial element made by bombarding uranium with neutrons in a nuclear reactor. Huge plants for separating U-235 were already under construction at Oak Ridge and plutonium reactors were being built at Hanford.

Separating U-235 and U-238 from Uranium Ore

Little Boy, the Hiroshima bomb, was made from Uranium-235, a rare Uranium isotope that had to be physically separated from the more plentiful Uranium-238 isotope that was not suitable for use in an explosive device. Since U-235 was only 0.6% of raw uranium and was chemically identical to the 99.4% of U-238, various physical methods were considered for separation.

In order for the US nuclear program to continue the expedited construction of facilities to produce enriched Uranium-235 in sufficient quantities to sustain a chain reaction was needed. Most of the Uranium enrichment work was to be performed at Oak Ridge where several methods of separating raw Uranium ore were developed. Only a complex mechanical method developed by Columbia University could be used for the initial separation of the isotopes U-235 and U-238 from raw ore.

To begin the separation of the two isotopes Dr. H.C. Urey and his associates at Columbia devised a system based upon gaseous diffusion developed by Jewish émigrés, Franz Simon and Nicholas Kurti, at Oxford University. Their method of gaseous diffusion using uranium hexafluoride (UF6) gas was deployed at a large separation plant at Oak Ridge. During the war this method was important primarily for producing partly enriched material to supply the electromagnetic separation process developed by Dr. Earnest Lawrence at the University of California, Berkeley. This method was implemented in Oak Ridge at the Y-12 Plant, employed devices known as calutrons, which were effectively mass spectrometers. Copper was originally intended for electromagnet coils but due to wartime shortages there was an insufficient amount available. The project engineers needed to have US Treasury lend them $70,000,000 of silver for use in the coils. Initially the method seemed promising for large scale production but was found to be expensive and produced insufficient material and was abandoned after the war. Following these two processes a gas centrifuge was used to further separate the slightly lighter fissionable U-235 from the heavier non-fissionable U-238. Once these procedures were completed the U-235 was molded inside the warhead.

Other techniques, such as thermal diffusion and the use of high speed centrifuges, were also tried. Thermal diffusion was not used to produce highly-enriched uranium but was used in the S-50 facility to begin Uranium enrichment process and its product fed other facilities.

Making an Atomic Bomb

In general usage the Atomic Bomb refers to the type of bombs used on Japan but to be accurate the Hydrogen Bomb is also an Atomic Bomb as both use the energy released from the nucleus of atoms. The earlier Atomic Bombs released energy by nuclear fission, the splitting of the atom, while the Hydrogen Bomb worked by nuclear fusion, the joining of small atoms together to make larger ones.

When a nucleus fissions it splits into several smaller fragments. These fragments, or fission products, are about equal to half the original mass. Two or three neutrons are also emitted. The sum of the masses of these fragments is less than the original mass. This "missing" mass (about 0.1 % of the original mass) has been converted into energy according to Einstein's equation. Fission can occur when a nucleus of a heavy atom captures a neutron or it can happen spontaneously.

The power of nuclear fission results from the forces holding each individual atom of a material together. Atoms are made up of three kinds of particles: protons and neutrons that form the nucleus of an atom and electrons that circle the nucleus. Most naturally occurring elements have very stable atoms and are virtually impossible to split but the metal uranium has atoms that are relatively easy to split because it is an extremely heavy metal with the largest atoms of any element. Its atoms have far more neutrons than protons and are not held together firmly, making the metal exceptionally liable for nuclear fission. The conversion of Uranium ore to Uranium metal was approximately 500 to 1 and then of that small fraction of Uranium metal extracted, 99.4% of it was the useless U-238 isotope and the small remaining fraction U-235 isotope. U-238 and U-235 are virtually similar in their chemical makeup: U-238 has 92 protons and 146 neutrons (92+146=238) while U-235 has 92 protons and 143 neutrons (92+143=235). U-238 being neutron heavy reflects neutrons while U-235 absorbs them. The natural radioactivity of U-235 (100,000 years to turn into lead) can be accelerated in a process known as a chain reaction. Instead of disintegrating slowly the atoms are forcibly split by neutrons forcing their way into the nucleus. A U-235 atom is so unstable that a hit from a single neutron is enough to split it causing a chain reaction. The Uranium atom splits into two smaller atoms of different elements such as Krypton and Barium creating energy in the form of heat and Gamma radiation, the most powerful and lethal of all radiation. When a chain reaction occurs the split atom also gives off two or three of its extra neutrons that are not needed to make Krypton or Barium. These extra neutrons fly out with sufficient force to split the other atoms they contact and this progression continues geometrically in a millionth of a second.

Theoretically, only one split U-235 atom should be needed to yield enough neutrons to split other atoms to create a chain reaction. But in practice, there has to be a certain weight of U-235, called the "critical mass," to be present to produce a chain reaction that will maintain itself. If there is less than this amount there will be too few atoms to ensure that the neutrons from every other atom that had split will hit other unsplit atoms. The weight of pure U-235 required 110 pounds for a critical mass. But U-235 is never quite pure and so 141.4 pounds was required; separated into 85 pounds (60%) for the subcritical projectile and 56.5 pounds (40%)

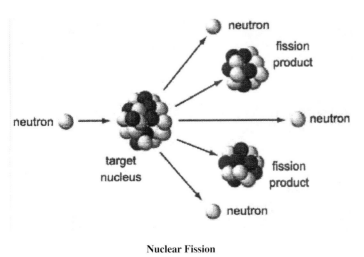

Nuclear Fission

for the subcritical target. The U-235 was named *Oralloy* for its **O**ak **R**idge **Alloy** secret manufacturing origin.

Uranium was not the only substance used in manufacturing Atomic Bombs; the other was the man-made element Plutonium in its isotope form, U-239. Plutonium in its isotope PU-239 was not found in nature except in miniscule traces and was always made from Uranium by processing U-238 in a nuclear reactor. After a time in the reactor the intense radioactivity caused the metal to pick up extra particles so that increasingly more of its atoms were converted into Plutonium. Plutonium can not begin a chain reaction by itself, but could by providing a neutron source to a highly radioactive material that emitted neutrons faster than Plutonium itself.

Of course, building an Atomic Bomb was far more complicated than placing a piece of Uranium larger than critical mass inside a bomb casing, as it would explode at once. Two pieces of fissionable material were placed safely apart inside the bomb casing and intricate mechanisms positioned the two together by either "shooting" them together or "assembling" them to start the chain reaction. The scientists at Los Alamos investigated various methods of assembling radioactive material to construct an Atomic Bomb. They focused on two specific means of reaching "critical mass" which was the minimum amount of active material required to achieve a nuclear detonation. The less complicated and most reliable of the two techniques was called the "gun method" which required one piece of active material to be loaded into a cannon and fired into another piece mounted in a plug in the cannon's muzzle. The two pieces were to combine to form a critical mass and stay intact long enough to detonate before the confined propellant blew the cannon barrel and its contents apart.

Although gun assembly was the simplest technique some Los Alamos theoreticians had considered the "implosion" method which used explosives to squeeze a single, subcritical mass to become dense enough to become "critical' and chain react into full scale detonation. Implosion required very precise timing and extreme reliability because the inwardly-focused explosions had to attain near-perfect symmetry. Their shock waves all had to converge upon the nuclear core at exactly at the right time, so that it would be compressed to the same degree on every point of its

Dr. Norman Ramsey was a physicist and talented engineer-organizer who would be responsible for managing and dealing with the problems of daily operations of the *Manhattan Project*. (AFHRC)

surface. Scientists compared this extremely intricate theoretical procedure to crushing an unopened pop can without spilling any of its contents and it would not be until late 1943 that implosion seemed to be attainable.

In summer 1943 Los Alamos anticipated that Plutonium would be the active material in the combat weapon using the gun method. Plutonium's rate of spontaneous natural fission would require the gun to have a muzzle velocity of about 3,000 feet per second as lower velocities risked the possibility of a drawn-out, low-yield reaction that would waste most of the Plutonium's energy potential. The calculations of the ordnance designers showed that accelerating the Plutonium projectile to the necessary speed would require extraordinary propellant pressures. Even with the use of special steel alloys, the gun barrel would need to be at least 17 feet long which was longer than existing bomb bays.

Early Work at NPG Dahlgren

The *Manhattan Project* was not only about the development of the Atomic Bomb but also developing a reliable method of delivering those bombs. Capt. William "Deke" Parsons, USN, and Dr. Norman Ramsey were appointed to manage the atomic weapon delivery system. Parsons had been instrumental in the Navy's deployment of the proximity fuse while Ramsey was a Los Alamos physicist and talented engineer-organizer, who would be responsible for managing and dealing with the problems of daily operations. Parsons would later closely collaborate with Col. Paul Tibbetts, CO of the 509th Composite Group, who was in charge of training and testing.

The first 14/23 scale models of the Plutonium Gun Bomb were created by cutting a standard 500 pound, 23 inch diameter GP bomb in half and welding a 12 foot length of 14 inch diameter, sewer pipe between the two halves. Beginning in August 1943 test drops were made from a Grumman TBF at the Naval Proving Ground (NPG), Dahlgren, VA. The ballistic characteristics of the "sewer pipe bomb" weren't even mediocre as upon release, the bomb consistently went into a flat spin, hitting the ground broadside, and breaking up. In October, scale models of the Plutonium Gun Bomb were revised by changing the center of gravity and the configuration of the tail fins and continued to be flight tested at Dahlgren. Meanwhile, Ramsey was investigating aircraft suitable for carrying either type of the proposed weapons shapes: the tubular gun-type fission weapon shape and the oval Plutonium implosion weapon shape.

In 1943, there were no aircraft in the US inventory with a bomb bay that could enclose a 17 foot bomb. Ramsey considered modifying

USN **Capt. William "Deke" Parsons** (right) was appointed to manage the atomic weapon delivery system while **Col. Paul Tibbetts** (left), CO of the 509th Composite Group was in charge of training and testing. (AFHRC)

a Consolidated B-24 bomber but abandoned the idea when he learned that the Navy had previously tried and failed to reengineer the B-24 for internal torpedo carriage. The Boeing B-29 was the only other possible American contender to carry the weapon. Ramsey measured the bomb bays of the Superfortress and found that it could be adapted for the purpose by combining its two 12 foot bomb bays into one but only if the bomb was no more than two feet in diameter. The reason was that the attachment box for the main wing spars was located between the bomb bays and the maximum distance between the lower side of the box and the bottom of the fuselage was two feet.

By the late fall of 1943, the ballistic problems of the Plutonium Gun Bomb had been largely solved with improved tail surfaces and better weight balance. As its internal arrangements became more definitely determined, the bomb casing's layout was modified to conform. The final "pod" or "Cornog" model (named after a design team member) highlighted a rounded, bulbous nose to house the fusing arrangements and the muzzle plug, ("anvil") that was to retain the plutonium target, and a long, slender body with an elongated box tail. The full size models were 18 feet long, and weighed about 7,500 pounds.

Scale model airdrops continued on into the winter at Dahlgren, but it became obvious that another location was required as the skies near Chesapeake Bay was chronically hazy and good visibility was important as full sized model testing would have to be conducted from as high as 30,000 feet. Security was also a concern in the populated coastal area and Parsons and Ramsey began looking for an alternative test site. Meanwhile, Los Alamos scientists and engineers made progress in developing a practical implosion bomb. Its dimensions would be very different from the Plutonium gun weapon, however, which meant that the search for a suitable bomber had to be expanded. In September, Ramsey was directed to locate an aircraft with a bomb bay that could carry a weapon weighing as much as 9,500 pounds and could be up to six feet in diameter. Unlike the long, slender plutonium gun, this new bomb had to be ball-shaped to contain the bulky explosive charges. Ramsey quickly decided that there were only two Allied bombers capable of carrying both weapons: a modified Boeing B-29 and the Avro Lancaster. The Lancaster had sufficient internal space and was known to carry extraordinary weights. Ramsey traveled to Canada in October 1943 to meet with Roy Chadwick, the Lancaster's chief designer and Ramsey showed Chadwick some preliminary sketches of both the gun and the implosion weapon casings. Chadwick assured Ramsey that the Lancaster could accommodate either bomb and agreed to provide the necessary support. When Ramsey returned to the US, he recommended that the Avro Lancaster should be seriously considered. When Gen. Hap Arnold heard of the Lancaster proposal he made it clear to Groves that, if any Atomic Bombs were to be dropped in combat, a USAAF-crewed B-29 would deliver them!

On 30 November 1943, Arnold sent instructions to the Air Materiel Command at Wright Field, OH, for a highly-classified B-29 modification project to be kept in greatest secrecy, code-named *Silver-Plated*. The *Manhattan Project* would deliver full sized mockups of the plutonium gun weapon (codenamed *Thin Man*) and the implosion weapon (codenamed *Fat Man*) to Wright Field by mid-December, where the AMC would modify the first aircraft and turn it over to the Project by 15 January 1944; and deliver it for use in bomb flight testing at Muroc Army Air Field, CA. A small number of combat-ready aircraft would follow later.

The AMC's engineering Division issued the B-29 modification work order on a separate internal code name, *Pullman* and a classified project reference number, MX-469. The word *Pullman* had been chosen to fit the overall cover story devised on 29 November: British Prime Minister Churchill (the *Fat Man*) would visit the US to tour defense plants with President Roosevelt (the *Thin Man*) in a specially-modified (*Silver-Plated*)

B-29 (the *Pullman*). Over time the overall code name was soon shortened to its more familiar form: *Silverplate*.

Silverplate: Building A Bomber to Carry the Bomb

Silverplate was the code reference for the USAAF participation in the *Manhattan Project* during World War II. It originally was the name for the aircraft modification project for the B-29 Superfortress to enable it to drop an atomic weapon but *Silverplate* eventually came to identify the training and operational aspects of the program as well. The aircraft modification project fell under the purview of *Project Alberta* after March 1945. The original directive for the project had as its subject line "*Silver Plated Project*" but continued usage of the term shortened it to the one word "*Silverplate*." Between February 1944 and December 1947 a total of 65 B-29s were modified to *Silverplate* specifications in five increments. Ultimately 53 of them served with the first nuclear weapons unit, the 509th Composite Group and only the *Enola Gay* and *Bockscar* remain as museum displays.

Boeing-Wichita completed its 58th B-29-5-BW, AAF serial number 42-6259, on 30 November 1943 and delivered it to the 468th Bomb Group at Smoky Hill AFB, KS that day and it was in Wright Field's modification shop two days later. Wright completed alterations requiring over 6,000 man-hours by hand and the prototype *Silverplate* B-29 was ready. The ventral fuselage skin and fuselage center structural section between the bomb bays and under the wing spar were removed between the two bomb bays to create one long opening and the four original 12 foot bomb bay doors were replaced by two 27 foot doors. The rear bay's forward bomb racks were fitted with a carrier frame and sway bracing and hoists were mounted at each of the four corners of the frame.

New bomb suspension was anchored in the aft bomb bay although its length protruded into the forward bay. Bomb suspensions and bracing were attached to accommodate three Atomic Bomb shape types (*Thin Man*, *Little Boy*, and *Fat Man*), with the gun-type suspended in the rear bay and the implosion type mounted in the forward bay. Separate twin-release mechanisms were mounted in each bay, using modified glider tow-cable attach-and-release mechanisms. To document the tests, motion picture camera mounts were installed in the rear bay. The *Thin Man* just barely fit with very little clearance as its pod nose was 23 inches in diameter. The B-29 modifications weren't completed until early February but chronic engine problems further delayed availability and it did not arrive at Muroc Field (now Edwards AFB), CA until 20 February 1944.

Silverplate **B-29 Prototype** (AAF)

Atomic Bomb Suspension

To carry the large Atomic Bombs the B-29 bomb bay doors had to be modified. The ventral fuselage skin was removed between the two bomb bays to create one long opening and the four 12 foot bomb bay doors were replaced by two 27 foot doors. (AAF)

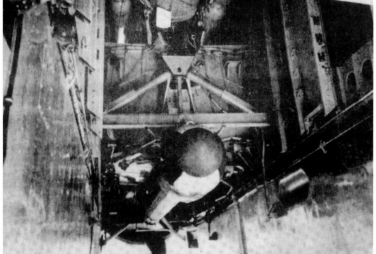

A new **bomb suspension apparatus** had be developed. Bomb suspensions and bracing were attached for the three Atomic Bomb shape types (*Thin Man*, *Little Boy*, and *Fat Man*). The suspension was anchored in the aft bomb bay although its length protruded into the forward bay. Separate twin-release mechanisms were mounted in each bay and the rear bay's forward bomb racks were fitted with a carrier frame and sway bracing, and hoists were mounted at each of the four corners of the frame. (AAF)

Thin Man prototype suspended in a *Silverplate* B-29 bomb bay. (AAF)

The *Thin Man* model tested at Muroc weighed about 8,000 pounds, was 17 feet long, had a nose section diameter of 38 inches, a diameter of 23 inches through the middle section, and a tail fin assembly of 38 inches from tip to tip. (AAF)

Flight and Bomb Shape Trials at Muroc

Several drop tests were conducted at Muroc AAF in March 1944 using the prototype *Silverplate* B-29. The *Thin Man* model tested at Muroc weighed about 8,000 pounds, was 17 feet long, had a nose section diameter of 38 inches, a diameter of 23 inches through the middle section, and a tail fin assembly of 38 inches from tip to tip.

The first Muroc flight test drop on 6 March used a standard *Thin Man* and was followed on 14 March by the drops of two *Fat Man* shapes fitted with circular tail shrouds designed by engineers at the National Bureau of Standards. The *Thin Man* functioned well as its ballistics had been mostly resolved during the previous scale model tests at Dahlgren. Conversely, the *Fat Man* shapes performed poorly, demonstrating yaw angles of as much as 19°; with the problem caused by poor workmanship and misalignment of the tail surfaces. The use of the glider tow releases also caused major problems as all three bombs failed to release immediately causing calibrations to be incorrect. During the fourth drop test several days later the *Thin Man* was released prematurely while the *Pullman* was still on the way to the test range. The bomb fell on the bay doors; severely damaging them and the B-29 was sent to Wright Field for repairs. Investigation showed that the weight of the bomb and twin glider release lugs were the source of the failure and the British method of suspending heavy bombs by single lug Type G attachments and Type F releases was adopted.

Testing resumed in mid-June, and twelve shapes were dropped from the *Silverplate* prototype between the 14th and the 27th: three *Thin Men* and nine *Fat Men*. In an effort to dampen the persistent yaw, various combinations of tail boxes and drag fins were tested on the implosion shape. The final solution combined a box tail with internal drag plates set at 45° to the line of flight which was dubbed the "California Parachute."

Thin Man Becomes *Little Boy*

Earlier theoretical studies had acknowledged a "possible problem" with gun-assembled Plutonium weapons. When the first Hanford plutonium samples arrived at Los Alamos in the spring 1944, that "possible problem" became a very real problem.

The *Thin Man* gun-type design was based on the fissibility of the very pure Pu-239 isotope which was produced only in microgram quantities by the Berkeley cyclotron. When the Hanford production reactors came online in the spring of 1944, the mix of Pu-239 and Pu-240 obtained contained

impurities which could not be removed by chemical methods. These impurities raised the "fissionability" of Hanford-produced plutonium such that the gun could not shoot pieces of it together fast enough; they would begin to interact well before they could be fully joined. To avoid this pre-detonation, the muzzle velocity would need to be greatly raised, making the bomb impractically long. The Thin Man project came to a dead end.

As a hedge against the failure of implosion bomb the gun model was refurbished to use U-235 instead of Plutonium. U-235 fissioned less efficiently than Plutonium but there was an advantage to this method in that the assembly speed could be greatly reduced. So, by lowering the gun's muzzle velocity to 1,000 feet per second, the barrel length could be reduced to less than ten feet which would easily fit into a standard B-29 bomb bay.

While the prototype *Silverplate* B-29 was undergoing repairs at Wright Field for its damaged bomb bay doors it was modified to replace the single bomb bay needed for the long *Thin Man* bomb with the original configuration of two separate bomb bays to carry the new shorter bomb. In addition, the suspension equipment for the *Thin Man* bomb was removed and new shackles and release mechanisms for mounting the *Fat Man* and *Little Boy* bomb shapes in the front bomb bay were installed. The *Pullman* B-29 was flown to Wendover and assigned to further drop testing in September 1944 with the 216th Base Unit until it was damaged in a landing accident in December.

Silverplate Production Versions

On 22 August 1944, to meet the requirements of the AAF group about to be formed to train in the atomic mission, the production phase of *Silverplate* B-29s was ordered under the designation Project 98146-S. The Glenn L. Martin Company's modification center at Omaha, NB, was contracted with the first three aircraft to be delivered by 30 September, followed by 11 more by 31 December. These 14 aircraft would be used for test and training purposes. The remaining 10 were due ASAP in 1945 to be outfitted with the latest changes and would be reserved for combat.

In mid-October the first three (42-65209, -216, and -217) of these second increment *Silverplate* B-29s were delivered to the AAF and flown to Wendover Army Airfield, UT. They were fitted with British single-point Type-F bomb releases mounted on a redesigned H-frame suspension rack fitted in the forward bomb bay, so that additional fuel tanks could be carried in the aft bay. A new crew position, called the "weaponeer's station," was created in the cockpit with a panel to monitor the release and detonation of the bomb during the actual combat drops. Fourteen production aircraft were assigned to the 393rd Bomb Squadron and three to the 216th Base Unit for bomb drop testing.

By February 1945 the 17 aircraft of the second increment required upgrades, principally those of the 216th Base Unit. Four of the bombers assigned to the 393BS which has been assigned to the 509th Composite Group were immediately transferred to the 216th to begin accelerated testing. Because of the time involved in attempting to modify existing aircraft a few at a time; a new production series was to be commenced. The first five of this third increment, known as Project 98228-S, also went to the test unit. The order totaled an additional 28 aircraft, with delivery of 15 designated combat models for the 393BS beginning in April; the final eight were not delivered until after the Atomic Bomb missions in August.

The final wartime *Silverplates* integrated all technical improvements to B-29 aircraft, as well as the final series of *Silverplate* modifications that included fuel-injected Wright R-3350-41 engines, Curtiss Electric reversible-pitch propellers, and pneumatic actuators for rapid opening and closing of bomb bay doors. Weight reduction was also accomplished by removal of all gun turrets and armor plating. These B-29s represented a significant increase in performance over the standard variants.

Silverplate Tests at Wendover

Muroc did not have the facilities necessary to support 12 to 14 B-29s and the 500 to 650 people required to operate and maintain them, so Wendover, UT was chosen for its clear weather and isolation for security purposes. In addition to a training site selection, the combat unit and its commanding officer was selected. The 393BS was detached from the newly-activated 504th Bomb Group (Very Heavy) and assigned to a new unit, the 509th Composite Group under new Commander Col. Paul Tibbetts. The 320th Troop Carrier Squadron was also assigned to provide the Group with its own internal airline.

Training and test work began in parallel at Wendover immediately upon arrival of the 509th and continued through the winter and on into spring. Long range missions were flown to test facilities established at Naval Weapons Station Inyokern, CA and later to ranges south of Albuquerque. The *Fat Man* design evolved considerably in sophistication, although its ballistic characteristics still remained less than satisfactory. The new *Little Boy* design also underwent continued development but it had far fewer teething problems than *Fat Man*.

Project Alberta

Project Alberta was officially established within the *Manhattan Project* in March 1945, although its functions had been executed by various Project offices for months. Simply, *Project Alberta's* purpose was to facilitate deployment of the bomb into the combat zone and to ensure that it was ready for delivery as early as possible. This would require the training of bomb assembly teams and technical support personnel that would provide logistic support for the 509th, assembling and testing weapons and practice equipment in the combat area.

One major consideration was to have the *Silverplate* bombers ready for combat. The original order for the replacement aircraft had specified 10 bombers to be delivered at two per month but by January 1945 what was considered high tech at the time had rapidly made many of the bombers delivered to Wendover in the Fall obsolete. Col. Tibbetts had the 509th fly for as many training hours as maintenance would support and the bombers were showing the wear and tear. In February, the standing order for modified bombers was doubled from a total of 24 to 48, and in April, an additional five were added to the order. The delivery schedule called for 13 aircraft to be delivered to the 509th in April and two more per month for the next four months.

These new aircraft included all of the latest technical changes made to recent B-29 aircraft as well as special modifications added only to *Silverplate* aircraft. In addition to the special equipment related to carrying and dropping atomic bombs, the latest *Silverplate* batch received fuel-injected engines and reversible-pitch propellers. Given that the final versions of the *Fat Man* and *Little Boy* weapons each weighed about 10,000 pounds, significant efforts were made to reduce aircraft weight. All the turrets were removed, as was a substantial amount of armor plate. As a result, the *Silverplate* aircraft were slightly faster, achieved better fuel economy, and could carry a heavier payload at higher altitudes. Ramsey later wrote that "...the performance of the 509th aircraft was exceptional ... they were without doubt the finest B-29s in the theater."

Deployment of crucial personnel to Tinian, including Parsons and Ramsey, was completed by mid-July, and the first *Little Boy* practice bomb, L1, was assembled and dropped on 23 July. Four more *Little Boys* were assembled and test-dropped before the Hiroshima mission on 6 August. The first test *Fat Man*, F13, was dropped on 1 August. Three additional *Fat Men* were dropped before the Nagasaki mission on 9 August. In addition, the 509th carried out many practice missions, both over nearby waters, and against Japanese targets. A practice bomb nicknamed *Pumpkin*, of about the same weight and ballistics and filled with conventional explosives as

Fat Man, was used for these missions and was described in the previous chapter.

Operation Centerboard and a Third Atomic Attack

The two atomic strikes on Japan, codenamed *Operation Centerboard*; *Little Boy*, weapon number L11, was dropped on Hiroshima on the morning of 6 August; and *Fat Man*, weapon number F31, was dropped on Nagasaki three days later. *Fat Man* F32 was held in reserve for the third strike, should President Truman direct its accomplishment, and 20AF "targeteers" were allegedly preparing for a night strike on Tokyo when the stand down order was issued. However, there are reports that indicate that the nuclear core for F32 was shipped from Albuquerque late on 12 August and that the aircraft was on its way to Hawaii when it received the return order. Fortunately, no further strikes were necessary.

Rational for the Atomic Bombing of Japan

The XXBC B-29s began their operations against the Japanese Homeland in August 1944 when the 58BW bombed the Yawata Steel Works. The XXBC overcame overwhelming logistical problems while operating from bases in India and advanced bases in China. Bombs were dropped on Manchuria, Korea and Thailand and 800 tons on Japan, a small amount in the future bombing scheme but a portent to the Japanese. In late November 1944, the B-29s of the XXIBC operating from the Marianas began a large-scale offensive against Japan. The offensive was based on the AAF's traditional daylight visual precision bombing ideology mainly against the Japanese aircraft industry, particularly engine manufacture. The offensive continued until early March with mixed results but Japanese fighter production did begin to decline from fall 1944. On 9 March 1945 LeMay made his significant decision to shift to low level firebombing and in 10 days 9,373 tons of incendiaries decimated four of Japan's largest cities and 31 square miles of urban and industrial area. In April and early May the XXIBC moved on to a tactical role in supporting the invasion and fierce fighting on Okinawa and disrupting the destructive kamikaze attacks at their bases on Kyushu. Once Okinawa was secured, the bomber offensive was continued utilizing mostly incendiary attacks but also precision bombing depending on the target. During May and June six more of Japan's largest cities were written off and the target lists included the enemy's secondary cities. By the time the Atomic Bombs were ready the B-29s delivered 91% (147,000 tons of 160,800 total tons) of all bombs dropped on Japan and 66 urban areas and 178 square miles were uninhabitable. This total bomb tonnage was one ninth that dropped on Germany but caused equivalent damage in terms of the effect on Japan's ability to wage war. Before the Atomic Bombs were dropped, statistically Japan was thoroughly beaten and unable to effectively wage war. Whether it was necessary to drop the Atomic Bombs remains an unending ethical and political question that is much more easily raised after the fact by today's revisionists of World War II history. But the reality of August 1945 was the specter of invading the Japanese islands with colossal casualties and of the Russian army that was about to enter the war, over running Manchuria and then taking easy spoils in Asia. After Hiroshima and Nagasaki, the collective Japanese military and civilian psyche changed and the Emperor was forced to stop the bleeding and end the war.

Preparing and Loading the Bombs

The *Pumpkin* bombs required slight preparation before they were moved to the loading pit area but the Atomic Bombs required much more. Both the test and live Atomic Bombs were assembled and tested in one of the assembly buildings before they were transported to one of the nearby loading pits. The two loading pits constructed on Tinian were similar to those built at Wendover and Inyokern; being concrete lined rectangular

Bomb Loading

The bomb loading pits were concrete lined rectangles, 20 feet long, ten feet wide, and eight feet deep. A hydraulic lift which was similar to those found in auto service stations was installed in the center of the bottom of the pit with the operating controls mounted on one wall. The custom trailer loaded with the bomb was then towed to the loading pit and positioned across the pit on rails. (AAF)

The trailer was raised about a foot and then the rails were removed. The trailer was then rotated so that it was aligned with the length of the pit. The trailer, with the bomb mounted on the cradle, was then lowered to the bottom of the pit. (AAF)

The pins holding the cradle to the frame of the trailer were removed so that the bomb and cradle were ready to be lifted up into the front bomb bay with the transport trailer remaining at the bottom of the pit. (AAF)

The bomber was positioned over the loading pit by backing it over the pit with the port and starboard main landing gears straddling the pit. (AAF)

Once the bomber was positioned over the loading pit, the cradle and bomb were raised up into the bomb bay by the hydraulic lift and the bomb bay shackle was attached to the lug on the bomb and sway braces were installed to keep the bomb securely mounted. (AAF)

boxes, 20 feet long, ten feet wide, and eight feet deep. A hydraulic lift which was similar to those found in auto service stations was installed in the center of the bottom of the pit with the operating controls mounted on one wall.

The first stage in loading the Atomic Bomb (or *Pumpkin*) was to transport the unit from the storage or assembly area to the loading pit under a special concealing tarp. The bomb was loaded on a cradle mounted on a transport trailer with four large pins which could be removed when the bomb and cradle were to be lifted off the trailer. The loaded trailer was then towed to the loading pit and positioned across the pit on rails. The second stage in loading the bomb was to raise the trailer about a foot and then remove the rails. The trailer was then rotated so that it was aligned with the length of the pit. The trailer, with the bomb mounted on the cradle, was then lowered to the bottom of the pit. The pins holding the cradle to the frame of the trailer were then removed so that the bomb and cradle were ready to be lifted up into the front bomb bay of the *Silverplate* B-29 with the transport trailer remaining at the bottom of the pit. The next stage was to position the bomber over the loading pit by backing it over the pit with the port and starboard main landing gears straddling the pit. The *Enola Gay* was moved into position for loading the *Little Boy* bomb by a ground service vehicle using a tow bar connected to the front landing gear structure. The *Bockscar* moved back over the loading pit for loading the *Fat Man* by using reverse pitch on its propellers for reverse thrust and its main landing gear brakes for steering. Once the bomber was properly positioned over the loading pit, the cradle and bomb were raised up into the bomb bay by the hydraulic lift. This step was an exacting procedure as there was little clearance in the bomb bay and the catwalks. A plumb bob was dropped from a bomb shackle as a guide to line up the bomb cradle jacks that then lifted the bomb up to the single shackle and adjustable sway braces. Once the bomb was in position, the bomb bay shackle was attached to the lug on the bomb and sway braces were installed to keep the bomb securely mounted. The final stage in the loading was to add any last pieces of paraphernalia to the bomb (e.g. contact fuses and radar antennas) and to attach the various electric cables from points in the bomb bay to the bomb. These cables provided aircraft power to the bomb and established circuits for monitoring the condition of the bomb and controlling equipment inside the bomb. The bomb loading procedure required 20 to 25 minutes.

Hiroshima Mission: *Operation Centerboard I*, 6 August 1945

Little Boy: The Gun-Type Uranium Nuclear Bomb

The *Little Boy* Uranium Bomb worked mechanically as a gun-type fission weapon assembling the critical mass from two subcritical masses: a "bullet" and a "target." At one end of the relatively conventional gun barrel was a "target" piece of U-235 that was slightly smaller than the critical mass. This piece of U-235 was spherical with a conical wedge removed from it. This conical wedge cut extended into the center of the sphere and faced toward the other end of the barrel. At the other end of the barrel there was another conical wedge of U-235, the "bullet" that was exactly the same size as the target conical wedge and was covered by a neutron reflector. This piece had its pointed end facing toward the conical cut in the target and the two pieces were just over critical mass. The smaller piece had a high explosive charge behind it that when discharged shoots the cone into the sphere and the force of the collision joined the two pieces solidly together and the bomb exploded in one millionth of a second.

The resulting chain reaction released tremendous energy, producing an explosion, and also blowing apart the critical mass and ending the chain reaction. The configuration of the critical mass determined how much of the fissile material reacted in the interval between assembly and dispersal, and therefore the explosive yield of the bomb. (The chain reaction actually started before complete assembly of the critical mass.) Even 1% fission of the material would result in a workable bomb, equal to thousands of tons of high explosive. A poor configuration, or slow assembly, would release enough energy to disperse the critical mass, but too quickly. Far less than 1% would react, and the yield would be equivalent to only a few tons of HE. The design was known to be inefficient with a potential yield of 15-16 kilotons of TNT. It was estimated that only about 15% of the fissile material went critical. The scientists were so convinced that this method would work that no test was conducted before the bomb was dropped over Hiroshima (however, extensive laboratory testing was undertaken to be positive that the fundamental assumptions were correct). Besides, the manufacture of the Hiroshima Bomb had used all the existing extremely highly purified U-235 so there was no U-235 available for such a test.

Little Boy measured 10 feet long by 28 inches in diameter and weighed 9,700 pounds. The outer ballistic case and tail sections were encased in a 0.375 inch armored blackened dull steel jacket The cast bomb casing was fitted with a box-frame tail cone and stabilizing fins and had

Little Boy measured 10 feet long by 28 inches in diameter and weighed 9,700 pounds. The outer ballistic case and tail sections were encased in a 0.375 inch armored blackened dull steel jacket. The *Little Boy* Uranium Bomb worked mechanically as a gun-type fission weapon. (AAF)

The photo shows the interior of the *Little Boy*. The center section contained the APS-13 radar unit, four radar unit battery boxes, clock box, and Yagi radar antennas. The rear section contained the gun tube and associated conduit tubes. The flat, rounded nose consisted mainly of the target case, U-235 target discs, and tamper material surrounding the U-235 comprised about half of the total weight of the bomb. (AAF)

airstream deflectors on the casing forward of the tail cone. The conical section was 0.187 inch thick steel and the square tail was constructed of 0.156 thick steel plate. Telemetry monitoring probes and associated batteries were placed on the outside of the forward bomb casing. The flat, rounded nose consisted mainly of the target case, U-235 target discs, and tamper material surrounding the U-235 comprised about half of the total weight of the bomb.

Fusing

The bomb had a triple fusing system to arm it, preventing an accidental detonation of both the conventional explosives and the nuclear payload. Outwardly there were short trailing radar whip antennae, clock wires threaded into holes in the bomb's upper casing toward the tail, and a hole in the tapered tail end that admitted external air for the barometric readings. The main fuse was a radar unit adapted from a tail warning IFF device, "*Archie*," developed to warn of aircraft approaching from the rear. Both *Little Boy* and *Fat Man* carried four *Archies* as a redundant safety measure. Instead of warning of an approaching aircraft this radar unit would transmit signals off the approaching ground. At a pre-determined altitude, agreement by any two of the four units would send a firing signal to the next stage of fusing. This phase consisted of a number of clock-activated switches that were activated after 15 seconds by arming wires that were pulled out of the clocks when the bomb was dropped out of the bomb bay. Their function was to prevent detonation in case the *Archie* units were activated by signals that were reflected from the bomber. A second arming device was a barometric pressure switch that was pre-set to close at a pressure corresponding to 7,000 feet. After this barometric arming a firing signal was sent directly to the primers that lit the cordite charges that initiated the "atomic gun" that shot the conical wedge into the sphere to start the chain reaction.

The Mission and the Bomb

On 6 August 1945, seven B-29s of the 509th Composite Group were scheduled to take part in the mission with three bombers in the strike force. Col. Paul Tibbets was the Group Commander and Airplane Commander of the lead B-29, the *Enola Gay* that he named after his mother. The two other B-29s, the *Great Artiste*, piloted by Maj. Charles Sweeney, and *Necessary*

Enola Gay carried the *Little Boy* bomb and was flown by 509th Composite Group Commander Paul Tibbetts who named the B-29 after his mother. (AAF)

Enola Gay **Crew** Kneeling (L-R) Stiborik, Caron, Nelson, Shumard, and Duzenbury. Standing (L-R) Porter, Van Kirk, Ferebee, Lewis, and Beser. (Parson and Jeppson not pictured) (AAF)

Evil piloted by Capt. George Marquand were assigned to the mission as photographic and scientific blast measurement escorts, respectively. Three other B-29s were to fly over three targets to determine which had the best weather for the mission: *Full House* (Pilot: Capt. Ralph Taylor, Target: Nagasaki), *Jabbitt III* (Maj. John Wilson/Kokura), and *Straight Flush* (Maj. Claude Eatherly/Hiroshima). A spare B-29, *Big Stink* was stationed at Iwo Jima (Note: *Big Stink* later would drop the Atomic Bomb in the *Crossroads*, Bikini tests in 1946).

Despite the previous great secrecy of the Atomic Bomb Project there were dozens of photographers and reporters on hand to record the 0245 predawn takeoff of Air Force Special Mission No. 13 (after 12 completed *Pumpkin* missions). Ten minutes after takeoff the *Enola Gay* climbed to 5,000 feet and the two weapons officers, Parsons and Jeppson, climbed into the cramped unpressurized, but relatively warm (at low altitude in the tropics) bomb bay. They placed green plugs into the bomb that blocked the firing signal and prevented accidental detonation. Then they removed the rear plate and the armored plate underneath and revealed the gun breech. A plug in the breech was unscrewed with a wrench and carefully stored on a rubber pad. Four sections of cordite were placed one at a time in the breech and the plug was replaced and a firing line was connected and the two plates replaced. This procedure required about a quarter hour and another 15 minutes were then spent checking the monitoring equipment at the panel at the weapons officer's station in the forward compartment. The bomb now only needed to be armed. At daybreak, just off Iwo Jima the bomber climbed to 9,300 feet to rendezvous with the two observation aircraft and flew on automatic pilot toward Japan. After about another hour and a half, just before the B-29 began its climb to bombing altitude, Parsons returned to the bomb bay to arm the bomb. He removed the green plugs and installed red plugs that activated the bomb's internal batteries. The bomber then began its 45 minute climb to the bombing altitude of 31,500 feet after being informed that Hiroshima was all clear. As the *Enola Gay* approached Hiroshima the two escort bombers dropped back and the crews donned their protective goggles. At 12 miles from the drop point, bombardier Ferebee took control of aircraft for a visual bomb run with Van Kirk giving him radar course corrections. Ferebee released *Little Boy* and immediately unclutched his bombsight. Once dropped the bomb fell forward and exploded several miles ahead of release point. If the B-29 continued to fly in the same direction it would fly too close to the explosion so it had to turn away quickly, banking at 155° to the rear

The first atomic mushroom cloud would appear when *Little Boy* exploded 1,900 feet above the center of Hiroshima at 0816; 43 seconds after it fell from the belly of the *Enola Gay*. (AAF)

to escape the shock wave. The 155° bank was determined as optimal as it pointed the tail of the bomber directly to the shock wave and not the side of the bomber that was considered to be dangerous. The first Atomic Bomb would explode 1,900 feet above the center of Hiroshima at 0816; 43 seconds after it fell from the belly of the *Enola Gay*. The explosion was equivalent to 15 to 16 kilotons of TNT and killed 75,000 people and destroyed 48,000 structures. The *Enola Gay* returned to Tinian without incident after flying for 12 hours, 13 minutes (0815 local time).

Nagasaki Mission: *Operation Centerboard II*, 9 August 1945
Fat Man: The Plutonium Nagasaki Bomb
Fat Man was 10.7 feet long but was a rotund 60 inches in diameter and weighed 10,265 pounds. Inside the 0.375 inch thick outer steel ballistic case was a large seven piece cast Dural sphere. The sphere had a 0.5 inch thick rubberized cork compression lining and contained 5,300 pounds of the high explosives Composition B and Baratol. Contained in the center of the high explosives was the "nuclear pit" consisting of the spherical aluminum pusher and tuballoy tamper with the Plutonium core.

The bombs used in the first test at Trinity Site on 16 July 1945, in New Mexico (the "gadget" of the Trinity test), and in *Fat Man*, the Nagasaki bomb, were made primarily of Plutonium-239, a synthetic element. Although Uranium-238 was useless as a fissile isotope for an Atomic Bomb, it was vital to producing Plutonium. The fission of U-235 released neutrons which were absorbed by U-238 becoming Uranium-239. U-239 which had a half-life of 23.45 minutes rapidly decayed to Neptunium-239 which then decayed (half-life 2.35 days) into Plutonium-239.

In 1943–1944, development efforts had been directed to a gun-type fission weapon using Plutonium, called *Thin Man* and once this was achieved, it was thought that the Uranium version (*Little Boy*) would require a relatively simple adaptation. Initial research on the properties of Plutonium was done using cyclotron-generated Plutonium-239, which was very pure, but could only be created in very small amounts. On 5

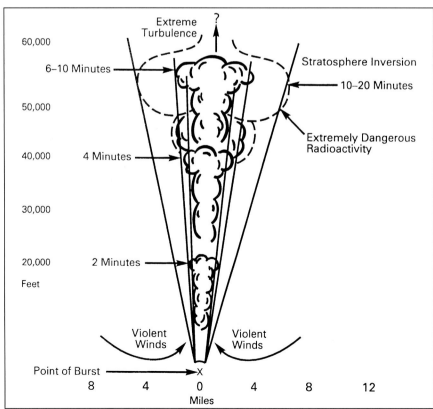

Anatomy of an Atomic Explosion

The ***Little Boy*** bomb was equivalent to 15 to 16 kilotons of TNT and killed 70,000-80,000 people and destroyed 4.7 square miles. (AAF)

Fat Man was 10.7 feet long but was a rotund 60 inches in diameter and weighed 10,265 pounds of which 5,300 pounds was high explosives. Contained in the center of the high explosives was the "nuclear pit" consisting of the spherical aluminum pusher and tuballoy tamper with the Plutonium core. (AAF)

April 1944, Emilio Segre received the first sample of Hanford-produced Plutonium at Los Alamos. Within ten days, he discovered a fatal flaw: reactor-bred Plutonium was far less isotopically pure than cyclotron-produced Plutonium. A higher concentration of Pu-240, formed from Pu-239 by capture of an additional neutron, gave it a much higher spontaneous fission rate than U-235. Pu-240 was even more difficult to separate from Pu-239 than U-235 was to separate from U-238, so no purification was attempted. The implications of this made the Hanford Plutonium unsuitable for use in a gun-type weapon.

In an incident of "disruptive technology," Oppenheimer recognized that a proposal by James Tuck in April 1944 to use explosive lenses to create spherical converging implosion waves was the best strategy to rapidly achieve a working Plutonium Bomb. In July 1944, Oppenheimer quickly canceled all ongoing work in order to reallocate resources in that new direction which would be the foundation of US nuclear research. *Thin Man* was cancelled but the gun method was further developed for Uranium only, which encountered only a few complications but most efforts were then directed to a different method for Plutonium.

Ideas for alternative detonation schemes had existed for some time at Los Alamos. One of the more innovative ideas was "implosion" which used chemical explosives so that a sub-critical sphere of fissile material could be squeezed into a smaller and denser form. When the fissile atoms were packed closer together, the rate of neutron capture would increase, and the mass would become a critical mass. The metal needed to travel

Fat Man Explosive Sphere The U-239 Plutonium Atomic Bomb was somewhat more complex and more fissionable than the U-235 bomb. It had a lower critical mass weight of 35.2 pounds. This weight could be further reduced to 22 pounds by forming a sphere of this weight of fissionable U-239 and then surrounding it with non-fissionable U-238. (AAF)

Bock's Car, flown by Maj. Charles Sweeney, carried *Fat Man* to Nagasaki. The B-29 was named after its usual commander, Capt. Frederick Bock. (AAF)

only very short distances, so the critical mass would be assembled in much less time than it would take to assemble a mass by a bullet impacting a target.

Initially, implosion had been considered as a possible, though improbable, method. But after Segre discovered that a gun-type bomb using reactor-bred Plutonium would not work and that Uranium-235 production could not be substantially increased; the Plutonium implosion bomb was the only practical solution for production of multiple bombs from the available fissionable material. The implosion project received the highest priority and by the end of July 1944, the entire project had been reorganized around building the implosion-type bomb.

The U-239 Plutonium Atomic Bomb was somewhat more complex and more fissionable than the U-235 bomb. It had a lower critical mass weight of 35.2 pounds. This weight could be further reduced to 22 pounds by forming a sphere of this weight of U-239 and then surrounding it with non-fissionable U-238. The outer U-238 shell would rebound neutrons back into the center of the fissionable U-239 sphere and reduced their loss to the outside. Plutonium was not easily exploded by the gun-type mechanism and needed to be "assembled" with much greater speed than U-235 or it would not explode. The Plutonium Atomic Bomb was assembled by "implosion." The Plutonium was shaped into a number of 32 wedge-shaped 45° sections that when placed together would form a sphere that resembled a soccer ball. This sphere surrounded a Beryllium/Polonium mixture. These wedges were grouped in a ring at equal intervals around a source of neutrons. Explosive charges of exactly equal weight were positioned behind each wedge. When the charges were detonated they fired each wedge towards the center of the ring and they collided at exactly the same instant to start the chain reaction and explosion within 1/10 millionth second.

The *Fat Man* design was was fraught with difficulties. The explosive lenses needed for perfect compression had to be manufactured perfectly and the Plutonium sphere needed to be compressed exactly equally on all sides as any error would result in a "fizzle" which would only waste the valuable Plutonium and not result in a large explosion. Because of the complexity of this implosion-style weapon, the *Manhattan Project* military administrator Gen. Leslie Groves and scientific director J. Robert Oppenheimer, decided that to test the concept before the weapon could be confidently used in combat. So it was decided that an initial test would be required, code name "*Trinity*," which took place on 16 July 1945, near Alamogordo, NM, under the supervision of Groves' deputy Brig.Gen.

Thomas Farrell and Test director Kenneth Bainbridge. The results of *Trinity* were eminently successful as after the bomb exploded Bainbridge turned to Oppenheimer and said; "Now we are all sons of bitches."

The Mission and the Bomb

Fat Man was originally scheduled for assembly by 11 August but this date was advanced two days as good weather was forecast for 9 August. On 8 August the bomb was loaded into the forward bomb bay of *Bockscar* that was named after its usual commander, Capt. Frederick Bock. The primary target of Air Force Special Mission No. 16 (there were two *Pumpkin* Special Missions on 8 August and the last two on 14 August) was to be Kokura Arsenal and the secondary was Nagasaki. The *Bockscar* (also referred to as Bock's Car) bombing crew for the mission was Maj. Charles Sweeney's *Great Artiste* crew with three additional members. The usual *Bockscar* pilot, Capt. Frederick Bock, was flying the *Great Artiste* that was the scientific aircraft on the mission. A third B-29, the *Big Stink*, piloted by Capt. James Hopkins was also assigned to the mission as the high speed photo aircraft. *Full House* piloted by Maj. Ralph Taylor was the *Bockscar* backup on Iwo Jima. Two weather B-29s, *Up n' Atom* (piloted by Capt. George Marquand to check Kokura) and *Laggin' Dragon* (Capt. Charles McKnight/Nagasaki) were sent out to recon the weather over the primary and secondary targets. Because a typhoon was threatening off the coast of Iwo Jima the rendezvous was to be off the Japanese coast of Kyushu.

The second A-Bomb mission was not to duplicate the smooth Hiroshima mission. Shortly before takeoff, the flight engineer (Kuharek) discovered that one of the fuel pumps was not functioning and the 600 gallons of gasoline in the bomb bay tank were unavailable. This would have been reason to cancel a normal mission but the Japanese had to be shown that Hiroshima could be quickly repeated and the weather after the ninth was to be socked in for at least five days. Again with great press fanfare Capt. Sweeney barely lifted the overweight *Bockscar* off from Tinian at 0347. All the aircraft on the mission ran into bad weather inbound but both weather aircraft reported good weather over the primary and secondary targets. Then the weapons officers, Ashworth and Barnes, discovered to their dismay that the red arming light on the black box connected to the bomb indicated that the firing circuit had closed. For a half-hour the two calmly traced the problem to a switch malfunction and the crew could breathe easier. The *Bockscar* and *Great Artiste* rendezvoused off Kyushu and after waiting for 40 minutes for the *Big Stink* the two B-29s continued on toward Kokura. When they reached Kokura the huge army arsenal

Bockscar **Crew** Kneeing (L-R) Buckley, Gallager, DeHart, and Spitzer. Standing (L-R) Beahan, Van Pelt, Albury, Olivi, and Sweeney. (Ashworth, Barnes, and Beser not pictured). (AAF)

Bockscar being backed over the pit holding *Fat Man*. (AAF)

The ***Fat Man*** bomb was equivalent to 21 kilotons of TNT and killed 40,000-50,000 Japanese and totally destroyed one square mile of Nagasaki. (AAF)

was obscured by smoke and haze and after three unsuccessful runs the prescribed visual bombing accuracy could not be attained. Also, the city's heavy AA fire was ranging in, fighters were seen in the distance and fuel was becoming a concern. Sweeney decided to head toward Nagasaki and against orders would use radar if visual bombing were impossible. The weather over Nagasaki was not much better and 90% of the bombing run was made by radar. At the last second, the bombardier (Beahan) saw a break in the clouds and dropped the bomb at 1058 local time. Sweeney banked the *Bockscar* out of danger and concentrated on returning to base. He had only 300 gallons of fuel left that was not enough to get them back to Tinian so Okinawa or ditching became the alternatives. Sweeney tried to contact the ASR units waiting for ditching who did not answer. Sweeney presumed the other three B-29s had already returned to Tinian and turned toward Okinawa. When he reached the island he tried to contact the tower without success. Running very low on fuel he could not afford to circle the field and as a last resort dropped flares and was given clearance to land at 1400 (local) with only seven gallons of fuel remaining. *Bockscar* was refueled and landed at Tinian at 2330 that night to little fanfare.

Fat Man had exploded at 1,650 feet above the hilly city with an estimated force of 22 kilotons. However, these steep hills confined the larger explosion of this atomic bomb and caused less damage and loss of life than *Little Boy*. The next morning the Japanese Inner Cabinet learned of the Nagasaki attack and heard a report on the extent of the Hiroshima damage and that the Russians had invaded Manchuria. However, the Samurai code of the Cabinet members would not allow them to surrender but Divine Emperor Hirohito intervened and Japanese Foreign Minister Togo contacted the Allies for surrender terms. Togo qualified the surrender demanding that the Emperor remain Japan's Sovereign Ruler. President Truman and the Allies agreed but the Emperor's rule would be subject to the Allied Commander in Japan and eventually the Japanese people would be free to choose the type of government they wanted as per the Potsdam Agreement. For three more days the Japanese military and civilian regimes could not agree to these surrender terms and finally on 14 August the Emperor acted again and commanded the divided factions to "bear the unbearable and accept the Allied reply." He also agreed to personally inform his subjects of his decision over the radio the next day. Before noon on the 15th, the Japanese people heard their Emperor for the time. Despite the fact that the Japanese people had previously only received propaganda that they were winning the war, and that the Emperor's speech was so formal and ambiguous and that he had used the word "surrender," they understood and were shocked that Japan was defeated and had surrendered.

Silverplate Becomes *Saddletree*

One year after V-J Day the USAAF had so completely demobilized that it had become practically useless as a combat entity. By early 1947 the Strategic Air Command was unable to locate much less verify the combat status of all its *Silverplate* bombers . SAC dispatched inspectors to locate and examine all of the remaining *Silverplate* bombers . They found that no two aircraft were identical as so many modifications and changes, official or in the field, had been made. Drawings and paperwork had been disposed of or misplaced and entirely new engineering drawings would have to be made before further improvements could be incorporated. The name *Silverplate* had become so compromised through overuse and negligence that on 12 May 1947; a new codeword, *Saddletree*, would replace it. Under *Saddletree* the Air Materiel Command authorized *Project DOM-595C* to modify 80 B-29s.

In January 1948 the Joint Chiefs of Staff issued a directive for the modification of 225 B-29, B-50, and B-36 bombers to carry nuclear weapons, known by the code name *Gem*, which was intended to be completed by December 1948. The project included "winterization" of 36 B-29s for operating from Arctic bases, and the modification of 36 others to have an air refueling capability under *Project DOM-599C (Ruralist)*. With the addition of the 80 *Saddletree* bombers , a total of 145 B-29s were modified to carry nuclear weapons, and 117 of these were assigned to operational units.

Silverplate Operational Units

Including the *Pullman* B-29, a total of 65 *Silverplate* B-29s were produced both during and after World War II. Twenty-nine of these were assigned to the 509th Composite Group during World War II, with 15 used to carry out the Atomic Bombings of Hiroshima and Nagasaki. An additional 24 were assigned to the group for post-war operations as the 509th Bomb Group. Fifty-seven *Silverplates* were produced by Martin-Omaha and eight by Boeing-Wichita. Thirty-two were eventually converted to other configurations, 16 were placed in storage and later scrapped, and 12 were lost in accidents (including four of the Tinian bombers). Only 65 of these *Silverplate* aircraft came into existence and only the *Enola Gay* and *Bockscar* exist today.

The only other USAF combat unit to use the *Silverplate* B-29 was the 97th Bomb Wing at Biggs AFB, El Paso, TX. In the summer of 1949 it received 27 of the aircraft from the 509th Bomb Wing when the latter transitioned to B-50D bombers , but within a year all were converted to TB-29 trainers. One other *Silverplate* B-29, on temporary assignment in the United Kingdom was converted into a weather reconnaissance aircraft (WB-29) and transferred to the 9th Bomb Wing at Travis Air Force Base, CA.

Mk-3 and Mk-4 Atomic Bombs

During the summer of 1945, Gen. Groves and Dr. Oppenheimer created a new division of the Los Alamos Laboratory, designated the Z Division, at Oxnard Field which adjoined Kirtland AAF outside of Albuquerque. The new Z Division area was named Sandia Base and would later form the basis for Sandia National Laboratories. The new organization was to stockpile existing *Fat Man* bombs and improve and test the existing and improved models. In late 1945, all existing *Fat Man* components were shipped to Sandia Base and stored in boxes and crates and these components became America's nuclear stockpile immediately after the war. In 1946, the *Fat Man* design was given improved detonators and a more reliable arming and firing system and this enhanced stockpile version was designated as an Mk-3. About 120 Mk-3 bombs were produced between April 1947 and April 1949 when the termination of Mk-3 began to be completed late in 1950. Although the Mk-3 had the same yield of about 21,000 tons of TNT it was an improvement over the *Fat Man* dropped on Nagasaki. However, it required substantial time and labor to assemble and after 48 hours the batteries had to be replaced. In the five years after the war the Mk-4 was assigned to the *Silverplate* B-29s at Walker AFB, Roswell, NM and Biggs AFB, El Paso, TX. By 1950 the Mk-3 was no longer in the inventory by 1950 and was replaced by the M-4 bomb.

Mk-4 Atomic Bomb

Before the end of war Los Alamos began the development of new components for a much improved version of the *Fat Man* bomb. The improvements were to include simplified production, better dependability and safety, easier field handling, and improved long term storage and ballistic performance. These improvements had to fall into the parameters of the bomb size remaining limited to the dimensions of the B-29 bomb bay in both *Silverplate* and *Saddletree* configurations.

The Mk-4 was an implosion-type bomb based on the same Plutonium fission model as used in the *Fat Man* and Mk-3 bombs but with significant

The **Mk-4** was a much improved version of the *Fat Man* bomb. It was an implosion-type bomb based on the same Plutonium fission model as used in the *Fat Man* and Mk-3 bombs but with significant changes in its vital components. (AAF)

changes in its vital components. The Mk-4's general dimensions were the same as the *Fat Man* and Mk-3 bombs: 128 inches long and 60 inches in diameter but it weighed about 10,800 pounds which was about 500 pounds more. The ballistic characteristics of the Mk-4 were improved when the box fin of the *Fat Man* and Mk-3 was replaced by four wedge-shaped fins with a span of 59 inches. The Mk-4's yield (21 kilotons) was about the same as the *Fat Man* and Mk-3 bombs

The most significant upgrades integrated into the Mk-4 were a composite core that was levitated in the center of the high explosive shell. This nuclear capsule could be carried separately from the bomb on takeoff and landing and could be inserted and after the bomb was carried in the aircraft. The levitated composite core consisted of a solid ball of seven pounds of Plutonium suspended at the center of a shell of 14.3 pounds of Uranium highly enriched with the U-235 isotope. The *Fat Man* and Mk-3 bombs used a core of plutonium that weighed about 13.6 pounds. Other improvements were better arming and firing components and circuitry, increased battery life, and the elimination of the four nose contact fuses. The deletion of joint fittings, external radar antennas, and the suspension lug improved the Mk-4's ballistics. The suspension lug was recessed and the antennas were flush-mounted in the nose.

The first Mk-4 entered the US nuclear stockpile in March 1949 and 550 Mk-4s of all types were produced between March 1949 and May 1951 when all were phased out between July 1952 and May 1953.

14

Poison Gas and Biological Bombs

Poison Gas Warfare: A Background

World War I

Chemical warfare was outlawed at the 1899 Hague Conference but after the Russo-Japanese War of 1904-5, France, Germany, and Britain experimented with tear gases which they did not consider to be a violation of the Hague agreements. During World War I trench warfare stalemated the battlefield and caused the combatants to turn again to chemical weapons. The French and British started with tear gas suffocates and the Germans escalated gas warfare stakes when they decided to release chlorine from industrial cylinders on the Eastern Front as an answer to the Allies use (limited) of tear gas. Again the Germans believed that chlorine did not violate the specific letter of the Hague agreement. After several abortive attempts to use chlorine gas on the Eastern Front the Germans made the decision to attack Ypres on the Belgian Flanders front on 22 April 1915. The effects were devastating as 800 to 1,400 French troops were killed and 2,000 to 3,000 injured and their lines were over run. However, the Germans rightly held back their counterattack as they could not be sure of the whims of the winds and concluded it would be impossible to carry out a mass attack behind a wall of released gas.

By the 11 November 1918 Armistice, Allied gas production had equaled Germany's and American industry was about to greatly tip the balance. American Expeditionary Force artillery fired their first mustard

An estimated million soldiers were killed or injured by gas during World War I but gas had not been dispersed by aircraft during the war. (US Army)

gas shells on 1 November in a bombardment of 36,000 shells north of Verdun. By November 1918, the Edgewood Arsenal had the capacity to fill 2.7 million 75mm gas shells per month (20% of all shells). US mustard gas production was projected to reach 200 tons a day by May 1919; compared to 18 tons in Germany. An estimated million soldiers were killed or injured by gas during World War I but gas had not been dispersed by aircraft.

Post-War

At the end of World War I, the Army Chief of Staffs unsuccessfully tried to disband the Chemical Warfare Service (CWS). In the inter-war years, especially after 1925 when the Geneva Protocol was signed banning chemical weapons, the CWS had particular problems surviving and justifying its role in poison gas manufacture.

Geneva Protocol

At the end of World War I, the Versailles Treaty of 1919 reaffirmed the prewar prohibition of the use of poisonous gases. At the Washington Disarmament Conference of 1922 the US employed the language of this treaty to introduce a similar provision into a treaty on submarines and noxious gases. The US Senate gave its advice and consent to the ratification of this treaty without a dissenting vote but it was never entered into force as the necessary French ratification was not made. At the 1925 Geneva Conference for the Supervision of the International Traffic in Arms, the United States took a similar initiative of seeking to prohibit the export of gases for use in war. The French suggested that a protocol on nonuse of poisonous gases be drafted and Poland extended the prohibition to bacteriological weapons. The Geneva Protocol was signed on 17 June 1925, thus restating the prohibition previously decreed by the Versailles and Washington Treaties and added the ban on bacteriological warfare. Before World War II the Protocol was ratified by many countries, including all the major powers except the United States and Japan. The United Kingdom, France, and Russia declared that the Protocol would cease to be binding on them if their enemies, or the allies of their enemies, failed to respect the prohibitions of the protocol. Although Italy was a party to the protocol, it used poison gas in the Ethiopian war.

The US Chemical Warfare Service in the Inter-war Years

During World War I, the CWS had relied on both Government factories and private industry for the manufacture of chemical weapons and equipment. However, from 1920 to 1939 the chemical industry which supplied the

Lt. Donald Grantham dropped the first air-dropped chemical weapons at Lake Onega, North Russia, in September 1919.

CWS with much of its toxic materials was reluctant to manufacture them not only because of the moral issue but also because it exposed them to possible unfavorable public opinion. During the late 1930s, the CWS wanted to build a chemical stockpile and estimated that it would need at least $15 million for the period 1939 through 1942 but it was only allocated $6 million as this figure assumed that there would be no war. The allocation was increased only after World War II broke out in September 1939.

Interwar Poison Gas Dispersion by Air
Allied Intervention in the Bolshevik Revolution 1919
Maj. Thomas Davies arrived at Archangel, Russia during the Allied intervention in the Bolshevik Revolution in 1919-1920 with 50,000 thermo-generators. The thermo-generator was a large hand-thrown grenade which produced a highly irritating arsenic smoke; designed to be thrown downwind by trained infantry as a prelude to an attack. Davies found the north Russian countryside too densely wooded for any chemical weapons that relied on the wind. So he adapted them for use as aerial bombs by adding fins and a padded nose cap and they were dropped on Bolshevik targets by the RAF in small numbers on about ten occasions in September 1919. Lt. Donald Grantham dropped the first air-dropped chemical weapons, "M Bombs" at Lake Onega, North Russia, in September 1919.

Suppressing Insurgent Forces
In 1919 the British shipped stocks of phosgene and mustard gas to India for use against rebels on the Northern Frontier (Afghanistan). There were unconfirmed reports that the Royal Air Force was alleged to have used gas bombs against the Afghans.

During the Third Rif War in Spanish Morocco between 1921 and 1927, the Spanish Army of Africa indiscriminately dropped phosgene, diphosgene, chloropicrin and mustard gas on rebellious civilian populations. In a telegram sent on 12 August 1921 by the Spanish Morocco High Commissioner, Damaso Berenguer, to the Spanish minister of War, Berenguer stated:

"I have been obstinately resistant to the use of suffocating gases against these indigenous peoples but after what they have done, and of their treasonous and deceptive conduct; I have to use them with true joy."

The Spanish surreptitiously obtained mustard gas from Germany which was prohibited from manufacturing such weapons as per the 1919 Treaty of Versailles of 1919. The first poison gas bomb delivery occurred in 1923 and Air Force General Hidalgo de Cisneros (in his autobiography) claims to have dropped a 100kg mustard gas bomb from his Farman F60 Goliath during the summer of 1924.

Also, during the 1930s mustard gas was dropped or sprayed from aircraft as a method to easily suppress insurgent factions by the Government of Manchuria and by Russia against the Basmatch tribes of Central Asia.

Italian-Ethiopian War 1935-1936
In 1935 and 1936, during the Italian invasion of Abyssinia, between 300 and 500 tons of mustard gas for use in both artillery and aerial bombardments was used. Savoia-Marchetti SM 81 and Caproni CA 133 tri-motor bombers dropped 500 pound torpedo-shaped, time-fused bombs. These bombs were set to burst about 200 feet above the ground, scattering spray over a large area but later, aerial spraying became the ideal method of dispersing poison gas. Groups of 10 to 15 aircraft followed one another so that the liquid issuing from them formed a continuous fog over soldiers, civilians, and farm animals; killing or wounding over 15,000 Abyssinians. Mussolini's sons, Bruno and Vittorio, flew CA 113 bombers with the Disperata and Quia Sum Leo Squadrons and indiscriminately bombed the Ethiopians as Vittorio's described in a brutal account in his book, Flight Over Ambas.

Mussolini personally authorized the use of gas in an order dated 27 October 1935 to General Graziani: "The use of gas….to overwhelm enemy resistance and in case of counterattack is authorized. Mussolini." In another order (28 December 1935) to General Badoglio he wrote: "Given the enemy system, I authorize Your Excellency the use even on a vast scale of any gas and flamethrowers. Mussolini."

Mussolini and his generals sought to conceal the use of gas warfare but the International Red Cross exposed the Italian use of gas to the world. The Italian reaction to these revelations consisted of at least 19 "erroneous" bombings of Red Cross encampments.

Japanese Late 1930s Invasion of China
Japan made use of poison gas in the battles at Hs-chou, Wuhan, and Canton in 1938; at the Hsiu-shui River and against the South China Summer

During the Italian-Ethiopian War of 1935-1936 the unrepentant Italians used mustard gas in aerial bombardments killing or wounding over 15,000 Ethiopians. (AFHRC)

Offensive in 1939; in the Central China winter campaign of 1939-40; during the Hyakudan campaign that began in August of 1940; and at I-ch' ang in Hopeh Province during 1941. Since the use of gas warfare was clandestine operation there is very little information available on the method of dispersion but it is probable that the Japanese used dispersion by aircraft as it could be used behind the lines in great quantities and safety to their troops.

The Imperial Army's use of gas during the war was motivated by its choice of victims. From 1938 onward the Japanese came to rely on poison gas as a necessity in order to overcome tough Chinese resistance, particularly in North China against Communist forces. No doubt, the Japanese hesitated to use these weapons against American units because the US had the technological capacity to retaliate in kind. Chinese forces, on the other hand, never presented such a concern. There is some evidence that Japan did use small amounts of poison gas against British Commonwealth forces during their drive on Singapore. A resolution adopted by the League of Nations on 14 May 1938 condemned the use of poison gas by Japan.

At the Tokyo War Crimes Trials it was alleged that Japan used poison gas in China on 1,312 separate occasions, producing 36,968 casualties of which only 2,086 were battle deaths. These figures were provided by the KMT government and did not include casualties incurred by Communist forces.

American Involvement with Poison Gases in World War II

The horrific deaths and maiming by gas in World War I was fixed in the nation's memory and acted as an incentive to prevent its future use. After the war Presidents Harding, Coolidge, Hoover, and Roosevelt all condemned gas as immoral and vowed to abide by the Geneva Protocol even though the US Senate never ratified it. Secretary of State Cordell Hull, a Democrat, and Secretary of the Navy Frank Knox, a Republican, each declared their opposition to the use of gas and recommend that US leaders unilaterally affirm America's condemnation of gas. However, Secretary of War Henry Stimson maintained that a public condemnation against gas could lead to a lengthy debate on the political and ethical concerns on the use of gas which could hamper the military production of gas. Stimson concluded that "the only deterrent (to gas use) is fear of our retaliation."

In 1940 England was under the threat of a Nazi invasion and Churchill thought he would have to reluctantly resort to poison gas if the invasion occurred despite Britain's affirming the Geneva Protocol. In late 1940, the neutral US secretly began to supply poison gas to Britain which was manufactured by private US companies contracted by the British and then shipped to the UK in foreign registered vessels. By summer 1941, 200 tons of American Phosgene gas per month was being accepted by the British.

Every city in Europe was vulnerable to gas attack by any of the combatants but the US was out of range of enemy bomber attack and could look at the use of poison gas more unemotionally and besides its Senate had not yet ratified the Geneva Protocol. In 1940 the US authorized $2.1 million for its Chemical Warfare Service; in 1941 when the chemical rearmament program was launched this figure was increased to over $60 million; and in 1942, once the US was in the war expenditure reached a billion dollars and 60,000 employees. The majority of this CWS disbursement was for incendiaries for bombing, flamethrowers, smoke, and other similar weapons but a covert amount went to the development of poison gas and BW weapons within CWS facilities.

The early beneficiaries of the increased allotment were the existing CWS facilities. The Edgewood Arsenal, MD, was part of the Aberdeen Proving Ground and the principal facility of the CWS in World War I.

Edgewood was awarded $34 million for renovations, including a new R&D building, a new Chemical Warfare School, and large new storage depots. During the war America built 13 new chemical warfare plants in conjunction with DuPont beginning with the largest, the $60 million, 15,000 acre, 10,000 employees, Pine Bluff Arsenal, AR in late December 1941. In 1942 the US opened the $60 million, 20,000 acre, 3,000 employees Rocky Mountain Arsenal near Denver which produced 87,000 tons of poisonous chemicals by the end of the war. Also in summer 1942 the CWS opened the 250,000 acre Dugway Proving Grounds (DPG) at the edge of the Great Salt Lake Desert in Utah, 80 miles southwest of Salt Lake City. Dugway would eventually cover 1,248 square miles (larger than Rhode Island) to become the world's largest gas weapons test area. During World War II, DPG tested toxic agents, flame throwers, chemical spray systems, biological warfare weapons, antidotes for chemical agents, and protective clothing. Gas testing was continued at the Dugway Proving Ground Mobile CWS Unit, located in Florida, and at the end of the war by a large project located in the Republic of Panama. With the increased production of gases, safe storage became a major part of the process. The CWS spent $12 million building new storage facilities and at Edgewood Arsenal 360,000 square feet was added including six new warehouses, 13 magazines, six igloos, and four miscellaneous buildings.

Testing and Development

At all of these stations, before carrying out the tests the NDRC and the Army worked together in developing testing methods in this new and dangerous area. Initially, the relationship of NDRC to the Chemical Warfare Service was contentious. The CWS was established and had existed from World War I while the newly created NDRC, staffed by strong-minded academic individualists, was suspect as it was an independent agency free from Army control. The NDRC regarded the Army as inflexible, uncooperative, and unwilling to accept any new developments which it had not originated. The rivalry between these two groups inevitably led to duplication of effort and a waste of time and funds but improved dramatically by the end of the war.

Many factors concerning the functioning of the gas bomb had to be recorded and analyzed. During tests correct fusing was required to prevent the bombs from burying themselves and therefore not properly distributing the gas. Equally important was that the burst of the bomb should not burn up the agent; determining what gas concentrations could be obtained; how many bombs needed to be placed on the target to obtain

During the US Army Maneuvers of March 1941 an A-17A simulates a gas attack. As of 1940 the US Senate had not yet ratified the Geneva Protocol and in 1940 authorized $2.1 million for its Chemical Warfare Service and $60 million in 1941 when the chemical rearmament program was launched. (AAF)

the desired effects; what effect meteorological factors such as wind speed and temperature had on the performance of the gas agents as well as on the susceptibility of personnel exposed to them.

In addition to the American test facilities, there were several others located in the United Kingdom, in Canada, in Australia, and in India. In March 1944 the Project Co-ordination Staff was formed at Edgewood Arsenal, as a central Allied agency to scrutinize the data from all of these facilities and to draw the best possible conclusions. Aided by the NDRC, various Divisions of the Chemical Warfare Service, and by several countries in the British Empire, this unit analyzed the field data and published several reports, among which was one summarizing the best considered conclusions gathered from all sources on the field use of chemical warfare material.

Although President Roosevelt was adamantly opposed to the use of poison gas; Japanese gas atrocity news stories against the Chinese in 1941 made good propaganda and after Pearl Harbor the US press advocated that America use gas in retribution. The threat of enemy gas warfare caused Congress to fund America's Chemical Warfare Program. In reality, Japan virtually stopped its manufacture and use of poisonous gas in 1942. Hitler would never use gas against the Allies because he feared retaliation and probably remembered his own painful gassing experience while fighting for the Kaiser in 1918.

Despite its huge budget, the CWS continued under the restraints imposed by President Roosevelt. In mid-December 1943 after the Marines suffered a horrific 3,400 casualties during the four day battle for Tarawa, Maj.Gen. William Porter, head of the CWS, implored America to begin using poison gas. Porter argued that American air superiority precluded Japanese retaliation and that "Properly used gas could shorten the war in the Pacific and prevent loss of many American lives." About three quarters of the American public was opposed to the use of gas and there were factions in the military that argued that American use of gas against the Japanese could give the Germans a justification to use it against the Allies in any invasion of the Continent.

By late June 1944 the Allied breakout from Normandy had bogged down and the fear that the war would stagnant into trench warfare. The threat of the slaughter of the Great War appeared and the use of poison gas was considered to be a method of breaking any stalemate. Also, the Germans had began the indiscriminate launching of their V-1 and V-2 Vengeance weapons which were considered a possible vehicle to eventually carry poison gas warheads if the Germans became desperate. On 5 July, the Joint Planning Staff, (JPS) recommended against using poison gas but the next day Winston Churchill wrote a remarkably callous memorandum on his position on poison gas:

"I want you to think very seriously over this question of using poison gas. I would not use it unless it could be shown either that it was life or death for us, or that it would shorten the war by a year.

"It is absurd to consider morality on this topic when everybody used it in the last war without a word of complaint from the moralists or the Church. On the other hand, in the last war the bombing of open cities was regarded as forbidden. Now everybody does it as a matter of course. It is simply a question of fashion changing as she does between long and short skirts for women.

"I want a cold-blooded calculation made as to how it would pay us to use poison gas, by which I mean principally mustard. We will want to gain more ground in Normandy so as not to be cooped up in a small area. We could probably deliver twenty tons to their one and for the sake of their one they would bring their bomber aircraft into the area against our superiority, thus paying a heavy toll.

"Why have the Germans not used it? Not certainly out of moral scruples or affection for us. They have not used it because it does not pay them; the greatest temptation ever offered to them was the beaches of Normandy. This they could have drenched with gas greatly to the hindrance of our troops. That they thought about it is certain and that they prepared against our use of gas is also certain. But the only reason they have not, used it against us is that they fear the retaliation. What is to their detriment is to our advantage.

"Although one sees how unpleasant it is to receive poison gas attacks, from which nearly everyone recovers, it is useless to protest that an equal amount of HE will not inflict greater cruelties and sufferings on troops or civilians. One really must not be bound within silly conventions of the mind whether they be those that ruled in the last war or those in reverse which rule in this.

"The bombardment of London really became a serious nuisance and great rockets with far-reaching and devastating effect fall on many centres of Government and labour, I should be prepared to do <i>anything</i> that would hit the enemy in a murderous place. I may certainly have to ask you to support me in using poison gas. We could drench the cities of the Ruhr and many other cities in Germany in such a way that most of the population would be requiring constant medical attention. We could stop all work at the flying bomb starting points. I do not see why we should always have all the disadvantages of being the gentleman while they have all the advantages of being the cad. There are times when this may be so but not now.

"I quite agree it may be several weeks or even months before I shall ask you to drench Germany with poison gas, and if we do it, let us do it one hundred per cent. In the meanwhile, I want the matter studied in cold blood by sensible people and not by that particular set of psalm-singing uniformed defeatists which one runs across now here now there. Pray address yourself to this. It is a big thing and can only be discarded for a big reason. I shall of course have to square Uncle Joe and the President, but you need not bring this into your calculations at the present time. Just try to find out what it is like on its merits."

Two days later, the Joint Planning Staff, met to discuss the Prime Minister's extraordinary proposal. The JPS stated that there was no doubt that if the Allies initiated chemical warfare the Germans would immediately retaliated both in the field and against the United Kingdom. After five years of war, with success appearing more assured, the British population would receive a particularly demoralizing blow if the Germans were forced to use poison gas in retaliation for the Allies first use of the weapon. Also the use of gas on occupied areas with unprotected civilians would critically damage relations with these civilians when it became commonly known that chemical warfare was first employed by their "friendly" Allies. The report also stated that it would be very difficult to lay down heavy concentrations of gas over large areas. Churchill received a copy of the JPS report on 27 July and the next day the Chiefs of Staff met and approved its contents and on the 29th, Churchill abandoned his stand on gas and biological warfare.

In March of 1943, the first gas warfare plan was developed for the Pacific and Mustard Gas canisters, spray tanks, and bomb casings were dispersed at six toxic storage yards in Australia. There were 14,000 empty 100 pound bomb casings available in Australia for filling only because they were not shipped to the Philippines which was their original destination. The CWS in the SWPA estimated that in the event of gas warfare initiated by the Japanese the pre-filled gas bomb stock at the Charters Towers yard would be sufficient for an immediate retaliatory strike. Then, within seven hours, the more effective aerial spray tanks could be filled and delivered for a 16 aircraft toxic gas spray mission. Four more spray missions could be flown using gas from other stocks. More missions could be flown only if some spray tanks were returned after the flights and this was not expected because spray tanks were normally jettisoned.

The *Lethbridge Report*, prepared by the US High Command concerning the use of poison gas in the Pacific, recommended the saturation of Iwo Jima with poison gas in 1944. The report concluded that "the employment of chemical warfare with complete ruthlessness and upon a vast scale would be decisive in winning the war against the Japanese." The Combined Chiefs of Staff and Adm. Chester Nimitz approved the report but President Franklin Roosevelt vetoed it.

As the war in the Pacific grew bloodier with the invasions of Peleiliu and Iwo Jima there were factions that advocated the use of gas in the Pacific, including Gen. George C. Marshall, Army Chief of Staff. Marshall urged its use after the huge casualties sustained at Iwo Jima and then proposed using gas on Okinawa before the invasion which was projected (correctly) to cost thousands of American casualties. Marshall felt that gas warfare would have caused the Okinawan civilians to move to an isolated part of the island and keep Japanese troops in gas masks for about a week, demoralizing and incapacitating them to such an extent that the invasion "could have been accomplished with little loss of life." Although Marshall valued American lives over the immorality of using gas he still did not authorize it use. Marshall later maintained that the primary reason for not using gas was the opposition of the British who feared that a desperate Nazi regime would have an excuse to use gas in the last weeks of war.

Once Germany surrendered on 8 May 1945 there no longer the chance of retaliation in Europe and the issue of using gas in the Pacific again arose. General Marshall once more advocated the use of gas "to cope with the ... last ditch defense tactics of the suicidal Japanese." Marshall, as callous as Churchill stated: "It did not need to be our newest and most potent (gas); just drench them and sicken them so that the fight would be taken out of them; saturate an area, possibly with mustard...." Marshall shrugged off public opinion by arguing that gas was "no less inhumane than phosphorus and flame throwers and need not be used against dense populations of civilians; merely against these last pockets of resistance which had to be wiped out but had no other military significance."

The ethical issues of gas warfare were superseded by the ethical issues of the Atomic Bomb and while Marshall was willing to breach the ethical code against gas warfare, he was reluctant to use the Atomic Bomb against civilians. He recommended its use against a purely military target or as a demonstration against a manufacturing center with an advanced warning to the population to leave. Soon, the Interim Committee, a high level advisory agency on the A-Bomb, recommended that "the most desirable target would be a vital war plant employing a large number of workers and closely surrounded by worker's houses." This would be, to all intents and purposes, terror bombing with the purpose of terrifying the Japanese into surrendering before they suffered a similar end. Of course, at the time the Committee did not know the true power of the Atomic Bomb which would wipe out an entire city of industrial plants.

Meanwhile, Marshall persisted in his desire to use gas and soon was joined by Gen. Douglas MacArthur who could find "no reason why we should not use gas right now against Japan proper. Any kind of gas." Assistant Secretary of War John McCloy also supported Marshall and wanted to reconsider the gas policy "in the face of the public pressure for the use of gas, which may develop as our casualties rise due to the Okinawa cave type of Japanese defense." In early June 1945, with casualties mounting on Okinawa, Marshall requested the Army's Operations Division (OPD) study old and new justifications for using gas in the Pacific. Their report stated that while the use of gas would save

American lives and that the British would no longer have to be concerned with German retaliation; there was the possibility that the Japanese could retaliate against civilian populations, especially in China and also in Manchuria and Korea. The OPD warned that the introduction of gas warfare by the US would abolish future ethical restraints against using gas but concluded that this would make no practical difference, because in any future war chemical and biological warfare would be directed against the United States "on the opening day." The OPD closed its report on an optimistic note concluding that American public opinion could be easily swayed to accept gas warfare: "A program of education, stressing that it is not worse than flamethrowers, phosphorus, or Napalm and that lives of... soldiers can be saved, will overcome this prejudice. Actually, there is considerable public demand to use gas." Since the media reported the huge casualties at Iwo Jima American support for gas warfare was near 40% and growing.

However, by mid-1945 circumstances decided that the military advantages of using gas against the Japanese would not merit the damage done to American prestige. There was no need for Truman, the new President, to reverse Roosevelt's anti-gas stand as he had been informed of the power of the Atomic Bomb and the distinct possibility that it could end the war. At no point during the war was the factor that chemical weapons were banned under international law a major consideration in the decision not to use them. The sine qua non was that gas was not used because at any particular point in the war there always were sufficient military and ethical deterrents to prevent any combatant from using it.

Poison Gases Available During World War II

As a rule the purpose of poison gas was not to kill but to disable large numbers of the enemy. A dead soldier was written off while wounded soldiers required many weeks to recover and when thousands of gassed casualties returned home the civilian population would become much more demoralized than by reading about unseen fatalities.

Mustard Gas

The original discovery of Mustard Gas is uncertain but French chemists M. Depretz in 1822 and Alfred Riche in 1854 described the reaction of sulfur dichloride and ethylene but neither mentioned any physiological reactions. It was not until 1886 that Vicktor Meyer described the irritating properties of the gas and its synthesis. In 1913 English chemist Hans Clarke working with German chemist Emil Fischer in Berlin changed ingredients in Meyer's synthesis. During his work a flask broke and Clarke was hospitalized for two months for severe burns. Fischer reported on his research to the German Chemical Society and the German military manufactured and stockpiled the gas which was first used in July 1917 against British infantry at the battle of Ypres and then in retaliation by the Allies in November 1917 at the battle of Cambrai using captured German gas shells. It was not until September 1918 that the British developed their own Mustard Gas.

The process of distilling Mustard Gas to improve its storage properties was fully developed during World War II. The first pilot plant for producing the new distilled Mustard (code named "HD") was brought online in 1944 at the Edgewood Arsenal which led to the construction of a full-scale plant at the Rocky Mountain Arsenal, near Denver which would produce 4,600 tons of this Mustard Gas by the war's end. Sulfur Mustard is also known as "Mustard Gas or Mustard Agent," or by the military designations H, HD, and HT.

Sulfur Mustard is a type of chemical warfare agent called vesicants or blistering agents, because they caused blistering of the skin and mucous membranes on contact. It can be a vapor (the gaseous form of a liquid), an oily-textured liquid, or a solid. Sulfur mustard vapor is heavier than air, so it will settle in low-lying areas. Mustard Gas was dispersed as a long-lasting, persistent, yellow-brown aerosol in a mixture of other chemicals which had a distinctive odor sometimes smelling like garlic, onions, or mustard. Wearing a gas mask was not effective as the gas was absorbed through the skin.

Exposure to Sulfur Mustard was usually not fatal as when it was used during World War I, it killed fewer than 5% of the individuals who were exposed and received medical care. Typically, signs and symptoms do not occur immediately and depending on the severity of the exposure and the sensitivity of the victim, symptoms may not occur for two to 24 hours. The symptoms included redness and itching of the skin occurring two to 48 hours after exposure and change eventually to yellow blistering of the skin. Irritation, pain, swelling, and tearing in the eyes may occur within three to 12 hours of a mild to moderate exposure. A severe exposure may cause symptoms within one to two hours and may include the symptoms of a mild or moderate exposure plus light sensitivity, severe pain, or blindness lasting up to 10 days. Runny nose, sneezing, hoarseness, bloody nose, sinus pain, shortness of breath, and cough occur within 12 to 24 hours of a mild exposure and within two to four hours of a severe exposure. Abdominal pain, diarrhea, fever, nausea, and vomiting affected the digestive tract. The gas causes damage to the DNA component of cells in the body.

Phosgene

Phosgene, from the Greek: *Phos* (light) and *gene* (born), was first synthesized by chemist John Davy in 1812 by exposing a mixture of carbon monoxide and chlorine in sunlight. The chemical was used during the 19th century in the dye industry and as an industrial reagent. It can be colorless or appear in a white or pale yellow and have a very unpleasant odor at high concentrations and is heavier than air. Its military designation is CG.

The first use of poison gas during World War I was by the Germans who released chlorine at the First Battle of Ypres on 22 April 1915. Soon Phosgene was introduced as a weapon that was more effective than chlorine which caused the victim to violently cough and choke. Phosgene was absorbed through the skin, eyes, breathing into the lungs and caused coughing; burning of the eyes and throat; difficulty in breathing and fluid in the lungs; and nausea and vomiting. Phosgene caused much less

coughing and so more of it was inhaled. Phosgene often had a delayed effect and apparently healthy soldiers were debilitated by Phosgene gas poisoning up to 48 hours after inhalation.

Lewisite

Lewisite was originally developed by Julius Nieuwland, a chemist at the Catholic University, Washington, DC, from synthesis by the combination of allowing arsenic trichloride to react with acetylene in the presence of hydrochloric acid solution of mercuric chloride. Nieuwland's thesis was discovered by soldier/chemist Winford Lewis in 1918 after whom the gas was named. It was developed into a secret weapon and given the name the "New G-34" so as to confuse its existence with Mustard Gas. It was not used in World War I but work continued on the gas under the military symbol of M-1 which was changed to "L" during World War II. Field trials during World War II showed that high casualties could not be attained as its characteristic odor and ease of producing tears caused troops to don their gas masks. It is classified as a vesicant or blistering agent as it caused blistering of the skin and mucous membranes on contact. Because it contains arsenic, Lewisite has some effects that are similar to arsenic poisoning, including stomach ailments and low blood pressure. Lewisite is an oily, colorless liquid in its pure form and can appear amber to black in its impure form. Lewisite has an odor like geraniums. It has no practical use other than as a military poisonous gas.

The Disaster at Bari

Although poison gas was not used during World War II a horrific unintended event involved the release of Mustard Gas from a shipment resulting in 628 American casualties from exposure and 69 deaths along with affecting an estimated 1,000 Italian civilians. On 28 November 1943, the American merchantman *John Harvey* arrived at the Italian port of Bari loaded with two thousand 100 pound Mustard Gas bombs each containing 60-70 pounds of Sulfur Mustard. American Mustard Gas was manufactured by the quick and inexpensive Levinstein H process which made it very unstable. Each bomb contained 30% impurities which caused gases to build up inside and possibly explode. The bombs had to be regularly vented and the casings inspected for corrosion.

On the night of 2/3 December 1943, 20 German Ju-88 bombers carried out a surprise air raid on Bari, that led to the destruction of 17 ships carrying around 90,000 tons of supplies and another eight were seriously damaged, for the worst maritime disaster suffered by the Allies since Pearl Harbor. Explosions tore through the congested harbor and the *John Harvey* suffered a hit and then a few minutes later a second explosion tore through the ship which then listed and began to sink. The Chemical Warfare contingent accompanying the shipment and the ship's captain frantically attempted to scuttle the ship but some of the gas bombs began to burn, some sank, but most of the bomb casings leaked gas out of the ship's ruptured hold and spread over the debris-filled harbor. The settling gas mixed with the many thousands of gallons of oil floating on the water's surface to form a lethal concoction. A dense black cloud of smoke mixed with the gas and began to roll across the harbor and over Bari. The worst casualties were not those inhaling the garlicky fumes but those exposed with their bodies immersed in a lethal solution of Mustard Gas.

Medical personnel treating the casualties were unaware of the existence of the gas, as it was diluted sufficiently not to be detected by odor. Also, the shipment of the banned Mustard Gas was secret and the Chemical Warfare Service officer and his crew and the *Harvey's* captain were killed while trying to scuttle the ship and thus it was not immediately recognized that Mustard Gas had been released. In treating the casualties covered with oil but showing no physical injuries; the diagnosis was that

On the night of 2/3 December 1943, German Ju-88 bombers carried out a surprise air raid on the port at Bari, Italy sinking 17 ships, one of which was carrying mustard gas. The escaping gas caused 628 American casualties and 69 deaths from exposure along with affecting an estimated 1,000 Italian civilians. (AAF)

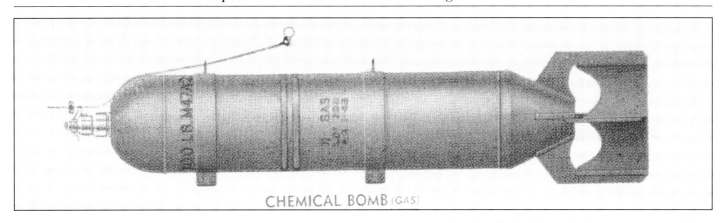

CHEMICAL BOMB (GAS)

they were suffering from exposure and immersion. The treatment was to wrap them in blankets, still in their oil-soaked clothing, given hot tea, and left for 12 to 24 hours while the more urgent blast injuries and surgical cases were attended to first. Those with the energy and will to clean the oil from their own bodies suffered no serious damage but the remainder suffered varying degrees of Mustard burns. Eyes began to burn about six hours after exposure, and were so badly swollen in 24 hours that many of the patients thought themselves blind. The first deaths occurred without warning 18 hours after exposure.

Initially, Eisenhower and the Combined Chiefs of Staff decided to keep the Bari disaster a secret for fear that the Germans believed that the Allies were preparing to use chemical weapons which might provoke them into preemptive use. Attempts were made for the cover up but the scale of the tragedy was so great that it could not be kept a secret. In February the Chiefs of Staff, after being informed that the rumor of the incident would soon become exposed as fact, prepared a statement reiterating that the "Allied policy is not (repeat not) to use gas unless or until the enemy does so first but that we are fully prepared to retaliate and do not deny the accident, which was a calculated risk." The US records of the incident were classified and the British amended all related documents to record Mustard Gas deaths as "burns due to enemy action." American records of the attack were declassified in 1959, but the episode remained obscure until the late 1960s. In 1986 the British government finally admitted to survivors of the Bari raid that they had been exposed to poison gas and revised their pension payments.

Types of Gas Bombs
Bomb, Gas, Persistent, H, 100 Pound, M47A2
This bomb was loaded with a 68.5 pound charge of Mustard Gas and the complete round weighed 98 pounds.

Authorized Fuses and Bursters
The M4 Burster was authorized for use in this bomb with H filling. As originally designed, this bomb was adapted for M108 nose fuse. If the AN-M126 or AN-M126A1 was available, it was preferred to the M108.

Other models
Bomb, Gas, Persistent, H, 100 Pound, M47A1 differed from the M47A2 only in that the interior was coated with acid-proof black paint instead of oil. The M47 was not used for H filling.

Bomb, Gas, Persistent, H, 115 Pounds, M70
The M70 was a round-nose, cylindrical-type; the complete round measuring 48.7 inches overall length and 8.1 inches in diameter and weighed 116.1 pounds and carried a charge of 57.1 pounds of Mustard Gas or Lewisite. The bomb body was 40.4 inches long and weighs 107

pounds. It was shipped unfused, with wooden lug protectors and without the fin or burster. The fin assembly, fuse, and burster were each shipped separately with the arming wire packed with the fin.

Authorized Fuses and Burster
The AN-M110A1 Fuse and M10 Burster were authorized for use in this bomb.

Bomb, Chemical, 500 Pound, M78
The M78 resembled the CC bomb described above except that the chemical charge consisted of approximately 205 pounds of Phosgene of the 485 pounds of the weight of the complete round.

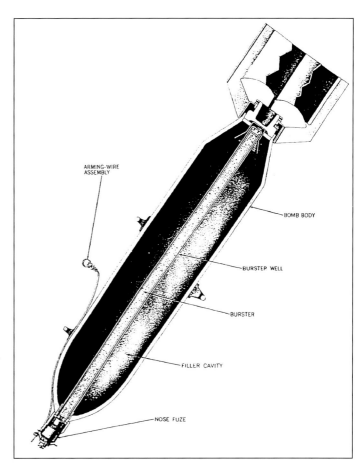

Chemical Bomb, 115 pound, M70A1 (AAF)

Bomb, Chemical, 1,000 Pound, AN-M79
This bomb was similar to the AC bomb described above except for the difference in filler and corresponding difference in weight. The chemical charge consisted of 417 pounds of Phosgene and the complete round weighed 939 pounds.

The Use of Poison Gas
There were two methods which aircraft could dispense poison gas over enemy infantry and armored units: bombs and spray dispensers. When using either method the attacking aircraft was more protected from enemy AA and small arms ground fire than when using conventional bombs. When dropping conventional bombs the pilot had to fly directly over the enemy but when spraying or dropping gas bombs the pilot had to fly upwind to have the gas flow over enemy positions. A smoke screen dropped in bombs or dispensed by sprayers just previous to the gas attack not only shielded the attacking aircraft but indicated the direction of the wind and the location of the target. Gas could also be laid in low-lying areas behind enemy lines where it would remain for hours and even days with the intent of either cutting off reinforcement and resupply to the front or avenues of retreat.

Tests showed that in laying a smoke screen or gas cloud a spray dispenser could be more effective than a conventional strafing attack under ideal circumstances. Tests demonstrated that a strafing aircraft could fire only a maximum of 3,400 (8 guns x 425 rpg) bullets over an area of two million square feet while the same aircraft could dispense 100 gallons of gas that formed a destructive cloud over the same mile long by quarter mile wide area. However, the major drawback to this technique was the difficulty in achieving the necessary concentration of gas, particularly in the presence of any wind.

Delivering gas in bombs became the method choice as a considerable quantity of gas could be accurately concentrated over a relatively large area and because standard bombs could be adapted to carry the gases. This technique was called thermal dissemination as the bomb contained a poison gas and a central burster charge which detonated to spread the gas laterally. This method was not considered particularly efficient as a large percentage of the gas was lost by incineration in the initial blast and by being forced into the ground. Also the sizes of the gas particles varied considerably because explosive dissemination produced a mixture of liquid droplets of variable and difficult to control sizes.

Because the infantryman could not march any distance in gas; he had to unpack and put on the impervious protective clothing that would ward off the flesh-burning mustard or Lewisite gas. During an airborne gas attack the infantryman on the ground had little time to don his gas mask, much less his protective clothing, and then fire at the fast-flying attacking aircraft which were gone in seconds. After the gas was laid; the engulfed infantry tried to move upwind as soon as possible but often were driven into planned enemy fire. Armored units were particularly vulnerable to poison gas as the occupants of a tank would choke on the fumes as they were unable to leave the tank for fear of being drenched with the blistering gas.

The major combatants in World War II expected that chemical weapons would be used and stockpiled them; especially Mustard Gas. During the war the Americans stockpiled 87,000 tons, the Russians 77,400 tons, the British 40,719 tons while the Germans had 27,597 tons on hand at the end of the war. Fortunately, neither side used poison gas, not because of moral motives but for the fear of retaliation.

Biological Warfare
The intent of Biological Warfare (BW) was seen as a way to annihilate such a large proportion of the enemy's population that his war making

capability would collapse. In 1932 Japan's Biological Warfare Unit was established under Shiro Ishii at the Army Medical College in Tokyo and with a production facility and test site in China. With reports of the Japanese interest in biological warfare in the previous decade, in 1940 the US Health and Medical Committee of the Council for National Defense initiated a study of "the offensive and defensive potential of biological warfare." Once the world was at war a Special Assignments Branch was created at the Edgewood Arsenal, Baltimore in August 1941 to continue biological research. Three months later the War Department formed the top secret War Bureau of Consultants (WBC) comprised of 12 nationally prominent scientists headed by Edwin Fred, professor of bacteriology at the University of Wisconsin to assess the threat of germ warfare. Members met for the first time on 18 November 1941 in Washington and decided they would perform a literature search on the subject. On 27 November the first reports of the Japanese bubonic plague attacks on the Chinese village of Changteh were received in Washington and then ten days later the Japanese bombed Pearl Harbor, which prompted the committee to increase their BW study efforts. On 17 February 1942, the WBC Committee issued its first official report on its literature search which ran an impressive 289 pages covering 55 articles discussing the use of animal, insects, sabotage of water supplies, and aerosols to spread pathogens while 16 additional articles mentioned dissemination by airplane and six proposed bacterial bombs. The WBC's report was received by the Secretary of War, Henry Stimson and on 29 April 1942 and he wrote to President Roosevelt outlining the committee's findings:

"The value of biological warfare will be a debatable question until it has been clearly proven or disproved by experiences. The wide assumption is that any method which appears to offer advantages to a nation at war will be vigorously employed by that nation. There is but one logical course to pursue, namely, to study the possibilities of such warfare from every angle, make every preparation for reducing its effectiveness, and thereby reduce the likelihood of its use."

In June, the WBC disbanded and issued its second and final report stating: "The best defense for the United States is to be fully prepared to start a wholesale offensive whenever it becomes necessary to retaliate," and then emphasizing that in biological warfare "the best defense is offense and the threat of offense." The WBC's final conclusion was: "Unless the United States is going to ignore this potential weapon, steps should be taken immediately to begin work on the problems of biological warfare."

In May 1942, President Roosevelt authorized Secretary Stimson to establish a civilian agency to take the lead on all aspects of bacterial warfare. Secretary Stimson had been privy to intelligence reports that clearly stated both Germany and Japan had a BW capability. He also knew of Germany's BW attack on the Rumanian Cavalry using Glanders Disease and that German saboteurs introduced the disease into the United States among horses and mules being shipped to Europe in World War I.

The new agency, the War Research Service (WRS) was assigned to the Federal Security Agency (FSA) to obscure its existence and George Merck (of Merck Drugs) was named its Director. It soon became evident to the WRS and Merck that the study of BW weapons by universities and private research institutions would be insufficient to meet the large scale effort required to develop the use of and the concomitant need for protection from biological agents. Merck then allocated overall BW responsibility to the Army's Chemical Warfare Service. Col. William Kabrich, Chief of the Technical Division of the Army's Chemical Warfare Service invited Dr. Ira Baldwin, a plant biologist and Chairman of the Bacteriology Department of the University of Wisconsin to oversee the program. Baldwin chose Detrick Field, a little-used National Guard airfield in Frederick, MD, as

In March 1943 **Fort Detrick**, MD, a former airfield, became the location for America's new Biological Warfare Laboratory with over $40 million invested in plant and equipment with approximately 4,000 personnel employed in BW research, testing, and production during the war. (AFHRC)

Extreme caution was exercised during research and production of botuinum toxin and anthrax bacterial spores at Fort Detrick. (AFHRC)

the location for the new BW laboratory in March 1943 and was given carte blanche for funding and personnel. Unless the researcher was required for the Manhattan Atomic Bomb Project, the priority of the BW gave Baldwin the personnel he sought.

Detrick Field was chosen because of its practically remote location and proximity to Washington, DC, as well as Edgewood Arsenal, the center of US chemical warfare research. The buildings and other facilities that remained from the airfield included the large hangar that provided the center of support that was needed at the start of operation. Detrick Field was formally acquired on 9 March 1943 and could be expanded from its original 92 acres by acquiring surrounding farmland. A small cadre of men arrived to begin the conversion process. Lt.Col. William Bacon, the first CO, and his successor, Col. Martin Chittick who directed the renovation and construction at an estimated to cost of $1.25 million.

The base was ringed by fences and towers with searchlights and guards with machine guns and orders to shoot first and ask questions later. The headquarters building at the center of the complex had its own armed guards on alert 24/7. Supposedly the scientists were issued pistols which they kept at their sides or nearby on workbenches. All personnel had identity passes with photos and persons transferring from Detrick surrendered their photo passes to the guards; and accidentally keeping one could lead to arrest and interrogation.

The British had been investigating biological warfare but were unable to afford the immense monetary and personnel outlay that a full-blown BW program would have required. The English, under bacteriologist Paul Fildes, head of the Biology Department, Porton (BDP) were far ahead of the US in BW research. They had conducted the world's first biological weapons test on 15 July 1942 at Gruinard Island located in a lake in the

Dr. Ira Baldwin was in charge of the US Biological Warfare program at Fort Detrick. (AFHRC)

English bacteriologist **Dr. Paul Fildes** was the head of the Biology Department at the Biological Warfare Research Station at Porton. (AFHRC)

Scottish Highlands. Caged sheep were exposed to anthrax spores which killed 13 of 15 sheep. The first BW air drop occurred on 26 September 1942 when a Vickers Wellington released a 30 pound anthrax bomb from 7,000 feet on 50 sheep. However, not one died as the bomb hit a peat bog and sank discharging the anthrax into the soft ground instead of the air. Using the "Green Book," a comprehensive manual composed by Fildes chronicling everything the British had learned about BW, Baldwin's team began work on the production of botuinum toxin and anthrax bacterial spores at Camp Detrick. So between 1942 and March 1945, with the British lending their previous expertise, America invested over $40 million in plant and equipment with approximately 4,000 personnel employed in BW research, testing, and production.

One of the projects the British had initiated and were unable to pursue was the use of anthrax (codenamed "N"). Anthrax is an ancient disease dating back to the Greeks. Sheep, cattle, pigs, horses, and goats can contract it by eating grass or drinking water that contains the bacillus. The microbe is fast acting and the acutely infected animal can die within a few minutes after the appearance of the first symptoms. Anthrax is easily transmissible to humans, with three modes of transmission:

Cutaneous anthrax is caused by the microbe entering the body through the skin. It has an incubation period of from one to five days after which the victim develops a skin rash at the site of entry and nasty black scabs developing on the skin. Cutaneous anthrax is treatable if it is diagnosed in time.

Gastrointestinal anthrax is contracted by eating undercooked infected meat. The symptoms are severe abdominal pain, fever, vomiting, and bloody diarrhea. Without treatment death occurs in about 50% of cases.

Inhalation or pulmonary anthrax is contracted by breathing the microbe from the fur or hides of infected animals. This was the most deadly form of anthrax as by the time the first symptoms appear it is too late for treatment and mortality rates are 95%, with or without treatment. The microbe enters the lungs, where it germinates and multiplies, and then invades the bloodstream, discharging toxins while the victim experiences basically the symptoms of a common cold: mild chest pains, malaise, cough, and fever. These symptoms continue for a day or two, after which there can be a short period of apparent improvement. Then, usually within 24 hours of this apparent remission, the victim dies of respiratory failure.

Bacillus anthracis is fast-acting and lethal but has a third characteristic that makes it an ideal biological weapon; its ability to sporulate. Specific bacterial organisms when confronted with unfavorable conditions such as lack of suitable nutrients or moisture can compress themselves into minute balls and extrude a durable and long-lasting protein coat around their outer surfaces known as a spore. Spores are impervious to light, heat, and radiation, and even to some noxious chemicals and have been known to survive for decades and even for hundreds of years and when conditions are appropriate they can germinate.

The British supplied America with the means to produce the anthrax and the so-called "*Black Maria*" anthrax production facility was built in May 1943 at Camp Detrick to produce laboratory quantities of anthrax. This facility was replaced in late 1943 by larger Pilot Plants which would lead to plants to mass produce the Anthrax spores. The early British bombs in use at Porton were inadequate large 30 pound canisters which were replaced by the Type F bomb. This bomb was a conventional incendiary device used to ignite wooden buildings but its canister could be converted to contain a biological filling. The bomb was a welded steel tube some 21 inches long and about 1.75 inches in diameter, closed at one end by a metal cap and at the other end by an explosive fuse. A thin shaft of high explosive ran down the center of the tube, with an axial burster, and the liquid biological agent poured around it. The cavity could hold about a pint of liquid pathogen slurry and on detonation the axial burster would

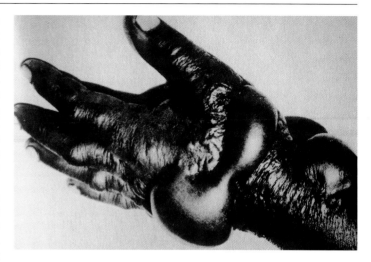

The severe effects of untreated **Cutaneous Anthrax**. (Author)

blow open the steel walls of the bomb; at the same time aerosolizing the anthrax spores and dispersing them as a homogeneous cloud.

In early 1943 Baldwin investigated locations for outdoor biological weapons testing that were similar to Gruinard Island in Britain and selected Horn Island, located off the Mississippi coast. The island was a narrow spit of land ten miles long and just a mile wide at its widest Within a year it was developed into the world's premier BW test facility. However, once in use it became apparent that Horn Island, due to its proximity to populated areas could not safely be used in live pathogen testing. In October 1943, the Army established separate biological warfare facilities in an isolated 250 square mile area in the Dugway Proving Grounds called the Granite Peak Installation. Dugway had previously been established as part of the chemical warfare section. The Army constructed the biological installation consisting of test grid, laboratory, and an incinerator for disposal of animal carcasses and the infrastructure including living quarters, roads, a landing strip, water supply system, sewers and septic tanks, power generators. The site was finally completed at the end of January 1945 at a total cost of $1,343,334.

Until this time biological warfare remained an academic possibility but not a clear and present threat as it had never been used in battle and nor had Allied intelligence uncovered any significant enemy BW effort. However, in December 1943, reports were received by Allied Intelligence that the Germans were preparing the pilotless V-1 to deliver a warhead filled with botulinum, the most toxic substance known, on England or against any invasion of the Continent. If that were the case then the Allies would have to defend their civilians or troops against the substance and then retaliate with a biological weapon of their own.

To defend the population against botulinum a toxoid would have to be developed and mass produced. In 1943 Harvard professors, Alvin Pappenheimer and Howard Mueller, had already developed and tested an effective toxoid against botulinum and later Pappenheimer developed a technique at Camp Detrick for mass producing the toxoid. By summer 1944 Detrick's D (Defensive) Division had manufactured and stockpiled more than 4,000 gallons of botulinum toxoid, enough to immunize approximately 700,000 personnel.

But in the spring of 1944 the work on a retaliatory biological weapon was lagging when Prime Minister Winston Churchill directed Ernest Brown, chairman of the British Bacteriological Warfare Committee, to place an order for 500,000 anthrax biological bombs from the Americans. Although American military contractors could mass produce that quantity of empty bombs easily enough, filling them all with anthrax spores was a problem. Camp Detrick's factories were pilot plants, not production plants; being test beds or prototypes rather than true mass production facilities. In the meantime, the Canadians had facilities for producing anthrax at Grosse Ile and the US government agreed to provide 75% of the operating expenses. But by the summer of 1944 the Canadian facility was producing only small quantities of anthrax under unsafe conditions and the facility was closed down. On 20 June 1944, with the British order for 500,000 filled anthrax bombs, the Special Projects Division of the Chemical Warfare Service ordered one million MkI bombs. These bombs, virtually the US copy of the British four-pound Type F bomb, were to be mass produced, filled with anthrax, and packed into clusters. The British were to receive their order and the other 500,000 would remain in the US for possible use.

With the promise of the mass production of anthrax bombs the British formulated a contingency plan to use anthrax in retaliation if Germany used germ warfare. Their estimates, based on field trials and experiments on monkeys, indicated that if six major German cities were simultaneously attacked by heavy bombers carrying forty thousand 500 pound anthrax cluster bombs, approximately 50% of the inhabitants who were exposed to the cloud of anthrax would be killed by inhalation, while many more would probably parish from the subsequent contamination of their skin. The affected region would be contaminated for years and would be uninhabitable as there was no effective method of decontamination or preventative inoculation. To attack these six cities would require 4.25 million four pound bomblets carried by 2,700 heavy bombers. Once mass production was achieved it would have taken eight months to accumulate 4.25 million bombs which would have caused three million fatalities and left the German cities uninhabitable for 40 to 50 years.

The bomb casings and other internal components were to be produced by bomb manufacturer, Electromaster Corporation of Detroit while the high explosives, the Pentolite pellets and Tetryl powder, would be manufactured by the Unexcelled Manufacturing Company of Cranbury, NJ. The anthrax spores would be manufactured by the US Army at its new production center located near the small farm town of Vigo, IN which was located six miles south of Terre Haute. The original 700 acre, $21 million facility was constructed in 1942 as a conventional HE bomb factory but had been decommissioned in July 1943 as the US had a large over capacity of HE bombs. In May 1944 the Army's Special Projects Division contracted the H.K. Ferguson Construction Company to build the necessary fermenter tanks, air compressors, refrigerators, and slurry heaters. Existing buildings were converted to biological laboratories and catalyst and separation buildings, a sewage decontamination plant, and an animal farm were also built.

Vigo was the largest bacterial mass production facility ever created with twelve 20,000 gallon anthrax fermenting tanks that measured about 20 feet wide and 40 feet high. Inserting 240,000 gallons of anthrax slurry into individual bombs was to prove a major problem as a safe mechanical filling apparatus was necessary. The M (Munitions) Division at Camp Detrick explored various commercial high speed filling machines used for loading bags, cans, and bottles with powders (e.g. flour, starch) or liquids (e.g. milk, beer) which needed to be "dustless" or "dripless." But onsite inspection of these filling machines found that a quart or a pound was commonly lost in filling and was considered dripless or dustless for commercial purposes but was not suitable for filling dangerous anthrax bombs. Even pharmaceutical filling machines used for filling bottles with drugs or vaccines emitted imperceptible amounts of spray.

The British, however, had developed a bomb filling machine to load a BW agent into its four pound Type F bomb. The American MkI bomb was nearly identical to the Type F bomb and the British sent a prototype

of its bomb filling machine to Camp Detrick for testing and development. The operator of this filling machine placed an empty bomb casing on the filling platform and the filling head was lowered onto the open end of the bomb when a foot pedal was depressed. The filling head created a small vacuum in the bomb chamber and also fed BW agent slurry into the bomb through a nozzle. Once the bomb chamber was filled, the operator released the foot pedal causing the filling head to rise and move away. The operator then removed the filled bomb off the filling platform. The British machine was fast; filling a bomb in 15 seconds (240 bombs per hour). However, this filling machine had a major disadvantage in that it was not spray proof with the slurry liquid foaming as it was poured into the bomb. The bubbles would burst; spraying particles out to a radius of 20 feet. Although the operator was dressed in protective clothing, gloves, and gas mask, this filling machine was deemed to be unacceptable.

There seemed to be three possible solutions to the filling machine problem: developing a non-foaming agent; carefully pouring the liquid without splashing; placing a rubber diaphragm over the open end of the bomb, puncture the diaphragm with a hollow needle, send the slurry in while simultaneously removing the air displaced by the slurry, and then withdraw the needle. The latter solution was thought to be the most promising from the critical safety aspect but it would require prolonged development and testing, as well as large quantities of rubber which was not readily obtainable during wartime. To get the BW bombs into mass production ASAP Detrick's M Division decided to use the British filling machine without modification but would add a hood and exhaust that would draw in the surrounding air and pathogen spray particles to a safe area. The operator was also placed in an airtight suit. Six British filling machines were built at Detrick and sent to Vigo. Once the bomb casings were filled they would go to the bomb assembly building, where each would be fitted with a detonator and were to be then sent to the separate cluster assembly building where 108 bombs were fitted into an M26 cluster adapter with the entire unit designated as the M33 biological cluster bomb which weighed 500 pounds. An explosive charge at one end would eject the 108 MkI bomblets at a predetermined altitude above the ground and scatter them over a large area. The question in a bomb-delivered BW attack was not how many pathogens were killed in the blast but how many survived and into what environment they were disseminated.

Once Vigo had received the six British-designed bomb-filling machines the safety and security of the Vigo bacterial mass-production system had to be extensively tested and proven. Ira Baldwin selected Walter Nevius, a specialist in pathogen containment methods, to get the Vigo facility certified for safe production of "*INK-B*," the Vigo codename for anthrax. The exacting and cautious safety tests continued slowly and in April 1945 the plant was finally declared air and watertight and in June the first simulated production runs were conducted. Toward the end of the war, the Allies were aware of the limitations of anthrax and the UK stocks of anthrax stored at Porton were incinerated.

The possibilities of other microbial agents were investigated during the war for BW use by many institutions including the National Institute of Health: cholera (HO) and typhus (YE), University of Cincinnati: tularemia (UL), Cornell: anthrax (N), Harvard Medical School: dysentery (Y), Michigan State College: brucellosis (US), Notre Dame: rickettsiae (RI), and Northwestern: mussel toxins (SS). The scientists at Fort Detrick began the investigation of the use of highly infectious Brucellosis which like Mustard Gas, had a low mortality rate of about 2% but could incapacitate a very large percentage of the exposed population. The bomb load required to attack a city was found to be less than one-tenth that of anthrax and the objective would be contaminated for only a matter of days. By VJ-Day, Fort Detrick was in an advanced stage of development of Brucellosis as a weapon. In 1946 the secret wartime testing of effects of the bubonic plague (LE) on 50 San Quentin convicts by the Naval Research Unit (University of California, Berkeley) was revealed. Over 200 men volunteered and after personal interviews and physical fitness examinations 50 were selected and injected with the plague organism. None of the volunteers became dangerously ill with only several having sore arms and headaches two days after the injections. There was no public hue and cry in 1946 over this human testing as there would have been decades later.

At the end of the war there had been some 200 individual projects investigated at Detrick including the priority anthrax spore production program and research on insect-spread diseases and the dissemination of plant diseases. At its peak Detrick employed 2,273 personnel including 1,702 Army, 562 Navy, and 9 civilians. In April 1943, the Chemical Warfare Service had authorized a modest $1.25 million for the required technical facilities, personnel housing, and administration buildings. But only three months later, the cost had risen to $4.3 million to include additional research facilities and equipment. By the end of the war the final cost of Camp Detrick was $12.27 million, not only for Laboratory buildings, the pilot plants, the water, air, and steam-sterilization plants,

the sewage sterilization system, animal incinerators but also for 245 other buildings including enough housing for 5,000 workers, a hospital, fire house, laundry, chapel, theater, library, post exchange, swimming pool, and several recreation halls. Between August 1943 and December 1945, 17 different species and 658,039 individual animals had been utilized in experiments at Detrick including 598,604 white mice, 32,339 guinea pigs, 16,178 rats, 5,222 rabbits, and 4,578 hamsters. The animals were bred on Detrick's own animal farm or supplied by outside facilities that raised animals for laboratory use.

Thankfully, biological warfare was not used during the war but it was evident that BW was a technology that almost any country or faction could successfully develop with little expense involved. Pathogens occurred in nature and someone with only college level biology laboratory proficiency could produce large volumes of dangerous agents quickly and economically with common equipment and ingredients. Development and production could be done in secret making detection virtually impossible. The pathogens did not require dispersal by bombs or explosions but could be spread surreptitiously from spray nozzles or introduced into water supplies with even minuscule quantities able to incapacitate or kill large numbers of people.

15

Psychological Weapons

Leaflets and Leaflet Bombs In the ETO
Organization and Functions

There were three organizations responsible for "white" or overt psychological warfare in the ETO: the Office of War Information (OWI) representing the US State Department, the Political Intelligence Department (PID) representing the British Foreign Office, and the Psychological Warfare Division (PWD) of SHAEF representing the Supreme Commander (Eisenhower). Subversive or "black" propaganda was a separate operation which was the joint responsibility of PID and the Office of Strategic Services (OSS) representing the US War Department. White propaganda, the most common type, originated from a source that identified itself correctly and the information in its message tended to be accurate. Black propaganda originated from a source that was often well concealed and contained a large number of distortions or complete falsehoods. Grey propaganda fell somewhere between. Various civilian agencies were responsible for the political aspects of propaganda and the PWD was responsible for the military aspects. Because there was no obvious dividing line between the two, close coordination was necessary between the Tri-Partite Committee that was composed of the Chiefs of the three organizations (OWI, PID, and PWD) and via direct liaison with the operational sections involved.

Before D-Day, all leaflets were produced by the civilian agencies but after D-Day, the PWD produced the great bulk of the leaflets with the civilian agencies acting in an advisory capacity and producing only a few leaflets of a purely political nature. An exception was the newspaper *Nachrichten fur die Truppe* which was produced for PWD by a special PID/OSS editorial team. To perform the detailed mechanics of production and distribution during the post D-Day period there were four echelons in effect, each with its own special aptitude for performing a particular task.

1) The Civilian Agencies (OWI, PID, OSS)

The Civilian Agencies were equipped with complete news gathering facilities, trained writing personnel, typographical and printing plants, as well as art and layout personnel. Their writing facilities produced news sheets and periodicals directed to the civilians of enemy occupied countries and for special strategic leaflets directed to enemy civilians. In addition, the special news gathering facilities available to PID and OSS made

them the logical group to edit *Nachrichten,* the daily "grey" newspaper in German which was originally designed exclusively for dropping on German troops but later was dropped to German civilians as well. A Joint Production Unit was established by these agencies to manage all leaflets printed in the UK

2) Psychological Warfare Division/Supreme Headquarters Allied Expeditionary Force

PWD/SHAEF was a special section of Gen. Eisenhower's staff set up to conduct all the psychological warfare activities of SHAEF. It worked in

PWD/SHAEF was a special section of Gen. Eisenhower's staff set up to conduct all the psychological warfare activities of SHAEF. It included its own writing and printing unit and controlled a special leaflet squadron of AAF heavy bombers. (AAF)

close co-ordination with other staff sections, particularly G-2, G-3, and G-5 and thus was able to plan psychological warfare campaigns as an integral part of military operations. The Leaflet Section of PWD/SHAEF included its own writing unit, controlled a special leaflet squadron of AAF heavy bombers , and a packing and trucking unit for providing British-based aircraft with leaflet bombs. Among PWD/SHAEF functions were:

1) Policy guidance of and coordination with the Leaflet Units at the Army Group level.

2) The production of general tactical and strategic leaflets with the exception of a few special strategic leaflets on political themes produced by the civilian agencies.

3) The distribution of all General Tactical Leaflets from the UK, and jointly with PID, the distribution of all Strategic Leaflets.

4) The production and delivery to the Army Groups of SHAEF leaflets required for their own distribution.

5) The preparation and distribution of reaction reports and similar material designed to facilitate and expand the leaflet operation by explaining its nature and emphasizing its importance.

6) Liaison with the Air Forces for the production or procurement of leaflet bombs, packing into bombs, and delivery of all leaflets to the airfields.

7) Co-ordination with the Joint Production Unit.

In actual practice, the Leaflet Section assumed an even greater proportion of the total Allied leafleting effort than had been originally planned. Its Special Leaflet Squadron was the only Air Force unit under the operational control of PWD and therefore, the only one available at all times for distribution where and when it was most necessary. Because production and trucking facilities in the UK were superior to those on the Continent the great proportion (approximately 90%) of all air-dropped leaflets, both tactical and strategic, were produced in the UK and dropped by UK-based heavy bombers .

3) Psychological Warfare Units of the Army Groups
Leaflet functions at Army Groups varied according to the equipment and personnel available to the Army Group and Army Teams, respectively. Two factors controlled Army Group leaflet activities: first, overall propaganda lines were determined at the SHAEF level, and second, the Army Teams because of their forward locations and better tactical intelligence, were the ideal agencies for the output of purely tactical propaganda.

4) Army Psychological Warfare Teams
Army Psychological Warfare Teams were best able, because of their forward location and rapid intelligence, to exploit local tactical situations with combat leaflets aimed at specific enemy units and positions. Much of the effectiveness of the Army Team resulted from its unique ability to produce and distribute these leaflets quickly and, in particular, to direct coordinated loudspeaker and leaflet missions at the request of local commanders.

These Teams, which functioned either under G-2 or as separate units, were hindered by initial shortages of personnel and equipment. They often improvised in the field, printing on mobile equipment and in local printing facilities when these were available. Near the end of the war Army Teams were responsible for the distribution by artillery shell and fighter bombers of a million or more leaflets daily.

Coordination between Echelons
After D-Day, as the leaflet operations became more tactical, SHAEF produced a larger percentage of the leaflets and the civilian agencies limited themselves to general policy supervision except in situations where political issues were involved and it was necessary for the leaflet and radio propaganda to be closely coordinated. They continued, however, to edit *Nachrichten* which became more important and in the closing months of the campaign accounted for about 60% of the available airlift space. The pattern of coordination between SHAEF and each of the Army Groups was basically similar.

Types of Leaflets
Leaflet Newspapers
Early in the war the distribution of news was found to be the most effective method to undermine enemy morale and to get his attention to read the underlying surrender offer.

Nachrichten fur die Truppe
Nachrichten fur die Truppe (*News for the Troops*) was the creation of famous English Black Propagandist, Sefton Delmer, and was produced in close cooperation with the Headquarters of the Supreme Commander by a joint British PID and American OSS body planned especially for D-Day and after. Its effectiveness was due to indirect propaganda focused on undermining the German soldier's belief in his leaders and convincing

Nachrichten fur die Truppe (*News for the Troops*) was a form of indirect propaganda focused on undermining the German soldier's belief in his leaders and convincing him of the inevitability of defeat. (AAF)

him of the inevitability of defeat. Originally it was intended to be solely a tactical newspaper but later was also dropped on civilians.

The newspaper was normally composed and printed at PID HQ outside London between 2200 hours of one day and 0600 hours of the next and would then be dropped at night 18 to 24 hours later (although daylight drops did take place at shorter intervals). The newspaper employed about 25 writers and editors and between 70 and 80 printers and distribution staff. The typical paper consisted of 10,000 to 12,000 words with several photographs and a half million daily copies and occasionally more. The finished newspapers were transported to airfields and packed in bombs and dropped by the Special Squadron of the 8AF on general and pinpoint targets selected in daily conferences between military and PWD staff. The initial run totaled 200,000 single sheet copies but soon reached one million. By the time of the last issue No. 381 on 9 May 1945, a total of 159,898,973 copies of *Nachrichten fur die Truppe* had been run.

This daily leaflet newspaper originally was printed on a two sided 13 x 9 inch page and later on two double-sided pages. On the front page and in columns on the back page, the German soldier read accurate news from all fronts with his own Western Front covered in detail. This news was usually received before the Germans received it from their own sources. The articles continually emphasized that before and during the Normandy campaign that the Russian Front was the only one considered important by the Nazi Party and the High Command and Western Front was characterized as an example of useless sacrifice and division of strength. On page two was the daily commentary by "Lt. von 0" who conveyed a critical and resentful attitude to the conduct of the war on both

the front and at home. He gave a rational for the German soldier to have no faith in the Nazi Party and to save himself by surrendering. On page three, the German soldier found disquieting news from home, suggesting the blatant inequality in the sacrifices made by the soldier at the front compared to the life lead by Party leaders and read of the disparity of the ordinary civilian and the Party member. He was told of conditions in the bombed out cities, of the food shortages, and black markets in the Homeland. As a further incentive to pick up and read the leaflet page three also featured a daily photo of a pin up girl. Often, *Nachrichten* provided the German soldier his first news of important military events such as the Allied landing in the south of France or the crossing of the Rhine. Because the newspaper gained a reputation for reliability in its war news many readers unconsciously transferred this reliability to its German home front news. *Nachrichten fur die Truppe* was able to combine the functions of a political leaflet, a strategic leaflet, and at times, of a tactical leaflet. Its main difference from other Allied leaflets was that in style; the newsy tone, sports news, and pin-up pictures, it was devised to persuade the German soldier that the paper was not just an obvious propaganda device.

L'Amerique en Guerre

The *L'Amerique en Guerre* (America in War) was a four page, 8.5x10.5, weekly newspaper dropped by the millions on France. The paper was intended to keep up the spirits of French population by informing them of the "true" course of the war. Similar newspapers were dropped on the populations of other occupied countries.

Frontpost

Frontpost was a weekly, semi-tactical newspaper produced in the field by the Twelfth Army Group without the benefit of the extensive civilian assistance that was available to the *Nachrichten* in the UK. *Frontpost*, usually slightly less timely than *Nachrichten*, was specially intended for the requirements of the particular Army Group front and similarly to a combat leaflet that stressed surrender. It was to be distributed by fighter bombers and medium bombers. An abridged version, called the *Feldpost*, was provided to the lower echelons for distribution by artillery shells.

General Tactical Leaflets

The General Tactical Leaflet was usually produced by PWD/SHAEF and dropped by the Special Leaflet Squadron from the UK. There were of two types of General Tactical Leaflets depending on the general status of the war at the time. All these leaflets emphasizing surrender were directed at the individual German soldier during the German's disheartening retreat as distinguished from leaflets written for particular units in locally limited situations.

During periods of static battle situations the General Tactical Leaflets dealt with general subjects; either with news in its largest strategic sense or exclusively with the surrender theme, the treatment of prisoners, and the prospects of the individual soldier reader in the future. General surrender propaganda comprised by far the largest portion of the General Tactical Leaflets dropped and were a documented success.

During times of rapid mobile warfare only the general aspects of the developing strategy could be included in the General Tactical Leaflets as they required several days to produce. However, due to close liaison with the Army Groups, the leaflets produced by SHAEF could exploit the main tactical developments during the movement east into a well coordinated series of leaflets; from then D-Day landings, the Normandy breakout, the battle of the Falaise pocket, the assault on the West Wall, the Battle of the Bulge, and finally, the crossing of the Rhine. After the Normandy breakout these leaflets could only be distributed in the required great quantities by bombers dropping them along the enemy's line of constant retreat.

WEEKLY NEWSPAPER, several million copies of which are dropped monthly over France by AAF planes, consists of four pages, 8½ by 10½ in. Similar issues are dropped on other occupied countries.

L'Amerique en Guerre (**America in War**) (AAF)

Local Tactical Leaflets

Local Tactical Leaflets included those produced in response to a temporary battle situation which needed to be exploited by a quickly produced and distributed leaflet. These leaflets were produced by a local Team and were dispensed by either artillery or fighter bombers .

Strategic Leaflets

Strategic Leaflets were wholly managed from the rear echelon where the necessary large production facilities were located and were distributed by heavy bombers except for a small quantity of fighter bomber disseminated Army leaflets directed to specific German communities in the final stages of the war. There were three main types of Strategic Leaflets:

1) General Leaflets were designed to undermine confidence in the government and in the outcome of the war. As soon as the Allies entered Germany, instructional-type leaflets required higher priorities and these leaflets were seldom used.

2) Civilian Instruction Leaflets consisted of warnings to specified communities, evacuation orders, instructions on how to save a town by surrender, on disbandment of the local Volkssturm, etc. They were exclusively produced by SHAEF and dropped by heavy bombers .

3) Foreign Worker Leaflets were produced by SHAEF and distributed by heavy bombers from the UK. These leaflets pursued the dual purpose of waging psychological warfare against the German authorities and of issuing practical instructions to the widely dispersed foreign worker component in Germany.

Official Instruction Leaflets

Official Instruction Leaflets were carefully produced with attention to the selection of type layout, reproduction of insignia, and in their printing these leaflets were intended to convey the official prestige of the Allied Governments and Eisenhower, the Supreme Commander personally.

The *Safe Conduct* leaflet was the most important of the Official Instructional Leaflets. It was designed as a document complete with the crests of Great Britain and the United States, the SHAEF insignia, and the signature of the Supreme Commander. This leaflet embodied the relevant provisions of the Geneva Convention and instructed the Allied outposts to take the bearer prisoner and treat him decently. This leaflet was so successful that throughout the leaflet campaign it was mixed in the proportion of 10% and later 15% with all other combat leaflets dropped. In tactically favorable situations bombs filled with only *Safe Conducts* were dropped on German troops. A study found that three quarters of the Germans who surrendered in the last months of the war carried or used *Safe Conduct* leaflets.

Even as defeatism spread through the German Army, it became increasingly obvious that exhortations and the reasons for surrendering

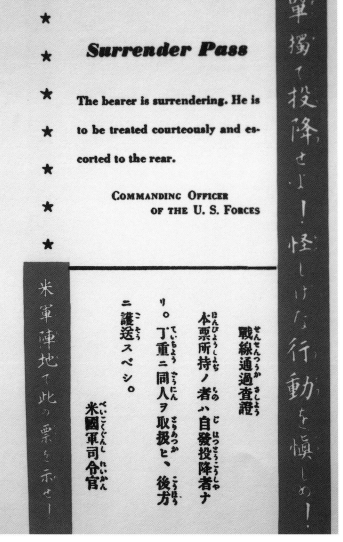

continued to be insufficient to overcome the dishonor and strong obedience to orders which prevented German soldiers from surrendering in large numbers. Consequently, the *Surrender Order* was designed to appear as an official order from the German Command to surrender. SHAEF issued orders to use the *Surrender Order* only in overwhelming tactical situations where there was a good probability that German soldiers would use it as a reason for surrendering.

Many of the civilian instruction leaflets, those directed to foreign workers, and the official instructions to specific occupational groups, such as to railroad workers came under this classification.

Black Leaflets

Black Leaflets were the joint top secret creation of the PID and the OSS and were designed to appear to originate from official enemy sources and were a very effective form of propaganda as they accomplished their aims by subtlety and misdirection. Black Leaflets included a large number of themes but, in general, were designed to undermine the soldier's confidence in the competence of the Nazi Party and the High Command (or the Emperor or Code of Bushido in the Pacific). Leaflets such as forged German food and clothing coupons, travel orders, etc. were intended to add to administrative difficulties and provide additional work for the SS and the Gestapo.

Combat Leaflet Content

All leaflets intended for the German soldier constantly dealt with the topic of captivity, incidentally or as a main theme. The theme of good treatment in captivity was a constant in the leaflets and many German soldiers kept the *Safe Conducts* leaflet on their person. Mention of the Allied adherence to the provisions of the Geneva Convention proved to be a great asset and was used throughout the campaign. It was found that the German soldier felt that surrender was tantamount to desertion and was dishonorable so the leaflets did not encourage surrender outright but used other suggestions to show that continued combat was futile. To appeal to his honor there was a deliberate policy to continuously highlight the great bravery of the German soldier but to also show how he was confronted by an overwhelming superiority of war material against which his soldierly qualities were useless.

As the leaflet program progressed and more intelligence on the German soldier accumulated, it became evident that a number of obvious propaganda ploys were either ineffective or could not be used for policy reasons. The suggestion of a revolt by either German soldiers or civilians was not considered as they both were under too much restraint to make this line of propaganda even remotely effective. Personal attacks on Hitler were ineffective as the German soldier's attachment to his Fuehrer was dedicated and often mystical. The objective became not to convert the soldier but to get him to surrender. In the final stages of the war the Allies unconditional surrender policy caused the German soldier to fight more rigorously to defend the Fatherland and made it necessary to concentrate on the futility of fighting on and to offer postwar Germany a democratic way of life.

Civilian Leaflet Content

As the Allies reached the Rhine, defeatism was widespread in Germany but the acceptance of Nazism was so complete and so effectively enforced by terror that many of the surrender leaflets were read and met with the answer "You are right, but what can we do?" The problem therefore, was to suggest measures the German population could do to speed the end of the war without immediately risking their lives. Incitements to revolution were not used except in the final collapse situation when they took the form of recommending steps to cause the surrender of towns or villages. Among the principal leaflet themes directed toward German civilians were to evacuate specified areas, designed as "danger areas" and to avoid the needless destruction of towns and villages by surrendering. There was an anti-Volksturm and talk-to-the-soldier campaign to save the needless loss of life and property.

Leaflet Dispersal

Ideally, a leaflet dispersal was to employ all means of distribution; artillery for pinpoint local tactical leaflets, fighter bombers for tactical targets out of the reach of artillery, medium bombers for close in strategic and semi-tactical leaflets and heavy bombers for strategic leaflets directed toward enemy civilians far behind the lines. In this campaign, however, due to the superior production facilities in the UK, and the fact that the only aircraft continuously under the operational control of the Psychological Warfare Division (PWD) were the Special Leaflet Squadron of the 8th Air Force, the great bulk of SHAEF leaflets, both strategic and tactical, were distributed by UK-based heavy bombers. 9AF medium bombers were used for a few weeks after D-Day for special tactical leaflet missions but as soon as they moved to the Continent, these operations ceased owing to lack of communications and transportation facilities. From then until the closing months of the war when arrangements were made for the distribution of the 12th Army Group weekly newspaper *Frontpost*, little use was made of 9AF medium bombers .

8AF Special Leaflet Squadron

The most effective leaflet distribution by PWA/SHAEF was done by a squadron of heavy bombers especially assigned for leaflet operations by the 8th Air Force. This Special Leaflet Squadron sent out an average of 10 aircraft per night, weather permitting. These aircraft went out individually, each covering as many as five targets per night selected by the Leaflet Section, PWA/SHAEF. This squadron accomplished the bulk of the leaflet distribution from the UK and was used primarily for the distribution of general tactical leaflets on targets on all sectors of the front, at the request of the Army Groups.

Leaflet Section, PWA/SHAEF, Rear

The Leaflet Section, PWA/SHAEF, Rear, which was located at Headquarters 8th Air Force, received wire requests direct from the Army Groups and Armies for *Nachrichten* and standard general tactical leaflets, such as *Safe Conduct, You are Surrounded, etc.*, on targets in their areas. Based on these requests, each morning the Leaflet Section made up a list of targets and loads for the available aircraft for that night and telephoned them direct to the Operations Officer of the Squadron. This was the only AAF unit which was permanently and directly under the operational control of a psychological warfare organization and it enabled the PWA to deliver leaflets to any targets they selected at the time when they were most needed.

The great advantages of the Leaflet Section and Special Leaflet Squadron are obvious. In addition to making it possible to direct leaflets to targets when they were most needed it also made it possible for the PWA to write and produce special leaflets with assurance that they were delivered where intended. This enabled them to write messages addressed specifically to the inhabitants of a particular town or region which greatly increases the effectiveness of the leaflets. In the closing days of the ETO campaign when the demand for leaflets on the demoralized enemy was at its height the 8th Air Force made an additional squadron available for leaflet operations.

The most effective leaflet distribution by PWA/SHAEF was done by a squadron of B-17s especially assigned for leaflet operations by the **8th Air Force Special Leaflet Squadron**. This B-17, *Mickey Finn* of the 422nd Leaflet Squadron and others were painted all black and survived 151 missions. (AAF)

Aircraft for Special Leaflet Missions

Heavy, medium, and fighter bombers were used for leaflet distribution in the ETO. Each possessed certain unique qualifications for the particular task performed and the use of all three types of aircraft was essential to the successful execution of the leaflet effort. In this campaign, however, due to the superior production facilities in the UK and due to the fact that the Special Leaflet Squadron was the only distributing unit continuously under the operational control of PWA the great bulk of SHAEF leaflets, both strategic and tactical, were distributed by that unit. This was not an ideal arrangement as much of this distribution could have been done more economically and with greater accuracy in daylight operations by medium and fighter bombers based on the Continent had these aircraft been made permanently available for special leaflet operations.

Heavy Bombers

Heavy bombers possessed the obvious advantages for leaflet operations with their superior range and load-carrying capacity. As used in the Special Leaflet Squadron of the 8AF, each B-24 could drop 960,000 leaflet units on as many as five separate targets per sortie. In the operations of the Special Squadron, the large number of targets covered per mission and the efficiency of enemy air defenses necessitated night operations by aircraft flying singly. Although the leaflet bombing was done from high altitude at night by instruments, the wide dispersion of leaflets after the bombs burst gave sufficient coverage, and prisoner reaction figures show conclusively that a large percentage of leaflets dropped by the Special Leaflet Squadron heavies reached their target areas.

At the request of PWA the 8th Air Force made available heavy bombers for special leaflet missions on several occasions. Regular bombing missions however obviously had priority and it was only on a few special occasions such as the attempt on Hitler's life on 20 July 1944 that the AAF was disposed to make this special lift available.

Medium Bombers

Leaflet missions by the Ninth Air Force B-26s were carried out in daylight at medium altitudes, with each aircraft dropping twenty T-3s or six T-1 leaflet bombs, or approximately 480,000 leaflet units. Daylight operations at lower altitudes permitted greater accuracy but of course the range of mediums was considerably less than that of heavies, and the daylight missions necessitated formation flying and fighter escort, which reduced flexibility to some extent.

Medium bombers of the 9AF based in the UK were made available for the special tactical leaflet missions but when the 9AF moved to the Continent the lack of communications and transportation facilities made it impossible to continue this operation. However, during the closing months of war these aircraft were also made available for special leaflet missions to distribute the Twelfth Army Group weekly newspaper *Frontpost*.

Fighter Bombers

Pinpoint low-altitude leafleting of tactical targets beyond the range of artillery was the job of the fighter bombers of the various tactical air commands. These missions were flown at the request of the Army Psychological Warfare liaison officer and made an extremely valuable contribution to the leaflet operation. Regular operational missions, however, had priority.

P-47s were able to carry six T-3 bombs (three clustered under each wing) and sometimes nine (with three additional in the belly tank position) giving them a maximum load of 135,000 leaflet units. The accuracy of their low level bombing and the proximity of their bases to Army teams producing tactical combat leaflets made fighter bombers the ideal instrument for dissemination of these leaflets to areas immediately behind the front lines. Distribution by fighter bombers was carried out by means of special leaflet missions arranged through the air commands.

Regular Bombing Missions Dropping Leaflets

Royal Air Force

The bombers of the RAF carried bundles of leaflets on their regular operational missions over enemy territory. These leaflets were released through the flare chute or bomb bay at or near the target and in this way very substantial quantities of leaflets were distributed over enemy territory. The disadvantages of this system were that the Political Intelligence Department (PID) which coordinated this operation had no information before the mission of the target to be attacked and therefore had no control over the selection of leaflets or the quantities of leaflets which were dropped on each target. Also leaflets dropped loose at bombing altitudes often drifted considerable distances before reaching the ground.

Eighth Air Force

On each major bombing mission of the 8AF, a maximum of 12 aircraft were loaded with leaflet bombs. Each aircraft carried 10 leaflet bombs so that on a mission a maximum of 9,600,000 leaflet units could be distributed. Arrangements were made with the 8th Air Force to inform the Leaflet Section, PWA/SHAEF Rear, of the targets when the mission was

The box located under the engine nacelle of this Special Leaflet Squadron B-17 was an **exhaust flame damper** to prevent the bomber's detection during the nighttime leaflet dropping operations. (AAF)

descended the same distance in three and a half minutes. The suggested altitude at which leaflets were to be dropped was from tree top level to 5,000 feet. A bundle limited to 500 leaflets or less was held together with a piece of string or rubber band near the end of the bundle. When dispensed from 25,000 feet the leaflet bundles thrown or dropped into the slip stream broke up immediately and the individual leaflets began their random descent and could land 40 to 50 miles from their intended target. It was estimated that an average of only 4% of the leaflets dropped by this method were picked up by the intended individuals.

Quick Release Leaflet Packs "Nickels"
In summer 1943 the 8AF began to deliver 45,000 pounds of leaflets weekly as part of its bombing missions. After 14 July, the five Bomb Groups of the First Air Wing were designated to drop 25 pound 8.5x10.5x7.25 inch bundles of 6,500 leaflets, code-named "*Nickels*," that were hand-dispensed through flare chutes and windows. This dispensing method was inefficient and special leaflet containers, adapted from hinged wood packing cases were developed to be carried in bomb bays to be released after a formation's bombs had been dropped. The cover of the case was held down to the bottom of the box by the four "traveling" cords which attached to the middle of the bottom leaflet container's four corners. The case was attached to the aircraft by a static line attached to the traveling cords. The wooden cases were inverted between the outboard and inboard bomb racks of a B-17 with a releasable shackle attached to the lid. The standard bomb control system released the shackle and the lid swung open and the leaflet bundles dropped out. Once out of the bomber the slip stream would cause pressure on the traveling cords and pull the lid off the box, scattering the leaflets. However, when released care had to be taken that the leaflet bundles would stay clear of the tail surfaces and the propellers or engines of following bombers .

Modified Quick Release Leaflet Pack
The next attempt at better leaflet release was the 25 pound Modified Quick Release Leaflet Pack which was specially fabricated from two heavy cardboard rectangular boxes with a top box acting as a cover that was as large as the bottom box. This large top box cover fit inside the bottom box instead of the outside. The cover box was secured to the outside bottom box by four cords attached to the side of the box and crossing the corners diagonally. The entire unit was attached by a static line secured to the center of the top box. When dropped or pushed out of carrying aircraft the static line would hold onto the top cover box and the leaflets in the free-falling bottom box were dispersed by falling through the air.

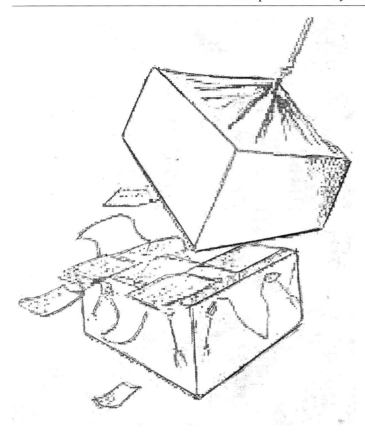

Modified Quick Release Leaflet Pack (AAF)

planned, so that they were able to specify the leaflet and the quantities which were to be dropped on each target. This had the obvious advantage of allowing PWA to specify a reasonable quantity and the proper leaflet for each target, and also, to avoid covering the same target with the same leaflet on successive missions. As the 8AF (and RAF) bombed targets deep in Germany which were beyond the range of the Special Leaflet Squadron, they were used primarily for the distribution of strategic leaflets addressed to the German civilian population.

Leaflet Bombs and Delivery
In early World War II the British developed a psychological warfare program which mainly consisted of dropping loose propaganda leaflets over German-occupied territory but these were considered only as providing toilet paper to the then victorious Germans. As defeat loomed Allied leaflet dropping warfare probably further demoralized the German soldiers and civilians and the leaflets aimed at civilians in occupied territories lifted their morale as they received news of the progress of the war.

The RAF initially hand-dropped packed leaflet bundles through the flare chute, an open door, or through the bomb bay to break open and scatter in the slip stream. Most of the leaflets were small so that the finder could conceal them into his pocket to read in private. The bulk leaflets arrived from the British printer and were packed into card wrapped bundles tied by a cord which had to be tied properly; not too tight nor too loose. Tied too tightly they fell like a brick to the ground and those too loosely tied came apart in the slipstream immediately after release and could clog engine air intakes of following bombers. A leaflet of one sheet was calculated to fall 1,000 feet in five minutes, a double-sheeted leaflet

Barometric Release Mechanism (AAF)

T-1 Monroe Leaflet Bomb being filled with leaflets. The T-1 was a strong laminated card container in which the M-17 Aimable Incendiary Clusters were shipped. These cylindrical containers were 48 inches long with a diameter of 16.5 inches and had two cardboard end caps. (AAF)

Later a barometric release mechanism was employed which was a four inch diameter canister containing a bellows which compressed when it reached heavier atmosphere and eventually pulled a pin that released the cord around the leaflet box.

T-1, -2, and -3 Leaflet Bomb Series

It was obvious that a leaflet bomb was required with a trajectory that would permit a reasonably accurate drop and which would open to release leaflets at a low altitude. Three types of leaflet bomb, the T-1, -2, to -3 series, were eventually accepted as standard for use in this theatre by the AAF.

T-1 Leaflet Bomb

The method of carrying and dispersing the leaflets continued to be unsatisfactory, so Capt. James Monroe, the 422nd Bomb Squadron's Armament Officer, explored the possibility of a new leaflet bomb that

would break apart to release its contents at lower altitudes, like the new M-17 Aimable Incendiary Cluster. While studying the M-17, he discovered the strong laminated card containers in which the M-17s were shipped. These cylindrical containers were 48 inches long with a diameter of 16.5 inches and had two cardboard end caps. Monroe added light steel bands and U-brackets to them so that a container could be easily adapted to hang from a standard bomb shackle to be carried and released like a conventional bomb carrying 300 pounds of leaflets. To release the leaflets Monroe drilled a series of 0.5 inch holes along the tube container, across one end cap, and then back on the opposite side of the tube. He then passed double strands of standard explosive primer cord through the holes, securing both ends to a T-39 time fuse, which was fitted into a wooden block on the other end cap. A static test of the explosive charge resulted in the container being split neatly in two. The first test drop took place over The Wash estuary on the English east coast on 21 January 1944 when a B-17 dropped the leaflet bomb from 30,000 feet. Monroe and Maj. Earle Aber, the 422BS CO, flew in an A-20 at 5,000 feet to observe the bomb that failed to release the leaflets. Two weeks later the next test over The Wash was very successful when the container with a five second fuse was dropped from 10,000 feet and opened as planned at 2,000 to 2,500 feet, theoretically concentrating 80,000 leaflets over a square mile. After several more test drops, four Norwegian towns were the targets for the first operational use which took place on the night of 18/19 April 1944. Subsequent intelligence reports revealed that the fuses had been set for too low release and the leaflet distribution had been poor.

T-2 Leaflet Bomb

The dropping technique was rapidly improved and the Monroe Bombs proved to be effective but there was a limited supply of the M-17 packing containers to meet the demand. The ordnance maintenance unit at Melchbourne Park was scheduled to mass produce the leaflet bomb but as a temporary expedient the chemical company in charge of the nearby Sharnbrook incendiary bomb dump was to manufacture as many of the Monroe Leaflet bombs as possible. Melchbourne Park began mass production of the newly designated T-2 in mid-May. In place of the scrap M-17 incendiary cases, specially-made laminated card cases 60 inches long by 18 inches in diameter were manufactured by a British contractor. Instead of being threaded through holes, the primer cord was now held

T-1 leaflet containers weighing 300 pounds being loaded into a 422nd Leaflet Squadron B-17. (AAF)

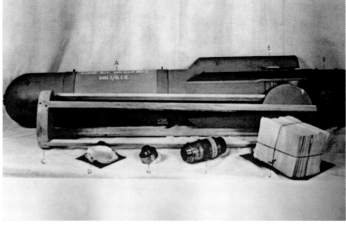

The **T-2 Leaflet Bomb** was a specially-made laminated card case 60 inches long by 18 inches in diameter were manufactured by a British contractor. (AAF)

under a paper strip with adhesive and a more suitable British 860A type fuse was used. Fins could also be attached to give the bomb better stability and accuracy when dropped. The T-2 was usually fused to burst at 2,000 to 2,500 feet setting off the primer cord which split the container releasing the leaflets which covered an area of 600 by 150 feet. It was first employed operationally on 20 June 1944 and thereafter became the standard leaflet container used by 8th Air Force heavy bombers. Melchbourne produced 75,277 T-2s of which approximately 55,000 were used operationally, carrying approximately 90% of the AAF leaflet total during the remainder of the war.

T-3 Bomb
The T3 Leaflet bomb was converted from the American M-26 Parachute Flare by an RAF officer for use by both British and American fighter and bomber aircraft. The bomb case was a 50 inch long and 8 inch diameter cylinder with a streamlined nose and tail to assist trajectory. It could hold between 14,000-15,000 standard sized 8.5 inch x 5.25 inch leaflets which were held in bundles inside a wooden frame which was inserted into the bomb. A small explosive charge set off by either an American M-111 clockwork fuse or a British 860A barometric fuse ejected this frame after the bomb's release. The bomb, whose first operational use was in July 1944, was to be used only over enemy troops or territory as the empty containers were a danger to anyone under them. The B-17 could carry 30 T-3s, the B-24 30+, and the B-25 or B-26 could carry up to 20, or three when included in a normal lethal bomb load, and a fighter bomber could carry up to nine.

422BG Leaflet Campaign
In late summer 1943 the 422BS of the 305BG at Chelveston experimented with the feasibility of using B-17s in night bombing operations. It was soon determined that the B-17 was not suited to conduct RAF-type night attacks but it was revealed that leaflet dropping could well be adapted to individual aircraft flying under the cover of darkness. The Special Leaflet Squadron (or later as the Night Leaflet Squadron), as the 422nd became known, commenced regular leaflet operations with a drop on Paris on the night of 7/8 October 1943. Occasionally, a few bombers in normal bomb groups continued to be required to carry and dispense leaflets on occasions, particularly over out of range German homeland targets.

The 422nd normally sent out between two and eight bombers during a night's operations during its first six months. The bombers operated individually, each often visiting four to seven locations to drop leaflets. Most sorties were flown at over 30,000 feet to enable the release to be made on a Gee navigation fix when possible. Flying at this high altitude, with the bomber's course planned to include frequent changes of direction, helped minimize the chance of interception by dangerous *Luftwaffe* night fighters.

During spring 1944 the 422BS was also employed as the Pathfinder unit for 1st Bomb Division, using different aircraft and crews for both the PFF and leaflet mission. Essentially, it became two squadrons in one but this circumstance was finally settled in June when the leaflet constituent, 14 B-17s and 16 crews, moved to Cheddington and became the 858BS. In August it was redesignated as the 406BS and converted from B-17s to B-24s, due to an anticipated shortage of B-17s. The B-24 could carry 12 leaflet bombs compared with nine in the B-17 but a fully-loaded B-24 was more difficult to fly at the high altitudes used by the Leaflet Squadron. The new B-24s would replace the Squadron's aging B-17s by natural attrition but two additional B-24s arrived in July to help the Squadron meet its increasing mission load. In October, with 12 B-17s and eight B-24s in inventory, the Squadron dispensed double the leaflet tonnage compared with the previous May. The Squadron's mission load continued to increase

and in November 1944 seven crews and aircraft from 492BG were detached to Cheddington for a month to aid the Night Leaflet Squadron. The number of B-17s in the 422nd gradually declined and by April 1945, the 422nd maintained a maximum inventory of 22 B-24s and six B-17s which were used for very high altitude releases over dangerous drop areas. When returning from his 51st mission in a B-17, Squadron CO, Lt. Col. Earle Aber was killed by friendly AA fire near Harwich during one of the last *Luftwaffe* air raids on England.

In July 1944 six regular 8AF heavy bomb groups (the 91st, 306th, 445th, 447th, 487th, and 491st), two in each division, were designated to carry leaflets when required. Beginning 5 July an average eight aircraft in every mission carried only leaflets to dispense over the target area. Until VE-Day these groups continued to provide one or two bombers per mission to carry only leaflet bombs. On 8 May 1945, the last 8AF heavy bomber mission of the war was flown by 12 B-17s of 306BG dropping leaflet bombs over German cities.

After D-Day the 422nd Squadron dropped 3,734 tons of leaflets (1,577,000,000 leaflets) during the war which compares with 2,086 tons (1,176,000,000 leaflets) delivered by regular 8AF heavy bomb groups on bombing missions.

Summary
A total of approximately 5,997,000,000 leaflet units were distributed over Europe by aircraft based in the UK which began when the RAF dropped leaflets over Kiel on 3/4 September 1939, and continued on an increasing scale until the unconditional surrender of Germany in May 1945. During this time, the objectives and methods of this leaflet distribution underwent considerable changes in order to keep pace with the developments of war.

In the pre-D-Day period, 2,750,000,000 leaflets were distributed; 2,151,000,000, by the RAF and 599,000,000 by the 8th Air Force which started leaflet operations in August 1943. In the early phases these leaflets were almost entirely of a long range political nature. After the Germans occupied most of Western Europe and the maintenance of morale and the spirit of resistance in these countries became of paramount importance, a large proportion of the leaflets were aimed at the inhabitants of these occupied countries. With the Allied landings on D-Day, the leaflet campaign became a closely integrated part of the military operations. From D-Day on, although the Army Groups and Army Psychological Warfare Units in the field produced substantial quantities of leaflets for local distribution by fighter bombers and artillery, the great bulk of the leaflets (approximately 90%) were produced by PWA/SHAEF and distributed by aircraft based in the UK. Primarily, leaflets fell into two types: tactical leaflets aimed at reducing the enemy's combat strength by impairing morale and persuading the individual soldier to stop fighting and strategic leaflets, designed to make civilians take action to aid Allied military operations. During this period, an astounding total of 3,240,000,000 leaflets were distributed; 405,000,000 by the RAF; 1,577,000,000 by the Special Leaflet Squadron; 1,176,000,000 by the 8AF on daylight bombing missions and 82,000,000 on special leaflet missions by medium bombers of the AEAF before they moved to the Continent.

Leaflet Bombs in the Pacific
The 100 Pound M104 and 500 Pound M105 Leaflet Bombs
In the Pacific the 20AF developed the special M104 and M105 leaflet bombs which were essentially the same as the 100 pound Fragmentation Bomb cluster adapter M15A2 and the 500 pound Fragmentation Bomb cluster adapter M16A1, respectively. The 100 pound M104 was 47.4 inches long and eight inches in diameter and weighed 75.1 pounds and carried 7,350 leaflets weighing 26 pounds. The 500 pound M105 was

59.4 inches long and 13.9 inches in diameter and carried 30,000 leaflets weighing 100 pounds.

These bombs were cylindrical sheet metal cans to which a fin assembly, fuse adapter, and nose locking cup were attached. One half of the cylindrical could be opened to allow the placement of the leaflets. The leaflet bombs were issued empty and unfused and once the leaflets were placed in the bomb and the bomb fused a complete round was created. The mechanical time nose fuse was set for air functioning in order to get the proper dispersal of the leaflets.

Preparation of the Leaflets for Loading
The method described applies to 6x8 inch leaflets but could be used for leaflets of any other size, provided they were folded so as to make up rolls of a correct size. Rolls of leaflets had to be 7.5 inches outside diameter by 5.125 inches high for the M104 and 13.5 inches outside diameter by

The **T3 Leaflet Bomb** was converted from the American M-26 Parachute Flare. The 50 inches long and 8 inches in diameter bomb case cylinder had a streamlined nose and tail to assist trajectory. (AAF)

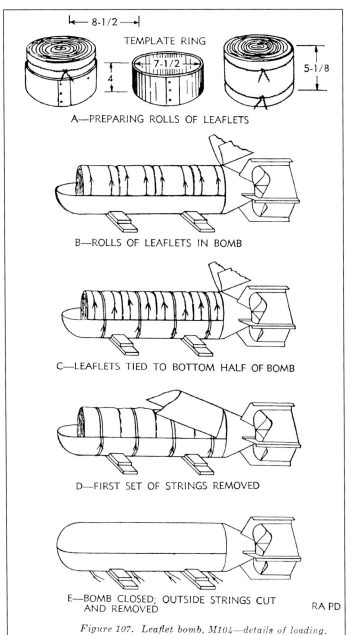

Figure 107. *Leaflet bomb, M104—details of loading.*

d. PREPARATION OF LEAFLETS FOR LOADING BOMB.

(1) *General.* The leaflets must be loaded into the bomb in the form of roll-like bundles (fig. 107). Each roll must be tied tightly and have a sliding fit in the bomb case. It is important that the bomb case be fully loaded. If there are not sufficient leaflets to load the bomb, then use some other filling material but leave the nose compartment empty (except for locking cup). Rolls of leaflets must be 7½ inches outside diameter for the M104 and 13½ inches outside diameter for the M105.

(2) *Preparation of roll.*

Note. The method described below applies to 5- by 8-inch leaflets. However, this same method can be used for leaflets of any other size, provided they are folded so as to make up rolls of a correct size, i.e., 5⅛ (height) x 7½ (diam) inches for the M104 and 5⅛ (height) x 13½ (diam) inches for the M105.

(a) Prepare template rings (fig. 107) made of sheet metal or cardboard. Each ring should be approximately two-thirds of leaflet height, with an inside diameter of 7½ inches for the M104 and 13½ inches for the M105.

(b) Prepare a quantity of cardboard disks (spacers) 7 inches in diameter for the M104 and from 12 to 13 inches in diameter for the M105.

(c) Fill each template ring carefully and tightly with leaflets.

(d) Tie a string tightly around one end of the roll of leaflets. Slide the template towards the string just tied and tie another around the other end of the roll.

(e) Place a cardboard disk on top of the roll upside down, remove the template ring, and store until ready for use.

Preparation of leaflets for Loading (AAF)

5.125 inches high for the M105. A sheet metal or cardboard template was formed to the dimensions listed above and the leaflets were loaded and a string was tightly tied to the newly made roll. The cover of the bomb was opened and the leaflet rolls were inserted in the compartments, placing a cardboard disk on each side of each roll. The leaflet rolls were to fit loosely in their compartments and not bind at the ends. A string was tied around the center of each roll and around the bottom half of the outside of the bomb. Then the strings with which the rolls were originally tied were cut; leaving the second set of strings tied around the bomb. It was important that the bomb case was fully loaded and if there were not enough leaflets to load the bomb some other filling material was to be used. The cover of the bomb was closed and securely locked. The strings on both sides of the bomb were cut near the edges of the cover; freeing all the leaflets so that when the bomb opened, the leaflets dispersed quickly and easily. A time fuse was installed and set for air functioning and an arming wire installed and the bomb was ready to drop. When the bomb was dropped the arming wire was withdrawn from the fuse, and after the set time elapsed, the fuse functioned and the locking mechanism was blown off and the cluster opened and the leaflets were dispersed.

Leaflet Missions and Leaflet Bombs in the Pacific

While not as proliferate as the leaflet operations over Europe, millions of leaflets and hundreds of thousands of newspapers were dropped on the Japanese Homeland in the final months of the war. Leaflet sorties were begun in February 1945 but it was not until May that Gen. Curtis LeMay ordered 100 tons of leaflets to be dropped monthly. The 73BW conducted the first leaflet drops in June 1945 when it combined leaflet bombs with conventional bombs during their weather reconnaissance/bombing missions. Soon only leaflet bombs were dropped as part of weather missions as the effectiveness of the dropping "mental" and "physical" bombs together was questioned. The first leaflets, approved by LeMay, were dropped on a city that was one of 10 listed in the leaflet that was scheduled to be bombed within 72 hours. The leaflets began by stating: "This advance notice will give your military authorities ample time to take the necessary defensive measures to protect you from our inevitable attack. Watch and see how powerless they are to protect you." It continued by warning that the "systematic destruction of city after city will continue as long as you blindly follow your military leaders whose blunders have placed you at the very brink of oblivion. It is your responsibility to overthrow the military government now and save what is left of your beautiful country," and ended by warning the population to evacuate. In

While not as proliferate as the leaflet operations over Europe, millions of leaflets and hundreds of thousands of newspapers were dropped on the Japanese Homeland in the final months of the war. (AAF)

June the 73WB dropped 508 bombs dispersing 15,200,000 leaflets and 101,000 newspapers over Japanese population centers.

In July the 313BW and 314BW joined the 73BW in leaflet missions. The 313BW combined its mining activities with leaflets that emphasized the starvation that would result from the mining blockade of Japanese ports. In July more cities were listed as potential bombing targets and of 31 listed on 5 August 14 were fire bombed by the last day of the war. These forewarnings concerned the B-29 crews but the Japanese AA and interceptor defenses were negligible at the time. In July 1,001 leaflet bombs were dropped dispersing 33,000,000 leaflets and 200,000 newspapers.

Food Drops
Operation Chowhound
On 17 September 1944, *Operation Market Garden* began with the drop of British and American paratroopers over southern Holland as Field Marshall Montgomery's grand plan to end the war before the end of the year. The Dutch Government in Exile called for a railway strike in occupied Holland to help bring about the quick end of the war as this strike would critically obstruct German transport preventing a rapid German response to *Market Garden* in its early stages. The strike did prevent a German counterattack but *Market Garden* failed as it overextended itself at the Bridge Too Far at Arnhem and the Dutch people faced another nine months of war.

As a reprisal for the strike the Nazis placed an embargo on shipments of food to Dutch cities where a large number of citizens relied on rationing for sustenance. Food shipments from neutral countries did help as the embargo was partially lifted in early November 1944, allowing restricted food transport over water. The onset of a particularly severe, cold winter led to the threat of widespread starvation by early 1945. Canals froze over and became impassable for barges and food stocks in the cities in the western Netherlands rapidly dwindled. From September 1944 until early 1945 approximately 30,000 people starved to death in the Netherlands.

Prince Bernhard of the Dutch Royal Family contacted Supreme Allied Commander Gen. Dwight Eisenhower asking him to negotiate a temporary truce so that food could be air dropped over the western Holland. Eisenhower did not have the authority to negotiate with the Germans and referred the Prince to Churchill and Roosevelt. As usual, once politicized, negotiations slowed as the Soviets got involved. Dutch Queen Wilhelmina (in exile in London) then wrote to President Roosevelt, British Prime Minister Churchill, and King George VI, predicting "if a major catastrophe, the like of which has not been seen in Western Europe since the Middle Ages, is to be avoided in Holland, something drastic has to be done now." In the emergency Eisenhower ordered Air Commodore Andrew Geddes to start the development of an aerial relief effort. Geddes was given access to three RAF Bomber Command Groups and three Wings from the US Eighth Air Force. On 23 April US Chief of Staff General George C. Marshall authorized Eisenhower to contact the Germans concerning a temporary truce in the Netherlands. Eisenhower authorized a message to be broadcast over the BBC and Radio Orange announcing that Allied bombers would be flying peaceful missions to deliver food. Upon, receiving the message, Reichskommissar Arthur Seyss-Inquart, the German governor of the Netherlands, initiated meetings with Dutch organizers to determine drop zones and food distribution. However, Seyss-Inquart did not have the authority to approve or discuss SHAEF's proposal but an unofficial truce was arranged. An agreement was reached on corridors of safe passage and where drop zones were to be located to prevent the German flak batteries from firing at the humanitarian aircraft. The Allies informed the Germans and Dutch that *Operation Manna* was to begin while the final details of the surrender of all German forces could be determined.

US Army "10-in-1" Rations were packed in durable rectangular cardboard boxes which were dropped without parachutes. The outer box was closed with sleeve and two metal straps. (AAF)

Long rows of B-29s on Saipan, Guam, and Tinian called **"Conga Lines"** were loaded with supplies to be dropped on American POWs held in Japanese camps. (AAF)

The relief operation, totaling about 11,000 tons, took place from 29 April to 8 May 1945, at the end of World War II. It was to be delivered by combined operations, one conducted by the British and another by the Americans, with the planning of the whole operation done initially by the Royal Air Force. The RAF operation was named after the food, manna, which miraculously appeared for the Israelites in the book of Exodus. The USAAF operation was coded *Chowhound*.

Officials calculated if each bomber dropped 5,000 pounds of emergency rations per trip, two million pounds could be delivered by 400 sorties. To ensure accuracy of the drop and that the food parcels hit the ground relatively undamaged, the Fortresses flew at very low altitude, typically 500 feet or less, and at very slow speed. In March, aircrews conducted trial runs over central England, dropping sand-filled bags from low altitudes at minimum airspeed. No parachutes were used as the ration boxes were stacked on the bomb bay doors which were opened over the designated drop zones so some of the cans inevitably dented. Ground crewmen often rode along on these missions to have their first view of the Continent.

US Army "10-in-1" rations were packed in durable rectangular cardboard boxes. The outer box was closed with a sleeve and two metal straps. The box contained two "first halves" and two "second halves." The first half boxes contained paper and cardboard packaged items such as teas, pre-mixed cereal, biscuits, flour, dried eggs, salt, candy bars, chewing gum, cigarettes and matches. The second half boxes contained canned items such as meat (e.g. corned beef hash, Spam), dehydrated items (e.g. meats and rice), jams, processed cheese, vegetables, condensed or powdered milk, instant coffee), water purifying tablets, a bar of soap, and paper towels. The box also included two small folding can openers and key openers.

On the ground, Dutch working parties assembled to gather and to distribute the rations to the starving population. A large white cross on the ground marked the center of the drop zone. Green flares were fired to indicate the supplies were landing within the agreed drop zones and red flares to indicate that they were straying into danger zones.

AAF B-17s were scheduled to fly a test mission on 28 April but were grounded by bad weather. The first relief flights began early morning

The "10-in-1" box contained two "first halves" and two "second halves." The first half boxes contained paper and cardboard packaged items while the second half boxes contained canned items. Shown are some of the contents of the first half box. (AAF)

on 29 April when two RAF Lancaster bombers flew a test flight at low altitudes and were not fired on by the Germans. Geddes then began the full scale operation later that day with aircraft from RAF Bomber Command Groups 1, 3, and 8 involving 242 Lancasters to drop the food and eight Mosquitoes from 105 and 109 Squadrons to find and mark four drop zones at Leiden, at The Hague, at Rotterdam, and at Gouda. During the mission 239 Lancasters dropped 500 tons of food. Both sides met again on 30 April with Seyss-Inquart, attending in person, and agreeing to an official truce and to increase the number of drop zones to 10 on 2 May.

USAAF *Chowhound* missions flown by the 13CBW, 45 CBW, and 93CBW Groups of the US Third Air Division:

1 May: 396 B-17s dispatched, 393 effective, dropping 767.1 tons on:
The Hague (Volkenburg): 77 B-17s dropped 148.3 tons
The Hague (Duindigt Horse Racetrack): 79 B-17s dropped 153.1 tons
The Hague (Ypenburg Airfield): 81 B-17s dropped 161.0 tons
Rotterdam: 156 B-17s dropped 313.7 tons

2 May: 401 B-17s dispatched, 393 effective, dropping 772.8 tons on:
Schipol Airfield: 250 B-17s dropped 491.7 tons
Vogelenzang: 40 B-17s dropped 79.0 tons
Alkmaar Airfield: 20 B-17s dropped 33.5 tons
Hilversam: 20 B-17s dropped 40.5 tons
Utrecht: 59 B-17s drooped 115.4 tons
Target of Opportunity: 4 B-17s dropped 7.0 tons
(Note: Four B-17s of the 385BG were fired on by German 20mm AA fire which ceased when a green flare was fired)

3 May: 399 B-17s dispatched, 395 effective, dropping 739.1 tons on:
Schipol Airfield: 251 B-17s dropped 472.5tons
Vogelenzang: 42 B-17s dropped 76.7 tons
Alkmaar Airfield: 20 B-17s dropped 37.7 tons
Hilversam: 21 B-17s dropped 37.7 tons
Utrecht: 58 B-17s dropped 108.8 tons
Target of Opportunity: 3 B-17s dropped 5.7 tons

5 May: 403 B-17s dispatched, 392 effective, dropping 737.9 tons on:
Schipol Airfield: 249 B-17s dropped 480.6 tons
Vogelenzang: 40 B-17s dropped 75.4 tons
Alkmaar Airfield: 21 B-17s dropped 37.7 tons
Hilversam: 18 B-17s dropped 30.2 tons
Utrecht: 60 B-17s dropped 113.1 tons
Other Targets: 4 B-17s dropped 7.5 tons

6 May: 383 B-17s dispatched, 381 effective, dropping 689.7 tons on:
Schipol Airfield: 249 B-17s dropped 454.3 tons
Vogelenzang: 37 B-17s dropped 61.8 tons
Alkmaar Airfield: 18 B-17s dropped 32.2 tons
Hilversam: 18 B-17s dropped 30.2 tons
Utrecht: 59 B-17s dropped 111.2 tons

7 May: 231 B-17s dispatched, 229 effective, dropping 406.2 tons on:
Schipol Airfield: 154 B-17s dropped 285.6 tons
Vogelenzang: 25 B-17s dropped 46.2 tons
Alkmaar Airfield: 10 B-17s dropped 18.8 tons
Hilversam: 12 B-17s dropped 22.8 tons
Utrecht: 28 B-17s dropped 52.8 tons

(Note: These flights were not considered combat sorties and the only credits given were to the crews of four 385th Bomb Group B-17s which mistakenly entered into a flak area on the 2 May mission.)

Though the Germans largely withheld their fire, Fortress crews landed at their bases in England to discover bullet holes in wings and fuselages. If enemy AA fire was encountered the bomber was to fire a green flare. Three B-17s were lost during *Chow Hound* operations. A collision claimed two B-17s during assembly and the fiery wreckage fell at Booking in Essex. On the final *Chow Hound* mission, the 95th Bomb Group's B-17 (44-8640) experienced an engine fire caused by ground fire from German infantry near Ijmuiden. The fire threatened to engulf the bomber and the pilot attempted to ditch in the North Sea. The bomber hit a swell causing it to break up and sink almost immediately. Air Sea Rescue retrieved two men but only one survived.

Operations Chowhound and *Manna* continued through the surrender of Germany on May 8. *Manna* delivered 6,680 tons in 3,298 sorties by 3,156 Lancasters (effective). *Chowhound*'s US Third Air Division flew 2,213 sorties by 2,183 B-17s (effective) delivering 4,113 tons. *Operations Chowhound* and *Manna* saved many lives and the drops gave the Dutch not only nourishment but the hope that the war would soon be over. On their first mission *Chowhound* crews observed a large message northwest of the drop zone at Rotterdam, saying "Many Thanks."

Pacific POW Supply Missions
When the Japanese surrendered on 15 August 1945, they held 70,000 Allied POW in 150 camps with two-thirds in Japan and the remainder in China, Formosa, Manchuria, and Korea. Until they could be liberated by occupation troops it was imperative that the sick and starving prisoners were supplied with food, clothing, and medicine. But first the locations of the camps had to be plotted, the logistics sorted out, and the supplies gathered. The 73BW based at Isley Field on Saipan was to administer the operation but B-29s from the other wings flew in supplies to be packed at Saipan from sub-depots at Guam and elsewhere. The B-29s participating in these missions had large capital letters spelling out "P.W. SUPPLIES" on the under surfaces of their wings. They were black letters on natural finish and white letters on B-29s painted with anti-glare black undersurfaces. The 315BW flew airlift missions to the Philippines to collect 24,000 supply parachutes but during a test drop made on Isley Field some of chutes failed to open and all 24,000 of the chutes had to be opened and repacked. The Air Service crews, who called themselves "*Saipan Samaritans*," worked three eight hour shifts to weld two barrels together to provide enough barrels for the drops. Over 1,800 supply drums were welded that looked like little blockbuster bombs and were to be hung from the bomb bay bomb shackles. More supplies were packed on pallets stacked on special bomb bay cargo platforms with parachutes on top. The B-29s carried sufficient supplies for 200 prisoners in 18 bundles or drums loaded in the bomb bays to be dropped at 1,000 feet. The camps were identified by "POW" painted on the roofs of the buildings or by panels on the ground.

The B-29s lined up in long rows called "Conga Lines" and everyone, including flight crews, helped to load the supplies. The first drop on each camp contained sufficient supplies for three days and if the camp were not liberated by that time then a second drop was made with supplies for seven more days. If a third drop were necessary then food for ten more days was dropped. The first POW supply drop was made on 8 August on the camp at Weisien on the Shantung Peninsula, China. All five Bomb Wings participated in the POW supply missions, the 58BW and 313BW on Tinian, the 314BW and 315BW on Guam and the 73BW on Saipan.

The B-29s participating in these missions had large capital letters spelling out "PW SUPPLIES" painted under their wings. The bombers carried sufficient supplies for 200 prisoners in bundles, pallets, or drums loaded in the bomb bay. (AAF)

B-29s flew into Isley to be loaded for these missions but sometimes also brought in additional supplies from sub depots at Tinian and Guam. The 315BW flew three of the longest missions of the war when it flew 4,000 mile round trips to Mukden, Manchuria. After a month there were only three camps that needed further supplies and the final drop was made on 20 September 1945. There were cases of Japanese civilians intercepting errant supplies but by and large the drops were accurate and timely and there were instances of these civilians returning the supplies to the camps. The wings flew 1,010 sorties dropping 4,104 tons of supplies on 154 camps to 63,500 POWs. Seven B-29s were lost in these mercy missions.

The last B-29 shot down in World War II was lost on 29 August 1945, during a POW supply drop on a camp near Hamhung, Korea. *Hog Wild* of the 500BG, piloted by 1Lt. Joseph Queen was in the area of the camp when a pair of Russian Yak fighters approached and signaled Queen to follow them. The B-29 followed and was led to a small landing strip about 10 miles from the camp. Queen turned back toward the POW camp but the Soviets fired across his nose and motioned him to land. Instead Queen turned toward Iwo Jima but after he reached the Korean coast the Yaks attacked and set the bomber's #1 engine on fire. Queen ordered the crew to bail out but after six had jumped the engine fire subsided somewhat and Queen decided to land on the Soviet strip. He landed safely and the Russians were able to extinguish the fire and took the remaining crew captive. Queen explained that their mission was a POW supply drop and were allowed to return to *Hog Wild* to pick up personal belongings. While they were in the aircraft they noticed that it had been stripped of papers and the aircraft commander's handbook and some equipment. At the end of the war the Russians were interested in duplicating the B-29 and *Hog Wild* was a late factory model. The next day Queen and his crew began to

The supplies were parachuted at 1,000 feet on the POW camps which were identified by "POW" painted on the roofs of the buildings or by panels on the ground. The wings flew 1,010 sorties dropping 4,104 tons of supplies on 154 camps to 63,500 POWs. (AAF)

walk toward the bomber and were forcibly detained. On 31 August, the six crewmen who had bailed out were returned and Queen was allowed to contact Saipan by his aircraft radio. He asked for spare parts to repair the bomber and on 11 September a C-47 flew in. Queen decided to salvage the bomber rather than repair it and all flight instruments, gunsights, bombsight radar and other sensitive equipment were removed and loaded in the C-47 and flown back to Saipan with the crew.

16

The War on Insects

The Japanese and the Germans were not the only deadly enemies during the war as mosquito armies causing malaria took their toll in casualties.

Before the advent of DDT, a method of combating mosquitoes was to attack their larval stage in the water in the Spring before they became the mature flying adult. A mixture of Paris Green, the common name for copper acetoarsenite and lye was the larvicide used. Paris Green which was used as a pigment, animal poison (mostly rodenticide), insecticide, and blue colorant for fireworks was placed in a large hopper mounted in the bomb bay of a medium bomber. The hopper was fitted with a small propeller-type agitator to break up any clumping of the larvicide to maintain it in the powdered form. At 10 to 20 foot altitude the pilot dispersed the powder through a venturi valve located in a door in the bottom of the hopper. A huge amount of Paris Green was sprayed by A-20s and B-25s in Italy, Sardinia, and Corsica during 1944 before DDT was available in large quantities.

Although DDT (**D**ichlor **D**iphenyl **T**richloroethane) was first synthesized in 1874, its effectiveness as a potent nerve poison against certain insects was only discovered in 1939 by chemist Paul Muller of J.R. Geigy, a Swiss company which manufactured and distributed it under the patented name of Gesarol. The company sent samples of the compound to the Orlando laboratories of the Department of Agriculture's Bureau of Entomology in October 1942 where it was demonstrated to be superior to other insecticides, especially as a larvicide for anopheline malarial mosquitoes. Within a year it was being distributed in quantity to the services and the War Production Board launched a program to increase the supplies of DDT in December 1943, by granting A-1 priorities to four companies to expand their manufacturing facilities. Production, which had totaled only 153,000 pounds in 1943, increased to 10,000,000 pounds by the end of 1944, and by the end of the war had reached 36,000,000 pounds a year.

Initially, it required 25 gallons of crude oil mixed with DDT sprayed by hand on the surface of an acre of water to be effective but later it proved to be even more effective when sprayed at the rate of only two quarts of a 5% solution per acre using a smaller particle size. The small volume of DDT solution now required led to testing its dispersal by spraying it from aircraft and automobiles. An aerial spraying project was initiated at the Bureau of Agriculture's Orlando laboratories, in co-operation with the Army and Navy Air Forces and the NDRC. Several methods of disseminating the DDT as a mist from an aircraft were finally developed,

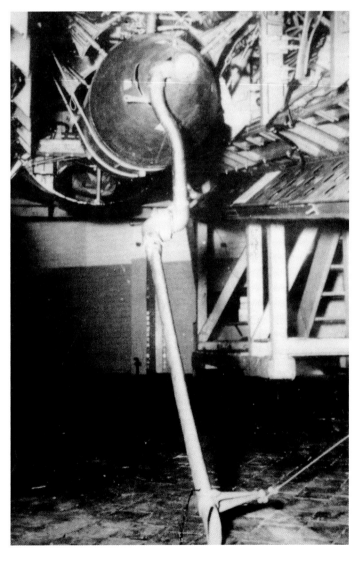

The most common method of **insecticide dispersal** was a 200 gallon drum filled with powdered DDT fitted into the aircraft's bomb bay. The solution was fed by gravity to a single nozzle spray exhaust dump valve hanging below the plane and was released through a three foot pipe.

Capt. Joe Foss, top USMC fighter ace, was hospitalized after losing 35 pounds during his bout with malaria while flying from Guadalcanal in 1942. (Author)

each having a common dependence on the slipstream from the propeller to produce distribution.

The most common aerial spraying method was using a 200 gallon drum filled with powdered DDT fitted into the aircraft's bomb bay. The solution was fed by gravity to a single nozzle spray exhaust dump valve hanging below the plane. The DDT was released through a three foot pipe extending 90° from the bomb bay that spread the insecticide over a 300 yard by seven mile swath. Another method used the bomb bay mounted 200 gallon drum containing a pump activated by a wind-driven propeller that delivered the DDT solution to a series of nozzles placed in long pipes located beneath the aircraft's wings. The spraying run had to be made in suitable wind conditions, from a specific altitude, and properly spaced during multiple runs over the area to be covered.

To slow down the Allied troops advance through Italy, the Germans breached the dikes in southern and central Italy which had been constructed to dry up the land and protect it from the anophelines mosquitoes which carried malaria. When this area was flooded the mosquitoes repopulated but the Allies sprayed DDT and were able to continue their advance through Italy. Spraying continued in 1945 and by 1948 and after spraying half a million pounds over 135,000 square miles, the malarial death rate in Italy was zero.

DDT was also extensively sprayed on Pacific beachheads by medium bombers in advance of and after infantry landings. Immediately after the Morotai invasion B-25s sprayed DDT to combat rampant typhus and malaria in the area. When Marines fell ill from mosquito-borne dengue fever after the 1944 invasion of Saipan, a DDT air strike was called and dengue was suppressed.

So effective was DDT during World War II, that its discoverer, Paul Muller, was awarded the Nobel Prize in 1948. In World War I typhus killed more servicemen than bullets but in World War II typhus was not a problem. A potentially deadly typhus outbreak in newly captured Naples was thwarted by the extensive use of DDT in January 1944. By the end of World War II, the availability of the malarial medication, Atabrine, and the use of DDT, led to the knowledge and experience gained through their use to revolutionize malaria control throughout the world and would lead to the development of the global malaria eradication strategy in the post-war years.

On the flip side of killing mosquitoes was to use them as killers. The War Bureau of Consultants Committee on biological warfare had an ingenious proposal that was to combine many diseases into a mosquito as a single live weapon. The WBC considered the mosquito as the perfect delivery system and suggested studies to find if mosquitoes could be infected with several diseases simultaneously with a view to using these insects as an offensive weapon. As much of the work on biological warfare during the war was classified there is no record of studies being done on the WBC's proposal.

17

Animal Aerial Weapons

Bat Bombs

In early December 1941, Dr. Lytle Adams, a dental surgeon and amateur chiropterogist from Irwin, PA was vacationing the Southwest and visited Carlsbad Caverns, which housed one of the world's largest bat colonies. During the drive back home he heard of the Japanese attack on Pearl Harbor and his creative mind, seeking revenge, settled on the thought of fitting miniature incendiary bombs on these tiny flying mammals. Adams thought the bats would have several advantages: they lived in huge colonies numbering in the millions; they could carry almost double their weight; they hibernated and while dormant were easy to handle and maintain, requiring no food; and they flew in darkness and when dropped away from their home colony would seek dark hiding places, such as flammable buildings, in the daytime. Previously, Adams had become known as an inventor as in the 1930s he had perfected an airmail pickup system for rural areas in which a package was suspended between two poles and swooped up by a low-flying aircraft.

Dr. Lytle Adams (center), who originated the idea of using bats for "bombs," is seen loading Mexican Free Tail Bats into stacked trays. The technician on the left is attaching the miniature incendiary bomb to a bat. (Author)

Adams composed a memorandum entitled, "The Use of Bats as Vectors of Incendiary Bombs," in which described his idea as:

"A very large numbers of bats, each carrying a small incendiary time bomb. The bats would be released at night from airplanes, preferably at high altitudes and the incendiaries would be timed to ignite after the bats had descended to low altitudes and taken shelter for the day. Since bats often roost in buildings, they could be released over settled areas with a good expectation that a large percentage would be roosting in buildings or other inflammable installations...when the incendiary material was ignited."

The memo was sent to President Roosevelt whose aides found it intriguing enough to have the President read it and he considered the idea good enough to be forwarded to William Donovan, then head of information and later would serve as the Chief of the OSS. Donovan, also impressed, passed it on to Earl Stevenson of the National Defense Research Committee of the National Inventors Council. Harvard Zoologist Donald Griffin, a special-research assistant was assigned to examine the bat bomb idea and for both aircraft and submarine release. On 16 April 1942, Griffin summarized Adam's proposal as seeming "bizarre and visionary at first glance... extensive experience with experimental biology convinces the writer that if executed competently it would have every chance of success." Griffin went on to recommend an investigation "with all possible speed, accuracy and efficiency" by the AAF who passed bomb development on to the Army Chemical Warfare Service (CWS).

Adams and a group of naturalists were sent to Texas and New Mexico where bats could be found in large numbers; mainly in caves and mines, but also under bridges and in barns. Because time was of the essence the teams searched for sleeping bats during the day and drove to the next prospective sites at night. The Western Mastiff Bat which was America's largest at 6.5 inches long with a 22 inch wingspan was studied first as it could carry a one pound load but there were not large enough populations available as their colonies numbered only about a 100. The Mule-eared or Pallid variety which measured 4.5 inches with a 15 inch wingspan, and could carry three ounces, also was found in small colonies of 10 to 100 bats but was determined not to be robust enough for the task. The Mexican Free Tail Bat which is the most common bat species in North America was chosen for the project as it formed huge colonies. It measured 4.5 inches long and had a 12.5 inch wingspan. Although it weighed only one-third of an ounce, experiments showed that it could fly satisfactorily with a half to two-third ounce load.

The Ney and Bracken limestone caves, near Bandera in southwest Texas had the largest colony of Free Tails which was an estimated 20 to 30 million. At the Ney cave the bat population was so large that it took five hours for all the hungry bats to leave the mouth of the cave. The stream of bats was fifteen feet in diameter that was so closely packed they could scarcely fly which made capturing them relatively easy. Fish nets attached to long poles were held in front of the mouth of the cave and the bats flew into the nets and captivity.

The captured bats were placed in a truck refrigerated to 40F° to force them into hibernation which alleviated the necessity of feeding the creatures that normally ate many times their own weight per day. The bats were transported to the Chemical Warfare Service headquarters at Aberdeen, MD but since the scientists had no experience in putting bats into hibernation; many did not wake up. The secret bat project was not immediately embraced by the CWS but in March 1943 the AAF authorized the project via a memo: Subject: "Test of Method to Scatter Incendiaries. Purpose: Determine the feasibility of using bats to carry small incendiary bombs into enemy targets."

The Army's Edgewood Arsenal in Maryland, near Washington, DC, was delegated to design an incendiary bomb weighing no more than two-thirds ounce. Harvard chemist Louis Fieser, the inventor of Napalm, was assigned as the project chief to design bombs light enough to be carried by the Free-Tails. The British had developed miniature Thermite bombs during World War I called "baby incendiaries" that weighed 6.4 ounces. From the British design Fieser created two sizes of incendiaries that were oblong celluloid cases filled with thickened Napalm gel and had a small 15 hour time delay igniter fuse attached along one side. One size weighed 0.6 ounces and burned for four minutes with a 10 inch flame while the second bomb weighed 0.78 ounces and would burn for six minutes with a 12 inch flame. The time delay igniter consisted of a firing pin held in tension against a spring by a thin steel wire. A copper chloride solution was injected into the bomb case cavity through which the steel wire passed. The copper chloride was to slowly corrode the wire which would then cause the firing pin to snap forward, striking the igniter head and lighting the kerosene. Specially trained technicians attached the bomb to the bat by attaching the case to the loose skin on the bat's chest with a surgical clip and a piece of string. The five foot bat "bomb" resembled a finned bomb casing and included 26 stacked trays each containing compartments holding 40 bats. The bombs were dropped from 5,000 feet when at a predetermined height of about 1,000 feet an altitude sensor

The five foot **"Bat Bomb"** resembled a finned bomb casing and included 26 stacked trays each containing compartments holding 40 bats. The bombs were dropped from 5,000 feet when at a predetermined height of at about 1,000 feet an altitude sensor (seen on the tail fin) would release a parachute and the trays would separate from the bomb but remain connected to a parachute. (Author)

would release a parachute and the trays would separate from the bomb but remain connected to a parachute. The trays were attached to the parachute upside down, one below the other and while slowly floating down the bats were released and would then fly into hiding in buildings. They would then chew through the string to get rid of the annoying bombs after which the firing pin wire continued to corrode to ignite the bomb. At the time there was the question as to the altitude at which to release the bats. If they were released too high they would freeze to death or be too groggy to fly while if they were released at lower altitudes the dropping aircraft would be subject to enemy AA fire. The scientific solution prevailed and the bats were to be released at 5,000 feet.

Approximately 3,500 bats were captured at Carlsbad Caverns in early May 1943, and flown to Muroc Dry Lake, CA for tests. At Muroc the bats were placed in refrigerators and forced to hibernate for storage and preparation for testing. On 21 May 1943, bats were placed in five prototype cardboard boxes (the metal "bat bomb" was not ready) and dropped from 5,000 feet by a B-25 but the test was unsuccessful because the cardboard boxes split open in the bomber's slipstream killing many of them while the remaining bats were not fully recovered from hibernation and were too groggy and unable to fly. The result was many dead bats feeding scavenging desert birds and animals

The project was transferred to the Army Auxiliary Airbase at Carlsbad where the bats were placed in ice cube trays and refrigerated to put them into hibernation. Technicians took 50 hibernating bats and folded about a one half inch of loose skin away from their chests and a technician attached the incendiary to the fold of skin on the bat's chest with the surgical clip. A B-25 and a L-4 Piper Cub were used to drop the bats in cardboard cartons but problems again developed: many bats didn't awaken from hibernation in time to be able to fly, the cardboard cartons didn't always open correctly, and the surgical clips were difficult to attach to the bat's chests. More bats were captured and the problems resolved with the bats waking in time to be released and fly away. The bats used at Carlsbad weighed an average of 0.32 ounces and could easily carry 0.39 ounces and up to 0.63 ounces satisfactorily but loads over 0.78 ounces were too heavy as these bats couldn't fly very far.

Tests continued using more than 6,000 bats and the results showed that a better time delay parachute-type container, new clips, and a simplified time delay igniter were required. The air-dropped test bats were never fitted with actual bombs but some ground-based bats were accidentally released and their bombs destroyed a large portion of the test buildings at Carlsbad but other buildings and a fuel tank outside the test area was also set on fire.

By August 1943, the AAF abandoned the project and Adams lobbied the Navy to take it over, which it did, and then assigned it to the Marine Corps as *Project X-Ray* at El Centro, CA. Adams continued his contentious association with those in charge which came to a head when he asked to release 10,000 bats over the Southern California desert. Adams' request was denied as too dangerous by William Young, NDRC supervising chemist, and Adams became so incensed that he was asked to leave the project. The first USMC tests began on 13 December 1943 at the Chemical Warfare Service Proving Grounds at Dugway where a simulated Japanese city had been built. The egg crate-style trays and bomb shells were improved and tests were moderately successful with 30 fires starting but 22 flamed out. The head of CWS at Dugway stated:

"A reasonable number of destructive fires can be started in spite of the extremely small size of the units. The main advantage of the units would seem to be their placement within enemy structures without the knowledge of the householder or fire watchers, thus allowing the fire to establish itself before being discovered."

In March 1944, a million bats were tentatively scheduled to be captured. The CWS Chief Chemist emphasized that the bat incendiaries were more effective than the conventional incendiary bomb bomber attack. The incendiary payload of a conventional bomber could start 167 to 400 fires per aircraft while the bats dropped from a single bomber could start 3,600 to 4,750 fires.

At this time another should-have-been anticipated problem arose. The gestation period of bats was seasonal and once female bats became pregnant the male bats did not eat properly; so the weapon-carrying capability of the bats was also seasonal. Comprehensive tests were planned for August 1944 could not be completed until mid-1945 when the Navy decided to cancel the 27 month, $2 million project: "not based on any shortcomings of the incendiary and time units developed....but rather upon the shortcomings of the fundamental idea and the opportunity of getting sufficient reliable data in order to plan a timely operation."

Pigeon Bombs

During the late 1930s Burrhus Frederic (B.F.) Skinner, a behavioral psychologist at Harvard University developed the concept of Operant Conditioning which simply was the theory that the reinforcement of a repeated negative stimulus (punishment) or positive stimulus (reward) formed the basis for learned behavior. For his studies Skinner identified the significance of constancy of conditions in his experiments and developed the "instrumental conditioning chamber" better known as the "Skinner Box" which typically contained one or more levers which an animal could press, one or more stimulus lights, and one or more places in which positive or negative "reinforcers" would be provided. The rat's or pigeon's pushes on the levers were sensed and recorded and a contingency between these pushes, the state of the stimulus lights, and the delivery of reinforcement was set up automatically. To teach the desired response Skinner developed the idea of "shaping" which was "the method of successive approximations." Shaping was initiated by reinforcing a behavior that was somewhat similar to the desired behavior. Once that behavior was established, when variations occurred that are closer to the desired behavior those were rewarded until the desired behavior was being carried out. The pigeons in Skinner's early trials could dance, spin, and play ping pong.

Once World War II in Europe began Skinner contemplated using pigeons to navigate bombs dropped from aircraft so they would hit their targets accurately. Pigeons had better vision than humans, had quicker movements and reactions, could distinguish colors, didn't get airsick, and were more easily managed than many other animals.

Dr. B.F. Skinner, a behavioral psychologist at Harvard, used his Operant Conditioning concept to train pigeons in his "Skinner Box." (Author)

The bound pigeon in the **Skinner Box**. The pigeon's eyes would pick out a target, movement of its neck would then generate signals to steer the missile, and its head and neck together would pick up grain as a reinforcement. (Author)

Using his Operant Conditioning and Shaping techniques Skinner started teaching the birds to earn kernels of grain by pecking at a specific target image on a screen. The birds had to be specially harnessed in a sock with its head and neck protruding through a hole in the big toe area and its wings and legs bound lightly in the sock by a shoestring. The bound pigeon was strapped to a wooden block and placed into the modified Skinner Box. The pigeon's eyes would pick out a target, the movement of its neck would then generate signals to steer the missile, and its head and neck together would pick up pieces of grain as a reinforcer. The pigeon steered by moving pairs of lightweight rods placed around its neck. When the pigeon lifted or lowered its head, it closed electrical contacts that operated a hoist. When it moved its head from side to side, it operated a motorized hoist back and forth on an overhead track.

Skinner placed a bull's-eye on a far wall of the room and placed a few grains of bird food in a small cup in the center. The bird was pushed toward it and by moving its head up or down and from side to side, the pigeon could move toward the wall to a position to reach and eat the grain. The pigeons were moved more quickly toward the target on successive runs and soon operated the hoist as fast as the hoist motors permitted.

Next Skinner devised a method that recorded pigeon pecks as an electronic signal which was transferred to a control system. If the image moved off center, the pigeon would peck quickly to bring the device back on track; and the resulting signals would operate the simulated missile control system to center the device on the target. With training the birds could easily differentiate one target from another and were able to hit the target almost flawlessly.

In mid-1941 Skinner submitted a proposal for his "guidance system" to both the National Inventors Council and the NDRC and was rejected. Once America entered the war Skinner restarted the project and sent a film of his pigeons in action to the NDRC which showed only slight interest.

A.D. Hyde, head of the mechanical division of General Mills, became interested in the project and was able to persuade company Headquarters to support the project with technical assistance until it could be transferred to the government. With General Mills' support Skinner was able to improve his system. The previous bird harness was discarded for a more practical lens and screen grid with a special servo-control mechanism. The force of the pigeon's pecking motion was increased by running a bomb's gyro and controls in a vacuum and by placing valves behind the top, bottom, and sides of the flexible screen. When the pigeon tapped one of these valves,

During the development of the SWOD MK7 *Pelican* a trained Skinner pigeon was to be harnessed inside the nose cone and navigate guided bomb using aerial photographs of the target and if it kept the crosshairs on the target, the pigeon was rewarded by a grain deposited in a tray in front of it. (Author)

it opened, permitting air pressure to build up in the system and operate the fins on the bomb. When the target image was at dead center and the pigeon pecked at dead center, all the valves opened an equal amount and the setting was unchanged.

By June 1943 the project had shown enough potential that the newly formed Office of Scientific Research and Development (OSRD) awarded Skinner a contract for a homing device designated as *Project Pigeon*. Skinner gathered 40 homing and 24 ordinary pigeons and began their training. The target for the Florida bombing trials was a white pyramid on a green field, so Skinner placed white triangles on a lightweight sheet of green paper in the bird's cage. Eventually the bird learned that pecking the white pyramids would produce a few kernels of grain and became conditioned to expect to be fed when he saw them. As soon as the bird had learned to break through the paper, heavier sheets were substituted until the bird would peck very forcefully.

After this primary training phase the pigeon was placed in a lightproof box mounted over a projection screen which had a moving picture of a ground target projected on it. Whenever the pigeon pecked the target on the screen; an electrical contact closed and a small drawer opened containing kernels of grain.

Soon, the pigeons learned they could get the grain no matter where they pecked the screen and began to disregard the target. Skinner outwitted the pigeons by crossing two beams of light at right angles in front of the image causing the pigeons to peck the target image directly in order to break both beams of light and actuate a photoelectric relay to release the food. Skinner then fed feed the birds at regular intervals or after a defined number of pecks. Eventually, the pigeons learned to peck

as fast as four pecks a second for more than two minutes without stopping; working industriously to prevent the target image from moving from being centered. One diligent pigeon pecked at the screen image 10,000 times in 45 minutes. All 64 pigeons in the tests performed successfully.

Tests continued to subject the pigeons to battle conditions. Skinner put the pigeons in a pressure chamber set at 10,000 feet and they were whirled around in a centrifuge subjecting them to large G-forces. Pistols were fired only a few inches from their heads but they didn't miss a peck or even look up. They were exposed to bright flashes that simulated shell bursts and high vibrations were also introduced. Skinner found that the pigeons were less easily disturbed under confusing circumstances if they were fed hemp (marijuana) seeds rather than grains!

Once trained Skinner's pigeons were ready to navigate guided bombs dropped from aircraft. The NDRC was developing its SWOD Mk7 *Pelican* guided missile (as described elsewhere) and interest was shown in Skinner's *Project Pigeon* guidance project. The pigeons were trained with slides of aerial photographs of the target and if they kept the crosshairs on the target, they were rewarded by a grain of food deposited in a tray in front of them. A pigeon was harnessed inside the nose cone of a guided bomb. Skinner's control system used a lens in the nose of the bomb to project an image of the approaching target on a ground glass screen. If the target's image moved off center, the pigeon's pecking tilted the screen, which moved the bomb's tail surfaces, which corrected the bomb's course.

After the successful completion of those experiments, Skinner placed pigeons in three, five, and even seven tandem positions to control the bomb's direction by majority rule. If one or more birds became stubborn, lazy, or distracted; the majority could override any incorrect signals and keep the missile on course. In a very large percentage of cases they pecked away at the target as hunger overcame any other needs.

Skinner sent the results to OSRD for evaluation and eventually he was asked to demonstrate a pigeon working in a box with the target screen. The demonstration was eminently successful as it exhibited the extraordinary predictability of the pigeon's behavior, its acute vision, the accuracy of its responses, and its freedom from distraction.

Nonetheless on 8 October 1944, Skinner was informed by the OSRD that "further prosecution of this project would seriously delay others which in the minds of the Division have more immediate promise of combat application" and *Project Pigeon*, like the bat bombs, quietly came to an end as an intriguing footnote which was classified until 1959.

After World War II, the US Navy became interested in using missiles against surface ships and in 1948 reopened the classified *Project Pigeon* and redesignated it as *Project Orcon* (for organic control) under the Naval Research Laboratory. Tests were conducted over the next five years, using a sophisticated trainer that simulated a missile. The tests repeatedly showed that the pigeons could guide missiles satisfactorily to score hits under ideal conditions, although clouds, waves, and shadows could cause them to deviate from course. *Project Orcon* was canceled in 1953, when electronic guidance systems for missiles were considered more reliable.

Bibliography

Magazine Articles and Press Releases

Air Classics, "Bat Victory (Letters to the Editor)," *Air Classics*, April 2007.

Air Force, "Guided Missiles," *Air Force*, March-April, 1946.

Army Ordnance, "Homing Missiles," *Army Ordnance*, May-June 1947.

Associated Press, "WW-II 'Bat Bombs' Went Bust for US," March 22, 1995.

ASME, "David Taylor Model Basin," *ASME*, 30 January 1998.

Baumann, Peter, "Lethal Sky Rockets," *Air Force*, November 1945.

Bye, Roger, "Man-Made *Earthquakes*," *Air Force*, September 1945.

Dailey, Owen, "*Tiny Tim*," *Skyways*, June 1945.

Daniels, George (ed.), "Know Your Bombs," *Flying Manual*, No.9, 1942.

Davis, Kenneth, "The Deadly Dust: The Unhappy History of DDT," *American Heritage*, February 1971.

Dyson, J.D., "Documentation and Diagrams of the Atomic Bomb," Pvt. Printing, n.d.

Fahrney, D.S., "Guided Missile: US Navy, the Pioneer," *AAHS Journal*, spring 1982.

Flight, "Bombs versus Concrete," *Flight*, 30 May 1946.

FlyPast, "The Flying Bombs of Rabaul," *FlyPast*, September 1982.

Fuller, Curtis, "Rockets and Aircraft," *Flying*, February 1945.

Gault, Owen, "Dive bombers : The Warplanes That Shaped Aircraft Evolution," *Sea Classics,* July 2007.

Glines, C.V., "The Bat Bombers ," *Air Force Magazine*, October, 1990.

Glines, C.V., "Top Secret World War II Bat and Bird Bomber Program," *Aviation History*, May 2005.

Gray, Edwin, "Operation *Aphrodite's* B-17 Smart Bomb," *Aviation History*, May 1996.

Hallstead, William, "The US Navy's Kamikazes," *Aviation History*, January 2004.

Helmick, F.F., "Our Search for Guided Missiles," *Air Force*, October 1945.

Impact, "Aerial Bombs Pollute Jap Waters," *Impact*, June 1945.

Impact, "American Buzz Bomb Now Gets Launched from 50 Foot Ramp," *Impact*, August, 1945.

Impact, "*AZON*," *Impact*, March 1945.

Impact, "Around the World with the Rocketeers," *Impact*, October 1944.

Impact, "Big Bombs for Big Bombers ," *Impact,* June 1945.

Impact, "Fire Bombs Turn the Trick against Holed-Up Nips in Luzon," *Impact*, August 1945.

Impact, "Kennedy Cocktails," *Impact*, January, 1944.

Impact, "Leaflets are Weapons of Attack," *Impact*, March 1944.

Impact, "Psychological Bombing by the AAF," *Impact*, March 1945.

Impact, "US Buzz Bombs," *Impact*, January 1945.

Kenyon, Gerald, "Bat Victory," *Air Classics*, March, 2007.

Knight, Charlotte, "Dress Rehearsal for drones," *Air Force*, March/April 1946.

Kopp, Carlo, "The Dawn of the Smart Bomb," *Air Power, Australia*, July, 2006.

Lewis, Jack, "The Bat Bombers ," *Air Combat*, November 1975.

Marshall, Charles, "Television Equipment for Guided Missiles," *Inter Avia*, January 1947.

Mets, David, "The Quest for a Surgical Strike: The Air Force and the Laser-guided Bombs," *Air and Space Case Study*, 1987.

Milford, Frederick, "US Navy Torpedoes, Part I: Torpedoes through the Thirties," *Submarine Review*, April, 1996.

Milford, Frederick, "US Navy Torpedoes, Part II: Great Torpedo Scandal, 1941-43," *Submarine Review*, October 1996.

Milford, Frederick, "US Navy Torpedoes, Part III: Development of Conventional Torpedoes, 1940-1946," *Submarine Review*, January, 1997.

Naval Aviation News, "Guided Missiles," *Naval Aviation News*, February, 1947.

O'Neil, John, "How H2X 'Mickey' Got Its Name*," 8th Air Force News*, March 2009.

Pearson, Lee, "Developing the Flying Bomb," *Naval Aviation News*, May 1968.

Peck, James. "Man-Made Meteors," *Air Force*, July 1946.

Powles, James, "Lytle Little Proposed One of America's Battiest Weapons," *World War II*, July 2002.

Puffer, Raymond, "Bombs with Wings," *Air Force Flight Center*, No Date.

Saberian, Michael, "The Flaming Sword: Napalm and Its Effects," University of Texas, 2004.

Scullin, Harry, and Morgan, Clyde, "The *Earthquake* Bomb," *Army Ordnance*, September-October, 1945.

Spark, Nick, "Classified: The Secret Weapons of World War II," *Wings*, October, 2004.

Spark, Nick, "Command Break," USNIP, Wash, DC.

Spark, Nick, "Secret Arsenal: Advanced American Weapons of WWII, *Wings*, October 2004.

Trimble, William, "When a Torpedo is Not a Torpedo," *Aerospace Historian*, Winter 1988.

USN, "Navy Pilot Sinks Three U-Boats," press release 28 September 1943.

Van Atta, Lee, "Strafe-Bombing Payoff in the South Pacific: How it Blasts Jap Shipping," *Air Force*, February 1944.

Waitt, Alden, "Gas," *Flying & Popular Aviation*, May 1942.

Wainwright, Marshall, "Mr. Stout's Torpedo-Bomber," *Air Classics*, November, 008

Wells, William, "Top Secret Mission: *Project Anvil*," *King's Cliffe Remembered*, January, 1984.

Werrell, Kenneth, "The Forgotten Missile: The Kettering-General Motors A-1," *AAHS Journal*, Spring 1985.

Wolf, William, "American Glide Bombs of WW-2: The GB Series," unpublished article.

Wolf, William, "Glider Borne Pattern Torpedo (GT-1)," unpublished article.

Wolf, William, "V for Vengeance," *Airpower*, March, 1978.

Books

Abramson, Albert, History of Television, 1942-2000, McFarland & Co, NC, 2003.

Althof, William, Sky Ships, Orion, NY, 1990.

Anderton, David, B-29 Superfortress at War, Scribner, NY, 1978.

Ayling, Keith, Bombardment Aviation, Military Service, PA, 1944.

Banks, Herbert, 379th Bombardment Group (H) Anthology, Volume 1, Turner, KY, 2000.

Barris, Ted, Days of Victory: Canadians Remember, 1939–45, Thomas Allen, Toronto, Canada, 1998.

Birdsall, Steve, Superfortress, Squadron/Signal. TX. 1980.

Bowman, Martin, The B-24 Liberator: 1939-1945, Wensum, UK, 1979.

Bridgeman, Leonard (Ed.), Jane's All the World's Aircraft, 1945-46, Arco, NY, 1970 (reprint).

Baldwin, Ralph, The Deadly Fuse, Presidio, CA, 1980.

Baxter, James, Scientists Against Time, MIT Press, MA, 1946.

Boyce, Joseph, New Weapons for Air Warfare, Little Brown, Boston. 1947.

Campbell. Richard, The Silverplate Bombers , McFarland, NC, 2005.

Carey, Alan, Above the Angry Sea, Schiffer, PA, 2001.

Carey, Alan, Reluctant Raiders, Schiffer, PA, 1999.

Carey, Alan, US Navy PB4Y-1 (B-24) Liberator Squadrons in Great Britain during World War II, Schiffer, PA, 2003.

Carpenter, D.M. and D'Alessandro, P.V., Thunderbug: WWII Flying Wing Bomb, Jet Pioneers, MA, n.d.

Chilstrom, John, Mines Away!: The Significance of USAAF Minelaying in WW-2, Air University, Al, 1993.

Christman, Albert, Sailors, Scientists, and Rockets, Naval History Division, Wash, DC, 1971.

Clarke, R.M., Fortress and Superfortress Portfolio, Brooklands, UK, n.d.

Coster-Mullen, John, Atomic Bombs: The Top Secret Inside Story of Little Boy and Fat Man, Pvt. Printing, WI, 2006.

Couffer, Jack, Bat Bomb: World War II's Other Secret Weapon, U. of Texas, TX, 1992.

Covert, Norman, Cutting Edge: A History of Fort Detrick, Maryland, US Army Garrison, MD, 1997.

DeJong, Ivo, Mission 376, Specialty Press, MN, 2004.

Delano, Jack et al, Superfortress Over Japan, Motor books, WI, 1996.

Dwiggins, Don, The Kennedy Courage, Pyramid, 1965.

Flower, Stephen, Barnes Wallis' Bombs, Tempus, UK, 2002.

Francis, Devon, Flak-Bait, Zenger, Wash. DC, 1948.

Freeman, Roger, B-26 Marauder at War, Scribner, NY, 1977.

Freeman, Roger, Mighty Eighth, Janes, UK, 1978.

Freeman, Roger, Mighty Eighth War Diary, Janes, UK, 1981.

Gannon, Robert, Hellions from the Deep, Penn State U, PA. 1996.

Gaylor, Walter, et.al., Revenge of the Red Raiders, IR, CO, 2006.

Gerrard-Gough, J.D. and Christman, Albert, Grand Experiment at Inyokern Vol. 2, Naval History Division, Wash. DC, 1978.

Gooderson, Ian, Airpower at the Battlefront, Cass, UK, 1998.

Ginter, Steve, Douglas TBD-1 Devastator, Ginter, CA, 2006.

Gray, Edwyn, The Devil's Device: Robert Whitehead and the History of the Torpedo, NIP, MD, 1991.

Hall, James, American Kamikaze, Pvt. Printing, 1984, FL.

Harris, Robert, and Paxman, Jeremy, A Higher Form of Killing, Hill & Wang, NY, 1982.

Henshall, Philip, Hitler's V-Weapon Sites, Sutton, UK, 2002.

Howeth, L.S., History of Electronics-Communications in the United States Navy, Bureau of Ships and Naval History, Washington, DC, 1963.

Infield, Glenn, Disaster at Bari, MacMillan, NY, 1971.

Kay, Anthony, Buzz Bomb: Close Up, Monogram, MA, 1977.

Kemp, Paul, U-Boats Destroyed, Arms & Armour, UK, 1999.

Kenney, George, The Saga of Pappy Gunn, Duell, Sloan and Pearce, NY, 1959.

Kinzey, Bert, B-24 Liberator in Detail, Squadron/Signal, TX, 2000.

Kinzey, Bert, TBF & TBM Avenger, Squadron/Signal. TX 1997.

Kinzey, Bert, SB2C Helldiver, Squadron/Signal, TX, 1997.

Kleber, Brooks, and Birdsell, Dale, <u>Chemical Warfare Service: Chemicals in Combat</u>, US Army, Wash, DC, 1964.

Kopenhagen, Wilfried, <u>V-1 and Its Soviet Successors</u>, Schiffer, PA, 2000.

Lloyd, Alwyn, <u>B-17 Flying Fortress in Scale & Detail, Part 1</u>, Aero, PA, 1985.

Lloyd, Alwyn, <u>B-17 Flying Fortress in Scale & Detail, Part 2</u>, Aero, PA, 1986.

Lloyd, Alwyn, <u>B-29 Superfortress in Scale & Detail, Part 1</u>, TAB, PA, 1986.

Lloyd, Alwyn, <u>B-29 Superfortress in Scale & Detail, Part 2</u>, TAB, PA, 1987.

McArthur, Charles, <u>Operations Analysis in the US Army Eighth Air Force in World War II</u>, American Mathematical Society, RI, 1990.

Mizrahi, J.V., <u>Dive and Torpedo Bombers</u>, Sentry, CA, 1967.

Neufeld, Jacob, <u>Development of Ballistic Missiles in the USAF: 1945-60</u>, Office of History, Wash. DC, 1990.

Nowarra, Heinz, <u>German Guided Missiles</u>, Schiffer, PA, n.d.

Onderwater, Hans, <u>Operation Manna/Chowhound</u>, Deboer, Holland, 1985.

Pons, Gregory, <u>8th Air Force</u>, Historie & Collections, France, 2006.

Price, Alfred, <u>Aircraft vs. Submarine</u>, Kimber, UK, 1973.

Regis, Ed, <u>The Biology of Doom</u>, Holt, NY, 1999.

Rhodes, Richard, <u>The Making of the Atomic Bomb</u>, Simon & Schuster, NY, 1986.

Rowland, Buford, and Boyd, William, <u>US Navy Bureau of Ordnance in World War II</u>, BuOrd, Wash, DC, 1948.

Sakaida, Henry, <u>Siege of Rabaul</u>, Phalanx, MN, 1996.

Scutts, Jerry, <u>North American B-25 Mitchell</u>, Crowood, UK, 2001.

Schmeelke, Karl-Heinz and Michael, <u>German U-Boat Bunkers: Yesterday and Today</u>, Schiffer, PA, 1999.

Schmitt, Vernon, <u>Controlled Bombs and Missiles of the World War II and Cold War Eras</u>, SAE, PA, 2002.

Shachtman, Tom, <u>Terrors and Marvels</u>, Morrow, NY, 2002.

Showell, J.P.M., <u>Hitler's U-Boat Bases,</u> Sutton, UK, 2002.

Smith, Peter, <u>Curtiss SB2C Helldiver</u>, Crowood, UK, 1998.

Smith, Peter, <u>Dive Bomber!</u>, Moorland, UK, 1982.

Smith, Peter, <u>Story of the Torpedo Bomber</u>, Altmark, UK, 1974.

Theismeyer, Lincoln and Burch and, John, <u>Combat Scientists</u>, Little Brown, Boston, 1947.

Thomas, Gordon and Morgan-Witts, Max, Enola Gay: Mission to Hiroshima, Dalton Watson, UK, 1995.

Thompson, Scott, <u>Douglas A-26 and B-26 Invader</u>, Crowood, UK, 2002.

Thompson, Scott, <u>Douglas Havoc and Boston</u>, Crowood, UK , 2004.

Tillman, Barrett, and Lawson, Robert, <u>US Navy Dive and Torpedo Bombers of WWII</u>, WI, 2001.

Tillman, Barrett, <u>Avenger at War</u>, Ian Allan, UK, 1979.

Tillman, Barrett, <u>Dauntless Dive Bomber of World War 2</u>, NIP, MD, 1978.

von Karman, Theodore and Edson, Lee, <u>Wind and Beyond: Theodore von Karman</u>, Little, Brown, Boston, 1967.

Willard, Lt. F. Willard, "VC-7 and the Development of Air-to-Ground Rockets: World War II Aviation Unit," Naval Aviation News, March-April, 2003.

Wolf, William, <u>Boeing B-29 Superfortress The Ultimate Look From Drawing Board to VJ-Day</u>, Schiffer, PA, 2005.

Wolf, William, <u>Consolidated B-32 Dominator: The Ultimate Look From Drawing Board to Scrapyard</u>, Schiffer, PA, 2006.

Wolf, William, <u>Douglas B-18 Bolo: The Ultimate Look From Drawing Board to U-Boat Hunter</u>, Schiffer, PA, 2006.

Wolf, William, <u>German Guided Missiles: Henschel Hs 293 and Ruhrstahl SD 1400X "Fritz,"</u> Merriam, VT, 1999.

Wolf, William, <u>North American B-25 Mitchell: The Ultimate Look From Drawing Board to Flying Arsenal</u>, Schiffer, PA, 2008.

Wolf, William, <u>Rockets and Guided Missiles of World War II</u>, Unpublished Manuscript.

Wolf, William, <u>USAAF Jabos in the MTO and ETO,</u> Schiffer, PA, 2003.

Wolf, William, <u>Victory Roll: The American Fighter Pilot and Aircraft,</u> Schiffer, PA, 2001.

Y'Blood, William, <u>Hunter-Killer, US Escort Carriers in the Battle of the Atlantic</u>, NIP, MD, 1983.

Young, Richard, <u>The Flying Bomb</u>, Sky Books, NY, 1977.

Zaloga, Steven, <u>German V-Weapon Sites 1943-45,</u> Osprey, UK, 2008.

Technical Manuals and Reports

AAFAC: <u>Anti-submarine Manual SOP</u>, 29 July 1943.

AAFAC: "Anti-Submarine Monthly Intelligence Report," August 1943.

AAFPGC: "Final Report GT-1," (to Gen. George Kenney), Eglin Field, FL, 13 October 1943.

AAFTC, <u>Student's Manual Bombing</u>, Wash. DC, c. 1945.

Air Materiel Command, <u>Case History of Controlled Missiles</u>, February 1945, National Archives, MD, ATSC, Historical Office, OH, 1945.

Air Materiel Command, <u>Development of Guided Missiles, Case Histories, 1941</u>-1946, Historical Division Intelligence, AMC, June 1946.

Air Materiel Command, <u>Case History of Controlled Guided Missiles: Vertical Bombs</u>, Assistant Chief of Air Staff, AMC, February 1945.

Air Materiel Command, <u>Case History of Controlled Guided Missiles: Aircraft</u>, Assistant Chief of Air Staff, AMC, February 1945.

Anthony, Alistair; Walker, Norman; and DeSocio; <u>Accuracy of the *AZON* Guided Bomb as Affected by Battle Conditions in World War II, US</u> Army Human Engineering Laboratories, MD, May 1964.

Bentz, W.H., "Penetration and Deceleration of 25,000 Pound Bombs in Massive Concrete Targets, Report No. 712," Aberdeen Proving Ground, 14 December 1949.

Department of the Army, British Explosive Ordnance, Washington, DC, July 1952.

Chilstrom, John, Mines Away!: The Significance of the USAAF's Minelaying in WW-II, School of Advanced Airpower Studies, AL. 1992.

Fifth Air Force HQ, "Ordnance Technical Report No.6: Parachute Demolition Bombs," Wash. DC. 1945.

458 Bomb Group History, "753rd Bombardment Squadron History: June-July-August 1944," Private printing, n.d.

Gordon, Grant, A Case Study of AZON: An Azimuth Guided Bomb, Air University, AL, July 1989.

HQ of the Commander, Aircraft, Northern Solomons, "Report on the Operations of STAG-1 in the Northern Solomons Area," 30 October 1944, Gen. Claude Larkin.

Lowrey Field, Department of Armament, Norden Bombsight: Maintenance and Calibration, CO, 1 September 1943.

Malina, F.J., Essays on the History of Rocketry and Astronautics, NASA, 1977.

MacIsaac, David, (ed.), United States Strategic Bombing Survey, (10 volumes), Garland, NY, 1976.

Naval Ordnance Laboratory, Mines Against Japan, NOL, MD, 1973.

Ninth Air Force, "Rocket Status in the 9th Air Force, Report (No. 59)," 19 Sept. 1944.

Northrop Aircraft, "Model Specification & Model Description: JB-1 (Report N8-16)," Northrop Aircraft, CA, 6 July 1944.

Pearson, Lee, "Development of the Attack Concept and the Attack Bomber," Naval Aviation Bulletins, 1951.

Sallagar, F.M., "Lessons From an Aerial Mining Campaign," Rand Corp., CA 1974.

SHAEF, Leaflet Operations in the Western European Theater, 1944-45, Psychological Warfare Division, UK, 1945.

STAG-1, War Diary: 5 June 1944 to 30 October 1944, Aircraft South Pacific Force, 30 October 1944.

388th Bomb Group, 388th Bomb Group: Fortress for Freedom, Newsfoto, TX, 1946.

20th Air Force, A Statistical Summary of Its Operations Against Japan, June 44-August 45, 20th AF HQ, October 1945.

US Army, Ballistic Data Performance of Ammunition, TM9-1907, July 1948.

US Army, Ballistic Data Performance of Ammunition, TM9-1907, 23 September 1944.

USAAF, "AAF Missile Documents," Maxwell AFB, MF Reel A2050.

USAAF, AAF Statistical Digest, Office of Statistical Control, December 1945.

USAAF, Anti-Submarine Command, AAFRH No. 7, April, 1945.

USAAF, "Bomber and Fighter Tactics in Combat," Office of the Assistant Chief of Staff, Wash. DC, c. 1943.

USAAF, Bombs for Aircraft, TM9-1980. Wash. DC, November 1944.

USAAF, Case History of Castor, Maxwell AFB, MF Reel A2082, A2083, and A2051.

USAAF, Case History of the GMA-1, Maxwell AFB, MF Reel A2082, A2083, and A2051.

USAAF, Case History of the GB-1, Maxwell AFB, MF Reel A2082, A2083, and A2051.

USAAF, Case History of the Hydrobomb, Maxwell AFB, MF Reel A2082, A2083, and A2051.

USAAF, Case History of Vertical Bombs: AZON, SPAZON, RAZON, Felix, ROC, Maxwell AFB, MF Reel A2082, A2083, and A2051.

USAAF, "Design Data for Aircraft Hydrobomb," 22 February 1943.

USAAF, "Final Report on Minimum Altitude Attack of Water-Borne Surface Vessels with Aircraft Bombs," No.1-42-12, Eglin AFB, FL, 7 December 1942.

USAAF, "Navy and Ordnance Guided Missile Projects," Maxwell AFB, MF Reel A2050.

USAAF, "Guided Missile Policy Documents," Maxwell AFB, MF Reel A2050.

USAAF, "JB-1 through JB-10 Series," Maxwell AFB, MF Reel A2051.

USAAF, "Power-Driven Weapons Developed by the Special Weapons Branch Equipment Laboratory," Maxwell AFB, MF Reel A2051.

USAAF Proving Ground Command, Eglin Field, FL, to Gen. George Kenney, CG 5th Air Force, 13 October 1943, "Final Report Glider Borne Pattern Torpedo."

USAAF, Commander of Air Forces in the Northern Solomons, "Report: Operations of STAG-1 Detachment in Northern Solomons Area," Brig.Gen. Claude Larkin to Adm. Halsey, 30 October 1944.

USAAF, "SWOD-7 Bat," Maxwell AFB, MF Reel A2051.

USAAF, "12,000 Lb. High Nagle RAZON Controlled Bomb (Tallboy)," Maxwell AFB, MF Reel A2051.

USAF, Bombs for Aircraft, TM9-1980. Wash. DC, 1950.

USN, Aircraft Bombs, Fuses, and Associated Components, Bureau of Naval Weapons, Wash, DC, 1 August 1960.

USN, Anti-Submarine Operations by CVE Based Aircraft, ASWORG 87, 1 April 1944.

USN, "Mark 24 Success in Combat," Navy OEG Study No. 289, 12 August 1946.

US Navy OEG Study No. 289, 12 August 1946

US Pacific Fleet, Psychological Warfare, US Pacific Fleet, August 1944.

War Department, bombardier's Information File (BIF), March, 1945.

War Department, "History of Launchers and Rockets," Bureau of Public Relations, Press Release, n.d.

War Department, "Rockets, Launchers, and Propellants," Bureau of Public Relations, Press Release, 24 September 1944.

War Department, OSRD, "US Rocket Ordnance Development and Use in World War II," n.d.

XXI Bomber Command, Combat Crew Manual, May 1945.

Websites

www.About.com; Operations Manna & Chowhound, Kennedy Hickman

www.almc.army.mil; Chemical Warfare Service Prepares for World War II," Wright, Burton

www.americanheritage.com; "Why We Didn't Use Poison Gas in World War II, Bernstein, Barton

www.biomicro.sdstate.edu/pederses/asmbat; "Family Tree & History of the ASM-N-2 *Bat* Glide Bomb," Pedersen, Scott.
www.bt.cdc.gov/agent/basic/facts; Phosgene, Mustard, Lewisite
www.cybermodeler.com; "Silverplate: The Aircraft of the Manhatten Project," Cully, George
www.designation-systems.net; Directory of US Military Rockets and Missiles.
www.eugeneleeslover.com/USNAVY
www.fas.org; "Magnetic Anomaly Detection (MAD)"
www.geocities.com/Pentagon; "US Navy Torpedoes"
www.history.navy.mil; Patrol Squadron (VP) Histories.
www.historynet.com; "German Raid on Bari," Niderost, Eric
www.historynet.com; "Lawrence Sperry: Autopilot Inventor and Aviation Innovator"
www.historywired.si.edu; "Nose Cone, Pigeon-Guide"
www.navweaps.com/Weapons; "USA Torpedoes of World War II"
www.psywar.org; Various articles
www.//vectorsite.net; Various articles
www.worldwarii.com/WorldWarII/articles; "US Torpedo Troubles"
www.ww2pacific.com; "Dud Torpedoes"
www.history.navy.mil.com; "Developing the Flying Bomb," Lee Pearson

Videos/DVD/Films
Dead Men's Secrets: "The Mysterious Death of Joe Kennedy", History Channel, n.d.
"RAZON," Office of Strategic Services, NDRC (Division 5), n.d.
"AZON," Office of Strategic Services, NDRC (Division 5), n.d.

Index

(Note: Pages in **Bold** type are photos of the subject)

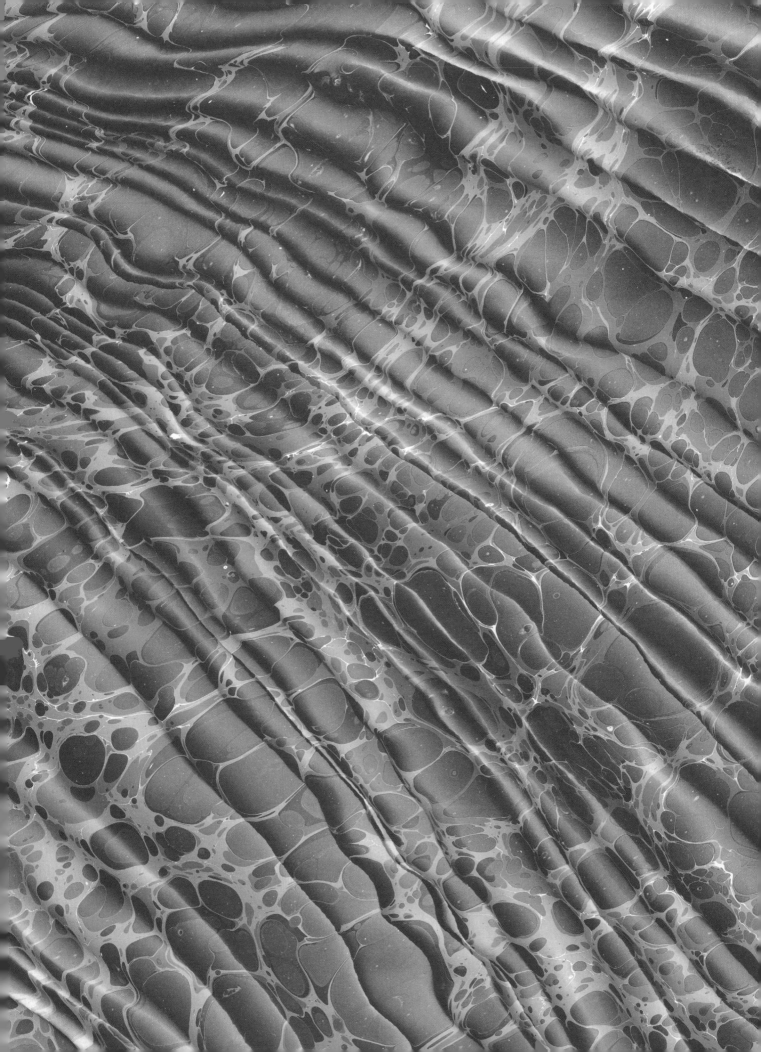